# Relating System Quality and Software Architecture

# Relating System Quality and Software Architecture

Edited by

**Ivan Mistrik**

**Rami Bahsoon**

**Peter Eeles**

**Roshanak Roshandel**

**Michael Stal**

**ELSEVIER**

AMSTERDAM • BOSTON • HEIDELBERG • LONDON
NEW YORK • OXFORD • PARIS • SAN DIEGO
SAN FRANCISCO • SINGAPORE • SYDNEY • TOKYO

Morgan Kaufmann is an imprint of Elsevier

**Acquiring Editor**: Todd Green
**Editorial Project Manager**: Lindsay Lawrence
**Project Manager**: Punithavathy Govindaradjane
**Designer**: Russell Purdy

*Morgan Kaufmann* is an imprint of Elsevier
225 Wyman Street, Waltham, MA, 02451, USA

**Library of Congress Cataloging-in-Publication Data**
Relating system quality and software architecture / edited by Ivan Mistrik, Rami Bahsoon, Peter Eeles, Roshanak
  Roshandel, Michael Stal.
    pages cm
Includes bibliographical references.
ISBN 978-0-12-417009-4
1.  Computer systems–Quality control. 2.   Software architecture.   I. Mistrik, Ivan.
  QA76.9.A43R45 2014
  005.1'2–dc23

                                                                                        2014014126

**British Library Cataloguing-in-Publication Data**
A catalogue record for this book is available from the British Library.

ISBN: 978-0-12-417009-4

For information on all MK publications
visit our website at www.mkp.com

This book has been manufactured using Print On Demand technology. Each copy is produced to order and is
limited to black ink. The online version of this book will show color figures where appropriate.

# Contents

# PART II    ANALYSIS, MONITORING, AND CONTROL OF SOFTWARE ARCHITECTURE FOR SYSTEM QUALITIES

# Acknowledgments

The editors would like to sincerely thank the many authors who contributed their works to this collection. The international team of anonymous reviewers gave detailed feedback on early versions of chapters and helped us to improve both the presentation and accessibility of the work. Finally, we would like to thank the Elsevier management and editorial teams, in particular Todd Green and Lindsay Lawrence, for the opportunity to produce this unique collection of articles covering a wide range of areas related to system quality and software architecture.

# About the Editors

**Ivan Mistrik** is an independent researcher in software-intensive systems engineering. He is a computer scientist who is interested in system and software engineering (SE/SWE) and in system and software architecture (SA/SWA), in particular, life cycle system/software engineering, requirements engineering, relating software requirements and architectures, knowledge management in software development, rationale-based software development, aligning enterprise/system/software architectures, value-based software engineering, agile software architectures, and collaborative system/software engineering. He has more than forty years' experience in the field of computer systems engineering as an information systems developer, R&D leader, SE/SA research analyst, educator in computer sciences, and ICT management consultant.

In the past 40 years, he has worked primarily at various R&D institutions in United States and Germany and has consulted on a variety of large international projects sponsored by ESA, EU, NASA, NATO, and the UN. He has also taught university-level computer sciences courses in software engineering, software architecture, distributed information systems, and human-computer interaction. He is the author or co-author of more than 90 articles and papers in international journals, conferences, books, and workshops, most recently a chapter, "Capture of Software Requirements and Rationale through Collaborative Software Development"; a paper, "Knowledge Management in the Global Software Engineering Environment"; and a paper "Architectural Knowledge Management in Global Software Development."

He has written a number of editorials and prefaces, most recently for the books *Aligning Enterprise, System, and Software Architecture* and, *Agile Software Architecture*. He has also written over 120 technical reports and presented over 70 scientific/technical talks. He has served on many program committees and panels of reputable international conferences and organized a number of scientific workshops, including two workshops on Knowledge Engineering in Global Software and Development at the International Conference on Global Software Engineering 2009 and 2010 and the IEEE International Workshop on the Future of Software Engineering for/in the Cloud (FoSEC) held in conjunction with IEEE Cloud 2011. He has been the guest editor of *IEE Proceedings Software: A special Issue on Relating Software Requirements and Architectures,* published by IEE in 2005, and the lead editor of the book *Rationale Management in Software Engineering,* published by Springer in 2006. He has been the co-author of the book *Rationale-Based Software Engineering,* published by Springer in May 2008. He has been the lead editor of the book *Collaborative Software Engineering,* published by Springer in 2010; the book *Relating Software Requirements and Architectures,* published by Springer in 2011; and the lead editor of the book *Aligning Enterprise, System, and Software Architectures*, published by IGI Global in 2012. He was the lead editor of the *Expert Systems Special Issue on Knowledge Engineering in Global Software Development* and co-editor of the *JSS Special Issue on the Future of Software Engineering for/in the Cloud,* both published in 2013. He was the co-editor for the book *Agile Software Architecture,* published by Elsevier in 2013. Currently, he is the lead editor for the book *Economics-driven Software Architecture*, to be published by Elsevier in 2014.

**Rami Bahsoon** is a senior lecturer in software engineering and founder of the Software Engineering for/in the Cloud interest groups at the School of Computer Science, University of Birmingham, UK. His group currently comprises nine PhD students working in areas related to cloud software engineering and architectures. The group's research aims at developing architecture and frameworks to support and reason about the development and evolution of dependable, ultra-large, complex, and data-intensive software systems, in which the investigations span cloud computing architectures and their economics. Bahsoon had founded and co-organized the International Software Engineering Workshop series on Software Architectures and Mobility held in conjunction with ICSE and the IEEE International Software Engineering for/in the Cloud workshop in conjunction with IEEE Services. He was the lead editor of two special issues of Elsevier's *Journal of Systems and Software*—one on the Future of Software Engineering for/in the Cloud and another on Architecture and Mobility. Bahsoon has co-edited a book on *Economics-driven Software Architecture*, published by Elsevier in 2014 and co-edited another book, *Aligning Enterprise, System, and Software Architectures*, published by IGI Global in 2012. He is currently acting as the workshop chair for IEEE Services 2014, the Doctoral Symposium chair of IEEE/ACM Utility and Cloud Computing Conference (UCC 2014), and the track chair for Utility Computing of HPCC 2014. He holds a PhD in Software Engineering from University College London (UCL) for his research on evaluating software architecture stability using real options. He has also read for MBA-level certificates with London Business School.

**Peter Eeles** is an IBM Executive IT Architect and Industry Lead for the Financial Services Sector in IBM Rational's Worldwide Tiger Team, where he helps organizations improve their software development and delivery capability. This work is often performed in conjunction with the adoption of the Rational Unified Process and associated IBM development tools. Peter has been in the software industry since 1985 and has spent much of his career architecting, project managing, and implementing large-scale, distributed systems. He has a particular interest in architecture-centric initiatives such as SOA, large-scale architecting, strategic reuse programs, and the like. Prior to joining Rational Software, which was acquired by IBM in 2003, Peter was a founding member of Integrated Objects, where he was responsible for the development of a distributed object infrastructure. This technology was used by System Software Associates (an ERP solutions provider) and by Mobile Systems International (a telecoms solutions provider) where Peter also held positions. Peter is co-author of *The Process of Software Architecting* (Addison-Wesley, 2009), *Building J2EE Applications with the Rational Unified Process* (Addison-Wesley, 2002), and *Building Business Objects* (Wiley, 1998).

**Roshanak Roshandel** is an associate professor in the Department of Computer Science and Software Engineering at Seattle University where she is also the Director of the Master of Software Engineering program. She received her M.S. and Ph.D. in Computer Science in 2002 and 2006 respectively from the University of Southern California, and her B.S in Computer Science from Eastern Michigan University in 1998. Her research is in the area of software architecture, software dependability, reliability and security analysis, and software product families. She is author of research papers on software architecture, software reliability, dependability, software product families, as well as software engineering education. She has served on the technical program committee of numerous conferences and workshops such as ICSE, QoSA, ISARCS, WADS, and CSEET and has served as reviewer for ACM Computing Surveys, IEEE TSE, ACM TOSEM, Elsevier's JSS and JIST among others. She has also served as the Program Co-chair for the First and Second International Workshop on the Twin Peaks of Requirements and Architecture. She is a member of ACM and SIGSOFT.

In his work, **Michael Stal** focuses on software architecture, distributed systems, and programming paradigms. Within Siemens he is responsible for coaching mission-critical projects on these topics as well as for education of (senior) software architects. As a professor, he is teaching software architecture at the University of Groningen, where he also obtained his Ph.D. on the use of patterns for analyzing the architecture of distributed systems paradigms. He has been co-author of the book series *Pattern-Oriented Software Architecture*. He is author of many papers on software engineering research and practice as well as speaker, invited speaker, and keynote speaker at many renowned conferences such as ECOOP, OOPSLA, and SPLE. In addition, he served as PC member and conference chair of many conferences such as ECOOP, SATURN, SEACON, and CUC. Michael has been Microsoft MVP for Solution Architecture and C# since 2003, editor-in-chief of the magazine *JavaSPEKTRUM*, and advisory board member of JOT (*Journal of Object Technology*). In a past life he was member of the OMG on behalf of Siemens as well as a member of the ISO/ANSI standardization committee for C++ (X3J16).

# List of Contributors

**Onur Aktuğ**
Aselsan, Ankara, Turkey

**Azadeh Alebrahim**
University of Duisburg-Essen, Essen, Germany

**Nour Ali**
University of Brighton, Brighton, UK

**Paris Avgeriou**
University of Groningen, Groningen, The Netherlands

**Rami Bahsoon**
University of Birmingham, Birmingham, UK

**Vilhelm Bergmann**
Saab Electronic Defense Systems, Gothenburg, Sweden

**Luigi Buglione**
ETS Montréal/Engineering.IT SpA, Rome, Italy

**Rafael Capilla**
Universidad Rey Juan Carlos, Madrid, Spain

**Laura Carvajal**
Universidad Politécnica de Madrid, Madrid, Spain

**Christine Choppy**
University Paris 13 - Sorbonne Paris Cité, LIPN CNRS UMR 7030, Villetaneuse, France

**Maya Daneva**
University of Twente, Enschede, The Netherlands

**Peter Eeles**
IBM Rational, London, UK

**Veli-Pekka Eloranta**
Tampere University of Technology, Tampere, Finland

**Özgü Özköse Erdoğan**
Aselsan, Ankara, Turkey

**Stephan Faßbender**
University of Duisburg-Essen, Essen, Germany

**Matthias Galster**
University of Canterbury, Christchurch, New Zealand

**Martin Große-Rhode**
Fraunhofer Institute for Open Communication Systems, Berlin, Germany

**Jörgen Hansson**
Chalmers University of Technology, Gothenburg, Sweden

**Neil Harrison**
Utah Valley University, Orem, UT, USA

**Maritta Heisel**
University of Duisburg-Essen, Essen, Germany

**Sebastian Herold**
Clausthal University of Technology, Clausthal-Zellerfeld, Germany

**Andrea Herrmann**
Herrmann & Ehrlich, Stuttgart, Germany

**Robert Hilbrich**
Fraunhofer Institute for Open Communication Systems, Berlin, Germany

**Christoffer Höglund**
Saab Electronic Defense Systems, Gothenburg, Sweden

**Christian Kop**
Alpen-Adria-Universität Klagenfurt, Klagenfurt, Austria

**Kai Koskimies**
Tampere University of Technology, Tampere, Finland

**Hui Lin**
Universidad Politécnica de Madrid, Madrid, Spain

**Stefan Mann**
Fraunhofer Institute for Open Communication Systems, Berlin, Germany

**Heinrich C. Mayr**
Alpen-Adria-Universität Klagenfurt, Klagenfurt, Austria

**Wilhelm Meding**
Ericsson AB, Sweden

**Ivan Mistrik**
Independent Consultant, Heidelberg, Germany

**Kent Niesel**
Volvo Car Corporation, Gothenburg, Sweden

**Andreas Rausch**
Clausthal University of Technology, Clausthal-Zellerfeld, Germany

**Roshanak Roshandel**
Seattle University, Seattle, WA, USA

**Vladimir A. Shekhovtsov**
Alpen-Adria-Universität Klagenfurt, Klagenfurt, Austria

**Carlos Solis**
Amazon, Dublin, Ireland

**Michael Stal**
Siemens AG, Munich, Germany and University of Groningen, Groningen, The Netherlands

**Miroslaw Staron**
University of Gothenburg, Gothenburg, Sweden

**Bedir Tekinerdogan**
Bilkent University, Ankara, Turkey

**Uwe van Heesch**
Capgemini, Düsseldorf, Germany

**Stephan Weißleder**
Fraunhofer Institute for Open Communication Systems, Berlin, Germany

**Antoine Widmer**
University of Applied Sciences Western Switzerland, Sierre, Switzerland

**Qian Zhang**
The National University of Defense Technology, Changsha, China

**Yanlong Zhang**
Manchester Metropolitan University, Manchester, UK

**Hong Zhu**
Oxford Brookes University, Oxford, UK

# Foreword by Bill Curtis
## Managing Systems Qualities through Architecture

As I begin writing this foreword, computers at the NASDAQ stock exchange have been crashing all too frequently over the past several weeks. Airline reservation system glitches have grounded airlines numerous times over the past several years. My friends in Great Britain are wondering when their banks will next separate them from their money for days on end. These disruptions account for a tiny fraction of the financial mayhem that poor software quality is inflicting on society. With the software disasters at RBS and Knight Trading running between a quarter and a half billion dollars, software quality is now a boardroom issue.

I hear executives complaining that it takes too long to get new products or business functionality to the market and that it is more important to get it delivered than to thoroughly test it. They tend to temper these opinions when it is their quarter billion dollars that just crashed. Nevertheless, they have a point in the need to deliver new software quickly to keep pace with competitors. We need faster and more thorough ways to evaluate the quality of software before it is delivered. Sometimes speed wins, and sometimes speed kills.

We are pretty good at testing software components and even at testing within layers of software written in the same language or technology platform. That is no longer the challenge. Modern business applications and many products are composed from stacks of technologies. Just because a component passes its unit tests and appears to be well-constructed does not guarantee that it will avoid disastrous interactions that the developer did not anticipate. Many of the worst outages are caused by faulty interactions among components with good structural characteristics. Our problems lie not so much in our components as in our architectures and their interconnections.

The complexity of our systems has now exceeded the capacity of any individual or team to comprehend their totality. Developers may be experts in one or two technologies and languages, but few possess expert knowledge in all the languages and technologies integrated into modern products and systems. Consequently, they make assumptions about how different parts of the system will interact. Generally, their assumptions are correct. However, their incorrect assumptions can create flaws from which small glitches become system outages. All too frequently it is not the small glitch, but the chain of events it instigated that led to disaster.

The challenge of modern software systems brings us ultimately to their architecture. As systems become larger and more complex, their architectures assume ever greater importance in managing their growing integrity and coherence. When architectural integrity is compromised, the probability for serious operational problems increases dramatically. Interactions among layers and subsystems will become increasingly more difficult to understand. The ability to assess unwanted side effects before implementing changes will become more laborious. The making of changes will become more intricate and tedious. Consequently, the verification of functional and structural quality becomes less thorough when speed is the priority. Architectural integrity enables safe speeds to be increased. Architectural disarray makes any speed unsafe.

Maintaining architectural quality across a continuing stream of system enhancements and modifications is critical for at least five reasons. First, it decreases the likelihood of injecting new defects into the system, some of which could be disastrous. Second, it reduces the time required to understand the software, which studies report to be 50% of the effort in making changes. Third, it shortens the time to implement changes because fewer components need to be touched if an optimal coupling-cohesion balance has been sustained. These two points combine to shorten the time it takes to release new products or features.

Fourth, it allows the system to scale, regardless of whether the scaling is driven by new features or increased load. Fifth, it allows the life of a system to be extended. Once the quality of an architecture can be described as "sclerotic," the system becomes a candidate for an expensive overhaul, if not an even more expensive replacement. Given that seriously degraded architectures are extremely hard to analyze, overhauls and replacements are usually fraught with errors and omissions that make you wonder if devil you knew wasn't better than the new devil you created.

Maintaining architectural integrity is not easy. Architectural quality requires investment and discipline. First, system architects must establish a set of architectural principles that guide the original construction and subsequent enhancement of the system. Second, managers must enforce a disciplined change process with specific practices to ensure the architecture does not degrade over time. Third, architects must have access to representations that support modeling and envisioning the architecture to be constructed, as well as undated as-is representations of the architecture throughout the system's lifetime. Fourth, automated tools should be used to analyze the system and provide insight into structural quality issues that are obscure to individual developers. Finally, management must be willing to invest in revising or extending the architecture when new uses or technologies require it. To this latter point, sustainable architectures can be transformed; degraded architectures leave organizations trapped in antiquity.

To meet these requirements for sustainable architectural quality, theoretical computer scientists must continue their exploration of architectural methods, analysis, and measurement. Experimental computer scientists must continue prototyping powerful new tools make these advances available to architects and developers. Empirical computer scientists must continue evaluating how these new concepts and technologies work in practical applications at industrial scale. The editors in this book have undertaken these challenges. While it is tempting to call such work "academic," we are doomed by the complexity of our systems unless at least some of these efforts produce the next generation of architectural technologies. Our thirst for size and complexity is unending. Our search to simplify and manage it must keep pace.

**Dr. Bill Curtis,**
Senior vice president and chief scientist at CAST,
Fort Worth, Texas
September 3, 2013

## ABOUT THE AUTHOR

Dr. Bill Curtis is a senior vice president and chief scientist at CAST. He is best known for leading development of the Capability Maturity Model (CMM), which has become the global standard for evaluating the capability of software development organizations. Prior to joining CAST, Curtis was a cofounder of TeraQuest, the global leader in CMM-based services, which was acquired by Borland. Prior to TeraQuest, he directed the Software Process Program at the Software Engineering Institute (SEI) at Carnegie Mellon University. Prior to the SEI, he directed research on intelligent user interface technology and the software design process at MCC, the fifth generation computer research consortium in Austin, Texas. Before MCC he developed a software productivity and quality measurement system for ITT, managed research on software practices and metrics at GE Space Division, and taught statistics at the University of Washington. Bill holds a Ph.D. from Texas Christian University, an M.A. from the University of Texas, and a B.A. from Eckerd College. He was recently elected a Fellow of the Institute of Electrical and Electronics Engineers for his contributions to software process improvement and measurement.

# Foreword by Richard Mark Soley
## Software Quality Is Still a Problem

Since the dawn of the computing age, software quality has been an issue for developers and end users alike. I have never met a software user—whether mainframe, minicomputer, personal computer, or personal device—who is happy with the level of quality of that device. From requirements definition, to user interface, to likely use case, to errors and failures, software infuriates people every minute of every day.

Worse, software failures have had life-changing effects on people. The well-documented Therac-25 user interface failure literally caused deaths. The initial Ariane-5 rocket launch failure was in software. The Mars Climate Orbiter crash landing was caused by a disagreement between two development teams on measurement units. Banking, trading, and other financial services failures caused by software failures surround us; no one is surprised when systems fail, and the (unfortunately generally correct) assumption is that software was the culprit.

From the point of view of the standardizer and the methodologist, the most difficult thing to accept is the fact that *methodologies for software quality improvement are well known.* From academic perches as disparate as Carnegie Mellon University and Queen's University (Prof. David Parnas) to Eidgenoessische Techniche Hochschule Zürich (Prof. Bertrand Meyer), detailed research and well-written papers have appeared for decades, detailing how to write better-quality software. The Software Engineering Institute, founded some 30 years ago by the United States Department of Defense, has focused precisely on the problem of developing, delivering, and maintaining better software, through the development, implementation, and assessment of software development methodologies (most importantly the Capability Maturity Model and later updates).

Still, trades go awry, distribution networks falter, companies fail, and energy goes undelivered because of software quality issues. Worse, correctable problems such as common security weaknesses (most infamously the *buffer overflow* weakness) are written every day into security-sensitive software.

Perhaps methodology isn't the only answer. It's interesting to note that, in manufacturing fields outside of the software realm, there is the concept of *acceptance of parts.* When Boeing and Airbus build aircraft, they do it with parts built not only by their own internal supply chains, but in great (and increasing) part, by including parts built by others, gathered across international boundaries and composed into large, complex systems. That explains the old saw that aircraft are a million parts, flying in close formation! The reality is that close formation is what keeps us warm and dry, miles above ground; and that close formation comes from parts that fit together well, that work together well, that can be maintained and overhauled together well. And that requires aircraft manufacturers to *test the parts when they arrive in the factory and before they are integrated into the airframe.* Sure, there's a methodology for building better parts—those methodologies even have well-accepted names, like "total quality management," "lean manufacturing," and "Six Sigma." But those methodologies do *not* obviate the need to test parts (at least statistically) when they enter the factory.

## QUALITY TESTING IN SOFTWARE

Unfortunately, that ethos never made it into the software development field. Although you will find regression testing and unit testing, and specialized unit testing tools like JUnit in the Java world, there has never been a widely accepted practice of software part testing based solely on the (automated) examination of software itself. My own background in the software business included a (non-automated) examination phase (the Multics Review Board quality testing requirement for the inclusion of new code into the Honeywell Multics operating system 35 years ago measurably and visibly increased the overall quality of the Multics code base) showed that examination, even human examination, was of value to both development organizations and systems users. The cost, however, was rather high and has only been considered acceptable for systems with very high failure impacts (for example, in the medical and defense fields).

When Boeing and Airbus test parts, they certainly do some hand inspection, but there is far more automated inspection. After all, one can't see *inside* the parts without machines like X-rays and NMR machines, and one can't test metal parts to destruction (to determine tensile strength, for example) without automation. That same automation should and must be applied in testing software—increasing the objectivity of acceptance tests, increasing the likelihood that those tests will be applied (due to lower cost), and eventually increasing the quality of the software itself.

## ENTER AUTOMATED QUALITY TESTING

In late 2009, the Object Management Group (OMG) and the Software Engineering Institute (SEI) came together to create the Consortium for IT Software Quality (CISQ). The two groups realized the need to find another approach to increase software quality, since

- Methodologies to increase software *process* quality (such as CMMI) had had insufficient impact on their own in increasing software quality.
- Software inspection methodologies based on human examination of code is an approach, which tend to be prone to errors, objective, inconsistent, and generally expensive to be widely deployed.
- Existing automated code evaluation systems had no consistent (standardized) set of metrics, resulting in inconsistent results and very limited adoption in the marketplace.

The need for the software development industry to develop and widely adopt automated quality tests was absolutely obvious, and the Consortium immediately set upon a process (based on OMG's broad and deep experience in standardization and SEI's broad and deep experience in assessment) to define automatable software quality standard metrics.

## WHITHER AUTOMATIC SOFTWARE QUALITY EVALUATION?

The first standard that CISQ was able to bring through the OMG process, arriving at the end of 2012, featured a standard, consistent, reliable, and accurate complexity metric for code, in essence an update to the Function Point concept. First defined in 1979, there were five ISO standards for counting function points by 2012, none of which was absolutely reliable and repeatable; that is, individual (human) function counters could come up with different results when counting the same piece of software twice! CISQ's Automatic Function Point (AFP) standard features a fully automatable standard that has absolutely consistent results from one run to the next.

That doesn't sound like much of an accomplishment, until one realizes that one can't compute a defect, error, or other size-dependent metric without an agreed sizing strategy. AFP provides that strategy, and in a consistent, standardized fashion that can be fully automated, making it inexpensive and repeatable.

In particular, how can one measure the quality of a software *architecture* without a baseline, without a complexity metric? AFP provides that baseline, and further quality metrics under development by CISQ and expected to be standardized this year, provide the yardstick against which to measure software, again in a fully automatable fashion.

Is it simply lines-of-code that are being measured, or in fact entire software designs? Quality is in fact inextricably connected to architecture in several places; not only can poor software coding or modeling quality lead to poor usability and fit-for-purpose; but poor software *architecture* can lead to a deep mismatch with the requirements that led to the development of the system in the first place.

## ARCHITECTURE INTERTWINED WITH QUALITY

Clearly software quality—in fact, system quality in general—is a fractal concept. Requirements can poorly quantify the needs of a software system; architectures and other artifacts can poorly outline the analysis and design against those requirements; implementation via coding or modeling can poorly execute the design artifacts; testing can poorly exercise an implementation; and even quotidian use can incorrectly take advantage of a well-implemented, well-tested design. Clearly, quality testing must take into account design artifacts as well as those of implementation.

Fortunately, architectural quality methodologies (and indeed quality metrics across the landscape of software development) are active areas of research, with promising approaches. Given my own predilections and the technical focus of OMG over the past 16 years, clearly modeling (of requirements, of design, of analysis, of implementation, and certainly of architecture) must be at the fore, and model- and rule-based approaches to measuring architectures are featured here. But the tome you are holding also includes a wealth of current research and understanding from measuring requirements design against customer needs to usability testing of completed systems. If the software industry—and that's every industry these days—is going to increase not only the underlying but also the perceived level of software quality for our customers, we are going to have to address quality at all levels, and an architectural, holistic view is the only way we'll get there.

**Richard Mark Soley, Ph.D.**
Chairman and Chief Executive Officer, Object Management Group
Lexington, Massachusetts, U.S.A.
30 August 2013

## ABOUT THE AUTHOR

Dr. Richard Mark Soley is Chairman and Chief Executive Officer of OMG ®. As Chairman and CEO of OMG, Dr. Soley is responsible for the vision and direction of the world's largest consortium of its type. Dr. Soley joined the nascentOMG as Technical Director in 1989, leading the development of OMG's world-leading standardization process and the original CORBA ® specification. In 1996, he led the effort to move into vertical market standards (starting with healthcare, finance, telecommunications, and manufacturing) and modeling, leading first to the Unified Modeling Language TM (UML®) and later the Model Driven Architecture (MDA®). He also led the effort to establish the SOA Consortium in January 2007, leading to the launch of the Business Ecology Initiative (BEI) in 2009. The Initiative focuses on the management imperative to make business more responsive, effective, sustainable, and secure in a complex, networked world through practice areas including Business Design, Business Process Excellence, Intelligent Business, Sustainable Business, and Secure Business. In addition, Dr. Soley is the Executive Director of the Cloud Standards Customer Council, helping end users transition to cloud computing and direct requirements and priorities for cloud standards throughout the industry.

Dr. Soley also serves on numerous industrial, technical, and academic conference program committees and speaks all over the world on issues relevant to standards, the adoption of new technology, and creating successful companies. He is an active angel investor and was involved in the creation of both the Eclipse Foundation and Open Health Tools.

Previously, Dr. Soley was a cofounder and former Chairman/CEO of A. I. Architects, Inc., maker of the 386 HummingBoard and other PC and workstation hardware and software. Prior to that, he consulted for various technology companies and venture firms on matters pertaining to software investment opportunities. Dr. Soley has also consulted for IBM, Motorola, PictureTel, Texas Instruments, Gold Hill Computer, and others. He began his professional life at Honeywell Computer Systems working on the Multics operating system.

A native of Baltimore, Maryland, U.S.A., Dr. Soley holds bachelor, master's, and doctoral degrees in Computer Science and Engineering from the Massachusetts Institute of Technology.

# Preface

Software architecture is the earliest design artifact that realizes the requirements of the software system. It is the manifestation of the earliest design decisions, which comprise the architectural structure (i.e., components and interfaces), the architectural topology (i.e., the architectural style), the architectural infrastructure (e.g., the middleware), the relationship among them, and their relation to other software artifacts (e.g., detailed design and implementation) and the environment. As an earliest design artifact, a software architecture realizes the *qualities* of the software system such as security, reliability, availability, scalability, and real-time performance. The architecture can also guide the evolution of these qualities over time, as stand-alone product or across a family of products. Those properties, whether structural or behavioral, can have global impact on the software system. Poor realization and architecting for qualities may "regress" the software system, threating its trustworthiness and slowing down its evolution. Quality is the degree to which a software product lives up to the modifiability, durability, interoperability, portability, security, predictability, scalability, and other attributes. These qualities translate stakeholders' expectations when procuring, using, maintaining, and evolving, or even "transacting" a software system. The realization of these qualities in the architecture and the software product has significant impact on users' satisfaction, value creation, sustainability, and durability of the software. They also determine the extent to which it can meet its business and strategic objectives. Realizing qualities in the architecture and engineering for qualities in a software product are therefore interlinked, intertwined, and interleaved activities cross-cutting technical, structural, behavioral, environmental, and business concerns.

As the field of software architecture enters its third decade of formal study, it finds itself moving from its traditional and foundational focus on the nature of an architecture in terms of its structure and behavior to the more general notion of software architecture as the set of design decisions made to ensure the software requirements will be met. Consistent with this view is the trend toward focusing software architecture documentation on meeting stakeholder needs and communicating how the software solution addresses their concerns and the business objectives. Often, a software system is not isolated, but a part of a larger system. When making decisions, not only is the quality of the software architecture itself important, but a consideration of the overall quality of the system is warranted. For example, quality attributes such as performance and reliability can only be realized through a combination of software, hardware, and the operating environment (and, if relevant to the system, people).

Quality concerns describe system-level attributes such as reliability, testability, usability, modifiability, performance, security, maintainability, and portability. In conjunction with functional requirements, these quality concerns drive and constrain a system's architectural design and often introduce significant trade-offs that must be considered and balanced.

The goal of this book is to expand the quality aspects of software architecture, focusing broadly on quality-related characteristics and how these relate to the design of software architectures. In addition to architectural qualities (conceptual integrity, correctness, and completeness), we are including three additional directions that distinguish our book from "classical" (however excellent) publications on quality of software architectures:

1. We are including Business Qualities (e.g., product lifetime, time to market, roll-out schedule, integration, cost, and benefit) as well as enterprise aspects such as Business Goals, Return on

Investment, Economics, and Value Creation, to ensure a comprehensive consideration of quality, thereby supporting the concept of "total quality management."

**2.** We are also including System Quality Attributes (those properties of a system that do not directly relate to the functionality of that system, e.g., modifiability, usability, security, availability, testability, performance) and Nonfunctional Requirements (specific, measurable properties of a system that relate to a quality attribute) in relation to software architecture. Their consideration ensures that the resulting software product addresses these quality attributes, which are strongly influenced by the architecture of the software.

**3.** From the perspective of technology platforms, we are including recent interest in "disruptive" technologies and approaches. In particular, we are including cloud, mobile, and ultra-large-scale/Internet-scale architecture as an application focus of this book.

In particular, this book addresses the key elements of System Quality and identifies current challenges in relating System Quality and Software Architecture:

– System Quality Attributes

Software quality, by definition, is the degree to which software possesses a desired combination of attributes [IEEE 19921]. To improve system quality, we pay attention to system quality attributes, such as usability, maintainability, flexibility, reliability, reusability, agility, interoperability, performance, scalability, security, testability, and supportability.

– Defining Quality Requirements

An oft-cited reason for failed software projects is incomplete and/or unclear requirements. This is especially true of nonfunctional requirements and quality requirements in particular. Our focus is on techniques for defining quality requirements. taxonomies of quality attributes. stakeholder interaction when gathering quality requirements. and approaches for prioritizing requirements.

– Addressing System Qualities

The following issues have been identified in addressing system qualities:
system patterns that improve quality: This encompasses tactics for meeting specific quality requirements; system anti-patterns that degrade quality; the tradeoffs necessary when addressing quality requirements (the classic case being a tradeoff between system performance and system flexibility); and different project lifecycles and how they contribute to ensuring that quality attributes are met. Waterfall, iterative, agile, and disciplined agile are examples of project lifecycles.

– Assessing System Qualities

Based on assumptions listed above of how to implement system quality, we are defining the metrics relating to system quality and how these are monitored and tracked throughout the software-development life cycle. The purpose of using metrics is to reduce subjectivity during monitoring activities and provide quantitative data for analysis. We are focusing on approaches for assessing different quality attributes and metrics relevant to an assessment of quality attributes. The IEEE Software Quality Metrics Methodology [IEEE 1992] is a framework for defining and monitoring system-quality metrics and analysis of measurements gathered through the implementation of metrics.

– Current Challenges

Over the past decade many different opinions and viewpoints have been expressed on the terms "quality of software architecture," "software quality," and "system quality." However, no clear consensus has yet emerged. Fundamental questions remain open to debate: how to align software specifications with quality and business goals; what impact the organization developing the software, architectural design decisions, and development processes has on software quality; what interdependencies software quality attributes have among each other; what the exact relationships are between quality of software architecture, software quality, and system quality; what extrinsic relations such as the increase of one property (e.g., performance) diminishing another property (e.g., maintainability) are; what intrinsic interdependencies are, because many quality attributes depend per definition on other quality attributes (e.g., reliability depends on the system's timing behavior in real-time systems); what additional factors (besides architectural design) are that influence software quality attributes; what impact organizational issues (e.g., team structuring and individual software development processes) have as well as implications of the software development process (e.g., quality assurance measures like reviews and the deployment of agile methods) for software quality; how to balance different quality attributes of a system so that they are best aligned to delivering business value for the organization; how to foster the exchange between several areas of research which have been historically divided into different communities (e.g., performance engineering, software reliability, software metrics); and how to assure the alignment of quality and business IT during the entire software development process.

This book provides a collection of perspectives marking one of the first detailed discussions on the theme of relating system quality, software quality, and software architecture. Through these viewpoints we gain significant insight into the challenges of relating system quality and software architecture from experienced software architects, distinguished academics, and leading industry commentators.

We have organized this book into three major sections, with an introductory editorial chapter providing an introduction to the topic of relating system quality and software architecture.

- **Part 1: Human-centric Evaluation for System Qualities and Software Architecture** explores several of the most basic issues surrounding the task of quality software delivery and the role of stakeholder's goals.
- **Part 2: Analysis, Monitoring, and Control of Software Architecture for System Qualities** considers how core architectural ideas impact other areas of quality software delivery such as knowledge management and continuous system delivery.
- **Part 3: Domain-specific Software Architecture and Software Qualities** offers deeper insight into how quality software architecture issues affect specific solution domains.

As we summarize below, each of the chapters of this book will provide you with interesting and important insights into a key aspect of relating system quality and software architecture. However, more importantly, the comprehensive nature of this book provides us with the opportunity to take stock of how the emergence of quality software delivery practices change our understanding of the critical task of architecting enterprise-scale software systems.

## PART 1: HUMAN-CENTRIC EVALUATION FOR SYSTEM QUALITIES AND SOFTWARE ARCHITECTURE

Software architecture not only embodies important design decisions about software systems, but also plays a critical role in facilitating communication among stakeholders. While the impact of these design decisions on system quality has been subject of much investigation, it is important to study the role of human stakeholders in evaluating and interpreting architectural design decisions. Over the past few years, specific emphasis on capturing design decisions for different stakeholders has driven much of the research in this area. This part includes three chapters that reflect on the role of stakeholders in capturing and evaluating system quality as it relates to software architecture. The key objectives of these chapters include:

- Studying how different quality-related design decisions are perceived by different stakeholders.
- Focusing on stakeholder perspectives when ensuring the consistency among different views and optimizing functional and quality requirements.

Chapter 2 reports on a study that assesses the perception of software engineers about Attribute Driven Development (ADD) method. Specifically, the authors have focused on the stakeholders' perception related to the usefulness, ease of use, and willingness to use the ADD method. Chapter 3 motivates the need to harmonize different stakeholders' views on software quality and present a conceptualized reference framework for the harmonization. Chapter 4 presents a methodology to obtain an optimal set of requirements that contain no conflicts and satisfy stakeholders' goals and quality requirements.

The Attribute Driven Design (ADD) method provides steps for designing software architecture for satisfying quality attributes. This method has not been explored in terms of users' perception on its usefulness and ease of use. The goal is to study the perceptions that software engineers with no or little experience industrially in designing software architecture using the ADD. In Chapter 2, Nour Ali and Carlos Solis describe an empirical study that they conducted on master students to measure their perceptions of the ADD after using it. Authors of this chapter performed two experiments: one with students enrolled in the Software Architecture module in 2010 and the second with the students of the same module in 2011. The main findings are that the subjects perceive the ADD method as useful and that there is a relationship between its usefulness and willingness of use. However, the subjects' opinion was that they did not agree that the ADD method is easy to use. They also discuss several problems that the subjects faced when using ADD.

Chapter 3 by Vladimir A. Shekhovtsov, Heinrich C. Mayr, and Christian Kop summarizes the related state-of-the-art and presents a conceptualization of the process of harmonizing the views on quality possessed by the different sides of the software process. These concepts are based on applying the empirical techniques to the qualitative data obtained from relevant IT companies and are grounded in the set of basic concepts provided by the Unified Foundational Ontology. In particular, the chapter deals with and conceptualizes the following dimensions: the software quality itself and the related aspects as well as their interrelations, in particular, the notion of quality assessment and the concepts utilized in the quality assessment activities; the knowledge about the various stakeholders and the differences in their perception of quality; the knowledge about the activities of the harmonization process and the capabilities of the process participants needed for performing these activities. The proposed conceptualizations could be used as a reference framework for the particular applications in the domain of harmonizing the views on quality; the conceptual models utilized by these tools could be based on these concepts to achieve higher degree of reuse and semantic interoperability.

High-quality software has to consider various quality issues and different stakeholders' goals. Such diverse requirements may be conflicting, and the conflicts may not be visible at first sight. Moreover, the sheer number of stakeholders and requirements for a software system make it difficult to select a set of requirements sufficient to meet the initial goals. In Chapter 4, Azadeh Alebrahim, Christine Choppy, Stephan Faßbender, and Maritta Heisel propose a method for obtaining an optimal set of requirements that contains no conflicts and satisfies the stakeholders' goals and quality requirements to the largest possible extent. At first, they capture the stakeholders' goals and then analyze functional and quality requirements using an extension of the problem frame approach. Afterward, they determine candidates for requirements interaction and derive alternatives in a systematic way. Then they assign values to the different requirements using the Analytic Network Process. Finally, they obtain an optimal set of requirements not containing any conflicting requirements. The authors illustrate their method with the real-life example of smart metering.

## PART 2: ANALYSIS, MONITORING, AND CONTROL OF SOFTWARE ARCHITECTURE FOR SYSTEM QUALITIES

As the earliest design artifact, a software architecture realizes the qualities of the software system such as security, reliability, availability, scalability, and real-time performance and manages their evolution over time. Those properties have a global impact on the software system, where any change in users' requirements or operating environment may "regress" these qualities, threatening system trustworthiness and slowing down its evolution.

Current research and practice pursue software architectures as the appropriate level of abstraction for evaluating, reasoning about, and managing change and evolution of qualities and their trade-offs in complex software systems. An architecture-based approach for analyzing, reasoning about, and monitoring a system's qualities is believed to offer the potential benefits of generality (i.e., the underlying concepts and principles are applicable to a wide range of application domains), appropriate level of abstraction to tackle the complexity (i.e., software architecture can provide the appropriate level of abstraction in describing dynamic changes as opposed to algorithmic level), potential for scalability (i.e., facilitating the use in large-scale complex applications), and providing opportunities to facilitate automated analyses benefiting from Architecture Description Languages analyses (ADLs).

Research into analysis, monitoring, and control of software architectures for qualities and their trade-offs has taken two forms: (A) static analysis, where a number of analysis techniques and ADLs have been proposed for modeling and analysis of architectures both within a particular domain and as general-purpose architecture modeling languages. Modeling has primarily been intended to analyze qualities concerned with large, distributed, and concurrent systems. Analysis of architectural qualities upstream, at the architectural level, can substantially lessen the costs of any errors and promote proactivity when designing for dependability. The usefulness of these techniques and ADLs has been directly related to the kind of analyses they tend to support. The ultimate goal is to establish confidence in systems qualities through various means. Examples include analysis of connectors for deadlocks; schedulability analysis for criticality and priority; relative correctness of architectures with respect to a refinement map; use of critics to establish adherence to style rules and design guidelines; enforcement of constraints implicit in types, nonfunctional attributes, component and connector interfaces, and semantic models, etc. Static analysis verifies that all possible executions of the architecture description conform to the specification. Such analyses help the developers to understand the changes that need to be made to satisfy the analyzed properties and to appraise the architecture for meeting its qualities. They span approaches such as reachability analysis, symbolic model checking, flow equations, and data-flow analysis. Dynamic analysis and monitoring for quality, where work has focused on the principles and foundations for enriching the architecture with primitives that can monitor, analyze, plan, and execute decisions that react to feedback loops, emerging from the system and its environment. The ultimate objective has been treating qualities as a moving target and maintaining them through runtime monitors and control. The influx of work on self-* including self-awareness, self-configuration, self-optimization, self-healing, self-protecting, and self-adaptive architectures in specific has advanced our understanding to means of achieving qualities at runtime. Rainbow project of SEI and the Autonomic Manager of IBM are classic examples.

The chapters in this part provide new perspectives and a set of practices and principles for analysis, monitoring, and control of software architecture for qualities.

Chapter 5 by Hong Zhu, Quian Zhang, and Yanlong Zhang proposes a model-based approach called HASARD for the analysis of software quality based on architectural designs. The name HASARD stands for *Hazard Analysis of Software Architectural Designs*. It adapts the HAZOP hazard identification technique and applies it to software architectural designs to systematically discover the potential quality issues. The identified hazards are then transformed into a graphic quality model to represent how quality attributes and quality carrying properties relate to each other in the particular system. A number of algorithms are developed to analyze the critical design decisions with respect to certain quality concerns, the impacts of a design decision to various quality attributes, the factors that influence a quality attributes, and the trade-off points between a number of contradiction quality properties. The chapter also presents a tool called SQUARE that supports the whole HASARD quality modeling and analysis process and implements the quality analysis algorithms. Finally, the chapter reports a case study with a real e-commerce software system to demonstrate the applicability of the method to real systems.

Software architecture provides the foundation upon which the most important qualities of a software product can be achieved. Thus, it is crucial to evaluate software architecture in the early stages of the software design to avoid expensive rework during later stages. Unfortunately, architecture evaluation methods rarely support the iterative and incremental nature of agile software development methods. A software architecture can be considered as a set of design decisions that are made incrementally as the architect gradually analyzes the problem and solution spaces. To enable the evaluation of the architecture during this process, an evaluation method should support incremental assessment of the design decisions, rather than the architecture as a whole. Furthermore, during development, some of the decisions may become invalid or deprecated; thus, decisions should be revisited and re-evaluated at certain periods. In Chapter 6, Veli-Pekka Eloranta, Uwe van Heesch, Kai Koskimies, Paris Avgeriou, and Neil Harrison present the Decision-Centric Architecture Review method (DCAR). DCAR uses architecture decisions as first-class entities to carry out lightweight, incremental, and iterative architecture evaluations. Additionally, this chapter describes how DCAR can be integrated in the Scrum framework.

The process of divergence between intended software architecture and its actual implementation, often called *architecture erosion* or *architectural drifts*, can have negative effects on the overall quality of the system. It is hence very important to check regularly whether the realization of a system conforms to its intended architecture. Checking architectural conformance and consistency is a difficult task because many types of artifacts can be affected by constraints that software architecture defines. Moreover, the broad range of sources for such constraints, which we call *architectural rules*, makes it difficult to provide flexible tool support. In Chapter 7, Sebastian Herold and Andreas Rausch describe an approach to flexible architecture conformance checking based on a formalization of architectural rules as logical formulas. The artifacts manifesting the intended software architecture and the realization of a software system are represented as knowledge base of logical knowledge representation and reasoning system that is utilized to check the validity of the required architectural rules. The approach is implemented prototypically and has been successfully applied in several case studies.

In Chapter 8, Miroslaw Staron, Wilhelm Meding, Jörgen Hansson, Christoffer Höglund, Kents Niesel, and Vilhelm Bergmann address the challenges of continuously monitoring of internal and external quality of products under development in modern large-scale software development. The challenges are related to the fact that modern software development utilizes the concepts of distributed, self-organized teams and decentralized responsibility for the product. The chapter introduces the concepts relevant for continuous measurement, elements of successful measurement systems, examples of how to visualize the measures, and a case study of three companies that successfully realized these concepts—Ericsson, Volvo Car Corporation, and Saab Electronic Defense Systems. The case study is concluded by a set of guidelines for other companies willing to follow Ericsson, Volvo Car Corporation, and Saab Electronic Defense Systems—for example, how to assess information quality and how to identify implicit architectural dependencies.

## PART 3: DOMAIN-SPECIFIC SOFTWARE ARCHITECTURE AND SOFTWARE QUALITIES

In commercial development projects, software architects face various challenges regarding technology and cost constraints. Stringent quality expectations of customers need to be balanced with cost/benefit aspects. The difficulty in dealing with such aspects is mainly caused by strategic requirements such as reliability, usability, safety, or real-time behavior, which tend to introduce many sensitivity and trade-off points. Hence, strategic quality attributes have a huge impact on sustainability and maintainability of a system. In addition, software and system engineers mostly address cost reduction through tactical qualities like reusability and modifiability. Getting modifiability and reusability right is hard, but achieving the combination of technical and business goals is even harder.

This particularly holds for industrial and enterprise domains where software development comprises only one constituent among other disciplines such as mechatronics or electronics. Consider, for example, medical imaging devices, automation, automotive applications, or railway control systems. When architects design such large-scale systems, application integration and system integration increase complexity and costs significantly. Desired capabilities such as connecting mobile and embedded devices in enterprise systems cause additional quality challenges.

Part 3 contains five chapters looking at addressing strategic and tactical qualities in different domains. The chapters in this section present perspectives how to ensure developmental qualities such as configurability and systematic reuse in product lines, as well as how to deal with operational quality in mobile systems and medical systems. The last chapter extracts experiences from real-world projects that reveal how software architects have addressed quality requirements and software architecture in practice.

Customers of products that include or are determined by software nowadays expect the product to be individually configurable. At the same time, high quality and short delivery times are expected. As a consequence, the producer of the software must be able to develop systems that can be easily configured according to the customers' needs in such a way that each individually configured system satisfies all quality requirements. Especially in the case of high numbers of possible configurations, it is obvious that it is not feasible to construct all system configurations and check the properties of each of them. Rather, there must be means to assure quality generically, which means once and for all configurations at the same time. Chapter 9 by Martin Große-Rhode, Robert Hilbrich, Stefan Mann, and Stephan Weißleder considers software product line engineering as the base technology for how to construct configurable systems and adds generic quality assurance means to this process. The mechanism can be understood as a general pattern describing how to carry over quality assurance techniques to configurable systems. This is done for two concrete techniques in the chapter: model-based testing as technique for the assurance of functional quality and model-based deployment as a technique for the assurance of real-time properties like responsiveness, availability, and reliability. The techniques are demonstrated on the example of a configurable flight management system as used in modern airplanes.

The increased size and complexity of software systems has led to the notion of multiple software product lines (MPL) in which products are composed from sub-products in separate software product lines. Thus it is important to identify the proper architectural decomposition of the MPL with respect to the stakeholders' concerns before large organizational resources are committed to the development. Designing MPL architectures is challenging due to the higher level of abstraction and the integration of different product lines. Different architecture analysis approaches have been introduced, but none of these focuses on the evaluation of multiple product line architectures. In Chapter 10, Bedir Tekinerdogan, Özgü Özköse Erdogan, and Onur Aktug propose the architecture analysis approach for multiple product line engineering, Archample, which has been particularly defined for the analysis of multiple product line architectures. Archample also introduces architectural viewpoints for modeling and documenting multiple product lines and likewise supporting the analysis of the decomposition of a multiple product line architecture. The approach has been designed and validated within a real industrial context of Aselsan REHİS Group (Aselsan REHİS), a leading high technology company in defense systems development in Turkey.

In Chapter 11, Matthias Galster and Antoine Widmer think that medical planning and simulation systems integrate resource-consuming computations (e.g., simulations of human tissue) and advanced interaction techniques (e.g., haptic devices and stereoscopic displays). Developing such systems is challenging and usually a specialized, time-consuming, and expensive activity. Achieving high quality for these systems is essential because such systems are often critical to human health and life. Throughout their experience with developing research and commercial medical planning and simulation systems over several years, they found that these systems impose specific constraints on "quality." Therefore, they elaborate on how quality attributes of medical planning and simulation systems are exhibited in the architecture and the architecting process for those systems and how we may achieve those quality attributes. In particular, their chapter (a) explores challenges related to quality attributes in the development of medical planning and simulation systems, (b) proposes a set of quality attributes that should be addressed in the software architecture of such systems, and (c) discusses some potential strategies on how to handle these quality attributes at the architecture stage.

Chapter 12 by Rafael Capilla, Laura Carvajal, and Hui Lin highlights the role of usability requirements in software architecture, and in particular how important usability concerns are addressed in the architecture of mobile software applications. Because mobile software demands stringent quality requirements, many times quality concerns are not properly addressed in the design, and usability is only described at the code level. Therefore, software designers cannot estimate properly the impact in the design of the usability mechanisms introduced in the system. Consequently, this chapter describes first which usability mechanisms are key for mobile software, and second, it guides software designers to determine the generic and concrete architectural responsibilities of such usability mechanisms including which classes describe the functionality pertaining to each mechanism. As a result, the software architect can use the concrete responsibilities of any usability mechanism such as the ones shown in this chapter to adapt and integrate them in any particular architecture of a mobile application, identifying which classes are necessary to support the functionality of the usability mechanism used and estimating the design effort to introduce or modify one or several usability mechanisms before implementation.

Chapter 13 by Maya Daneva, Andrea Herrmann, and Luigi Buglione describes the involvement of software architects in the process of engineering quality requirements in large contract-based system delivery projects. It also seeks to understand how architects viewed their work in relation to other project stakeholders involved in quality requirements engineering. The chapter presents findings from an exploratory study based on interviews with 21 software architects from European project organizations. Special attention is paid to the roles that these architects played in quality requirements' activities; their interactions with other project roles; the ways in which the architects coped with elicitation, documentation, prioritization, quantification, negotiation, and validation of quality requirements; and the role of the contract in orchestrating the quality requirements engineering activities and in encouraging the architects to do what they did. Some interesting findings that emerged from the research in contract-based project contexts include (1) the notion of the contract as a vehicle for reinforcing the cost-consciousness of software architects when reasoning about quality requirements, (2) the notion of the project business cases as the key driver for making quality requirements trade-offs, and (3) the notion of quality requirements validation as a socially constructed process and not merely a technical tool-based one.

**Ivan Mistrik**
**Rami Bahsoon**
**Peter Eeles**
**Roshanak Roshandel**
**Michael Stal**

# Relating System Quality and Software Architecture

## Foundations and Approaches

**Peter Eeles[1], Rami Bahsoon[2], Ivan Mistrik[3], Roshanak Roshandel[4], and Michael Stal[5,6]**

[1]*IBM Rational, London, UK*
[2]*University of Birmingham, Birmingham, UK*
[3]*Independent Consultant, Heidelberg, Germany*
[4]*Seattle University, Seattle, WA, USA*
[5]*Siemens AG, Munich, Germany*
[6]*University of Groningen, Groningen, The Netherlands*

## INTRODUCTION

In this section, we set the stage for the ensuing discussion and define some of the most important terminology used in this book.

## Quality

Quality is a fundamental property of software systems and generally refers to the degree to which a software system lives up to the expectation of satisfying its requirements. Quality is often characterized in terms of attributes such as modifiability, durability, interoperability, portability, security, predictability, scalability, and so on. Some of these properties are software properties while others are system properties.

Despite a focus on software, IEEE Std 1061 (the IEEE Standard for a Software Quality Metrics Methodology) provides a definition of quality and also a useful distinction between quality and quality attributes (QAs) (such as performance, usability, and maintainability):

> *Software quality is the degree to which software possesses a desired combination of attributes (IEEE Computer Society, 1998).*

## Architecture

There is no shortage of definitions when it comes to architecture. The definition used in this book is that taken from IEEE 1471-2000, IEEE Recommended Practice for Architectural Description of Software-Intensive Systems (IEEE 1471-2000), which has since evolved into an ISO standard (ISO/IEC/IEEE 42010, 2010):

> *[An architecture is] the fundamental organization of a system embodied in its components, their relationships to each other, and to the environment, and the principles guiding its design and evolution (IEEE Computer Society, 2000).*

## System

The IEEE 1471-2000 standard also defines the term *system*:

> *[A system is] a collection of components organized to accomplish a specific function or set of functions. The term* system *encompasses individual applications, systems in the traditional sense, subsystems, systems of systems, product lines, product families, whole enterprises, and other aggregations of interest. A system exists to fulfill one or more missions in its environment (IEEE Computer Society, 2000).*

## Architectural scope

The concept of architecture is prevalent in many disciplines, but perhaps is best known in civil and structural engineering and building architecture. Even in the field of software engineering, we often come across different forms of architecture. For example, in addition to the concept of software architecture, we may encounter notions such as enterprise architecture, system architecture, information architecture, hardware architecture, application architecture, infrastructure architecture, data architecture, and so on. Each of these terms defines a specific scope of the architecting activities within the software domain.

Unfortunately, there is no agreement in the industry on the meaning of all of these terms. However, the scope of some of these terms, as used in this book, can be inferred from Figure 1.1, where we place a focus on the architecture of software-intensive systems (those in which software is an indispensable element). In particular, it should be noted that a system (even a software-intensive system) is comprised not only of software but also of hardware (that the software executes upon), information (that the software manipulates), and workers (that represent any humans that are considered to be part of the system—such as a pilot in an aircraft).

## System quality and software quality

A particular focus of this book is on system quality, which is related to, but distinct from, software quality. Consequently, high-quality systems rely on high-quality software. Certain QAs, such as code portability, are confined to software. Other QAs, such as performance and reliability, are realized through a combination of software, hardware, and (possibly) human interactions. Yet other QAs, such as safety, are exclusively a system property because they can only be measured by considering the system as a whole.

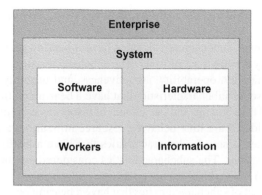

**FIGURE 1.1**

Relating the scope of various types of architectures.

As implied earlier, architectural design decisions directly impact software system quality. These design decisions further influence system deployment (onto hardware resources), as well as the human interactions with the system. High-quality software deployed and executed on poor quality or under-specified hardware cannot operate satisfactorily. At the same time, high-quality hardware cannot always compensate for poorly designed and implemented software. Given the complexity, scale, and heterogeneity of today's software systems, it is imperative to study, design, and develop approaches, tools, and techniques that intentionally study the relationships and trade-offs between design choices that influence both software and system quality.

## 1.1 QUALITY ATTRIBUTES

Given that quality is the manifestation of the exhibited QAs, it makes sense for us to have a thorough understanding of which specific attributes are being considered. Fortunately, there are several existing frameworks that can assist in this regard. Such frameworks, for example, provide a useful checklist that can be used when gathering stakeholder requests or when reviewing requirements.

The international standard ISO/IEC 9126, Software engineering—Product quality (ISO/IEC 9126-1, 2001), classifies software quality within a taxonomy of characteristics and subcharacteristics. The characteristics considered are functionality, reliability, usability, efficiency, maintainability, and portability. Each of these characteristics is further subdivided into subcharacteristics that themselves are subdivided into QAs that can be measured and verified.

- **Functionality** considers a set of subcharacteristics that have a bearing on the function of the system in addressing the needs of stakeholders. The subcharacteristics considered are suitability, accuracy, interoperability, security, and functionality compliance.
- **Reliability** considers a set of subcharacteristics that have a bearing on the ability of the software to maintain its level of performance under stated conditions for a stated period of time.

The subcharacteristics considered are maturity, fault tolerance, recoverability, and reliability compliance.

- **Usability** considers a set of subcharacteristics that have a bearing on the ease with which the software can be used by a known set of users. The subcharacteristics considered are understandability, learnability, operability, attractiveness, and usability compliance.
- **Efficiency** considers a set of subcharacteristics that have a bearing on the relationship between the level of performance of the software and the amount of resources used under given conditions. The subcharacteristics considered are time behavior, resource utilization, and efficiency compliance.
- **Maintainability** considers a set of subcharacteristics that have a bearing on the effort needed to make specified modifications. The subcharacteristics considered are analyzability, changeability, stability, testability, and maintainability compliance.
- **Portability** considers a set of subcharacteristics that have a bearing on the potential for the software to be moved from one environment to another. The subcharacteristics considered are adaptability, installability, coexistence, replaceability, and portability compliance.

Another framework is the "FURPS+" classification (Grady, 1992), where the FURPS acronym stands for "functionality, usability, reliability, performance, and supportability" and the "+" represents any additional considerations that the system must accommodate. The subcharacteristics are taken from Eeles and Cripps (2008).

- **Functionality** considers the functions that the system should exhibit when used under defined conditions. Functionality is often specific to the system under consideration, is based on the specific needs of the end users and other stakeholders, and varies from system to system. However, there are functional requirements that are commonly found among systems. This includes a consideration of feature set, capabilities, generality, and security.
- **Usability** considers the degree to which the system is understood and used. This includes a consideration of human factors, esthetics, consistency, and documentation.
- **Reliability** considers the degree to which the system provides a defined level of operational performance. This includes a consideration of frequency/severity of failure, recoverability, predictability, accuracy, and mean time to failure.
- **Performance** considers the degree to which the system provides a defined level of execution performance. This includes a consideration of speed, efficiency, resource consumption, throughput, and response time.
- **Supportability** considers the degree to which the system can be supported. This includes a consideration of testability, extensibility, adaptability, maintainability, compatibility, configurability, serviceability, installability, and localizability.
- The "+" category is rather open-ended but, in practice (Eeles and Cripps, 2008), is often used to capture additional constraints that must be considered. This includes a consideration of business constraints such as compliance, cost, and schedule; architecture constraints such as those that constrain the mechanisms used in the solution, such as a mechanism for storing persistent data; development constraints such as the implementation languages to be used; and physical constraints such as size and weight (which might be relevant when producing a mobile phone, for example).

The previous example of considering physical constraints is most definitely touching on systems thinking and, therefore, the emphasis on system QAs and not simply software QAs. Taking this view further, a consideration of nontechnical system QAs such as alignment with business goals, return-on-investment, as well as recent technology innovations considerations such as cloud, mobile, social, ultra-large scale, and big data that are relevant to the system as a whole, is also beneficial. We anticipate further research on such topics in both industry and academia.

It should also be noted that some QAs are appropriate to particular solution domains. For example, in a regulated environment, such as in the financial services sector and pharmaceuticals, the ability for the system to support auditability in terms of its execution is, clearly, a measure of the quality of the system.

## 1.2 STATE OF THE PRACTICE

A significant bearing on the success (or failure) of any development initiative is not simply being aware of the various relevant QAs and accordingly managing them. The approach taken to producing the solution takes a fundamental role in this regard. This section considers some of the key factors of this approach.

### 1.2.1 Lifecycle approaches

A consideration of QAs through the lifecycle of a project varies with the specific approach applied. This section touches on a number of lifecycle approaches, discusses their pros and cons, and focuses on their relevance in terms of achieving the specified QAs.

#### 1.2.1.1 Waterfall

A traditional waterfall development process is shown in Figure 1.2. In this approach, each discipline is deemed to be complete when all of the appropriate work products for that discipline have been created and signed off. For example, the requirements discipline may be considered complete when all of the requirements have been identified, defined in detail, and reviewed. The output from requirements then "flows" into the architecture discipline. This process continues until the system has been designed in detail, coded, tested, and made available to its end users. Changes to earlier work products (shown with the backward-pointing arrows) are typically handled through a formal change process. Development may therefore return to a previous process step in order to redo work products when the current step has revealed problems with the work products provided as input.

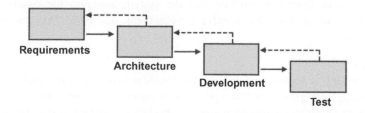

**FIGURE 1.2**

Pure Waterfall: In the pure waterfall model phases have a fixed time sequence and do not overlap.

This approach is widely used, especially on projects that represent minor enhancements to an existing system, systems that are based on a proven reference architecture or the development of systems where there is a relatively small amount of risk. However, on "greenfield" projects, or projects that are extensively changing, this approach can be problematic for several reasons:

- Project progress cannot be accurately measured, because it is based on the creation of work products, rather than the achievement of results. For example, completing the requirements for a system doesn't give an accurate indication of how long the project will take, because the feasibility of a solution has yet to be considered.
- User feedback cannot be obtained until late in the project, when the system is available to use. This delays ultimate convergence on the real requirements.
- Resolution of certain risks is deferred until late in the project, once the system has been built, integrated, and tested. Such activities often identify flaws in the design and in the stated requirements, which is one of the main reasons why many projects that follow a waterfall approach are prone to schedule slippage.

This last point is particularly relevant when addressing system qualities that represent cross-cutting concerns and, thus, cannot be simply "bolted on" at the end. For example, an auditability or maintainability requirement might require the system to log its state during execution. This is necessary for fault diagnosis, or regulatory reporting, pervades the entire system, and may even require a rethink of the architecture of the system itself.

### 1.2.1.2 Incremental

According to the architecture and patterns community, software architecture and its implementation should be subject to piecemeal growth. They evolve piece by piece instead of being defined in their entirety in one large step, as characterized by the aforementioned waterfall lifecycle. Due to inherent complexity of most systems, a one-step-design is not feasible and mostly results in overly complex and poorly defined solutions. In an incremental approach, each increment produces an executable and tested system.

In this approach, the system is grown incrementally, albeit in large chunks. Each increment adds functionality to the previous increments and addresses additional QAs. An increment always yields an executable and testable implementation that exhibits the required product quality, but only contains a subset of the envisaged product, in terms of both functionality and qualities exhibited. The individual increments can be built using a waterfall model or any other process model. As opposed to the waterfall model, the development team can validate that the system achieves the required qualities after each increment. Combining this with iterative development, discussed next, creates an "iterative-incremental" approach.

### 1.2.1.3 Iterative

An alternative approach is to use an iterative development process. It is similar to an incremental approach, but is much finer-grained in that a project undergoes a series of iterations before any product is released, unlike an incremental approach where a product is released at the end of each increment.

Within an iteration, a pass is made through each of the disciplines, including requirements, architecture, development, and test. An iteration is a distinct, time-boxed sequence of activities that results in an internal or external of an executable product. As the project progresses, releases provide incremental improvements in capability until the final system is complete. An iterative development process is similar to "growing" software, where the end product matures over time. Each iteration results in a better understanding of the requirements, a more robust architecture, a more experienced development organization, and a more complete executable implementation.

Figure 1.3 illustrates how the focus of a project shifts across successive iterations. In this figure, we can see that each discipline is addressed in every iteration. The size of the box within each of the disciplines illustrates the relative emphasis spent on the discipline. In this simple example, we can see that iteration 1 is focused on requirements definition. However, we can also see that some architecting is performed (which focuses on the highest priority requirements to be considered in the iteration), together with some development and testing. In this example, iteration 2 is focused on stabilizing the architecture, which is why we see the emphasis on the architecting activities. Iteration 3 is focused on completing the solution based on a relatively stable set of requirements and architecture, which is why there is an emphasis on development and testing.

An iterative development approach is particularly appealing to the architect because it specifically acknowledges that adjustments to the architecture will need to be made as the project progresses. Of course, the number of architectural changes should reduce over time, but the point is that such changes are not an afterthought but are considered to be an essential aspect of the project lifecycle. In particular,

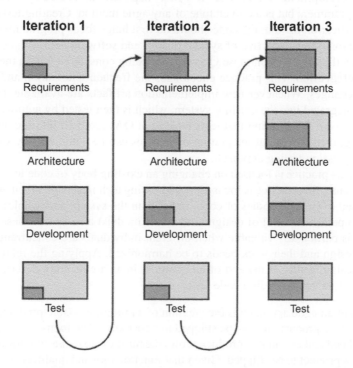

**FIGURE 1.3**

The focus of a project changes from iteration to iteration.

system qualities are addressed early on in the project and not left until it is too late to ensure that they have been adequately addressed.

Applying an iterative approach to system integration environments, where hardware is part of the solution, can be somewhat problematic. For example, we can't always create the physical manifestation of, say, a mobile phone or aircraft. In these cases, an emphasis can be placed on how such elements are simulated.

### 1.2.1.4 Agile

So what is so different about agile? Specifically, how does it differ from iterative or incremental development? The key distinction is that, while practices such as iterative or incremental development are a cornerstone of an agile approach, agile methods take the notions of continuous delivery, team development, and stakeholder interaction to a new level. They also emphasize on additional practices such as test-driven development, continuous integration, or refactoring.

While many agile practices are focused on the "project management" aspects of a project (such as a "Whole Team" practice as exemplified by Scrum's Daily Standup meeting), others are of great relevance when considering QAs, as discussed below.

- **Test-Driven Development (TDD)**. The "test first" approach advocated by TDD is primarily targeted at programmers but is a cornerstone of any agile method. Creating tests that, essentially, define the specification of what the code should do first helps focus programmers on meeting this specification. From the perspective of system quality and software architecture, test cases can be created that specifically focus on those QAs that are being considered within the current iteration.
- **Continuous Integration**. This practice encourages the frequent integration and testing of programming changes. Whenever new implementation artifacts are available, they are continuously integrated into the existing system, which is then tested by automatically running all applicable test cases. By ensuring that tests looking at QAs are built into the iterative and agile way of working, then successful integration of changes can be automatically validated through this regression testing approach.
- **Refactoring**. This practice is focused on changing an existing body of code to improve its internal structure. In a sense, this practice is focused on addressing technical debt, albeit at a local level (it is typically applied to isolated bodies of code, rather than the system as a whole). In practice, any teams that also perform a level of design (and create models) also update these designs where relevant. This is particularly valuable when different individuals are concurrently updating an architectural design and their work needs to be harmonized. Applying the refactoring practice to architectural design results, at the end of an iteration, in an architecture description that is representative of its corresponding code base.

A particular focus of an agile approach is the creation of a minimum viable product, which represents (as its name suggests) a product that can be shipped to a customer. The focus of an agile approach on a continuously validated and executable product allows the business to make an informed decision about the "readiness" of a product to be shipped. Given that functionality and qualities are integrated step by step starting with the most important requirements down to less important ones as part of an agile approach, it is guaranteed that in case of time or budget slips, the most important qualities are already implemented while only less important qualities are missing.

### 1.2.2 **Defining requirements**

Given the previous discussion, it should be obvious why most qualities should be considered through-out the life of a project, starting with a clear understanding of what qualities the system must exhibit. "Many development methods often capture this understanding using a 'nonfunctional requirements' work product or something similar." Unfortunately, the definition of nonfunctional requirements is often uncharted territory (when contrasted with the elicitation of more domain-specific requirements) for those responsible for their definition, such as business analysts, for a number of reasons:

- In most (although not all) systems, from an end user perspective, domain-specific requirements are more visible than their architectural counterparts. Consequently, emphasis is placed on the gathering of these domain-specific requirements, because they are perceived as being the most valuable.
- Stakeholders are not usually familiar with the majority of nonfunctional requirements. They feel more comfortable with specifying domain-specific features such as "Order Processing" and "Stock Control," while neglecting qualities such as "Reliability" and "Usability." Such qualities are often considered technical issues that lie outside of their area of concern.
- Techniques for gathering nonfunctional requirements are generally less well known than techniques for gathering domain-specific requirements. Systematic approaches to the gathering of domain-specific requirements are much more prevalent such as use case-driven development or user story-driven development.

The first step in the development process should be the creation of a common language all stakeholders agree to. A domain model supports engineers and stakeholders in providing or obtaining in-depth knowledge about the problem domain. It documents the essential concepts and relationships within a particular problem domain without referring to the solution domain. Usage of domain models helps avoid common traps and pitfalls such as two stakeholders that have completely different perspectives on the same requirement. Sometimes, the domain model can even be formalized within a DSL (domain-specific language).

One technique for capturing nonfunctional requirements, especially those related to system quality, is to detail appropriate scenarios that allow QAs to be expressed (all nonfunctional qualities are referred to as "quality attributes" in this context). This is discussed in Bass et al. (2013), where each quality is partitioned into one or more concrete QA scenarios, which may be identified in a Quality Attribute Workshop (QAW) (Barbacci et al., 2003). In this approach, Business and IT work together to create a utility tree with quality-relevant scenarios that they jointly prioritize depending on business relevance and implementation complexity, using this quality tree as the more concrete specification of nonfunctional requirements. Architects can subsequently define design tactics that introduce these qualities in the architecture and its implementation.

### 1.2.3 **Defining the architecture**

Architecture design is the process of making strategic architectural decisions. Each decision must address one or more concrete requirements, which should themselves align with the organization's business goals. Clearly, new decisions should not adversely impact earlier decisions, and one mechanism for helping determine any impact is the traceability defined from the design to the requirements.

A number of approaches to deriving an architectural solution exist and several are worthy of note. The commonality between several approaches is discussed in Hofmeister et al. (2000) where five approaches are considered. Three are listed here.

- Attribute Driven Design (ADD) method developed at the Carnegie Mellon Software Engineering Institute (Bass et al., 2013). In this approach, QAs (such as "availability") are used to drive the derivation of the architecture and design, at successive levels of decomposition, through the use of architectural tactics and patterns that satisfy QA scenarios. Tactics are design decisions that decide how a functional requirement will be met or how a QA will be resolved. For example, a tactic that addresses availability might be to introduce redundancy into the system.
- Siemens' 4 Views (S4V) method developed at Siemens Corporate Research (Hofmeister et al., 2000). This approach starts with a global analysis of the factors that influence the architecture, such as functional requirements, desired system qualities, organizational constraints, and technical constraints. The key architectural challenges are identified, and strategies are derived for iteratively addressing these challenges across four views (conceptual, execution, module, and code architecture).
- The Rational Unified Process (RUP) developed at Rational Software, now IBM Rational (Kruchten, 2000). This approach is driven by the architecturally significant use cases, nonfunctional requirements, and risks. Each iteration considers the key architectural elements of the solution before realizing the requirements using these solution elements. The solution is validated in executable software.

### 1.2.3.1  Documenting an architecture

The primary purpose of documenting a software architecture design is, of course, to communicate the architecture. This communication is important to ensure that all stakeholders understand the architecture, at least those parts they are involved in or responsible for, and can provide feedback. This is of particular relevance when it comes to demonstrating how, for example, qualities and other requirements are addressed in the solution. In particular, a documented architecture can help us explore alternative architectural solutions and the pros and cons of each. As mentioned earlier, the design process should also enforce requirements traceability, allowing the traceability from design to requirements to be specified. For QAs it is particularly important to explain any options and trade-off points, as well as points of sensitivity in the architecture.

There are some simple concepts that can be applied when documenting an architecture. In particular, a viewpoint specifies the conventions and techniques for describing the architecture from a particular perspective. This concept is clearly important when it comes to explaining how QAs are accommodated in the architecture description. For example, a performance-related QA may be made visible through the application of a requirements viewpoint (that is applied to communicate any architecturally significant performance requirements), a functional viewpoint (that is applied to communicate those functional components of the solution that contribute to addressing any performance requirement), and a deployment view (that is applied to communicate any deployment elements that contribute to addressing any performance requirement).

In larger companies, mandatory guidelines and conventions are often available, primarily for implementation artifacts. More mature companies define mandatory guiding principles for all roles in a project as well as for the development process. For instance, 1 of the 12 guiding principles at Siemens defines architecture design as covering the whole lifecycle, not just the short timespan where design has its greatest emphasis. A well-balanced level of architecture governance also needs to be enforced, so that problems can be detected and addressed early.

## 1.2.4 Assessing an architecture

Architecture assessments are essential for avoiding, identifying, or mitigating risks. Additional code and design reviews support the identification of design flaws and architecture drift. Organizations leverage different quantitative and qualitative approaches for architecture assessment. The choice of specific techniques depends on the current phase of overall project lifecycle and the current state of the architecture. For example, early in the project, the architecture may be best evaluated by simply presenting the architecture to the key stakeholders. Later in the project, we may perform a more rigorous and systematic walkthrough of the architecture. Evaluation of a physical architecture (one that has accommodated technology considerations) may also consider characteristics of the executing system.

### 1.2.4.1 Quantitative versus qualitative approaches

In quantitative approaches the techniques include metrics, benchmarks, simulators, and prototypes. A major benefit of quantitative approaches is that they typically yield hard facts such as concrete quantities. On the other hand, quantitative approaches have serious liabilities. They are often expensive and only applicable when sufficient parts of the implementation are available. In addition, they are tightly coupled to one or few qualities that become an obstacle when additional qualities need to be checked. Thus, quantitative approaches are often applied only for the most critical qualities.

Qualitative approaches require experts who are capable of assessing an architecture design even in the absence of an implementation. Such architecture reviews typically consist of workshops and interviews in which (a subset of) architecture decisions and their relationship to the defined requirements are considered. Reviews can reveal where design and requirements are not in sync with each other. Specifically, one goal of a review is to expose areas where there is architectural drift or unnecessary complexity.

### 1.2.4.2 Scenario-based evaluation

In order to "divide and conquer" the task of evaluating the architecture, it is often useful to consider a set of key scenarios that are used to walk through the architecture and that allow the architect to demonstrate the architecture in action in terms of, for example, the decisions that have been made, the elements that comprise the architecture and their collaboration, and the qualities that the architecture exhibits.

A well-known scenario-based approach is the architecture trade-off analysis method (ATAM) from the SEI (Clements et al., 2002), as well as its predecessor, the software architecture analysis method (Clements et al., 2002). The ATAM considers a set of scenarios where each scenario is either focused on the functionality offered by the system or the qualities exhibited by the system. In either case, this approach affords the architect the opportunity to convey the architecture in the context of each scenario.

### *1.2.4.3 Experience-based evaluation*

In practice, qualitative experience-based reviews are frequently used in organizations rather than scenario-based methods. Such reviews typically comprise four phases:

- In the definition phase, the review topic and the review goals are defined by experienced reviewers and the organization asking for the review.
- In the collection phase, all required information is collected by the reviewers. This may include documents, code, test plans, interviews, and any other information essential for the review.
- The Evaluation phase covers the actual review. From the collected material, problems and potential solutions are derived.
- In a final workshop, the reviewers present their findings to the stakeholders and answer questions.

The liability of experience-based reviews is that their results may be less concrete, especially if they are merely based on architecture design. Their success depends heavily on the experience of the reviewers. Also, as opposed to quantitative approaches, qualitative reviews cannot yield lots of hard facts.

On the positive side, they are much more lightweight than scenario-based methods. Additionally, they provide recommendations on how to address the findings of the review. Their applicability is also broader than that of methods that emphasize an assessment of qualities only. For example, they allow architects to address several qualities simultaneously instead of only a few, albeit with less detail.

In practice, various qualitative and quantitative techniques are combined to a hybrid best-of-breed approach where reviewers address each problem with an appropriate technique. For example, at Siemens experience-based reviews are often enriched with quantitative and scenario-based techniques. The configuration of such reviews depends on the review topic.

## 1.3 STATE OF THE ART

Before software architecture gained broader attention in the 1990s, commercial software development focused mainly on building software that was tightly coupled with the business domain at which the solution was targeted. This often resulted in one-off applications with an *ad hoc* software architecture with limited or no potential for reuse of knowledge or artifacts. Over the subsequent years, design reuse became more prominent. In turn, this resulted in emergence of reusable, high-quality design solutions for recurring problems. Methodologies and tools supporting architectural patterns, frameworks, reference architectures, and product lines were developed to support and promote design reuse. Moreover, architecture served as an important foundation for managing change both at design and runtime. The emergence of self-adaptive systems and new approaches such as value-driven approaches demonstrates the promotion of the role of architecture and its relation to system quality. Several of these themes are discussed below.

### 1.3.1 Loose coupling

Software systems are no longer treated as monolithic systems, and the typical tight coupling between domain- and technology-specific elements of the system has diminished. Software architects explicitly and strictly enforce separation of concerns by introducing layers of abstraction. This allows for domain-specific logic to be better modularized and encapsulated instead of being interwoven with each other as well as with elements of the solution space.

## 1.3.2 Designing for reuse

Challenges associated with reuse are exacerbated when considering software and system quality. For example, generic reusable components that also support a variety of quality requirements are rare. Reuse is much more achievable when there is some constraining context within which reusable elements exist. For example, code reuse is most effective and feasible when components are integrated into a greater context such as a product line platform, implementation framework, or library.

There therefore needs to be an element of forethought when designing and implementing for reuse. The software engineering community has learned from failure that software architecture needs to be designed in a systematic and planned way; an architecture should not emerge from an implementation, but an implementation should emerge from an architecture. Even in the most agile of projects there needs to be an element of upfront design.

## 1.3.3 Quality-centric design

As a software engineering body of knowledge began to emerge, the focus on quality expanded. Functionality is no longer considered to be the only driving force in design and development of large and complex systems. Meeting system QAs such as usability, modifiability, performance, and security has surfaced as the primary challenge in architecting complex software systems and as an indicator of project success.

## 1.3.4 Lifecycle approaches

As iterative and agile methodologies have gained popularity and prominence over the past decade, the notion of completely defining an architecture upfront has been recognized as impractical. This initially resulted in an interpretation that architectural design and agile approaches are inconsistent. This naïve interpretation stems from the outdated perspective on architecture in which architectural design is considered to be a "phase" of development. Treating architectural design as a phase is simply ineffective: Software architecture is a temporal artifact that evolves through a series of executable releases of software that in turn may validate or invalidate previous architecture assumptions. Architecture plays a focal point throughout the development lifecycle, and treating the architecture as a cornerstone of the development process provides a team with greater intellectual control of their products and sets the foundation for managing evolution and change.

While some agile approaches ignore the centrality of architecture and design modeling and analysis, successful agile practices do indeed capture and highlight the central role that architecture plays in developing and maintaining high-quality software systems. The key observation is that architecture should be a central focus throughout the iterative process. A prescriptive approach for architecture design, building on the description of an agile approach given earlier, can be outlined as follows:

- **Requirements selection**. In each iteration, the architect focuses on one or a few use cases, user stories or scenarios, starting with the highest priority requirements. Scrum introduces a "sprint backlog" for this purpose.

- **Architecture design**. The architecture evolves in a piecemeal manner as requirements and business goals are considered in each current iteration. Each decision has a rationale based upon requirements and business goals. In an agile development process, the creation of an architecture, even one that is lightweight and skeletal, typically precedes the detailed design and implementation activities. Failure to perform any level of architectural thinking upfront often results in a need to reverse engineer the architecture from a fast moving target that is overly complex due to a lack of forethought from an architecture perspective.
- **Architecture assessment**. At the end of each iteration, the architecture is evaluated to identify design flaws, bugs, inefficient design decisions, quality defects, and other issues early. If such issues are found, they are addressed before the following iteration, otherwise design erosion will increase, resulting in a loss of intellectual control and effective management of subsequent changes. In agile circles, the failure to address such issues results in what is known as "technical debt." Architecture sustainability helps to avoid this. In the context of agile processes, TDD and refactoring support architecture assessment.
- **Iteration planning**. Architecture sustainability is an important driver for architecture evolution and maintenance. Before continuing with detailed design or the next iteration, the detected issues need to be prioritized and finally resolved by architecture restructuring or architecture refactoring activities, so that functionality is not built on an unstable foundation. Some refactoring necessities may be postponed to the next iterations, either because the issues are less critical or would require substantial rework shortly before important events such as product release. However, all postponed issues should be explicitly documented as architectural debt that must be paid back later in the project.

The "Twin Peaks" model (Nuseibeh, 2001) suggests that the requirements and architects should be developed and refined in parallel (Cleland-Huang et al., 2013). As the project starts, architects may not understand the requirements, while other stakeholders may not understand the technical implications and feasibility of their requirements. The major benefit of the Twin Peaks model is that it yields both requirements and software architectures with higher stability because both are converged. Such an approach also helps with defining an appropriate risk-based testing strategies and determining the need for any proof-of-concept prototypes. If requirements and architecture evolve in parallel, the risk-based testing strategy can evolve, too.

Another advantage of this approach is that it is often not known beforehand, at least not in concrete quantitative estimations, how architecture decisions and technologies will affect requirements related to qualities. Therefore, requirements not only influence the architecture but the technology choices and architecture decisions may influence the requirements.

This approach is particularly beneficial when the system will contain technologies from third-party vendors, open-source communities, or offshoring suppliers—the operating system also represents such a critical constituent. Consequently, architects have to take the implications of these components on system quality into account, for example, by quality assurance of components delivered by suppliers. Careful vendor and technology selection are therefore additional considerations in this context and may be refined to accommodate any perceived or actual risk. For example, if a delivery from a supplier has quality issues, then the organization should have a second source or a contractual agreement with the supplier concerned requiring that such issues are resolved within a specific time span.

### 1.3.5 **Architecture representation**

The book *Software Architecture in Practice* (Bass et al., 2013) emphasizes system quality. QAs such as security have a high impact on software architecture and are described using QA scenarios, such as "when a user provides the wrong user credentials to the login dialog three times in a row, the system denies access for one minute after the last retry." Such descriptions are precise and contain concrete metrics like "three times" and "within 1 min." Thus, vague system quality requirements are made more concrete by introducing specific scenarios that both business stakeholders and architects can understand and that they can prioritize with respect to business value and technical complexity. For documentation, architects use utility trees, a hierarchical description of system qualities with quality scenarios becoming the leaves.

In addition, design tactics provide adequate solutions for recurring design solutions with respect to specific quality facets. For example, scenarios such as web searches that yield a large result set from which clients only extract a small subset of results often cause high performance penalties. To improve efficiency, the Lazy acquisition pattern helps increase performance and reduce memory consumption by delivering only the information the user is currently interested in, instead of obtaining all the information the user might need later. Lazy acquisition is an example of a performance design tactic. In particular, the specification of tactics and patterns can reduce the amount of effort in documenting an architecture because these elements can be defined once but then referred to where appropriate. Using quality-attribute-driven design, architects can trace from initial system requirements to architectural decisions. With additional efforts they can relate and document architectural decisions and implementation artifacts.

Some classes of applications need special consideration with regard to the architecture representation:

- **Embedded systems development**. In embedded systems development, system functions are typically split across various disciplines (such as electrical engineering, software engineering, mechatronics, and building construction). System engineers therefore decide how to split functions across software engineering and other disciplines. But how can we document the mapping of system qualities, such as the constraints software engineering must adhere to, as well as the technical end economic feasibility of theses constraints? How can software even be tested in the absence of hardware?
- **Product line architectures**. In a product line, commonality and variability are the main drivers for design. Handling variability in domain-specific functionality is one side of the coin, while variability in system qualities is the other. For example, suppose that a low-end application is supposed to use only one single processor core, while the high-end variant may leverage all available cores in the CPU and the GPU. How can an architect design and describe the impact of binding a particular quality parameter? What is the impact of other variation points on system qualities?

There is, of course, a relationship between design tactics and design patterns and how these can be applied to address system quality requirements. In general terms, some pattern systems already provide design solutions for specific qualities. Existing books address security, high availability, fault tolerance, usability, and small systems, to name just a few domains. In essence, patterns are an appropriate means to document design tactics, although not every design tactic qualifies to become a pattern description. Unfortunately, there is no uniform mapping between design tactics and system quality patterns that makes the transition seamless and traceable. Also, most of the literature does not consider trade-off points or other points of sensitivity, such as dependencies between different system qualities. This could be and should be addressed by future work.

Patterns are idiomatic solutions for recurring design problems in specific problem contexts. Pattern languages, in contrast to pattern systems, introduce languages that completely cover particular domains. One possible solution for addressing system qualities, therefore, could be to use DSLs that help describe system qualities in the problem domain. Automation tools could automatically generate appropriate implementations based on design tactics from these DSLs. Again, this area should be addressed by future work.

## 1.3.6 Qualities at runtime through self-adaptation

Self-adaptation in software architecture has been driven by the desire to achieve or maintain stability and the desirable qualities for the runtime configuration in the presence of varying stimuli. These stimuli may be environmental (in the form of workload, failure of external components, security attack on the system, changes in compliance standards, etc.) or internal (failure of internal components, changed target states, etc.). Given that the range of stimuli that affect a software system is wide, self-adaptation has come to mean an umbrella term that covers multiple aspects of how a system reacts: (1) self-awareness, (2) context awareness, (3) self-configuration, (4) self-optimization, (5) self-healing, and (6) self-protection among the other self-* categories.

Research into self-adaptive software architecture has focused on principles and foundations for enriching the architecture with primitives that can monitor, analyze, plan, and execute decisions that react to feedback loops emerging from the system and its environment. The ultimate objective has been treating qualities as a moving target and maintaining them through runtime monitors and control. The influx of work on self-*, including self-awareness, self-configuration, self-optimization, self-healing, self-protection in particular, has advanced our understanding of the means required to achieving qualities at runtime.

MAPE and MAPE-K have been widely adopted as an autonomic architecture style. Most approaches to self-adaptation have followed a common pattern building on MAPE's components: monitor-analyze-plan-execute, connected by a feedback loop. The (K)nowledge component is shared by the (M)onitor, (A)nalyzer, (P)lanner, and (E)xecutor components. MAPE-K provides primitives for encoding experts' knowledge about a domain in K. This knowledge is used to reason about runtime adaptation.

There are two approaches to self-adaptation: centralized and decentralized. In a centralized self-adaptive system, the analysis and planning parts are concentrated in one entity. This form of self-adaptation has the advantage of cohesiveness and low communication overheads as when compared to a decentralized mechanism. The analysis and the plan can be communicated to the effectors, and feedback from obeying the plan is communicated back through the monitors (or sensors).

Rainbow (Cheng et al., 2004) and The Autonomic Manager (Kephart and Chess, 2003) are classic examples of centralized self-adaptation. Decentralized self-adaptation, on the other hand, distributes the analysis, planning, or the feedback mechanism among different parts of the adapting system. This automatically implies a communication overhead, because all constituent parts must coordinate their actions. However, it also provides for robustness in the presence of node failure and scalability of application size. Henceforth, the decision for adopting either a centralized or decentralized self-adaptation has been driven by qualities and trade-offs. It is worth noting that most decentralized self-adaptation systems are typically realized as multiagent systems wherein the agents are autonomous in their environments and implement strategies that collectively move the entire system into a desirable state for the sought qualities and their trade-offs. Cheng et al. (2009) have advocated that the feedback loop, which is a critical part of the adaptation, be elevated to a first-class entity in terms of modeling, design, and implementation. Again, the motivation has been primarily driven by better "appraisal" for qualities and the associated trade-offs.

Elkhodary et al. (2010) proposed FUSION, a framework for tuning self-adaptive software system at runtime. FUSION uses a feature-based approach and online learning for analysis and adaptation. The approach is capable of coping with uncertainty, unanticipated changes in runtime qualities, and their trade-offs through learning and feature adaptation. The unit of adaptation is a feature, i.e., a functional or quality abstraction of a capability provided by the system.

The approach proposed by Abbas et al. (2010) is motivated by the observation that goals and context continuously evolve at runtime in product line architecture. The context of adaptation is a "product" with dynamic variants. An MAPE-K architecture is adopted for self-managing variability. The adaptation mechanism continuously learns which variants to bind given the current context and system goals that can include quality goals.

Contemporary software systems are becoming increasingly large, heterogeneous, and decentralized. They operate in dynamic environments, and their architectures exhibit complex trade-offs across dimensions of goals, time, and interaction, which emerge internally from the systems and externally from their environment (Faniyi et al., 2014). This motivates the need for research for self-aware architecture, where design decisions and execution strategies for these concerns and associated quality trade-offs are dynamically analyzed and seamlessly managed at runtime. In particular, future research shall provide explicit focus for managing such trade-offs in highly dynamic, uncertain, and unpredictable environments, where adaptation strategies are mere difficult to anticipate and plan for at runtime. The focus shall explicate scale, multiple feedback loops leading to more precise adaptation when maintaining and/or achieving qualities at runtime.

### 1.3.7 A value-driven perspective to architecting quality

Boehm and Sullivan (2000) noted that the seminal work, *Software Architecture—Perspectives on an Emerging Discipline* by Shaw and Garlan begins, "As the size and complexity of software systems increase, the design and specification of overall system structure become more significant issues than the choice of algorithms and data structures . . . ." They added, "This statement is true, without a doubt. The problem in the field is that no serious attempt is made to characterize the link between structural decisions and value added." Indeed, the traditional focus of software architecture, and so current practices, has been to a big extent focus on structural and technical perfection for qualities rather than on architecting with explicit focus on interlinking qualities to cost and value creation.

Economics-driven software architecting adopts the view that software design and engineering activity is one of investing valuable resources under uncertainty with the goal of maximizing the value added. This perspective views evolving software as a value-seeking and value-maximizing activity. The implicit focus has been on deriving value through supporting qualities. Means for adding value are typical architectural mechanisms or strategies that are built in or adapted into the architecture with the objective of facilitating change and delivering on the desired qualities which the architecture is designed to support. This could be in response to changes in functional (e.g., changes in features) or nonfunctional requirements (e.g., changes in scalability demands). Optimally, an architecture that shall continue to add value to the enterprise and the system as the requirements evolve. The value-driven perspective provides the architect/analyst with a useful tool for reasoning about a crucial but previously intangible source of value. This value can be then used for deriving "insights" into architectural stability with respect to qualities and investment decisions related to maintain and evolving long-lived software. The perspective has been effective in providing a compromise through linking technical issues to value creation.

Research in architecture adoption and evaluation, for example, has attempted to link architecture design decisions and qualities to economics and value creation. The focus had been primarily concerned with the ability of the architecture to support change and continues to deliver an added value through meeting its desirable qualities and as the system evolves. Research has been fundamentally motivated by the universal "design for change" philosophy, where the architecture is conceived and developed such that evolution is possible (Parnas, 1976, 1979). "Design for change" has been promoted as a value-maximizing strategy provided one could anticipate changes (Boehm and Sullivan, 2000).

However, the challenge is that there is a general lack of adequate models and methods that connect this technical engineering philosophy to value creation under given circumstances. From an economic perspective, a change is a source of uncertainty that confronts an architecture during the evolution of the software system and could regress the qualities it supports. Regressing qualities may place the investment in a particular architecture at risk. The challenge is to accommodate the change without compromising qualities that the system is supposed to deliver. Conversely, designing for change incurs upfront costs and may not render future benefits. The benefits are uncertain because future changes—their nature and their probability of occurrence—are uncertain. The worthiness of designing or re-engineering architecture for change and qualities should involve a trade-off between the upfront cost of enabling the change and the future value added by the architecture, if the change materializes. The value added, as a result of enabling the change on a given architecture, is a powerful heuristic that can provide a basis for analyzing the sustainability of the architecture and can inform retiring and replacement decisions of the architecture and/or the decisions of selecting an architecture, architectural style, and middleware with the potential of delivering better value through supporting quality.

The cost benefit analysis method (CBAM) (Asundi and Kazman, 2001) is an architecture-centric method for analyzing the costs, benefits, and schedule implications of architectural decisions. The CBAM builds upon the ATAM to model the costs and benefits of architectural design decisions and to provide means of optimizing such decisions. Conceptually, CBAM continues where the ATAM leaves off; it adds a monetary dimension to ATAM as an additional attribute to be traded off. The CBAM consists of the following steps: (i) choosing scenarios and architectural strategies (AS), (ii) assessing QA benefits, (iii) quantifying the Architectural Strategies, (iv) costs and schedule implications, (v) calculating desirability, and (vi) making decisions. Upon completion of the evaluation using CBAM, CBAM could have guided the stakeholders to determine a set of architectural strategies that address their highest priority scenarios. These chosen strategies furthermore represent the optimal set of architectural investments. They are optimal based upon considerations of benefit, cost, and schedule within the constraints of the elicited uncertainty of these judgments and the willingness of the stakeholders to withstand the risk implied by uncertainty.

Bahsoon and Emmerich (2008) have pursued an economics-driven software architecting to value the flexibility of an architecture in enduring likely changes in quality requirements. They contributed to a model that builds on an analogy with real options theory. The model examines some likely changes in nonfunctional requirements and values the extent to which the architecture is flexible to endure these changes. They have shown how the model can be used to assess the worthiness of re-engineering a "more" stable architecture in face of likely changes in future requirements; the value of refactoring relative to likely changes in requirements; and inform the selection of a "more" stable middleware-induced software architecture in the face of future changes in nonfunctional requirements.

Future research in economics-driven software architecting shall take the multioptimization view to software design and qualities as modeling the cost/value implications on multiple qualities is not straightforward. In this context, utilizing the NFR framework (Mylopoulos et al., 1992), for example, could be a promising starting point to model the interaction of various nonfunctional requirements, their corresponding architectural decisions, and the negative/positive contribution of the architectural decisions in satisfying these nonfunctionalities. The framework could be then complemented by means for measuring (i) the corresponding cost of implementing the change itself and (ii) the additional cost due to the impact of the change on other contributing or conflicting nonfunctionalities.

Future research shall investigate how to cope with the coevolution of both the architecture and the nonfunctional requirements as we change domains. This poses challenges in understanding the evolution trends of nonfunctional requirements; designing architectures that are aware of how these requirements will change over the projected lifetime of the software system and tend to evolve through the different domains. From an economics perspective, such is necessary to reduce the future "switching cost," which could hinder the success of evolution. In this perspective, engineering requirements and designing architectures need to be treated as value-maximizing activities in which we can maximize the net benefits (or real options) by minimizing the future "switching costs" while transiting across different domains. This necessitates amending the current practice of engineering requirements and brings a need for methods and techniques that explicitly model the domain, the "vertical" evolution of the software system within the domain itself, and how the domain is likely to change over the projected lifetime of the software system.

# References

Abbas, N., Andersson, J., Lowe, W., 2010. Autonomic software product lines (ASPL). In: Proceedings of the Fourth European Conference on Software Architecture: Companion Volume ECSA '10, pp. 324–331.

Asundi, J., Kazman, R., 2001. A foundation for the economic analysis of software architectures. In: Proceedings of the Third Workshop on Economics-Driven Software Engineering Research, in Affiliation with the 23rd International Conference on Software Engineering, Toronto, Canada.

Bahsoon, R., Emmerich, W., 2008. An economics-driven approach for valuing scalability in distributed architectures. In: Proceedings of the 7th Working IEEE/IFIP Conference on Software Architecture (WICSA 2008). IEEE Computer Society Press, Vancouver, Canada.

Barbacci, M.R., Ellison, R., Lattanze, A.J., Stafford, J.A., Weinstock, C.B., Wood, W.G., 2003. Quality Attribute Workshops (QAWs). Carnegie Mellon University, Pittsburgh, CA.

Bass, L., Clements, P., Kazman, R., 2013. Software Architecture in Practice, third ed. Addison-Wesley, Upper Saddle River, NJ.

Boehm, B., Sullivan, K.J., 2000. Software economics: a roadmap. In: Finkelstein, A. (Ed.), The Future of Software Engineering. ACM Press, New York, NY, pp. 320–343.

Cheng, S.-W., Huang, A.-C., Garlan, D., Schmerl, B., Steenkiste, P., 2004. Rainbow: architecture-based self-adaptation with reusable infrastructure. In: Proceedings of International Conference on Autonomic Computing, pp. 276–277.

Cheng, B.H., de Lemos, R., Giese, H., Inverardi, P., Magee, J., Andersson, J., Becker, B., Bencomo, N., Brun, Y., Cukic, B., et al., 2009. Software Engineering for Self-adaptive Systems: A Research Roadmap. Springer, New York, NY.

Cleland-Huang, J., Hanmer, R.S., Supakkul, S., Mirakhorli, M., 2013. The Twin Peaks of requirements and architecture. IEEE Softw. 30 (2), 24–29.

Clements, P., Kazman, R., Klein, M., 2002. Evaluating Software Architectures—Methods and Case Studies. Addison Wesley, Los Alamitos, CA.

Eeles, P., Cripps, P., 2008. The Process of Software Architecting. Addison Wesley, Boston, MA.

Elkhodary, A., Esfahani, N., Malek, S., 2010. Fusion: a framework for engineering self-tuning self-adaptive software systems. In: Proceedings of the Eighteenth ACM SIGSOFT International Symposium on Foundations of Software Engineering (FSE '10), pp. 7–16.

Faniyi, F., Bahsoon, R., Yao, X., Lewis, P.R., 2014. Architecting self-aware software systems (to appear). In: The 11th Working IEEE/IFIP Conference on Software Architecture (WICSA 2014), Sydney, Australia.

Grady, R.B., 1992. Practical Software Metrics for Project Management and Process Improvement. Prentice Hall, Englewood Cliffs, NJ.

Hofmeister, C., Nord, R., Soni, D., 2000. Applied Software Architecture. Addison Wesley, Boston, MA.

IEEE Computer Society, 1998. IEEE Std 1061. Standard for a Software Quality Metrics Methodology. IEEE Computer Society, New York.

IEEE Computer Society, 2000. IEEE 1471-2000. Recommended Practice for Architectural Description of Software-Intensive Systems. IEEE Computer Society, New York.

ISO/IEC 9126-1, 2001. Software engineering—product quality. ISO/IEC 9126-1. TBD: ISO.

ISO/IEC/IEEE 42010, 2010. Systems and software engineering—architecture description. ISO.

Kephart, J.O., Chess, D.M., 2003. The vision of autonomic computing. Computer 36 (1), 41–50.

Kruchten, P., 2000. The Rational Unified Process—An Introduction, second ed. Addison Wesley, Boston, MA.

Mylopoulos, J., Chung, L., Nixon, B., 1992. Representing and using nonfunctional requirements: a process-oriented approach. IEEE Trans. Softw. Eng. 18 (6), 483–497.

Nuseibeh, B., 2001. Weaving together requirements and architecture. Computer 34 (3), 115–119.

Parnas, D.L., 1976. On the design and development of program families. IEEE Trans. Softw. Eng. 1 (1976), 1–9.

Parnas, D.L., 1979. Designing software for ease of extension and contraction. IEEE Trans. Softw. Eng. 5 (2), 128–138.

# Human-Centric Evaluation for Systems Qualities and Software Architecture

# Exploring How the Attribute Driven Design Method Is Perceived

2

**Nour Ali[1] and Carlos Solis[2]**
*[1]University of Brighton, Brighton, UK*
*[2]Amazon, Dublin, Ireland*

## INTRODUCTION

Software architecture is a coordination tool among the different phases of software development. It bridges requirements to implementation and allows reasoning about satisfaction of systems' critical requirements (Kazman et al., 2006). Quality attributes (Gorton, 2006) are one kind of nonfunctional requirements that are critical to systems. The Software Engineering Institute (SEI) defines a quality attribute as "a property of a work product or goods by which its quality will be judged by some stakeholder or stakeholders" (Software Engineering Institute, 2010a). They are important properties that a system must exhibit such as scalability, modifiability, or availability (Wojcik et al., 2006).

A method for designing software architecture based on quality attributes is defined by the SEI and called the attribute driven design (ADD) method (Bardram et al., 2005; Wojcik et al., 2006). The ADD method is based on an iterative process for designing software architecture based on applying architectural tactics and patterns that satisfy quality attributes. This method has been applied in different domains such as fault-tolerant systems (Wood, 2007), adopted in companies as stated in Kazman et al. (2006), and composes part of curricula for training software architects (Software Engineering Institute, 2010b).

Research has been performed to evaluate the different artifacts and activities of ADD (Kannengiesser and Zhu, 2009; Lee and Shin, 2008). However, not much scientific research has reported on experiences using this method (Falessi et al., 2007). We investigate how software engineers with no or little industrial experience in software architecture design and quality attributes perceive the usefulness and ease of use of the ADD method. Design methods can only be effective if users adopt and accept them. Although novice software engineers are not experienced software architects, it is interesting to understand how they perceive these kinds of methods to be part of their training and if they are willing to adopt them in the future. In addition, we are interested in understanding the problems they face when applying the ADD.

This chapter presents an empirical study to explore ADD method users' perception. We apply the technological acceptance model (TAM) (Davis, 1989), which investigates people's attitudes and behavior toward accepting an innovation. We designed a survey with questions that follow the TAM in order to measure perceived usefulness, ease of use, and willingness to use for the ADD method. We performed an experiment in 2010 with 12 participants, and repeated it in 2011 with 7 participants.

All the participants were postgraduate students in the software engineering master program, enrolled in the software architecture module of each year. After they received 8 h of training on the ADD method and designed and documented a software architecture following the ADD method for six weeks, they were asked to fill a survey.

Our findings reveal that the subjects found ADD method useful and that this had a positive influence on their willingness of using it. However, the subjects had a neutral/negative opinion on its ease of use and a neutral opinion on their willingness to use it. We also discuss the problems that the subjects faced when using the ADD that have influenced their opinions.

This chapter is structured as follows: In Section 2.1, we describe the ADD method and the TAM. Section 2.2 explains the empirical study. Section 2.3 describes the data and the results of the study. Section 2.4 presents a discussion about the problems faced by the subjects when using ADD method, an analysis of the results, several lessons learned from the study, and the validity threats. Finally, Section 2.5 presents conclusions and implications for further work.

## 2.1 BACKGROUND

In this section, we provide an overview of the ADD method and the TAM.

### 2.1.1 ADD method

The ADD method is an iterative approach, proposed by the SEI, for designing software architecture to meet functional and quality requirements (Bardram et al., 2005). The ADD method uses a recursive decomposition process based on the quality attributes that a system needs to fulfill. At each stage, tactics and architectural patterns are chosen to satisfy some qualities, and functionality is allocated to instantiate the architectural element types. A practical example applying ADD is presented in Wood (2007).

In the following, we give a brief explanation of each ADD step based on Wojcik et al. (2006) (see Figure 2.1). In the *first step*, a list of stable and prioritized requirements including functional constraints and quality attributes must be available to start ADD. Functional requirements are expressed as use cases, and quality attributes are expressed as quality attribute scenarios templates (stimulus-response) (Bardram et al., 2005). In the *second step*, the iterative process can start. If you are in the first iteration, your system is the element to be decomposed. If not, you choose an architectural element to start decomposing.

In the *third step*, the ranking of the requirements by stakeholders is combined with rankings based on their impacts on the architecture. Five to six high-priority requirements are chosen and are called candidate architectural drivers. *In the fourth step*, the architectural element types and their relationships are chosen. To identify them, the design constraints and quality attributes (candidate architectural drivers) are used to identify patterns and tactics (design options for achieving quality attributes) that satisfy them, and architectural views are partially captured.

In the *fifth step*, the chosen architectural element is decomposed into children elements. Responsibilities are allocated to the children elements with use cases, and architectural views from step 4 are complemented. In the *sixth step*, the services and properties that are provided and required for each element are defined. Finally, in *step 7*, architects verify that the functional requirements, quality

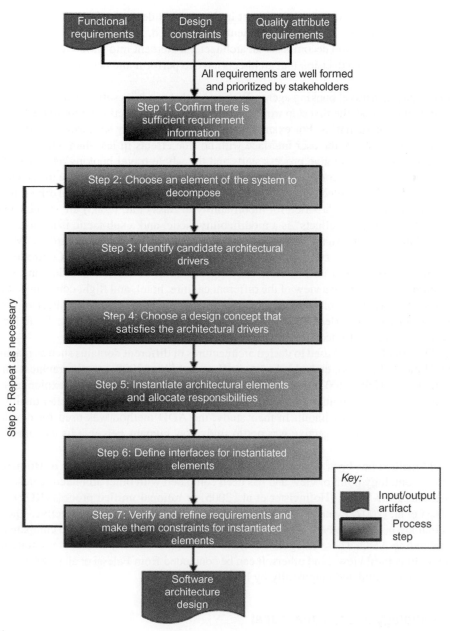

**FIGURE 2.1**

Steps of ADD.

*Taken from Wojcik et al. (2006).*

attributes, and design constraints have been met in the element decomposition and that the child element's functional and quality attribute requirements are allocated. After the last step, a new iteration of ADD can begin. Each iteration decomposes an architectural element into children elements. The number of iterations applied is a decision that architects have to perform and depends on the abstraction of the architecture.

*Example*: Imagine a travel booking agency Web portal that needs its software architecture designed. By using the ADD method, the first step would be to identify stable functional requirements and quality attributes expressed as scenarios. For example, a modifiability quality scenario is "The system shall allow a developer to modify the user interface with no side effects in less than 3 h."

In the second step, the iterative process starts and the whole travel booking agency system is the architectural element to be decomposed. In the third step, based on the importance to stakeholders and its relative impact on the architecture, modifiability is the most ranked architectural driver. In the fourth step, the architectural tactics classified for modifiability in Bass et al. (2003) are studied and chosen. For example, "prevent ripple effects" is a modifiability tactic, and a sub-tactic is to "use an intermediary." An architectural pattern that satisfies these tactics is the Model View Controller (MVC). In the fifth step, the travel booking system is separated into the Model, View, and Controller elements. For example, a customer will have a view showing details of his or her booking and profile, and the agency employee will have a view of the different car hire, hotel, and flight companies. In the sixth step, the services of properties of the MVC are defined. In the seventh step, the architect verifies that the MVC has met modifiability. Because MVC is a well-documented pattern, it does. Then, the architect can start another iteration to decompose the Model element.

The ADD method has been used to design architectures of different domains such as machine learning (Dulva Hina et al., 2006), embedded systems (Lee and Shin, 2008), or geographical information systems (Habli and Kelly, 2007). Ferrari and Madhavji (2008) performed an exploratory study to research whether architects with requirements engineering knowledge develop better quality software architectures than architects without. In their study, the ADD method was used for developing the architecture. However, their objective was not to study how humans perceive its usefulness and ease of use.

The ADD method has been evaluated in Kannengiesser and Zhu (2009) and in Hofmeister et al. (2007) from an ontology point of view and has been compared with other architecture design methods such as Siemens Four Views (Hofmeister et al., 2005) or rational unified process (RUP) (Kruchten, 2004). Falessi et al. (2007) evaluate ADD from software architects' needs perspective. They use nine categories that are believed to be real needs of software architects and use them to compare the design methods, including ADD. These categories include tool support, ability to react to requirements, and support for architectural views, and others. It can be concluded from Falessi et al. (2007) that the ADD has been minimally validated empirically by humans.

## 2.1.2 Technology acceptance model

The TAM (Davis, 1989) is used to explain the individual acceptance of new technology or innovations. In the TAM, accepting or rejecting an innovation is measured through two variables, "perceived usefulness" and "perceived ease of use." An innovation is perceived as useful when its users believe that it would help them perform their job. However, if an innovation is useful, it might not be adopted because its use requires too much. An innovation is perceived as easy to use when people believe that its use would be effortless. The third TAM variable is "willingness of use," which represents people's intention to use an innovation.

TAM has been used for assessing perceived usefulness and ease of use of technologies such as Web tools in education (Toral et al., 2007) and software engineering techniques such as business process modeling (Eikebrokk et al., 2010). In this chapter, we adopt the TAM to evaluate the acceptance of the ADD method by the students.

## 2.2 THE EMPIRICAL STUDY

In this section, we describe the study that was conducted to explore how users perceive the ADD method.

### 2.2.1 Research questions

In this study, our objective is to investigate on the following research questions.

*RQ*: How do students perceive the ADD method?

To answer this question, we have divided it into these two sub-questions:

*RQ1*: How do students perceive the usefulness and ease of use of the ADD method?

The hypotheses to be contrasted to answer this research question are the following:

H1: ADD is perceived as useful.
H2: ADD is perceived as easy to use.
H3: There is willingness to use ADD.
H4: The perceived usefulness of ADD is correlated with willingness to use.
H5: Perceived ease of use of ADD is correlated with willingness to use.
H6: Perceived usefulness of ADD is correlated with ease of use.
*RQ2*: What are the problems that users face when applying the ADD?

To answer this question, we will ask the subjects about their problems and understand the practices they have used.

### 2.2.2 Experiment design and study variables

The design of this study is a survey design and a nonexperimental design (Kitchenham and Pfleeger, 2007; Mitchell, 2004). Given that we performed the same study in two different years, the one performed in 2011 is considered to be a closed replication (Lindsay and Ehrenberg, 1993). For the study, we designed a questionnaire to contrast the hypotheses that is composed of three sets of questions (items) in order to measure the three TAM variables: perceived usefulness, perceived ease of use, and willingness of use (see Table 2.1).

The questionnaire consists of 12 questions using a 7-point (1-7) Likert scale (1, extremely unlikely; 2, quite unlikely; 3 slightly unlikely; 4, neither; 5, slightly likely; 6, quite likely; 7, extremely likely). We deal with Likert scale as ordinal data, because the answers to the questions can be meaningfully

**Table 2.1** Items to Measure ADD Method Perceived Usefulness, Perceived Ease of Use, and Willingness to Use

| **Items Regarding "Perceived Usefulness" (PU)** | |
|---|---|
| PU1 | Using ADD would improve my *performance*[a] in architecture design |
| PU2 | Using ADD would increase my *productivity* in architecture design |
| PU3 | Using ADD would enhance my *effectiveness*[b] in architecture design |
| PU4 | Using ADD would enable me to accomplish architecture design tasks *more quickly* |
| PU5 | I find that ADD would be *useful* in architecture design |
| PU6 | Using ADD would *make it easier* to design architecture |
| **Items Regarding "Ease of Use" (PEU)** | |
| PEU1 | *Learning* to use ADD is easy for me |
| PEU2 | It will be possible to use ADD without *expert help* |
| PEU3 | It is easy for me to become *skilful* at using ADD |
| PEU4 | It is easy to *remember* how to perform the ADD |
| PEU5 | I would find ADD *easy to use* |
| **Items Regarding "Willingness to Use" (WU)** | |
| WU1 | I *will use* ADD for designing software architectures |

[a]*Performance: effort expended to achieve results.*
[b]*Effectiveness: doing the right thing without mistakes.*

ordered from lowest to highest, but the intervals between the scoring are not equal psychological intervals (Jamieson, 2004).

We adapted the items of the TAM. The items of perceived usefulness are the same as TAM, but we focused the questions on the ADD method and architecture design. In the case of perceived usefulness, some of the original TAM items were focused on users interacting with tools or technologies. We removed the items as "*I would find it easy to get X to do what I want it to do,*" "*My interaction with X would be clear and understandable,*" or "*I would find X to be flexible to interact with*" (Christensen and Hansen, 2010). We left the items shown in Table 2.1. To measure the willingness to use, we have one question that asks the users if they will use ADD for designing software architectures.

### 2.2.3 Participants and training

We used availability (or convenience sampling) (Mitchell, 2004), where the participants were all graduate students in the Software Architecture module of software engineering master program of the University of Limerick. In the first experiment, conducted in 2010, they were 12 participants, divided into four architecting teams. In the experiment conducted in 2011, they were 7 participants, divided into three groups. One group had three members, and the two other groups had two members each.

The students had some background in requirements engineering, including use cases or viewpoints, and Software Design including the knowledge of several design patterns and modeling in UML. They did not have previous knowledge in specifying quality attribute scenarios, which is needed for using the

ADD method or using a pattern-driven method. Previous to receiving training in ADD, the students had some experience using artifact-driven architecture design and use-case-driven methods, which they used in other projects. They had also previous knowledge in RUP.

The students were given the following training background as part of the ADD:

- 2-h lecture reviewing definitions about software architecture, its concepts, elements, and architectural views
- 2-h lecture about quality attribute scenarios that included understanding quality attributes by using the quality attribute scenarios and achieving quality attributes through tactics. The contents of the lecture were based on chapters 4 and 5 of Bass et al. (2003) and Wojcik et al. (2006).
- 2-h lecture about architectural styles/patterns that presented many options found in the literature. The contents of this lecture were based on styles/patterns presented in Chapters 4 and 11 of Taylor et al. (2010) and Chapter 3 of Shaw and Garlan (1996).
- 2-h lecture about designing architectures using the ADD method; contents were based on Chapter 7 of Bass et al. (2003). In addition, a few minutes were also dedicated to explaining documentation of architectures using templates.

### 2.2.4 **The architecting project**

In the two times this study has been performed, we used two different projects but tried to keep their requirements size and difficulty similar. This was decided so as not to allow students in 2011 to be able to copy the solutions of students of previous years. In 2010, the system to be architected was about a Web portal for the university library that allows users to search for different kinds of publications. The Web page should be accessible from desktops or mobile devices. In 2011, the project was about a travel agency Web portal that allows users to search for hotels and flights and book them.

These projects were chosen because both of them are Web portals; needed integration with different kinds of external systems such as payment systems; and needed to satisfy many quality attributes such as security, modifiability, scalability, performance, and availability. At the same time, the students are familiar with both the library and travel agency Web portals; this would minimize the possibility of having problems in understanding their requirements.

All teams were responsible for designing and documenting the software architecture using the ADD method independently of the other teams. Each team was given the option to decide on the number of iterations. Each was also asked to use a template for documenting the software architecture. This template was adapted from Gorton (2006), which included sections for documenting quality attribute scenarios (Bass et al., 2003), use cases, constraints, architectural styles and patterns, rationale, views, assumptions, architectural elements, interfaces, risks, and implementation. We also asked each team to fill in a template for each iteration of the ADD, documenting the decisions and the rationale taken in each step. This allowed us to ensure that they were following the ADD method correctly and to understand the rationale behind the decisions that they took.

### 2.2.5 **Data collection**

The teams were given six weeks for handing in software architecture documentation, and a list of problems they faced when applying the ADD method in designing the architecture. There was no interaction between the students and the instructor during this period of time.

**Table 2.2** Validation of Questionnaire Using Cronbach's $\alpha$

| Dimension | 2010 | 2011 |
| --- | --- | --- |
| Perceived Usefulness | 0.834 | 0.843 |
| Perceived Ease of Use | 0.625 | 0.666 |

Later, the questionnaire of Table 2.1 was given to each of the students who were asked to fill it during a 20-min period. Each participant was asked to respond to each statement in terms of his or her own degree of agreement or disagreement. The questionnaire was filled in anonymously in order not to provoke doubt between the subjects that their answers would affect their module marks.

## 2.3 RESULTS

In the following, we describe the results of the two studies that were conducted.

### 2.3.1 Questionnaire reliability

To measure the reliability of the questionnaire, we calculated the Cronbach's $\alpha$ reliability index for each dimension (Mitchell, 2004). Cronbach's $\alpha$ indicates the internal consistency of a set of questions. When Cronbach's $\alpha$ value is above 0.70, it is an acceptable value, although in exploratory studies a threshold of 0.60 is also acceptable (George and Mallery, 2009).

In the case of perceived usefulness, the Cronbach's $\alpha$ values for 2010 and 2011 are above 0.70 (see Table 2.2), which indicates that the items are a highly reliable measure for the dimension. The Cronbach's $\alpha$ values for perceived ease of use are higher than 0.60, and below 0.70 (see Table 2.2). This indicates that the reliability of the questions in this dimension is acceptable because this is an exploratory study.

### 2.3.2 Descriptive statistics

According to Stevens (1946), means and standard deviations cannot be used to describe ordinal data. Instead, medians and percentile measures should be applied (Jamieson, 2004; Stevens, 1946). We describe the items using the median, inter-quartile range, and the mode. Table 2.3 summarizes the results for items dealing with the usefulness, ease of use, and willingness to use dimensions for both experiments, 2010 and 2011.

#### 2.3.2.1 Usefulness of ADD method

For the 2010 experiment, notice that the median of all items is equal to or higher than 5. For the 2011 experiment, the median of the items is equal to 5 except for item PU4, which indicates a slight disagreement that ADD enables to accomplish Architecture Design tasks *more quickly*. In conclusion, we can notice that there is a positive agreement for perceived usefulness of the ADD method.

**Table 2.3** Usefulness, Ease of Use, and Willingness to Use Results

|  | Median | | Interquartile Range | | Mode | | | |
|---|---|---|---|---|---|---|---|---|
|  | 2010 | 2011 | 2010 | 2011 | 2010 | 2011 | | |
| Performance (PU1) | 5.5 | 5 | 1 | 3 | 6 | 5 | | |
| Productivity (PU2) | 5 | 5 | 2 | 2 | 5 | 6 | | |
| Effectiveness (PU3) | 5 | 5 | 1 | 1 | 5 | 5 | | |
| More Quickly (PU4) | 5 | 4 | 1 | 1 | 5 | 3 | | |
| Useful (PU5) | 6 | 5 | 1 | 2 | 6 | 5 | | |
| Make It Easier (PU6) | 5 | 5 | 2 | 1 | 5 | 5 | | |
| Learning (PEU1) | 3 | 3 | 3 | 3 | 3 | 5 | | |
| Expert Help (PEU2) | 4 | 4 | 2 | 3 | 4 | 4 | | |
| Skillful (PEU3) | 4 | 2 | 3 | 3 | 4 | 2 | | |
| Remember (PEU4) | 4 | 3 | 3 | 1 | 4 | 3 | | |
| Easy to Use (PEU5) | 4 | 2 | 2 | 1 | 4 | 2 | | |
| Willingness to Use (WU1) | 4 | 4 | 2 | 2 | 4 | 3 & 5 | | |

### 2.3.2.2 Ease of use of ADD method

Notice that for the 2010 experiment, the median is equal to 4 for all items excluding PEU1 (Learning), which is 3. The medians for the 2011 experiment are different from those of 2010 except for the items PEU1 and PEU2. The medians of 2011 subjects' opinions are negative about items PEU3, PEU4, and PEU5.

### 2.3.2.3 Willingnes of use

For the 2010 experiment, the median and mode were neutral (4), and for the 2011 experiment the median was also neutral, but its mode had the values of 3 and 5.

### 2.3.3 Hypotheses tests

In statistical terms, H1 is defined as the median of usefulness that is greater than 24 (which is the sum of 6 answers in the Likert scale with a value of 4), H2 is defined as the median of ease of use greater than 20, and H3 as the median of willingness of use greater than 4. These hypotheses can be checked with a one-tailed Wilcoxon signed rank test (Table 2.4).

The test has a significance of 0.05. Our hypotheses are accepted if $W-$ is less than or equal to the Wilcoxon statistic for $N =$ sample size $-$ ties. In both experiments, H1 is accepted, and H2 and H3 are rejected.

To check the hypotheses H4, H5, and H6 and to study the relationships between the variables, we used Spearman's $\rho$ correlation coefficient (see Table 2.5). Notice that the Spearman's $\rho$ coefficient for the relationship between perceived usefulness of ADD and the willingness to use ADD is 0.681 in 2010 and 0.963 in 2011, and the $p$-values are positive and significant for both years. Therefore, hypothesis

**Table 2.4** Results of the Wilcoxon Signed Rank Test

|  | H1 | | H2 | | H3 | |
|---|---|---|---|---|---|---|
|  | 2010 | 2011 | 2010 | 2011 | 2010 | 2011 |
| W− | 1 | 3 | 28.5 | 26 | 28.5 | 10.50 |
| W+ | 54 | 25 | 26.5 | 2 | 23 | 10.50 |
| Ties | 2 | 0 | 2 | 0 | 5 | 1 |
| Wilcoxon (one-tailed 0.05) | 10 | 3 | 10 | 3 | 3 | 2 |

**Table 2.5** Spearman $\rho$ Correlations Among the Dimensions

|  |  | 2010 | | | 2011 | | |
|---|---|---|---|---|---|---|---|
|  |  | PU | PEU | WU | PU | PEU | WU |
| Perceived usefulness (PU) | Correlation coefficient | 1 | 0.210 | 0.681 | 1 | 0.655 | 0.963 |
|  | Sig. (two-tailed) |  | 0.512 | 0.015 |  | 0.111 | 0.001 |
| Perceived ease of use (PEU) | Correlation coefficient | 0.210 | 1 | 0.208 | 0.655 | 1 | 0.523 |
|  | Sig. (two-tailed) | 0.512 |  | 0.797 | 0.111 |  | 0.228 |
| Willingness to use (WU) | Correlation coefficient | 0.681 | 0.208 | 1 | 0.963 | 0.523 | 1 |
|  | Sig. (two-tailed) | 0.015 | 0.797 |  | 0.000 | 0.228 |  |

*A correlation is significant at the 0.05 level (two-tailed).*
*(George and Mallery, 2009)*

H4 is accepted in both experiments. H5 and H6 hypotheses are rejected because the Spearman correlations between perceived ease of use and willingness to use and perceived ease of use and perceived usefulness are not significant.

## 2.4 DISCUSSION

In this section, we discuss issues that the subjects faced when using the ADD method, we interpret and analyze the results, and we discuss lessons learned and the validity threats.

### 2.4.1 ADD issues faced by subjects

In this section, we discuss the problems that the teams reported facing when using the ADD method and relate them to the current literature. The 2011 teams did not report any new problems not mentioned by the 2010 teams. We have classified the issues into four main categories.

### 2.4.1.1 Team workload division and assignment

The ADD method does not explicitly give guidelines on how a team of architects should divide their workload (Wojcik et al., 2006). This can be emphasized on the first iteration. One 2010 team reported, "*Attribute Driven Design presented a conceptual challenge in terms of dividing workload within the group initially.*" It has to be noted that none of the teams that participated in the 2011 experiment explicitly reported this problem. A reason for this could be due to the fact that two of the teams had only two members.

According to the practical example reported in Wood (2007), the architecture team perform the first iteration. However, no details are given on how the team divided its workload in the first iteration. In the later iterations of ADD, architects with expertise in specific qualities are assigned to perform the architecting of specific iterations (architectural elements), and iterations that are independent of each other can be performed in parallel by different architects. For example, an architect with expertise in fault tolerance is assigned to perform iterations for fault tolerance components and another architect to perform the ones related to start-up. However, even this practice is not documented as a guideline or practice in the ADD steps. As future improvement of ADD, specific practices for team workload division and assignment can be explicitly included.

### 2.4.1.2 No consensus in terminology

ADD method terminology used to refer to its artifacts is different from the rest of the literature. The problems of communicating among themselves, looking for appropriate patterns, and determining tactics were faced by the subjects. A clear example is the use of the words *architectural patterns* and *architectural styles* interchangeably in the literature. A 2010 team reported, "*It was found that several institutions use identical terms to refer to the same object (such as diagrams, patterns, tactics etc.). This was found by the group to be quite frustrating as we often found ourselves looking at that same material and referring to it using different terms.*" A 2011 team also reported, "*The terminology surrounding software architecture can be ambiguous at times and is used with varying meanings across the literature surveyed.*"

Related to this problem is the issue that the different architecture design methods proposed by different organizations or researchers use different terminology. This discourages the reuse of other researchers' experiences, practices, and guidelines in the software architecture field. An effort toward addressing this problem is the architecture design model proposed by Hofmeister et al. (2007), which is a result of comparing and contrasting the different architecture design methods, including the ADD. This kind of work can help in finding out the commonalities and differences in the architecture design methods based on the activities and artifacts and to identify methods that can complement each other.

Another team reported that they had difficulty in finding patterns to satisfy quality attributes because the language used in patterns did not directly indicate the quality attributes. They reported as follows, "*The language used in patterns and ADD greatly differs and patterns don't always immediately identify what quality attributes they support.*" This problem has been indicated in the literature in Gross and Yu (2001) and Harrison and Avgeriou (2007). Although this problem does not only affect the ADD method, it affects in general software architecture designs that are based on quality attributes.

### 2.4.1.3 ADD first iteration

The teams reported that during the first iteration they found difficulties. A 2010 team reported, "*The first iteration is very confused and it is hard to decompose the system into elements,*" and a 2011 team reported, "*As the system was the element to decompose in this iteration, the scope was very wide and so it was a challenge to determine where to start.*" An obvious flaw is that there is no complete example of ADD where the first iteration is demonstrated (Wood, 2007). In this iteration the number of architectural drivers and requirements is the highest. For the subjects it was difficult to determine which architectural drivers to choose at the first iteration.

For example, in steps 2 and 3, when choosing the architectural element to decompose and the candidate architectural drivers, in the second and later iterations of ADD, the subjects chose the architectural element to decompose based on criticality of the functional and quality attribute scenarios associated with it or based on the quality attributes. In the first iteration, it is hard to understand which are the most critical functional and quality attributes and from where to start.

### 2.4.1.4 Mapping quality attributes to tactics, and tactics to patterns

This problem is specific to step 4 where the types of elements and their relationships based on tactics, architectural styles, or both are identified. We have noticed that the users performed the following practices in this step to map the quality attributes to tactics or patterns: They used tactics and defined their own patterns; they chose existing patterns and then verified that each pattern satisfied a set of tactics and quality attribute scenarios, or they reflected on several tactics to satisfy a quality scenario and then chose a pattern. To identify the elements and their relationships, they added elements responsible for a quality attribute and the functionality or elements that had been defined in the architectural style.

The teams found it complicated to choose or find tactics that satisfied quality attributes. In addition, they found complicated defining, evaluating, and assessing which architectural patterns were suitable to implement the tactics and quality attributes. A 2010 team reported, "*Difficulty in locating suitable patterns to fulfill tactics identified for a quality attribute*"; another reported, "*It was not clear how to relate the tactics to components.*" In 2011, a team reported, "*It is difficult to find one style to fit every aspect of the software architecture. It is also difficult to identify architectural pattern combinations to the context.*"

In the literature, these problems have been reported and considered, but still much has to be performed. Bachman et al. (Bachmann et al., 2003) describe steps for deriving architectural tactics. These steps include identifying candidate reasoning frameworks that include the mechanisms needed to use sound analytic theories to analyze the behavior of a system with respect to some quality attributes (Bachmann et al., 2005). However, this involves that fact that architects need to be familiar with formal specifications that are specific to quality models. Research tools are being developed to aid architects in integrating their reasoning frameworks (Diaz-Pace et al., 2008), but still reasoning frameworks have to be implemented, and tactics descriptions and their applications have to be indicated by the architect. It has also been reported in Remco and Van Vliet (2009) that some quality attributes do not have a reasoning framework.

Architecture prototyping is an experimental approach for determining whether architecture tactics provide desired quality attributes and to observe conflicting qualities (Bardram et al., 2005). This technique can be complementary to the ADD method. However, it has been found to be quite expensive, and "substantial" effort must be invested to adopt architecture prototyping (Christensen and Hansen, 2010).

Harrison and Avgeriou analyze the impact of architectural patterns on quality attributes and how patterns interact with tactics (Harrison and Avgeriou, 2007, 2010). The documentation of this kind of analysis can aid in creating repositories for tactics and patterns based on quality attributes. ADD depends on these kinds of repositories, which currently do not exist.

### 2.4.2 **Analysis of the results**

In both years, we can *accept* our hypothesis "*H1: ADD is perceived as useful.*" This emphasizes literature reviews such as (Falessi et al., 2007) where the ADD method is one of the best methods for meeting software architects' needs. This can be attributed to the fact that it deals with quality attributes in an explicit way.

On the other hand, we *reject* the hypothesis "*H2: ADD is perceived as easy to use.*" Notice that the median for the item PU5 in 2010 was neutral; however, for the 2011 subjects, the median is 2. In other words, they answered that they were quite unlikely to perceive the ADD method as easy. In addition, if we compare $W+$ to the Wilcoxon statistic, we can determine if the median of ease of use is less than the neutral value. We can confirm that for 2010, H2 is rejected with a neutral opinion, and for 2011, H2 is rejected with a negative tendency, indicating ADD is not perceived as easy. These results can be interpreted to mean that a good number of the 2010 subjects felt they needed more training in ADD method steps or they needed to practice it more times to decide if it was easy or not. The 2011 subjects felt it was difficult, and they expressed that, when explaining their problems, they would be required to be more professional and knowledgeable, specifically in understanding quality attributes and applying architectural patterns.

Willingness of use received a neutral value on the Likert scale, and comparing it with hypothesis test, we reject the hypothesis "*H3: There is willingness to use ADD.*" Many interpretations for having a high percentage for neutral answers exist. One of them can be that, due to the fact that our subjects were not practicing as industrial software architects at the time of the study, they could not predict if they would use ADD or not. Another possible interpretation is that the subjects did not know other methods for designing architectures other than the ADD method, and they believed that they needed to have knowledge in other methods to make an appropriate choice.

We found out there is a positive correlation between usefulness and willingness to use in both years. In addition, the study points out that there is no significant correlation between perceived ease of use and willingness to use, as well as no significant correlation between usefulness and ease of use. Therefore, we accept hypothesis: "*H4: Perceived usefulness of ADD has a positive incidence over willingness to use.*" Hypotheses "*H5: ADD's perceived ease of use has a positive incidence over its willingness of use*" and "*H6: Perceived usefulness of ADD has a positive incidence over its ease of use*" are rejected.

Our results could indicate that users of the ADD method are driven to adopt it primarily because of its usefulness in architecting rather than on how hard or easy it is to use. The issues reported in the previous section could have influenced the perceived usefulness and ease of use in the following ways:

- *Team workload division and assignment:* This issue could have influenced the perceived usefulness to the subjects, because workload and assignment can affect the productivity in architecture design (PU3) and in accomplishing the tasks quicker (PU4).
- *No consensus in terminology:* This issue could have influenced the perceived ease of use for the subjects. Specifically, the learning of the terminology of ADD could have been perceived hard (PEU1), the subjects believed they needed expert help (PEU2), and they were not skillful enough (PEU3). In addition, the usefulness of the ADD could have been slightly influenced negatively due to this issue because the subjects perceived that they would not be doing the right things (effectiveness PU3).

- *Attribute driven design first iteration:* This problem could have influenced the ease of use negatively. Specifically, learning (PEU1) the ADD was difficult, and the subjects felt they needed expert help (PEU2). Also, the usefulness of ADD has been affected negatively due to the lack of instruction about how to make decisions as users felt that ADD was not effective in providing guidance in choosing the architectural drivers in the first iteration (PU3).
- *Mapping quality attributes to tactics, and tactics to patterns*: This problem could have negatively affected the perception of the usefulness of the ADD method. Given that students had problems identifying patterns and tactics, they could have perceived that they were less effective (PU3) and that the design of their architecture was not easy to be performed using ADD (PU6). In addition, users responded negatively to each item used to measure ADD perceived ease of use (learning, expert help needed, or being skillful).

### 2.4.3 Lessons learned

Several of the lessons we learned from this study can be applied in training software architects and in focusing research directions. From a training perspective, we have learned that:

- Students perceive that ADD is useful and that ADD enhances their effectiveness in Architecture Design (PU3). From this, we can learn that ADD can be an appropriate part of the software architecture curriculum because the students value its usefulness in giving them guidelines that they can follow when architecting.
- To increase the ease of use of the ADD, more training has to be given to students by concentrating on the problems they faced. These problems can be software architecture technical as well as other aspects. For example, more training in software architecture concerning tactics and the use of architectural styles has to be performed. In addition, although many of the students received previous training in requirements engineering, they did not have a clear idea what quality attributes are and had not previously specified quality attribute scenarios.

From a research perspective, we have learned that:

- Although the ADD does not cover behavioral aspects, the software architecting process is human related, involving assembling teams and teamwork with other architects. Much research should concentrate in this direction. The SEI has also recognized this and is working on combining ADD with a team software process (Nord et al., 2010).
- Detecting the practices that students/users perform in each ADD step and the specific challenges they face aids in improving its teaching and practical application. As we discussed previously, we have analyzed some of the practices related to some of the problems. It would be interesting to understand how the combination of the different practices chosen at each step can affect the later steps and the resulting architecture.
- Tools for supporting the ADD steps: An integrated tool that supports the ADD step by step would be of great value. This can include verifying that each step has been performed correctly, suggesting recommended practices, and facilitating the voting and the design decision making. In addition, the tool can contain a repository of well-known and available tactics and patterns related to quality attributes. This would reduce the effort of users to look for the scattered knowledge.

### 2.4.4 **Threats to validity**

As our research design is nonexperimental and we cannot make cause-effect statements, internal validity is not contemplated (Mitchell, 2004).

Face validity: The questions were shown to two researchers who were not involved in this research. They indicated that the terms *efficiency* and *productivity*, which are often used in TAM questions, are not easy to understand. As a result, the terms were explained in the introduction of the questionnaire.

Content validity: The questionnaire used is based on the established model of TAM for measuring usefulness and ease of use. The items in the questionnaire are similar to the questions used in several studies that have followed TAM.

Criterion validity: We checked whether the results behave according to the theoretical model (TAM). In this case, the criterion validity can be checked by the Spearman's $\rho$ correlation. The correlations among the variables behave in the theoretical expected way. In addition, other TAM studies have also found similar correlations (Davis, 1989).

Construct validity: The internal consistency of the questions was verified with the Cronbach's $\alpha$. For minimizing bias errors, the researchers did not express to the participants opinions nor have any expectation. The surveys were collected anonymously. In addition, the researchers are not related to the creation of the ADD, and the results of the study do not affect them directly.

Conclusion validity: The main threat is the small sample used. However, in order to have more meaningful results, we used nonparametric tests instead of parametric tests. Because this is an exploratory study, the hypotheses built into this study can be used in future studies to be validated with a richer sample. In respect to the random heterogeneity of subjects, the participants have more or less the same design experience and have received the same training about software architecture design.

External validity: The results can be generalized to novel software architects who have received formal training in software architecture design and in the ADD method. We have repeated the experiment in order to confirm our initial findings with students. The domain of the project was changed in the two experiments, but both of them are Web applications with similar characteristics. Untrained architects and experienced architects in practice may have different perceptions than the ones found in this study. However, we believe there are practices common to all business-related (not critical or real time) domains. There is a threat that the academic context is not similar to industrial. In our case, we did not restrict the teams to work in specific hours and times such as in a lab. The development of the tasks was flexible. They were also given a deadline as in the real world to deliver the architecture documentation.

Ethical validity: The questionnaire questions and the study method were approved by The Research Ethics Committee of the University of Limerick.

## 2.5 CONCLUSIONS AND FURTHER WORK

This chapter describes an exploratory study to evaluate the perceived usefulness, ease of use, and willingness to use of the ADD method. The evaluation performed follows the TAM. The study was performed in an experiment in 2010, and was replicated in 2011 in order to verify the results obtained in 2010. We have achieved similar results in both experiments, indicated by the fact that the acceptance or rejection of our hypotheses did not change.

The subjects are students who had no previous industrial experience in designing software architecture and who received basic training on the ADD method. They have perceived the ADD software architecture design as useful and believe that it made it easier for them to design architectures. In addition, they have not perceived ADD as easy to use. In both years, the hypothesis "ADD is perceived as easy" was rejected, but in 2010 the students had a neutral opinion while the students in 2011 found the ADD was not easy to be used. In both years, the students had a neutral opinion about their willingness to use it. We have also found that perceived usefulness has a positive correlation with willingness to use. However, ease of use is not correlated to willingness to use nor usefulness.

We have also discussed the problems that the subjects faced when designing with ADD. These problems concern: (1) No explanation of team workload division and assignment, (2) no consensus in terminology, (3) the first iteration of ADD was difficult to understand, and (4) mapping quality attributes to tactics, and tactics to patterns was not clear. These problems could have affected the subjects' opinion in determining their neutral answers to perceived easiness and their slight agreement with the usefulness of ADD.

In the near future, we would like to replicate this study in order to increase our sample and improve our questionnaire. We are also planning to replicate this study in an industrial setting to take into account more experienced architects and compare their perception with the students' results.

One of our objectives is to research whether our findings in ADD can be generalized to other software architecture design methods. In this way, we can compare and contrast the different methods from software architects' perspective. In addition, we would like to understand which people hold the appropriate skills for applying ADD. This is important for the software architecture community in order to improve the training and further research in the field of design methods.

# References

Bachmann, F., Bass, L., Klein, M., 2003. Deriving architectural tactics: a step toward methodical architectural design. CMU/SEI-2003-TR-004. ESC-TR-2003-004.

Bachmann, F., Bass, L., Klein, M., Shelton, C., 2005. Designing software architectures to achieve quality attribute requirements. Softw. IEE 152 (4), 153–165.

Bardram, J.E., Christensen, H.B., Corry, A.V., Hansen, K.M., Ingstrup, M., 2005. Exploring Quality Attributes Using Architectural Prototyping. Proceedings of First International Conference on the Quality of Software Architectures, September. In: Lecture Notes in Computer Science, vol. 3712. Springer-Verlag, Berlin, Heidelberg, pp. 155–170, September.

Bass, L., Clements, P., Kazman, R., 2003. Software Architecture in Practice, second ed. Addison-Wesley Professional, Boston, MA.

Christensen, H.B., Hansen, K.M., 2010. An empirical investigation of architectural prototyping. J. Syst. Softw. 83 (1), 133–142.

Davis, F.D., 1989. Perceived usefulness, perceived ease of use, and user acceptance of information technology. MIS Q. 13 (3), 319–340.

Diaz-Pace, A., Kim, H., Bass, L., Bianco, P., Bachmann, F., 2008. Integrating Quality-Attribute Reasoning Frameworks in the ArchE Design Assistant. Proceedings of the 4th International Conference on Quality of Software-Architectures: Models and Architectures. In: Lecture Notes in Computer Science, vol. 5281. Springer, Berlin, pp. 171–188.

Dulva Hina, M., Tadj, C.K., Ramdane-Cherif, A., 2006. Attribute-driven design of incremental learning component of a ubiquitous multimodal multimedia computing system. In: Canadian Conference on Electrical and Computer, Engineering, pp. 323–327, May.

Eikebrokk, T.R., Iden, J., Olsen, D.H., Opdahl, A.L., 2010. Determinants to the use of business process modeling. In: 43rd Hawaii International Conference on System Sciences, pp. 1–10, January.

Falessi, D., Cantone, G., Kruchten, P., 2007. Do architecture design methods meet architects' needs? In: Sixth Working IEEE/IFIP Conference on Software, Architecture (WICSA'07), pp. 44–53.

Ferrari, R., Madhavji, N., 2008. Software architecting without requirements knowledge and experience: what are the repercussions? J. Syst. Softw. 81 (9), 1470–1490.

George, D., Mallery, P., 2009. SPSS for Windows Step by Step: A Simple Study Guide and Reference, 170 Update, tenth ed. Allyn & Bacon.

Gorton, I., 2006. Essential Software Architecture. Springer-Verlag, New York.

Gross, D., Yu, E., 2001. From non-functional requirements to design through patterns. Requir. Eng. 6 (1), 18–36, February.

Habli, I., Kelly, T., 2007. Capturing and Replaying Architectural Knowledge through Derivational Analogy. In: Proceedings of the Second Workshop on Sharing and Reusing Architectural Knowledge Architecture, Rationale, and Design Intent.

Harrison, N.B., Avgeriou, P., 2007. Leveraging Architecture Patterns to Satisfy Quality Attributes. European Conference on Software Architecture. In: Lecture Notes in Computer Science, vol. 4758. Springer, Berlin, Heildelberg, pp. 263–270.

Harrison, N.B., Avgeriou, P., 2010. How do architecture patterns and tactics interact? A model and annotation. J. Syst. Softw. 83 (10), 1735–1758.

Hofmeister, C., Nord, R.L., Soni, D., 2005. Global analysis: moving from software requirements specification to structural views of the software architecture. IEE Proc. Softw. 152 (4), 187–197.

Hofmeister, C., Kruchten, P., Nord, R.L., Obbink, H., Ran, A., America, P., 2007. A general model of software architecture design derived from five industrial approaches. J. Syst. Softw. 80 (1), 106–126.

Jamieson, S., 2004. Likert scales: how to (ab)use them. Med. Educ. 38 (12), 1217–1218. [Online] Available:http://dx.doi.org/10.1111/j.1365-2929.2004.02012, December.

Kannengiesser, U., Zhu, L., 2009. An ontologically-based evaluation of software design methods. Knowl. Eng. Rev. 24 (1), 41–58, December.

Kazman, R., Bass, L., Klein, M., 2006. The essential components of software architecture design and analysis. J. Syst. Softw. 79 (8), 1207–1216.

Kitchenham, B., Pfleeger, B.A., 2007. Personal opinion surveys. In: Shull, F., Singer, J., Sjøberg, D.I.K. (Eds.), In: Guide to Advanced Empirical Software Engineering. Springer-Verlag, London, pp. 63–92.

Kruchten, P., 2004. The Rational Unified Process: An Introduction. Addison-Wesley.

Lee, J., Shin, G.S., 2008. Quality attribute driven architecture design and evaluation for embedded operating system. In: Advanced Communication Technology, pp. 367–371.

Lindsay, R.M., Ehrenberg, A.S.C., 1993. The Design of Replicated Studies. Am. Stat. 47 (3), 217–228, August.

Mitchell, M.I., 2004. Research Design Explained, fifth ed. Thomson-Wadsworth.

Nord, R., McHale, J., Bachman, F., 2010. Combining Architecture-Centric Engineering with the Team Software Process, Technical report CMU/SEI-2010-TR-031, December 2010.

Remco, C., Van Vliet, H., 2009. QuOnt: an ontology for the reuse of quality criteria. In: ICSE Workshop on Sharing and Reusing Architectural Knowledge, pp. 57–64.

Shaw, M., Garlan, D., 1996. Software Architecture Perspectives on an Emerging Discipline. Prentice Hall, Upper Saddle River, NJ.

Software Engineering Institute, 2010a. Software Architecture Glossary. http://www.sei.cmu.edu/architecture/start/glossary/.

Software Engineering Institute, 2010b. Architecture Training. http://www.sei.cmu.edu/architecture/start/training/index.cfm.

Stevens, S.S., 1946. On the Theory of Scales of Measurement. Science, New Series, vol. 103, No. 2684. , pp. 677-680 (June 7, 1946).

Taylor, R., Medvidovic, N., Dashofy, E., 2010. Software Architecture, Foundations, Theory, and Practice. Wiley Publishing, Hoboken, NJ.

Toral, S.L., Barrero, F., Martínez-Torres, M.R., 2007. Analysis of utility and use of a web-based tool for digital signal processing teaching by means of a technological acceptance model. Comput. Educ. 49 (4), 957–975, December.

Wojcik, R., Bachmann, F., Bass, L., Clements, P., Merson, P., Nord, R., Wood, B., 2006. Attribute-Driven Design (ADD), Version 2.0, Technical report CMU/SEI-2006-TR-023, SEI.

Wood, W.G., 2007. A practical Example of Applying attribute-Driven Design (ADD), Version 2.0, Technical report CMU/SEI 2007-TR-005, SEI.

# Harmonizing the Quality View of Stakeholders

**Vladimir A. Shekhovtsov, Heinrich C. Mayr, and Christian Kop**

*Alpen-Adria-Universität Klagenfurt, Klagenfurt, Austria*

## INTRODUCTION

A software development process typically has many stakeholders: the prospective end users, business actors, architecture and software designers, software developers and integrators, database engineers, test engineers, and others. All these should agree at an early stage on the same—or close enough—view of quality to make a software development process successful. Only then quality requirements can be determined reliably, implemented during software development, and thus met by the resulting system.

Failure to establish an appropriate common understanding of the prospective system's quality leads to the problems in the late stages of the development lifecycle that are very difficult and expensive to fix. In particular, the end users' opinions and expectations on software quality tend to be neglected or at least handled incompletely; as a result, the understanding of system quality becomes biased toward the view of the software developers—a problem known as "the inmates are running the asylum" (Cooper, 2004). This is supported by evidence of the practice of development: For example, a study of the current practice of the Quality Aware Software Engineering (QuASE) partner companies revealed that in the early stages of their software lifecycles, mainly usability is addressed, including handling performance and other issues is often postponed until system deployment. Clearly, that approach comes with negative consequences for all parties, because fixing the problems with unsatisfied stakeholder expectations on the late stages of the software process is difficult and expensive and may even lead to the failure of the whole project (Walia and Carver, 2009; Westland, 2002).

Thus it is necessary to harmonize the different stakeholder views of quality from the beginning throughout the complete development process, addressing requirements engineering via architectural design, specification to implementation, test, and rollout. This applies for both traditional structured and lightweight agile development processes.

For this purpose, an appropriate communication channel between the stakeholders has to be established, allowing them to discuss all relevant quality issues from their respective views.

This chapter presents a conceptualization of quality view harmonization and summarizes the related state of the art in research and development. In detail, we identify the dimensions of knowledge that are relevant for view harmonization, propose a set of concepts for each dimension, and align these where possible with concepts offered by other approaches. Our concepts will be grounded in the Unified Foundational Ontology (UFO) (Guizzardi, 2005) and materialized by applying them to the empirical data in a given software development venture. Thus, our conceptualization is intended to be a key constituent of a common ontology of stakeholder perception and assessment (QuOntology). This ontology can be used to support the organization of the interaction process following the ontology-based software engineering paradigm.

The following dimensions of quality view harmonization will be addressed:

1. The quality of system under development (SUD) itself and the related aspects as well as their interrelations, in particular, the notion of quality assessment and the concepts utilized in the quality assessment activities.
2. The knowledge about the various stakeholders, the differences in their perception of quality, and the amount of knowledge about the software quality issues.
3. The knowledge about the activities of the harmonization process and the capabilities of the process participants needed for performing these activities.

The harmonization process will be dealt with on three levels:

1. Terminology harmonization: The stakeholders seek an agreement on the common quality-related terminology, the language constructs used for expressing expectations and opinions on quality. These can emerge in natural, domain-specific, or even formal language. The purpose of harmonization is to make them understandable to all stakeholders of the process.
2. View harmonization: The stakeholders seek an agreement on the sets of objects and the types of their qualities they are interested in, as well as the procedures of assessment.
3. Quality harmonization: The stakeholders seek an agreement on the evaluation schemes and the particular qualities they are interested in.

In this chapter, we concentrate on the view and quality harmonization.

The concepts presented here are consolidated by a study that is part of the ongoing QuASE project. We carried out detailed interviews with various members of the four industrial QuASE partners. The answers have been transcribed using the basic techniques of coding and conceptualization stages of the grounded theory (Adolph et al., 2011; Coleman and O'Connor, 2008). The obtained evidence then was combined with our own experience and with the body of knowledge inherent in the software quality standards such as ISO/IEC 25010 (ISO, 2011). A detailed description of this empirical study and an outline of the upcoming industrial application of the proposed conceptualization are presented in Section 3.4.

The chapter is structured as follows: In Section 3.1, we present the concepts we adopt from the UFO for grounding our approach. Section 3.2 introduces the conceptualization of quality assessments to be used as a foundation for the conceptualization of the harmonization process that is discussed in Section 3.3 on the three aforementioned levels supplemented with a running example of instantiating the proposed concepts. In Section 3.4, we describe the conducted empirical study and show how to apply the proposed concepts in practice. The chapter closes with a conclusion and directions for future research.

## 3.1 ADOPTED CONCEPTS OF THE UFO

We follow a multilevel approach to conceptualization where upper-level (more generic) concepts form the foundation for the concepts belonging to the lower levels. Such frameworks are called *foundational ontologies* in the literature. We start with making specific foundational choices, the most important among them being the selection of the foundational framework providing upper-level generic concepts. Such ontologies define a set of basic concepts that reflect the particular world view. They can be extended and reused by the lower-level conceptual frameworks.

There are several foundational ontologies providing the concepts that could serve as a fundament for our venture: GFO (Herre, 2010), DOLCE (Masolo et al., 2003), and UFO (Guizzardi, 2005). For our purposes, we choose to adapt UFO; the reasons of that choice will be discussed at the end of this section.

Figure 3.1 depicts the subset of adapted UFO concepts that are useful for our conceptualization. The right-hand side represents the type level; according to extensional semantics, each of these concepts spans a set of instances that materialize the respectful type. The left-hand side represents the instance level and, as result, conceptualizes the materialization of the type level.

The root of the relevant UFO concept hierarchy is *Thing,* which generalizes the concepts *Individual, Type,* and *Abstract.* Individuals are Things that exist in the real world and possess a unique identity; Types can be seen as "templates of features," which may be materialized in a number of Individuals.

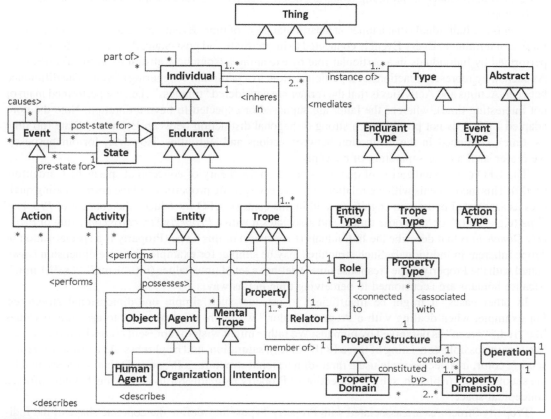

**FIGURE 3.1**

Fragment of the Unified Foundational Ontology.

*Adapted from Guizzardi and Zamborlini (2013).*

In other words, they are *instantiated* by Individuals; Abstracts are not materialized in the real world and therefore cannot be instantiated.

Individuals are specialized to *Endurants* or *Events*. Endurants are Individuals that exist, for a certain period, continuously in time. They are further categorized into *Entities* and *Tropes*: Entities are Individuals that may exist on their own. In contrast to this, Tropes can only exist in dependence with their "bearers," which are (instances of) Things. Entities are materializations (*instance_of*) Entity Types; Tropes are materializations of Trope Types. Following the object-oriented paradigm, Entities corresponds to objects, Tropes to attributes, and Entity Types to classes.

*Relator* is a special kind of Trope that defines a connection between two or more Individuals. As an example, think of a person assessing a particular quality. Following the object-oriented paradigm, Relators correspond to associations. One could question if the UFO explanation as a specialization of Trope is appropriate. In our opinion, it would be preferable to define Relators more generally as Entities; *inter alia*, this would allow for "objectified associations."

*Roles* are Entity Types associated to Entities where this association may change in time. In other words, the Individuals instantiating Roles are determined by their relationships (via Relators) to other Individuals.

Events are Individuals that happen at a particular point of time. Events are related to *States* that they initiate or terminate: Every Event is connected to its pre-State and post-State. *Actions* and *Activities* are performed by Individuals in a particular role by executing a (somehow abstractly defined) operation. As such, they represent reactions of a particular Role to a particular (triggering) Event. The difference between Actions and Activities is that the former are considered "timeless" (i.e., are performed in no or not interesting time), whereas the latter are supposed or expected to have a duration. Note the non-adapted UFO does not provide such strong orthogonal distinction between Event and State (no time vs. time), continued in the distinction between actions and Activities. However, for our purposes, we prefer such a clear separation of concepts.

The UFO conceptualization of quality is based on the theory of conceptual spaces by Gärdenfors (2000). This theory deals with the relationship between specific properties and the corresponding qualities as associated by human cognition. Within this context, UFO introduces the concept of *Property Type* (e.g., "color" or "response time") and associates it with a *Property Structure* consisting of *Property Dimensions* that describe the Individuals (*Properties*) of this Type (Property is a specialization of Trope inherent in Individual). Such structures may be simple; for example, the time dimension (associated with the Property Type "response time") defines a set of time values (i.e., "1 ms," "2 s," "1 min") because humans are accustomed to perceiving time in this way.

In other cases, it might be insufficient to use just such simple one-dimensional structures. For example, when dealing with a Property "color," we might want not only to use simple values like "red," "green" as perceived by humans. We rather might wish to represent colors by three values: hue (again possibly consisting of three RGB values), saturation, and brightness. As a result, for representing color, it is necessary to use a three-dimensional structure: a Property Domain represented by the set of defined triples (h, s, b). A collection of Property Domains forms, according to Gärdenfors, a conceptual space.

Property Structures are associated with Property Types; they define the concrete shape of the Individuals of these Property Types, otherwise known as the Properties. Property Types conceptualize quality characteristics and the relevant metrics as defined by such standards as ISO/IEC 9126 (ISO, 2001, 2003a,b, 2004) and ISO/IEC 25010 (ISO, 2011).

A specific subset of UFO (UFO-C) (Guizzardi et al., 2008) is devoted to conceptualizing the human social context. Among these concepts, we limited ourselves to adopting the concept of *Agent* describing active Entities that can respond to Events by performing Actions or Activities; passive Entities that cannot respond to Events are *Objects*. We further distinguish *Human Agents* and *Organizations*. UFO-C distinguishes *Mental Trope* as a subtype of Trope. Mental Tropes are related to Human Agents and reflect their capacity to respond to situations emerging in reality. In this chapter, we are interested in one category of such Mental Tropes, namely, *Intentions*. Intentions can be understood as "internal commitments" of the Agents to do something according to their will and, eventually, to start Activities or Actions.

### 3.1.1 Selection of the Foundational Ontology

We considered UFO, DOLCE, and GFO as the alternatives for the choice of the foundational ontology. Although all these ontologies provide the conceptual notions suitable for representing qualities of software artifacts and the process of their assessment by quality subjects, they apply different approaches to deal with these notions:

1. DOLCE treats all qualities as particulars (actually, this ontology positions itself as the "ontology of particulars"). There is no notion corresponding to the quality characteristic as understood by industry standards as a type (template) for the particular qualities, it also lacks concepts representing human social contexts.
2. GFO is an ontology that also lacks components related to human social context and the detailed representation of quality-related concepts.
3. UFO provides both particulars (Qualities) and generics (Quality Types); it also includes concepts related to quality and human social contexts.

As a result, we can justify the selection of UFO by the fact that it provides the most complete set of foundational concepts related to the representation of object and system qualities and the classification of such qualities.

As an alternative to using foundational ontology as the base for the presented set of concepts, it is possible to consider using meta-modeling approach such as SPEM (OMG, 2008) or ISO/IEC 24744 (ISO, 2007) targeting software development processes. These solutions, however, also do not provide concepts related to the representation of object and system qualities and the classification of such qualities.

## 3.2 ASSESSMENT AND RELATED CONCEPTS

Informally, quality assessment consists of associating Qualities (that conceptualize the assessment results) to Properties; this induces a ranking if the set of instances of the respective Quality Type is partially or fully ordered. Such ranking may be implicit if no other comparison object is explicitly mentioned.

Quality assessment is done by the Quality Subjects (stakeholders) according to their particular viewpoints, appraisals, preferences, and priorities—and thus requires a subsequent harmonization. As a consequence, quality assessment can be seen and formalized from two levels: the *specification level* (dealing with specification of assessments) and the *execution level* (dealing with the execution of assessments).,Conceptualizing the specification level means to describe the way of performing assessments and the capabilities of the subjects who perform the assessments; conceptualizing the execution level means to capture the relevant aspects of assessment execution along its specification, including the assessed values, the results of the assessments, the time needed and consumed for assessments. In this section, we will describe the relevant concepts for both levels.

### 3.2.1 Specification-level concepts

Figure 3.2 depicts the specification-level concepts; our extensions to UFO are shaded in gray.

We start by introducing the concepts that reflect the human way to assess Properties, namely to associate *Quality Types* (e.g., "color quality" or "response time quality") with Property Types and to assign instances ("*Qualities,*" e.g., "good," "bad," "interesting") of the former to the latter. Note that in the case of Property Structures, such associations and assignments may occur on different levels and include aggregations.

*Software Artifacts* are Objects that are produced in a software process; their qualities are of interest to the involved *Quality Subjects. Quality Assessment Functions* conceptualize the association of Qualities (or combinations of those) to Software Artifacts. More specifically, Qualities are assigned to the related Properties of the given artifact. This leads to the following definition:

**Definition 1:** Let SA be a Software Artifact, $PT_{SA}$ the set of Property Types, instances of which are inherent in (components of) SA. For $pt \in PT_{SA}$, let $I_{pt}$ be the set of instances of pt and $I_{qt}$ the set of instances of the Quality Type qt associated with pt. Then a Property-Level *Quality Assessment Function* is formally defined as $f_{SApt}: I_{pt} \rightarrow I_{qt}$.

Note that, depending on the related Quality Structure definition, Qualities may be scalar as well as structured. In a concrete application, the Quality Assessment function may be both

- *ad hoc* defined by a Quality Subject in such a manner that he/she directly assigns Qualities to the Properties at hand.

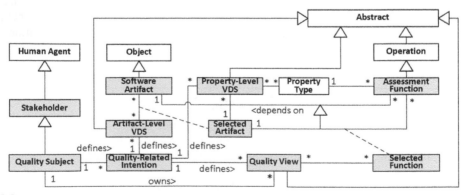

**FIGURE 3.2**

Specification-level concepts for Property-Level Assessments.

| $f_{\text{SA,response time}}$ | |
|---|---|
| $I_{\text{response\_time}}$ | $I_{\text{response\_time\_quality}}$ |
| <1 s | Good |
| [1s, 2s] | Satisfying |
| >2 s | Bad |

**FIGURE 3.3**

Tabular definition of a Quality Assessment Function.

- predefined by means of a functional definition that can be used to calculate a concrete value assignment. As an example, consider Figure 3.3, which depicts a tabular definition of a Quality Assessment Function that associates the Qualities "Good," "Satisfying," and "Bad" with Quality Type "response_time_quality" depending on the current Individual of Property Type "response time."

Artifact-Level Quality Assessment Functions associate Qualities with Artifacts based on (sub)sets of their Properties. Such function can be defined as $f_{\text{SA PT}'_{\text{SA}}} : \{I_{\text{pt}}|\text{pt} \in \text{PT}'_{\text{SA}} \subseteq \text{PT}_{\text{SA}}\} \to I_{\text{SA}}$, where $I_{\text{SA}}$ is the set of instances of the Quality Type associated with the Entity Type of the particular Software Artifact. Clearly, the SUD itself is such an artifact.

As depicted on Figure 3.4, it is possible to distinguish:

- *System-Level Qualities,* which belong to the whole system and cannot be derived from the Qualities of its parts (e.g., its total cost).

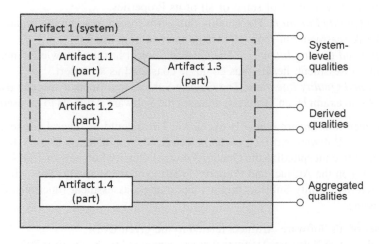

**FIGURE 3.4**

The relationships between the qualities of the system and the qualities of its parts.

- *Derived Qualities,* which depend on the Qualities of the parts of the system (e.g., the value of latency depends on the Quality Type related to the particular component such as hardware and software performance).
- *Aggregated Qualities* (e.g., the user-interface-related Qualities of the whole system could be considered as the aggregated Qualities of its user-interface-related components).

All these categories of Qualities need to be taken into account in the System-Level Assessment Function.

In general, because Software Artifacts are Individuals that can be part of other Individuals, we can reduce the System-Level and Artifact-Level Functions to the generic version of the Artifact-Level Function, which could perform aggregation over the parts of their corresponding Software Artifact.

*Stakeholders* are Human Agents participating in the software development process. Quality Subjects are Stakeholders capable of performing Quality Assessments and thus parties in the harmonization process. They apply Quality Assessment Functions driven by their Individual Intentions.

Not all Stakeholders are necessarily Quality Subjects. For example, if we consider the Stakeholder instances "hardware supplier," "developer," and "end user" and assume that hardware supplier has delivered the best of the market so no optimization of hardware is possible, in case of a performance issue in the SUD, the Quality Subjects who have to harmonize their views are "developer" and "end user," whereas "hardware supplier" can be filtered out in this situation. If dealing with quality issues related to the response time of data accesses, then the involved Quality Subjects will be "end user," "database backend developer," and "database supplier," whereas "UI developer" might be filtered out. On the other hand, while doing a usability check, "UI developer" and "end user" will more likely serve as Quality Subjects.

*Quality-Related Intentions* characterize the Intentions of Quality Subjects when performing Quality Assessment. Given that different Quality Subjects may have different attitudes toward performing the Assessment, we need to distinguish between several categories of *Quality-Related Intentions:*

- *Interest-Related Quality Intention*: The Quality Subject is interested in the Assessment of a particular Software Artifact or of some or all of its Properties.
- *Force-Related Quality Intention*: The Quality Subject is forced (e.g., by the organizational duties) to perform the Assessment but probably has no interest in doing this.
- *Knowledge-Related Quality Intention:* The Quality Subject has the knowledge needed for performing the Assessment; he/she thus could be consulted as an expert.
- *Viewpoint-Related Quality Intention:* The Quality Subject represents a specific user group (viewpoint). As an example, an IT person assesses the Software Artifacts to be used by IT persons.

Quality-Related Intentions are not mutually exclusive: There could be several connections between a Quality Subject and a Software Artifact, each characterized by a different Quality-Related Intention.

We now proceed to conceptualize the Quality Views of Quality Subjects by first introducing *View-Defining Sets* (VDS) on the Artifact and Property Type Level, respectively. This will lead us to those Properties to which the Quality Subjects might want to apply assessment functions. For that purpose assume the following:

- $A_{\text{UoD}}$ is the set of all Software Artifacts related to the given UoD.
- $A_u \subseteq A_{\text{UoD}}$ is the set of Software Artifacts that are connected to the Quality Subject $u$ by means of Quality Intentions (*Subject-u-related Artifacts*).

- $PT_a$ is the set of all Property Types defined for the Software Artifact $a \in A_u$.
- $PT_{au} \subseteq PT_a$ is the set of Subject-$u$-related Property Types of $a \in A_u$.
- $P_u$ is the set of all Quality-Related Intentions of $u$.
- $VDS_i \subseteq A_u$ is the Artifact-Level "View-Defining Set" = set of Software Artifacts related to Intention $i \in P_u$.
- $VDS_{ia} \subseteq PT_{au}$ is the Property-Level "View-Defining Set" = (sub)set of Property Types associated with Software Artifact and related to the Intention $i$.

Then the *Quality View* of a Quality Subject $u$ for a particular Intention $i$ may be defined as the total of Quality Assessment Functions that this Quality Subject applies to the elements of the VDS for Intention $i$:

$$QV_i = \{f_{at} | t \in VDS_{ia}, a \in VDS_i\} \cup \{f_{aVDS_{ia}} | a \in VDS_i\}$$

A Quality Subject may have different Quality Views at the same time connected to his/her different Quality-Related Intentions; for example, a developer could deal with different Business Stakeholders. In this situation, he/she can utilize a specific Quality View for the purpose of communication with every Stakeholder.

### 3.2.2 Execution-level concepts

After conceptualizing what and how it is assessed, we now have to define the concepts that will enable us to capture the process of performing the assessments. The schema illustrating these concepts is shown on Figure 3.5.

The key execution-level quality-related concept is *Quality Assessment*. Again we differentiate between Software Artifact and Property-Type Level. On the latter, Assessment is viewed as an Activity depending on the following Individuals:

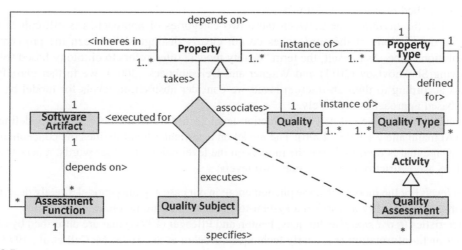

**FIGURE 3.5**

Execution-level concepts for Property-Type Level Assessment.

1. The Property of the particular Software Artifact to be considered for assessment.
2. The Quality Subject performing the assessment.
3. The Quality that is assigned to the particular Property as a result of assessment.

Artifact-Level Assessment is viewed as the Activity depending on the following Individuals:

1. The Software Artifact to be assessed.
2. The (sub)set of its Properties to be considered for assessment.
3. The Quality Subject performing the assessment.
4. The Quality that is assigned to the particular Artifact as a result of assessment.

To establish the connection between execution-level and specification-level concepts, Quality Assessment Functions are used to perform particular assessments. The Property-Level Quality Assessment operation takes a particular Property $p \in I_{pt}$, applies the corresponding Quality Assessment Function $f_{SA\,pt}$, thus associating the Quality $q \in I_{qt}$ to Property $p$ according the specification of $f_{SA\,pt}$.

The Artifact-Level Quality Assessment operation takes a particular version of SA represented by a (sub)set of its Properties, $P_{SA\,PT'_{SA}} = \{p | p \in I_{pt}, pt \in PT'_{SA} \subseteq PT_{SA}\}$, and applies the corresponding Quality Assessment Function $f_{SA\,PT'_{SA}}$.

## 3.2.3 State of the Art: Addressing basic quality-related concepts

We published a detailed literature review of the *quality conceptualization techniques* in Shekhovtsov (2011). Among these techniques, following Aßmann and Zschaler (2006) and Pastor and Molina (2007), we distinguish:

There are survey papers devoted to *model-based approaches,* which conceptualize software quality in a solution space (prescriptively defining the system-to-be) under the "closed-world" assumption (everything not explicitly described is assumed nonexistent) (Carvallo, 2005; Deissenboeck et al., 2009).

*Ontology-based approaches* conceptualize software quality in a problem space (describing the real-world problem domain addressed by the SUD) under the "open-world" assumption (everything not explicitly described is assumed unknown).

In practice, the dividing line between these two categories of approaches is difficult to define, because the descriptions of the approaches do not clearly distinguish between the problem space and the solution space. As a result, the term "quality model" often refers to ontology-based solutions.

Following Shekhovtsov (2011) and Wagner and Deissenboeck (2007), we further classify these techniques according to their abstraction level; we consider abstraction levels for model-based and ontology-based approaches separately.

For quality models, we define the abstraction level according to the notion of a modeling meta-pyramid (Aßmann and Zschaler, 2006): The model on a particular level defines the conceptualization of the language that is used to define the models on the level below. In other words, it acts as a meta-model. Here, we restrict ourselves to only two levels:

1. *Model level*: For the models of some phenomenon; in our case a quality model directly describes the phenomenon of quality as used in a system-to-be; examples are taxonomies of quality characteristics (*fixed model* techniques; Fenton and Pfleeger (1997)) that are described by example without meta-information (e.g., early techniques, Boehm et al., 1978; McCall et al., 1977, standards, ISO, 2001, 2011). Such approaches are criticized due to the arbitrary choice of quality characteristics (Deissenboeck et al., 2009; Kitchenham and Pfleeger, 1996).

2. *Meta-model level*: For the meta-models (models of languages used for describing the models); in our case a quality meta-model is used to define quality models; we further distinguish *implicit* and *explicit quality meta-models*. The former are introduced "bottom-up," via *custom* or *mixed model* QMT (Fenton and Pfleeger, 1997) and allow modification of the model structure; they often omit quality characteristics from the model descriptions (Dromey, 1996; IEEE, 1998). The latter are introduced "top-down" with the explicit purpose of describing the set of possible quality models (Burgués et al., 2005; Cachero et al., 2007; Jureta et al., 2009b; Susi et al., 2005). Industry examples are *UML quality profiles* adding support for new modeling concepts to UML via an extension of the UML meta-model (Aagedal et al., 2004; Apvrille et al., 2004; OMG, 2003; Rodríguez et al., 2006).

For *ontological approaches*, the abstraction level refers to the concepts being described, not the description approach (all ontologies of different levels can be defined using the same ontology language).

Before elaborating the description of these two levels, it is necessary to mention that basic concepts for representing qualities could be found in most foundational ontologies (we have already discussed this issue in Section 3.2). Different approaches to the definition of concepts for representing properties, qualities, and their perception in the human mind are surveyed in Masolo and Borgo(2005).

The two ontological levels based on foundational ontologies are as follows:

1. The *quality upper ontologies* level covers the techniques describing the concepts (universals) for concrete quality ontologies (e.g., by defining concepts for quality characteristic, quality metric, describing their relationships) (Bertoa et al., 2006; Falbo et al., 2002; Jureta et al., 2009a; Magoutas et al., 2007). Some of these techniques are based on the so-called foundational ontologies; in particular, UFO is applied for the ontologies of software requirement management (de Almeida Falbo and Nardi, 2008), software measurement (Barcellos et al., 2010), and agent-oriented software development (Guizzardi and Wagner, 2005);
2. The *quality ontologies* level covers the techniques directly describing the phenomenon of quality (via particulars; with concepts for performance, reliability, etc.) (Al Balushi et al., 2007; Boehm and In, 1996).

## 3.3 THE HARMONIZATION PROCESS

### 3.3.1 Quality Subjects' positions in the harmonization process

Prior to elaborating the conceptualization of the harmonization process, we introduce the following concepts describing the positions of Quality Subjects within the harmonization process (Figure 3.6):

1. The *Organizational Side* is an Organization participating in the software process.
2. The *Process Side* is a Role possessed by a Quality Subject with reference to his/her affiliation with the Organizational Side.

We define two concretizations of the Organizational Side:

1. The *Business Side* is the Organizational Side ordering the software product (e.g., the customer company).

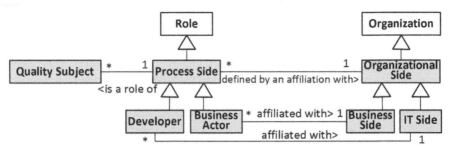

**FIGURE 3.6**

Process Side role and its related concepts.

**2.** The *IT Side* is the Organizational Side responsible for developing this product (e.g., the developing company).

The concretizations of the Organizational Side define the concretizations of the Process Side role:

**1.** The *Business Stakeholder* role is a Process Side that is taken by a Quality Subject (e.g., a person) affiliated with the responsible Business Side.
**2.** The *Developer* role is a Process Side taken by a Quality Subject (e.g., a person) affiliated with the IT Side.

In some projects, there could be additional roles extending the Process Side.

### 3.3.2 Process definition and harmonization levels

We define a *Harmonization Process* as *the entirety of interactions between involved Process Sides targeting at a set of Terminology Means, Quality Views, and Qualities that satisfies all these Process Sides.*

Such processes affect the following *harmonization levels* (which also could be seen as process stages):

**1.** *Terminology Harmonization*: The sides agree on the terminology used to describe quality-related concepts.
**2.** *View Harmonization*: The sides align their Quality Views.
**3.** *Quality Harmonization*: The sides agree on the Qualities for the particular version of the system or its component.

These activities are supposed to be enacted with different frequencies. In particular, it could be sufficient to harmonize terminology at the beginning of a particular software development project, whereas Quality harmonization, for example, should be enacted on every change in the system implementation that affects the current SUD state.

As mentioned in the section "Introduction," we restrict ourselves to the detailed description of the View and Quality harmonization activities; Terminology Harmonization is left to a separate publication.

### 3.3.3 **Running example**

For a better understandability of our description, we introduce first a running example for the harmonization process to be conceptualized that involves, for reasons of simplicity, only two persons and relates to one particular software artifact:

1. David (the Developer) and Sean (the Business Stakeholder) negotiated the quality of the software component called Financial Report Generator (FRG).
2. Initially, David considered also the Database Subsystem (DBS) and the Hardware Subsystem (HWS) as relevant artifacts, because the quality of FRG depended on their characteristics. Sean, however, only dealt with FRG because he did not see the other components of the system. As a result of negotiation, David agreed not to discuss DBS and HWS with Sean.
3. David was going to deal with the metrics for FRG internal and external quality characteristics (according to ISO/IEC 9126-2, ISO, 2003a, and ISO/IEC 9126-3, ISO, 2003b), in particular I/O utilization, memory utilization, and response time. Sean restricted himself to quality in use metrics (according to ISO/IEC 9126-4; ISO, 2004), namely FRG task efficiency. After negotiation, David agreed not to discuss I/O utilization and memory utilization; whereas Sean agreed to discuss response time instead of task efficiency because this external quality metric was understandable to him. As a result, the parties agreed to consider only FRG response time.
4. Before discussing FRG response time, the sides agreed that they will assess it using the following scale: {very bad, bad, satisfactory, good, very good} ordered from "very bad" to "very good." Also, Sean felt that very good response time would be immediately satisfactory to him so that he would accept FRG immediately; on the other hand, very bad would lead him to stop dealing with David; all other assessment results were negotiable to him.
5. Initially, David produced three FRG prototypes (starting from 1 ms response time) until he felt that the response time of 0.25 ms was good. Then he showed the prototype to Sean, who did not like it and felt this response time was bad.
6. As a result, David reconsidered his judgment and changed it from good to satisfactory. Then he continued producing prototypes until he obtained a response time of 0.1 ms, which he considered good even taking new insights into account. Then he again showed the prototype to Sean; this time Sean also felt the response time was good.
7. As a result, the parties agreed on FRG response time of 0.1 ms.

### 3.3.4 **View harmonization process**

At this level, the parties agree on their views on quality; we refer to the process of such agreement as View Harmonization Process.

In the treatment of this and the subsequent process, we assume that the parties share a common Quality-Related Intention of communicating with each other (omitting this Intention from the notational representations.)

#### 3.3.4.1 *Stage 1: Harmonizing artifacts*

The sides agree on the set of software artifacts to be included in $VDS^H$, forming the harmonized Artifact-Level VDS. Suppose that the external quality-related Properties of the Software Artifact included in $VDS^{BS}$ (i.e., the Developer's view) depend on internal quality-related Properties of other Software Artifacts included in $VDS^D$. Then, in a process of negotiation, the Developer could

1. Agree to discuss only the Software Artifact included in $VDS^{BS}$, or not to include other Software Artifacts from $VDS^D$ into $VDS^H$.
2. Propose that the other party to discuss external quality-related Property Types related to Software Artifacts from $VDS^D$, including these Artifacts in $VDS^H$.

### 3.3.4.1.1 Artifact harmonization example
The part of the running example related to artifact harmonization is conceptualized as follows:

1. David in a process of dealing with FRG considers $VDS^{David} = \{FRG, HWS, DBS\}$.
2. At the same time, Sean only deals with FRG: $VDS^{Sean} = \{FRG\}$.
3. As a result of negotiation, David agrees not to include DBS and HWS into $VDS^H$.
4. Subsequently, the parties agree on $VDS^H = \{FRG\}$.

### 3.3.4.2 *Stage 2: Harmonizing property types*
For every Software Artifact $a$ in $VDS^H$ as agreed on the previous stage, the sides agree on the set of its Property Types to be included into $VDS_a^H$, the harmonized Property-Level VDS.

It is important to emphasize that the harmonized Property Types conceptualize quality characteristics and the relevant metrics belonging to different categories, in particular, Business Stakeholders usually include Property Types conceptualizing quality in use metrics (ISO, 2004) into their VDS, whereas Developers usually include Property Types conceptualizing external (ISO, 2003a) and internal (ISO, 2003b) metrics.

Suppose the Business Stakeholder considers the set of external quality-related Property Types whereas the Developer additionally considers the set of internal quality-related Property Types for the particular artifact. In a process of negotiation, the Developer could

1. Agree to discuss only Property Types included in $VDS_a^{BS}$, or not to include other Property Types from $VDS_a^D$ in $VDS_a^H$.
2. Propose that the Business Stakeholder discuss additional Property Types, or *external quality*-related Types derived from *internal quality*-related $VDS_a^D$ Property Types; these new Property Types have to be included into $VDS_a^H$, possibly instead of some Property Types from $VDS_a^{BS}$.

### 3.3.4.2.1 Example of harmonizing property types
The part of the running example related to property type harmonization is conceptualized as follows:

1. Having agreed on FRG as the artifact under discussion, the sides have different views concerning the relevant Property Types:
   a. David is going to deal with the Property Types related to internal and external quality:
      $VDS_{FRG}^{David} = \{I/O\,utilization, memory\,utilization, response\,time\}$
   b. Sean restricts himself to Property Types related to the quality in use:
      $VDS_{FRG}^{Sean} = \{task\,efficiency\}$.
2. As a result of negotiation:
   a. David agrees not to include $\{I/O\,utilization, memory\,utilization\}$ into $VDS_{FRG}^H$
   b. Sean agrees to include response time instead of task efficiency into $VDS_{FRG}^H$.
3. As a result the parties agree on $VDS_{FRG}^H = \{response\,time\}$.

### 3.3.4.3 Stage 3: Aligning quality views

The sides now align their Quality Views to these View Definition Sets by selecting the appropriate Quality Assessment Functions. For simplicity, we assume here that the sides align Quality Views containing only Artifact-Level Functions; in this case, these views could be represented as follows:

$$\text{QV}^{\text{DH}} = \left\{ f^{\text{D}}_{a\text{VDS}^{\text{H}}_a} \middle| a \in \text{VDS}^{\text{H}} \right\}, \quad \text{QV}^{\text{BSH}} = \left\{ f^{\text{BS}}_{a\text{VDS}^{\text{H}}_a} \middle| a \in \text{VDS}^{\text{H}} \right\}$$

To align Quality Views, the following activities are performed:

1. The Developer adjusts Quality Assessment Functions belonging to $\text{QV}^{\text{D}}$ to deal with the Properties of types belonging to $\text{VDS}^{\text{H}}$; in particular the following activities for every $a \in \text{VDS}^{\text{H}}$ are performed:
   a. If $a \notin \text{VDS}^{\text{D Old}}$ (new artifact has been taken into account as a result of harmonization) a new $f^{\text{D}}_{a\text{VDS}^{\text{H}}}$ is formed and added to the Quality View $\text{QV}^{\text{DH}}$ (here $\text{VDS}^{\text{D Old}}$ is the Developer's original non-harmonized VDS).
   b. If $a \in \text{VDS}^{\text{D Old}}$, but the corresponding $\text{VDS}^{\text{D Old}}_a \neq \text{VDS}^{\text{H}}_a$ (it has been changed as a result of harmonization, e.g., by omitting internal quality-related Property Types not understood by Business Stakeholder), the corresponding $f^{\text{D}}_{a\text{VDS}^{\text{H}}_a}$ is adjusted to deal with modified $\text{VDS}^{\text{H}}_a$.
2. The same activities are performed by Business Stakeholder.
3. Both sides explicitly agree on Quality Types for corresponding Quality Assessment Functions. For $f^{\text{D}}_{a\text{VDS}^{\text{H}}_a}$ and $f^{\text{BS}}_{a\text{VDS}^{\text{H}}_a}$, $a \in \text{VDS}^{\text{H}}$, this means that these functions assign Qualities of the same Quality Types: $I^{\text{DH}}_{\text{aqt}} = I^{\text{BSH}}_{\text{aqt}}$. This can be also performed based on the available historical information about the Quality Types involved in the past.

As a result, the sides agree on harmonized $\text{VDS}^{\text{H}}$ and $\text{VDS}^{\text{H}}_a$, $a \in \text{VDS}^{\text{H}}$ and the aligned $\text{QV}^{\text{DH}}$ and $\text{QV}^{\text{BSH}}$.

### 3.3.4.3.1 Quality view alignment example

The part of the running example related to quality view alignment is conceptualized as follows:

1. Prior to harmonization the parties had the Quality View configurations:
   a. $\text{QV}^{\text{David}} = \left\{ f^{\text{David}}_{a\text{VDS}^{\text{David}}_a} \middle| a \in \text{VDS}^{\text{David}} \right\}$; this view included the Quality Assessment Function: $\bar{f}^{\text{David}}_{\text{FRG,VDS}^{\text{David}}_{\text{FRG}}}$ where $\text{VDS}^{\text{David}}_{\text{FRG}} = \{\text{network latency, cache capacity, response time}\}$ as defined above; this function reflected his ability to assess FRG based on three of its Properties. David's Quality View also included $\bar{f}^{\text{David}}_{\text{HWS,VDS}^{\text{David}}_{\text{HWS}}}$ and $\bar{f}^{\text{David}}_{\text{DBS,VDS}^{\text{David}}_{\text{DBS}}}$ but we omit their description here.
   b. $\text{QV}^{\text{Sean}} = \left\{ f^{\text{Sean}}_{a\text{VDS}^{\text{Sean}}_a} \middle| a \in \text{VDS}^{\text{Sean}} \right\}$; this view included only $f^{\text{Sean}}_{\text{FRG,VDS}^{\text{Sean}}_{\text{FRG}}}$ where $\text{VDS}^{\text{Sean}}_{\text{FRG}} = \{\text{efficiency}\}$ as defined above; this function reflected his ability to assess FRG based on its perceived efficiency.
2. Now after agreeing on $\text{VDS}^{\text{H}} = \{\text{FRG}\}$ and $\text{VDS}^{\text{H}}_{\text{FRG}} = \{\text{response\_time}\}$ both David and Sean adjust (implicitly, maybe unknowingly for them) their Quality Assessment Functions to reflect their abilities to assess the Software Artifacts belonging to these VDS. In particular,

a. David's assessment functions for HWS and DBS are dropped and his function for FRG is changed to reflect his ability to assess it based on only one Property, as a result, his adjusted Quality View is as follows: $QV^{David\,H} = \left\{ f^{David}_{FRG,VDS^H_{FRG}} \right\}$. Now it reflects his ability to assess FRG based only on its response time.

b. Sean's Assessment Function for FRG is changed to reflect his ability to rank FRG based on the different Property: $QV^{Sean\,H} = \left\{ f^{Sean}_{FRG,VDS^H_{FRG}} \right\}$; now it also reflects his ability to assess FRG based on the response time (and not on the perceived efficiency).

3. Both David and Sean agree that all Qualities to be associated by their Assessment Functions have to belong to the same Quality Type: $I^{David\,H}_{FRG\,qt} = I^{Sean\,H}_{FRG\,qt} = \{\,\text{very bad, bad, satisfactory, good, very good}\,\}$.

4. To sum it up, as a result of performing Quality View Alignment activities the sides formed $QV^{David\,H}$ and $QV^{Sean\,H}$ reflecting their common (harmonized) abilities to assess the quality of FRG by associating a common Quality Type to its response time.

It is important to note that the results of the assessments performed by the parties after completing all the steps of the View Harmonization Process can be different as the functions forming both views are different; aligning the assessment results (associated Qualities) is the subject of the subsequent quality harmonization activities.

## 3.3.5 Quality harmonization process

After completing the View Harmonization Process, the parties are able to assess the harmonized set of Software Artifacts; this is based (1) on using Properties that are instantiated from the harmonized sets of Property Types and (2) on using Qualities to represent assessment results that instantiate harmonized Quality Types. Thus is these parties can agree on the instances of Property Types (particular Properties) based on the instances of Quality Types (particular associated Qualities); we refer to the process of such agreement as *Quality Harmonization Process*.

### 3.3.5.1 Substitution artifacts

Quality harmonization activities are treated as being based on either the particular versions of the Software Artifacts or *Substitution Artifacts*. Substitution Artifacts are, for example, mockups, software prototypes, and simulation models; they allow for proposing particular Properties (stimuli) to the Stakeholders as arguments in negotiation *instead of* Properties of the original Software Artifact under harmonization and allow for collecting Stakeholders' reactions to these stimuli (associated Qualities) in place of the Qualities associated to the original Artifact. The Properties of the Substitution Artifact have to properly represent the Properties of the original Artifact; as a result, it should be possible to make decisions regarding the Qualities associated to the original Artifact based on those associated to the Substitution Artifact.

We conceptualize the Substitution Artifact as *the one that inherits the relevant Properties from the original Software Artifact and makes the original Artifact inherit its associated Qualities in turn*.

To simplify the subsequent treatment, we describe Quality Harmonization Process as operating with different *versions* of the Software Artifact $a \in VDS^H$, where each version is represented by the set of Properties $P_{aVDS^H_a} = \{p | p \in I_{pt}, pt \in VDS^H_a\}$ possibly inhering in a Substitution Artifact for a;

we refer to such set as *a particular version of Quality Harmonization Object* referred to as $a^{val} = P_{a\text{VDS}_a^H}$. We also restrict ourselves to only Artifact-Level Assessments.

### 3.3.5.2 Rank-oriented and property-oriented harmonization. Expected property state

We conceptualize two possible approaches to the quality harmonization process:

1. *Rank-oriented harmonization:* Both sides perform assessments of the particular version of $a^{val}$ (according to their own Quality Views) and perform negotiations based on the ranks over Qualities associated by these assessments. In particular,
   a. The Developer assesses every produced version of $a^{val}$ before submitting it to the Business Stakeholder associating Quality $q_{a^{val}}^D$.
   b. Ranking over Qualities is introduced; according to this rank if $r\left(q_{a^{val}}^{BS}\right) < r\left(q_{a^{val}}^D\right)$ (the Business Stakeholder ranks the provided $a^{val}$ less favorable than Developer) the sides try to eliminate the reasons of these rank differences.
   c. In producing $a_{i+1}^{val}$ the Developer is guided by both $r\left(q_{a_i^{val}}^{BS}\right)$ and $r\left(q_{a_i^{val}}^D\right)$.
2. *Property-oriented harmonization*: Both sides perform negotiations based on Properties and not the ranks over associated Qualities. In particular:
   a. The Developer makes Business Stakeholder experience $a_i^{val\,D}$.
   b. The Business Stakeholder executes Quality Assessment for $a_i^{val\,D}$ obtaining Quality $q_{a_i^{val\,D}}^{BS}$, and provides $q_{a_i^{val\,D}}^{BS}$ back to the Developer.
   c. The Developer derives $a^{val}$ implicitly desired for Business Stakeholder (his *Expected Property State*, $a_i^{val\,BS}$) from $a_i^{val\,D}$ experienced by Business Stakeholder and his/her associated Quality $q_{a_i^{val\,D}}^{BS}$.
   d. In producing $a_{i+1}^{val\,D}$ the Developer takes into account revealed Expected Property State $a_i^{val\,BS}$.

The Expected Property State thus can be defined as *the set of $a^{val}$ Properties that is conceived by the Individual Business Stakeholder as those he/she wants the final version of $a^{val}$ to provide and that can be the subject of negotiation*. The Expected Property State can change throughout the Quality Harmonization Process as a result of the evolution of Business Stakeholder's quality vision.

In this subsection, we will describe Quality Harmonization Process only for the case of rank-oriented harmonization due to the space restrictions.

### 3.3.5.3 Stage 1: Producing an initial example property state

We define our conceptualization for the case when the interaction with Business Stakeholder is performed from the Developer side by *making the Business Stakeholder experience a version of $a^{val}$: $a_i^{val\,D}$ that could be the subject of subsequent negotiations*.

We call $a_i^{val\,D}$ the *Example Property State*. It reflects the current state of $a^{val}$ development, although it should not necessarily be originated from the implemented version of $a^{val}$. The only requirement for $a_i^{val\,D}$ is that it should *represent* the set of Properties $a^{val}$ is expected to have *if implemented exactly as defined at the given development stage* (e.g., according to the set of requirements, as specified by its accepted design specification, as perceived by the Developers). In practice, the Example Property State can be produced based on a Substitution Artifact.

At this stage, for every Production iteration $j$:

1. Developer produces the particular development (internal) version of the Example Property State: $a'^{val\,D}_j$.

2. Developer executes Quality Assessment based on his/her Quality Assessment Function for $a'^{\mathrm{val\,D}}_j$ producing Quality $q^D_{a'^{\mathrm{val\,D}}_j}$.

3. If $r\left(q^D_{a'^{\mathrm{val\,D}}_j}\right) \geq \mathrm{CPB}^D$ Developer provides $a'^{\mathrm{val\,D}}_j$ to Business Stakeholder as its external version $a^{\mathrm{val\,D}}_0$; he/she also takes into account the last $q^D_{a'^{\mathrm{val\,D}}_j}$ as the Quality related to the version shown: $q^D_{a^{\mathrm{val\,D}}_0} = q^D_{a'^{\mathrm{val\,D}}_j}$. Here $\mathrm{CPB}^D$ is the *Conditional Production Boundary* reflecting the fact that some level of quality is good enough for the Developer to make him/her stop producing iterations and show the current $a^{\mathrm{val\,D}}_j$ to the Business Stakeholder.

### 3.3.5.3.1 Example for producing the initial example property state

As stated in the previous section, as a result of completing View Harmonization process, David and Sean agreed on $\mathrm{VDS}^H = \{\mathrm{FRG}\}$ and $\mathrm{VDS}^H_{\mathrm{FRG}} = \{\text{response\_time}\}$ and adjusted their Quality Views. As a result, the Quality Harmonization Object is instantiated as $\mathrm{FRG}^{\mathrm{val}} = P_{\mathrm{FRG},\mathrm{VDS}^H_{\mathrm{FRG}}} = \{p \in I_{\text{response\_time}}\}$. The relevant activities of the running example are conceptualized as follows:

1. David agrees with Sean the rank over {very bad, bad, satisfactory, good, very good} (i.e., they agree that $r(\text{very bad}) < r(\text{bad}) < r(\text{satisfactory}) \ldots$).
2. David defines for himself his conditional boundary for providing $\mathrm{FRG}^{\mathrm{val\,David}}$ version to Sean: $\mathrm{CPB}^{\mathrm{David}} = r(\text{good})$.
3. David produces the internal version of the Example Property State $\mathrm{FRG}'^{\mathrm{val\,David}}_j$. This state could look as follows: $\mathrm{FRG}'^{\mathrm{val\,David}}_j = \{1\,\mathrm{ms}_{\text{response\_time}}\}$; here we denote by $\mathrm{val}_{\mathrm{pt}}$ the property val of type pt. This process is repeated for several iterations until he ranks its associated Quality (resulting from the Assessment) as good or higher: $r\left(q^{\mathrm{David}}_{\mathrm{FRG}'^{\mathrm{val\,David}}_j}\right) \geq r(\text{good})$; it happens on third iteration so it is satisfied with $\mathrm{FRG}'^{\mathrm{val\,David}}_3 = \{0.25\,\mathrm{ms}_{\text{response\_time}}\}$.
4. David provides $\mathrm{FRG}'^{\mathrm{val\,David}}_3$ to Sean as $\mathrm{FRG}^{\mathrm{val\,David}}_0$ and takes into account $q^{\mathrm{David}}_{\mathrm{FRG}'^{\mathrm{val\,David}}_3}$ as $q^{\mathrm{David}}_{\mathrm{FRG}^{\mathrm{val\,David}}_0}$.

### 3.3.5.4 Stage 2: Executing initial assessment and deciding on a negotiation

The initial version of the Example Property State has to be assessed by Business Stakeholder by performing the following steps:

1. Business Stakeholder experiences the initial version of the Example Property State $a^{\mathrm{val\,D}}_0$ provided by Developer.
2. Business Stakeholder assesses $a^{\mathrm{val\,D}}_0$ (applying his/her Assessment Function) and produces the Quality $q^{\mathrm{BS}}_{a^{\mathrm{val\,D}}_0}$.
3. Prior to making the negotiation decision, two negotiation boundaries for Business Stakeholder (inside of his mind) have to be established: *Unconditional Acceptance Boundary* ($\mathrm{UAB}^{\mathrm{BS}}$) and *Unconditional Rejection Boundary* ($\mathrm{URB}^{\mathrm{BS}}$); the decision-making process then has the following form:

   **a.** If $r\left(q^{\mathrm{BS}}_{a^{\mathrm{val\,D}}_0}\right) > \mathrm{UAB}^{\mathrm{BS}}$, $a^{\mathrm{val\,D}}_0$ is *unconditionally accepted* as completely satisfying the Business Stakeholder; no additional interactions are necessary in this case. Such experience can be of the great service to the project because it establishes the feeling of trust between Business Stakeholders and Developers.

**b.** If $r\left(q_{a_0^{\text{val D}}}^{\text{BS}}\right) < \text{URB}^{\text{BS}}$, the harmonization process has to be aborted immediately without any attempt to perform negotiation and $a_0^{\text{val D}}$ is *unconditionally rejected* as dissatisfying the Business Stakeholder; such experience can be damaging to the whole project.

**c.** If $r\left(q_{a_0^{\text{val D}}}^{\text{BS}}\right)$ falls between $\text{URB}^{\text{BS}}$ and $\text{UAB}^{\text{BS}}$, the negotiation process has to be initiated.

### 3.3.5.4.1 Example of a negotiation decision

The relevant activities of the running example are conceptualized as follows:

**1.** Sean defines $\text{UAB}^{\text{Sean}} = r(\text{good})$ and $\text{URB}^{\text{Sean}} = r(\text{bad})$.

**2.** Sean experiences $\text{FRG}_0^{\text{val David}} = \{0.25\,\text{ms}_{\text{response\_time}}\}$ provided by David.

**3.** Sean assesses $\text{FRG}_0^{\text{val David}}$ and produces $q_{\text{FRG}_0^{\text{val David}}}^{\text{Sean}} = \text{bad}$.

**4.** Sean checks the negotiation boundaries; as $\text{URB}^{\text{Sean}} \leq r(\text{bad}) \leq \text{UAB}^{\text{Sean}}$ he decides to initiate the negotiation process.

### *3.3.5.5 Stage 3: Performing negotiations*

The negotiation process is performed iteratively; we denote its iteration as $i$. For every $i$, the following activities are performed:

**1.** Developer takes into account two Qualities associated with $a_{i-1}^{\text{val D}}$: his/her own Quality $q_{a_{i-1}^{\text{val D}}}^{\text{D}}$ and the Quality associated by Business Stakeholder $q_{a_{i-1}^{\text{val D}}}^{\text{BS}}$.

**2.** If $r\left(q_{a_{i-1}^{\text{val D}}}^{\text{BS}}\right) < r\left(q_{a_{i-1}^{\text{val D}}}^{\text{D}}\right)$ the Developer adjusts Assessment Functions in his QV to come closer to those of the Business Stakeholder: now getting $r\left(q_{a_{i-1}^{\text{val D}}}^{\text{D New}}\right) < r\left(q_{a_{i-1}^{\text{val D}}}^{\text{D}}\right)$. This adjustment can be useful for the subsequent executions of the harmonization process (Assessment Functions can stay adjusted); also the set of adjusted Assessment Functions can be the input to the knowledge base.

**3.** Developer (after reaching his $\text{CPB}^{\text{D}}$ with $r\left(q_{a'_j^{\text{val D}}}^{\text{D New}}\right)$) makes Business Stakeholder experience the new version of Example Property State $a_i^{\text{val D}}$ and Business Stakeholder assesses his/her experience again producing $q_{a_i^{\text{val D}}}^{\text{BS}}$; in doing this, every side tries to insist on some preferable Qualities, in particular:

   **a.** Developer tries to keep the ranks for Quality closer to the initial $\text{CPB}^{\text{D}}$ or even to $\text{URB}^{\text{BS}}$ to spend fewer resources.

   **b.** Business Stakeholder tries to keep the ranks for Quality closer to the $\text{UAB}^{\text{BS}}$ as it is better correspond to what he/she had in mind initially.

**4.** The negotiation process eventually ends with agreeing upon a version of the Example Property State shown to the Business Stakeholder: the *Accepted Property State* $a^{\text{val D}*}$.

### 3.3.5.5.1 Example of negotiations

For the first negotiation iteration ($i = 1$) the relevant activities of the running example are conceptualized as follows:

1. David takes into account $q_{\mathrm{FRG}_0^{\mathrm{val\,David}}}^{\mathrm{David}} = \text{good}$ and $q_{\mathrm{FRG}_0^{\mathrm{val\,David}}}^{\mathrm{Sean}} = \text{bad}$.

2. As $r\left(q_{\mathrm{FRG}_0^{\mathrm{val\,David}}}^{\mathrm{Sean}}\right) < r\left(q_{\mathrm{FRG}_0^{\mathrm{val\,David}}}^{\mathrm{David}}\right)$ David adjusts his QV to make possible obtaining

   $q_{\mathrm{FRG}_0^{\mathrm{val\,David}}}^{\mathrm{David\,New}} = \text{satisfactory}$ (so it is ranked closer to the Quality provided by Sean).

3. David produces $\mathrm{FRG}_1^{\mathrm{val\,David}} = \{0.1\,\mathrm{ms}_{\mathrm{response\_time}}\}$, which he again assesses as $q_{\mathrm{FRG}_1^{\mathrm{val\,David}}}^{\mathrm{David\,New}} = \text{good}$
   (but with adjusted QV) and makes Sean experience and assess it.

4. Sean now obtains $q_{\mathrm{FRG}_1^{\mathrm{val\,David}}}^{\mathrm{Sean}} = \text{good}$.

5. The sides agree on the Accepted Quality State $\mathrm{FRG}^{\mathrm{val\,David\,*}} = \{0.1\,\mathrm{ms}_{\mathrm{response\_time}}\}$.

### 3.3.6 State of the art: Addressing harmonization process activities

#### 3.3.6.1 Addressing organization sides

We start from approaches that provide generic conceptualizations of the organizational Entities. There are several approaches to such conceptualizations besides UFO-C, in particular, Boella and van der Torre (2006) introduces a foundational ontology of organizations and roles, Bottazzi and Ferrario (2005) define a basic ontology of organizations that is grounded in DOLCE foundational ontology, and Dietz and Habing (2004) describe a meta-ontology for organizations. Other approaches are grouped under the umbrella title of Enterprise ontology; they address different components of the real-world enterprise. Generic enterprise ontologies are presented in Abramowicz et al. (2008), Albani et al. (2006), and Almeida and Cardoso (2011). Another approach is grounded in UFO (Barcellos and de Almeida Falbo, 2009), and the practical ontology-based implementation of the set of such concepts is defined for the Jade agent development framework (Baldoni et al., 2010).

#### 3.3.6.2 Addressing quality subjects

Most of the ontologies of organizations and social aspects (in particular UFO-C, the foundational ontology from Boella and van der Torre, 2006 and the practical implementation from Baldoni et al., 2010) include notions for the organizational roles that could be applied to Quality Subjects; more specific conceptualization approaches include an ontology of social roles (Boella and Van Der Torre, 2007). Baldoni et al. (2006) treat these roles as affordances.

While dealing with the approaches that address the abilities and intentions of Quality Subjects, first of all, it is necessary to categorize those addressing the actors who participate in the software process. Some conceptualization approaches include the notion of stakeholder, but do not connect this notion to the quality assessment process by disallowing per-stakeholder assessments (Gilb, 1988; Kim and Lee, 2005); other techniques allow such assessments (Chung and do Prado Leite, 2009; Chung et al., 1999; Jureta et al., 2009a). A generic attempt to define the foundation of knowledge-related abilities of stakeholders can be based on a knowledge-management ontology (Holsapple and Joshi, 2006). For the field of requirements engineering, the most detailed treatment of stakeholder capabilities is provided in CORE (Jureta et al., 2009a); this treatment is discussed below.

The closest notion to UFO intentions and the derived concepts introduced in this chapter is the concept of *stakeholder speech mode* introduced by the CORE ontology (Jureta et al., 2009a), which represents an uttered stakeholder intention with reference to some aspects of the UoD.

We categorize the techniques addressing stakeholder intentions according to these modes:

1. Directive mode defines explicit goals also addressed, for example, in Chung and do Prado Leite (2009), Kassab et al. (2009), Zhu and Gorton (2007), or in Boehm and In (1996), Krogstie (1998) as quality constraints. See also the notion of a soft goal in Chung et al. (1999) and derived works for a goal that could be only satisfied to some degree.
2. Declarative/assertive mode defines assumptions or the values of attributes (Kayed et al., 2009).
3. Expressive mode is used to declare evaluations also addressed, for example, in Choi et al. (2008) and Tian (2004).

### 3.3.6.3 Generic process-based techniques

Prior to aligning the state-of-the-art approaches to harmonization levels, we need to briefly consider generic process-level techniques aimed at conceptualizing software quality negotiation.

*Software process conceptualization techniques* (Acuna and Sanchez-Segura, 2006; Adolph et al., 2012; Münch et al., 2012) propose conceptual foundations for formalizing software process activities, in particular those involving business stakeholders. Some of these approaches are grounded in foundational ontologies. In particular, UFO-based software process conceptualizations are defined in Guizzardi et al. (2008). The most relevant among these techniques is an approach by Adolph et al. (2012) that proposes a conceptualization of the development activities aimed at reaching common understanding between the parties in this process. We discuss this approach in more detail at the end of this section while addressing the treatment of harmonization levels.

*Quality-driven process support approaches* aim at using quality to drive the whole software process or its particular tasks. Among these approaches are Quality-Driven Re-Engineering (Tahvildari et al., 2003) approaches targeting quality-driven development restricted to the architectural design phase (Kim et al., 2010) and techniques that aim at making the entire software process driven by quality without organizing direct interaction with stakeholders (de Miguel et al., 2008; Grambow et al., 2011; Hummel et al., 2010; Matinlassi, 2005).

### 3.3.6.4 Addressing harmonization activities

There are several categories of methods addressing the issue of involving stakeholders in the development process as a means for performing the harmonization activities; in describing them, we follow the classification of the methods to represent the quality of the prospective system proposed by Bosch (Bosch, 2000), which includes request- and scenario-based techniques, prototyping, and simulation.

*Request-centered techniques* implement the way of questioning the business stakeholders and processing their opinions. Empirical techniques (Drew et al., 2006) such as surveys, interviews, brainstorming, questionnaires, or checklists are used (Lauesen, 2002; McManus, 2004) together with software engineering-specific techniques such as CRC cards (Bellin and Suchman-Simone, 1997).

*Scenario-centered techniques* (Carroll, 1995) organize scenarios of stakeholder interaction with software under development to harmonize qualities; they often rely on request-centered techniques to process the opinions of business stakeholders. In the manual scenario-centered approach, the stakeholders are requested to go through the scenarios (without interacting with the prospective software or its executable model) and express their opinions. The techniques of this kind are widely used to evaluate software architectures (Kazman et al., 1999; Williams and Smith, 2002) and to elicit quality requirements (Barbacci et al., 2003; Gregoriades and Sutcliffe, 2005; Lassing et al., 2002; Sindre and Opdahl, 2005). In industry, such scenarios are often based on user stories (Cohn, 2004): Together they form an approach to gather user requirements in the agile software process (Leffingwell, 2011).

*Prototyping techniques* use system prototypes as an aid for business stakeholders (Arnowitz et al., 2007), helping them to express their quality preferences. The notion of traditional prototype refers to a scaled-down version of the final system running in its intended context (Floyd, 1984; Lim et al., 2008). They are used in requirement engineering, being embedded into scenarios (Sutcliffe and Ryan, 1998; Tolstedt, 2002) and during the software design activities (Hartmann, 2009). In industry, prototypes are often supplemented by mockups that are simplified versions of prototypes not integrated into usage scenarios and often not requiring writing any code (Schneider, 2007). Implementing mockup-like solutions exclusively as sketches on paper is also known as *paper prototyping* (Snyder, 2003).

*Simulation-based techniques* use simulation in a sense of "the process of designing and creating a computerized model of a real or proposed system for the purpose of conducting numerical experiments" (Kelton et al., 2004) to model quality characteristics in a way that can be used to support stakeholder involvement. Performance prototyping techniques (Hennig et al., 2003) allow performance simulations to be used as alternatives for prototypes. Other performance simulation solutions are described in Bause et al. (2008), Cortellessa et al. (2008), and Driss et al. (2008). Reliability simulations are proposed in Gokhale et al. (1998), Grishikashvili Pereira and Pereira (2007), and Looker et al. (2007). Some solutions embed quality simulations in context of usage scenarios (Egyed, 2004; Haumer et al., 1999) or complete business processes (Fritzsche et al., 2008, 2009; Jansen-Vullers and Netjes, 2006; Marzolla and Balsamo, 2004; Rozinat et al., 2009; Tewoldeberhan and Janssen, 2008).

An important generic approach addressing different levels of harmonization is provided by Adolph et al. (2012). In this work, the harmonization process is treated in detail: It is oriented at reconciling perspectives, where the perspectives refer to the views of different process participants. However, the authors propose the approach for language and view harmonization but not specifically related to quality issues. Consequently, our work may be considered as a specialization of this approach targeting the harmonization of quality-related perspectives.

## 3.4 PRACTICAL RELEVANCE

In this section, we describe how our research relates to the practice of software development. First, we describe the empirical studies that formed the starting point for our conceptualizations. These studies have been carried out in cooperation with industrial partners in the framework of the QuASE project. After that, we outline the practical application of our conceptualizations in knowledge-oriented solutions.

### 3.4.1 Empirical studies

We conducted empirical studies from March 2012 to July 2013 in cooperation with five IT organizations having the following diverse characteristics:

1. A: middle-sized product-oriented IT company targeting the healthcare sector that follows the product line approach in organizing its development projects.
2. B: smaller-sized solution-oriented IT company also offering consulting services.
3. C: small consulting and solution development company targeting SAP applications.

4. D: middle-sized consulting and solution development company with an expertise in quality assurance and management.
5. E: IT service department of a large service-providing company.

### 3.4.1.1 Conducting interviews

The main data collection method was to conduct structured and semi-structured interviews. Twenty-nine interviews were conducted in two time intervals: 14 interviews in March-June 2012 and 15 interviews in April-July 2013. In the first period, the interviews involved staff of A and B; in the second period the three other companies were involved. The total duration of the interviews was about 40 h; all the interview conversations have been digitally recorded and then transcribed. In total, about 150 questions were discussed (3-4 per hour).

For every company, we interviewed people belonging to three main categories: top managers (CEO/CIO), project managers, and software engineers; the latter group has been subdivided into line developers, software architects, analysts, and requirement engineers. For some companies, such as company B, it was not possible to put the people (except top managers) into a particular category because this company expects from its staff the ability to perform different software engineering and project management activities.

Prior to an interview, its plan has been agreed with the participant, but interviewers were allowed to ask additional questions that were generated by the answers on previous questions. Three sets of questions (related to top managers, project managers, and developers) were discussed with the relevant staff members of all five companies; the questions belonging to these sets were adjusted as a result of the previous interviews, but core questions remained the same. This allowed for the comparison of the results obtained in different contexts.

Three interviews with staff members of A were of a different kind: They were devoted to discussing the issues arising in the company's ongoing projects; consequently, both project managers and involved developers participated. One of the projects under discussion was in trouble, so the possible reasons for such situation were discussed, too.

### 3.4.1.2 Postmortem analysis

In addition to the interviews, a postmortem analysis of already finished projects was performed in A, B, and D. Prior to performing the analysis, a documentation meeting was held with the responsible staff members. The documents available for analysis included requirement specifications, meeting minutes, excerpts from the data collected in the company IMS or wiki.

### 3.4.1.3 Data processing

After transcription of the interviews and performing postmortem analysis, the collected data was processed as follows:

1. We started from performing open coding (Corbin and Strauss, 2008; Strauss and Corbin, 1998) of the transcripts with a goal of obtaining an initial set of concepts based on the indicators presented in the data.
2. After the initial set of concepts was established (as a result of the first period's interviews), we compared the indicators from the new interview transcripts with the existing concepts and revised

these concepts if necessary; the exact sets of questions for the interviews belonging to the second time interval was based on the answers of the previous interviews.

3. We performed axial coding (Strauss and Corbin, 1998) with the goal of establishing the relationships between the concepts belonging to the initial set.
4. The obtained preliminary set of concepts and their relationships was validated by the staff of the relevant company-partner; during that validation, necessary modifications were proposed and discussed.

### 3.4.1.4 Soundness factors
The following factors contributed to the soundness of the empirical studies and, as a result, the soundness of their results:

1. Diversity of the represented companies, ability to ask compatible interview questions in different contexts and compare the results.
2. Ability to interview company staff workers belonging to different groups with the sets of questions specifically targeting the particular group.
3. Ability to supplement the interview data with the data obtained as a result of postmortem analysis.
4. Using sound qualitative research principles in conducting the interviews and processing their results. In particular, by sampling of the people involved in the interviews and by defining the scope of the interviews we followed the principles of theoretical sampling that are part of the grounded theory approach (Strauss and Corbin, 1998).
5. Ability to validate the obtained set of concepts by the partner companies.

## 3.4.2 Practical application
A software tool based on the presented conceptualizations of the harmonization process is currently under development as a part of the QuASE project. It aims at providing support for

1. Acquiring and formalizing domain knowledge about handling quality-related issues in software processes (we conceptualize such issues as the triggers for launching quality harmonization processes).
2. Collecting the raw information about such issues from the involved parties and converting it into operational knowledge (using available domain knowledge to ensure conversion correctness).
3. Using the collected knowledge for establishing a quality-related communication basis for the involved parties, supporting decision making, reusing quality-related experience, and predicting future quality-related requirements of the involved parties.

### 3.4.2.1 The QuASE process
We established a four-stage *QuASE process* (Figure 3.7).

1. The *elicitation stage* is devoted to acquiring the raw information about quality-related issues and the relevant harmonization processes from the different parties in a software process and converting this information into a set of semantic knowledge structures that reflect the views of these parties.
2. The *integration stage* is devoted to converting and integrating (including conflict resolution) the results of stage 1 into a "global view."

**FIGURE 3.7**

Stages of the QuASE process.

3. During the *analysis stage* the analytical tasks such as facilitating knowledge reuse or predicting the handling of the future issues are solved based on the global view.
4. The *dissemination stage* is devoted to converting and externalizing the global view back into the form that reflects the views of the different parties.

Due to space restrictions, we will describe in detail only the elicitation stage of the QuASE process.

### 3.4.2.2 QuOntology and QuIRepository

The process is based on managing the knowledge about quality-related issues and relevant harmonization processes in a repository that serves as an experience base (*QuIRepository*) and is structured along an ontology (*QuOntology*). QuOntology incorporates, among others, the set of concepts presented in the previous sections. It aims at sharing the conceptual knowledge about software quality, supplying the semantics to supplement the information about quality-related issues and relevant harmonization processes before converting it into the knowledge structures to be stored into QuIRepository; it serves as a foundation of the QuIRepository by defining its structure.

*QuIRepository* is intended for storing the operational knowledge about quality-related issues as instances of the QuOntology concepts. For the general principles of establishing the QuIRepository, the concept of experience-knowledge base (Basili et al., 1994; Schneider, 2009) is extended to enable collecting and sharing quality-related experience. QuIRepository has to be organized into subsections corresponding to the knowledge supporting the various stages of the QuASE approach by applying knowledge modularization techniques (Stuckenschmidt et al., 2009). In this, we follow Babar (2009) and Feldmann et al. (1999), who propose a knowledge base that facilitates software engineering activities on different stages.

### 3.4.2.3 Elicitation stage

This stage is devoted to (1) acquiring the raw information on quality-related issues and the relevant harmonization processes from the different parties of the software process, (2) supplementing it by semantics obtained from QuOntology, and (3) storing the resulting knowledge into QuIRepository. We concentrate on collecting *party-dependent knowledge* based on the views and understanding of the particular party (i.e., its specific language) from the following sources:

1. The systems deployed at the developer side to support the software process (IMS, wikis etc.).
2. The process of *instrumented stakeholder interaction,* where business stakeholders interact with QuASE-enhanced substitution artifacts (e.g., prototypes and mockups) in the usual way; but the information about stakeholders' reactions to stimuli (e.g., mouse clicks or selected control paths) is transparently captured and collected into QuIRepository.
3. Direct stakeholder communication specifying the assessments of quality characteristics, such as usability assessments expressed while interacting with a substitution artifact such as mock-up or prototype.

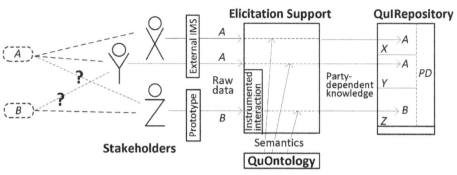

**FIGURE 3.8**

QuASE process elicitation stage knowledge conversions.

Figure 3.8 illustrates an exemplary situation. Suppose that the stakeholders X (*project manager*) and Y (*developer*) state their knowledge on the harmonization process related to issue A (*a particular performance issue*) in their terminology, whereas stakeholder Z (*business person on the customer side*) uses his terminology for stating his knowledge on the harmonization process related to issue B (*a particular usability issue*). Neither Y knows the terminology of business stakeholder Z, nor does Z understand the terminology of the IT-persons X and Y. These problematic links are denoted by question marks in Figure 3.8.

X and Y provide their knowledge about issue A via an external IMS, Z provides his knowledge about issue B via instrumented interaction with a prototype. This raw data is supplemented with the semantics from QuOntology (comprised, in particular, of the concepts defined in this chapter). The results are stored into the party-dependent knowledge section PD of QuIRepository, where each view has its separate subsection. Knowledge about a particular issue and the relevant harmonization process can be found in different subsections corresponding to the respective views.

To establish a theoretical basis for the acquisition of the raw information from the parties and converting it into knowledge, it is necessary to conceptualize the data to be collected. The set of concepts presented in this chapter are the basis of this conceptualization. In addition, the concept of *quality-related issue* has to be defined generalizing the artifacts available in existing IMS; in particular, it is necessary to treat software requirements as specific categories of issues (Shekhovtsov et al., 2013; Weinreich and Buchgeher, 2010) and associate conceptualized harmonization processes such as defined in Section 3.3 with the particular issues triggering them. To formalize the process of acquiring party-dependent knowledge with a support of QuOntology, we apply the techniques of ontology-based knowledge acquisition (Abecker and Elst, 2009; Aroyo et al., 2006; Lebbink et al., 2002; Wang et al., 2002) and experience-knowledge transformation (Sanin et al., 2007).

## 3.5 CONCLUSIONS AND FUTURE RESEARCH DIRECTIONS

### 3.5.1 Basic conclusions

In this chapter, we presented a set of concepts describing the process of harmonizing the views on quality possessed by the different sides involved in a software process. These concepts

1. Are based on applying empirical techniques to the qualitative data obtained from the business partners in the framework of the QuASE project.
2. Are grounded in a set of basic concepts provided by the UFO.

Combining these two characteristics of the provided conceptualizations allowed us

1. To supply these conceptualizations with real-world semantics supported by empirical evidence and, as a result, more truthful to the view harmonization domain.
2. To make explicit their ontological commitments.

Our conceptualizations could be used as a reference framework for applications in the domain of harmonizing the views on quality; the conceptual models utilized by these tools could be based on these concepts to achieve a higher degree of reuse and semantic interoperability. Reaching the above two goals contributes to the effectiveness of these practical applications as allows conceptual models to be at the same time based on reality, verifiable and conceptually clear.

### 3.5.2 Future research and implementation directions

Future directions of research include reaching a deeper degree of grounding in the existing foundational and upper-level ontologies, in particular, UFO-C as an ontology of social connections between the actors, ontologies of organizations and roles, and ontologies related to knowledge acquisition and representation.

From the implementation point of view, we are in a process of applying the proposed conceptualizations by implementing a complete common ontology of quality-related stakeholder interactions (QuOntology) that is intended for sharing the conceptual knowledge about the domain and for supporting the harmonization process. In particular, the QuASE tool will support the following stages of a harmonization process based on QuOntology:

1. Acquiring the raw information about quality-related issues (in a sense of issue management systems such as JIRA) from the different parties in a software process and converting this information into a set of semantic knowledge structures reflecting the views of these parties (with a process of conversion here and during the following stages supported by the necessary semantics available from QuOntology).
2. Converting and integrating (including conflict resolution) the results of the previous stage into a "global view" (separating party-independent and party-specific knowledge).
3. Converting and externalizing the global view back into the form that reflects the views of the different parties.

## Acknowledgment

The QuASE Project is sponsored by the Austrian Research Promotion Agency (FFG) in the framework of the Bridge 1 program (http://www.ffg.at/bridge1); Project ID: 3215531.

# References

Aagedal, J., de Miguel, M.A., Fafournoux, E., Lund, M.S., Stolen, K., 2004. UML Profile for Modeling Quality of Service and Fault Tolerance Characteristics and Mechanisms, Technical report TR 2004-06-01, Object Management Group.

Abecker, A., Elst, L., 2009. Ontologies for knowledge management. In: Staab, S., Studer, R. (Eds.), Handbook on Ontologies (International Handbooks on Information Systems). Springer, Berlin/Heidelberg, pp. 713–734.

Abramowicz, W., Filipowska, A., Kaczmarek, M., Pedrinaci, C., Starzecka, M., Walczak, A., 2008. Organization structure description for the needs of semantic business process management. In: 3rd International Workshop on Semantic Business Process Management Colocated with 5th European Semantic Web Conference.

Acuna, S.T., Sanchez-Segura, M.I. (Eds.), 2006. New Trends in Software Process Modeling. World Scientific Publishing, Singapore.

Adolph, S., Hall, W., Kruchten, P., 2011. Using grounded theory to study the experience of software development. Empir. Softw. Eng. 16, 487–513.

Adolph, S., Kruchten, P., Hall, W., 2012. Reconciling perspectives: a grounded theory of how people manage the process of software development. J. Syst. Softw. 85, 1269–1286.

Al Balushi, T.H., Sampaio, P.R.F., Dabhi, D., Loucopoulos, P., 2007. ElicitO: a quality ontology-guided NFR elicitation tool. In: Sawyer, P., Paech, B., Heymans, P. (Eds.), REFSQ 2007. In: Lecture Notes in Computer Science, vol. 4542. Springer, Berlin/Heidelberg, pp. 306–319.

Albani, A., Dietz, J.L., Zaha, J.M., 2006. Identifying business components on the basis of an enterprise ontology. In: Interoperability of Enterprise Software and Applications. Springer, Berlin/Heidelberg, pp. 335–347.

Almeida, J.P.A., Cardoso, E., 2011. On the elements of an enterprise: towards an ontology-based account. In: Proceedings of the 2011 ACM Symposium on Applied Computing. ACM, New York, pp. 323–330.

Apvrille, L., Courtiat, J.-P., Lohr, C., de Saqui-Sannes, P., 2004. TURTLE: a real-time UML profile supported by formal validation toolkit. IEEE Trans. Softw. Eng. 30 (7), 473–487.

Arnowitz, J., Aretn, A., Berger, N., 2007. Effective Prototyping for Software Makers. Morgan Kaufmann, San Francisco, CA.

Aroyo, L., Denaux, R., Dimitrova, V., Pye, M., 2006. Interactive ontology-based user knowledge acquisition: a case study. In: ESCW'06.

Aßmann, U., Zschaler, S., 2006. Ontologies, meta-models, and the model-driven paradigm. In: Calero, C., Ruiz, F., Piattini, M. (Eds.), Ontologies for Software Engineering and Software Technology. Springer, Berlin/Heidelberg, pp. 255–279.

Babar, M.A., 2009. Supporting the software architecture process with knowledge management. In: Babar, M.A., Dingsøyr, T., Lago, P., van Vliet, H. (Eds.), Software Architecture Knowledge Management. Springer, Berlin/Heidelberg, pp. 69–86.

Baldoni, M., Boella, G., Genovese, V., Mugnaini, A., Grenna, R., van der Torre, L., 2010. A middleware for modeling organizations and roles in jade. In: Programming Multi-Agent Systems. Springer, Berlin/Heidelberg, pp. 100–117.

Baldoni, M., Boella, G., Van Der Torre, L., 2006. Modelling the interaction between objects: roles as affordances. In: Knowledge Science, Engineering and Management. Springer, Berlin/Heidelberg, pp. 42–54.

Barbacci, M., Ellison, R., Lattanze, A., Stafford, J., Weinstock, C.B., Wood, W.G., 2003. Quality Attribute Workshops (QAWs), third ed. Carnegie Mellon University, Pittsburgh, PA.

Barcellos, M.P., de Almeida Falbo, R., 2009. Using a foundational ontology for reengineering a software enterprise ontology. In: Advances in Conceptual Modeling-Challenging Perspectives. Springer, Berlin/Heidelberg, pp. 179–188.

Barcellos, M.P., Falbo, R.D.A., Dalmoro, R., 2010. A well-founded software measurement ontology. In: Proceedings of the 6th International Conference on Formal Ontology in Information Systems (FOIS 2010), Toronto-Canadá.

Basili, V., Caldiera, G., Rombach, D.H., 1994. Experience factory. In: Marciniak, J.J. (Ed.), Encyclopedia of Software Engineering. Wiley, New York, pp. 469–476.

Bause, F., Buchholz, P., Kriege, J., Vastag, S., 2008. A framework for simulation models of service-oriented architectures. In: SIPEW 2008. In: Lecture Notes in Computer Science, vol. 5119. Springer, Berlin/Heidelberg, pp. 208–227.

Bellin, D., Suchman-Simone, S., 1997. The CRC Card Book. Addison-Wesley, Reading, MA.

Bertoa, M., Vallecillo, A., Garc¡a, F., 2006. An ontology for software measurement. In: Calero, C., Ruiz, F., Piattini, M. (Eds.), Ontologies for Software Engineering and Software Technology. Springer, Berlin/Heidelberg, pp. 175–196.

Boehm, B., Brown, J.R., Kaspar, H., Lipow, M., MacLeod, G.J., Merritt, M.J., 1978. Characteristics of Software Quality. North Holland, New York.

Boehm, B., In, H., 1996. Identifying quality-requirements conflicts. IEEE Softw. 13 (2), 25–35.

Boella, G., van der Torre, L., 2006. A foundational ontology of organizations and roles. In: Baldoni, M., Endriss, U. (Eds.), Declarative Agent Languages and Technologies IV. Lecture Notes in Computer Science, vol. 4327. Springer, Berlin-Heidelberg, pp. 78–88.

Boella, G., Van Der Torre, L., 2007. The ontological properties of social roles in multi-agent systems: definitional dependence, powers and roles playing roles. Artif. Intell. Law 15 (3), 201–221.

Bosch, J., 2000. Design and Use of Software Architectures. Addison-Wesley, Reading, MA.

Bottazzi, E., Ferrario, R., 2005. A path to an ontology of organizations. In: Guizzardi, G., Wagner, G. (Eds.), VORTE'05, pp. 9–16.

Burgués, X., Franch, X., Ribó, J.M., 2005. A MOF-compliant approach to software quality modeling. In: Delcambre, L., Kop, C., Mayr, H.C., Mylopoulos, J., Pastor, O. (Eds.), Conceptual Modeling—ER 2005. In: Lecture Notes in Computer Science, vol. 3716. Springer, Berlin/Heidelberg, pp. 176–191.

Cachero, C., Calero, C., Poels, G., 2007. Metamodeling the quality of the web development process' intermediate artifacts. In: Baresi, L., Fraternali, P., Houben, G.-J. (Eds.), WISE 2007. In: Lecture Notes in Computer Science, vol. 4607. Springer, Berlin/Heidelberg, pp. 74–89.

Carroll, J.M. (Ed.), 1995. Scenario-Based Design. Wiley, New York.

Carvallo, J.P., 2005. Systematic construction of quality models for COTS-based systems (Ph.D. thesis). Universitat Politècnica de Catalunya, Barcelona.

Choi, Y., Lee, S., Song, H., Park, J., Kim, S.H., 2008. Practical S/W component quality evaluation model. In: 10th IEEE International Conference on Advanced Communication Technology (ICACT'08). IEEE Press, New York, pp. 259–264.

Chung, L., do Prado Leite, J., 2009. On non-functional requirements in software engineering. In: Borgida, A.T., Chaudhri, V.K., Giorgini, P., Yu, E.S. (Eds.), Conceptual Modeling: Foundations and Applications. Lecture Notes in Computer Science, vol. 5600. Springer, Berlin/Heidelberg, pp. 363–379.

Chung, L., Nixon, B.A., Yu, E., Mylopoulos, J., 1999. Non-Functional Requirements in Software Engineering. Kluwer Academic Publishers, Boston, MA.

Cohn, M., 2004. User Stories Applied: For Agile Software Development. Addison Wesley, Reading, MA.

Coleman, G., O'Connor, R., 2008. Investigating software process in practice: a grounded theory perspective. J. Syst. Softw. 81, 772–784.

Cooper, A., 2004. The Inmates are Running the Asylum. Sams, Indianapolis, IN.

Corbin, J., Strauss, A., 2008. Basics of Qualitative Research, third ed. Sage Publications, Thousand Oaks, CA.

Cortellessa, V., Pierini, P., Spalazzese, R., Vianale, A., 2008. MOSES: modeling software and platform architecture in UML 2 for simulation-based performance analysis. In: QoSA 2008. In: Lecture Notes in Computer Science, vol. 5281. Springer, Berlin/Heidelberg, pp. 86–102.

de Almeida Falbo, R., Nardi, J.C., 2008. Evolving a software requirements ontology. In: XXXIV Conferencia Latinoamericana de Informática, Santa Fe, Argentina, pp. 300–309.

de Miguel, M.A., Massonet, P., Silva, J.P., Briones, J., 2008. Model based development of quality-aware software services. In: ISORC'08. IEEE, New York, pp. 563–569.

Deissenboeck, F., Juergens, E., Lochmann, K., Wagner, S., 2009. Software quality models: purposes, usage scenarios and requirements. In: 7th International Workshop on Software Quality (WoSQ 09). IEEE Press, New York, pp. 9–14.

Dietz, J.L., Habing, N., 2004. A meta ontology for organizations. In: On the Move to Meaningful Internet Systems 2004: OTM 2004 Workshops. Springer, Berlin/Heidelberg, pp. 533–543.

Drew, P., Raymond, G., Weinberg, D. (Eds.), 2006. Talk and Interaction in Social Research Methods. Sage Publications, Thousand Oaks, CA.

Driss, M., Jamoussi, Y., Jezequel, J.-M., Hajjami, H., Ghezala, B., 2008. A discrete-events simulation approach for evaluation of service-based applications. In: ECOWS'08. IEEE, New York, pp. 73–78.

Dromey, R.G., 1996. Cornering the chimera. IEEE Softw. 13, 33–43.

Egyed, A., 2004. Dynamic deployment of executing and simulating software components. In: Component Deployment. Lecture Notes in Computer Science, vol. 3083. Springer, Berlin/Heidelberg, pp. 113–128.

Falbo, R.A., Guizzardi, G., Duarte, K.C., 2002. An ontological approach to domain engineering. In: 14th International Conference on Software Engineering and Knowledge Engineering (SEKE'02). ACM Press, New York, pp. 351–358.

Feldmann, R.L., Geppert, B., Rößler, F., 1999. An integrating approach for developing distributed software systems—combining formal methods, software reuse, and the experience base. In: ICECCS'99. IEEE, New York, pp. 54–63.

Fenton, N., Pfleeger, S.L., 1997. Software Metrics: A Rigorous and Practical Approach. PWS Publishing, Boston, MA.

Floyd, C., 1984. A systematic look at prototyping. In: Approaches to Prototyping. Springer, Berlin/Heidelberg, pp. 1–17.

Fritzsche, M., Gilani, W., Fritzsche, C., Spence, I., Kilpatrick, P., Brown, J., 2008. Towards utilizing model-driven engineering of composite applications for business performance analysis. In: ECMDA-FA'08, pp. 369–380.

Fritzsche, M., Picht, M., Gilani, W., Spence, I., Brown, J., Kilpatrick, P., 2009. Extending BPM environments of your choice with performance related decision support. In: BPM 2009. In: Lecture Notes in Computer Science, vol. 5701. Springer, Berlin/Heidelberg, pp. 97–112.

Gärdenfors, P., 2000. Conceptual Spaces: A Geometry of Thought. MIT Press, Cambridge, MA.

Gilb, T., 1988. Principles of Software Engineering Management. Addison Wesley, Reading, MA.

Gokhale, S.S., Lyu, M.R., Trivedi, K.S., 1998. Reliability simulation of component-based software systems. In: ISSRE'98, pp. 192–201.

Grambow, G., Oberhauser, R., Reichert, M., 2011. Contextual injection of quality measures into software engineering processes. Int. J. Adv. Softw. 4 (1–2), 76–99.

Gregoriades, A., Sutcliffe, A., 2005. Scenario-based assessment of nonfunctional requirements. IEEE Trans. Softw. Eng. 31 (5), 392–409.

Grishikashvili Pereira, E., Pereira, R., 2007. Simulation of fault monitoring and detection of distributed services. Simul. Model. Pract. Theory 15, 492–502.

Guizzardi, G., 2005. Ontological foundations for structural conceptual models, University of Twente.

Guizzardi, G., Falbo, R., Guizzardi, R.S., 2008. Grounding software domain ontologies in the unified foundational ontology (UFO): the case of the ODE software process ontology. In: Proceedings of the XI Iberoamerican Workshop on Requirements Engineering and Software Environments, pp. 244–251.

Guizzardi, G., Wagner, G., 2005. Towards ontological foundations for agent modelling concepts using the unified fundational ontology (UFO). In: Bresciani, P., Giorgini, P., Henderson-Sellers, B., Low, G., Winikoff, M. (Eds.), Agent-Oriented Information Systems II. In: Lecture Notes in Computer Science, vol. 3508. Springer, Berlin/Heidelberg, pp. 110–124.

Guizzardi, G., Zamborlini, V., 2013. A common foundational theory for bridging two levels in ontology-driven conceptual modeling. In: Software Language Engineering. Springer, Berlin/Heidelberg, pp. 286–310.

Hartmann, B., 2009. Gaining design insight through interaction prototyping tools (Ph.D. dissertation), Stanford University.

Haumer, P., Heymans, P., Jarke, M., Pohl, K., 1999. Bridging the gap between past and future in RE: a scenario-based approach. In: RE'99. IEEE CS Press, New York, pp. 66–73.

Hennig, A., Hentschel, A., Tyack, J., 2003. Performance prototyping—generating and simulating a distributed IT-system from UML models. In: ESM'2003. IEEE, New York.

Herre, H., 2010. General formal ontology (GFO): a foundational ontology for conceptual modelling. In: Poli, R., Healy, M., Kameas, A. (Eds.), Theory and Applications of Ontology: Computer Applications. Springer, Netherlands, pp. 297–345.

Holsapple, C.W., Joshi, K., 2006. Knowledge management ontology. In: Encyclopedia of Knowledge Management. Idea Group Reference, Hershey, PA, pp. 397–402.

Hummel, O., Momm, C., Hickl, S., 2010. Towards quality-aware development and evolution of enterprise information systems. In: Proceedings of the 2010 ACM Symposium on Applied Computing. ACM, Sierre, Switzerland, pp. 137–144.

IEEE, 1998. IEEE 1061-1998: IEEE Standard for Software Quality Metrics Methodology. IEEE Press, New York.

ISO, 2001. ISO/IEC 9126-1:2001: Software Engineering—Product Quality—Part 1: Quality Model. International Organization for Standardization, Geneva.

ISO, 2003a. ISO/IEC 9126-2:2003: Software Engineering—Product Quality—Part 2: External Metrics. International Organization for Standardization, Geneva.

ISO, 2003b. ISO/IEC 9126-3:2003: Software Engineering—Product Quality—Part 3: Internal Metrics. International Organization for Standardization, Geneva.

ISO, 2004. ISO/IEC 9126-4:2004: Software Engineering—Product Quality—Part 4: Quality-in-Use Metrics. International Organization for Standardization, Geneva.

ISO, 2007. ISO/IEC 24744:2007: Software Engineering—Metamodel for Development Methodologies. International Organization for Standardization, Geneva.

ISO, 2011. ISO/IEC 25010:2011: Systems and Software Engineering—Systems and Software Quality Requirements and Evaluation (SQuaRE)—System and Software Quality Models. International Organization for Standardization, Geneva.

Jansen-Vullers, M., Netjes, M., 2006. Business process simulation—a tool survey. In: CPN Tools Workshop.

Jureta, I., Mylopoulos, J., Faulkner, S., 2009a. A core ontology for requirements. Appl. Ontol. 4 (3–4), 169–244.

Jureta, I.J., Herssens, C., Faulkner, S., 2009b. A comprehensive quality model for service-oriented systems. Softw. Qual. J. 17, 65–98.

Kassab, M., Ormandjieva, O., Daneva, M., 2009. An ontology based approach to non-functional requirements conceptualization. In: 4th International Conference on Software Engineering Advances (SEA'09). IEEE Press, New York, pp. 299–308.

Kayed, A., Hirzalla, N., Samhan, A.A., Alfayoumi, M., 2009. Towards an ontology for software product quality attributes. In: 4th International Conference on Internet and Web Applications and Services (ICIW '09). IEEE Press, New York, pp. 200–204.

Kazman, R., Barbacci, M., Klein, M., Carriere, S.J., 1999. Experience with performing architecture tradeoff analysis. In: ICSE'99. ACM, New York, pp. 54–63.

Kelton, W.D., Sadowski, R.P., Sadowski, D.A., 2004. Simulation with Arena, second ed. McGraw-Hill, New York.

Kim, E., Lee, Y., 2005. Quality Model for Web Services 2.0. OASIS.

Kim, S., Kim, D.-K., Park, S., 2010. Tool support for quality-driven development of software architectures. In: ASE'10. ACM, Antwerp, Belgium, pp. 127–130.

Kitchenham, B., Pfleeger, S.L., 1996. Software quality: the elusive target. IEEE Softw. 13 (1), 12–21.

Krogstie, J., 1998. Integrating the understanding of quality in requirements specification and conceptual modeling. ACM SIGSOFT Softw. Eng. Notes 23 (1), 86–91.

Lassing, N., Bengtsson, P., Bosch, J., Vliet, H.V., 2002. Experience with ALMA: architecture-level modifiability analysis. J. Syst. Softw. 61 (1), 47–57.

Lauesen, S., 2002. Software Requirements: Styles and Techniques. Addison-Wesley, Reading, MA.

Lebbink, H.-J., Witteman, C.L.M., Meyer, J.-J.C., 2002. Ontology-based knowledge acquisition for knowledge systems. In: Blockdeel, H., Denecker, M. (Eds.), BNAIC'02, pp. 195–202.

Leffingwell, D., 2011. Agile Software Requirements. Addison-Wesley, Reading, MA.

Lim, Y.-K., Stolterman, E., Tenenberg, J., 2008. The anatomy of prototypes: prototypes as filters, prototypes as manifestations of design ideas. ACM Trans. Comput.-Hum. Interact. 15 (2)Article 7.

Looker, N., Xu, J., Munro, M., 2007. Determining the dependability of service-oriented architectures. Int. J. Simulation Process Model. 3 (1–2), 88–97.

Magoutas, B., Halaris, C., Mentzas, G., 2007. An ontology for the multi-perspective evaluation of quality in E-government services. In: Wimmer, M.A., Scholl, J., Grönlund, Å. (Eds.), EGOV 2007. Lecture Notes in Computer Science, vol. 4656. Springer, Berlin/Heidelberg, pp. 318–329.

Marzolla, M., Balsamo, S., 2004. UML-PSI: the UML performance simulator. In: QEST'04. IEEE, New York, pp. 340–341.

Masolo, C., Borgo, S., 2005. Qualities in formal ontology. In: Hitzler, P., Lutz, C., Stumme, G. (Eds.), Workshop on Foundational Aspects of Ontologies (FOnt 2005), pp. 2–16.

Masolo, C., Borgo, S., Gangemi, A., Guarino, N., Oltramari, A., 2003. The WonderWeb Library of Foundational Ontologies. WonderWeb Deliverable D18. Ontology Library (final). ISTC-CNR, Trento.

Matinlassi, M., 2005. Quality-driven software architecture model transformation. In: Proceedings of the 5th Working IEEE/IFIP Conference on Software Architecture. IEEE Computer Society, New York, pp. 199–200.

McCall, J.A., Richards, P.K., Walters, G.F., 1977. Factors in Software Quality, NTIS.

McManus, J., 2004. Managing Stakeholders in Software Development Projects. Butterworth-Heinemann, London.

Münch, J., Armbrust, O., Kowalczyk, M., Soto, M., 2012. Software Process Definition and Management. Springer, Berlin/Heidelberg.

OMG, 2003. UML Profile for Schedulability, Performance, and Time, version 1.0, Object Management Group.

OMG, 2008. Software Process Engineering Metamodel (SPEM) 2.0, Object Management Group.

Pastor, O., Molina, J.C., 2007. Model-Driven Architecture in Practice. Springer, Heidelberg.

Rodríguez, A., Fernández-Medina, E., Piattini, M., 2006. Capturing security requirements in business processes through a UML 2.0 activity diagrams profile. In: Roddick, J.F., Benjamins, V.R., Cherfi, S., Chiang, R., Claramunt, C., Elmasri, R., Grandi, F., Han, H., Hepp, M., Lytras, M., Mišic, V.B., Poels, G., Song, I.-Y., Trujillo, J., Vangenot, C. (Eds.), ER 2006 Workshops and Tutorials. Lecture Notes in Computer Science, vol. 4231. Springer, Berlin/Heidelberg, pp. 32–42.

Rozinat, A., Wynn, M., van der Aalst, W., ter Hofstede, A., Fidge, C., 2009. Workflow simulation for operational decision support. Data Knowl. Eng. 68, 834–850.

Sanin, C., Szczerbicki, E., Toro, C., 2007. An OWL ontology of set of experience knowledge structure. J. Universal Comput. Sci. 13, 209–223.

Schneider, K., 2007. Generating fast feedback in requirements elicitation. In: Sawyer, P., Paech, B., Heymans, P. (Eds.), REFSQ 2007. In: Lecture Notes in Computer Science, vol. 4542. Springer, Berlin/Heidelberg, pp. 160–174.

Schneider, K., 2009. Experience and Knowledge Management in Software Engineering. Springer, Berlin/Heidelberg.

Shekhovtsov, V.A., 2011. On the evolution of quality conceptualization techniques. In: Kaschek, R., Delcambre, L. (Eds.), The Evolution of Conceptual Modeling. Lecture Notes in Computer Science, vol. 6520. Springer, Berlin/Heidelberg, pp. 117–136.

Shekhovtsov, V.A., Mayr, H.C., Kop, C., 2013. Towards conceptualizing quality-related stakeholder interactions in software development. In: Mayr, H.C., Kop, C., Liddle, S., Ginige, A. (Eds.), Information Systems:

Methods, Models, and Applications. Lecture Notes in Business Infomation Processing, vol. 137. Springer, Berlin/Heidelberg, pp. 73–86.

Sindre, G., Opdahl, A.L., 2005. Eliciting security requirements with misuse cases. Req. Eng. 10 (1), 34–44.

Snyder, C., 2003. Paper Prototyping: The Fast and Easy Way to Define and Refine User Interfaces. Morgan Kaufmann, San Francisco, CA.

Strauss, A.L., Corbin, J.M., 1998. Basics of Qualitative Research: Grounded Theory Procedures and Techniques, second ed. Sage Publications, Thousand Oaks, CA.

Stuckenschmidt, H., Parent, C., Spaccapietra, S. (Eds.), 2009. Modular Ontologies: Concepts, Theories and Techniques for Knowledge Modularization. Springer, Berlin/Heidelberg.

Susi, A., Perini, A., Mylopoulos, J., 2005. The tropos metamodel and its use. Informatica 29 (4), 401–408.

Sutcliffe, A., Ryan, M., 1998. Experience with SCRAM: a scenario requirements analysis method. In: ICRE'98. IEEE CS Press, New York, pp. 164–171.

Tahvildari, L., Kontogiannis, K., Mylopoulos, J., 2003. Quality-driven software re-engineering. J. Syst. Softw. 66 (3), 225–239.

Tewoldeberhan, T., Janssen, M., 2008. Simulation-based experimentation for designing reliable and efficient web service orchestrations in supply chains. Electron. Commerce Res. Apps. 7, 82–92.

Tian, J., 2004. Quality-evaluation models and measurements. IEEE Softw. 21 (3), 84–91.

Tolstedt, J.L., 2002. Prototyping as a means of requirements elicitation. In: SAE International Off-Highway Congress (SAE Technical Paper Series), vol. 2002-01-1466.

Wagner, S., Deissenboeck, F., 2007. An integrated approach to quality modelling. In: WoSQ'07. ACM, New York.

Walia, G.S., Carver, J.C., 2009. A systematic literature review to identify and classify software requirement errors. Inf. Softw. Technol. 51, 1087–1109.

Wang, X., Chan, C.W., Hamilton, H.J., 2002. Design of knowledge-based systems with the ontology-domain-system approach. In: SEKE'02. ACM, New York, pp. 233–236.

Weinreich, R., Buchgeher, G., 2010. Integrating requirements and design decisions in architecture representation. In: Babar, M.A., Gorton, I. (Eds.), ECSA'10. In: Lecture Notes in Computer Science, vol. 6285. Springer, Berlin/Heidelberg, pp. 86–101.

Westland, J.C., 2002. The cost of errors in software development: evidence from industry. J. Syst. Softw. 62, 1–9.

Williams, L.G., Smith, C.U., 2002. PASA: a method for the performance assessment of software architecture. In: 3rd Workshop on Software Performance, Rome, Italy. ACM Press, New York, pp. 179–189.

Zhu, L., Gorton, I., 2007. UML profiles for design decisions and non-functional requirements. In: Proceedings of ICSE Workshop on Sharing and Reusing Architectural Knowledge (SHARK'07). IEEE Press, New York.

# Optimizing Functional and Quality Requirements According to Stakeholders' Goals

**Azadeh Alebrahim[1], Christine Choppy[2], Stephan Faßbender[1], and Maritta Heisel[1]**

[1]*University of Duisburg-Essen, Essen, Germany*
[2]*University Paris 13 - Sorbonne Paris Cité, LIPN CNRS UMR 7030, Villetaneuse, France*

## INTRODUCTION

Nowadays, for almost every software system, various stakeholders with diverse interests exist. These interests give rise to different sets of requirements. The combination of these requirements may lead to interactions among them. But interactions may not only stem from requirements of different stakeholders, but also from different qualities that are desired by the stakeholders. In such a situation it is hard to select those requirements that serve the different stakeholders in an optimal way, even if all requirements are elicited. First of all, it is a necessary quality of a system to be free of unwanted requirements interactions. Hence, some requirements might have to be removed. But removing requirements might have a huge impact on each stakeholder's perceived quality regarding the expected functionality and qualities, such as performance or security. In order to select the overall optimal set of requirements, one that is free of unwanted interactions, considering the expectations of all stakeholders, one has to discover the interactions, decide whether there are alternatives for problematic requirements, and prioritize and/or valuate requirements with respect to the involved stakeholders.

The analysis of interactions and dependencies among requirements is called *requirements interaction management*. Robinson et al. (2003) define it as the "set of activities directed towards the discovery, management, and disposition of critical relationships among sets of requirements." In this chapter, we not only aim at giving a structured method for requirements interaction management, but also at extending it by further steps toward an optimal set of requirements. We not only strive for detecting and documenting interactions, but also for resolving negative interactions in such a way that the resulting requirements are optimal regarding the stakeholders' expectations.

Our general approach for optimizing functional and quality requirements regarding stakeholder goals (see Figure 4.1) consists of the preparatory phases **Understanding the Purpose** and **Understanding the Problem** and the phase **Reconciliation**. To cover the Reconciliation phase, we propose the **QuaRO** (Quality Requirements Optimization) method, which is our main contribution for this chapter. An overview of the method is given in Figure 4.1. The first step for reconciliation is to discover the interactions between the requirements (Detection of Interactions in Figure 4.1). Then, we need to generate alternatives for interacting requirements (Generation of Alternatives). For optimization, the requirements need a value to which the optimization can refer. The relations between requirements also

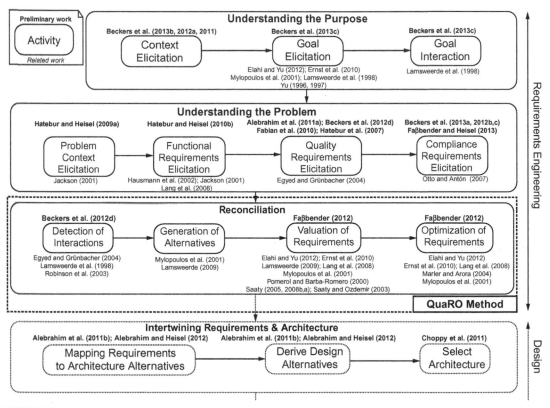

**FIGURE 4.1**

The QuaRO method and its context in a software engineering process.

need to be valuated. This is achieved in the third step (Valuation of Requirements). Finally, we set up an optimization model that uses the input information from previous steps to compute the optimal set of requirements regarding the optimization goals and the valuation of the requirements (Optimization of Requirements). QuaRO can be integrated into existing software engineering methods.

The optimal set of requirements obtained by QuaRO forms the basis of the subsequent steps of software development, in particular architectural design. The phase **Intertwining Requirements & Architecture** in Figure 4.1 gives an overview of the further steps. Given that architectural decisions may have repercussions on the requirements, requirement descriptions and architectural descriptions have to be considered as intertwining artifacts to be developed concurrently, as proposed by the Twin Peaks model (Nuseibeh, 2001).

Note that in the literature references given above the different steps refer to our own previous work, whereas the literature references given below the different steps refer to related work of other authors. In our previous work regarding detection of interactions (Beckers et al., 2012b), we performed a threat analysis to find interactions among various stakeholder goals regarding privacy. In this chapter, we focus on detecting interactions among security and performance requirements. In another previous work (Faßbender, 2012), we sketched our first ideas to obtain an optimal set of requirements that is compliant and secure.

The remainder of the chapter is organized as follows. In Section 4.1, we introduce the smart grid example, which we use to illustrate the application of the QuaRO method. We present the background on which our method is built in Section 4.2. Section 4.3 is devoted to illustrating the preparatory phases, including understanding the purpose of the system and understanding the problem. We describe the QuaRO method in Sections 4.4–4.7. After detecting interaction candidates among quality requirements in Section 4.4, we generate alternatives for conflicting requirements in Section 4.5. Subsequently, all the requirements and their relations have to be valuated (Section 4.6) in order to provide input for the optimization model we set up in Section 4.7. Related work is discussed in Section 4.8, and conclusions and perspectives are given in Section 4.9.

## 4.1 SMART GRID

To illustrate the application of the QuaRO method, we use the real-life example of smart grids. As sources for real functional and quality requirements, we consider diverse documents such as "Application Case Study: Smart Grid" and "Smart Grid Concrete Scenario" provided by the industrial partners of the EU project NESSoS,[1] the "Protection Profile for the Gateway of a Smart Metering System" (Kreutzmann et al., 2011) provided by the German Federal Office for Information Security,[2] "Smart Metering Implementation Program, Overview Document" (Department of Energy and Climate Change, 2011a) and "Smart Metering Implementation Program, Design Requirements" (Department of Energy and Climate Change, 2011b) provided by the UK Office of Gas and Electricity Markets,[3] and "D1.2 Report on Regulatory Requirements (Remero et al., 2009b)" and "Requirements of AMI (Advanced Multi-metering Infrastructure") (Remero et al., 2009a) provided by the EU project OPEN meter.[4]

### 4.1.1 Description of smart grids

To use energy in an optimal way, smart grids make it possible to couple the generation, distribution, storage, and consumption of energy. Smart grids use information and communication technology (ICT), which allows for financial, informational, and electrical transactions.

Figure 4.2 shows the simplified context of a smart grid system based on the protection profile (Kreutzmann et al., 2011). We first define the terms specific to the smart grid domain taken from the protection profile:

*Gateway* represents the central communication unit in a *smart metering system*. It is responsible for collecting, processing, storing, and communicating *meter data*.
*Meter data* refers to meter readings measured by the meter regarding consumption or production of a certain commodity.
*Meter* represents the device that measures the consumption or production of a certain commodity and sends it to the gateway.

---

[1]http://www.nessos-project.eu/.
[2]www.bsi.bund.de.
[3]http://www.ofgem.gov.uk.
[4]http://www.openmeter.com/.

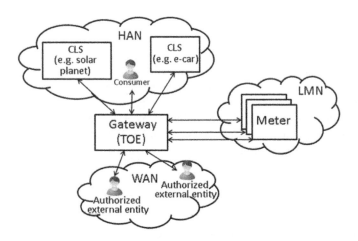

**FIGURE 4.2**

The context of a smart grid system based on Kreutzmann et al. (2011).

> *Authorized external entity* could be a human or IT unit that communicates with the gateway from outside the gateway boundaries through a *Wide Area Network* (WAN). The roles defined as external entities that interact with the gateway and the meter are *consumer, supplier, gateway operator, gateway administrator, etc.* (For the complete list of possible external entities see the protection profile (Kreutzmann et al., 2011)).
>
> *WAN (Wide Area Network)* provides the communication network that interconnects the gateway with the outside world.
>
> *LMN (Local Metrological Network)* provides the communication network between the meter and the gateway.
>
> *HAN (Home Area Network)* provides the communication network between the consumer and the gateway.
>
> *LAN (Local Area Network)* provides the communication network that interconnects domestic equipment or metrological equipment.[5]
>
> *Consumer* refers to the end user or producer of commodities (electricity, gas, water, or heat).

For the smart grid, different quality requirements have to be taken into account. Detailed information about consumers' energy consumption can reveal privacy-sensitive data about the persons staying in a house. Hence, we are concerned with privacy issues. A smart grid involves a wide range of data that should be treated in a secure way. Additionally, introducing new data interfaces to the grid (smart meters, collectors, and other smart devices) provides new entry points for attackers. Therefore, special attention should be paid to security concerns. The number of smart devices to be managed has a deep impact on the performance of the whole system. This makes performance of smart grids an important issue.

Due to the fact that different stakeholders with diverse and partially contradicting interests are involved in the smart grid, the requirements for the whole system contain conflicts or undesired mutual influences. Therefore, the smart grid is a very good candidate to illustrate our method.

---

[5]In the protection profile, LAN is referred to as hypernym for LMN (Local Metrological Network) and HAN (Home Area Network).

### 4.1.2 **Functional requirements**

The use cases given in the documents of the open meter project are divided into three categories: *minimum*, *advanced*, and *optional*. Minimum-use cases are necessary to achieve the goals of the system, whereas advanced-use cases are of high interest, but might not be absolutely required, and optional-use cases provide add-on functions. Because treating all 20 use cases would go beyond the scope of this work, we decided to consider only the use case *Meter Reading for Billing*. This use case is concerned with gathering, processing, and storing meter readings from smart meters for the billing process. The considered use case belongs to the category *minimum*.

The protection profile (Kreutzmann et al., 2011) states that *"the Gateway is responsible for handling Meter Data. It receives the Meter Data from the Meter(s), processes it, stores it and submits it to external parties"* (p. 18). Therefore, we define the requirements *RQ1-RQ3* to receive, process, and store meter data from smart meters. The requirement *RQ4* is concerned with submitting meter data to authorized external entities. The gateway shall also provide meter data for consumers for the purpose of checking the billing consistency (*RQ5*). Requirements with their descriptions are listed in Table 4.1.

**Table 4.1** Requirements for Smart Metering

| Requirement | Description | Related Functional Requirement |
|---|---|---|
| *RQ1* | Smart meter gateway shall receive meter data from smart meters | – |
| *RQ2* | Smart meter gateway shall process meter data from smart meters | – |
| *RQ3* | Smart meter gateway shall store meter data from smart meters | – |
| *RQ4* | Smart meter gateway shall submit processed meter data to authorized external Entities | – |
| *RQ5* | The gateway shall provide meter data for consumers for the purpose of checking the billing consistency | – |
| *RQ6* | The gateway shall provide the protection of integrity when receiving meter data from a meter via the LMN | RQ1 |
| *RQ7* | The gateway shall provide the protection of confidentiality when receiving meter data from a meter via the LMN | RQ1 |
| *RQ8* | The gateway shall provide the protection of authenticity when receiving meter data from a meter via the LMN | RQ1 |
| *RQ9* | Data shall be protected from unauthorized disclosure while persistently stored in the gateway | RQ3 |
| *RQ10* | Integrity of data transferred in the WAN shall be protected | RQ4 |
| *RQ11* | Confidentiality of data transferred in the WAN shall be protected | RQ4 |
| *RQ12* | Authenticity of data transferred in the WAN shall be protected | RQ4 |
| *RQ13* | The gateway shall provide the protection of integrity when transmitting processed meter data locally within the LAN | RQ5 |
| *RQ14* | The gateway shall provide the protection of confidentiality when transmitting processed meter data locally within the LAN | RQ5 |
| *RQ15* | The gateway shall provide the protection of authenticity when transmitting processed meter data locally within the LAN | RQ5 |

*Continued*

**Table 4.1** Requirements for Smart Metering—cont'd

| Requirement | Description | Related Functional Requirement |
|---|---|---|
| RQ16 | Data shall be protected from unauthorized disclosure while temporarily stored in the gateway | RQ1 |
| RQ17 | Privacy of the consumer data shall be protected while the data is transferred in and from the smart metering system | RQ1, RQ4, RQ5 |
| RQ18 | The time to retrieve meter data from the smart meter and publish it through WAN shall be less than 5 s (together with RQ20, RQ22, RQ24) | RQ1 |
| RQ19 | The time to retrieve meter data from the smart meter and publish it through HAN shall be less than 10 s (together with RQ21, RQ23, RQ25) | RQ1 |
| RQ20 | The time to retrieve meter data from the smart meter and publish it through WAN shall be less than 5 s (together with RQ18, RQ22, RQ24) | RQ2 |
| RQ21 | The time to retrieve meter data from the smart meter and publish it through HAN shall be less than 10 s (together with RQ19, RQ23, RQ25) | RQ2 |
| RQ22 | The time to retrieve meter data from the smart meter and publish it through WAN shall be less than 5 s (together with RQ18, RQ20, RQ24) | RQ3 |
| RQ23 | The time to retrieve meter data from the smart meter and publish it through HAN shall be less than 10 s (together with RQ19, RQ21, RQ25) | RQ3 |
| RQ24 | The time to retrieve meter data from the smart meter and publish it through WAN shall be less than 5 s (together with RQ18, RQ20, RQ22) | RQ4 |
| RQ25 | The time to retrieve meter data from the smart meter and publish it through HAN shall be less than 10 s (together with RQ19, RQ21, RQ23) | RQ5 |

### 4.1.3 Security and privacy requirements

To ensure security of meter data, the protection profile (Kreutzmann et al., 2011, pp. 18, 20) demands protection of data from unauthorized disclosure while received from a meter via the LMN (*RQ7*), while temporarily or persistently stored in the gateway (*RQ9, RQ16*), while transmitted to the corresponding external entity via the WAN (*RQ11*), and while transmitted locally within the LAN (*RQ14*). The gateway shall provide the protection of authenticity and integrity when receiving meter data from a meter via the LMN to verify that the meter data have been sent from an authentic meter and have not been altered during transmission (*RQ6, RQ8*). The gateway shall provide the protection of authenticity and integrity when sending processed meter data to an external entity, to enable the external entity to verify that the processed meter data have been sent from an authentic gateway and have not been changed during transmission (*RQ10, RQ12, RQ13, RQ15*). Privacy of the consumer data shall be protected while the data is transferred in and from the smart metering system (*RQ17*).

### 4.1.4 Performance requirements

The report "Requirements of AMI" (Remero et al., 2009a, pp. 199-201) demands that the time to retrieve meter data from the smart meter and publish it through WAN shall be less than 5 s. Due to the fact that we decompose the whole functionality from retrieving meter data to publishing it into requirements *RQ1-RQ4*, we also decompose this performance requirement into requirements *RQ18* (complementing *RQ1*), *RQ20* (complementing *RQ2*), *RQ22* (complementing *RQ3*), and *RQ24* (complementing *RQ4*). The requirements *RQ18, RQ20, RQ22,* and *RQ24* shall be fulfilled in a way that in total they do not need more than 5 s.

Further, the report "Requirements of AMI" states that for the benefit of the consumer, actual meter readings are to be provided to the end consumer device through HAN. It demands that the time to retrieve meter data from the smart meter and publish it through HAN shall be less than 10 s. Similar to the previous requirement, we decompose this requirement into requirements *RQ19* (complementing *RQ1*), *RQ21* (complementing *RQ2*), *RQ23* (complementing *RQ3*), and *RQ25* (complementing *RQ5*). These requirements together shall be fulfilled in less than 10 s.

Figure 4.3 shows five quality requirements *RQ10, RQ11, RQ12, RQ17,* and *RQ24* that complement the functional requirement *RQ4*.

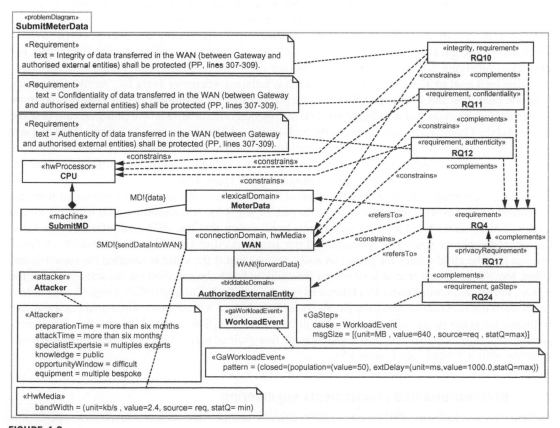

**FIGURE 4.3**

Problem Diagram for submitting meter data to external entities.

## 4.2 BACKGROUND, CONCEPTS, AND NOTATIONS

This section outlines concepts and terminologies our method relies on. In the preparatory phase **Understanding the Purpose**, we make use of the goal notation *i\**, introduced in Section 4.2.1. The problem frames approach and our enhancements described in Section 4.2.2 are used in the preparatory phase **Understanding the Problem**. Subsequently, we give a brief overview of the analytical network process (ANP), which is used in the **Reconciliation** phase in the step **Valuation of Requirements**. Finally, the relevant concepts in the field of optimization to be used in the step **Optimization of Requirements** of the **Reconciliation** phase are introduced in Section *4.2.4*.

### 4.2.1 The *i\** framework

In the *i\** framework (Yu, 1996, 1997), goal graphs serve to visualize the goals of an actor. Hence, the first element of a goal graph is the actor visualized by the actor boundaries (see Figure 4.5: light gray rectangles with rounded corners). Actor boundaries indicate intentional boundaries of a particular actor. All of the elements within a boundary for an actor are explicitly desired by that actor. For our use case, the consumer, the billing manager, and the grid operator Tesla Inc. are actors. A goal of an actor represents an intentional desire of this actor. The *i\** framework distinguishes between hard goals, soft goals, and tasks. A hard goal defines a desire for which the satisfaction criteria are clear, but the way of satisfying it is unspecified. Hard goals are visualized as ellipses (see Figure 4.5). An example is the hard goal of Tesla Inc.: "Get Money." It is satisfied whenever Tesla Inc. receives its money from the consumer but is not specific about the process to get the money. A soft goal is even more underspecified, because for a soft goal no clear satisfaction criteria are known. Soft goals are denoted as clouds (see Figure 4.5). An example is the high-level goal "Performance," because at this level one cannot give a process for achieving performance nor can one give an overall criterion when a consumer perceives a system as performant. In contrast, a task defines both the criteria for fulfilling the goal and the process to do so. Tasks are denoted as hexagons (see Figure 4.5).

Goals are connected by links. The first kind of link is the contribution link. Contribution links are visualized using arrows with filled arrowheads (see Figure 4.5). A contribution link between a child goal (tail of the arrow) and a parent goal (arrow head) means that the child goal influences the satisfaction of the parent goal. The annotation of the arrow specifies the kind of contribution. A *break* denotes that the child denies the parent. A *make* denotes that if the child is satisfied the parent is satisfied, too. An *or* means that at least one of the children has to be satisfied for the satisfaction of the parent. For an *and* contribution all children have to be satisfied. *Hurts* specifies a negative influence, which does not necessarily break the parent goal. *Helps* is used whenever the child goal has a positive influence but is not necessarily needed to fulfill the parent goal. The second kind of link is the decomposition link. It is used to decompose a goal to more fine-grained parts. A decomposition link is denoted as arrow with a T-head (see Figure 4.5).

### 4.2.2 Problem-oriented requirements engineering

Problem frames (Jackson, 2001) are a means to describe and classify software development problems. A problem frame represents a class of software problems. A problem frame is described by a *frame diagram*, which basically consists of *domains*, *interfaces* between them, and a *requirement*.

Domains describe entities in the environment. Michael Jackson distinguishes the domain types *biddable domains* that are usually people, *causal domains* that comply with some physical laws, and *lexical domains* that are data representations. *Interfaces* connect domains, and they contain *shared phenomena*. Shared phenomena may be events, operation calls, messages, and the like. They are observable by at least two domains, but controlled by only one domain, as indicated by the name of that domain and "!". In Figure 4.3 the notation *MD!{data}* (between *MeterData* and *SubmitMD*) means that the phenomenon *data* is controlled by the domain *MeterData* and observed by the machine *SubmitMD*.

When we state a requirement, we want to change something in the world with the software to be developed. Therefore, each requirement constrains at least one domain. Such a constrained domain is the core of any problem description, because it has to be controlled according to the requirements. A requirement may refer to several other domains. The task is to construct a *machine* (i.e., software) that improves the behavior of the environment (in which it is integrated) in accordance with the requirements.

Requirements analysis with problem frames proceeds as follows: First the environment in which the machine will operate is represented by a *context diagram*. A context diagram consists of machines, domains, and interfaces. Then, the problem is decomposed into sub-problems, which are represented by *problem diagrams*. A problem diagram consists of one submachine of the machine given in the context diagram, the relevant domains, the interfaces between these domains, and a requirement.

We represent problem frames using UML class diagrams, extended by a new UML profile (UML4PF) as proposed by Hatebur and Heisel (2010c). Using specialized stereotypes, the UML profile allows us to express the different diagrams occurring in the problem frame approach using UML diagrams. Figure 4.3 illustrates one subproblem expressed as a problem diagram in UML notation in the context of our smart grid example. It describes that smart meter gateway submits meter data to an authorized external entity. The submachine *SubmitMD* is one part of the smart meter gateway. It sends the *MeterData* through the causal domain *WAN* to the biddable domain *AuthorizedExternalEntity*. The requirement *RQ4* constrains the domain *WAN*. This is expressed by a dependency with the stereotype ≪constrains≫. It refers to the domains *MeterData* and *AuthorizedExternalEntity* as expressed by dependencies with the stereotype ≪refersTo≫.

Requirements analysis based on the classical problem frames does not support analyzing quality requirements. So, we extended it by explicitly taking into account quality requirements, which complement functional requirements (Alebrahim et al., 2011a). Figure 4.3 shows five quality requirements *RQ10*, *RQ11*, *RQ12*, *RQ17*, and *RQ24* that complement the functional requirement *RQ4*. This is expressed by dependencies from the quality requirements to the functional requirement with the stereotype ≪complements≫. We use a UML profile for dependability (Hatebur and Heisel, 2010c) to annotate problem diagrams with security requirements. For example, we apply the stereotypes ≪integrity≫, ≪confidentiality≫, and ≪authenticity≫ to represent integrity, confidentiality, and authenticity requirements as it is illustrated in Figure 4.3. To annotate privacy requirements, we use the privacy profile (Beckers et al., 2012b) that enables us to use the stereotype ≪privacyRequirement≫. To provide support for annotating problem descriptions with performance requirements, we use the UML profile MARTE (Modeling and Analysis of Real-time and Embedded Systems) (UML Revision Task Force, 2011). We annotate each performance requirement with the stereotype ≪gaStep≫ to express a response time requirement. Note that for each type of quality requirement, a new UML profile should be created if not existing. This needs to be done only once.

As a basis for our QuaRO method, we use the problem frames approach, because it allows us to obtain detailed information from the structure of problem diagrams. Such information is crucial for our proposed approach, because it enables us to perform interaction analysis and optimization, whereas other requirements engineering approaches such as scenario-based approaches and use cases do not contain detailed information for such analyses.

### 4.2.3 **Valuation of requirements**

For valuating and comparing alternatives among each other, several methods are known, such as direct scoring (Pomerol and Barba-Romero, 2000), Even Swaps (Mustajoki and Hämäläinen, 2007), win-win negotiating, the analytical hierarchy process (AHP) (Saaty, 2005; Saaty and Ozdemir, 2003) or the ANP (Saaty, 2008a, 2005). They all support decision making (process of selecting a solution among a set of alternatives) by either eliminating alternatives successively or ranking them. For the QuaRO method, we decided to use the ANP (reasons for the decision are discussed in Section 4.6), which will be explained in the following.

The *ANP* is a generalization of the more widely known *AHP* (Saaty, 2008a, 2005). Both rely on *goals*, *criteria*, and *alternatives*. These *elements* are grouped by *clusters*, which can be ordered in *hierarchies* (AHP, ANP) or *networks* (ANP) (see Figure 4.4). A goal in this context is the desired outcome of a decision process, otherwise known as the "best system" or the "optimal marketing strategy." A criterion is one important property, which has an influence on the decision regarding the goal. An alternative is one possible solution (part) to fulfill the goal and is compared to other alternatives with respect to the criteria. Hierarchy means that there is a strict order of influence between elements of different hierarchy levels. So, sub-criteria are compared with respect to criteria but not the other way around. The top level of the hierarchy is formed by the elements not influenced by any other element. The bottom level forms the elements that do not influence other elements. In contrast to AHP, which only allows influential relations between elements of adjacent hierarchy levels and only from the higher level to the lower one (see Figure 4.4, left-hand side), ANP allows one to consider influential relations between elements within one level and bidirectional relations between all hierarchy levels forming a network (see Figure 4.4, right-hand side). Note that ANP allows a mixture of hierarchy and (sub-) networks

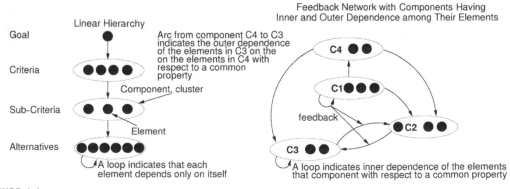

**FIGURE 4.4**

Hierarchy compared to a network based on Saaty (2005).

(see Figure 4.9 in Section 4.6). Hence, ANP allows one to model more complex decision makings more accurately than AHP. The downside of ANP compared to AHP is the increasing number of comparisons to be made and the complex calculations to be executed (Saaty, 2005). On the one hand, ANP takes more time and the final decision is more difficult to understand, but on the other hand, ANP allows a much deeper problem understanding and modeling and avoids errors due to oversimplification, which often occur when using AHP (Saaty, 2005; Saaty and Ozdemir, 2003). The steps of ANP are as follows (Saaty, 2008a,b, 2005; Saaty and Ozdemir, 2003):

1. **Describe the decision problem**. The first step of ANP is to understand the decision problem in terms of stakeholders, their objectives, the criteria and sub-criteria, alternatives, and the influential relations among all those elements. ANP gives no guidance for this step, but it is crucial for the success of the whole process.

2. **Set up control criteria**. In addition to the criteria and sub-criteria relevant for the decision, Saaty recommends using control criteria for many decisions. He suggests benefits, opportunities, costs, and risks (BOCR) as control criteria (Saaty, 2008b). Using control criteria allows one to model different dimensions of a decision problem and to combine negative and positive dimensions. Using control criteria is optional.

3. **Set up clusters**. To structure the (sub-)criteria and alternatives and to make the network and the later comparisons better manageable, the (sub-)criteria and alternatives can be merged into clusters, regarding, for example, their relation to a parent criterion. It is also allowed to have elements that represent sub-networks to the network the element resides in within a cluster. In this way very complex networks can be handled in a "divide-and-conquer" style.

4. **Relate elements of the network**. The (sub-)criteria and alternatives have to be related according to their influence on each other. At this point the relation is undirected. Only the elements of one cluster are allowed to be directly related (inner dependence influence). Clusters are related whenever at least one element of the first cluster is related to at least one element of the second cluster (outer dependence influence).

5. **Determine the influence direction**. For each relation it has to be decided whether it is an unidirectional or bidirectional relation. One has also to decide whether a direction means "influences target element" or "is influenced by target element." The first option is recommended.

6. **Set up supermatrix**. For each control criterion a supermatrix has to be constructed. Each element has to have a row and column representing it. Rows and columns are grouped according to the clusters. The cells of the supermatrix are marked whenever the element of the column influences the element of the row or the cluster the column element belongs to influences the cluster of the row element.

7. **Compare elements**. In this step, the pairwise comparison of elements, according to the inner and outer dependences of the cluster they belong to, has to be carried out. This results in an unweighted supermatrix.

8. **Compare clusters**. To weight the different clusters, all clusters are compared pairwise with respect to a (control/sub-)criterion or goal. The resulting weights are then used to weight the cells of the columns whose elements belong to the cluster. In this way, one obtains the weighted supermatrix.

9. **Compute limited supermatrix**. The limited supermatrix is computed by raising the weighted supermatrix to a certain power $k$. The constant $k$ can be freely chosen. For a low $k$ the limited

supermatrix might not be stable in the sense that for some elements, given by their row, the actual value does not converge to the final value. Hence, the priority of the element is not stable and cannot be determined. For a high $k$ small priorities might drop to zero.

10. **Synthesize results to the control level.** Set up a formula and weights for relating the control criteria. The result is the weighted prioritization of alternatives regarding the control criteria.

## 4.2.4 Optimization

The process of optimizing systematically and simultaneously a collection of objective functions is called *multi-objective optimization (MOO)* or *vector optimization* (Marler and Arora, 2004). MOO is used whenever certain solutions or parts of solutions exist, the values of the solutions with respect to objectives are known, there are some constraints for selecting solutions, but the complexity of the optimization problem hinders a human to figure out the optimum or an automated selection is desired. The optimization problem can be complex due to the sheer number of solutions, the number of constraints, and/or the number of relations between solution parts. The following definitions are used in the rest of the chapter:

| | | |
|---|---|---|
| $\mathbf{F}$ | Vector of objective functions (point in the criterion (problem) space) | (1) |
| $F_i \in \mathbf{F}$ | The $i$th objective function | (2) |
| $\mathbf{F}^{\circ}$ | Vector of utopia points (optimizing the collection of objective functions) | (3) |
| $F_i^{\circ} \in \mathbf{F}^{\circ}$ | The utopia point for the $i$th objective function | (4) |
| $\mathbf{G}$ | Vector of inequality constraints | (5) |
| $g_j \in \mathbf{G}$ | The $j$th inequality constraint | (6) |
| $\mathbf{H}$ | Vector of equality constraints | (7) |
| $h_k \in \mathbf{H}$ | The $k$th equality constraint | (8) |
| $\mathbf{x}$ | Vector of design (decision) variables (points in design (solution) space) | (9) |
| $\mathbf{w}$ | Vector of weighting coefficients/exponents | (10) |
| $w_l \in \mathbf{w}$ | The $l$th weighting coefficient/exponent | (11) |

The general MOO problem is posed as follows (Note that $\geq$ constraints can be easily transformed to $\leq$ constraints. The same is true for maximization objectives.):

$$\text{Minimize} \, \mathbf{F}(\mathbf{x}) = [F_1(\mathbf{x}), F_2(\mathbf{x}), \dots, F_m(\mathbf{x})]^{\mathrm{T}} \tag{12}$$

$$\text{subject to} \, g_j \leq 0, \quad j = 1, 2, \dots, n \tag{13}$$

$$\text{subject to} \, h_k = 0, \quad k = 1, 2, \dots, o \tag{14}$$

where $m$ is the number of objective functions, $n$ is the number of inequality constraints, and $o$ is the number of equality constraints. $x \in E^q$ is a vector of design variables (also called decision variables), where $q$ is the number of independent variables $x_i$ with type $E$, which can be freely chosen. $F(\mathbf{x}) \in E^k$ is a vector of objective functions $F_i(\mathbf{x}) : E^q \to E^1$. $F_i(\mathbf{x})$ are also called objectives, criteria, payoff functions, cost functions, or value functions. The feasible design space $\mathbf{X}$ (often called the feasible decision space or constraint set) is defined as the set $\{x|g_j(x) \leq 0, j = 1, 2, \ldots, n \wedge h_i(x) = 0, i = 1, 2, \ldots, o\}$. $x_i^*$ is the point that minimizes the objective function $F_i(\mathbf{x})$. An $F_i^o$ utopia point is the value attainable at best for $F_i(\mathbf{x})$ respecting the constraints. The total optimum is the value attainable at best for $F_i(\mathbf{x})$ not respecting the constraints.

*Definition* Pareto Optimal: A point, $x^* \in X$, is Pareto optimal if there does not exist another point, $x \in X$, such that $F(\mathbf{x}) \leq F(\mathbf{x}^*)$, *and* $F_i(\mathbf{x}) < F_i(\mathbf{x}^*)$ for at least one function from $F$.

## 4.3 PREPARATORY PHASES FOR QuaRO

In the following, we outline the preparatory phases before we describe the QuaRO method in detail.

### 4.3.1 Understanding the purpose of the system

The phase **Understanding the Purpose** aims at understanding the purpose of the system-to-be, its direct and indirect environment, the relevant stakeholders, and other already established systems, assets, and other entities that are directly or indirectly related to the system-to-be. In the first step *Context Elicitation*, we consider all relevant entities of the environment. The second step *Goal Elicitation* captures the goals to be considered for optimization. Hence, we have to analyze the goals of each stakeholder in relation to the system-to-be. Detecting requirements interactions early at the goal level will eliminate some interactions among requirements related to those goals, which we would face later at the requirements level. Detecting and eliminating conflicts on the goal level is the purpose of the third step *Goal Interaction*.

For the elicitation of the context, we introduced so-called *context elicitation patterns* in earlier work of ours (Beckers et al., 2013b, 2012a, 2011). Such patterns exhibit typical elements occurring in the environments such as cloud computing systems or service-oriented architectures. For a structured elicitation of information about the context of a smart grid software, we adapted the existing patterns for smart grids, conducting an in-depth analysis of several documents as described in Section 4.1. The resulting pattern is not shown for reasons of space. Using the pattern, we identified three major stakeholders. The consumer, the grid provider, and the billing manager, as authorized external entity, were described in detail in terms of a general description, their motivation and top-level goals, such privacy, performance, economy, and so forth.

For refining the top-level goals, we used the $i^*$ notation (Mylopoulos et al., 2001; Yu, 1996, 1997). We refined the top-level goals for each stakeholder independently, obtaining three actor boundaries containing the goal graphs. In the end we got 67 softgoals, like "Responsive User Interface" or "Maximize Number of Sold Products," 9 hard goals, like "Pay Bill in time," and 47 tasks, like "Analyze Consumption" or "Send Bill." In step *goal interaction*, we discovered 37 positive goal interactions, such as "Collect Grid Information" helps "Offer Attractive Products and Services," and 4 cases where a goal hurts another goal, like "Collect Maximum of Information"(grid provider) and "Authorized Parties get Needed Data" (consumer). For reasons of space and readability the full goal graphs cannot be shown. A small part, which is sufficient for the rest of this chapter, is shown in Figure 4.5.

The goal graphs serve two purposes. First, to refine the top-level goals to the leaves. For example, refine "Privacy" to "Private Data not Disclosed" to "Authorized Parties get Needed Data." For the further procedure the leaves (goals without sub-goals) are of specific interest. For Tesla Inc. these are

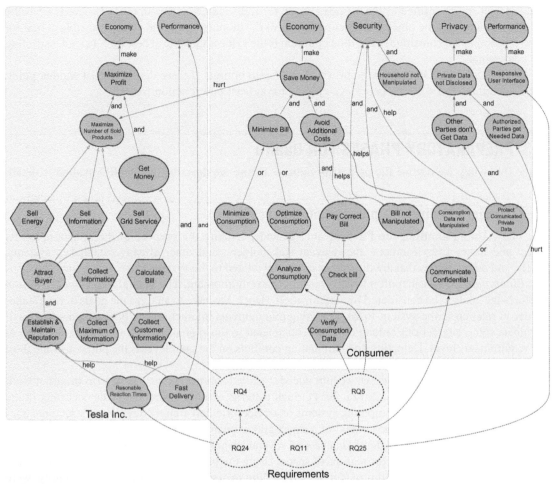

**FIGURE 4.5**

Goal tree (part) with relation to requirements.

"Establish & Maintain Reputation," "Collect Maximum of Information," "Collect Customer Information," "Reasonable Reaction Times," and "Fast Delivery." "Household not Manipulated," "Responsive User Interface," "Authorized Parties get Needed Data," "Bill not Manipulated," "Consumption Data not Manipulated," "Analyze Consumption," "Communicate Confidential," and "Verify Consumption Data" are the leaves for the consumer. The leaves will serve as criteria for the valuation.

The second purpose is the use of the graphs for the optimization. The graphs already contain alternatives for fulfilling the goals. Every *or* contribution like "Minimize Consumption" and "Optimize Consumption" for the soft goal "Minimize Bill" is an option for optimization. Additionally, whenever a goal cannot be fulfilled, all of its sub-goals do not have to be fulfilled. Hence, all requirements related to these sub-goals can be ignored. As result, the goal graphs serve for constraining the optimization and adding alternatives.

### 4.3.2 Understanding the problem

The phase **Understanding the Problem** aims at understanding the system-to-be and the problem it shall solve, and therefore understanding the environment it should influence according to the requirements. In the first step *Problem Context Elicitation*, we obtain a problem description by eliciting all domains related to the problem to be solved, their relations to each other, and the software to be constructed. The step *Functional Requirements Elicitation* is concerned with decomposing the overall problem into sub-problems that describe a certain functionality, as expressed by a set of related requirements. The functionality of the software is the core, and all quality requirements are related in some way to this core. Eliciting quality requirements and relating them to the system-to-be is achieved in the step *Quality Requirements Elicitation*. Once eliciting the functional and quality requirements is accomplished, one has to ensure that the system-to-be complies to regulations such as laws. To this end, we derive requirements from laws, standards, and policies in the step *Compliance Requirements Elicitation*.

To elicit the problem context, we set up a context diagram consisting of the machine *Gateway*, the domains *LMN*, *HAN*, *WAN*, *MeterData*, *AuthorizedExternalEntities*, *Consumer*, etc. and interfaces between these domains. To provide billing information to external parties and also to the consumer, the gateway receives the meter data from the meter(s) (*RQ1*), processes it (*RQ2*), and stores it (*RQ3*). The gateway submits the stored data to external parties (*RQ4*). The stored data can also be provided to the consumer to allow the consumer to verify an invoice (*RQ5*). We set up problem diagrams to model the functional requirements *RQ1-RQ5*. Figure 4.3 shows the problem diagram for the functional requirement *RQ4*. Besides the functionalities that the gateway has to provide, it is also responsible for the protection of authenticity, integrity, and confidentiality of data temporarily or persistently stored in the gateway, transferred locally within the LAN and transferred in the WAN (between gateway and authorized external entities). In addition, as stated by the protection profile (Kreutzmann et al., 2011), the privacy of the consumer shall be protected. Furthermore, it is demanded that functional requirements shall be achieved within a certain response time.

Hence, we annotate all problem diagrams with quality requirements as proposed in earlier work of ours (Alebrahim et al., 2011a). For example, we annotate the problem diagram for submitting meter readings (Figure 4.3) with security requirements *RQ10* (integrity), *RQ11* (confidentiality), *RQ12* (authenticity), which complement the functional requirement *RQ4*. The privacy requirement *RQ17* and the performance requirement *RQ24* also complement the functional requirement *RQ4*.

## 4.4 METHOD FOR DETECTING CANDIDATES FOR REQUIREMENTS INTERACTIONS

The first step for reconciliation is to discover interactions between requirements. Interactions can be positive or negative. In this section, we deal with negative interactions involving quality requirements, leading to undesirable effects among requirements. In the following, we propose a method to detect candidates for negative interactions based on pairwise comparisons between quality requirements. Figure 4.6 illustrates the phases of our method, input, and output of each phase.

To restrict the number of comparisons, we perform a preparation phase, in which we investigate which two types of quality requirements may be in conflict in general. In doing so, we consider different types of quality requirements. The preparation phase results in a table containing all types of

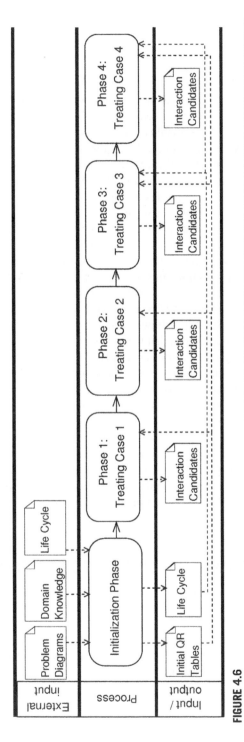

**FIGURE 4.6**

Method for detecting candidates for interactions among quality requirements.

quality requirements to be considered. We compare each two types of quality requirements regarding potential conflicts. If conflicts are possible, we enter a cross in the cell, where the two quality requirements cross, otherwise a minus. For example, no interactions between a confidentiality requirement and a privacy requirement are expected. Therefore, the cell crossing these two requirement types in the table contains a minus. In contrast, a confidentiality requirement might be in conflict with a performance requirement. Hence, the corresponding cell contains a cross. Table 4.2 shows possible interactions among security (confidentiality, integrity, authenticity), performance, and privacy requirements in general.

Interactions among quality requirements of different types can occur either between quality requirements related to the same functional requirement or among those related to different functional requirements. We classify quality requirements and their relations to the functional requirements into four cases (see Table 4.3). Case one arises when we consider two quality requirements of the same type related to the same functional requirement. The second case is concerned with considering two quality requirements of different types that are related to the same functional requirement. Case three occurs when two quality requirements of the same type but related to different functional requirements must be achieved in parallel. In the fourth case, two quality requirements of different types and related to different functional requirements must be achieved in parallel. We treat each case in a separate phase in our method. The result of this classification is represented in Table 4.3. The abbreviations FRQ and QRQ stand for "Functional Requirement" and "Quality Requirement," respectively.

**Table 4.2** Possible Interactions among Types of Quality Requirements in General

|                   | Confidentiality | Integrity | Authenticity | Performance | Privacy |
|-------------------|-----------------|-----------|--------------|-------------|---------|
| *Confidentiality* | –               | –         | x            | x           | –       |
| *Integrity*       | –               | –         | –            | x           | –       |
| *Authenticity*    | x               | –         | –            | x           | –       |
| *Performance*     | x               | x         | x            | x           | x       |
| *Privacy*         | –               | –         | –            | x           | –       |

**Table 4.3** Classification Table

| Case     | FRQ, Type of QRQ                    | Condition   | Row in QRQ Table                                    | Method's Phase |
|----------|-------------------------------------|-------------|-----------------------------------------------------|----------------|
| *Case 1* | Same FRQ, same type of QRQ          | –           | Rows related to same FRQ in same QRQ table          | Phase 1        |
| *Case 2* | Same FRQ, different types of QRQ    | –           | Rows related to same FRQ in different QRQ tables     | Phase 2        |
| *Case 3* | Different FRQ, same type of QRQ     | In parallel | Rows related to different FRQ in same QRQ table      | Phase 3        |
| *Case 4* | Different FRQ, different types of QRQ | In parallel | Rows related to different FRQ in different QRQ tables | Phase 4        |

The general principle of our method for detecting interactions among requirements is using the structure of problem diagrams to identify the domains where quality requirements might interact. Such domains are trade-off points. When the state of a domain can be changed by one or more sub-machines at the same time, their related quality requirements might be in conflict. We express this situation in the problem diagrams by dependencies that constrain such domains. Therefore, to detect interactions we set up tables where the columns contain information about quality-relevant domains (possible trade-off points) from the problem diagrams, and the rows contain information about quality requirements under consideration. We enter crosses in the cells whenever the state of a domain can be changed for the achievement of the corresponding quality requirement. In the following, we describe the method and its application to the smart grid example in more detail.

## 4.4.1 Initialization phase: Initial setup

In this phase, we make use of the structure of the problem diagrams and contained information regarding quality requirements (domain knowledge, see input in Figure 4.6) to set up the *initial QRQ tables*. These tables are used for the identification of interactions among quality requirements in later phases. Furthermore, we set up life cycle expressions that represent the order in which the requirements must be achieved.

### 4.4.1.1 Set up initial tables

For each type of quality requirement, we identify which domains are constrained by it. This results in *initial QRQ tables*, where the columns contain information about quality-relevant domains from the problem diagrams, and the rows contain information about quality requirements under consideration. We enter a cross in each cell, when a domain—given by the column—is relevant for the quality requirement under consideration—given by the row. For each type of quality requirement, we set up such a table. The second column in each table names the functional requirement related to the quality requirement given in the first column.

When we deal with performance, we need domain knowledge that is necessary to achieve performance requirements. As mentioned in Section *4.2.2*, we apply the MARTE profile to annotate performance requirements accordingly.

Performance is concerned with the *workload* of the system and the available *resources* to process the workload (Klein, 2000). The workload is described by triggers of the system, representing requests from outside or inside the system. Workload exhibits the characteristics of the system use. It includes the number of requests (e.g., number of concurrent users) and their arrival pattern (how they arrive at the system). The arrival pattern can be periodic (e.g., every 10 ms), stochastic (according to a probabilistic distribution), or sporadic (not to capture by periodic or stochastic characterization) (Bass et al., 2003). To model workload, we make use of the stereotype ≪GaWorkloadEvent≫, which may be generated by an *ArrivalPattern* such as the *ClosedPattern* that allows us to model a number of concurrent users and a think time (the time a user waits between two requests) by instantiating the attributes *population* and *extDelay*.

Processing the requests requires resources. Each resource is modeled by its type, such as CPU, memory, I/O device, network, utilization, and capacity (e.g., the transmission speed for a network). In order to elicit relevant resources required for performance analysis as domain knowledge, we have to check whether each domain represents or contains any hardware device that the system is executed on or any resource that can be consumed to achieve the corresponding performance requirement. If the domain is a performance-relevant resource, it has to be annotated as such a resource. To this end, we make use of stereotypes provided by MARTE. For example, for a hardware memory, MARTE provides the stereotype ≪HwMemory≫. Other possible stereotypes from MARTE are ≪DeviceResource≫, ≪HwProcessor≫, and ≪HwMedia≫. In our example, the domains *LMN*, *HAN*, and *LAN* represent communication resources. Hence, we annotate them with the stereotype ≪HwMedia≫. The domain *smartMeter* represents a device resource and is annotated with the stereotype ≪DeviceResource≫.

In some cases, it is possible that the domain itself represents no resource, but it contains a hidden resource with performance-relevant characteristics that has to be modeled explicitly. For example, it may contain a CPU, which is relevant when talking about performance issues. In this case, the hidden resource has to be modeled explicitly as a causal domain. It additionally has to be annotated with a stereotype from the MARTE profile representing the kind of resource it provides. In the smart grid example, *Gateway* is the machine (software we intend to build) that contains the resource CPU. Hence, all sub-machines from problem diagrams contain the resource CPU, which we model explicitly as a causal domain with the stereotype ≪HwProcessor≫.

So far, we have elicited and modeled the domain knowledge that we need to set up the initial performance table. In this table, similarly to other initial QRQ tables, columns contain information about quality-relevant domains from problem diagrams (resources in case of performance requirements) and rows contain information about quality requirements under consideration. Table 4.4 presents the initial performance table.

Initial tables for integrity, authenticity, and confidentiality for our example are given in Tables 4.5 and 4.6. Note that we have to consider *CPU* as a domain whenever we want to detect interactions

**Table 4.4** Initial Performance Table

| QRQ | Related FRQ | LMN | WAN | HAN | SmartMeter | CPU |
|-----|-------------|-----|-----|-----|------------|-----|
| RQ18 | RQ1 | x | | | x | x |
| RQ19 | RQ1 | x | | | x | x |
| RQ20 | RQ2 | | | | | x |
| RQ21 | RQ2 | | | | | x |
| RQ22 | RQ3 | | | | | x |
| RQ23 | RQ3 | | | | | x |
| RQ24 | RQ4 | | x | | | x |
| RQ25 | RQ5 | | | x | | x |

**Table 4.5** Initial Integrity (Left) and Authenticity (Right) Table

| QRQ | Related FRQ | LMN | WAN | HAN | CPU | QRQ | Related FRQ | LMN | WAN | HAN | CPU |
|-----|-------------|-----|-----|-----|-----|-----|-------------|-----|-----|-----|-----|
| RQ6 | RQ1 | x | | | x | RQ8 | RQ1 | x | | | x |
| RQ10 | RQ4 | | x | | x | RQ12 | RQ4 | | x | | x |
| RQ13 | RQ5 | | | x | x | RQ15 | RQ5 | | | x | x |

**Table 4.6** Initial Confidentiality Table

| QRQ | Related FRQ | LMN | MeterData | Temporary Storage | WAN | HAN | CPU |
|------|------|------|------|------|------|------|------|
| *RQ7* | RQ1 | X | | | | | X |
| *RQ16* | RQ1 | | | X | | | X |
| *RQ9* | RQ3 | | X | | | | X |
| *RQ11* | RQ4 | | | | X | | X |
| *RQ14* | RQ5 | | | | | X | X |

among performance and security requirements. The reason is that CPU time is consumed for the achievement of security requirements.

### 4.4.1.2 Set up life cycle

In this step, we use lightweight *life cycle expressions* to describe the relations between the functional requirements of the corresponding sub-problems to be achieved to solve the overall problem. The life cycle contains information about the order in which the requirements must be achieved. The following expression represents the life cycle for our example: *LC = (RQ1; RQ2; RQ3)\* ‖ RQ4\* ‖ RQ5\*.*

The expression *RQ1; RQ2* indicates that *RQ1* has to be achieved before *RQ2* is achieved. The expression *RQ4 ‖ RQ5* describes that *RQ4* and *RQ5* have to be achieved concurrently. *RQ4\** indicates that *RQ4* has to be achieved for 0 or more times. The complete life cycle *LC* stipulates that *RQ1, RQ2,* and *RQ3* must be achieved sequentially for 0 or more times, while *RQ4* and *RQ5* must be achieved in parallel to each other and to the sequence of *RQ1; RQ2; RQ3* for 0 or more times. This means, the meter readings have to be received first (*RQ1*). Then they have to be processed (*RQ2*) before storing them (*RQ3*). This can be achieved for 0 or more times. In parallel, the meter readings can be sent to external entities (*RQ4*) and consumers (*RQ5*) for 0 or more times.

### 4.4.2 Phase 1: Treating case 1

In this phase, we compare the rows in each table to identify potential conflicts among quality requirements concerning the first case of Table 4.3. The aim is to detect conflicts among the same type of quality requirements that are related to the same functional requirement. To deal with this case of requirements conflicts, we consider each table separately.

**Step 1.1:Eliminating irrelevant tables.** To eliminate irrelevant tables, we make use of the *initial interaction table* (Table 4.2) we set up before. According to this table, interactions among quality requirements of the same type can only happen when considering two performance requirements. Therefore, we mark Tables 4.5 (left), 5 (right), and 6 as irrelevant for requirements interactions and continue only with Table 4.4 for the treatment of first case.

**Step 1.2: Eliminating irrelevant rows.** In each table under consideration, we perform a pairwise comparison between quality requirements related to the same functional requirement. We check, if such quality requirements constrain the same domains (contain crosses in the same columns). We consider the rows related to such quality requirements as relevant and remove the irrelevant rows from Table 4.4. Doing so, we obtain Table 4.7. We also removed the columns *WAN* and *HAN*, because they did not contain any entry after removing irrelevant rows.

**Table 4.7** Phase 1, Step 1.2: New Performance Table

| QRQ | Related FRQ | LMN | SmartMeter | CPU |
|-----|-------------|-----|------------|-----|
| RQ18 | RQ1 | x | x | x |
| RQ19 | RQ1 | x | x | x |
| RQ20 | RQ2 | | | x |
| RQ21 | RQ2 | | | x |
| RQ22 | RQ3 | | | x |
| RQ23 | RQ3 | | | x |

**Step 1.3: Detecting interaction candidates**. Considering the new performance table from the previous step, we look at each two rows sharing the same functional requirement. We determine that the requirements *RQ18* and *RQ19* share the same domains *LMN*, *SmartMeter*, and *CPU*. Further, the requirements *RQ20* and *RQ21* share the same domain *CPU*. The same is the case for the requirements *RQ22* and *RQ23*. We identify these requirements as candidates for requirement interactions. Table 4.8 summarizes all detected interaction candidates.

### 4.4.3 Phase 2: Treating case 2

This phase is concerned with the second case of Table 4.3, dealing with possible conflicts among different types of quality requirements related to the same functional requirement. Hence, we compare quality requirements related to the same functional requirement in each two tables to identify potential conflicts.

**Step 2.1: Eliminating irrelevant tables**. To eliminate irrelevant tables, we make use of the *initial interaction table* (Table 4.2) to determine which two tables should be compared with each other. For our example, we can reduce the number of table comparisons to four: 4.5 (left) and 4.4, 4.6 and 4.5 (right), 4.6 and 4.4, 4.5 (right) and 4.4.

Note that in each phase, we have to consider the initial QRQ tables such as Table 4.4 and not the new reduced tables such as 4.7. The reason is that in each phase, we eliminate different rows from the initial QRQ tables according to Table 4.3.

**Step 2.2: Detecting interaction candidates**. To identify interactions among quality requirements related to the same functional requirement, we have to look in different tables at the rows with the same related functional requirement and check, if same the domains (columns) contain crosses. Such requirements are candidates for interactions.

This is mostly the case for performance and security requirements. The reason is that solutions for achieving security requirements are time-consuming and this is at the expense of performance. As an example, we describe how we compare the Tables 4.5 (left) and 4.4. We consider the rows related to the same functional requirement. The rows related to the functional requirement RQ1 contain entries in the columns *LMN* and *CPU*. This implies that we might have a conflict between the integrity requirement *RQ6* and the performance requirements *RQ18* and *RQ19*. Comparing each further two rows results in the following potential conflicts: *RQ10* with *RQ24*, and *RQ13* with *RQ25*. Table 4.8 summarizes all detected interaction candidates.

**Table 4.8** Candidates of Requirements Interactions

| Method's Phase | Comparison Between Tables | Interaction Candidates |
|---|---|---|
| *Phase 1* | Table 4.4 with itself | *RQ18* and *RQ19*, *RQ20* and *RQ21*, *RQ22* and *RQ23* |
| *Phase 2* | Table 4.4 with Table 4.5 (left) | *RQ6* and *RQ18*, *RQ6* and *RQ19*, *RQ10* and *RQ24*, *RQ13* and *RQ25* |
| | Table 4.5 (right) with Table 4.6 | ~~*RQ7* and *RQ8*, *RQ11* and *RQ12*, *RQ14* and *RQ15*, *RQ16* and *RQ8*~~ |
| | Table 4.4 with Table 4.5 (right) | *RQ8* and *RQ18*, *RQ8* and *RQ19*, *RQ12* and *RQ24*, *RQ15* and *RQ25* |
| | Table 4.6 with Table 4.4 | *RQ7* and *RQ18*, *RQ7* and *RQ19*, *RQ11* and *RQ24*, *RQ14* and *RQ25*, *RQ16* and *RQ18*, *RQ16* and *RQ19*, *RQ9* and *RQ22*, *RQ9* and *RQ23* |
| *Phase 3* | Table 4.4 with itself | *RQ18* and *RQ24*, *RQ18* and *RQ25*, *RQ19* and *RQ24*, *RQ19* and *RQ25*, *RQ20* and *RQ24*, *RQ20* and *RQ25*, *RQ21* and *RQ24*, *RQ21* and *RQ25*, *RQ22* and *RQ24*, *RQ22* and *RQ25*, *RQ23* and *RQ24*, *RQ23* and *RQ25*, *RQ24* and *RQ25*, *RQ18* and *RQ20*, *RQ19* and *RQ20*, *RQ18* and *RQ21*, *RQ19* and *RQ21*, *RQ18* and *RQ22*, *RQ19* and *RQ22*, *RQ18* and *RQ23*, *RQ19* and *RQ23*, *RQ20* and *RQ22*, *RQ21* and *RQ22*, *RQ20* and *RQ23*, *RQ21* and *RQ23* |
| *Phase 4* | Table 4.5 (left) with Table 4.4 | *RQ6* and *RQ20*, *RQ6* and *RQ21*, *RQ6* and *RQ22*, *RQ6* and *RQ23*, *RQ6* and *RQ24*, *RQ6* and *RQ25*, *RQ10* and *RQ18*, *RQ10* and *RQ19*, *RQ10* and *RQ20*, *RQ10* and *RQ21*, *RQ10* and *RQ22*, *RQ10* and *RQ23*, *RQ10* and *RQ25*, *RQ13* and *RQ18*, *RQ13* and *RQ19*, *RQ13* and *RQ20*, *RQ13* and *RQ21*, *RQ13* and *RQ22*, *RQ13* and *RQ23*, *RQ13* and *RQ24* |
| | Table 4.6 with Table 4.4 | *RQ7* and *RQ24*, *RQ7* and *RQ25*, *RQ16* and *RQ24*, *RQ16* and *RQ25*, *RQ9* and *RQ24*, *RQ9* and *RQ25*, *RQ11* and *RQ18*, *RQ11* and *RQ19*, *RQ11* and *RQ20*, *RQ11* and *RQ21*, *RQ11* and *RQ22*, *RQ11* and *RQ23*, *RQ11* and *RQ25*, *RQ14* and *RQ18*, *RQ14* and *RQ19*, *RQ14* and *RQ20*, *RQ14* and *RQ21*, *RQ14* and *RQ22*, *RQ14* and *RQ23*, *RQ14* and *RQ24*, *RQ9* and *RQ18*, *RQ9* and *RQ19*, *RQ9* and *RQ20*, *RQ9* and *RQ21*, *RQ7* and *RQ20*, *RQ7* and *RQ21*, *RQ7* and *RQ22*, *RQ7* and *RQ23*, *RQ16* and *RQ20*, *RQ16* and *RQ21*, *RQ16* and *RQ22*, *RQ16* and *RQ23* |
| | Table 4.5 (right) with Table 4.4 | *RQ8* and *RQ20*, *RQ8* and *RQ21*, *RQ8* and *RQ22*, *RQ8* and *RQ23*, *RQ8,* and *RQ24*, *RQ8* and *RQ25*, *RQ12* and *RQ18*, *RQ12* and *RQ19*, *RQ12* and *RQ20*, *RQ12* and *RQ21*, *RQ12* and *RQ22*, *RQ12* and *RQ23*, *RQ12* and *RQ25*, *RQ15* and *RQ18*, *RQ15* and *RQ19*, *RQ15* and *RQ20*, *RQ15* and *RQ21*, *RQ15* and *RQ22*, *RQ15* and *RQ23*, *RQ15* and *RQ24* |

### 4.4.4 **Phase 3: Treating case 3**

In this phase, we deal with case three of Table 4.3. In other words, we consider different functional requirements complemented with the same type of quality requirement. Table 4.2 enables us to eliminate irrelevant tables. Additionally, we make use of the information contained in the life cycle expression regarding the concurrent achievement of requirements.

**Step 3.1: Eliminating irrelevant tables**. According to Table 4.3, we have to consider each table separately. According to Table 4.2, no interactions will occur among different integrity, confidentiality, and authenticity requirements. Hence, we mark Tables 4.5 (left), 4.5 (right), and 4.6 as irrelevant. The only type of quality requirements to be considered are performance requirements as given in Table 4.4.

**Step 3.2: Eliminating irrelevant rows**. In each table under consideration, we perform a pairwise comparison between the rows. According to Table 4.3, interactions can only arise when quality requirements must be satisfied in parallel. We make use of the life cycle expression to identify requirements that must be achieved in parallel. According to the life cycle, we cannot eliminate any row in Table 4.4, because although the requirements *RQ1*, *RQ2*, and *RQ3* can be satisfied sequentially, they must be achieved in parallel with the requirements *RQ4* and *RQ5*.

**Step 3.3: Detecting interaction candidates**. In this step, we check if the requirements with parallel satisfaction contain entries in the same column. We see in Table 4.4 that all requirements concern the same domain *CPU*. Therefore, we identify a number of interaction candidates as given in Table 4.8.

### 4.4.5 Phase 4: Treating case 4

This phase is concerned with case four of Table 4.3, which deals with different functional requirements complemented with different types of quality requirements. Table 4.2 enables us to eliminate irrelevant tables. Additionally, we take the life cycle expression into account to reduce the number of comparisons within each table.

**Step 4.1:Eliminating irrelevant tables**. According to Table 4.2, we can reduce the number of table comparisons to three: 4.5 (left) and 4.4, 4.6 and 4.4, 4.5 (right) and 4.4.

**Step 4.2: Eliminating irrelevant rows**. According to the life cycle, although the requirements *RQ1*, *RQ2*, and *RQ3* must be achieved sequentially, they must be achieved in parallel to requirements *RQ4* and *RQ5*. Therefore, we cannot remove any row from the tables under consideration.

**Step 4.3: Detecting interaction candidates**. According to Table 4.2 and the results obtained from the previous steps, we only have to compare the rows in the following three tables: 4.5 (left) and 4.4, 4.6 and 4.4, 4.5 (right) and 4.4. We get a large number of interaction candidates between the integrity and performance requirements, confidentiality and performance requirements, as well as authenticity and performance requirements. Table 4.8 presents the overall result of applying the method.

**Discussion of the results**. At this point, we have to check if we can reduce the number of interaction candidates. Looking at the result, we see that most interactions might be among performance and security requirements and among different performance requirements. Additionally, we identified three pairs of interaction candidates among authenticity and confidentiality requirements (Table 4.8, phase 2). We figure out that the interaction depends on the order of applying confidentiality and authenticity solution mechanisms. If we sign the data first and then encrypt it, we can achieve both confidentiality and authenticity. The other way around, if we encrypted the data first and then signed it, the confidentiality and authenticity requirements would interact with each other. Under this condition, we can exclude interactions among requirement pairs *RQ7* and *RQ8*, *RQ11* and *RQ12*, *RQ14* and *RQ15* (crossed out in Table 4.8). Of course, we have to document this condition for the design and implementation phases. All other candidates have to be taken into account in the subsequent phases of the QuaRO method.

## 4.5 METHOD FOR GENERATION OF ALTERNATIVES

To enable the optimization for obtaining a final set of requirements that is as near to the optimal solution for every stakeholder as possible, we need to generate alternatives for the problematic requirements. Hence, an original requirement might be excluded from the final set, but a weaker variant of this requirement might be included in the optimal set of requirements. For example, for security requirements there can be certain kinds of attackers we want to be secured against. However, we maybe cannot address a strong attacker with certain properties such as the given time and resource limits. Hence, we propose a method for relaxing such properties in order to generate alternatives for problematic requirements. Generated alternatives are used as recommendations for stakeholders. Those alternatives that are not acceptable for stakeholders are excluded before they are used as input for the next step of the method. Figure 4.7 illustrates the steps of our method, input, and output of each step.

Based on the type of requirement we want to generate alternatives for, there are different properties, which are candidates to be relaxed. The qualities addressed by different requirements are very different, and as a result, so are the properties, which can be used to relax a requirement. But for particular kinds of qualities those properties are the same. Hence, it is possible to define a property template for a quality, which can be instantiated for a requirement belonging to this quality. For each quality, we capture the following information in the template (see Tables 4.9 and 4.10): *Property* describing the quality-relevant properties, *Possible Values* describing the range of values the property can take, *Rank* representing the property that can be most likely relaxed according to stakeholder preferences, *Value Original Requirement* representing the value of property for the original requirement before relaxing, *Upper/Lower Bound* describing the lower or upper bound (depending to the property) each property can take when relaxing, and *Value RQ* representing the values of the relaxed properties for requirements alternatives. In the following, we present the templates for the qualities security and performance before we introduce our method for generating alternatives.

### 4.5.1 Relaxation template for security

For security it is the type of attacker that influences the restrictiveness of a security requirement. How much resources and effort to spend on a requirement, how much influence security has on the behavior of the overall system-to-be, and which solution has to be chosen to fulfill the requirement later on all depend on the abilities of the attacker. While it is almost impossible to secure a system against an almighty attacker, defending against a layman (see International Organization for Standardization (ISO) and International Electrotechnical Commission (IEC), 2009) can be easily achieved without big impact on the rest of the system.

To describe the attacker, we use the properties as described by the Common Methodology for Information Technology Security Evaluation (CEM) (International Organization for Standardization (ISO) and International Electrotechnical Commission (IEC), 2009) for vulnerability assessment of the TOE (target of evaluation i.e., system-to-be). How to integrate this attacker description into problem frames is described in earlier work of ours (Hatebur and Heisel, 2009b, 2010a). The properties to be considered (according to CEM) are (International Organization for Standardization (ISO) and International Electrotechnical Commission (IEC), 2009):

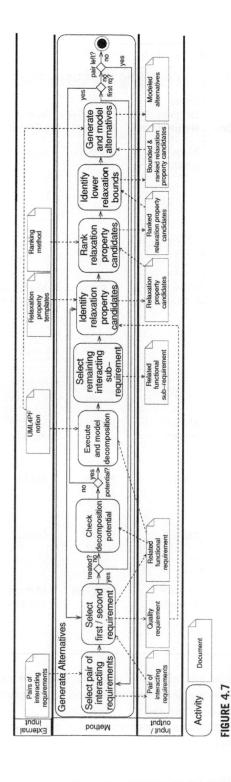

**FIGURE 4.7**

Method for alternative generation.

**Table 4.9** Security Relaxation Template and Its Instantiation for RQ11

| Quality: Security, Requirement RQ11, Alternatives RQ11.2, RQ11.3, RQ11.4 | | | | | | | |
|---|---|---|---|---|---|---|---|
| **Property (CEM)** | **Possible Values** | **Rank** | **Value Original Requirement** | **Upper/ Lower Bound** | **Value RQ11.2** | **Value RQ11.3** | **Value RQ11.4** |
| Preparation time | 1 day, 1 week, 2 weeks, 1 month, 2 months, 3 months, 4 months, 5 months, 6 months, more than 6 months | 3 | More than 6 months | 1 month | 4 months | 2 months | 1 month |
| Attack time | 1 day, 1 week, 2 weeks, 1 month, 2 months, 3 months, 4 months, 5 months, 6 months, more than 6 months | 5 | More than 6 months | 1 month | More than 6 months | 3 months | 1 month |
| Specialist expertise | Laymen, proficient, expert, multiple experts | 6 | Multiple experts | Proficient | Multiple experts | Expert | Proficient |
| Knowledge of the TOE | Public, restricted, sensitive, critical | 1 | Public | Public | Public | Public | Public |
| Window of opportunity | Unnecessary/ unlimited, easy, moderate, difficult | 2 | Difficult | Difficult | Difficult | Difficult | Difficult |
| IT hardware/ software or other equipment | Standard, specialized, bespoke, multiple bespoke | 4 | Multiple bespoke | Bespoke | Multiple bespoke | Multiple bespoke | Bespoke |

**Elapsed time** "Elapsed time is the total amount of time taken by an attacker to identify a particular potential vulnerability ..., to develop an attack method and ... to mount the attack ..." We distinguish between the *preparation time* and the *attack time*.
**Specialist expertise** "Specialist expertise refers to the level of generic knowledge of the underlying principles, product type or attack methods ...."

**Table 4.10** Performance Relaxation Template and Its Instantiation for RQ24

Quality: Performance, Requirement RQ24, RQ24.2, RQ24.3, RQ24.4

| Property (MARTE Profile) | Property Description | Possible Values | Rank | Value Original Requirement | Upper/Lower Bound | Value RQ24.2 | Value RQ24.3 | Value RQ24.4 |
|---|---|---|---|---|---|---|---|---|
| GaWorkloadEvent. pattern (closed. population) | Number of concurrent users | NFP Integer | 1 | 50 | 1 | 30 | 10 | 1 |
| DeviceResource. resMult | Number of devices | NFP Natural | 3 | Not relevant | Not relevant | Not relevant | Not relevant | Not relevant |
| DeviceResource. speedFactor | Speed of the device | NFP Real[0..1] | 6 | Not relevant | Not relevant | Not relevant | Not relevant | Not relevant |
| HwMemory. memorySize | Memory capacity | NFP DataSize (bit, Byte, kB, MB, GB) | 7 | Fixed | Fixed | Fixed | Fixed | Fixed |
| HwMemory. timing | Memory latency | NFP Duration (s, ms, min, h, day) | 8 | Fixed | Fixed | Fixed | Fixed | Fixed |
| HwMedia. bandWidth | Network bandwidth | NFP DataTxRate (b/s, kb/s, Mb/s) | 5 | 2.4 kb/s | 250 Mb/s | 576 kb/s | 50 Mb/s | 250 Mb/s |
| HwMedia. packetTime | Network latency | NFP Duration (s, ms, min, h, day) | 4 | Not known | Not known | Not known | Not known | Not known |
| HwProcessor. frequency | Processor speed | NFP Frequency (Hz, kHz, MHz, GHz) | 10 | Fixed | Fixed | Fixed | Fixed | Fixed |
| HwProcessor. nbCores | Processor cores | NFP Natural | 9 | Fixed | Fixed | Fixed | Fixed | Fixed |
| GaStep. msgSize | Data size | NFP DataSize (bit, Byte, kB, MB, GB) | 2 | 640 MB | 40 kB | 100 MB | 10 MB | 40 KB |

**Knowledge of the TOE** "Knowledge of the TOE refers to specific expertise in relation to the TOE."

**Window of opportunity** "Identification or exploitation of a vulnerability may require considerable amounts of access to a TOE that may increase the likelihood of detection. . . . Access may also need to be continuous, or over a number of sessions."

**IT hardware/software or other equipment** ". . . the equipment required to identify or exploit a vulnerability."

The resulting relaxation template is shown in Table 4.9.

## 4.5.2 Relaxation template for performance

As described in Section *4.4.1*, in the *initialization phase*, analyzing the context of performance requires a focus on two issues, namely the workload behavior, described by an arrival pattern, and the number of requests and the resources, described by utilization and capacity. For modeling this information we use the MARTE profile (UML Revision Task Force, 2011), which is integrated into UML4PF in our previous work (Alebrahim et al., 2011b).

**GaWorkloadEvent** represents the kind of arrival pattern. A *ClosedPattern* is one kind of arrival pattern. It contains the attribute *population* that represents a fixed number of active users (UML Revision Task Force, 2011, pp. 308, 503).

**DeviceResource** represents an external device. It contains the attribute *resMult* that represents the maximum number of available instances of a particular resource (UML Revision Task Force, 2011, p. 613). The attribute *speedFactor* gives the relative speed of the unit as compared to the reference one (UML Revision Task Force, 2011, p. 506).

**HwMemory** contains the attributes *memorySize* that specifies the storage capacity and *timing* that specifies timings of the *HwMemory* (UML Revision Task Force, 2011, p. 597).

**HwMedia** is a communication resource that represents a means to transport information from one location to another. It contains the attributes *bandWidth* specifying the transfer bandwidth and *packetTime* specifying the time to transmit an element (UML Revision Task Force, 2011, p. 598).

**HwProcessor** is a generic computing resource symbolizing a processor. It contains the attributes *nbCores*, which specifies the number of cores within the HwProcessor and *frequency* (not contained in the specification, but in the implementation) (UML Revision Task Force, 2011, p. 670).

**GaStep** is part of a scenario and contains the attribute *msgSize*, which specifies the size of a message to be transmitted by the Step (UML Revision Task Force, 2011, p. 306).

The used types NFP _. . . are complex data types defined in the MARTE profile (UML Revision Task Force, 2011). The resulting relaxation template for performance is shown in Table 4.10.

In the following, we describe our method to generate alternatives for interacting requirements to be used in further steps of QuaRO method (see Figure 4.7).

1. **Select pair of interacting requirements**. Table 4.8 is the input for the generation of alternatives. We have to analyze each pair for possible alternative requirements, which resolve or relax the interaction.

    *For our example, we select the requirements pair RQ11 and RQ24.*

2.  **Select first/second requirement**. For the selected pair, we have to check each of the two requirements for possibilities to resolve the interaction. Hence, we have to execute the next steps for both requirements.

    *Both requirements provide the possibility to be relaxed in order to resolve the interaction. Hence, we perform the next steps for both requirements RQ11 and RQ24. In Tables 4.9 and 4.10, we fill the column "value original requirement" for these two requirements. Because there is no information in the Protection Profile about the attacker that the system must be protected against, we assume that the system must be protected against the strongest attacker. Hence, we select for each property the strongest one to obtain values for original requirement RQ11. To fill the properties for the column "value original requirement" for the performance requirement RQ24, we need additional information that is missing in the Protection Profilep (Kreutzmann et al., 2011) and Open Meter (Remero et al., 2009a) documents. Hence, we looked for the necessary domain knowledge in the existing literature (Deconinck, 2008; Stromanbieter Deutschland, 2013). Based on this search, we assume the values given in column "value original requirement" in Table 4.10. The rest of properties is fixed (cannot be relaxed), unknown or irrelevant for the requirement RQ24.*

3.  **Check decomposition potential of requirements**. In the case of a complex requirement, it might help to separate the source of interaction from the rest of the requirement. The separated requirements can be treated differently. It might happen that an interaction would lead to a rejection of the whole complex requirement. In contrast, for the decomposed set of requirements, some parts of the original requirement might remain in the solution.

    *The quality requirements R11 and R24 complement the functional requirement R4, which is concerned with submitting meter data to external entities. This is not a complex problem and cannot be decomposed further. Hence, the related quality requirements cannot be decomposed further.*

4.  **Execute and model decomposition**. If a decomposition is possible, it has to be executed, and the result has to be modeled.

    *The selected requirements R11 and R24 cannot be decomposed.*

5.  **Select remaining interacting sub-requirements**. In case of a decomposition, only the sub-requirement, which is the source of the interaction, has to be analyzed further.

    *We did not decompose the requirements R11 and R24. Hence, they have to be considered in next steps.*

6.  **Identify relaxation property candidates**. Based on the type of requirement, there are different properties, which are candidates to be relaxed. These candidates are fixed for each kind of requirement. Hence, we can use predefined templates to identify these properties. For each property the actual value regarding the interacting requirement has to be stated. Next, it has to be decided if this value for the property is a hard constraint, which cannot be changed, or a soft constraint, which might be relaxed. In the second case, we identified a relaxation candidate.

    *For the security requirement RQ11 (Table 4.9), we figure out that the properties "knowledge of the TOE" and "window of opportunity" are fixed and cannot be relaxed. The rest of properties can be relaxed to generate alternatives for the original requirement RQ11. For the performance requirement RQ24 (Table 4.10) the characteristics of memory, namely "HwMemory.memorySize" and "HwMemory.timing" and the characteristics of processor, namely "HwProcessor.frequency" and "HwProcessor.nbCores" for the gateway are fixed. The rest of the properties can be used for relaxation, if they are known and relevant.*

7.  **Rank relaxation property candidates**. When talking about reasonable relaxations, it is also important to know which properties are more important to the overall requirement than others.

*The ranks to the requirements RQ11 and RQ24 can be found in Tables 4.9 and 4.10.*

**8. Identify upper/lower relaxation bounds**. For each property, the upper/lower bound, which is still acceptable, has to be identified. The upper/lower bounds of all properties form the worst-case scenario, which is still acceptable for a requirement.

*To identify "upper/lower bounds" for the requirement RQ11, we have to assume values from the possible values, because we have no information about the strength of the attacker. Hence, we assume that the system has to be protected at least against an attacker who is a "proficient," has "1 month" for preparing the attack, has "1 month" for the attack itself, and has a "bespoke" equipment for performing the attack. To identify "upper/lower bounds" for the requirement RQ24, we begin with the property "GaWorkloadEvent.pattern(closed.population)," which represents the number of concurrent users. For the case that the gateway sends meter readings to the external entities via a concentrator, there is only one user. Hence, we take 1 for the column "upper/lower bound." As "upper/lower bound" for the property "HwMedia.bandWidth," we take the bandwidth of Power Line Communication (PLC) that can be up to 250 Mb/s. The "upper/lower bound" for the property "GaStep.msgSize" is assumed to be 40 kB (Deconinck, 2008).*

**9. Generate and model alternatives**. The first alternative is the requirement realizing the worst-case scenario. Between the original requirement and this lower bound requirement, several other requirements can be generated by varying the relaxation candidates. For each generated requirement, it has to be checked, regardless of whether it eliminates the interaction. If it does not, further relaxation is needed. The generated alternatives have to be modeled.

*To relax the properties and thus generate alternatives for the requirements RQ11 and RQ24, we choose values between the "value original requirement" and "upper/lower bound" for properties that can be relaxed. For example, for the requirement RQ24 the properties "GaWorkloadEvent. pattern (closed.population)," "HwMedia.bandWidth," and "GaStep.msgSize" can be relaxed. The rest of the properties are either fixed or irrelevant for the corresponding requirement or unknown and thus cannot be considered for the relaxation process. Relaxing possible properties results in requirements alternatives RQ11.2, RQ11.3, and RQ11.4 for the original requirement RQ11 and in requirements alternatives RQ24.2, RQ24.3, and RQ24.4 for the original requirement RQ24. In this way, we cannot say that we assuredly resolve interactions between quality requirements, but we can weaken them for sure or even resolve them ideally.*

## 4.6 VALUATION OF REQUIREMENTS

For optimization, the requirements need a value to which the optimization can refer. The relations between requirements also need to be valuated. This can be achieved by prioritization in the form of cost estimations or statistical metrics. The valuating measure or method has to be selected in this step, and the values for the requirements have to be elicited. Furthermore, the valuation has to be documented for later use. The valuation of a requirement can differ from stakeholder to stakeholder.

For the QuaRO we decided to use ANP for valuation of requirements. There are several reasons for this decision:

**Capture complexity of the decision problem**. As we see from the goal model and the relations between goals, requirements, and requirement alternatives, we have a very complex decision problem. Even the decision about the value or rank of a requirement is not straightforward. ANP allows one to model the decision problem coherently to the real problem as described and modeled by the preliminary steps. For AHP, Even Swaps, or simple ranking, simplifications would be needed, making the outcome unreliable (Saaty, 2008b).

**Reduce complexity of decisions**. In ANP decisions are reduced to pairwise comparison. This has been proven to be the most natural decision a person can make (Saaty, 2005).

**Coping with fuzzy values**. ANP does not require giving concrete numbers for a value of a requirement or goal but relies on relative comparisons (Saaty, 2005). This is an important property because giving fixed numbers can hardly be achieved in the early phases of software engineering. Furthermore, ANP has proven to be one of the most reliable decision techniques for fuzzy environments (Saaty, 2008b).

**Detecting and handling inconsistencies**. ANP allows one to compute and check the consistency of the different comparisons. Thus, inconsistencies can be avoided. However, ANP even works for comparisons with small-scale inconsistencies (Saaty, 2005).

**Merging of different views and dimensions for a decision**. ANP allows one to merge results for different dimensions, like benefits and costs, of a decision. Furthermore, it is easy to integrate different views of different stakeholders (Saaty, 2005; Saaty and Ozdemir, 2003).

**Tool support**. For ANP, there are different support tools.[6]

Up to this point, we covered only step 1 of ANP as described by Saaty (2008b) (Section *4.2.3*). The steps for setting up the QuaRO-ANP-Network (see sketch in Figure 4.9), covering steps 2-4 of ANP, are as follows (see Figure 4.8).

1. **Set up top-level network**. For the top-level we set up the goal cluster containing the goal "Overall best system." The goal cluster is influenced by the control criteria cluster. For the control criteria, we stick to the BOCR criteria as suggested by Saaty (Saaty and Ozdemir, 2003). But nevertheless, it is possible to choose other strategic criteria here. Strategic criteria do not influence each other. Hence, for this network we have a hierarchy from the goal to the criteria (see Figure 4.9, upper left-hand side). *For our example, we decide to use only benefits and costs* (see Figure 4.10, left-hand side).

2. **Set up control criteria sub-networks**. For each control criterion we add a sub-network. A sub-network consists of a goal cluster with a goal like "Best system regarding benefits." The goal cluster is influenced by a stakeholder cluster, which contains a node for each stakeholder of the system-to-be. We assume the stakeholders to be independent, because the goals a stakeholder wants to achieve are not based on the perception of these goals by other stakeholders. Thus, we do not have any inner dependence influence. *For our example, we have the three stakeholders billing manager, Tesla Inc., and Consumer* (see Figure 4.10, right-hand side).

3. **Set up stakeholder sub-networks**. The stakeholder sub-networks are the real ANP networks, while the top-level and control criteria level just serve for the integration of dimensions and views on the system-to-be. Hence, we split up the setup of stakeholder sub-networks into some sub-steps. Note that these steps directly apply for the benefits criterion. For other criteria they might have to be modified. For risk and opportunity the steps can be performed without modifications, but for

---

[6]For example superdecisions (http://www.superdecisions.com/) or ANPSolver (http://kkir.simor.ntua.gr/anpsolver.html).

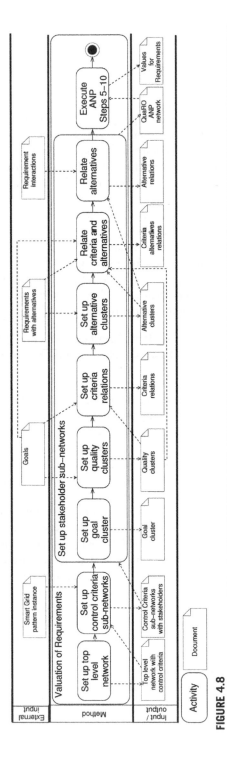

**FIGURE 4.8**

Method for valuation of requirements.

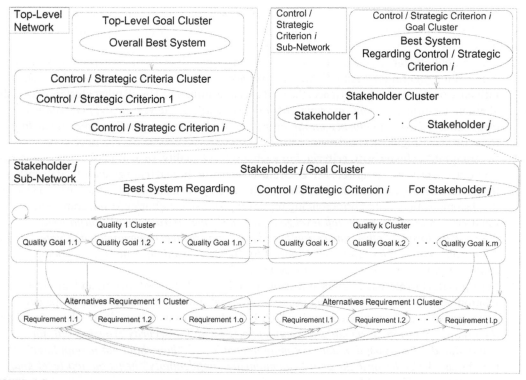

**FIGURE 4.9**

The QuaRO-ANP-Network.

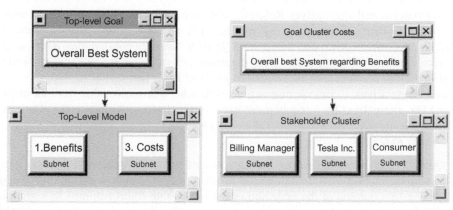

**FIGURE 4.10**

Top-level network (left) and control criterion sub-network for benefits (right) modeled in superdecisions.

costs, we removed the quality clusters and only introduced the clusters "fixed costs" and "running costs." *The resulting stakeholder sub-network for the Consumer regarding benefits is shown in* Figure 4.11.

a. **Set up goal cluster**. Add a goal cluster containing a goal like "Best system for stakeholder A regarding control criterion C." All top-level goals and their satisfaction level have an influence on the overall goal. Hence, the goal cluster is influenced by all other clusters except the alternative clusters. *For our example, the top-level goals privacy, security, performance, and economy have an influence on the overall goal "Best system for Consumer regarding Benefits"* (see Figure 4.11).

b. **Set up quality cluster with criteria**. For each top-level quality, such as performance, security, economy, or privacy, set up a cluster. Each cluster contains the leaf (hard goals/soft goals/tasks) of the goal model for a stakeholder as criteria. A cluster only contains those leaves that are a result of the decomposition of the corresponding top-level goal using and/or/makes/decomposition relations. *For example, for the top-level goal "privacy" there is a decomposition path via "private data not disclosed," "other parties don't get data," and "protect communicated private data" to "communicate confidentially"* (see Figure 4.5). *Hence, we add the criterion "communicate confidentially" to the privacy cluster* (see Figure 4.11).

c. **Set up criteria relations**. For each helps/hurts relation of the goal model, add an influence relation between the corresponding criteria. Note that those goal relations are propagated down transitively from a parent goal, which is the target, to its sub-goals. *We have to relate the privacy criterion "communicate confidentially" with the security criteria "bill not manipulated," "consumption data not manipulated," and "household not manipulated"* (see Figure 4.11), *because the goal "communicate confidentially" helps the top-level goal "security"* (see Figure 4.5).

d. **Set up alternative clusters**. For each requirement, add a cluster containing the alternatives for this requirement as nodes. Note that for some ANP software having several clusters for alternatives is not allowed. In this case, merge them to one. This does not influence the outcome, only the comprehensibility. Figure 4.11 *shows the alternative cluster (the cluster at the bottom). For superdecisions, the tool we use is the case that only one alternative cluster is allowed.*

e. **Relate criteria and alternatives**. Relate the criteria of the quality clusters with the requirements that influence their fulfillment. *Based on* Figure 4.5, *we relate "responsive user interface" with RQ25 and its alternatives, and we relate RQ5 with "analyze consumption data" and "verify consumption data." For the stakeholder Consumer, there is no relation between a criterion and RQ4 or RQ24, because they are related to goals of Tesla Inc.*

f. **Relate alternatives**. Relate the alternatives with other alternatives that have an impact on them. The alternatives for a requirement have to be related according to the relations of the original requirement. *According to* Table 4.8, *we have to relate RQ11 and RQ24, as well as RQ24 and RQ25.*

When the QuaRO-ANP-Network is set up, one can proceed with the regular ANP process starting with step 5 as described in Section *4.2.3*. Example results for a valuation with ranking are shown in Figure 4.12. The first column of the table shows the total value (third column) in a graphical way. The second column contains the name of the alternative. The third column shows the value of the

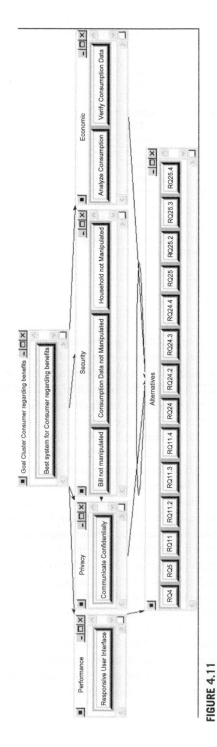

**FIGURE 4.11**

Stakeholder consumer sub-network modeled in superdecisions.

| Graphic | Alternatives | Total | Ranking |
|---------|-------------|-------|---------|
|         | RQ4         | 0.0000 | 14 |
|         | RQ5         | 0.0000 | 13 |
|         | RQ11        | 0.1652 | 3 |
|         | RQ11.2      | 0.3174 | 1 |
|         | RQ11.3      | 0.1302 | 4 |
|         | RQ11.4      | 0.0609 | 6 |
|         | RQ24        | 0.0086 | 8 |
|         | RQ24.2      | 0.0086 | 9 |
|         | RQ24.3      | 0.0086 | 10 |
|         | RQ24.4      | 0.0086 | 11 |
|         | RQ25        | 0.0066 | 12 |
|         | RQ25.2      | 0.0189 | 7 |
|         | RQ25.3      | 0.0636 | 5 |
|         | RQ25.4      | 0.2027 | 2 |

(a)   Values for RQs regarding consumer and benefits

| Graphic | Alternatives | Total | Ranking |
|---------|-------------|-------|---------|
|         | RQ4         | 0.0000 | 14 |
|         | RQ5         | 0.0000 | 13 |
|         | RQ11        | 0.0290 | 12 |
|         | RQ11.2      | 0.0358 | 11 |
|         | RQ11.3      | 0.0722 | 5 |
|         | RQ11.4      | 0.2627 | 1 |
|         | RQ24        | 0.0841 | 3 |
|         | RQ24.2      | 0.0627 | 7 |
|         | RQ24.3      | 0.0566 | 8 |
|         | RQ24.4      | 0.0668 | 6 |
|         | RQ25        | 0.0410 | 10 |
|         | RQ25.2      | 0.0501 | 9 |
|         | RQ25.3      | 0.0740 | 4 |
|         | RQ25.4      | 0.1652 | 2 |

(b)   Values for RQs regarding Tesla and benefits

| Graphic | Alternatives | Total | Ranking |
|---------|-------------|-------|---------|
|         | RQ4         | 0.0000 | 14 |
|         | RQ5         | 0.0000 | 13 |
|         | RQ11        | 0.3153 | 5 |
|         | RQ11.2      | 0.5681 | 3 |
|         | RQ11.3      | 0.3424 | 4 |
|         | RQ11.4      | 0.5959 | 2 |
|         | RQ24        | 0.1736 | 7 |
|         | RQ24.2      | 0.1329 | 9 |
|         | RQ24.3      | 0.1214 | 11 |
|         | RQ24.4      | 0.1407 | 8 |
|         | RQ25        | 0.0884 | 12 |
|         | RQ25.2      | 0.1250 | 10 |
|         | RQ25.3      | 0.2410 | 6 |
|         | RQ25.4      | 0.6337 | 1 |

(c)   Values for RQs overall

**FIGURE 4.12**

ANP Result computed using superdecisions.

alternative with respect to ANP. The ranking column orders the alternatives with respect to the total column. Note that requirements having no alternatives always valuate to 0 (RQ4, RQ5).

From the rankings we see that the consumer prefers to be secured against a rather strong attacker, which is indicated by high values for RQ11 and RQ11.2, and low ones for RQ11.3 and RQ11.4 (see Figure 4.12a). As a trade-off, the consumer is willing to relax the setting in which the performance expectations are guaranteed, which is indicated by a high value for RQ25.4. The consumer does not care about the performance regarding the external request (RQ24–24.3). In contrast, Tesla is willing to relax the attacker strength and the performance setting for internal requests, which is indicated by high values for RQ11.4 and RQ25.4 (see Figure 4.12b). For the external requests, Tesla prefers the strongest requirement RQ24. For RQ24 the values are not very distributed, which is due to the fact that Tesla does care about the requirements from the consumer. Hence, Tesla did some compromise balancing while comparing the alternatives. But overall, we see that the two stakeholders, consumer and Tesla, have different preferences, especially regarding security. These different views are then synthesized into one value for each requirement (or alternative) using the different levels of the QuaRO-ANP-Network (see Figure 4.9). First, the different views of the stakeholder regarding one control criterion are aggregated using the "Control Criterion Sub-Network for Benefits" (see Figure 4.10, right-hand side). Then, the different control criteria are aggregated using the top-level network (see Figure 4.10, left-hand side). The aggregation of the different views of consumer, Tesla, and the billing manager, and the two dimensions benefits and costs, is almost identical to the preferences of Tesla. RQ11.4 is the first option for security, RQ24 for the performance of the external communication, and RQ25.4 for the internal communication (see Figure 4.12c compared to Figure 4.12b). This happens not due to a discrimination of the consumers' wishes. When coming to costs, the consumer preferences change due to the increased costs for measurements against a strong attacker. Note that the billing manager has hardly any influence on the presented requirements. The only requirement the billing manager is concerned with is RQ24, and even for this requirement, the manager is not really interested in the performance setting. In the end, we get a meaningful ranking. Nevertheless, for RQ11 and RQ24 it is not as clear-cut as for RQ25.

## 4.7 OPTIMIZATION OF REQUIREMENTS

In this step, all the requirements, their relations and the corresponding values are prepared in such a way that they can form the input to an optimization model. We describe the setup of the optimization model and how to transform the input information into the optimization model. Using the optimization model, it is possible to compute the optimal set of requirements regarding the optimization goals and the valuation of the requirements automatically.

The parameters of the optimization model are described in the following:

Parameters: Sets

| | | |
|---|---|---|
| $G = \{G1, G2, \ldots, Gz\}$ | Set of goals | (15) |
| $FR = \{R1, R2, \ldots, Ry\}$ | Set of functional requirements | (16) |
| $QR = \{Q1, Q2, \ldots, Qx\}$ | Set of quality requirements | (17) |
| $R = FR \cup QR$ | Set of requirements | (18) |

Parameters: Relations/Value Coefficients

| | | |
|---|---|---|
| $G^{must}_{i \in G} \in \{0,1\}$ | Determines whether a goal $i$ has to be in the solution (1) or not (0) | (19) |
| $R^{initial}_{k \in R} \in \{0,1\}$ | Determines whether a requirement $k$ is part of the initial set of requirements (1) or not (0) | (20) |
| $R^{must}_{k \in R} \in \{0,1\}$ | Determines whether a requirement $k$ has to be in the solution (1) or not (0) | (21) |
| $R^{value}_{k \in R} \in R$ | Determines value of a requirement $k$ | (22) |
| $G2G^{and/or/xor}_{i,j \in G} \in \{0,1\}$ | Determines whether a goal $j$ is sub-goal to goal $i$ in an (AND/OR/XOR)-relation (1) or not (0) | (23) |
| $G2G^{deny}_{i,j \in G} \in \{0,1\}$ | Determines whether a goal $j$ denies goal $i$ (1) or not (0) | (24) |
| $G2R^{and/or/xor}_{i \in G, k \in R} \in \{0,1\}$ | Determines whether a requirement $k$ is required to fulfill goal $i$ in an (AND/OR/XOR)-relation (1) or not (0) | (25) |
| $R2R^{deny}_{k,l \in R} \in \{0,1\}$ | Determines whether a requirement $l$ denies requirement $k$ (1) or not (0) | (26) |
| $R2R^{complement}_{k \in FR, l \in QR} \in \{0,1\}$ | Determines whether quality requirement $l$ complements functional requirement $k$ (1) or not (0) | (27) |
| $R2R^{alternative}_{k,l \in R} \in \{0,1\}$ | Determines whether requirement $l$ is an alternative for requirement $k$ (1) or not (0) | (28) |

The inputs to this optimization model are the goal model with interactions (see Figure 4.5) and the requirements with interactions and alternatives (see Tables 4.8–4.10). The goals are collected in G. The information about AND, OR, XOR relations between goals is added to the corresponding coefficients $G2G^{and/or/xor}$. For the goal interactions, we only add the information about goals denying each other, using the coefficient $G2G^{\text{deny}}$. The other positive or negative interactions are already considered when valuating a requirement using ANP. For the requirements, we capture the information about denying requirements in $R2R^{\text{deny}}$, the information about complementing requirements in $R2R^{\text{complement}}$, and whether a requirement is an alternative for another requirement in $R2R^{\text{alternative}}$. If a goal or requirement has to be in the solution, is expressed using $G^{\text{must}}/R^{\text{must}}$. For the requirements we also model the information, if a requirement was already in the initial set of requirements or not using $R^{\text{initial}}$. Last, we have to relate goals and requirements using $G2R^{\text{and/or/xor}}$.

Decision variables

| | | |
|---|---|---|
| $g_{i \in G} \in \{0,1\}$ | Determines whether goal $i$ is part of the solution (1) or not (0) | (29) |
| $r_{k \in R} \in \{0,1\}$ | Determines whether requirement $k$ is part of the solution (1) or not (0) | (30) |

The target of our optimization is to minimize the difference between the initial set of requirements, which contains some unresolved conflicts but is ideal in the sense that all goals and requirements of each stakeholder are completely covered, and the compromise set of requirements, which contains no conflicts but relaxed original requirements or even excludes some goals and requirements. The solution is given with respect to the decision variables $g_i$ and $r_k$, which indicate whether a goal or requirement is in the solution or not.

Target function

| | | |
|---|---|---|
| Minimize $\left( \left( \sum_{k \in R} R_k^{\text{initial}} * R_k^{\text{value}} \right) - \left( \sum_{k \in R} r_k * R_k^{\text{value}} \right) \right)$ | Minimize difference between ideal solution with conflicts and compromise solution | (31) |

Note that the target function does not look like the regular form for MOO (see Section **4.2.4**). Indeed, the target function only optimizes the values of the requirements. The reason is that we moved the aggregation of different objectives and stakeholders to ANP. Hence, the value for a requirement already reflects the views of different stakeholders on different dimensions, such as benefits and costs. As a result, we do a hidden MOO, regarding the target function. This simplifies the optimization, but a more fine-grained and detailed optimization model might produce even better results. This is a topic for future research.

Because the solution has to assure several properties, there are some constraints. For example, it is not allowed to have two requirements in the solution that deny each other. Another example is the property that a goal is only allowed in the solution if at least one parent is in the solution and it is fulfilled with respect to related sub-goals or requirements. All constraints are formulated in the following.

Constraints

| | | |
|---|---|---|
| Assures that goal $i$ is in the solution whenever it is a must goal | | (32) |
| $\overbrace{G_i^{\text{must}}} - g_i \leq 0$ | $\forall i \in G$ | |

*Continued*

$g_i$ has to be 0 if any other goal denying it is in the solution. Otherwise free choice. (33)

$$\left(1 - \prod_{j \in G}^{} \left(1 - \overbrace{\underbrace{\left(g_j * G2G_{i,j}^{\text{deny}}\right)}_{\text{1 if no goal denying } i \text{ is in solution}}}^{\text{1 if } j \text{ denies } i \text{ and } j \text{ is in the solution}}\right)\right) * g_i = 0 \qquad \forall i \in G$$

$g_i$ has to be 0 if an AND sub–goal is not in the solution. Otherwise free choice. (34)

$$\left(1 - \prod_{j \in G}^{} \overbrace{\underbrace{\left(\left(1 - G2G_{i,j}^{\text{and}}\right) + \left(G2G_{i,j}^{\text{and}} * g_j\right)\right)}_{\text{1 if all AND sub–goals are in the solution}}}^{\text{1 if } j \text{ is not an AND sub–goal of } i \text{ or } j \text{ is an AND sub–goal and } j \text{ is in the solution}}\right) * g_i = 0 \quad \forall i \in G$$

$$\left(1 - \overbrace{\prod_{j \in G}^{}\left(1 - G2G_{i,j}^{\text{or}}\right)}^{\text{0 if } i \text{ has at least one OR sub–goal}}\right) * \left(g_i - \overbrace{\sum_{j \in G}\left(G2G_{i,j}^{\text{or}} * g_j\right)}^{\text{Sum of OR sub–goals in the solution}}\right) \leq 0 \;\; \forall i \in G \tag{35}$$

$g_i$ is free to choose when at least 1 OR sub–goal of $i$ is in the solution, otherwise 0.

$$\left(1 - \overbrace{\prod_{j \in G}^{}\left(1 - G2G_{i,j}^{\text{xor}}\right)}^{\text{0 if } i \text{ has at least one XOR sub–goal}}\right) * \left(g_i * \left(1 - \overbrace{\sum_{j \in G}\left(G2G_{i,j}^{\text{xor}} * g_j\right)}^{\text{Sum of XOR sub–goals in the solution}}\right)\right) = 0 \;\; \forall i \in G \tag{36}$$

$g_i$ is free to choose when exactly 1 XOR sub–goal of $i$ is in the solution, otherwise 0.

$g_i$ has to be 0 if an AND requirement is not in the solution. Otherwise free choice. (37)

$$\left(1 - \prod_{k \in R}^{} \overbrace{\underbrace{\left(\left(1 - G2R_{i,k}^{\text{and}}\right) + \left(G2R_{i,k}^{\text{and}} * r_k\right)\right)}_{\text{1 if all AND requirements of } i \text{ are in the solution}}}^{\text{1 if } k \text{ is not an AND requirement of } i \text{ or } k \text{ is an AND requirement and in the solution}}\right) * g_i = 0 \;\; \forall i \in G$$

$$\left(1 - \overbrace{\prod_{k \in R}^{}\left(1 - G2R_{i,k}^{\text{or}}\right)}^{\text{0 if } i \text{ has at least one OR requirement}}\right) * \left(g_i - \overbrace{\sum_{k \in R}\left(G2R_{i,k}^{\text{or}} * r_k\right)}^{\text{Sum of OR requirements in the solution}}\right) \leq 0 \;\; \forall i \in G \tag{38}$$

$g_i$ is free to choose when at least 1 OR requirement of $i$ is in the solution, otherwise 0.

*Continued*

$$
\overbrace{\left(1-\prod_{k\in R}^{k\in R}(1-G2R_{i,k}^{xor})\right)}^{\text{1 if }i\text{ has at least one XOR requirement}} * \left(g_i * \overbrace{\left(1-\sum_{k\in R}(G2R_{i,k}^{xor}*r_k)\right)}^{\text{0 if one XOR requirement is in the solution}}\right) \le 0 \quad \forall i \in G \tag{39}
$$

$g_i$ is free to choose when exactly 1 XOR requirement of $i$ is in the solution, otherwise 0.

Assures that a requirement $k$ is in the solution, when it is a must requirement $\qquad$ (40)

$$
R_k^{must} - r_j \le 0 \qquad \forall k \in R
$$

$r_k$ has to be 0 if any other requirement denying it is in the solution. Otherwise free choice. $\qquad$ (41)

$$
\overbrace{\left(1-\prod_{l\in R}\left(1-\overbrace{(r_l*R2R_{k,l}^{deny})}^{\text{1 if }l\text{ denies }k\text{ and }l\text{ is in the solution}}\right)\right)}^{} *r_k = 0 \qquad \forall k \in R
$$

1 if no requirement denying $k$ is in solution

$r_k$ has to be 0 if any other alternative requirement is in the solution. Otherwise free choice. $\qquad$ (42)

$$
\left(1-\prod_{l\in R}\left(1-\overbrace{(r_l*R2R_{k,l}^{alternative})}^{\text{1 if }l\text{ is an alternative for }k\text{ and }l\text{ is in the solution}}\right)\right) *r_k = 0 \quad \forall k \in R
$$

1 if no requirement, which is an alternative for $k$, is in solution

$$
\overbrace{\left(1-\prod_{l\in R}(1-R2R_{l,k}^{complements})\right)}^{\text{0 if }k\text{ complements no other requirement}} * \left(r_k - \overbrace{\sum_{l\in R}\left(R2R_{l,k}^{complements}*r_l\right)}^{\text{Sum of complement requirements in the solution}}\right) \le 0 \quad \forall k \in R \tag{43}
$$

$r_k$ has to be 0 if no requirements it complements is in the solution. Otherwise free choice

$r_k$ has to be 0 if no goal, it is related to, is in the solution $\qquad$ (44)

$$
r_k - \underbrace{\sum_{i\in G}\left(g_i*(G2R_{i,k}^{and} + G2R_{i,k}^{or} + G2R_{i,k}^{xor})\right)}_{\text{1 if }i\text{ is in the solution and }k\text{ is related to it.}} \le 0 \quad \forall k \in R
$$

For the five requirements of our example, the solution is as follows. We used LP-Solve[7] with the Zimpl[8] plugin for solving the optimization. The optimizer selected RQ11.4 for the confidential communication, RQ24 for the performance of the external communication, and RQ25.4 for the performance of the internal communication. Both functional requirements RQ4 and RQ5 are also in

---

[7]http://lpsolve.sourceforge.net/5.5/.
[8]http://zimpl.zib.de/.

the solution. Thus, every initial requirement is covered by itself or an alternative. Hence, all goals are also fulfilled.

The result looks somewhat trivial, because the optimization produces the same result as naively picking the requirements according to their ranks. But this is due to the nature of our example and the preferences. The alternatives preferred most for RQ11 and RQ25 are the most relaxed ones. Thus, the fulfillment of RQ24 is not a problem. But keeping in mind that for the full-use case, many more requirements have to be considered, it is not that easy any more. Then, a highly preferred requirement RQX might deny two other preferred (bus less preferred than RQX). Adding the two other requirements and replacing RQX by one of its alternatives might result in an overall better solution. Considering the goal tree the situation gets even more complicated. Whenever a goal is not satisfied, all of its sub-goals are also removed as long as they have no other parent. This also leads to a removal of the related requirements. Managing all of these goal and requirement interactions is hardly possible for a human for bigger scenarios. But using the optimization model, all balancing and managing of interactions is achieved automatically.

## 4.8 RELATED WORK

For related work, we consider topics related to the steps of our QuaRO method, namely *detection of requirements interactions*, *generation of requirements alternatives*, *valuation of requirements*, and *optimization of requirements*, reflecting the references at the bottom of each step of the QuaRO method given in Figure 4.1. Additionally, we discuss work in the field of smart metering.

Egyed and Grünbacher (2004) introduce an approach to identify conflicts and cooperations among requirements based on software quality attributes and dependencies between requirements. After categorizing requirements into software attributes such as security, usability, etc. manually, the authors identify conflicts and cooperations between requirements using dependencies among requirements. In a final step, they filter out requirements, the quality attributes of which are conflicting, but there is no trace dependency among them. Our method is similar to this method in a sense that both methods rely on dependencies between requirements. We make use of the existing problem diagrams to find the dependencies by taking the constrained domains into account.

As opposed to our problem-driven method, Hausmann et al. (2002) introduce a use-case-driven approach to detect potential consistency problems between functional requirements. A rule-based specification of pre- and post-conditions is proposed to express functional requirements. The requirements are then formalized in terms of graph transformations. Conflict detection is based on the idea of independence of graph transformations. In contrast to our method for detecting interactions among quality requirements, this approach detects interactions between functional requirements.

Lamsweerde et al. (1998) use different formal techniques for detecting conflicts among goals based on KAOS. One technique to detect conflicts is deriving boundary conditions by backward chaining. Every precondition yields a boundary condition. The other technique is selecting a matching generic pattern. The authors provide no tool support. Additionally, they elicit the domain knowledge relatively late, namely during the conflict analysis and not before as it is the case in our method.

Mylopoulos et al. (2001) propose a goal-oriented analysis to explore and evaluate alternatives for achieving a goal with regard to its objectives (softgoals). The authors first decompose functional goals into and/or hierarchies and quality goals into softgoal hierarchies. Next, they correlate the goals with all the softgoals in order to use this correlation for comparison and evaluation of goals later on. Subsequently, the authors select a set of goals and softgoals that meets all functional goals and best satisfies softgoals. In contrast to our approach, the softgoals (quality requirements) analysis is not performed with regard to the goals (functional requirements).

Elahi and Yu (2012) present work on comparing alternatives for analyzing requirements trade-offs. They start by modeling the goals in $i*$ to determine the important properties for deciding which solution should be selected. Then they propose a pairwise elimination of alternatives using the Even Swaps method. Our approach is different, because Elahi and Yu only compare complete systems as alternatives. Hence, they do not propose a method for requirements reconciliation but solution picking. And Even Swaps is not preferable whenever one has many alternatives or goals (Mustajoki and Hämäläinen, 2007).

Ernst et al. (2010) propose a method for reasoning about optional and preferred requirements. First. they model the requirements using goal graphs. Then they use a SAT solver to compute all possible goal graphs, which contain no interactions and satisfy the mandatory goals. Then they eliminate some of the generated solutions using a dominance decision strategy. As an alternative, they propose a method using tabu search and solution pruning for improving the runtime of executing their method. However, using that alternative no longer guarantees optimality. In contrast, our approach guarantees optimality, because no solution is discarded. Moreover, we always identify one solution, whereas the dominance approach is so strict that sometimes no solution can be removed from the set of possible solutions. Thus, the decision problem might not be solved.

Lang et al. (2008) present an optimization model for the selection of services according to customers' needs. Needs are represented as business processes that have to be supported by service selection. The optimization takes communication costs, platform costs, and a monetarized utility value into consideration. Hence, Lang et al. only do an optimization for functional requirements, indirectly expressed by the process, and they do not target services to be developed but only existing ones.

Stegelmann and Kesdogan (2012) treat privacy issues in the context of smart metering. The basis of the analysis is the protection profile (Kreutzmann et al., 2011); we also used in this work. They propose a security architecture and a non-trusted $k$-anonymity service. In contrast to our work, Stegelmann and Kesdogan only consider privacy issues and do not attempt to reconcile these with other quality requirements.

## 4.9 CONCLUSIONS AND PERSPECTIVES

In this chapter, we have presented a comprehensive method to systematically deal with quality requirements. In particular, we give guidance how to

— model quality requirements.
— find interactions involving quality requirements.
— relax quality requirements in order to ameliorate requirements interactions.
— use the relaxations to generate requirements alternatives.
— valuate requirements (and alternatives) according to stakeholders' preferences.
— obtain an optimal set of requirements to be implemented.

In the different steps of the QuaRO method, we bring together a number of established techniques and show how they can be applied together in an advantageous way. In particular, we combine goal- and problem-based requirements engineering methods, UML, ANP, and optimization techniques. The steps of the QuaRO method provide the "glue" between the different techniques.

Distinguishing features of our method are that it (i) explicitly takes into account different stakeholders with possibly conflicting interests and (ii) explicitly models the environment in which the software to be built will be operating. Using domain knowledge is crucial for adequately dealing with quality requirements. In contrast to other work, we remain in the problem space when expressing domain knowledge and do not yet consider possible solutions for quality requirements.

While for the smart grid example we deal with security and performance, of course our method is applicable to other quality requirements for which a UML profile, relaxation templates, etc. should be defined. Using our method, we obtain a set of requirements that satisfies the different stakeholders' goals to the largest possible extent. Those requirements are modeled in such a detailed way that they are an excellent starting point for the design of the software to be built.

In the future, we plan to elaborate further on the different steps of the QuaRO method, to provide an extension for our general approach to take into account further phases of software development, and to provide tool support for its application. As far as the refinement of the QuaRO method is concerned, we intend to further develop the requirements interaction method so as to obtain as few interaction candidates as possible. Furthermore, we want to elaborate more fine-grained optimization models and also investigate different optimization approaches. Considering uncertainty in the optimization process is another worthwhile goal, as well as developing strategies to minimize the number of comparisons needed for ANP.

Concerning the connection of the QuaRO method with further phases of software development, we plan to explicitly support the twin peaks model. Here, requirements are supposed to be the architectural drivers, whereas decisions made in the architectural phase might constrain the achievement of initial requirements, thus changing them. Such feedback loops should be supported by methods and tools.

As far as tool support is concerned, we envisage an integrated tool chain based on the UML4PF tool. The tool support reduces the complexity of the method for practical application. The envisaged tool should support the requirements engineer in applying the QuaRO method. In particular, the step "detection of interactions" can be performed automatically, using the information contained in the problem diagrams. The steps "generation of alternatives" and "valuation of requirements" are planned to be interactive involving stakeholders to exclude inappropriate alternatives and to compare different alternatives for valuation. We can then transform the input information contained in the model to compute the optimal set of requirements automatically using the optimization model.

## Acknowledgment

This research was partially supported by the German Research Foundation (DFG) under grant number HE3322/4-2 and the EU project Network of Excellence on Engineering Secure Future Internet Software Services and Systems (NESSoS, ICT-2009.1.4 Trustworthy ICT, Grant No. 256980).

# References

Alebrahim, A., Heisel, M., 2012. Supporting quality-driven design decisions by modeling variability. In: Proceedings of the International ACM Sigsoft Conference on the Quality of Software Architectures (QoSA). Springer, pp. 43–48.

Alebrahim, A., Hatebur, D., Heisel, M., 2011a. Towards systematic integration of quality requirements into software architecture. In: Crnkovic, I., Gruhn, V. (Eds.), Proceedings of the 5th European Conference on Software Architecture (ECSA). Lecture Notes in Computer Science, vol. 6903. Springer, pp. 17–25.

Alebrahim, A., Hatebur, D., Heisel, M., 2011b. A method to derive software architectures from quality requirements. In: Dan Thu, T., Leung, K. (Eds.), Proceedings of the 18th Asia-Pacific Software Engineering Conference (APSEC). IEEE Computer Society, pp. 322–330.

Bass, L., Clemens, P., Kazman, R., 2003. Software Architecture in Practice. Addison-Wesley.

Beckers, K., Küster, J., Faßbender, S., Schmidt, H., 2011. Pattern-based support for context establishment and asset identification of the ISO 27000 in the field of cloud computing. In: Proceedings of the International Conference on Availability, Reliability and Security (ARES). IEEE Computer Society, pp. 327–333.

Beckers, K., Faßbender, S., Heisel, M., Meis, R., 2012a. Pattern-based context establishment for service-oriented architectures. In: Heisel, M. (Ed.), Software Service and Application Engineering. Lecture Notes in Computer Science, vol. 7365. Springer, pp. 81–101.

Beckers, K., Faßbender, S., Küster, J., Schmidt, H., 2012b. A pattern-based method for identifying and analyzing laws. In: Proceedings of the International Working Conference on Requirements Engineering: Foundation for Software Quality (REFSQ). Lecture Notes in Computer Science, vol. 7195. Springer, pp. 256–262.

Beckers, K., Faßbender, S., Schmidt, H., 2012c. An integrated method for pattern-based elicitation of legal requirements applied to a cloud computing example. In: Proceedings of the International Conference on Availability, Reliability and Security (ARES)—2nd International Workshop on Resilience and IT-Risk in Social Infrastructures (RISI 2012). IEEE Computer Society, pp. 463–472.

Beckers, K., Faßbender, S., Heisel, M., Meis, R., 2012d. A problem-based approach for computer aided privacy threat identification. In: APF 2012. Lecture Notes in Computer Science, vol. 8319. Springer, pp. 1–16.

Beckers, K., Côté, I., Faßbender, S., Heisel, M., Hofbauer, S., 2013a. A pattern-based method for establishing a cloud-specific information security management system. In: Requirements Engineering. Springer, pp. 1–53 ISSN 0947-3602.

Beckers, K., Faßbender, S., Heisel, M., 2013b. A meta-model approach to the fundamentals for a pattern language for context elicitation. In: Proceedings of the European Conference on Pattern Languages of Programs (Euro-PLoP), To appear.

Beckers, K., Faßbender, S., Heisel, M., Paci, F., 2013c. Combining goaloriented and problem-oriented requirements engineering methods. In: Proceedings of the International Cross Domain Conference on Availability, Reliability and Security (CD-ARES). IEEE Computer Society, pp. 178–194.

Choppy, C., Hatebur, D., Heisel, M., 2011. Systematic architectural design based on problem patterns. In: Avgeriou, P., Grundy, J., Hall, J., Lago, P., Mistrik, I. (Eds.), Relating Software Requirements and Architectures. Springer, pp. 133–159 (chapter 9).

Deconinck, G., 2008. An evaluation of two-way communication means for advanced metering in Flanders (Belgium). In: Instrumentation and Measurement Technology Conference Proceedings (IMTC), pp. 900–905.

Department of Energy and Climate Change, 2011a. Smart Metering Implementation Programme, Response to Prospectus Consultation, Overview Document. Technical report, Office of Gas and Electricity Markets.

Department of Energy and Climate Change, 2011b. Smart Metering Implementation Programme, Response to Prospectus Consultation, Design Requirements. Technical report, Office of Gas and Electricity Markets.

Egyed, A., Grünbacher, P., 2004. Identifying requirements conflicts and cooperation: how quality attributes and automated traceability can help. IEEE Softw.. 21 (6), 50–58, ISSN 0740-7459.

Elahi, G., Yu, E., 2012. Comparing alternatives for analyzing requirements trade-offs in the absence of numerical data. Inf. Softw. Technol. 54 (6), 517–530.

Ernst, N., Mylopoulos, J., Borgida, A., Jureta, I., 2010. Reasoning with optional and preferred requirements. In: Parsons, J., Saeki, M., Shoval, P., Woo, C., Wand, Y. (Eds.), Conceptual Modeling ER 2010. In: Lecture Notes in Computer Science, vol. 6412. Springer, pp. 118–131.

Fabian, B., Gürses, S., Heisel, M., Santen, T., Schmidt, H., 2010. A comparison of security requirements engineering methods. Requirements Eng. 15 (1), 7–40.

Faßbender, S., 2012. Model-based multilateral optimizing for service-oriented architectures focusing on compliance driven security. In: Proceedings of the 1st SE Doctorial Symposium, SE-DS. Brandenburg University of Technology, Cottbus, pp. 19–24, Computer Science Reports.

Faßbender, S., Heisel, M., 2013. From problems to laws in requirements engineering—using model-transformation. In: International Conference on Software Paradigm Trends ICSOFT-PT.pp. 447–458.

Hatebur, D., Heisel, M., 2009a. Deriving software architectures from problem descriptions. In: Software Engineering 2009—Workshopbandpp. 383–392, GI.

Hatebur, D., Heisel, M., 2009b. A foundation for requirements analysis of dependable software. In: Buth, B., Rabe, G., Seyfarth, T. (Eds.), Proceedings of the International Conference on Computer Safety, Reliability and Security (SAFECOMP). In: Lecture Notes in Computer Science, vol. 5775. Springer, pp. 311–325.

Hatebur, D., Heisel, M., 2010a. A UML profile for requirements analysis of dependable software. In: Schoitsch, E. (Ed.), Proceedings of the International Conference on Computer Safety, Reliability and Security (SAFE-COMP). In: Lecture Notes in Computer Science, vol. 6351. Springer, ISBN 978-3-642-15650-2, pp. 317–331.

Hatebur, D., Heisel, M., 2010b. Making pattern- and model-based software development more rigorous. In: Proceedings of 12th International Conference on Formal Engineering Methods (ICFEM). In: Lecture Notes in Computer Science, vol. 6447. Springer, pp. 253–269.

Hatebur, D., Heisel, M., 2010c. A UML profile for requirements analysis of dependable software. In: Schoitsch, E. (Ed.), Proceedings of the International Conference on Computer Safety, Reliability and Security (SAFE-COMP). Lecture Notes in Computer Science, vol. 6351. Springer, pp. 317–331.

Hatebur, D., Heisel, M., Schmidt, H., 2007. A pattern system for security requirements engineering. In: Proceedings of the International Conference on Availability, Reliability and Security (ARES). IEEE TransactionsIEEE, pp. 356–365.

Hausmann, J., Heckel, R., Taentzer, G., 2002. Detection of conflicting functional requirements in a use case-driven approach: a static analysis technique based on graph transformation. In: Proceedings of the International Conference on Software Engineering, ICSE '02. ACM, ISBN 1-58113-472-X, pp. 105–115.

International Organization for Standardization (ISO) and International Electrotechnical Commission (IEC), 2009. Common Evaluation Methodology 3.1. ISO/IEC 15408.

Jackson, M., 2001. Problem Frames. Analyzing and Structuring Software Development Problems. Addison-Wesley, Boston, MA.

Klein, M., Bachmann, F., Bass, L., 2000. Quality attributes design primitives. Technical report, Software Engineering Institute.

Kreutzmann, H., Vollmer, S., Tekampe, N., A. Abromeit, 2011. Protection profile for the gateway of a smart metering system. Technical report, BSI.

Lamsweerde, A., 2009. Reasoning about alternative requirements options. In: Borgida, A., Chaudhri, V., Giorgini, P., Yu, E. (Eds.), Conceptual Modeling: Foundations and Applications. Lecture Notes in Computer Science, vol. 5600. Springer, pp. 380–397.

Lamsweerde, A., Letier, E., Darimont, R., 1998. Managing conflicts in goal-driven requirements engineering. IEEE Trans. Softw. Eng.. 24 (11), 908–926, ISSN 0098-5589.

Lang, J., Widjaja, T., Buxmann, P., Domschke, W., Hess, T., 2008. Optimizing the supplier selection and service portfolio of a SOA service integrator. In: Proceedings of the Annual Hawaii International Conference on System Sciences, HICSS '08. IEEE Computer Society, p. 89, ISBN: 0-7695-3075-8.

Marler, R., Arora, J., 2004. Survey of multi-objective optimization methods for engineering. Struct. Multidiscip. Optim. 26 (6), 369–395.

Mustajoki, J., H¨am¨al¨ainen, R., 2007. Smart-swaps a decision support system for multicriteria decision analysis with the even swaps method. Decis. Support. Syst.. 44 (1), 313–325. http://dx.doi.org/10.1016/j.dss.2007.04.004, ISSN 0167–9236.

Mylopoulos, J., Chung, L., Liao, S., Wang, H., Yu, E., 2001. Exploring alternatives during requirements analysis. IEEE Softw. 18 (1), 92–96.

Nuseibeh, B., 2001. Weaving together requirements and architectures. IEEE Comput. 34 (3), 115–117.

Otto, P., Antón, A., 2007. Addressing legal requirements in requirements engineering. In: Proceedings of the International Conference on Requirements Engineering. IEEE.

Pomerol, J.C., Barba-Romero, S., 2000. Multicriterion Decision in Management: Principles and Practice. In: International Series in Operations Research & Management Science: ISOR. Kluwer Academic Publishers, ISBN 9780792377566.

Remero, G., Tarruell, F., Mauri, G., Pajot, A., Alberdi, G., Arzberger, M., Denda, R. Giubbini, P., Rodrguez, C., Miranda, E., Galeote, I., Morgaz, M., Larumbe, I., Navarro, E., Lassche, R., Haas, J., Steen, A., Cornelissen, P., Radtke, G., Martnez, C., Orcajada, A., Kneitinger, H., Wiedemann, T., 2009a D1.1 Requirements of AMI. Technical report, OPEN meter project.

Remero, G., Tarruell, F., Mauri, G., Pajot, A., Alberdi, G., Arzberger, M., Denda, R., Rodrguez, C., Larumbe, I., Navarro, E., Lassche, R., Haas, J., Martnez, C., Orcajada, A, 2009b D1.2 report on regulatory requirements. Technical report, OPEN meter project.

Robinson, W., Pawlowski, S., Volkov, V., 2003. Requirements interaction management. ACM Comput. Surv. 35, 132–190, ISSN 0360-0300.

Saaty, T., 2005. The analytic hierarchy and analytic network processes for the measurement of intangible criteria and for decision-making. In: Figueira, J., Greco, S., Ehrgott, M. (Eds.), Multiple Criteria Decision Analysis: State of the Art Surveys. Springer, pp. 345–408.

Saaty, T., 2008a. Decision making with the analytic hierarchy process. Int. J. Serv. Sci.. 1, 83–98.

Saaty, T., 2008b. The analytic network process. Iranian J. Operat. Res. 1.

Saaty, T., Ozdemir, M., 2003. Negative priorities in the analytic hierarchy process. Math. Comput. Model. 37, 1063–1075.

Stegelmann, M., Kesdogan, D., 2012. Gridpriv: a smart metering architecture offering k-anonymity. In: Proceedings of the TrustCom 2012. IEEE Computer Society, pp. 419–426.

Stromanbieter Deutschland, June 2013. http://www.strom-pfadfinder.de/stromanbieter/.

UML Revision Task Force, 2011. UML Profile for MARTE: Modeling and Analysis of Real-Time Embedded Systems. http://www.omg.org/spec/MARTE/1.0/PDF.

Yu, E., 1996. Modelling strategic relationships for process reengineering (Ph.D. thesis).

Yu, E., 1997. Towards modeling and reasoning support for early-phase requirements engineering. In: Proceedings of the 3rd IEEE International Symposium on Requirements Engineering, RE '97. IEEE Computer Society, ISBN 0-8186-7740-6, p. 226.

# Analysis, Monitoring, and Control of Software Architecture for System Qualities

# HASARD: A Model-Based Method for Quality Analysis of Software Architecture

5

**Hong Zhu[1], Qian Zhang[2], and Yanlong Zhang[3]**

[1]*Oxford Brookes University, Oxford, UK*
[2]*The National University of Defense Technology, Changsha, China*
[3]*Manchester Metropolitan University, Manchester, UK*

## INTRODUCTION

An extraordinarily powerful means of software engineering is architecture analysis, which enables the early prediction of a system's quality at design stage. As Bass et al. (1998, 2012) pointed out, *without them, we would be reduced to building systems by choosing various structures, implementing the system, measuring the system's quality, and all along the way hoping for the best.* This chapter presents such a method for analyzing software architectural designs to predict their quality.

## Motivation

Software architecture is a structural model of software system at a very high level of abstraction. In this structural model, a software system is represented as a collection of components interconnected through connectors (Bass et al., 1998; Bosch, 2000; Hofmeister et al., 2000; Shaw and Garlan, 1996; Taylor et al., 2010). Being at a high level of abstraction, the implementation details of the components and the connectors are hidden, but the focus is on their characteristic features and/or the assigned functionality. For a given software system, a number of architectural models can be constructed to represent different views of the system in order to achieve different engineering purposes.

For example, to demonstrate that a system correctly satisfies its functional requirements, a *conceptual view* depicts the system in terms of how functions are decomposed and assigned to conceptual components and how these components are controlled and interact with each other through conceptual connectors. In order to provide instructions for further detailed design and implementation, a *module view* focuses on how the functionality of the system is mapped to the implementation environment, such as how the system uses the facilities and resources in the underlying software platform. It depicts software structures in terms of software modules and characterizes them with implementation-related features. In order to facilitate the construction, integration, installation, and testing of the system, a *code view* describes how the source code that implements the system is organized. To assist organizational management of the development process, a *development view* depicts a software system in terms of a repository of software artifacts that are created, modified, and managed by the programmers, maintainers, testers, etc. In order to understand the dynamic behavior of a system, a *behavior view* (or *execution view*) describes the system's execution in terms of its runtime platform elements, concurrency, communication, and the physical resources used.

One of the most important engineering purposes of software architecture is to predict the system's quality. To achieve this purpose, a *quality view* manifests the architectural design decisions made specifically to address quality requirements (Bass et al., 2012). Usually, a quality view builds on top of a conceptual view with the relevant elements characterized by properties that are either directly or indirectly related to quality attributes. Such properties are referred to as *quality-carrying properties* in the sequel. However, how to use such a quality view to predict software quality remains an open problem. This is the subject of this chapter.

## Related works and open problems

The approach reported in this chapter is model-driven: that is, we will first construct a quality model based on the architectural design, then infer the quality of the system based on the model. In this section, we review the current state of art in the related areas and discuss the open problems.

### Software quality models

Software quality is one of the most elusive concepts (Kitchenham and Pfleeger, 1996). A great amount of effort has been made since the 1970s to define software quality models in order to understand the concept, to measure software systems' quality, and to guide software development activities in order to improve software quality (Deissenboeck et al., 2009).

A software quality model defines a set of properties that are relevant to software quality and the relationships between them. Such a relationship can be either *quantitative* or *qualitative*. The former is the subject of research on software metrics. The latter is widely used in the literature on software quality models and often combined with metrics for the evaluation of software quality.

Existing qualitative software quality models fall into two types: hierarchical models and relational models.

A *hierarchical model* defines a set of aspects of software quality, then decomposes each aspect into a number of factors, which are in turn decomposed into a number of attributes, and further decomposed into several metrics. In this way, the abstract notion of software quality is characterized by a set of quality-related properties that are organized into a hierarchical structure to express the positive relationships between them. Some properties are more abstract, thus are at a higher level of the hierarchical structure. Some are more concrete, even directly measurable in a quantitative way, thus at a lower level of the hierarchy. The lower level properties have a positive contribution to the parent property. Here, a positive relationship from property A to B in a hierarchical model means that improving a software system's quality on property A implies an improvement of its quality on property B. Typical examples of such hierarchical models include the McCall model (1977), the Boehm model (1978), the ISO model (1992, 2012), the Dromey model (1995), the Bansiya-Davis model of OO software (2002), the Goeb-Lochmann model for service-oriented systems (2011), and the Franke-Kowalewski-Weise model for mobile software (2012). One of the main weaknesses of such models is that they are incapable of expressing negative relations between quality attributes.

A *relational model* overcomes this problem by defining a number of stereotypes of relationships between quality attributes, such as positive, negative, and neutral relations. Typically, a positive relation between two quality attributes indicates that a software system that is good on one attribute will also be good on the other. A negative relation means that a software system is good on one attribute implies that it is inevitably bad on the other. A neutral relation means that the attributes are not logically interrelated. Typical examples of relational quality models include the Perry Model (1991) and the Gillies Model (1992, 1997). There are also a number of such quality models of information systems (Zhang, 2005). Such models have significantly improved our understanding of software quality.

Both hierarchical and relational quality models can help software developers to improve software quality by providing guidelines for software development activities, such as in the elicitation of quality requirements. However, as Deissenboeck et al. (2009) pointed out, despite successes and standardization efforts, quality models do not live up to expectations and disappointed practitioners. In particular, they fail to take software structures into account (Dromey, 1995, 1996). Moreover, they are incapable of dealing with complicated relationships between quality attributes that are difficult to stereotype. They provide little help to the design of software systems, especially the architectural design. These problems will be addressed in this chapter by proposing a new quality modeling approach, that is, graphic quality modeling.

### Quality analysis of software architecture

Two types of quality analysis activities are often performed at software design stage: *quality assessment and evaluation* and *quality exploration*.

- *Quality assessment and evaluation* aims at evaluating software architecture with regard to a set of well-defined criteria and in a set of well-defined usages or scenarios. It assesses the software to determine whether the design meets the given design goals.
- *Quality exploration* intends to explore the architecture in order to discover problems in a design, where the problems are normally unknown and there are no fixed criteria and/or usage scenarios.

Each of these types of quality analysis has its own uses in software development. The former has its value in software validation and verification against known users' quality requirements, while the latter manifests its importance to software engineers by discovering and predicting unintended side effects of design decisions. This is particularly important for software that has large user bases and long lifespan such as systems software and utility software, where usages are complicated and may change significantly in the future.

In the past decade, a significant progress has been made in the research on the quality analysis of software architectures. A number of methods have been advanced in the literature to evaluate and assess the quality of software architectural designs. The existing architecture quality analysis techniques and methods can be classified into two types: *scenario-based* and *model-based*.

- *Scenario-based methods* examine software architecture in the context of a set of scenarios, although the ways that scenarios are elicited and used vary. Among the most well-known scenario-based methods are SAAM (Bass et al., 1998, 2012; Kazman et al., 1996) and ATAM (Clements et al., 2002); see Dobrica and Niemela (2002) for a survey and Babar and Gorton (2004) for a comparison of them. They have been applied to the evaluation and assessment of architectural designs on various quality attributes, such as modifiability (Kazman et al., 1994, 1996), usability (Folmer and Bosch, 2005), and security (Alkussayer and Allen, 2010). They have a number of advantages, including the examination of software behavior in real situations and reduction of complexity of analysis through focusing on typical scenarios. Each method is suitable for one specific quality attribute/factor. They are applicable to the evaluation and assessment type of quality analysis. However, there are difficulties in building an overall picture of the system's quality, especially when there are intensive and complicated interactions between scenarios. The elicitation of a complete and representative set of scenarios is by no means a trivial task, which currently still relies on brainstorming. The result of quality analysis heavily depends on the selection of the most representative scenarios as reported in practices (see Kostelijk, 2005). It was also perceived as complicated and expensive to use in industrial context (Woods, 2012).

• *Model-based methods* start the analysis of software architecture with the construction of a model of the software system and then systematically deduce the quality based on the model. Typical examples of such quality analysis techniques are used in performance evaluation, reliability estimation, and security analysis. Such methods are good at exploring the unknown quality problems in a design. However, each of them also aims at a single quality attribute.

Therefore, it is highly desirable to develop a method that enables software engineers to systematically explore software architecture in order to discover and predict quality problems, especially when multiple quality attributes are involved.

### *Hazard analysis methods and techniques*

For constructing quality models, we will adapt existing system hazard analysis methods and techniques that are widely used for safety engineering.

Hazard analysis techniques have been widely used in the development and deployment of safety critical systems. Originally, hazard analysis aims at systematically identifying, assessing, and controlling hazards before a new work process, piece of equipment, or other activity is initiated. In such a context, a *hazard* is a situation in which there is actual or potential danger to people or to the environment. Associated with each hazard is a risk, which is the product of the likelihood of the event occurring and its consequences. Once the hazards are identified and analyzed, safety requirements can be specified for each component. Risks can be avoided or reduced ultimately through technical design, management, and organizational means. Consequently, the safety of the system is improved (Leveson, 1995; Neumann, 1995; Storey, 1996).

Here, we adapt the methods of hazard analysis and extend the concept of hazard in order to cover all quality aspects besides safety. In our context, the word *hazard* has its widest meaning, which means *any situation that may cause harm as designed or due to a deviation from the design decision*. The more likely a hazard occurs and the more serious the consequences of the hazard, the higher the risk, and thus the more important the corresponding quality attribute is with the system in question.

There are a number of hazard analysis techniques available in the literature of safety engineering. These techniques fall into two types: (a) *hazard identification* techniques and methods and (b) *cause-effect analysis* techniques and methods. The former aims at discovering hazards systematically while the later aims to find out the causes and consequences of the hazards.

One of the most effective hazard identification technique is HAZOP (MoD, 2000), which has been adapted to the analysis of software safety. In order to deal with a wider range of quality attributes rather than just safety, in this chapter we will extend the method and interpret the technique in a wider context.

A typical example of cause-effect analysis techniques is the FMEA technique, which stands for *Failure Modes and Effects Analysis*. It is a mature and well-defined safety analysis technique.

Its engineering principle and process are similar to what software engineers are familiar with. It progressively selects the individual components or functions within a system and investigates their possible modes of failure. It then considers possible causes for each failure mode and assesses their likely consequences. In the original FMEA, the effects of the failure of a component are first determined for the unit itself, then for the complete system. Possible remedial actions are also suggested. It requires engineers to identify the potential failure modes and to link each failure mode to its possible causes and the consequences. This process is also adapted with some minor changes in order to make it closer to what software engineers familiar with and more suitable for software engineering.

## Overview of the proposed approach

This chapter presents a model-based method for exploratory quality analysis of software architecture. It aims at systematically analyzing an architectural design through building a quality model for the system under scrutiny. The method consists of the following technical elements.

- *A graphical quality modeling notation*. In this graphical notation, detailed and complex relationships between quality attributes and/or design decisions can be represented in the context of a given architecture design.
- *A software hazard analysis method*. It identifies the potential hazards in the development, operation, and maintenance of the software and the causes and effects of such hazards.
- *A quality model construction technique*. It transforms software hazard analysis results into a software quality model represented in the graphic notation.
- *A set of algorithms* for automatically analyzing quality models. They are applied in order to identify critical quality issues, trade-off design decision points, the impacts of a design decision and the factors that influence a quality attribute.
- *A software tool*. It supports the software hazard analysis process and the construction of graphic quality model and implements quality analysis algorithms.

The proposed quality analysis process is illustrated in Figure 5.1, which consists of the following activities.

- *Hazard identification*: Identifies the potential quality hazards of the software system as the consequences of the software architectural design decisions. The result is a list of quality hazards.
- *Hazard cause-consequence analysis*: Recognizes the cause-consequence relationships between software quality hazards and design decisions. The result is the causal relations between hazards. It may also result in additional hazards added into the list of hazards.
- *Hazard classification*: Associates each identified hazard to a quality attribute or a quality-carrying property that the hazard is concerned with. The result is a set of classified design hazards.
- *Quality model assembling*: Transforms the results of the above steps into a graphic quality model represented in the graphic quality modeling notation.
- *Quality concern analysis*: Analyzes the graphic quality model constructed through the above steps to infer quality concerns of the whole system, such as to find the critical design decisions that affect certain quality attributes, to recognize the trade-off points for certain conflict quality attributes, and to discover the consequences of a design decision on various quality attributes.

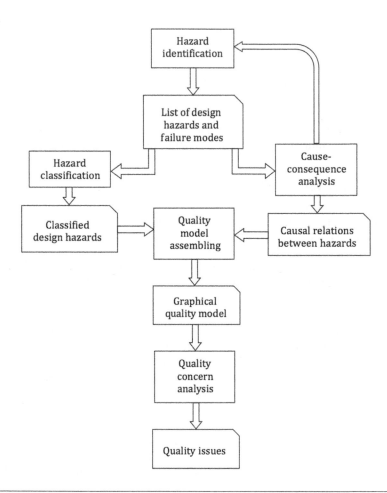

**FIGURE 5.1**

Process of model-based quality analysis.

## Organization of the chapter

The remainder of the chapter is organized as follows.

Section 5.1 is devoted to the hazard analysis of software systems. It is an adaptation and extension of the hazard analysis methods and techniques of system engineering.

Section 5.2 proposes the diagrammatic notations for graphical modeling of software quality and the technique for constructing such models from the results of hazard analysis of software architecture.

Section 5.3 presents the algorithms for the derivation of system quality features from graphic quality models.

Section 5.4 describes a software tool called SQUARE that supports the whole process of HASARD analysis and implements the quality analysis algorithms.

Section 5.5 reports a case study with the method and the tool.

Section 5.6 concludes the chapter with a comparison with related work and a discussion of future work.

## 5.1 HAZARD ANALYSIS OF SOFTWARE ARCHITECTURAL DESIGNS

This section introduces the software hazard analysis method. It takes an architectural model of a software system as input. It systematically explores observable quality-related phenomena of the system and then seeks to establish the causal relationships between the phenomena. Here, a *phenomenon* is a property or event that is observable and concrete in the development, operation, maintenance, and evolution of the software system. The process consists of two phases: The first is the identification of design hazards. The second is the discovery of causal relationships between such hazards and design decisions. The following subsections present each of these phases.

### 5.1.1 Identification of design hazards

The process of hazard analysis starts with the identification of hazards. In systems engineering disciplines, one of the most effective methods of hazard identification is the so-called *Hazard and Operability Studies* (or *HAZOP* for short) (MoD, 2000). The method relies on asking and answering questions of *what-if* nature.

For example, in the analysis of a design of a chemical reactor, a typical what-if question is: *What would happen if temperature in the reaction container is higher than the designed range?* An answer to this question could be: *The reactor will explode.* Consequently, the engineer will identify that controlling the temperature is a critical issue in the design of the reactor.

Similarly, such what-if questions are effective to identify quality issues in a software architectural design. For example, one may ask the what-if question: *What would happen if the authentication of the user is not checked before granting an access to the database?* An answer could be: *The integrity of the database will be broken.* In such a way, the importance of authentication to system security can be identified.

The effectiveness of HAZOP method heavily depends on systematically asking such what-if questions. In HAZOP technique, this is achieved by designing and applying a set of *guide words* to cover all aspects of the design in question.

For example, *more* and *less* are typical examples of guide words that are applicable to a quantitative attribute in the design of a system. Applying such a guide word to a quantitative attribute prompts the engineer to ask the what-if questions of what will happen if the actual value of the quantitative attribute is *more* than the designed value or *less* than the designed value. For instance, suppose that a design decision of a chemical reactor is that *the temperature of the reaction container is to be controlled in the range of $650 \pm 10\,°C$.* The what-if questions corresponding to these two guide words are:

- *More*: What will happen if the temperature of the reactor container is *higher* than $650 + 10\,°C$?
- *Less*: What will happen if the temperature of the reactor container is *lower* than $650 - 10\,°C$?

The same method can be applied to the identification of software hazards.

For example, the guide word *No* can be applied to a type of data produced by a component in the software system under analysis. In such a context, it means *no data* is produced by the component. In hazard identification, the analyst will ask the what-if question, *What would happen if the data is not produced by the component?*

Worth noting: First, each guide word may be applied to more than one type of design features and architectural design decisions. Its meaning depends on the type of design decisions and the context in the system. For example, the same guide word *No* can also be applied to an architectural component. In such a context, it means that the component is not contained in the system. For example, a dynamic link library is not available when the system is initialized at runtime. A what-if question can be asked to identify the consequences of missing such a component.

Second, not all what-if questions will lead to a hazard. However, systematically asking all such what-if questions reduces the chance of omitting serious hazards during hazard identification.

In order to identify hazards hidden in a software architectural design, we have developed a set of guide words for software engineers to systematically develop a collection of what-if questions. They are applied to the elements in an architectural design, where a design element can be a property or function assigned to a component and/or a connector, the component or connector itself, the configuration of the system, or other choices. If a deviation from the design is credible, the corresponding behavior of the element is considered as a potential hazard. Then, its causes, effects, and recommendations of the further investigation are documented. Table 5.1 lists the guide words for analyzing software architectural designs.

For example, consider the Internet connection between the client and server in a web-based application. As shown in Table 5.2, by applying these guide words, we can identify all of the most well-known hazards of web-based applications related to Internet connection.

A HAZOP study requires the analyst identify not only the hazards but also their effects and causes. Table 5.2 also shows the possible causes and the consequences of each hazard. Such analysis is preliminary but indicates which hazard is important and deserves further investigation in cause-consequence analysis.

## 5.1.2 Cause-consequence analysis

The cause-consequence analysis of hazards aims at deepening the understanding of the hazards. For example, consider the hazard *more messages are delivered to the server than the clients sent out* in Table 5.2. There are several possible causes of the hazard, which include that (a) the traffic on the Internet results in duplicated packages being generated, (b) a malicious source generates false request messages on purpose. A direct consequence of a large number of false request messages is a high workload on the server. This, in turn, could lead to (a) a poor performance of the system, even (b) the clash of the system. Consequently, the clients cannot get the requested services responsively. In the above analysis, we can see a sequence of hazardous phenomena or events is identified as a cause-effect chain.

The cause-consequence analysis can be performed in the backward or forward direction or a combination of both. Forward analysis extends from a hazard in search of potential effects, or the consequences. Backward analysis starts with a hazard to search for its causes.

In forward analysis, the consequences of a hazard are identified and added into the list of identified hazards until the consequence is *terminal*. A hazard is terminal if it does not affect any other component of the system or does not cause any other hazards/failures. In many cases, we consider a hazard as terminal simply because we are not interested in its further consequence. For example, the phenomenon that a user cannot find required information could be considered as terminal if we are not interested in what would happen afterwards. However, in certain context, what happens afterwards may become a serious

**Table 5.1** Guide Words for Software Hazard Identification

| Guide | Applicable Attribute | Interpretations |
|---|---|---|
| No | Data or control signals | No data or control signals are exchanged through a connector |
| | | No data or control signals produced by a component |
| | | No data or control signals received from input |
| | Property or function of a component or connector | The component (or connector) does not have the designed property (or function) |
| | Component or connector | The system does not contain the component (or connector) |
| More | Quantitative parameters of a component, connector or the whole system | The value of the parameter is too large |
| Less | Quantitative parameters of a component, connector or the whole system | The value of the parameter is too small |
| As well as | Event or activity | The intended event (or activity) occurs, but another event (or activity) also occurs in addition to this. For example, redundant data are sent to the designated receiver in addition to intended value |
| | | Data are sent to the designated receiver as well as an unintended receiver |
| | Property or function of a component or connector | In addition to the intended property (or function), the component (or connector) also has other additional properties (or functions) |
| | Component or connector | In addition to the intended component (or connector), the system contains other components and connectors |
| Part of | Structured data | Only a part of the data produced, stored, or received |
| | Structured events | Only a part of the events happened |
| Reverse | Direction of information flow | The information flows in the opposite direction |
| | Event | The opposite event happened |
| Other than | Data or control signals | Incorrect data or control signals produced |
| | Quantitative and qualitative parameters | The parameter has a value different from the designed one |
| | Property or function of a component, connector, or the whole system | The component (or connector, or the whole system) has a property (or function) different from the designed one |
| | Component or connector | The component (connector) is replaced by another kind of component (or connector). For example, a session bean is used instead of an entity bean |
| Early | Periodical events | The event happened earlier than expected |
| Late | Periodical events | The event happened later than expected |
| Before | Temporal orders between events | Two events happened in a different temporal order as designed |

**Table 5.2** Example of HAZOP Analysis: The Application of Guide Words to Identify the Hazards of the Internet Connection Between Client and Server

| Guide | Hazard | Causes | Consequences |
|---|---|---|---|
| No | The Internet connection passes no messages between the client and server | Physically disconnected; Traffic jam; Software failure; Network server is down | Client cannot communicate with the server |
| More | More messages are delivered to the server than what the clients sent out: duplicated messages | Hacker's attack; Heavy traffic on the Internet caused resending packages | System clash; Overload on the server |
| Less | Fewer messages are delivered than what the server (or the client) sent out: lost messages | Discontinued Internet connection; Heavy traffic on the Internet; Software failure | Incomplete transactions; System crash; Damage the data integrity of the server (and/or client) |
| As well as | Messages are delivered to other destinations in addition to the designated receiver | Hacker's attack; Software failure | Leak of sensitive information |
| Part of | Only a part of the packets of a message is delivered to the destination client (or server) | Discontinued Internet connection; Heavy traffic on the Internet; Software failure | Software failure; Production of incorrect computation results if incompleteness is not detected |
| Other than | A message not from the client (or the server) is passed to the server (or client) | Hacker's attack; Other software system's failure | System failure; Damage the integrity of the data and the program |
| Other than | The message is in a different format | The client (or the server) is modified; Fault in the software | System failure |

problem. For example, suppose that the system stores patients' medical records. The situation that a doctor cannot find a patient's record may lead to serious consequences in the treatment of the patient.

In backward analysis, the causes of a hazard are identified and added into the list of identified hazards until the hazard is *primitive*. A hazard is primitive if its causes cannot be further identified without additional knowledge of the system. A hazard can also be considered as primitive if we are not interested in its causes. For example, in most cases a broken link in a HTML file can be considered as primitive. However, in a different context, we may well be interested in its causes and want to find out why the hyperlink is broken.

The cause-consequence relationships between hazards can be recorded in a form as the results of cause-consequence analysis. They are used for the construction of a graphic quality model at the next step. Figure 5.2 shows the structure of the form with some examples of the hazards associated to web-based applications.

Most hazards should have already been identified in the initial hazard identification step. However, some new hazards may still be discovered in cause-consequence analysis. These new hazards are then added into the hazard list and assigned with a unique identification number.

| System: Webpage | | | | | | | |
|---|---|---|---|---|---|---|---|
| Analyists: HZ, QZ, YZ | | | | | | | |
| Date: April 14, 2009 | | | | Version: 1.0 | | | |
| **Ref** | **Cause** | | | **Consequence** | | | **Explanation** |
| | Hazard Ref. | Description | | Hazard Ref. | Description | | |
| | | Comp. | Phenomenon | | Comp. | Phenomenon | |
| R1 | W2 | HTML file | Contains a broken link | U8 | The user | Cannot download required HTML file | No file associated to the hyperlink |
| R2 | S1 | Web server | Server is down | U8 | The user | Cannot download required HTML file | The file cannot be retrieved and transmitted |
| R3 | U8 | The user | Cannot download required HTML file | Y1 | System | Cannot be used | The user is frustrated in finding required information |

**FIGURE 5.2**

Cause-consequence analysis form.

# 5.2 GRAPHICAL MODELING OF SOFTWARE QUALITY

In this section, we present the graphic notation for modeling software quality and the process of constructing such quality models based on hazard analysis.

## 5.2.1 Graphic notation of quality models

As shown in Figure 5.3, our proposed diagrammatic representation of quality models is a directed graph that consists of two principal elements: the *nodes* and *links*. Each node contains three basic elements:

1.  A design element in the architectural design
2.  Quality-carrying properties of the design element
3.  An observable phenomenon of the property

where a design element can be a component, a connector, or any design decision. An observable phenomenon could be a *positive indicator* of the quality-carrying property or a *negative indicator*. When it is a negative indicator, the property is marked with the symbol "−." The positive indicator is omitted, and it is the default.

It is worth noting that although there may be more than one observable phenomenon that reveals a quality-carrying property for a design element, each node can only have one such phenomenon. This is to enable different causal relationships between phenomena to be easily represented without transforming the graphic model and to enable the causal relationships to be validated separately.

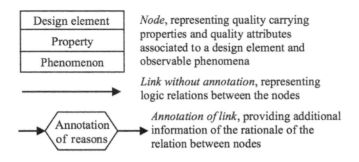

**FIGURE 5.3**

Graphic notation of quality models.

The links are directed arcs between the nodes. Each link must contain an *impact factor*, which can be either *positive* or *negative*. A positive link from node *A* to node *B* means that the occurrence of the phenomenon of node *A* implies the occurrence of the phenomenon on node *B*. A negative link means that the occurrence of the phenomenon of node *A* prevents the occurrence of the phenomenon on node *B*. When a link has a negative impact, the arc is marked with the symbol "−" on the arrow. It is omitted when the impact factor is positive, and it is the default.

Each link can also contain an optional annotation for the reasons why the two nodes are related. This enables manual validation of the model.

Figure 5.4 shows a fragment of a quality model of web-based information systems. This fragment of a quality model shows that the usability of a web-based system is related to the correctness of the HTML files, the load and performance of the server, the sizes of HTML files, the compatibility of client-side platform, and the availability of the online helps. It described in detail how these properties are related to each other and affect whether the user can find the required information.

For example, if the sizes of HTML files are large as shown in node *a* of Figure 5.4, the Web Server will need a long time to transmit a file from the server side to the client side. This results in Web Server's long response time as link *b* and node *c* shown. When the response time is longer than the time-out setting, the browser will regard the requested file as unavailable. This implies that the required information cannot be found, which is a negative phenomenon of the system's usability. This is depicted in Figure 5.4 by link *d* and node *e*. Therefore, using this quality model, we can infer that to achieve a good usability, the software designer should make each web page a reasonable size to avoid excessive response time.

Similarly, Figure 5.4 also shows how the compatibility of the client side (node *f*) and the broken links in the HTML files (node *h*) will affect the usability of the system through links *g* and *k*, and so on.

It is worth noting that the links between the nodes must be understood as the implications of one phenomenon to another, rather than simply the relationship between two quality attributes. For example, a collection of large-sized HTML files may contain fewer hyperlinks between them than a collection of smaller-sized files that contain the same information. This makes the navigation between the files easier, which is a positive observable phenomenon of the navigability of the HTML files (node *i*). Consequently, the user may find it easier to locate required information, which is a positive phenomenon of system's usability (node *j*). Therefore, the property that the HTML files are of large size is positively related to the usability of the system. On the other hand, as discussed above, large-sized HTML files will increase the response time and in extreme cases may cause poor usability.

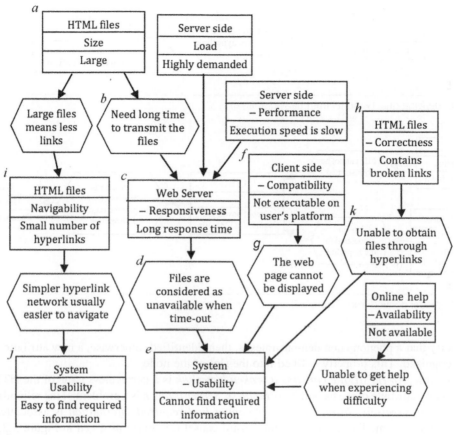

**FIGURE 5.4**

Example of quality model.

Such complexity cannot be represented in a quality model that only relates two abstract quality attributes as in hierarchical and relational models.

## 5.2.2 Construction of a quality model

The construction of a quality model takes the information charted in the cause-consequence analysis form as input. Each hazard in the chart forms a node with the component and phenomenon as specified in the form. Each row in the chart forms a link from the node that represents the cause to the node that represents the hazard. The explanation column of the row forms the reason of the link. For example, from the first row in Figure 5.2, the nodes and the link in Figure 5.5 are generated.

The nodes and links representing the hazards and their causal relationships are thus assembled together to form a diagram. However, such a diagram generated from a hazard analysis chart may be incomplete. The property slots of the nodes need to be filled in. In some cases, the quality-carrying property is the same as the property that the guide word is applied to. Otherwise, the observable phenomenon is compared with the definitions of a set of quality attributes and quality-carrying properties.

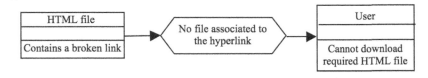

**FIGURE 5.5**

Example of deriving quality model from hazard analysis.

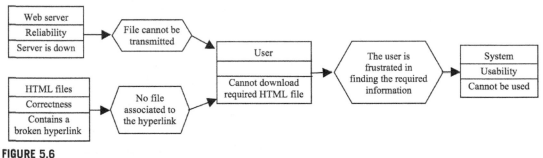

**FIGURE 5.6**

The quality model derived from Figure 5.2.

The property that a phenomenon demonstrates is, then, identified; otherwise, a new attribute or property is recognized. This property is filled into the slot of the node.

For example, *An HTML file contains a broken hyperlink* is a correctness issue of the HTML file, thus the quality attribute of the hazard is *correctness*. *Server is down* is a problem of the reliability of the server, or more precisely, *availability. User cannot find required information* is associated to the *usability* of the system. Therefore, from the hazard causal relationships given in Figure 5.2, we can derive the quality model shown in Figure 5.6.

## 5.3 REASONING ABOUT SOFTWARE QUALITY

In this section, we discuss various tasks of quality analysis at the software design stage and how they can be supported by automated tools. The algorithms for such tool support are presented.

### 5.3.1 Contribution factors of a quality attribute

In the analysis of a software architectural design, we often want to know how a quality issue is addressed. We want to know which components, connectors, or properties of the configuration are related to the quality issue and how they collectively provide the solution to meet quality requirements. The contribution factors of a quality attribute is a set of properties of the components and/or connectors or other design decisions such as the configuration of the architecture that affect the quality issue according to the design.

For example, consider the quality model given in Figure 5.4. We can derive the sub-graph shown in Figure 5.7 for the contribution factors of a server's responsiveness.

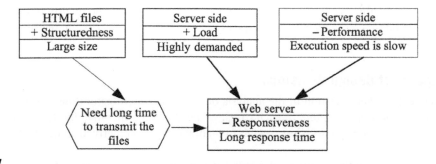

**FIGURE 5.7**

Factors contributing to server's responsiveness.

This quality analysis task can be automatically performed by using the following algorithm. Note that, given link *L* from node *A* to node *B* in a quality model, we say that node *A* is the *tail* of the link *L* and *B* are the *head* of *L*.

```
ALGORITHM A1
    INPUT:
        QualityModel (* which is < NodeList, LinkList >*);
        Component; (* the name of the component *)
        QualityAttribute; (* the quality attribute *)
    OUTPUT:
        RelatedNodeList;
        RelatedLinkList;
    BEGIN
        RelatedNodeList := { };
        RelatedLinkList := { };
        FOR each node N in NodeList DO
            IF (N's component name ==Component) AND (N's property ==QualityAttribute)
            THEN add N into RelatedNodeList;
        END_FOR;
        REPEAT
            FOR each link L in LinkList DO
                IF (L's head is in RelatedNodeList) AND (L's head is not equal to L's tail)?
                THEN
                    IF L is not in RelatedLinkList
                    THEN Add link L to RelatedLinkList;
                    IF L's tail is not in RelatedNodeList
                    THEN Add L's tail to RelatedNodeList;
                END_IF
            END_FOR;
        UNTIL no more element is added into RelatedLinkList or RelatedNodeList;
        OUTPUT RelatedLinkList and RelatedNodeList;
    END
END_ALGORITHM
```

Informally, Algorithm A1 searches for all the nodes and the links in the quality model that link to the nodes containing the component and its quality attribute that the user is interested in.

## 5.3.2 Impacts of design decisions

Another frequently asked question in the analysis of a software architectural design is *What are the consequences of a design decision*? In such cases, we need to find out what are the quality attributes that are affected by the design decision. Such information can also be derived from a well-constructed quality model.

For example, consider the quality model depicted in Figure 5.4. We can obtain the sub-graph shown in Figure 5.8 that represents the impacts of the quality-carrying property of HTML file's size on other quality attributes. It shows that the size of HTML files affects the navigability and responsiveness of the system, which in turn affects the usability of the whole system.

This analysis task can be automated by using the following algorithm.

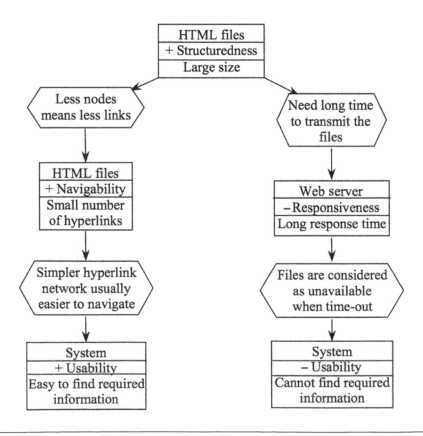

**FIGURE 5.8**

Example of the impacts of a design decision on system quality.

```
ALGORITHM A2
   INPUT:
      QualityModel (* which is < NodeList, LinkList >*);
      Component (* the name of the component *),
      QualityAttribute (* the property of the component *),
   OUTPUT:
      EffectedNodeList;
      EffectedLinkList;
   BEGIN
      EffectedNodeList := { };
      FOR each node N in NodeList DO
         IF (N's component name ==Component) AND (N's property== QualityAttribute)
         THEN add N into EffectedNodeList;
      END_FOR;
      EffectedLinkList := { };
      REPEAT
         FOR each link L in LinkList DO
            IF (L's tail is in EffectedNodeList) AND (L's head is not equal to L's tail)?
            THEN
               IF L is not in EffectedLinkList THEN Add link L to EffectedLinkList;
               IF L's head is not in EffectedNodeList
               THEN Add L's head to EffectedNodeList;
            END_IF
         END_FOR;
      UNTIL no more element is added into EffectedLinkList or EffectedNodeList;
      OUTPUT EffectedLinkList and EffectedNodeList;
   END
END_ALGORITHM
```

Informally, Algorithm A2 searches for the subset of nodes and links in the quality model to which the node(s) with user interested component and quality are directly or indirectly linked.

### 5.3.3 Quality risks

A design decision may have positive as well as negative effects on a quality attribute. The negative effects may impose quality risks to the system. Therefore, it is often desirable to know what are the quality risks. This can also be derived from a quality model.

A negative effect of a design decision can be recognized by searching for the links and nodes in the quality model that have a negative effect on the quality attribute. Such a negative effect could be in one of the following two forms.

First, there is a negative indicator in a node while there is a positive influence factor on the link. In this case, if the phenomenon of the node is observed, the quality will be worse on that attribute.

Second, there is a negative influence factor on the link while there is a positive indicator on the node. In this case, the phenomenon that indicates a better value of the quality attribute will be prohibited from happening.

For example, in the quality model depicted in Figure 5.4, there is a link from the node HTML files with the property of large size to the node Web Server with a property of responsiveness. There is a positive influence factor marked on the link between the large size of HTML file and the phenomenon of long response time. This is because that the larger the HTML file size is, the longer the response time will be. Because the phenomenon of long response time is a negative indicator on usability, a large file size has a negative effect on usability. Therefore, a design decision of large file size is a risk to the quality attribute of responsiveness. The further effects of a quality risk can be identified and analyzed. In certain cases, a negative effect, such as a quality risk, is not the consequence of a single design decision. Instead, it can be the consequence of a number of design decisions. In that case, all the causes must be identified so that a better design can be made. These causes can also be automatically derived from graphic quality models using the following algorithm.

```
ALGORITHM A3
   INPUT:
      QualityModel (* which is < NodeList, LinkList >*).
   OUTPUT:
      RelatedNodeList;
      RelatedLinkList;
   BEGIN
      RelatedNodeList := { };
      RelatedLinkList := { };
      FOR each node N in NodeList DO
         IF (N's influence indicator is negative)
         THEN add N into RelatedNodeList;
      END_FOR;
      FOR each link L in LinkList DO
         IF (L's influence factor is negative) AND (The indicator of L's head is positive)
         THEN add L into RelatedLinkList
      END_FOT;
      OUTPUT RelatedNodeList, RelatedLinkList;
   END
END_ALGORITHM
```

Informally, Algorithm A3 searches for all nodes that have negative phenomena of quality attributes and implications that prevent positive quality phenomena.

## 5.3.4 Relationships between quality issues

An important question to be answered in quality analysis is the interrelationship between two quality issues. For example, how is a server's performance related to the system's usability? Answers to such questions can be found from the quality model by searching for all paths from a node that represents one quality issue to the nodes that represent the other quality issue. The algorithm for this purpose is given below.

```
ALGORITHM A4
   INPUT:
      QualityModel (* which is < NodeList, LinkList >*),
      Component1 (* the name of the first component *),
      Component2 (* the name of the second component *),
      QualityAttribute1 (* the first quality attribute *),
      QualityAttribute2 (* the second quality attribute *),
```

```
OUTPUT:
    RelatedNodeList;
    RelatedLinkList;
BEGIN
    RelatedNodeList := { };
    RelatedLinkList := { };
    Node1 := NULL;
    Node2 := NULL;
    TemptNodeList := { };
    TemptNode := NULL;
    FOR each node N in NodeList DO
       IF (N's component name == Component1)
          AND (N's property == QualityAttribute1)
       THEN Node1=N;
       ELSE IF (N's component name == Component2)
               AND (N's property == QualityAttribute2)
       THEN Node2 := N
       END_IF;
    END_FOR;
    Add Node1 to TemptNodeList;
    CurrentNode := Node1;
    Search(CurrentNode, Node1, Node2, QualityModel,
          TemptNodeList, RelatedLinkList, RelatedNodeList);
    OUTPUT RelatedLinkList and RelatedNodeList;
   END
END_ALGORITHM.
```

In Algorithm A4, the following function of depth-first search is used.

```
FUNCTION Search (Component, Component1, Component2, QualityModel,
                CurrentNodeList, ResultLinkList, ResultNodeList)
(* Depth-First Search *)
    BEGIN
      TemptNode=NULL;
      FOR each link L in LinkList that L's head == Component DO
         Add L's tail to CurrentNodeList;
         IF L's tail == Component2
         THEN (* Find a path and record it*)
            TemptNode := L's tail;
            REPEAT
               Add TemptNode to ResultNodeList;
               TemptNode := TemptNode's previous node of CurrentNodeList;
               Add link TemptL( whose head == TemptNode's Next node of
                  CurrentNodeList AND whose tail == TemptNode)
                  to ResultLinklist;
            UNTILL TemptNode == Component1;
            Remove L's tail From CurrentNodeList;
         ELSE (* Depth first *)
            Search (L's tail, Component1, Component2, QualityModel,
               CurrentNodeList, ResultLinkList, ResultNodeList);
```

```
        END_IF
      END_FOR;
      remove Component from TemptList;
    END_FUNCTION
```

Informally, Algorithm A4 uses a depth-first search algorithm to search for a sub-graph of the quality model that contains all paths between two input nodes.

## 5.3.5 Trade-off points

In many situations, a quality risk cannot be resolved without compromising on another or a number of other quality issues because these quality issues are conflicting with each other. In such cases, a trade-off between the quality attributes must be made and a balance between them must be achieved through appropriate design decisions.

For example, consider the quality model depicted in Figure 5.4. The size of HTML files positively affects the navigability of the hypertext network but negatively affects responsiveness of the web server. Therefore, navigability is in conflict with responsiveness. A trade-off between them must be made so that responsiveness is within a tolerable range while navigability is also acceptable. Such a trade-off occurs in the form of deciding on a suitable size of HTML file. In other words, HTML file size is a *trade-off point*.

From this example, we can see that a trade-off point is a node in the quality model that has a negative effect on one or more quality attributes and at the same time it has positive effects on one or more other quality attributes. Trade-off points can also be derived from quality models automatically. The algorithm is given below.

```
ALGORITHM A5
  INPUT:
    QualityModel (* which is < NodeList, LinkList >*);
  OUTPUT:
    RelatedNodeList (* the set of trade-off points *);
  BEGIN
    RelatedNodeList := { };
    TemptNodeList := result from calling A3;
    FOR each node N in TemptNodeList DO
      FOR each link L in LinkList AND ( L's head == N OR L's tail ==N) DO
        IF ( L's head !=N AND (L's head's indicator == L's influence factor))
        THEN Add L's head to RelatedNodeList;
        IF (L's tail !=N AND (L's tail's indicator == L's influence factor))
        THEN Add L's tail to RelatedNodeList;
      END_FOR
    END_FOR
    OUTPUT RelatedNodeList;
  END
END_ALGORITHM
```

Informally, Algorithm A5 first searches for those nodes of negative quality by employing Algorithm A3. Then for each of such nodes of negative quality, it searches for the nodes that link to this node of negative quality as well as a node of positive quality.

## 5.4 **SUPPORT TOOL SQUARE**

To support the construction of quality model and the quality analysis of software architectural designs using HASARD method, we have developed a software tool called SQUARE, which stand for Software QUality and ARchitecture modeling Environment. It provides the following functions.

- Modeling software architecture in the visual notation proposed by Bass et al. (1998).
- Analyzing software architecture models using HASARD method.
- Constructing software quality models in the graphical notation.
- Reasoning about the system's quality using the quality model.

As shown in Figure 5.9, the SQUARE tool consists of the following components.

- The *Architecture Model Editor* supports software architecture modeling through an interactive graphical user interface and represents software architectural models in the *Software Architecture Visual Notation* proposed by Bass et al. (1998). Figure 5.10 shows the graphic user interface of the architectural modeling tool.
- The *Hazard Analysis Tools* help the developers to analyze software architecture using HASARD method. It records the analysis results and automatically transforms them into the graphic representation of quality models. It consists of three tools. The *hazard identification tool* helps the users to apply guide words to various attributes of components/connectors in software architecture models so that hazards are systematically identified. The *cause-consequence analysis tool* helps the user to identify the causal relationships between the hazards. The *quality model generation tool* automatically transforms the results of hazard analysis into a quality model in graphical notation. Figure 5.11 shows the interfaces of the hazard analysis tools.
- The *Quality Model Editor* provides an interactive graphical user interface to the users for the display and modification of software quality models.

**FIGURE 5.9**

Architecture of SQUARE.

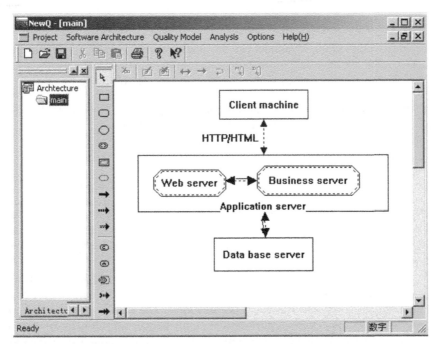

**FIGURE 5.10**

Interface of software architectural modelling.

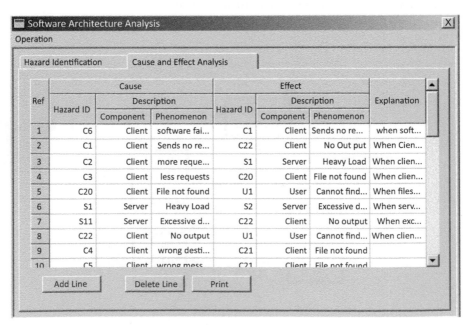

**FIGURE 5.11**

Graphic user interface of the cause-consequence analysis tool.

- The *Quality Model Analysis Tools* automatically recognize and identify the quality features of the software designs from a quality models when invoked by the user. The results of the analysis are also displayed as a diagram in the graphical notation of software quality models.
- The *Model Repository* stores the information about the architecture and quality models as well as the quality analysis results to enable them to be managed within a project and reused across different development projects.
- The *Project Manager* provides a graphic user interface to software engineers for managing the artifacts used and generated in the quality analysis process through accesses to the Model Repository.

## 5.5 CASE STUDY

A case study has been conducted with a real e-commerce application to evaluate the usability of the approach. This section reports the main results of the case study.

### 5.5.1 Research questions

The research question addressed in this case study is to test whether the proposed method and the supporting tools are practically applicable. This research question is decomposed into the following sub-questions:

- Can a quality model be constructed for a real-world software system with acceptable effort?
- How complex will a quality model be for a real software system?
- Can the quality model for such a real software system adequately cover the quality issues that a developer would be interested in?
- Can the automated quality analysis technique and the support tools derive the right quality predictions from the quality model?
- How well will the predictions of quality problems by the HASARD method match the real situation?

### 5.5.2 The object system

The object of the case study is an e-commerce system for online trading of medicine. The system is operated by the Medicine Trading Regulation Authority of the Hunan Province, P. R. China, to supply medicines to all state-owned hospitals in the province. Its main functions include (a) customer relationship management, (b) product catalogue management, (c) online trade management, (d) online auction of medicine supply bids, (e) order tracking and management, (f) advertisement release, and (g) a search engine for medicine information. The system was implemented in the J2EE technology.

The system includes the following functional components.

- *Management component*: Supports the management activities, including the management of information release, trading centers, users' membership, manufacture membership, permission of trade and/or production of medicine, and log information of online activities.

- *Content management*: Manages information contents stored, processed, and displayed by the system, such as medicine catalogues, prices, geographical information, and sales information.
- *Online trading*: Provides an interface and facilities for online trading activities and the links to other information contents such as catalogue, product information, and contract templates.
- *Public relationship*: Maintains the public relationship between the organization and its various types of customers, including sending out invitations to the public to bid on auctions, and so on.
- *Order tracking*: Provides the interface and facilities to track the business process of each deal.
- *Communication management*: Provides the secure communications facilities for sending messages and manages the mails sent and received by the system.
- *Report generation*: Answers queries from managers about various statistical data of the online trading and generates financial reports.

The case study was conducted after the object system was released and in operation for more than 1 year. However, the problems in the operation of the system were not revealed to the analysts involved in the case study before the predictions of the system's problems were made. This enables us to see how well the result of quality analysis matches the reality.

### 5.5.3 Process of the case study

The case study consists of the following activities.

- *Construction of the architectural model of the system through reverse engineering.* The system's design and implementation were fairly well documented. Access to the chief developers were available. The design documents as well as parts of the source code were reviewed. An architectural model of the system was constructed, which was reviewed by some of the chief developers of the system for approval of its accuracy. Figure 5.12 shows a part of the architectural model for the user management sub-system.
- *Application of HASARD method and construction of quality model.* The architectural model of the system was then analyzed using the HASARD method. The quality hazards of the system were identified. The cause-consequence relationships between the hazards were recognized. The information was then transformed into a quality model in the graphical notation. The quality model contains 70 nodes and 64 links between the nodes. For the sake of space, the details of the quality model are omitted in this paper.
- *Analysis of the quality model.* The quality model developed in the previous step was analyzed by applying the SQUARE analysis tools to identify quality risks and quality trade-off points and to derive the impacts of design decision on certain quality attributes and the contribution factors to certain quality attributes. More details are given in the next subsection.
- *Validation of analysis results.* The results obtained from quality analysis of the system were fed back to the developers of the e-commerce system. A workshop was run to validate whether the outcomes of the quality analysis matched the reality in the development and operation of the system. It was found that all our findings were consistent with what was observed in the operation of the system. Some of the phenomena observed in the operation of the system were satisfactorily explained through the architecture and quality models of the system. Based on the analysis results, a number of specific suggestions on the improvement of the system's architecture were made. Some

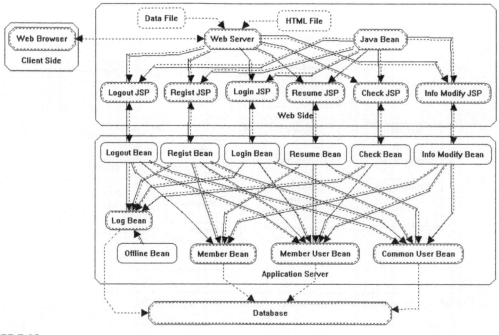

**FIGURE 5.12**

The architecture of the case study system.

of them were taken by the development team in the development of the new release of the system. Some would result in major changes of system's architecture and regrettably cannot be implemented within the budget of the new releases.

The following provides some details of the main findings of the case study to illustrate the kinds of quality issues that the method can discover and the kinds of analysis activities that the automated tools can support. Some sensitive issues related to the privacy of the system are carefully removed because the main purpose here is to validate our quality analysis method and tool.

### 5.5.4 Main results of quality analysis

In the case study, we discovered a number of quality issues of the system. The following are some examples.

- *Critical quality attributes.* One observation made during the operation of the system is that the some users complained that they cannot find desired information. In the case study, we analyzed the causes of the problem by finding the factors that affect the system's usability. The tool generated a sub-diagram that contains 35 nodes out of the 70 nodes in the quality model. This means that most components affect usability of the system. Consequently, we concluded that usability is a very

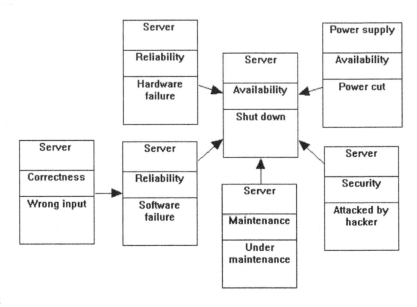

**FIGURE 5.13**

Example 1 of QA results in the case study: factors affecting server's availability.

sensitive quality issue in the design of the system. The generated sub-diagram provided detailed information about how properties of various components affect the usability of the whole system. Our case study provided useful guides to the developers for how to enhance the usability.

- *Contribution factors of a quality attribute.* Intuitively, the server's availability is of particular importance to a number of other quality attributes. To find out what are the factors that affect server's availability, we applied the tool and generated the sub-diagram shown in Figure 5.13. The diagram shows that the factors affecting this quality attribute include hardware reliability, software reliability, power supply, system security, and maintenance. Therefore, we can conclude that necessary measures must be adopted to prevent hackers from attacking the server, to ensure a reliable power supply and the stability of server's hardware and software system to avoid the server crashes, and to implement tools to enable online maintenance in order to reduce the time that the system has to be shut down for maintenance tasks.
- *Relationships between two quality attributes.* Our quality model can help us to understand the relationships between quality attributes. For example, the quality model demonstrated that usability of the client side is affected by performance of the web server. So we must consider carefully the system's hardware configuration and the deployment of software components onto the hardware cluster to balance the communication and computation workload according to the operation profiles.
- *Quality trade-off points.* In the case study, quality trade-off points were also identified. For example, we found that the size of HTML files is a trade-off point, because when the size is large, it has two different impacts on other quality attributes. On one side, the large-size HTML files will make users find necessary information through fewer clicks. On the other side, the large-size HTML

files also make the response time longer. Both of these are related to the usability of the system, but one has a positive impact while the other is negative. Therefore, it is a trade-off point. Another trade-off point identified in the case study is the granularity of session beans. A small-sized session bean can only implement relatively simpler functions in comparison to larger-sized session beans. Therefore, to complete a task, smaller session beans need to invoke more methods of other beans. This results in more execution time to complete a task. Consequently, the performance of the whole system declines due to the time spent on creating instances of session beans. On the other hand, if session beans are of a larger size, to serve the same number of clients, more memory will be consumed. Therefore, the granularity of session beans is a trade-off point between the response time of the system and the consumption of the memory space.

- *Impacts of a design decision.* As discussed in the previous sections, the impacts of a design decision can be easily identified by using our quality model. In the case study we derived a large amount of such information. For example, if the component of Internet has heavy traffic, the usability and performance of the whole system will be affected.
- *Key quality issues.* In the analysis of the impact of a quality attribute, quality risk points and critical quality issues can be recognized if the quality attribute has significant impacts on a wide range of other quality attributes. For example, in the case study, we found that the impacts of database's performance are extensive as shown in the sub-diagram in Figure 5.14, which is created by the SQUARE tool. It has the impact on a wide range of issues ranging from business layer to presentation layer. So it is necessary to take some measures to avoid a vicious attack and to ensure the stability of hardware and software of the database server.

### 5.5.5 Conclusions of the case study

From the findings of the case study, we answer the research questions asked in Section 5.5.1 as follows.

- *Can a quality model be constructed for a real-world software system with acceptable effort?*

In the case study, a quality model was successfully constructed by applying the HASARD method with the assistance of the automated tool SQUARE. Two persons (one PhD student and one MSc student of Computer Science) worked on this quality model construction task. It took them 1 month, including the reverse engineering effort. These two analysts were familiar with the method and the uses of the tools before they started the case study. We can draw the conclusion that quality models for such real-work software can be constructed with reasonable efforts.

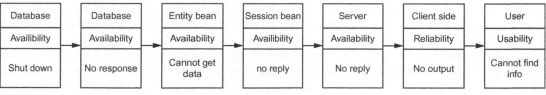

**FIGURE 5.14**

Example 2 of QA analysis in the case study: impact of database failure.

It is worth noting that the reverse engineering including the construction of the architectural model of the system takes about half of the time. It lays a foundation for the construction of the quality model. It is necessary to have a good understanding of the design of the system and to have good domain knowledge of the application. Hazard analysis of a design heavily depends on such knowledge as well as the knowledge about how the software system operates.

- *How complex will a quality model be for a real-world software system?*

The quality model of the system consists of 70 nodes, which is the largest and the most complicated quality model that we have ever seen in the literature. However, we found that the model is readable. The developers of the system validated the model by checking the information contained in each node and link. It is worth noting that we believe that a quality model of such a scale cannot be constructed without a structured method. Our HASARD method is capable of handling such a complexity and scale due to the structured approach based on hazard analysis techniques and the tool support.

- *Can the quality model for such a real-world software system adequately cover the quality issues that a developer would be interested in?*

Our case study found that the quality model adequately covered all quality attributes in existing quality models. Quantitative analysis of the quality issues were not covered because the original requirements and design document do not contain such information. Whether the proposed method can deal with quality issues quantitatively remains an open question that is not tested by the case study. It is one of the main limitations of the case study.

- *Can the automated quality analysis technique and the support tool derive the right quality concerns from the quality model?*

As reported in the previous subsection, the tool SQUARE was used to derive the quality concerns for each type of the quality concerns discussed in Section 5.3 and produced meaningful output. The use of SQUARE tool to derive quality concerns after the construction of the quality model took little effort, much less than 1 week by two analysts. For each query input to the tool, SQUARE responded within 1 s. The main time that the analysts spent on is reading and interpreting the output.

- *How well do the predictions of quality problems by the HASARD method match the real situation?*

The main findings reported in the previous subsection were all checked by the developers of the system. All these findings were confirmed and agreed upon by the development team, who are also responsible for the maintenance of the e-commerce system. Note that the quality problems of the system in the operation were unknown to the analysts before the predictions were made. Therefore, we can conclude from the case study that the predictions made by analyzing the quality model by employing our method were correct.

During the validation workshop of the case study, the development team were also asked if they had observed any quality problems in the operation of the system that were not predicted by the analysts. They answer was negative. Therefore, we can conclude that the predictions were also precise in the sense there no serious issues were missed in the quality analysis.

## 5.6 CONCLUSION

In this section, we conclude the chapter with a comparison of our approach with related work and a discussion of the limitations and open problems that deserve further research.

### 5.6.1 Comparison with related work

The work reported in this chapter is related to three groups of research: (a) software quality models, (b) hazard analysis methods and techniques, and (c) software architecture evaluation and assessment. The following subsections compare our approach to the related work in these three areas, respectively.

#### 5.6.1.1 Software quality models

The development of software quality models can be backdated to the 1970s such as the Boehm model (1978) and the McCall model (1977). Research on traditional quality models has been carried out in more recent years. Al-qutaish (2010) studied five hierarchical quality models, which are the McCall model, the Boehm model, the Dromey model, the FURPS model (Grady, 1992), and the ISO 9126 model. He compared the structure as well as the coverage of quality attributes in these models. Kayed et al. (2009) applied ontology extraction and analysis techniques to the definitions of software product quality attributes. They studied 67 most commonly discussed software product quality attributes and concluded that *there is a lack of consensus on the concepts and terminologies used in this field.*

The weaknesses of such quality models discussed in section "Related works and open problems" have been addressed successfully in our graphical quality modeling approach. In particular, graphic quality models make full use of the knowledge of the system's structure, where a node in the quality model associates an architectural design element, including the components, connectors, and configuration features, with an observable phenomenon of its quality-carrying property. The complicated relationships between various quality attributes can be represented by multiple links between the nodes. Our case study shows that such a quality modeling approach can represent complicated quality models of real software system adequately.

In this chapter, we demonstrated our graphical quality models as qualitative models. How to combine our graphical model with quantitative metrics is an interesting topic for further research. However, we believe that it should not be a major problem to include quantitative information in our graphic quality models. How to obtain and use such quantitative data in the analysis of software architecture is the key problem to be solved.

A closely related work on software quality modeling is the so-called activity-based approach proposed by Deissenboeck et al. (2007). In the activity-based approach, quality models are constructed based on two notions: the *facts* and the *activities*. A *fact* is a property of an entity in the system under consideration. It is represented in the form of [*entity | attribute*]. For example, the fact that *a class C is complex* can be represented as [ *C | Complex*]. An *activity* is an action that can be performed on or with the support of the system under consideration. Typical examples of activities are *attacking the system* related to system's security and *modifying the code of a class* related to the modifiability. In this approach, the quality of the system is manifested by how facts affect activities, where the impact of a fact on an activity can be either *positive* or *negative* depending on whether the fact contributes to the action positively or negatively. Therefore, the elements of a quality model are represented in the form of

$$[entity \mid attribute] \xrightarrow{+|-} [activity].$$

A model can therefore be depicted in the form of a two-dimensional matrix where the entity-attribute pairs are the rows, the activities are the columns, and the impacts are the cells in the matrix. The activity-based quality modeling approach was first proposed by Deissenboeck et al. (2007) for the quality of maintainability. It is generalized by Wagner and Deissenboeck (2007) and Lochmann and Goeb (2011), applied to security by Luckey et al. (2010), to usability by Winter et al. (2008), to service-oriented architecture by Goeb and Lochmann (2011), and combined with Bayesian network to assess and predict software quality by Wagner (2010). In 2011, Deissenboeck et al. (2011) and Wagner et al. (2012) reported a tool called Quamoco that supports the construction of such quality models. An evaluating of the Quamoco meta-model and the tool was reported in Klas et al., (2011).

Both the activity-based approach (and its extensions) and our approach are concerned with the properties of entities in a software system. However, we further include phenomena as an important part of quality models. The main difference between the activity-based approach and our approach is that we emphasize the relationships between quality-carrying properties while the activity-based approach is concerned with how such properties affect the actions to be performed on the system. Thus, the complicated relationships between the quality attributes cannot be modeled in the activity-based approaches. More importantly, our method covers the model construction process and automated analysis of the models, while their work does not.

### 5.6.1.2 Hazard analysis

Our software hazard analysis method is an adaptation of existing system hazard analysis methods and techniques for safety engineering (Leveson, 1995; Neumann, 1995; Storey, 1996).

In particular, we extended the concept of hazard in order to cover all quality factors besides safety in the construction of quality models of software systems. In our context, the word *hazard* has its widest meaning, which means any situation that may cause harm as designed or due to a deviation from the design decision.

One of the most effective hazard identification technique is HAZOP (MoD, 2000), which has already been adapted to analysis of software safety. Here, we further extended it for a wider range of software quality by redefining the guide words.

From software engineering point of view, the original FMEA method has a number of weaknesses when applied to software systems. First, the original FMEA chart is ambiguous about which component causes the failure. However, it is important to clearly identify the component that causes the failure in order to enable the construction of a quality model of the software. Therefore, we modify the format of FMEA chart to include information about the component that causes the failure. Note that by the word *component* we meant both software architectural components and connectors.

Our second modification to FMEA is that the indirect effects of a failure mode are not charted. There are two reasons for this: First, we found that for a complicated software system, the indirect effects such as those at system level may not be so clear when a component fails. Second, information about indirect effects are redundant because they will be analyzed subsequently as the effect of other failures. The system-level effects of a component failure will eventually emerge from such a chain of cause-effect.

Our third modification to FMEA is that we also included an explanation column in the chart so that the reasons why a failure mode causes another can be provided. This is for the purpose of validating the analysis results. Such reasons are usually obvious in physical systems, but we find that they are sometimes less obvious for software systems.

Finally, in addition to what hazard analysis techniques and methods do, our approach also links the results of hazard analysis to quality attributes. In particular, each cause of a failure mode indicates a quality attribute that the developers are usually concerned with. The corresponding consequences of the failure mode indicate what quality attributes the users are usually most concerned with. Note that both causes and consequences of a failure mode are stated as observable phenomena of the system. The abstract quality attributes that a phenomenon manifested must be identified. Consequently, the relationships between the quality attributes or quality-carrying properties can be established through such concrete phenomena. This enables engineers to reason about quality at a high level of abstraction.

### 5.6.1.3 Evaluation and assessment of software architecture

In the past decade, significant progress has been made in the research on the analysis of software architectures. A number of methods have been advanced in the literature to evaluate and assess the quality of software architectural designs. Among the most well-known are SAAM (Kazman et al., 1996) and ATAM (Clements et al., 2002); see (Dobrica and Niemela, 2002) for a survey.

Existing scenario-based methods are for the assessment and evaluation of software quality as exhibited in architectural design. They examine software architectures in the context of a set of scenarios, although the ways that scenarios are elicited and used vary. The set of scenarios serves as the criteria or benchmarks of the assessment and evaluation. A remarkable advantage of such methods is that the examination of software behavior can be performed in realistic situations. Moreover, the complexity of analysis can be reduced through focusing on typical scenarios. However, it is difficult to build an overall picture of the system's quality, especially when there are intensive and complicated interactions between scenarios. The elicitation of a complete and representative set of scenarios is by no means a trivial task, which is currently still a brainstorming and negotiation process. The result of quality analysis may heavily depend on the selection of scenarios as reported in practical experiences (Kostelijk, 2005).

Existing model-based techniques focus on one single quality attribute, such as performance and reliability, rather than relationships between various quality attributes. Moreover, they are mostly quantitative models.

Our method is fundamentally different from these existing works.

### 5.6.2 Limitations and future work

The work reported in this chapter has some limitations, and there are a number of open problems that deserve further studies.

First, the quality models exemplified in this chapter are qualitative. We believe that the quality models can be extended to include quantitative data. For example, a phenomenon may occur with certain probability, and the impact of one phenomenon on another can also be quantitative as in quantitative hazard analysis in systems engineering. The key open problem for quantitative quality modeling and quality analysis is how to use such quantitative data to predict software quality. This deserves further research and will significantly improve power of quality analysis of software architectures.

Second, architectural designs can be represented in two different approaches: (a) in the form of an architectural model or (b) as a set of design decisions (Jansen and Bosch, 2005; Shahin et al., 2009). The case study was carried out with an architectural model. Further investigation could be conducted to see how the approach can be adapted to analysis architecture represented in the form of a set of design decisions.

Another problem that is worthy of investigating is combining the activity-based approach with our approach. It will be interesting to see how hazard analysis can be applied to a software process model to derive the activities. Deriving activities related to a quality issue is a problem that has not been solved in the existing work of the activity-based approach.

Moreover, the automation techniques can only be applied once a quality model is constructed. The quality model construction process depends on (a) the knowledge of analysts and (b) good definition/specification of the architecture. This model construction process is a structure process, but still a manual activity. Further tool support for this process is worth further investigating.

It is also worth further investigation to integrate existing architectural analysis methods and techniques with the approach presented in this chapter. For example, a hazard can be considered as a scenario. Can scenario-based approach be adapted and integrated with our approach? For example, can scenario identification and specification be used to replace hazard analysis? Or, on the other hand, can hazard analysis be used to replace scenario identification in scenario-based techniques? Hazard analysis techniques have the advantages of being a structured and systematic process, while scenarios are concrete and easy to understand.

Finally, when quality analysis of software architectural design is performed in the context of software evolution, it is of great importance to study how the method presented in this chapter applies when the system is restructured, re-engineered, or integrated to another system. The particular research questions that deserve further investigation include: Can quality models be incrementally modified? Can analysis algorithms be revised to be an incremental algorithm?

## Acknowledgments

The work reported in this chapter is partly supported by China High-Technology R&D Programme (863 Programme) under the grant 2002AA11607. The authors are grateful to our colleague Dr. Sue Greenwood and Mr. Qingning Huo at Oxford Brookes University, UK, for their contribution to the research and Mr. Jian Wu of the National University of Defence Technology, China, for the participation in the development of the tools.

## References

Alkussayer, A., Allen, W.H., 2010. A scenario-based framework for the security evaluation of software architecture. In: Proceedings of the 3rd IEEE International Conference on Computer Science and Information Technology (ICCSIT 2010).

Al-qutaish, R.E., 2010. Quality models in software engineering literature: an analytical and comparative study. J. Am. Sci. 6 (3), 166–175.

Babar, M.A., Gorton, I., 2004. Comparison of scenario-based software architecture evaluation methods. In: Proceedings of the 11th Asia-Pacific Software Engineering Conference (APSEC 2004).

Bansiya, J., Davis, C.G., 2002. A hierarchical model for object-oriented design quality assessment. IEEE Trans. Softw. Eng. 28 (1), 4–17.

Bass, L., Clements, P., Kazman, R., 1998. Software Architecture in Practice, first ed. Addison Wesley, Reading, MA.

Bass, L., Clements, P., Kazman, R., 2012. Software Architecture in Practice, third ed. Addison Wesley, Reading, MA.

Boehm, B.W., Brown, J., Kaspar, H., Lipow, M., MacLeod, G., Merrit, M., 1978. Characteristics of Software Quality. North-Holland, New York.

Bosch, J., 2000. Design and Use of Software Architectures: Adopting and Evolving a Product-Line Approach. Addison-Wesley, London, UK.

Clements, P., Kazman, R., Klein, M., 2002. Evaluating Software Architectures: Methods and Case Studies. Addison Wesley, Reading, MA.

Deissenboeck, F., Wagner, S., Pizka, M., Teuchert, S., Girard, J.F., 2007. An activity-based quality model for maintainability. In: Proceedings of the 2007 IEEE International Conference on Software Maintenance (ICSM'07).

Deissenboeck, F., Juergens, E., Lochmann, K., Wagner, S., 2009. Software quality models: purposes, usage scenarios and requirements. In: Proceedings of the 2009 ICSE Workshop on Software Quality (WOSQ '09).

Deissenboeck, F., Heinemann, L., Herrmannsdoerfer, M., Lochmann, K., Wagner, S., 2011. The QUAMOCO tool chain for quality modeling and assessment. In: Proceedings of the 33rd International Conference on Software Engineering (ICSE'11).

Dobrica, L., Niemela, E., 2002. A survey on software architecture analysis methods. IEEE Trans. Softw. Eng. 28 (7), 635–638.

Dromey, R.G., 1995. A model for software product quality. IEEE Trans. Softw. Eng. 21 (2), 146–162.

Dromey, R.G., 1996. Cornering the chimera. IEEE Softw. 13 (1), 33–43.

Folmer, E., Bosch, J., 2005. Case studies on analyzing software architectures for usability. In: Proceedings of the 31st EUROMICRO Conference on Software Engineering and Advanced Applications (EUROMICRO 2005).

Franke, D., Kowalewski, S., Weise, C., 2012. A mobile software quality model. In: Proceedings of the 12th International Conference on Quality Software (QSIC'12).

Gillies, A., 1992. Modelling software quality in the commercial environment. Softw. Quality J. 1, 175–191.

Gillies, A., 1997. Software Quality: Theory and Management. International Thomson Computer Press, London, UK.

Goeb, A., Lochmann, K., 2011. A software quality model for SOA. In: Proceedings of the 8th International Workshop on Software, Quality (WoSQ'11).

Grady, R.B., 1992. Practical Software Metrics for Project Management and Process Improvement. Prentice-Hall, Englewood Cliffs, NJ.

Hofmeister, C., Nord, R., Soni, D., 2000. Applied Software Architecture. Addison-Wesley, Reading, MA.

ISO, 1992. Information Technology—Software Product Evaluation—Quality Characteristics and Guidelines for Their Use (ISO 9126). International Organisation for Standardization.

ISO/IEC, 2012. Systems and Software Quality Requirements and Evaluation (SQuaRE), ISO/IEC Standard, BS ISO/IEC 25021.

Jansen, A., Bosch, J., 2005. Software architecture as a set of architectural design decisions. In: Proceedings of the 5th Working IEEE/IFIP Conference on Software, Architecture (WICSA'05).

Kayed, A., Hirzalla, N., Samhan, A.A., Alfayoumi, M., 2009. Towards an ontology for software product quality attributes. In: Proceedings of the Fourth International Conference on Internet and Web Applications and Services (ICIW'09).

Kazman, R., Bass, L., Abowd, G., Webb, M., 1994. SAAM: a method for analyzing the properties of software architectures. In: Proceedings of the 16th International Conference on Software, Engineering (ICSE'94).

Kazman, R., Abowd, G., Bass, L., Clements, P., 1996. Scenario-based analysis of software architecture. IEEE Softw. 13 (6), 47–55.

Kitchenham, B., Pfleeger, S.L., 1996. Software quality: the elusive target. IEEE Softw. 13 (1), 12–21.

Klas, M., Lampasona, C., Munch, J., 2011. Adapting software quality models: practical challenges, approach, and first empirical results. In: Proceedings of the 37th EUROMICRO Conference on Software Engineering and Advanced Applications (SEAA'11).

Kostelijk, T., 2005. Misleading architecting tradeoffs. IEEE Computer 38 (5), 20–26.

Leveson, N.G., 1995. Safeware: System Safety and Computers. Addison Wesley, Reading, MA.

Lochmann, K., Goeb, A., 2011. A unifying model for software quality. In: Proceedings of the 8th international workshop on Software, quality (WoSQ'11).

Luckey, M., Baumann, A., Mendez, D., Wagner, S., 2010. Reusing security requirements using an extended quality model. In: Proceedings of the 2010 ICSE Workshop on Software Engineering for Secure Systems (SESS'10).

McCall, J., Richards, P., Walters, G., 1977. Factors in Software Quality, (Technical report CDRL A003, Vol. 1.), US Rome Air Development Center.

MoD, 2000. HAZOP Studies on Systems Containing Programmable Electronics, Part 1 Requirements; Part 2: General Application Guidance (MoD 0058). Ministry of Defence.

Neumann, P.G., 1995. Computer-Related Risks. ACM Press, New York.

Perry, W.E., 1991. Quality Assurance for Information Systems: Methods, Tools and Techniques. John Wiley and Sons, New York.

Shahin, M., Liang, P., Khayyambashi, M.R., 2009. Architectural design decision: existing models and tools. In: Proceedings of the Joint Working IEEE/IFIP Conference on Software Architecture, 2009 and European Conference on Software Architecture (WICSA/ECSA 2009).

Shaw, M., Garlan, D., 1996. Software Architecture: Perspectives on an Emerging Discipline. Prentice Hall, Englewood Cliffs, NJ.

Storey, N., 1996. Safety-Critical Computer Systems. Addison Wesley, Reading, MA.

Taylor, R.N., Medvidovic, N., Dashofy, E.M., 2010. Software Architecture: Foundations, Theory, and Practice. Wiley, New York.

Wagner, S., 2010. A Bayesian network approach to assess and predict software quality using activity-based quality models. Inform. Softw. Technol. 52 (11), 1230–1241.

Wagner, S., Deissenboeck, F., 2007. An integrated approach to quality modelling. In: Proceedings of the 5th International Workshop on Software, Quality (WoSQ'07).

Wagner, S., Lochmann, K., Heinemann, L., Klas, M., Trendowicz, A., Plosch, R., et al., 2012. The QUAMOCO product quality modelling and assessment approach. In: Proceedings of the 2012 International Conference on Software Engineering (ICSE'12).

Winter, S., Wagner, S., Deissenboeck, F., 2008. A comprehensive model of usability. In: Gulliksen, J., et al., (Eds.), Engineering Interactive Systems. Springer, Berlin, Heidelberg, pp. 106–122.

Woods, E., 2012. Industrial architectural assessment using TARA. J. Syst. Softw. 85 (9), 2034–2047.

Zhang, Y., 2005. Quality Modelling and Metrics of Web Information Systems. PhD Thesis, Oxford Brookes University, Oxford, UK.

# Lightweight Evaluation of Software Architecture Decisions

# 6

**Veli-Pekka Eloranta[1], Uwe van Heesch[2], Paris Avgeriou[3], Neil Harrison[4], and Kai Koskimies[1]**

*[1]Tampere University of Technology, Tampere, Finland*
*[2]Capgemini, Düsseldorf, Germany*
*[3]University of Groningen, Groningen, The Netherlands*
*[4]Utah Valley University, Orem, UT, USA*

## INTRODUCTION

Software architecture plays a vital role in the software engineering lifecycle. It provides a stable foundation upon which designers and developers can build a system that provides the desired functionality, while achieving the most important software qualities. If the architecture of a system is poorly designed, a software project is more likely to fail (Bass et al., 2003). Because software architecture is so important, it is advisable to evaluate it regularly, starting in the very early stages of software design. The cost for an architectural change in the design phase is negligible compared to the cost of an architectural change in a system that is already in the implementation phase (Jansen and Bosch, 2005). Thus, costs can be reduced by evaluating software architecture prior to its implementation, thereby recognizing risks and problems early.

Despite these benefits, many software companies do not regularly conduct architecture evaluations (Dobrica and Niemelä, 2002). This is partially due to the fact that architecture evaluation is often perceived as complicated and expensive (Woods, 2011). In particular, the presumed high cost of evaluations prevents agile software teams from considering architecture evaluations. Agile development methods such as Scrum (Cockburn, 2007; Schwaber, 1995; Schwaber and Beedle, 2001; Sutherland and Schwaber, 2011) do not promote the explicit design of software architecture. The Agile manifesto (Agile Alliance, 2001) states that best architectures emerge from teams. Developers using Scrum tend to think that while using Scrum, there is no need for up-front architecture or architecture evaluation. However, this is not the case. If there is value for the customer in having an architecture evaluation, it should be carried out. This tension between the architecture world and the agile world has been recognized by many authors (see Abrahamsson et al., 2010; Kruchten, 2010; Nord and Tomayko, 2006). The fact that many popular architecture evaluation methods take several days when being carried out in full scale (Clements et al., 2002; Maranzano et al., 2005) amplifies this problem. There have been some efforts (Leffingwell, 2007) to find best practices for combining architecture work and agile design, but they do not present solutions for architecture evaluation. In this chapter, we will address this problem by proposing a decision-centric software architecture evaluation approach that can be integrated with Scrum.

157

In the last few years, the software architecture community has recognized the importance of documenting software architecture decisions as a complement to traditional design documentation (e.g., UML diagrams) (Jansen and Bosch, 2005; Jansen et al., 2009; Weyns and Michalik, 2011). In general, software architecture can be seen as the result of a set of high-level design decisions. When making decisions, architects consider previously made decisions as well as various other types of decision drivers, which we call *decision forces* (see van Heesch et al., 2012b). Many of the existing architecture evaluation methods focus on evaluating only the outcome of this decision-making process, namely, the software architecture. However, we believe that evaluation of the decisions behind the software architecture provides greater understanding of the architecture and its ability to satisfy the system's requirements. In addition, evaluation of decisions allows organizational and economic constraints to be taken into account more comprehensively than when evaluating the resulting software architecture.

Cynefin (Snowden and Boone, 2007) provides a general model of decision making in a complex context. According to this model, in complex environments one can only understand why things happened in retrospect. This applies well to software engineering and especially software architecture design. Indeed, agile software development is said to be at the edge of chaos (e.g., Cockburn, 2007; Coplien and Bjørnvig, 2010; Sutherland and Schwaber, 2011). With respect to software architecture, this means that one cannot precisely forecast which architecture decisions will work and which will not. Decisions can only be evaluated reliably in retrospect. Therefore, we believe that there is a need to analyze the architecture decisions after the implications of a decision can be known to at least some extent, but still at the earliest possible moment.

If a decision needs to be changed, the validity of the decision has to be ensured again later on in retrospect. Additionally, because decisions may be invalidated by other decisions, a decision may have to be re-evaluated. Because of the need to re-evaluate the decisions, an iterative evaluation process of the decisions is required.

This chapter is an extension of the previously published description of the decision-centric software architecture evaluation method, DCAR by van Heesch et al. (2013b). In this chapter, we describe the method in more detail and describe how it can be aligned with the Scrum framework.

This chapter is organized as follows. Section 6.1 discusses the existing architecture evaluation methods and how those methods take architecture decisions in to account. Suitability of these methods for agile development is also briefly discussed. Section 6.2 presents the concept of architecture decisions. The decision-centric architecture review (DCAR) method is presented in Section 6.3. Section 6.4 summarizes the experiences from DCAR evaluations in industry. Possibilities for integrating DCAR as a part of Scrum framework are discussed in Section 6.5, based on observed architecture practices in Scrum. Finally, Section 6.6 presents concluding remarks and future work.

## 6.1 ARCHITECTURE EVALUATION METHODS

Software architecture evaluation is the analysis of a system's capability to satisfy the most important stakeholder concerns, based on its large-scale design, or architecture (Clements et al., 2002). On the one hand, the analysis discovers potential risks and areas for improvement; on the other hand, it can raise confidence in the chosen architectural approaches. As a side effect, architecture evaluation also can stimulate communication between the stakeholders and facilitate architectural knowledge sharing.

Software architecture evaluations should not be thought as code reviews. In architecture evaluation, the code is rarely viewed. The goal of architecture evaluation is to find out if made architecture decisions support the quality requirements set by the customer and to find out signs of technical debt. In addition, decisions and solutions preventing road-mapped features from being developed during the evolution of the system can be identified. In other words, areas of further development in the system are identified.

In many evaluation methods, business drivers that affect the architectural design are explicitly mentioned, and important quality attributes are specified. Given that these artifacts are also documented during the evaluation, the evaluation may improve the architectural documentation (AD) as well. In addition, as evaluation needs AD, some additional documentation may be created for the evaluation, contributing to the overall documentation of the system.

The most well-known approaches to architecture evaluation are based on scenarios, for example, SAAM (Kazman et al., 1994), ATAM (Kazman et al., 2000), ALMA (Architecture-level Modifiability Analysis) (Bengtsson, 2004), FAAM (Family-architecture Assessment Method) (Dolan, 2002), and ARID (Active Review of Intermediate Designs) (Clements, 2000). These methods are considered mature: They have been validated in the industry (Dobrica and Niemelä, 2002), and they have been in use for a long time.

In general, scenario-based evaluation methods take one or more quality attributes and define a set of concrete scenarios concerning them, which are analyzed against the architectural approaches used in the system. Each architectural approach is either a risk or a nonrisk with respect to the analyzed scenario. Methods like ATAM (Kazman et al., 2000) also explicitly identify decisions being a trade-off between multiple quality attributes and decisions that are critical to fulfill specific quality attribute requirements (so-called sensitivity-points).

Many of the existing architecture evaluation methods require considerable time and effort to carry out. For example, SAAM evaluation is scheduled for one full day with wide variety of stakeholders present. The SAAM report (Kazman et al., 1997) shows that in 10 evaluations performed by SEI where projects ranged from 5 to 100 KLOC (1,000 Lines of Code) the effort was estimated to be 14 days. Also, medium-sized ATAM might take up to 70 person-days (Clements et al., 2002). On the other hand, there are some experience reports indicating that less work might bring results as well (Reijonen et al., 2010). In addition, there exist techniques that can be utilized to boost the architecture evaluation (Eloranta and Koskimies, 2010). However, evaluation methods are often so time consuming that it is impractical to do them repeatedly. Two- or three-day evaluation methods are typically one-shot evaluations. This might lead to a situation where software architecture is not evaluated at all, because there is no suitable moment for the evaluation. The architecture typically changes constantly, and once the architecture is stable enough, it might be too late for the evaluation because much of the system is already implemented.

Many scenario-based methods consider scenarios as refinements of the architecturally significant requirements, which concern quality attributes or the functionality the target system needs to provide. These scenarios are then evaluated against the decisions. These methods do not explicitly take other decision drivers into account, for example, expertise, organization structure, or business goals. CBAM (Cost Benefit Analysis Method) (Kazman et al., 2001) is an exception to this rule because it explicitly regards financial decision forces during the analysis.

The method presented in this chapter holistically evaluates architecture decisions in the context of the architecturally significant requirements and other important forces like business drivers, company culture and politics, in-house experience, and the development context.

Almost all evaluation methods identify and utilize architecture decisions, but they do not validate the reasoning behind the decisions. Only CBAM operates partially also in the problem-space. The other methods merely explore the solution space and try to find out which consequences of the decisions are not addressed. In DCAR, the architecture decisions are a first-class entity, and the whole evaluation is carried out purely on considering the decision drivers of the made decisions.

Architectural software quality assurance (aSQA) (Christensen et al., 2010) is an example of a method that is iterative and incremental and has built-in support for agile software projects. The method is based on the utilization of metrics, but it can be carried out using scenarios or expert judgment, although the latter option has not been validated in industry. It is also considered to be more lightweight than many other evaluation methods, because it is reported to take 5 h or less per evaluation. However, aSQA does not evaluate architecture decisions, but rather uses metrics to assess the satisfaction of the prioritized quality requirements.

Pattern-based architecture review (PBAR) (Harrison and Avgeriou, 2010) is another example of a lightweight method that does not require extensive preparation by the company. In addition, PBAR can be conducted in situations where no AD exists. During the review, the architecture is analyzed by identifying patterns and pattern relationships in the architecture. PBAR, however, also focuses on quality attribute requirements and does not regard the whole decision-making context. It also specializes on pattern-based architectures and cannot be used to validate technology or process related decisions, for instance.

Many of the existing evaluation methods focus on certain quality attribute (such as maintainability in ALMA, Bengtsson, 2004, interoperability and extensibility in FAAM, Dolan, 2002, or some other single aspect of the architecture such as economics (CBAM), Kazman et al., 2001). However, architecture decisions are affected by a variety of drivers. The architect needs to consider not only the wanted quality attributes and costs, but also the experience, expertise, organization structure, and resources, for example, when making a decision. These drivers may change during the system development, and while a decision might still be valid, new more beneficial options might have become available and these should be taken into consideration. We intend to support this kind of broad analysis of architecture decisions with DCAR. Further, we aim at a method that allows the evaluation of software architecture iteratively decision by decision, so that it can be integrated with agile development methods and frameworks such as Scrum (Schwaber and Beedle, 2001).

## 6.2 ARCHITECTURE DECISIONS

When architects commence the design of a new system or design the next version of an existing system, they struggle on the one hand with a large number of constraining factors (e.g., requirements, constraints, risks, company culture, politics, quality attribute requirements, expectations) and on the other hand with possible design options (e.g., previously applied solutions, software patterns, tactics, idioms, best practices, frameworks, libraries, and off-the-shelf products). Typically, there is not a well-defined, coherent, and self-contained set of problems that need to be solved, but a complex set of interrelated aspects of problems, which we call *decision forces* (van Heesch et al., 2012b) (decision forces are explained in detail in the next section). The same holds for solutions: There is not just one way of solving a problem, but a variety of potential solutions that have relationships to each other and consequences; those consequences include benefits and liabilities and may in turn cause additional problems once a solution is applied.

When architects make decisions, they choose solution options to address specific aspects of problems. In the literature, these decisions are often referred to as *architecture decisions* (van Heesch et al., 2012b; Ven et al., 2006). The architecture decisions together with the corresponding design constitute the software architecture of a system. They establish a framework for all other, more low-level and more specific design decisions. Architecture decisions concern the overall structure and externally visible properties of a software system (Kruchten, 2004). As such, they are particularly important to make sure that a system can satisfy the desired quality attribute requirements. Decisions cannot be seen in isolation; they are rather a Web of interrelated decisions that depend on, support, or contradict each other. For example, consider how the selection of an operating system constrains other solutions that have to be supported by the operating system. Sometimes multiple decisions have to be applied to achieve a desired property; sometimes decisions are made to compensate the negative impact of another decision.

In his ontology of architectural design decisions, Kruchten differentiates between existence decisions, property decisions, and executive decisions (Kruchten, 2004). *Existence decisions* concern the presence of architectural elements, their prominence in the architecture, and their relationships to other elements. Examples for existence decisions are the choice of a software framework, the decision to apply a software pattern, or an architectural tactic (see, e.g., Harrison and Avgeriou, 2010; Kruchten, 2004). *Property decisions* concern general guidelines, design rules, or constraints. The decision not to use third-party components that require additional license fees for redistribution is an example for a property decision. These decisions implicitly influence other decisions and they are usually not visible in the architecture if they are not explicitly documented. Finally, *executive decisions* mainly affect the process of creating the system, instead of affecting the system as a product itself. Mainly financial, methodological, and organizational aspects drive them. Example executive decisions are the number of developers who are assigned to a project, the software development process (e.g., RUP or Scrum), or the tool suite used for developing the software.

Existence decisions are of highest importance concerning a system's ability to satisfy its objectives. However, during architecture evaluation, property decisions are also important because they complement the requirements and form a basis for understanding and evaluating the existence decisions. Executive decisions are of less importance in architecture evaluation, because they usually do not have an important influence on the system's ability to satisfy its goals, nor are they important to evaluate other decisions.

As one of the first steps in the DCAR method, presented in this chapter, the participants identify the architecture decisions made and clarify their interrelationships. Understanding the relationships helps to identify influential decisions that have wide-ranging consequences for large parts of the architecture. Additionally, when a specific decision is evaluated, it is important to also consider its related decisions, because—as described above—decisions can seldom be regarded in isolation.

In their previous work, some of the authors of this chapter developed a documentation framework for architecture decisions, following the conventions of the international architecture description standard ISO/IEC/IEEE 42010 (Avgeriou et al., 2009; ISO/IEC, 2011). The framework comprises five architecture decisions viewpoints that can be used to document different aspects of decisions for different stakeholders concerns. These viewpoints can offer support for making rational architecture decisions (van Heesch et al., 2013a). One of the viewpoints, the so-called *decision relationship viewpoint* is used in DCAR to describe the various relationships between the elicited decisions.

Figure 6.1 shows an example of a relationship view. The ellipses represent decisions. Each decision has a name (e.g., "Connection Solver") and a state. The state of a decision can be one of the following:

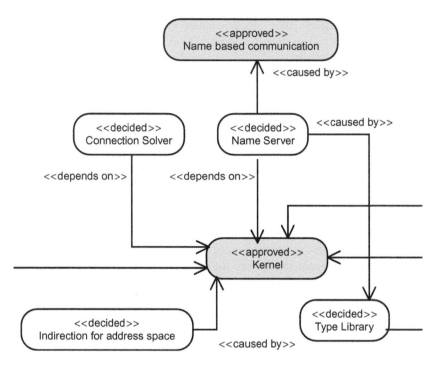

**FIGURE 6.1**

Excerpt from a decision relationship view model.

- **Tentative**: A considered solution that has not been decided so far.
- **Discarded**: A decisions that is tentative, but not decided for a specific reason.
- **Decided**: A chosen design option.
- **Approved**: A decision that was approved by a review board.
- **Challenged**: A formerly made decision that is currently put into question.
- **Rejected**: A formerly made decision that became invalid.

Theoretically, each of these decision states can be identified during a DCAR session; however, in most cases, a review is either done to approve decisions in the "decided" state (e.g., in a Greenfield project) or to challenge decisions that were already in the "approved" state (during software evolution).

Apart from decisions, the decision relationship view shows relationships between decisions, depicted by a directed arrow. Relationships can have one of the following types:

- **Depends on**: A decision is only valid as long as another decision is valid. As an example, the decision to use the Windows Presentation Foundation Classes depends on the decision to use a .NET programming language.
- **Is caused by**: A decision was caused by another decision without being dependent on it. An example is the use of a third-party library (decision 1) because it is supported out-of-the-box by a chosen framework (decision 2).

- **Is excluded by**: A decision is prevented by another decision.
- **Replaces**: A decision was made to replace another decision. In this case, the other decision must be rejected.
- **Is alternative for**: A tentative decision is considered as an alternative to another decision.

During a DCAR session, all types of relationships can be identified. As described above, it is important to identify decision relationships, because decisions cannot be evaluated in isolation. A decision relationship view makes explicit all other decisions that have to be considered as forces during the evaluation of a specific decision. The next subsection elaborates on the concept of forces in general. The use of the decision relationship view is described in its own section later.

### 6.2.1 Decision forces

When architects make decisions, many forces influence them. Here, a force is "any aspect of an architectural problem arising in the system or its environment (operational, development, business, organizational, political, economic, legal, regulatory, ecological, social, etc.), to be considered when choosing among the available decision alternatives" (van Heesch et al., 2012b). Forces are manifold, and they arise from many different sources. For instance, forces can result from requirements, constraints, technical, and domain risks; software engineering principles like high cohesion or loose coupling; business-related aspects like a specific business model, company politics, quick time to market, low price, or high innovation; but also tactical considerations such as using new technologies to avoid vendor lock-in, although the old solution has proven to work reliably.

Architects consciously or unconsciously balance many forces. It is quite common that forces contradict each other; therefore, in most situations a trade-off between multiple forces needs to be found. Conceptually, decision forces have much in common with physical forces; they can be seen as vectors that have a direction (i.e., they point to one of the considered design options) and a magnitude (the degree to which the force favors the design option). The act of balancing multiple forces is similar to combining force vectors in physics, as shown in the following example.

Figure 6.2 illustrates the impact of two forces on the available options for a specific design problem. The architect narrowed down a design problem to three design options for allowing the user to configure parts of an application. Option one is to develop a domain-specific language (DSL) from scratch; option two is to extend an existing scripting language like Ruby to be used as a DSL; the third option is to use an XML file for configuration purposes. Force one, providing configuration comfort for end users, attracts the architect more toward option one, because the configuration language could be streamlined for the application, leaving out all unnecessary keywords and control structures. Force two attracts the architect more toward option three, because this requires the least implementation effort. None of the forces favors option two, because extending an existing language requires some implementation effort, but on the other hand, it is not possible to streamline the language for the exact needs in the application domain.

Figure 6.3 shows the resulting combined force for the design problem. This means that, considering only configuration comfort and implementation effort as decision forces, the architect would decide to use XML as configuration language.

In more realistic scenarios, more forces would need to be considered. This is particularly true for architecture evaluations, in which the reviewers try to judge the soundness of the architecture. In DCAR,

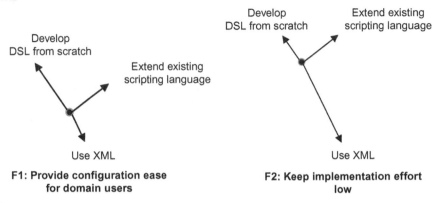

**FIGURE 6.2**

Two forces for a design problem.

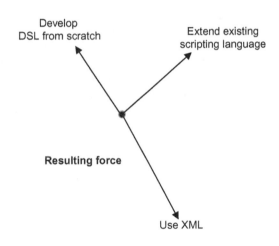

**FIGURE 6.3**

Resulting force for the design problem.

in order to get to a solid judgment, the reviewers elicit all relevant forces that need to be considered in the context of a single decision. Then the balance of the forces is determined. To help the reviewers to get a thorough overview of the forces that influence single decisions, but also to get an overview of the decisions impacted by single forces, a decision forces view (van Heesch et al., 2012b) is created.

Table 6.1 shows a forces view for the three design options mentioned above together with a few forces. The forces view lists decision topics (in this case "How do we describe configuration data?") and decision options for each decision topic in the top row, while the first column lists forces that have an impact on the decision topic. For each decision option and force, the intersection cell shows the estimated impact of the force on the decision option. This impact can be very positive (++), positive (+), neutral (0), negative (−), or very negative (− −).

**Table 6.1** Excerpt from a Forces View

| | How to Describe Configuration Data? | | |
|---|---|---|---|
| Forces\Decisions | Develop DSL from Scratch | Extend Scripting Language | Use XML |
| Usage comfort for domain users | + | 0 | − |
| Implementation effort | − | 0 | ++ |
| Error proneness | − − | − | ++ |
| Required developer skills | − | + | ++ |

When evaluating decisions in DCAR, the reviewers compare the weights of all forces impacting a decision option to judge its soundness. In the example shown in Figure 6.3, using XML as configuration option is a good choice in the context of the considered forces, while creating a DSL from scratch seems to be a suboptimal choice; extending an existing scripting language is neutral. Note that it is not always realistic to elicit other design options originally considered as alternatives to the chosen solution. The more common case is that decisions are evaluated against new design options or without considering alternatives at all. In such a case, extending an existing scripting language could be approved because there are no strong forces against it. We would argue that in both up-front design and in architecture evaluations, it always makes sense to consider multiple decision alternatives to form a thorough judgment on the soundness of design options.

Section 6.3 describes the DCAR method in detail.

## 6.3 DECISION-CENTRIC ARCHITECTURE REVIEW

DCAR comprises 10 steps; 8 of these steps take place during the evaluation session itself. The steps of the method with corresponding outputs are presented in Table 6.2. In the following subsections, participants of evaluation session and evaluation team roles are presented. Then each of the steps is explained in detail.

### 6.3.1 Participants

The participants of the DCAR evaluation session can be divided into two main groups: stakeholders and evaluation team. The evaluation team is responsible for facilitating the session and carrying out DCAR steps in schedule. Stakeholders are persons who have a vested interest in the system being evaluated. While it is beneficial to have people from different stakeholder groups present, DCAR requires only the lead architect and some of the other designers present. Typically, other stakeholders join the session when their expertise is needed. For example, during the analysis phase of the project under evaluation, it is beneficial to have requirements engineers, representatives of subcontractors, and the testing team available as participants.

**Table 6.2** DCAR Steps and Outputs of Each Step

| Step | Outputs |
| --- | --- |
| 1. Preparation | Material for evaluation |
| 2. DCAR presentation | – |
| 3. Business drivers and domain presentation | Decision forces |
| 4. Architecture presentation | Architecture decisions, decision forces |
| 5. Decision completion | Revised list of decisions, decision relationship graph |
| 6. Decision prioritization | Prioritized decisions |
| 7. Decision documentation | Documentation of most important decisions |
| 8. Decision analysis | Potential risks and issues, forces mapped to decisions, revised decision documentation, decision approval |
| 9. Retrospective | Input for process improvement |
| 10. Reporting | Evaluation report |

The evaluation team has the following roles: *evaluation leader*, *decision scribe*, *forces scribe,* and *questioner*. The roles can be combined, but it might require more experience from the evaluators, if they need to handle multiple roles. The roles are described in the following.

The *evaluation leader* facilitates the evaluation sessions and makes sure that the evaluation progresses and does not get stuck on any specific issue. The evaluation leader also opens the session and conducts the retrospective (step 9) in the end.

The *decision scribe* is the main scribe for the evaluation session. The decision scribe's responsibility is to write down the initial list of architecture decisions, elicited by the evaluation team during the presentations (steps 3 and 4). In the decision completion phase (step 5), the decision scribe will prepare a decision relationship view showing the decisions and their relationships. If necessary, the names of decisions and their relationships are rephrased. During the analysis (step 8), the decision scribe will write down stakeholders' arguments in favor or against decisions. In other words, the decision scribe continuously revises the decision documentation produced.

The *force scribe* captures the forces during the presentations (steps 3 and 4) and is responsible for producing a decision forces view during the review session. The force scribe also challenges the decisions during the analysis phase (step 8), using the elicited forces list.

The *questioner* asks questions during the analysis phase (step 8) and tries to find new arguments in favor and against the reviewed decisions. External domain experts can also act as questioners during the evaluation.

## 6.3.2 Preparation

In the preparation phase (step 1), the evaluation team is gathered, and each review team member is assigned to one or more roles. The date for the DCAR evaluation session is settled, and stakeholders are invited to participate. A preparation meeting is a good way to communicate the preparations needed. The architect is asked to prepare a 45-min architecture presentation for the evaluation. In the preparation phase, the representative of the stakeholders decides who is a suitable person to give the business and domain presentation. Typically, the product manager or product owner is instructed to prepare short 15-min presentation. Templates of both presentations can be found on the DCAR Web site.[1]

The initial schedule is also created during the preparation, so meeting rooms and other facilities can be reserved. If some of the stakeholders cannot attend the whole session, they can be informed when their input is needed and when they need to be present.

Presentations are sent to the review team before the actual evaluation so they can check if there are important topics not covered in the presentation and if a presentation needs to be revised. Additionally, the evaluation team members familiarize themselves with the system and read the existing AD. That way they can already recognize architecture decisions and forces and write down questions prior to the evaluation session. The evaluation team also prepares a tentative version of decision relationship graph. Additionally, the DCAR method description is sent to the stakeholders before the session, so they know what to expect in the evaluation session.

In the preparation phase, the target of the evaluation is also discussed. In some cases, the system is so large that it can't be covered in one DCAR session, so the evaluation is limited to certain subsystems or parts of the system. Additionally, the objectives for the evaluation are set. For example, if the system is to be replaced, the purpose of the evaluation can be to find out which decisions are valid in the old system and the same approach could be taken in the new system. The goal of the evaluation might also be to find areas in the system that need to be designed in more detail (aka boxes where the magic happens).

### 6.3.3 DCAR method presentation

The first DCAR step carried out during the evaluation session is the method presentation. However, it is advisable to start the session by having an introductory round in which all participants introduce themselves and their roles in the system development. The evaluation team records this information for the report. In this step, the evaluation leader gives a presentation on the DCAR method. The presentation is kept short. Later, in the beginning of the other steps, certain parts of the presentation might be recapped if necessary. The aforementioned DCAR Web site contains a template for this presentation.

### 6.3.4 Business drivers and domain overview presentation

In this step, the product manager or someone else who represents the business and customer perspective gives a short 15- to 20-min presentation. More time can be allocated for the presentation if the schedule allows it. The main goal of this step is to allow reviewers to elicit business-related decision drivers (forces). Typical forces identified during this step relate to time-to-market, costs, standards, contracts, subcontracting, or licensing models. The force scribe writes down the forces identified during this presentation.

### 6.3.5 Architecture presentation

The lead architect presents the architecture using the slides from the preparation step, following the given template. Typically, this presentation is 45 min in length, but sometimes it might take even 1 h. The goal is to give a good overview of the architecture for all participants and share architecture

---

[1]DCAR Web site: http://www.dcar-evaluation.com.

knowledge. The presentation is supposed to be interactive, and stakeholders and reviewers should ask questions to clarify issues that were left open after reading the documentation in the preparation step. The evaluation team should, however, avoid doing an analysis of the decisions on this step.

In this step, the reviewers complete the initial list of architecture decisions that were identified prior to the evaluation. Newly identified decisions are added to the list and names of decisions are rephrased if necessary. Additionally, the list of forces is continuously extended. The evaluation team also completes the decision relationship view created in step 1, but the focus should be on identifying the decisions.

Identifying architecture decisions might be challenging during the presentation and requires some experience from the reviewers. As a general rule, technologies to be used, such as servers, frameworks, or third-part libraries, are typical architecture decisions and should be recorded. Additionally, the application of a design or architectural pattern is also an architecture decision (Harrison and Avgeriou, 2010), so patterns can be used as a basis for identifying decisions, too.

### 6.3.6 Decisions and forces completion

In this step, the evaluators present the identified decisions to all participants. At first, the decisions are presented as a numbered list. The reviewers briefly present their understanding of each of the identified decisions. The decision names are rephrased if necessary to correspond to the vocabulary that the stakeholders are used to. In our experience the naming of decisions is crucial for the success of the following steps. If stakeholders misunderstand what is meant by the decision name, they struggle with the documentation step or they will document wrong decision. Generally, it is crucial to regularly include mutual feedback in the session in which participants explain their understanding of a force or a decision, instead of simply stating that they understood everything correctly. The question "Is it clear to you what I described?" is risky; it is better to ask "Could you please quickly recap what I just explained?"

During this step, one of the evaluators completes the decision relationship view (van Heesch et al., 2012a). The view is still refined in the following steps, but during this step the relationships of the decisions should be elicited. There are many types of connections between architecture decisions as stated by van Heesch et al. (2012a,b), but in DCAR mainly *caused by* and *depends on* types are used. The relationship view gives an overview of the decisions for the evaluators, and it can be seen from the view which one of the decisions has the most connections and thus are the most central ones. It also helps the evaluators to ask questions during the analysis. For example, using the view, the evaluators can question if another decision is a driving force behind a decision. Decision relationship views can be created using any UML tool or any other graph-drawing tools. Examples of a decision relationship view can be found on the DCAR Web site.

During this step forces are presented to the stakeholders as a bullet list. Stakeholders can complete the list if they feel that some significant decision driver is missing from the forces list. Forces can be freely described using the domain-specific vocabulary. For example, a music-streaming service could have forces like *"The software is developed by three development teams"* and *"The system should support A/B testing so that different advertisement locations in UI can be easily tested."*

### 6.3.7 Decision prioritization

If DCAR is carried out for the first time for the system, the number of elicited decisions is typically too large to analyze all of them during one review session. Therefore, the stakeholders need to prioritize the decisions; only the most important ones are documented and analyzed during the review session.

The other decisions can be documented and analyzed later in another DCAR session, if necessary. Typically, about 30 decisions are identified, but sometimes even more. According to our experiences, a realistic number of decisions to be reviewed in one DCAR session is between 7 and 12.

The criteria for the prioritization may vary from evaluation to evaluation. The criteria can be quickly negotiated between stakeholders in the evaluation session, or they can be previously decided in the preparation phase. The criteria could be anything from selecting mission-critical decisions to decisions known to bear high risks or decisions that potentially generate costs.

Basically, the prioritization can be carried out using any method, but we will present here the method we have used successfully. We have used two-step prioritization method. First, each stakeholder can mark one-third of the decisions as interesting ones. This is done so that the stakeholders do not know each other's choices. Then stakeholders state which of the decisions they would like to analyze. Different stakeholders may select the same decision. Every decision that receives a vote in this step is taken to the second round. Table 6.3 shows the results of the first prioritization round. Gray cells indicate the decision that was voted for the second round by the stakeholder. Global time did not receive any votes during the first prioritization round, so it is not available on the second prioritization round.

On the second round, each stakeholder has 100 points that he or she can divide for the decision in any way they like. On this round stakeholders can only vote for the decisions that were selected by some stakeholder on the first round. The purpose of this second round is to order the selected decisions regarding the assigned priorities. The goal is to analyze all the decisions selected on the first round, but if analysis falls behind the schedule for some reason, the second prioritization round should ensure that the most critical decisions still get evaluated.

## 6.3.8 Decision documentation

In this step, the lead architect and other stakeholders document the decisions that were taken to the second round in the prioritization step. Stakeholders should start the documenting from the decisions prioritized highest. Each of the stakeholders selects two or three decisions that they are familiar with and documents them using the decision documentation template (see DCAR Web site). Other decision documentation formats, which are presented, for example, in Harrison and Avgeriou (2010) and Tyree and Akerman (2005), can be used alternatively. The outcome of the decision is documented accompanied by the problem solved and considered alternative approaches. Additionally, arguments in favor of the decision and against it are documented. The list of forces collected during the previous steps is given to the stakeholders to help them to find arguments in favor and against the decision.

**Table 6.3** Decision Prioritization

| Decision | Stakeholder1 | Stakeholder2 | Stakeholder3 | Stakeholder4 |
|----------|--------------|--------------|--------------|--------------|
| Microkernel | 100 | 50 | 50 | 10 |
| QT for GUI | | 25 | | 90 |
| CANopen | | 25 | 50 | |
| Global time | | | | |
| *Gray background shows the first round votes.* | | | | |

Evaluators help the stakeholders document the decisions by guiding how the template should be used and asking questions about the decision. One evaluator can support two or three stakeholders by circulating and overseeing the documentation process. Usually support in the documentation step is needed because typically the decision concept is new to the stakeholders and the documentation quality affects the successfulness of the analysis—if the decision is documented well, the analysis will be shorter.

## 6.3.9 Decision evaluation

The documented decisions are subsequently evaluated, starting from the decision with the highest ranking. The stakeholder who documented the decision presents it to other stakeholders and to evaluators. During and after this presentation, the evaluators and other stakeholders challenge the decisions by coming up with new forces in favor of and against the decision. The decision scribe will add these new forces to the decision document during the analysis. These forces are then addressed by the architect, who explains why the decision is still valid or if it is not. These rationales are also recorded to the decision documentation by the decision scribe.

The force scribe uses the forces list to come up with questions that try to find out benefits and liabilities of the decision. The force scribe also marks how the decision interacts with different forces and creates a matrix with decisions as columns and forces as rows and marks in each column $++, +, -,$ or $--$ depending on how the decisions interact with the identified force. Pluses mean that the decision supports the elicited force while minuses mean that the decision is contradicting the force. The number of pluses or minuses indicates the magnitude of the force. Other markings like a question mark can be used to indicate that the relationship of the force and decision is unclear. This could be the case, for example, if the stakeholders are unable to articulate whether there a relationship between the force and decision.

Evaluators also use a decision relationship graph to find out how the decisions interact and how the some decisions might function as a driving force for other decisions. This graph is also constantly updated during this step.

The discussion on the decision and its forces continues for 15-20 minutes. If a particular decision seems to require more discussion, it can be flagged for future discussion, so the evaluation won't focus too much on a single decision. After the time has elapsed or when the discussion ends, the evaluation leader asks the stakeholders to vote on the decision, indicating whether they consider the status of the decision as "good," "unclear," or "needs to be reconsidered." Stakeholders vote by placing thumbs up, in the middle, or down simultaneously. The votes for the decision document are recorded as traffic light colors: green for good, yellow for acceptable, and red for needs reconsidering. Additionally, stakeholders are asked to give a brief rationale for their votes. This is also recorded to the decision documentation. After the voting, next decision is taken into analysis.

## 6.3.10 Retrospective

The last step of DCAR evaluation is retrospective where the evaluation process is briefly discussed. The evaluation team presents the deviations from the method and how the evaluation kept on schedule. Stakeholders give feedback on the DCAR process and make suggestions for improvement. Using this feedback is important, especially when DCAR is used multiple times, for example, as a part of Scrum. Scrum retrospective techniques can be used to facilitate the retrospective step, or the retrospective can be carried out just by having an open discussion.

## 6.3.11 **Reporting the results**

After the evaluation, the evaluation team collects all notes and artifacts created during the evaluation session. These are inputs for the evaluation report. Typically, the artifacts created during the evaluation session contribute directly to the evaluation report, and the report writing phase is merely stylizing the already produced artifacts as a report. The evaluation report is written within 2 weeks of the evaluation. In our experience, the best alternative is to reserve the next day after the evaluation for the report writing because the discussions are still fresh in mind. Normally, the report writing takes only several hours of the evaluation team's time. The report follows the table of contents presented in Listing 6.1.

When the report is finished, it is sent to the stakeholders, and a feedback session is arranged. If the evaluators have misunderstood some part of the system, it is made visible in this feedback session and the report can be corrected. After the feedback session, the evaluation report is revised and the final version is delivered to the stakeholders.

## 6.3.12 **Schedule**

A DCAR evaluation is carried out in 5 h, including lunch. The typical schedule for the evaluation is presented in Table 6.4. In our experience 30 min for the decision documentation may not suffice if the stakeholders are not familiar with the documentation template. So, when carrying out DCAR for the first time in a company, more time could be reserved for this step. Additionally, depending on the system size and how familiar participants are with the system, additional time for the architecture presentation is needed. In our experience, one and half hours for architecture presentation might not be too much in some cases.

1. Glossary
2. Table of Contents
3. Introduction
    1. Purpose and scope
    2. Review participants and roles
        1. Company Stakeholders
        2. Review Team
    3. DCAR description
4. System overview
5. Architecture decisions
    1. Decision relationship view
    2. Prioritization of decisions
    3. Decision forces
    4. Detailed decision documentation
    5. Traceability matrix for decision forces and decisions
6. Potential risks, issues and indicators for technical debt
7. Conclusions
8. Appendices

**LISTING 6.1**

DCAR evaluation report structure

| **Table 6.4** Typical Schedule of DCAR Evaluation | |
|---|---|
| 09:45 | Opening words, coffee |
| 10:00 | Presentation of DCAR method |
| 10:15 | Business presentation |
| 10:30 | Architecture presentation |
| 11:15 | Break |
| 11:30 | Decision overview and prioritization |
| 12:00 | Lunch |
| 12:45 | Decision documentation |
| 13:15 | Decision evaluation |
| 14:00 | Break |
| 14:15 | Decision evaluation |
| 15:00 | Feedback and retrospective |
| 15:15 | Session ends |

## 6.4 INDUSTRIAL EXPERIENCES

DCAR was developed to serve the need for a lightweight, but still effective, architecture evaluation method that can be conducted within the strict time constraints of software architects and domain experts, while producing artifacts that can be reused as AD.

Especially in early phases of the method development, we cooperated closely with industrial partners to refine DCAR and make it more accessible to a larger population of architects and reviewers. Later, we started using DCAR in our own industrial and academic software projects, where it has proven to work efficiently in several cases.

In this section, we first report on three small case studies that we conducted as external reviewers in different projects at Metso Automation in Tampere, Finland. Then we describe some additional observations we made when using DCAR in our own software projects.

### 6.4.1 Industrial case studies

The first industrial experiences with DCAR were made in projects from the process automation domain.[2] Table 6.5 presents descriptive statistics about the three projects. The company kindly allowed us to present aggregated statistics about the DCAR session but has not allowed the presentation of specific numbers.

All three evaluations were conducted within 5 h on one working day. All three systems were comparably large projects, reflected by SLOCs (Source Lines of Codes) greater than 500,000. The average number of decisions elicited during the architecture and management presentations, and completed in

---

[2]It is noteworthy that these systems are not regulated by law. Later we found that DCAR is particularly effective in regulated projects, which require detailed documentation and traceability between requirements, architecture, and design (for instance, in medical software that has to be approved by the U.S. Food and Drug Administration (FDA)).

**Table 6.5** Descriptive Statistics of DCAR Evaluations

| Variable | Value |
| --- | --- |
| Average system size | 600,000 SLOC |
| Average number of elicited decisions after Step 5 | 21 decisions |
| Average number of decisions documented in Step 7 | 9 decisions |
| Average number of decisions evaluated in Step 8 | 7 decisions |
| Average number or reviewers | 4 persons |
| Average number of company stakeholders | 4 persons |
| Average effort for reviewer team | 50 person-hours |
| Average effort for company stakeholders | 23 person-hours |

DCAR step 5 was 21. Roughly half of these decisions (nine decisions) made it through the decision prioritization in step 6 and were documented using the decision templates. Within the timeframe of the evaluations, and depending on the lengths and intensities of discussions, we evaluated seven decisions on average in DCAR step 8. We found it a good practice to stop the discussion of single decisions when we noticed that no new arguments were brought up.[3] We also observed a learning effect: We managed to evaluate more decisions from DCAR session to DCAR session.

The company stakeholders' effort sums up the time spent by the participants for preparation, taking part in the evaluation sessions, and reviewing the evaluation report. The effort for the review team is higher, because they need more time for preparation and for writing the review report. While the effort for company stakeholders is more or less stable, the reviewers' effort naturally varies from time to time, for instance, because templates for presentations and documentation can be reused and the process becomes more efficient.[4]

To gather qualitative feedback on DCAR, in addition to collecting quantitative statistical data, we carried out interviews with some of the DCAR participants from the company. The following list summarizes the main points we found:

- **Participants got a good overview of the system**: Especially in large projects, it is not uncommon that designers and developers only know the part of the system that they were working on. A positive effect of DCAR was that the participants were able to grasp the big picture and understand the role of their subsystems much better.
- **The open discussion of the entire system was appreciated**: A phenomenon that frequently occurs in software projects is that experienced senior members of the project team have such strong opinions on specific design problems and their solutions that it becomes impossible to have an objective discussion of other options. The participants of the DCAR session appreciated that all decisions, even if they were considered stable, were put into question again and could be discussed openly. The prioritization procedure in DCAR step 6 made sure that bias on behalf of the decision maker or the responsible architect was reduced. Our experience from many evaluations shows that

---

[3]If the participants realize that they are missing important information to form a thorough judgment, then the decision evaluation has to be postponed to another evaluation session. This, however, has not happened in our own evaluations so far.
[4]We publish some of these templates on the DCAR Web site www.dcar-evaluation.com.

the discussions are most fruitful if the review team is staffed with persons from outside the evaluated projects, ideally even outside of the organizational unit responsible for the project.

- **Decision discussions help to understand different points of view of the stakeholders**: Discussing decisions in a larger group of technical, nontechnical, internal, and external participants also helped the company stakeholders to understand different points of view that need to be considered in the context of a decision.
- **The review report is a valuable supplement to the system documentation**: The chief architects pointed out that the review report, which includes information about the architecture, elicited decisions, decision forces, and risks and issues, nicely complements the system documentation. It is even more effective to systematically use DCAR as a means to produce a part of the system documentation, rather than using the review report only as a supplement to existing documentation.
- **Good coverage of elicited decisions**: The interviewees estimated that the decisions elicited during the evaluation roughly covered the most important 75% of all significant architecture decisions; they called this an unexpected and excellent result given the short amount of time invested in the evaluation.
- **Identifying forces can be challenging**: Some participants mentioned that the documentation of reasoning, that is, forces in favor or against a specific solution, was challenging. This was particularly the case for stakeholders who had not taken part in the original decision-making process and for stakeholders who were inexperienced in architecture decision making in general. In subsequent DCAR sessions we found that providing decision examples to the participants with typical decision forces in the domain at hand alleviated the problem.

This subsection presented some empirical data we gathered in early DCAR sessions, in which we conducted the method with industrial partners and systematically gathered feedback afterward. The next subsection presents some additional observations we made in our own software projects when conducting DCAR.

## 6.4.2 Additional observations made in our own projects

In addition to the projects described above, one of the authors used DCAR in his own industrial software projects in the medical application domain. In one case, the author was the responsible software architect for the project under evaluation. In the other case, the author organized a DCAR review for a neighbor project in the same domain, developed for the same customer. Both projects have a runtime of multiple years (2 and 5 years) with peaks of 20 and 22 developers and testers. Empirical data was not collected during these projects, thus the following observations must rather be treated as experience reports that complement the earlier empirical studies.

DCAR has turned out to be a useful approach for performing lightweight and low-barrier evaluations in different types of software projects. We found that it is particular efficient in projects that require a consistent and complete documentation. This is, for instance, the case in regulated software projects that need to be approved by a government agency (e.g., the U.S. FDA for medical applications). In such systems, DCAR can be conducted not only to review the architecture, but also to systematically close documentation gaps in the architecture description (most importantly, the architecture decision documentation and the mapping to forces). To tap the full potential, DCAR should be planned as a project activity in the project management plan from the beginning on. Ideally, it is conducted after the architectural design is finished but before the architecture specification document is created as a project deliverable. The DCAR session can then use architecture views (e.g., different UML diagrams) and conceptual design documents as input, while the DCAR report is written in a form that its subsections can be taken over in the architecture specification document without further changes.

Another observation we made is that DCAR can be conducted in significantly less time (2-4 h) if the decision relationship view and the forces view are prepared by the architects as part of the architectural design process, rather than being created from scratch during the DCAR session. Apart from saving time during the evaluation, creating decision views during the design process can help architects make more rational decisions up front (see van Heesch et al., 2012a).

In Section 6.5, we describe how DCAR can be integrated in agile software projects using Scrum as an example.

## 6.5 INTEGRATING DCAR WITH SCRUM

Scrum is iterative and incremental framework for software development (Schwaber and Beedle, 2001; Sutherland and Schwaber, 2011). Scrum is one of the most widely adopted agile software development methods and has 54% market share, or 72% market share if Scrum hybrids are taken into account (VersionOne, 2013). In Scrum, all features that will be implemented in the software are organized as product backlog. A team takes product backlog items and splits them into tasks that are taken into the development sprint where these tasks are implemented. Sprints last for 2-4 weeks and produce potentially shippable product increments at the end of the sprint. This product increment is accepted by the product owner, who is responsible for the product being developed. If there are multiple teams, all the teams are working from the same product backlog and creating product increments simultaneously.

The architecture work in Scrum is not explicitly mentioned in many of the Scrum descriptions (e.g., Sutherland and Schwaber, 2011). However, the original Scrum paper (Schwaber, 1995) describes a pregame phase where the product backlog is collected and the items are analyzed. If this pregame incorporates architectural design, the natural place for the architecture evaluation would be at the end of the pregame phase just before the implementation sprints start. Recently, however, it is stated by Scrum originators (Harrison and Sutherland, 2013) that the pregame phase is part of the Value Stream (Poppendieck and Poppendieck, 2003) of Scrum. This implies that architecture work is carried out at two stages: up front before sprints start or during the development. This is in line with a recent study (Eloranta and Koskimies, 2013), where four different architecture work practices from the industry were identified. These four practices are up-front architecture, sprint 0, in sprints, and separate architecture team. Sprint 0 and separate architecture team are not in line with Scrum framework because there is no mention of sprint 0 in Scrum guide (Sutherland and Schwaber, 2011), and separate architecture team violates the principle of cross-functional team. Therefore, we will focus on how DCAR can be integrated with the up-front architecture approach and in sprints approach. DCAR integration with these approaches is described in the following subsections.

### 6.5.1 Up-front architecture approach

In up-front architecture design, the architecture design mostly takes place in the pregame phase of the Scrum (Eloranta and Koskimies, 2013; Schwaber, 1995). So the natural phase to evaluate the architecture is at the end of the pregame phase. ATAM or other scenario-based evaluation method might be the most suitable to use in this approach because at this stage it might be good idea to involve the developers and other stakeholders and evaluate the architecture. On the other hand, if there is need to document the made architecture decisions and forces behind these decisions, DCAR might be used as well, especially if the architects will not be part of the development teams implementing the software. Additionally, if there is a need to revisit the decisions made during the implementation sprints, DCAR could be used to revalidate the decisions.

In many cases, the up-front approach is used in large projects, where there are several development teams working on the project. So it is important to involve all stakeholders in the evaluation to gather decisions forces comprehensively. This also helps the product owner to make sure that product backlog items are enabling and the right ones. In other words, this process helps to increase confidence that the teams will be building the right product.

If DCAR is used in the up-front architecture approach, all steps of DCAR need to be used. However, the decision documentation step can be omitted if the architecture decisions are already documented during the architecture design. In authors' experience, this rarely still is the case, and the decisions need to be documented during the evaluation. Because DCAR will be used only once during the project in this approach, the retrospective and discussion on lessons learned stage is optional. Still, retrospective is strongly encouraged because it is a good opportunity to improve the process.

## 6.5.2 In sprints approach

Another option is to carry out DCAR within Sprints. However, this requires the team or other stake-holders to convince the product owner that performing DCAR will create value. If the product owner sees that there is value in DCAR, it is put into product backlog as product backlog Item. In this way, DCAR becomes something to be done within a sprint (a sprint backlog Item) and is carried out as a part of normal work during a Sprint. Because DCAR takes only half a day, it does not fill the whole sprint, but just part of the sprint backlog. This is the most practical approach and lets the product owner decide if there is enough value in DCAR evaluation. If multiple evaluations are required, then after the first evaluation, DCAR evaluation is put back to the product backlog after carrying it out. In this way, DCAR can be used after every sprint if the product owner sees that there is value for the customer to have continuous evaluation of architecture decisions.

In sprints approach, the architecture is designed by the team(s) in sprints (Eloranta and Koskimies, 2013) and the architecture decisions are made within one team or between multiple development teams. The decisions should be documented and evaluated within the sprint with stakeholders and other teams.

The most important and the biggest architecture decisions are typically made in the beginning of the project; these need to be discussed with other teams (Fairbanks, 2010). The rest of the decisions build on these earlier decisions, and in many cases concern only a part of the system. So, in this approach, the importance of architecture evaluation decreases gradually after each sprint. However, the evaluation should be carried out whenever architecture decisions are made in sprint or new information and decisions to be made emerge that might affect the forces in other decisions as well. Of course, there also has to be value in the evaluation for the customer. In addition, evaluation sessions enable the communication between teams on the architectural issues, so their value might come from information sharing.

In this approach, DCAR presentation (step 1) is needed only in the first DCAR session, if the participants are not familiar with the method. Business presentation (step 2) is needed once in the beginning of the project and it might be necessary to recap once in a while to see that all the business goals are met with the architecture. Architecture presentation (step 3) is optional and needed only when the participants are not familiar with the architecture being evaluated. However, if the system is very large and there are a lot of stakeholders and teams, introduction to the architecture is highly recommended.

Decisions and forces should be recorded as they are encountered during the design. Other teams might help in this identification process, and this step could also be carried out as a first step of iterative DCAR, for example, discussing what kind of things have occurred during the sprint that affected the decisions and what kind of constraints there have been. This can also contribute to the "lessons learned" session of the sprint.

Because DCAR is carried out incrementally, there should be small enough number of decisions per one session; a separate prioritization (step 6) is not usually needed. Of course, if in some sprint there are a lot of decisions that need to be discussed, some prioritization might be needed.

In this approach DCAR is carried out incrementally and iteratively, so in the spirit of agile methods, the team should also seek ways to improve the architecture evaluation process. After each DCAR session, the team should discuss in retrospective session (step 9) how the evaluation went and if was it useful. This discussion aims at finding ways to improve the method and the way it is applied in the organization. It also serves as an input for the product owner to see if there is a need for another DCAR session.

The method should be adapted to fit the needs of the current project. If any steps do not seem to be sensible in the context of current project, the step should be skipped.

## 6.6 CONCLUSIONS

In this chapter, we have presented DCAR, a lightweight method to evaluate architecture decisions. In contrast to scenario-based methods, DCAR focuses on the evaluation of individual decisions, rather than on a holistic evaluation of the whole architecture. This makes DCAR suitable for agile software development, because architecture decisions can be validated as they emerge in the process, decision by decision. The method uses forces as a key concept to capture the drivers of architecture decisions. If the decision does not balance the forces, it should be reconsidered. Similarly, if the forces are significantly changed, the decision should be revisited.

The main benefit of DCAR method is that the architecture decisions and their motivation are analyzed in detail. On the other hand, because DCAR focuses on the made decisions or on decisions to be made, the method might not be as suitable as scenario-based methods to elicit new trends and potential change areas from the stakeholders.

We have proposed different ways to integrate the DCAR method as an integral part of the Scrum software development framework, based on the observed real-life software architecture practices in Scrum. Adaptation will be required still, but this work is expected to give practitioners a good basis to build upon. Experiences from the industrial evaluations presented in this chapter demonstrate that architecture evaluation of a realistic system can be carried out using DCAR method in half a day. The future work will include reporting experiences from the practice how architecture evaluation can be used iteratively and incrementally.

## Acknowledgments

The authors would like to thank industrial participants of Sulava project: Metso Automation, Sandvik Mining and Construction, Cybercom, Wapice, Vincit, and John Deere Forestry. This work has been funded by the Finnish Funding Agency for Technology and Innovation (TEKES).

# References

Abrahamsson, P., Babar, M., Kruchten, P., 2010. Agility and architecture: can they coexist? IEEE Softw. 27 (2), 16–22.

Agile Alliance, 2001. Manifesto for Agile Software Development. Retrieved May 9, 2012, from, http://agilemanifesto.org.

Avgeriou, P., Lago, P., Kruchten, P., 2009. Towards using architectural knowledge. ACM Sigsoft Softw. Eng. Notes. 34 (2), 27–30.

Bass, L., Clements, P., Kazman, R., 2003. Software Architecture in Practice, second ed. Addison-Wesley, Boston, MA.

Bengtsson, P.-O., 2004. Architecture-level modifiability analysis (ALMA). J. Syst. Softw. 69 (1-2), 129–147.

Christensen, H., Hansen, K.M., Lindström, B., 2010. Lightweight and continuous architectural software quality assurance using the aSQA technique. In: Proceedings of the Fourth European Conference on Software Architecture (ECSA), pp. 118–132.

Clements, P., 2000. Active Reviews for Intermediate Designs. Carnegie-Mellon University, Pittsburgh.

Clements, P., Kazman, R., Klein, M., 2002. Evaluating Software Architectures. Addison-Wesley, Boston, MA.

Cockburn, A., 2007. Agile Software Development: The Cooperative Game, second ed. Addison-Wesley, Boston, MA.

Coplien, J.O., Bjørnvig, G., 2010. Lean Architecture for Agile Software Development. Wiley, Chichester.

Dobrica, L., Niemelä, E., 2002. A survey on software architecture analysis methods. IEEE Trans. Softw. Eng. 28 (7), 638–653.

Dolan, T., 2002. Architecture assessment of information-system families. Eindhoven (Ph.D. thesis), Department of Technology Management, Eindhoven University of Technology.

Eloranta, V.-P., Koskimies, K., 2010. Using domain knowledge to boost software architecture evaluation. In: Proceedings of the Fourth European Conference on Software Architectures (ECSA). Springer-Verlag, Berlin, Heidelberg, pp. 319–326.

Eloranta, V.-P., Koskimies, K., 2013. Software architecture practices in agile enterprises. In: Teoksessa, A., Mistrik, I., Tang, A., Bahsoon, R., Stafford, J. (Eds.), Aligning Enterprise, System, and Software Architectures. IGI Global, pp. 230–249.

Fairbanks, G., 2010. Just Enough Software Architecture: A Risk-Driven Approach. Marshall & Brainerd, Boulder, CO.

Harrison, N., Avgeriou, P., 2010. Pattern-based architecture reviews. IEEE Softw. 28 (6), 66–71.

Harrison, N., Sutherland, J., 2013. Discussion on value stream in scrum. In: ScrumPLoP 2013, May 23.

ISO/IEC, 2011. WD4 42010, IEEE P42010/D9. Standard draft. Retrieved December 12, 2012, from, http://www.iso-architecture.org/ieee-1471/docs/ISO-IEC-IEEE-latestdraft-42010.pdf.

Jansen, A., Bosch, J., 2005. Software architecture as a set of architectural design decisions. In: Fifth Working IEEE/IFIP Conference on Software Architecture (WICSA). IEEE, pp. 109–120.

Jansen, A., Avgeriou, P., Ven, J., 2009. Enriching software architecture documentation. J. Syst. Softw. 82 (8), 1232–1248.

Kazman, R., Bass, L., Webb, M., Abowd, G., 1994. Saam: a method for analyzing the properties of software architectures. In: Proceedings of the 16th International Conference on Software Engineering (ICSE). IEEE Computer Society Press, pp. 81–90.

Kazman, R., Bass, L., Northrop, L., Abowd, G., Clements, P., Zaremski, A., 1997. Recommended Best Industrial Practice for Software Architecture Evaluation. Software Engineering Institute/Carnegie-Mellon University, Pittsburgh.

Kazman, R., Klein, M., Clements, P., 2000. ATAM: Method for Architecture Evaluation. Software Engineering Institute, Carnegie Mellon University. Haettu April 22, 2013 osoitteestahttp://www.sei.cmu.edu/publications/documents/00.

Kazman, R., Asundi, J., Klein, M., 2001. Quantifying the costs and benefits of architectural decisions. In: Proceedings of 23rd International Conference on Software Engineering (ICSE). IEEE Computer Society, pp. 297–306.

Kruchten, P., 2004. An ontology of architectural design decisions in software intensive systems. In: Proceedings of second Groningen Workshop on Software Variability, Groningen, pp. 54–61.

Kruchten, P., 2010. Software architecture and agile software development: a clash of two cultures? In: Proceedings of 32nd International Conference on Software Engineering (ICSE). ACM/IEEE, pp. 497–498.

Leffingwell, D., 2007. Scaling Software Agility: Best Practices for Large Enterprises. Addison-Wesley Professional, Boston, MA.

Maranzano, J., Rozsypal, S., Zimmerman, G., Warnken, P., Weiss, D., 2005. Architecture reviews: practice and experience. IEEE Softw. 22 (2), 34–43.

Nord, R., Tomayko, J., 2006. Software architecture-centric methods and agile development. IEEE Softw. 47-53.

Poppendieck, M., Poppendieck, T., 2003. Lean Software Development: An Agile Toolkit. Addison-Wesley Professional, Boston, MA.

Reijonen, V., Koskinen, J., Haikala, I., 2010. Experiences from scenario-based architecture evaluations with ATAM. In: Proceedings of 4th European Conference on Software Architectures (ECSA), pp. 214–229.

Schwaber, K., 1995. Scrum development process. In: Proceedings of the 10th Annual ACM Conference on Object Oriented Programming Systems, Languages and Applications (OOPSLA). ACM, pp. 117–134.

Schwaber, K., Beedle, M., 2001. Agile Software Development with Scrum. Prentice-Hall, Upper Saddle River, NJ, USA.

Snowden, D., Boone, M., 2007. A leader's framework for decision making. Harv. Bus. Rev. 69-76.

Sutherland, J., Schwaber, K., 2011. The Scrum Guide—The Definitive Guide to Scrum: The Rules of the Game. Haettu June 7, 2012 osoitteesta, http://www.scrum.org/storage/scrumguides/Scrum_Guide.pdf.

Tyree, J., Akerman, A., 2005. Architecture decisions: demystifying architecture. IEEE Softw. 22 (2), 19–27.

van Heesch, U., Avgeriou, P., Hilliard, R., 2012a. A documentation framework for architecture decisions. J. Syst. Softw. 85 (4), 795–820.

van Heesch, U., Avgeriou, P., Hilliard, R., 2012b. Forces on architecture decisions—a viewpoint. In: Proceedings of Joint Working IEEE/IFIP Conference on Software Architecture (WICSA) and European Conference on Software Architecture (ECSA), pp. 101–110.

van Heesch, U., Avgeriou, P., Tang, A., 2013a. Does decision documentation help junior designers rationalize their decisions?—a comparative multiple-case study. J. Syst. Softw. 86 (6), 1545–1565.

van Heesch, U., Eloranta, V.-P., Avgeriou, P., Koskimies, K., Harrison, N., 2013b. DCAR—decision centric architecture reviews. IEEE Softw.

Ven, J.S., Jansen, A.G., Nijhuis, J.A., Bosch, J., 2006. Design decisions: the bridge between rationale and architecture. In: Teoksessa, A., Dutoit, H., McCall, R., Mistrík, I., Paech, B. (Eds.), Rationale Management in Software Engineering. Springer, Berlin/Heidelberg, pp. 329–348.

VersionOne, 2013. 7th Annual State of Agile Survey. VersionOne. Haettu May 15, 2013 osoitteesta, http://www.versionone.com/pdf/7th-Annual-State-of-Agile-Development-Survey.pdf.

Weyns, D., Michalik, B., 2011. Codifying architecture knowledge to support online evolution of software product lines. In: Proceedings of the 6th International Workshop on SHAring and Reusing Architectural Knowledge (SHARK'11). ACM, New York, NY, USA, pp. 37–44.

Woods, E., 2011. Industrial architectural assessment using Tara. In: Proceedings of the 9th Working IEEE/IFIP Conference on Software Architecture (WICSA). IEEE Computer Society, pp. 56–65.

# A Rule-Based Approach to Architecture Conformance Checking as a Quality Management Measure

7

**Sebastian Herold[*] and Andreas Rausch**

*Clausthal University of Technology, Clausthal-Zellerfeld, Germany*

## INTRODUCTION

The intended software architecture of a system captures the most far-reaching design decisions that are made during the development of a software system (Bass et al., 2003). It influences and determines very strongly the quality attributes of a software system. However, especially in complex and long-living software systems, it is likely that the realization of a system diverges from the intended software architecture. This effect is also known as *architectural erosion* or *architectural drift* (Perry and Wolf, 1992) and is hard to detect manually due to the size and complexity of software systems. These effects threaten quality properties of the system such as maintainability, adaptability, or reusability (Van Gurp and Bosch, 2002). Uncontrolled architecture erosion can lead to irreparable software systems that need to be replaced (Sarkar et al., 2009).

Software architecture erosion can be seen as a consistency problem between artifacts of software development processes. Consistency between artifacts has been intensively investigated in model-driven software development (MDSD) research, especially in the subfields of model transformations and inter-model consistency (Lucas et al., 2009). Nevertheless, Biehl and Löwe (2009) were among the first who showed that architecture erosion also might occur in MDSD approaches.

Model transformations describe the relationship between models, more specially the mapping of information from one model to another. Thus models are converted from one particular perspective to another and from one level of abstraction to another—usually from more to less abstract—by adding more detail supplied by the transformation rules.

It could be assumed that model transformations ensure that high-level artifacts, for example, UML models, are consistently transformed into low-level artifacts, for example, source code. However, the transformations in general do not create the entire set of low-level artifacts. Instead, they create skeletons that need to be manually extended and completed. Due to this semi-automation, projects developed with MDSD are also prone to the problem of drifts between the various models on different levels of abstraction and views with different perspectives. Such inter-model drifts can be introduced for various reasons, such as manual additions or incomplete or incorrect transformations (Biehl and Löwe, 2009).

Moreover, general purpose consistency checking approaches common in MDSD are difficult to use for erosion detecting in typical development scenarios. In these approaches, the specification of

---

*Lero - The Irish Software Engineering Research Centre, University of Limerick, Ireland

consistency constraints depends on the syntax of the participating models, and hence have to be repeatedly defined for each kind of model in which architectural erosion might appear. This redundancy limits the usability of these approaches for detecting erosion.

The focus and contribution of this chapter is in the area of architectural design within MDSD approaches. We will present an approach that allows integrating effective architecture erosion detection into MDSD more easily than existing solutions. Different models are represented as instances of a common ontology and architectural consistency constraints, which are called *architectural rules* in the following, are expressed as logical formulas over these structures. These are rules defined by architectural aspects like patterns that restrain the detailed design or the implementation of the system. The approach enables us to support a broad variety of architectural aspects in architectural conformance checking due to the formalization by first-order logics and allows us to integrate new meta-models easily because architectural rules are largely meta-model-independent.

The remainder of this chapter is structured as follows. Section 7.1 describes the necessity and the challenges of architectural conformance checking in more detail. Section 7.2 will give an overview of related work and approaches. The proposed approach is described in Section 7.3. In Section 7.4, the application of the approach in a detailed scenario as well as further case studies is described. Section 7.5 will address the contribution of the approach and its limitations.

## 7.1 CHALLENGES IN ARCHITECTURAL CONFORMANCE CHECKING

Software design activities can be separated into three groups (see Figure 7.1): software architecture, detailed design, and implementation (Clements et al., 2010). Artifacts created by those activities provide different views on the inner structures of a system with different levels of abstraction, adding more and more details starting at the most abstract view of the software architecture. As stated in the most common definitions of the term, the software architecture contains components and their externally visible interfaces (Bass et al., 2003; Hofmeister and Nord, 1999). These structures are refined during the detailed design and complemented by the inner structures of the components. The implementation, finally, provides the complete and executable system.

Current large-scale systems have up to several hundred million lines of code; large object-oriented systems are made of several thousand classes. Ensuring architectural conformance manually for

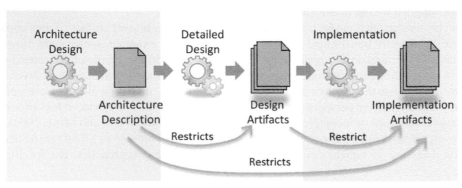

**FIGURE 7.1**

Architectural design, detailed design, and implementation in software development.

systems of that size and complexity is impossible and, even for smaller systems, time-consuming and error-prone. It is obvious for such settings that conformance checking cannot be performed manually. The software architect clearly requires tool support.

Figure 7.1 illustrates typical software development phases and the relationships between them. An architectural description, a model in MDSD, defines architectural rules that restrict the content of models worked with during detailed design and implementation. This is complex with regard to two aspects:

1. The set of artifact types—in MDSD the set of meta-models—used to describe the system that can be affected by architectural rules is heterogeneous and differs from project to project.
2. There is a large variety of architectural rules. Different architectural concepts, like patterns, reference architectures, or design principles can define rules that need to be checked in design and implementation.

Tool support that does not support these two complexity issues does not allow flexible and exhaustive architectural conformance checking. As a result, a probably expensive and hard-to-handle tool chain is needed for architectural conformance checking.

The inherent complexity of architecture conformance checking is tightened by the observation that the separation between the steps in the design process—architectural design, detailed design, and implementation—is most often unclear in both practice and research.[1]

Informal attempts to define a clear separation of concerns between architectural design and detailed design are made in software architecture literature with moderate clarifying contributions. Many definitions are along the lines of the one in Kazman (1999), which states that "Architecture [...] is design at a higher level of abstraction," without explaining whether there is a "threshold abstraction level" that distinguishes the two steps—and, if there is one, how it is defined. In Clements et al. (2010), the definition of software architecture makes a distinction: If software architecture is about the externally visible properties of components, detailed design is about the internal hidden properties. This definition does not help the effort to select an appropriate granularity for software architecture. Essentially, it says architectural things are those that the software architect defines to be architectural; everything else is subject to detailed design.

A clear distinction, however, is important for architectural conformance checking in order to clearly characterize architectural rules and to decide on the required expressive power to describe them. Theoretical work on the distinctions of architecture, design, and implementation, as described in Eden et al. (2006), exists but is not widely applied in practice.

In the following, we will see that the state of the art in architectural conformance checking does not provide solutions for MDSD approaches that provide the required flexibility.

## 7.2 RELATED WORK

As outlined in the section "Introduction," general transformation and conformance checking techniques from MDSD, like xlinkit, ECL/EVL, or similar approaches (Lucas et al., 2009; Nentwich et al., 2002; Rose et al., 2008) could be used to check architecture conformance, but they do not provide the required flexibility. Let us assume that a software architect wants to enforce the hierarchical layering of a system defined in an architectural model. He could define transformation rules that create

---

[1]The following explanations focus on the separation of architectural design from detailed design. In general, the confusion about this separation is much greater than that over the separation of detailed design from implementation.

for each layer a package in a UML model (for the detailed design of a system) with attached constraints allowing only dependencies in a way that the layering is followed.

The constraints, as part of the target side of a transformation rule, naturally refer to elements of the target meta-model and are hence meta-model-specific. In realistic scenarios with different meta-models in use for one software development project, a single architectural rule has thus to be manifested in many different sets of transformation rules. The constraint would have to be defined repeatedly for different meta-models, creating overhead in the process of maintaining the set of architectural rules.

On the other hand, there specialized approaches for architectural conformance checking. Passos et al. (2010) distinguish Dependency Structure Matrices (DSM), Code Query Languages (CQLs), and Reflexion Models as different techniques. *DSM* are a technique to represent and analyze complex systems in general (Steward, 1981). Regarding architectural conformance checking, approaches based on DSM represent the simplest form of checking approaches. The main idea is to represent a system as a square matrix. The value $e_{ij}$ denotes a dependency between the element $i$ and the element $j$ of the system, for example, modules and components.

*Lattix LDM* (Sangal et al., 2005) is a tool to create, analyze, and control a software architecture in terms of allowed dependencies based on DSM. In Hinsman et al. (2009), a case study is described in which Lattix LDM is successfully applied to manage the architecture of a real-life system and to execute refactorings.

That case study also shows what DSM focuses on and what kind of architectural rules are supported: Basically only dependency rules can be explicitly formulated. Hence, more complex architectural rules—for example, for different patterns—cannot be captured. Moreover, the dependency rules inside the LDM tool have to be kept manually consistent with an existing architectural model, causing additional maintenance efforts.

*Source CQLs* allow one to formulate queries upon a base of source code and retrieve single elements or more complex substructures from it. Such query languages can also be used to define queries retrieving elements that adhere to or violate architectural rules. In a similar way, constraint languages check constraints on a pool of data and can be used for architecture conformance checking. Examples of languages that can be used for this purpose are, for example, the CQL, .QL (de Moor et al., 2007), SCL (Hou and Hoover, 2006), or LogEn (Eichberg et al., 2008). Approaches based on such languages have in common that they often allow conformance checking for a small set of programming languages only and do not provide a high-level architecture model. However, given that these languages are mostly based on a relational calculus or first-order logics, they allow expressive architectural rules.

*Reflexion modeling* was introduced in Murphy et al. (2001) as a technique supporting program and system comprehension. Here the assumed or intended software architecture of a system is described by a high-level model, containing elements and dependencies as they are expected to be. After that, a dependency graph is automatically extracted from the existing system artifacts, source code in most cases. The graph created is also called the source model. In the following step, a mapping between elements of the high-level model and the source model is created manually, capturing the "common" elements of the intended high-level architecture and the actual structure of the system. As a next step, the actual comparison of both is presented in a reflexion model.

Reflexion modeling is implemented in many approaches and tools. The Fraunhofer *Software Architecture Visualization and Evaluation* tool follows the reflexion modeling approach (Knodel et al., 2006; Lindvall and Muthig, 2008) as does the tool *ConQAT* (Deissenboeck et al., 2010) and the Bauhaus tool suite (Raza et al., 2006), to name a few.

All reflexion-based approaches have in common that a mapping between architecture and source code elements (in fact, they all check source code but not detailed design artifacts) is required to keep track of how architectural elements are realized in code. In model-driven development, this information could be partially retrieved from persisted transformation information, such that manual creation of mappings could be easier or completely omitted. This redundancy of information is therefore a minor but not unsolvable drawback in the context of MDSD. The particular approaches illustrate that flexibility of conformance checking with regard to different artifact types is possible using reflexion modeling. However, compared with query language-based approaches or constraint-based approaches, their expressiveness to architectural rules is limited because they do not allow the specification of arbitrary constraints about the structures they define but focus on dependencies.

## 7.3 A FORMAL FRAMEWORK FOR ARCHITECTURAL CONFORMANCE CHECKING

The proposed approach consists of a conceptual framework that is based upon the formalization of models and other system descriptions as first-order logic formulas describing which properties a conforming system must have. Figure 7.2 illustrates the approach graphically.

A model $M$ (such as an architecture A, a detailed design D, or an implementation I) is transformed into a set of first-order logic statements $\phi_M$ that represents $M$ formally. The interpretations satisfying $\phi_M$, depicted as $S(\phi_M)$, represent those systems that conform to the model $M$. Formally, the elements of $S(\phi_M)$ are relational structures, consisting of a universe of entities and relations between them. Based on the sets $S(\phi_M)$, we can apply the two formal classification criteria by Eden et al. (2006), that is, intensionality/extensionality and locality/non-locality. We are thus able to formally distinguish models of those three development steps and to define precisely what architectural rules are. As a consequence,

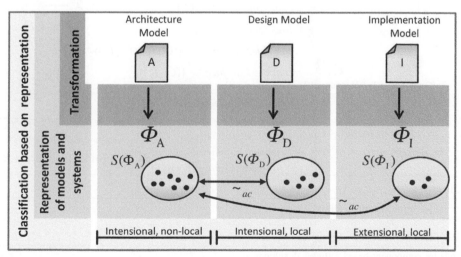

**FIGURE 7.2**

Overview of the proposed approach.

the term *architectural conformance* can be interpreted as relation $\sim ac$ between the sets of satisfying systems for an architectural model and one of its refining models.

In the following, we will first describe the formalization of component-based systems as logical structures conforming to a signature $\tau_{CBSD}$ of relation symbols that forms, together with an axiomatic system $\Phi_{CBSD}$, an ontology for component-based systems.[2] After that, the representation of models and their transformation into logical formulas will be described. The term *architectural conformance* will be defined. Finally, we will describe the implementation of the approach by a prototype based on a logical knowledge representation system.

### 7.3.1 Formal representation of component-based systems

As already mentioned, component-based systems are formalized by a kind of ontology defined by a set of relation symbols, the signature $\tau_{CBSD}$, and an axiomatic system $\phi_{CBSD}$. $\tau_{CBSD}$ defines which relation symbols can be used as predicates to form logical statements about component-based systems; $\phi_{CBSD}$ defines general constraints that pertain in such systems. A dedicated component-based system is therefore represented by a set of entities representing elements of the system and a mapping of the available relation symbols of $\tau_{CBSD}$ onto relations over the set of entities. In the following, we speak of $\tau_{CBSD}$-structures as relational structures using relation symbols from $\tau_{CBSD}$, and of *systems* if a structure additionally conforms to the axioms from $\phi_{CBSD}$.

The upper part of Figure 7.3 shows a relational structure modeling a very simple component-based system. The relation $Component^s$, for example, is the corresponding relation for the relation symbol $Component$ in the system $s$ and reflects the set of components in the system.[3]

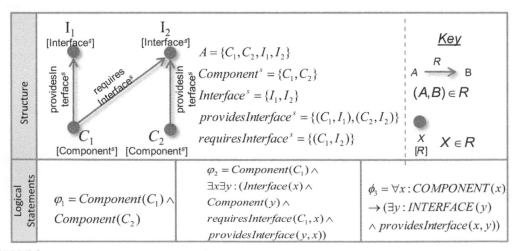

**FIGURE 7.3**

Example of $\tau_{CBSD}$-structure and -statements.

---

[2]CBSD stands for component-based software development.
[3]In the remaining text, we will refer to the concrete relation of a system with the relation symbol of equal name without adding the system as index.

Figure 7.4 illustrates a cutout of $\tau_{CBSD}$ graphically as a UML class diagram. Classes can be interpreted as unary relation symbols of $\tau_{CBSD}$, whereas associations are interpreted as having a binary relationship. Furthermore, the diagram also visualizes "typing" axioms of $\phi_{CBSD}$ by specialization and the types at association ends. For example, the specialization between Class and OOClassifier represents the axiom

$$\forall x : Class(x) \rightarrow OOClassifier(x)$$

and the association *providesInterface* implies the axiom

$$\forall x \forall y : providesInterface(x,y) \rightarrow Component(x) \wedge Interface(y)$$

The multiplicities of associations can also be translated into axioms for the minimal or maximal number of tuples in a relation for a fixed tuple component.

The depicted cutout of $\tau_{CBSD}$ models the organization of components and interfaces into packages, as well as the internal structures. *Component* and *Interface* stand for components and interfaces, respectively, and are contained in packages (*Package*). Interfaces contain a set of signatures (*Signature*), indicating the methods that an implementation must provide, and members (*Member*), or attributes. As these features are also provided by classes (*Class*), they are defined in a common superclass *OOClassifier*. The different relations modeled by *hasX*, *definesX*, and *inheritsX* reflect the different possibilities for relating signatures or members to classifiers by inheritance or defining; the set of all available signatures of one classifier, for example, is addressed by *hasSignature*, which is the union of *definesSignature* and *inheritsSignature*. Interfaces are provided and required by components, as modeled by *providesInterface* and *requiresInterface*.

Classes are interpreted as component-local classifiers that implement those interfaces that the component provides. The internal structure of components is reflected in parts (*Part*, related by *encapsulates*) that can be typed by components or classes (because *Component* and *Class* are specializations of *Type*). Special parts are *Ports*. Provided ports (*ProvidedPort*) are parts that are accessible from the environment of a component; required ports can be understood as place holders usable in the specification of a component, indicating a reference to a port that has to be provided by a different component at runtime. In contrast to ports, inner parts (*InnerPart*) are not accessible from outside a component. Ports are connected by connectors (*Connector*), which represent links between objects at runtime. Connectors are directed from *connectorSource* to *connectorTarget*, which are also parts. If the connected parts are ports, for example, the location of the parts where the ports are located must be idenfitified prior to connecting two component-typed inner parts of a component. This is modeled by *sourceContext* and *targetContext*. The specification of a whole system is done by *SystemConfigurations* that are structured the same way as components by parts (see relation *configurationParts*), only differing in the fact that all parts must be typed by components, not classes.

Constraints like this are also part of $\Phi_{CBSD}$. The example of system configuration parts that need to be typed by components can be expressed by the following axiom:

$$\forall x \forall y : (InnerPart(x) \wedge SystemConfiguration(y) \wedge configurationPart(y,x) \rightarrow \forall z : (hasType(x,z)$$
$$\rightarrow Component(z)))$$

$\tau_{CBSD}$ and $\Phi_{CBSD}$ furthermore define the behavior specification of component-based systems contained in *MethodBody*. The relevant relation symbols formalize control flow graphs (Allen, 1970) and different types of statement nodes such as instance creation and destruction, asynchronous and synchronous

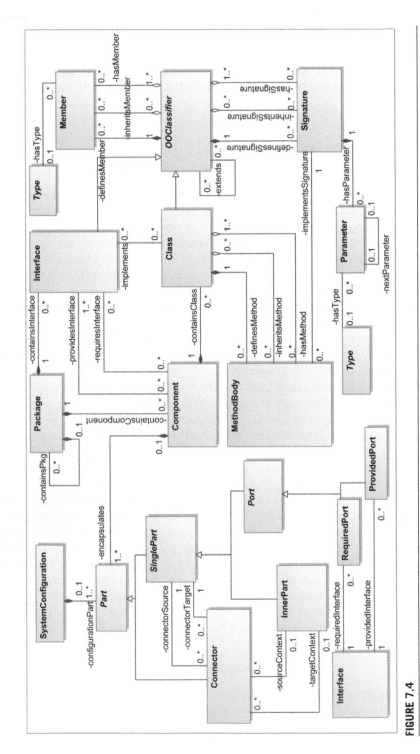

**FIGURE 7.4**

Cutout of $\tau_{CBSD}$ to describe components, their internal structure, and interfaces.

communication, and the assignment of references. For the sake of brevity, we omit the details and refer the reader to Herold (2011).

## 7.3.2 Formal representation of models

As mentioned above, models are represented as first-order logic $\tau_{CBSD}$-statements; these are statements that use relation symbols from $\tau_{CBSD}$ among others. This means that additional relation symbols can be defined and used if necessary. As an example of a statement representing a model, consider the UML design model cutout of Common Component Modeling Example (CoCoME) depicted in Figure 7.8. It shows that the component StoreGUI requires the interface StoreIF. This informal statement can be translated to a first-order logic statement over $\tau_{CBSD}$-structures:

$$Component(e_{StoreGUI}) \wedge Interface(e_{StoreIF}) \wedge requiresInterface(e_{StoreGUI}, e_{StoreIF})$$

whereas $e_x$ is the entity representing the element $x$ in the model. In the following, we will denote with $\phi_M$ the set of $\tau_{CBSD}$-statements for a model $M$. Logical statements are evaluated over relational structures as introduced, and we will denote by $S(\phi_M)$ the set of systems that fulfill the set of formulas $\phi_M$.

### 7.3.2.1 Classification of models

According to the classification scheme by Eden et al. (2006), we can distinguish architectural models, design models, and implementations by their sets of statements and properties of their sets of satisfying structures. A statement is called *extensional* if and only if each of the structures satisfying the statement is closed when addition and removal of elements. This means that

- adding entities or tuples containing new entities to the structure and
- removing entities or tuples that are not directly referenced in the statement

lead to structures satisfying the statement as well.

Statements that are not extensional are called intensional. Consider the statement examples in Figure 7.3. The depicted structure satisfies them all. Only the leftmost example is extensional, and neither adding entities nor removing other entities than $C_1$ or $C_2$ from the structure will change the evaluation of $\varphi_1$. $\varphi_2$ would evaluate to false if all interfaces were removed; $\varphi_3$ would evaluate to false if we added a component providing no interface.

Moreover, we call statements that are at least closed under addition *local*; such statements claim properties of systems that, once established, cannot be lost. Statements that are not local are called *non-local*; a system that satisfies such a statement can in general be extended in a way that the resulting system does not satisfy the statement any more. In Figure 7.3, only $\varphi_3$ is non-local.

Eden argues that statements being both intensional and non-local are those defined by architectures; such statements define constraints that are "system-global" constraints in the sense that their impact cannot be locally isolated. For example, the layering of a system is non-local; although a system may be correctly layered at some point, a component could be integrated and related to other components such that dependencies would form a cycle and the layering would be violated. We call constraints like that *architectural rules*. In contrast, consider two classes/components realizing an observer-observable relationship. The constraint about what makes them a "valid" observer or observable is local to the two components; it describes the interaction between these two alone, which stays the same if further components are added to the system in any case (see Eden et al., 2006 for details).

Hence, we define two partitions $\Phi_M := \phi_M^{ext} \uplus \phi_M^{int}$ for the set of statements for a model $M$, which contain the extensional and intensional statements of $M$, respectively. Furthermore, we call a model $M$(a) *architectural* if its set of intensional statements contains non-local statements (architectural rules), (b) a design model if its set of intensional statement contains only local statements, and (c) an implementation if its set of intensional statements is empty.

### 7.3.2.2 Transformation of models

The transformation of models into $\tau_{CBSD}$ expressions can be specified by transformation definition depending on a model's meta-model. Formally, we can express the transformation definition $T^L$ for a given meta-model $L$ as

$$T^L : Class^L \rightarrow \wp(\text{EXT}^{\tau_L}) \times \wp(\text{INT}^{\tau_L})$$

whereas $Class^L$ denotes the set of meta-classes defined in $L$ and $\text{EXT}^{\tau_L}$ denotes the set of extensional first-order logic expressions containing navigable expressions over $\tau_L \subseteq \tau_{CBSD}$ and $\text{INT}^{\tau_L}$ the set of intensional statements. Navigable expressions mean that the structure of the meta-model can be exploited to refer to objects in the model that has to be transformed. For example,

$$T^{UML}(Component) :=$$
$$(\{Component(this), providesInterface(this.provides), requiresInterface(this.requires)\}, \varnothing)$$

$$T^{UML}(Interface) := (\{Interface(this)\}, \varnothing)$$

that for each component in a UML model according tuples of *providesInterface* and *requiresInterface* are generated for each interface that is referred to in the model by *this.provides* (whereas "this" refers to the current component, see also OMG (Object Management Group), 2010).

## 7.3.3 Conformance of models

It is obvious that conformance between architecture and design cannot be defined as classical refinement relation stating that every satisfying system of the design model must also satisfy the architectural model. The statements for the design model are local, hence every extension of a satisfying system $s$ satisfies the design model, too. If $s$ also satisfies the architectural model, this does not necessarily have to be the case for every extension. Consider an architectural design model describing components $A$, $B$, and $C$ that are correctly dependent on each other with regard to the layer modeled by the architecture. A component $D$ can be added to the system,[4] destroying the correct layering.

Instead of claiming that every satisfying system of the design is also a system for the architecture, the constraint for conformance is weakened to a certain subset of satisfying systems: Only the minimal systems of the design (or the implementation) have to also satisfy the statements of the architecture (see Figure 7.5). A system is called minimal for a set of logical statements if it satisfies the set of statements, and no element or relationship could be removed from the system without losing this property.

Unfortunately, the set of minimal systems can be infinitely large. Consider the extensional statement *Component(StoreGUI)*. There is a single minimal satisfying *structure*, containing only one entity

---

[4]The design model, in this case, is an underspecification of the system.

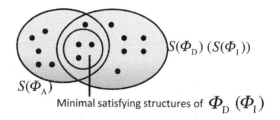

$$S(\Phi_D)\,(S(\Phi_I))$$

$$S(\Phi_A)$$

Minimal satisfying structures of $\Phi_D\,(\Phi_I)$

**FIGURE 7.5**

Relationships between the sets of satisfying systems in case of architectural conformance.

in the set of components. But unfortunately, the axioms of $\Phi_{CBSD}$ mention that components must be nested in packages, hence every *system* consisting of the single component StoreGUI in a package is a minimal system—infinitely many.

Therefore we make three restricting assumptions that have to be valid for models that can be checked for conformance. If all of these are valid for a model $M$, there is a unique minimal system for $M$, as follows:

1. Extensional statements of $M$ are conjunctions of facts. This means that they are conjunctions of terms of the form $Pred(e_1, \ldots, e_n)$ where $Pred$ is an $n$-ary predicate and $e_i$ refers to entities.
2. A structure that satisfies $\phi_M^{ext}$ also satisfies $\phi_M^{int}$. This means that a model satisfies its own constraints.
3. Every minimal structure satisfies the axioms of $\Phi_{CBSD}$, that is, minimal structures are also minimal systems.

There is at most one minimal structure for statements described in (1). Assumption (2) ensures that if this unique minimal model for the extensional part of a model exists, it is also a satisfying structure for the whole model. Assumption (3) finally ensures that the minimal structure is a minimal system.

The prototype presented in the following section implements conformance checking following this definition and these assumptions. Note that a minimal model for the extensional statement can be generated and that the assumptions can be checked by model checking.

### 7.3.4 Prototypical implementation

To evaluate the approach to architectural conformance checking, a prototypical tool called *ArCh* has been implemented. It is based on a realization using logic knowledge representation systems like Prolog or Powerloom (Information Sciences Institute, 2006). The overall structure and functionality of ArCh is depicted in Figure 7.6. The tool concept is integrated into Eclipse.[5]

The main component of ArCh is the *Architecture Conformance Checking Framework*. It realizes the functionality of conformance checking based upon the definition explained in Section 7.3.3. It also defines an internal representation of relational structures as used in the proposed approach. This is used by the wrapper interface to define a standardized interface to structures conforming to $\tau_{CBSD}$. Another interface, the backend interface, encapsulates the specific knowledge representation system and keeps the implementation interchangeable.

---

[5]The prototype currently has alpha status. Interested readers can contact the authors for a free demo version.

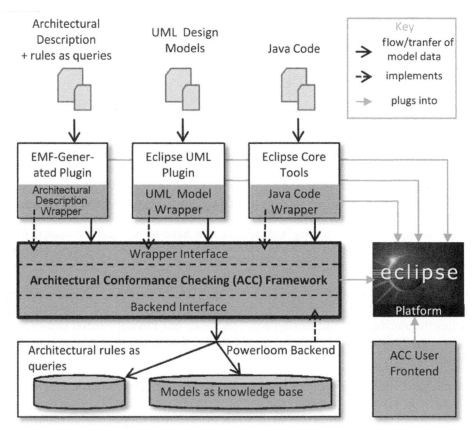

**FIGURE 7.6**

The ArCh prototype for architectural conformance checking.

Different wrappers encapsulate instances of different meta-models (or programming languages) and provide a $\tau_{\text{CBSD}}$-view onto models (or source code) that need to be checked. Currently, UML and Java are supported as well as simple examples of architecture description languages. Note that in the scenario described in this chapter, no separate meta-model for an architectural model of CoCoME has been defined; instead, two instances of a UML wrapper have been used, one responsible for the architectural model written in UML.[6] For arbitrary meta-models following the MOF (OMG (Object Management Group), 2006), plugins generated by EMF can be used to access models (Steinberg et al., 2009).

At the moment, the transformation of MOF-conforming meta-models is realized programmatically by navigating the model's structure through the API provided by EMF. One of the next development steps will be to replace the programmatic transformation with model transformations that create the internally used data model from EMF models. The transformation for Java has been realized as a

---

[6]In fact, previous versions of the architectural model expressing only the layering were using a domain-specific language to describe the architecture.

programmatic transformation using the Eclipse development tools that provide an API to the abstract syntax tree of Java source code.

The transformation definitions, that is, the queries representing the logical sentences for the architectural rules that a meta-model element implies, are stored separately and serve as input for the corresponding wrapper. The framework also supports loading queries from libraries in which common queries can be stored for reuse.

The framework forwards the relational structures representing the models as merged structure to the connected backend that represents it specifically for the implementation as logical knowledge base. As of yet, an implementation for third-party system Powerloom has been realized. Architectural rules are represented as logical queries and executed by the knowledge representation system in the process of conformance checking. The source for rule definitions can be any source for strings. In the case of the wrapper for layered architectures, a simple text file is attached to wrapper instances during their initialization. It contains a comma-separated list of entries of the form

```
<meta model element>,<rule-def>,<rule-desc>
```

`<meta model element>` refers to the element of the meta-model for which the rule is generated, `<rule-def>` contains the rule definition, and `<rule-desc>` is an informal description of the rule definition. The actual rule definition is PowerLoom query code. For example, the entry

```
"Layer",
"(illegalLayerDependencies ?this ?toLayer ?srcElem ?trgElem)",
"Actual layer dependencies are not compliant with intended ones!"
```

reflects basically the top-level statement of the architectural rule described in Section 7.4.1.2. Figure 7.7 shows the result dialog of ArCh checking a modified CoCoME system in which a logging

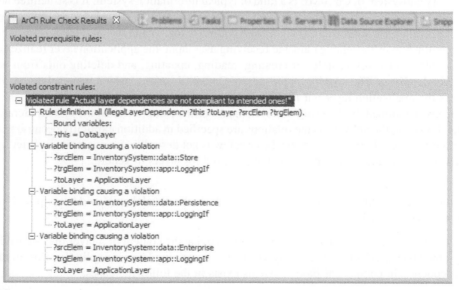

**FIGURE 7.7**

ArCh screenshot: violated layer structure.

component was added to the application layer. As the logging component is used in the entire inventory subsystem, the dependencies cause architectural violations.

The prototype can either be used interactively or in a batch-like mode as part of an automated process. In the first mode (also shown by the screenshot in Figure 7.7), the user can configure the set of related artifacts, for example, the architecture of the system and the folder of Java source code, and check this set for architectural conformance. In batch mode, ArCh can be integrated into an automatic build process, such as a nightly build, and generate reports about architectural conformance of the system. This allows continuous and effective checking of architectural conformance.

## 7.4 APPLICATION OF THE PROPOSED APPROACH

In this section, we describe the application of the proposed approach in different case studies. The first case study on the *CoCoME* will be covered in detail and the formalization of architectural rules will be explained. The further case studies will be summarized briefly and informally.

### 7.4.1 The common component modeling example

The *CoCoME* is a system that has been developed for a comparative study of component-based development approaches (Rausch et al., 2008). The system, also called *Trading System* for short, supports basic business processes in retail stores like supermarkets. The Trading System covers two functional areas: It supports the process of selling goods at cash desks, and it helps with the management of inventory, including ordering new goods, determining low stocks, and so forth.

#### 7.4.1.1 Architectural aspects of CoCoME

The Inventory subsystem of CoCoME is a kind of typical information system. It is structured according to the common Three-Layer-Architecture (Fowler, 2002) that defines a data layer, an application layer, and the graphical user interface (GUI) layer from bottom to top. While the GUI layer is responsible for user interaction, that is, presenting data and receiving user input, the application layer realizes business logic. The data layer is responsible for creating, reading, updating, and deleting data from persistent storages like databases. The layering in the case of CoCoME is strict, which means that the GUI layer may access the application layer but not the persistence layer directly.

As already mentioned, the layering of a system groups the components of the system hierarchically. In general, however, the allowed usage relations are specified in addition explicitly because normally a general right for upper layers to use every layer below is not desirable, for example, in strict layerings. Hence, the following informal constraints have to hold for layers in general:

- A layer $L$ may only use functionality of $L$ itself *or*
- $L$ may use functionality of layer $M$ ($L \neq M$) if $L$ is at a higher level than $M$ *and* $L$ is explicitly modeled to be allowed to use $M$.

Hence, a layer in general imposes the architectural rule that the content of a layer may depend only on content of the layer itself, or content in layers that the containing layer is explicitly allowed to depend on. A dependency in component-based systems exists in the following cases:

- *Usage between components and interfaces*, that is, components providing or requiring an interface, makes a component depend on the interface signature.

- *Specialization between interfaces* leads to a usage relation between the specializing and the generalized interface.
- *Usage of interfaces.* An interface using another interface as method argument type or return type, or as type of a reference.
- *Method calls.* The implementation of a component calls a method at another component (e.g., connected via a connector to a required port) *synchronously.* Because of the non-blocking behavior of asynchronous communication, the calling component does not depend on the "correct" behavior of the method invoked.

Figure 7.8 depicts a cutout of the CoCoME architecture and design models and shows a violation of this architectural aspect.

Another architectural aspect affects the application layer interface that is accessed via a network in the CoCoME system. One way of accessing a remote interface is via remote method invocation using middleware that includes marshaling and unmarshaling of calls. Due to these mechanisms, each call of a remote object's method, like reading object attribute values or navigating references to associated objects, causes overhead for this kind of communication (Fowler, 2002).

A common solution to this problem is the use of *data transfer objects* (Fowler, 2002). Instead of passing references to the web of persisted objects to the GUI layer, the required fragment of this web is copied into transfer objects. These copies are transferred to the GUI layer via the network; the GUI,

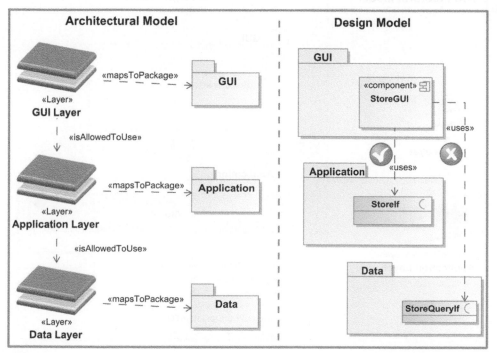

**FIGURE 7.8**

Layers of CoCoME.

running at a remote client computer, gets its own local and hence efficiently accessible copy of persisted data. We therefore also say that a component handling the passing of data the manner described provides an interface with *copy semantics* (in contrast to *reference semantics*). This concept is also an important part of service-oriented architectures (Krafzig et al., 2004).

The informal architectural rule defined by this concept is:

- The client of a *service-oriented* layer may connect only to interfaces that are declared *service interfaces*.
- A service interface is an interface providing *service methods* only. Those methods use only *transfer object classes* or primitive types as parameter types or result types. Each call of a service method returns a new copy of data, that is, a new instance of the transfer object class. This ensures that two different clients do not share a single instance as returned value.
- A transfer object class contains only attributes of primitive types or other transfer objects classes; a transfer object never refers to an object that is *not* a transfer object. Especially objects from the domain model are not allowed.

Figure 7.9 shows a fictitious violation of this concept in the CoCoME system.

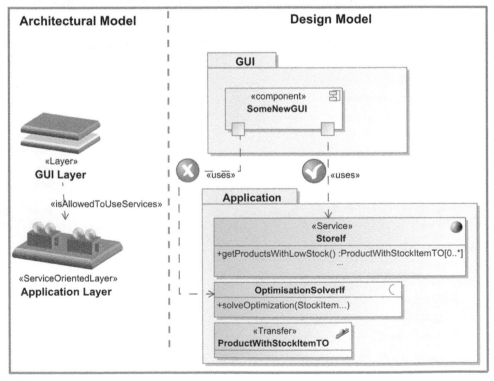

**FIGURE 7.9**

Service-oriented layer in CoCoME.

As mentioned above, the components of the Cash Desk System interact by causing and reacting to events. The event of scanning a product bar code (which is raised by the bar code scanner) causes reactions of other components: The running total is updated and visualized on the cash box display, and the receipt printer prints another entry of the sale. Such a system is also said to have an *event-driven architecture* (Yochem et al., 2009). A common way of realizing an event-driven architecture is to use the *Event Channel* pattern (Buschmann et al., 1996), a special variant of the Publisher-Subscriber pattern (Gamma et al., 1995).

In CoCoME, there are actually two kinds of event channels. Each single cash desk has a separate channel connecting the software controllers for the single devices; the channel is for the communication among them and the communication with the cash desk application. For the whole cash desk line, there exists an event channel with which the single cash desk applications register as publishers; the already mentioned application layer component StoreApp of the inventory system registers as subscriber. The cash desks publish SaleRegisteredEvents onto this channel, indicating that a sale process is finished. As a reaction to this event, the inventory system updates the amounts of goods in the inventory. Figure 7.10 depicts this structure and shows also a violation of the following rules that apply:

- There are two kinds of components in the considered subsystem: event channels and participants. The latter are publishers or subscribers (or both).
- Components interact by raising events modeled as a specific kind of type and reacting to them.

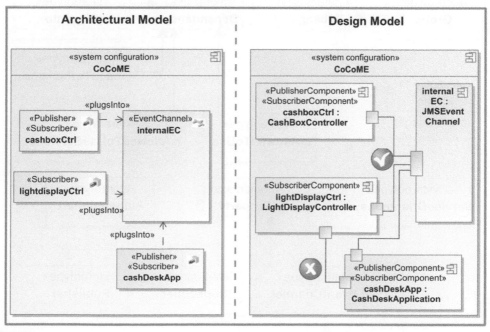

**FIGURE 7.10**

Event channels in CoCoME.

- Participants connected to the same event channel are not allowed to communicate directly with each other.
- Participants commit events to the event channel, which ensures that these events are forwarded to the other participants at some point. This happens decoupled from the original commit call to provide an asynchronous communication between participants.

### 7.4.1.2 The architectural rules of CoCoME

The proposed architecture conformance checking approach has been applied to check a design model of CoCoME described in Rausch et al. (2008) and refined in Herold (2011). The architecture of CoCoME was modeled using UML with architectural profiles that captured the relevant concepts. Figure 7.11 depicts the stereotypes used for CoCoME. The stereotype Group extends packages and reflects "virtual" groups of elements as outlined in Zdun and Avgeriou (2008). The Layer stereotype specializes Group and adds a level attribute reflecting the position of the stereotyped package in the layer hierarchy. A further specialization of Layer is ServiceOrientedLayer marking layers with copy semantics interface. The allowed usage relationships can be modeled by dependencies stereotyped with isAllowedToUse. The stereotype mapsToPackage extends the meta-class Dependency of the UML meta-model. It indicates which packages' contents are part of the "virtual group"; in our example, this relationship indicates by which packages a layer is manifested. The stereotypes EventChannel, Subscriber, and Publisher are used to model the event-based architecture; they extend Property because

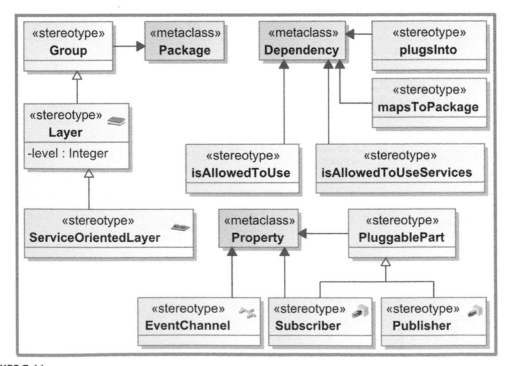

**FIGURE 7.11**

The architecture profile for UML.

they label parts of subsystems modeling the single component instances of a subsystem playing one or more of the three roles in event-based architectures.

For the sake of brevity, we will only consider the architectural layer aspect and will give a detailed description of the transformation for this aspect only. The stereotype Layer is transformed as follows:

$$T^{UML,arch}(Layer) := (\{Layer(this)\}, \{\neg illegalDependenciesFromLayer(this)\})$$

whereas the second statement constitutes an architectural rule, it basically states that there are no dependencies allowed that are not covered by parallel isAllowedToUse dependencies in the architectural model (see Figure 7.8), that is, there exist dependencies that do not conform to an existing *isAllowedToUse* tuple:

$$illegalDependenciesFromLayer(g) :=$$

$$\exists g' : \left( group\ Dependency(g, g') \land \overline{isAllowedToUse(g, g')} \land g \neq g' \right)$$

A group dependency between $g$ and $g'$ exists if $g$ contains an element that depends on an element contained in $g'$.

$$groupDependency(g, g') := \exists e \exists e' : (inGroup(e, g) \land inGroup(e', g') \land dependsOn(e, e'))$$

Whereas *inGroup* reflects the containment relationship. An element is contained in a group if it is directly contained in a package that the group maps to, or one of the package's subpackages. This also means that elements of groups are either components or interfaces, the only elements that are contained in packages by the definitions of $\tau_{CBSD}$:

$$inGroup(e, g) := \exists p$$

$$: (mapsToPackage(g, p) \land (containsComponent^+(p, e) \lor containsInterface^+(p, e)))$$

$dependsOn(e, e')$ is a container for the different possibilities of how single elements in a component-based system can depend on each other. It is defined as

$$dependsOn(e, e') := \bigvee_{i=1,...,8} dependsOn_i(e, e')$$

The complete refinement of this sentence and the overall rule for layers can be found in Herold (2011). For example, to express that an interface $e$ depends on another interface $f$ if it uses $f$ as type of a member, we can define

$$dependsOn_1(e, f) := Interface(e) \land Interface(f) \land \exists m : (hasMember(e, m) \land hasType(m, f))$$

### 7.4.1.3 Results of checking the architectural rules of CoCoME

The architectural layering of CoCoME implies the following architectural rules that need to be checked:

$$\{\neg illegalDependenciesFromLayer(e_{GUILayer}),$$
$$\neg illegalDependenciesFromLayer(e_{ApplicationLayer}),$$
$$\neg illegalDependenciesFromLayer(e_{DataLayer})\}$$

We will not go into the details of the evaluation of these rules. But informally, every layer is mapped onto one package in a design model or code. GUI layer components, that is, components contained in the GUI package, use only other GUI components or transfer object interfaces and services that are both defined at the application layer. No dependencies can be detected between elements of a layer and any layer above, and therefore no illegal dependencies can be detected. Moreover, event channels are properly used and are the only communication path in the cash desk subsystem.

However, an architectural violation has been detected for the application layer interface. This is the case because of the component StoreApp depicted in Figure 7.12, which is instantiated in the application layer. A component instantiated in the GUI layer connects to this component via its port storeIf. However, this port also provides the interface connecting the component to an event channel. Hence, it does not hold that the all components in the application layer are accessible by services only. In fact, the result that the approach notices a violation of the architecture makes sense. The accessed object, the port storeIf, appears as a service implementation by the fact that only the interface StoreIf is visible to the GUI; however, the non-service methods of the object could be retrieved, for example, by reflection.

### 7.4.2 Further case studies
#### 7.4.2.1 Checking layers
In another case study, we investigated a medium-sized information system of about 1600 classes and 130,000 lines of third-party code and a given logical layer architecture that was determined together with the provider of the system. In Deiters et al. (2009), we applied a preliminary version of this approach not using a common ontology. Instead, it could only represent UML models formally and was hence only able to check a reverse-engineered UML model of the Java code. Moreover, there was no explicit architectural model, but architectural facts had to be entered manually.

After this first experiment, we applied the proposed approach and the rules for layers as developed in the CoCoME application scenario. With our prototype and the existing UML and Java wrappers, we were able to detect the same points of erosion/architectural rule violations independently in the UML model of the system as well as in the Java implementation. Several hundred violations were detected that

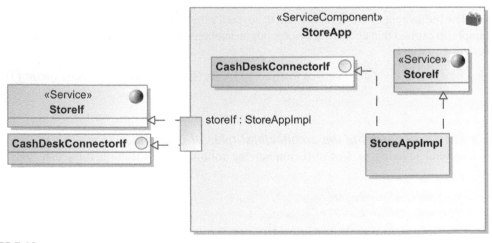

**FIGURE 7.12**

The component StoreApp causing a architecture violation (UML component diagram).

could be distinguished into five groups of different pairs of participating layers. Most of these violations could be reduced to conceptual problems like conceptually wrong placement of classes with a dedicated functionality. This case study has shown that the implementation of the approach was able to handle medium-sized systems with an architecture at a level of detail common in industrial practice.

Furthermore, we analyzed the layered architecture of the open source tool JEdit. In Patel et al. (2006), a reverse engineering approach detected 14 layers in the JEdit system that we used as input as intended architecture for ArCh. Checking the implementation of JEdit—consisting of about 300 KLOC of Java Code—against this architecture with ArCh revealed about 350 violations. Structure 101, for example, detects a similar but slightly higher number of violations due to technical reasons in the way ArCh transforms Java source code into logical facts; it does not transform all available constructs of the Java language correctly yet.

However, the advantage of ArCh is its flexibility, which enables it to detect violations other than layer violations due to its expressiveness. This, of course, comes with a higher complexity of the checking process, which, however, is not a problem so far. After transforming the source code of JEdit into a factbase, which takes about one minute, the current implementation of ArCh is able to check the layering of the system in less than 2 s.

### 7.4.2.2 Checking domain-specific reference architectures

In this case study, we enabled architecture erosion detection for a domain-specific reference architecture at the German Federal Office of Administration (BVA). The BVA supports German ministries and their departments by providing administrative tasks centrally, such as payments of salaries, time and attendance recording, and many more. It recently introduced a reference architecture called *Register Factory*[7] as a reference architecture for IT systems carrying out tasks around all different kinds of registering in the public administration.

The reference architecture provides guidelines for technical platforms as well as the logical structure of application systems. Given a detailed but informal description of the main aspects of the Register Factory, we developed a domain-specific modeling language such that instances of the reference architecture—hence, architectures for dedicated application systems—could be modeled. We analyzed six different architectural aspects including layers but also patterns regarding the prescribed component structure and formalized them as architectural rules.

The conformance checks revealed about 10 violations of the reference architecture in a register application consisting of about 900 classes and 60,000 lines of Java code. Details about the case study can be found in Herold et al. (2013).

### 7.4.3 Results

The case studies have shown us encouraging results. The approach provided the required flexibility to express very different aspects of software architecture from general patterns such as layering to domain-specific concepts of a reference architecture. We were able to check architectural for different architecture meta-models as well as different "implementations" of the architecture in forms of UML models or Java source code.

---

[7]www.register-factory.de.

The detected architecture violations were in all cases relevant matches that revealed more or less severe cases of eroded architectures. In a single case we found false positives that in all cases were results of incomplete or wrong formalizations of informally described architecture concepts that could be corrected together with the responsible software architects of the software system.

The applied prototype showed satisfying performance in the case studies. It took about one minute to check the mentioned Register Factory application or to check large layered systems. This performance is sufficient for a batch-like checking process, for example, as an integrated part of a nightly build of a software system. If a more interactive mode of operation is required, for example, for instant feedback to the programmer from getting shown compiler errors in modern IDEs, the performance must be improved.

## 7.5 CONCLUSION

As outlined in Section 7.1, adequate tool support for architectural conformance checking requires flexibility with respect to the heterogeneous set of architectural concepts used in a software architecture as well as with respect to the large number of different artifact types, or meta-models, that need to be checked. In MDSD approaches, furthermore, an approach to architectural conformance checking should integrate smoothly with existing techniques and models used to describe software systems.

### 7.5.1 Contribution and limitations

The ontology defined by $\tau_{\text{CBSD}}$ and $\Phi_{\text{CBSD}}$ describes component-based systems in great detail, such that architectural rules have great expressiveness. It enables software architectures to describe rules restricting type structures like inheritance; the inner structure of types such as components, interfaces, and classes; the configuration of component-based systems; and the control flow graphs of methods as specifications of component behavior. The framework, however, allows this ontology to be extended by relation symbols to introduce new architectural concepts such as layers. Extensions to $\tau_{\text{CBSD}}$ are considered in the definition of conformance and can be introduced technically through wrappers. We implemented a prototype that is able to check architectural rules as defined above applying the logical knowledge representation system, PowerLoom.

Compared with existing approaches (cf. Section 7.2), the proposed approach combines the advantages of query language-based approaches and reflexion modeling. While the first have great expressiveness, their integration into model-based approaches is not provided by current tool support. This is improved by the proposed approach because the definition of architectural rules can be easily integrated with arbitrary meta-models. Other query-based approaches, to our best knowledge, do not have this property.

On the other hand, reflexion modeling approaches already provide high-level models of systems but are limited in their expressiveness to components and dependencies. The proposed approach allows software architects to add full first-order logic rules in a customizable way to arbitrary high-level models of software systems. Rules like those regarding the usage of transfer objects are not possible with reflexion modeling approaches.

From the perspective of architecture modeling, the proposed approach makes a practical contribution insofar as it allows extending the extensional description that existing architecture description or modeling languages provide by intensional constraints requiring checking across a set of refining artifacts of arbitrary types. Hence, the proposed approach supports the requirements of architectural conformance checking as described in Section 7.1 more exhaustively than does the state of the art.

The approach provides a potentially powerful solution with regard to the support for different meta-models. At the *conceptual level*, we can conclude that different meta-models are supported by the approach as far as there can be given a meaningful transformation definition specifying how to transform an instance of the meta-model into a set of corresponding $\tau_{\text{CBSD}}$-statements. The effort of defining such a transformation is low in cases in which the modeling language itself contains component-based concepts and the mapping onto the $\tau_{\text{CBSD}}$-ontology is simple. However, in every case, the architectural rules are defined independently of any meta-model to be checked, providing flexibility in this point.

At the *implementation* level, the effort of implementing a document wrapper must be achieved, which adds to the effort of defining the conceptual transformation. Although the transformation is implemented manually and procedurally, and the effort could probably be reduced by using model transformation techniques, the effort involved in wrapper development is relatively small: The implemented UML wrapper takes about 800 lines of code.

As always with common ontologies, there is a certain trade-off in the definition of $\tau_{\text{CBSD}}$. Special characteristics and less strict constraints of single component models might not be expressed in $\tau_{\text{CBSD}}$. For example, UML allows both providing and requiring ports at the same time (which is not allowed in $\tau_{\text{CBSD}}$). As consequence, architectural rules must abstract from such component model-specific properties.

The representation of behavior as control flow graphs and the transformation of behavioral models into such structures might also limit the field of application of the proposed approach. The representation is strongly influenced from object-oriented systems in which behavior is specified by implementing methods. A mapping of other behavior specification techniques, for instance, contract specifications, might be difficult to realize.

The formulation of logical rules and their expressiveness is always limited by the applied logic and the set of available predicates, that is, the signature. First-order logics have proved expressive enough for the analyzed architectural rules; nevertheless, the developed ontology $\tau_{\text{CBSD}}/\Phi_{\text{CBSD}}$ lacks a certain expressiveness, especially for rules/statements referring to the behavioral aspects. In fact, concepts like program traces, call sequences, and other runtime constructs are missing.

Moreover, this approach does not check quality attributes of the software architecture directly because there is no way to specify them. As mentioned in the introduction, however, the quality of a system is influenced negatively by architecture erosion that can be detected and avoided by architecture conformance checking. Hence, the proposed approach can help to enforce a software architecture that ensures certain quality attributes and, hence, to indirectly support these quality attributes.

PowerLoom provides good query performance with respect to execution time. To evaluate performance for larger systems, some test series were executed. The tests included the implementation of the architectural rules for layers as discussed above. The checked models were UML design models and a layered architecture defining three layers with strict layering. The design models consisted of a defined number of components as depicted in Table 7.1; for each test series, randomly generated models of different sizes were generated. In addition to the components, the same number of interfaces was generated that provided and required relations in such a way that components were providing one to two interfaces and requiring two interfaces on average; these connected components and interfaced

**Table 7.1** Time Consumption to Check the Architectural Rules for Layers in Design Models of Different Size Measured in Number of Components

| #Components | Test Series | | | | | Average |
|---|---|---|---|---|---|---|
| | 1 | 2 | 3 | 4 | 5 | |
| 10 | 0.13 | 0.16 | 0.17 | 0.16 | 0.16 | 0.156 |
| 20 | 0.25 | 0.31 | 0.22 | 0.28 | 0.27 | 0.266 |
| 50 | 0.53 | 0.52 | 0.50 | 0.52 | 0.55 | 0.524 |
| 100 | 1.08 | 1.05 | 1.06 | 1.05 | 1.00 | 1.048 |
| 500 | 18.20 | 18.58 | 18.17 | 18.03 | 17.61 | 18.118 |
| 1000 | 78.67 | 75.27 | 81.06 | 76.11 | 80.33 | 78.288 |
| 2500 | 514.66 | 503.19 | 503.55 | 502.94 | 510.99 | 506.886 |

*Measured times in seconds.*

randomly. Moreover, components and interfaces were uniformly distributed to packages, and hence indirectly to layers. Tests were executed on a common desktop PC.

The results show that the worst-case complexity of PowerLoom in querying, which is exponential, does not affect checking the rule for layers; time consumption exhibits a quadratic growth with the size of the design model. The absolute numbers, however, show that the prototype delivers checking results in a reasonable time, at least for use cases in which checks are not permanently required (such as "in-line conformance checking" during programming).

The prototypical realization shows that, although the approach can be applied in practical relevant cases, it will be extended to support more requirements from real-life industrial projects. Currently, we are working on a better integration of third-party components into the conformance checking process that includes development of a wrapper for Java bytecode, definition of exceptions of rules, for example, to allow single (third-party) components to "violate" architectural rules, and a prioritization/classification of rules to distinguish different level of strictness for architectural rules. These features will require more information to be given in the specification of architectural rules, such as a list of exceptions or strictness classification, but will not affect the applied formalisms.

## 7.5.2 Future work

To further improve the practical relevance of the approach, architectural rules (and also design rules) should be defined and collected in a reusable catalogue of rules. This catalogue could be used by developers of document wrappers and would in general reduce the barriers to the application of architectural conformance checking. A reasonable starting point might be the formalization of the rules that patterns of popular pattern catalogues define (see, e.g., Buschmann et al., 1996). Of course, such general catalogues will be specialized in general in projects and companies applying them and tailoring them to specific needs. Hence, it is important that architects are equipped with good methodical knowledge and tools to specify architectural rules. What notation could be used to intuitively formulate architectural rules requires further investigation.

Checking architectural compliance and detecting violations of rules are only the first step in exhaustive conformance management tool support. Hence, this approach can and should be extended by refactoring and reengineering techniques. Given that software systems are large and inherently complex, resolving violations and re-establishing compliance are difficult tasks, too. Experiences from consistency management show that automatic resolution of inconsistencies is possible only to a certain degree and must often be complemented by opportunities to manually influence inconsistency repairing (Becker et al., 2007).

Further investigations can be made into the logical formalism that should be applied to architectural conformance checking. So far, first-order logics are applied whose principal undecidability leads to some restriction in the applied PowerLoom knowledge representation and reasoning system. There is always a trade-off between the expressiveness of the language and the efficiency of checking logical statements. We will investigate whether description logics (Baader et al., 2010) would be an appropriate alternative. We will also investigate temporal logics (Gabbay et al., 2000) that could be applied to address behavioral aspects of architectural rules more efficiently. Tools like Maude (Clavel et al., 2007), which allows rewriting logic specification and programming, could be interesting alternatives for integrating flexible logics into architectural conformance checking, especially when it comes to behavioral aspects. Maude could thus be an interesting backend implementation alternative for ArCh.

### 7.5.3 Summary

The proposed approach allows the realization of architecture conformance checking tools that are flexible with regard to supported meta-models and to variability of architectural rules. An implementation framework allows such tools to be easily adapted to new meta-models, such that existing compliance checking functionality can be easily enhanced to new models without the need to modify existing architectural rules. It is not only possible to easily integrate meta-models whose instances need to conform to some architectural model; meta-models for architecture description *defining* rules can also be easily integrated.

The solution enables the specification and checking of architectural rules with the expressiveness of full first-order logics. In combination with the easy integration of models into the process of checking, the resulting basis allows significantly more powerful support for architectural conformance checking in MDSD in the future compared with the state of the art. It can hence help better to avoid architecture erosion and the loss of quality that might come with this effect.

## References

Allen, F.E., 1970. Control flow analysis. In: ACM SIGPLAN Notices, vol. 5. ACM, New York, NY, pp. 1–19.

Baader, F., Calvanese, D., McGuinness, D.L., Nardi, D., Patel-Schneider, P.F., 2010. The Description Logic Handbook: Theory, Implementation and Applications, second ed. Cambridge University Press, Cambridge.

Bass, L., Clements, P., Kazman, R., 2003. Software Architecture in Practice, second ed. Addison-Wesley Longman, Amsterdam.

Becker, S., Herold, S., Lohmann, S., Westfechtel, B., 2007. A graph-based algorithm for consistency maintenance in incremental and interactive integration tools. Softw. Syst. Model. 6 (3), 287–315.

Biehl, M., Löwe, W., 2009. Automated architecture consistency checking for model driven software development. In: Proceedings of the 5th International Conference on the Quality of Software Architectures: Architectures for Adaptive Software Systems. Springer-Verlag, Berlin/Heidelberg, pp. 36–51.

Buschmann, F., Meunier, R., Rohnert, H., Sommerlad, P., 1996. first ed. In: A System of Patterns: Pattern-Oriented Software Architecture, vol. 1. John Wiley & Sons, Hoboken, NJ.

Clavel, M., Durán, F., Eker, S., Lincoln, P., Martí-Oliet, N., Meseguer, J., Talcott, C., 2007. All About Maude—A High-Performance Logical Framework: How to Specify, Program and Verify Systems in Rewriting Logic. Springer-Verlag, Berlin/Heidelberg.

Clements, P., Bachmann, F., Bass, L., Garlan, D., Ivers, J., Little, R., Nord, R.L., 2010. Documenting Software Architectures: Views and Beyond, second ed. Addison Wesley, Reading, MA.

de Moor, O., Verbaere, M., Hajiyev, E., Avgustinov, P., Ekman, T., Ongkingco, N., Tibble, J., 2007. Keynote address: .QL for source code analysis. In: Proceedings of the Seventh IEEE International Working Conference on Source Code Analysis and Manipulation. IEEE Computer Society, Washington, DC, pp. 3–16.

Deissenboeck, F., Heinemann, L., Hummel, B., Juergens, E., 2010. Flexible architecture conformance assessment with ConQAT. In: Proceedings of the 32nd ACM/IEEE International Conference on Software Engineering, vol. 2. ACM, New York, NY, pp. 247–250.

Deiters, C., Dohrmann, P., Herold, S., Rausch, A., 2009. Rule-based architectural compliance checks for enterprise architecture management. In: Proceedings of the 13th IEEE International Conference on Enterprise Distributed Object Computing. IEEE Press, Piscataway, NJ, pp. 158–167.

Eden, A.H., Hirshfeld, Y., Kazman, R., 2006. Abstraction Classes in Software Design. IEE Proc. Softw. 153 (4), 163–182.

Eichberg, M., Kloppenburg, S., Klose, K., Mezini, M., 2008. Defining and continuous checking of structural program dependencies. In: Proceedings of the 30th International Conference on Software Engineering. ACM, New York, NY, pp. 391–400.

Fowler, M., 2002. Patterns of Enterprise Application Architecture. Addison-Wesley Longman, Amsterdam.

Gabbay, D.M., Finger, M., Reynolds, M., 2000. In: Temporal Logic: Mathematical Foundations and Computational Aspects, vol. 2. Oxford University Press, Oxford.

Gamma, E., Helm, R., Johnson, R.E., Vlissides, J., 1995. Design Patterns: Elements of Reusable Object-Oriented Software. Addison-Wesley Longman, Amsterdam.

Herold, S., 2011. Architectural Compliance in Component-Based Systems. Foundations, Specification, and Checking of Architectural Rules, TU Clausthal.

Herold, S., Mair, M., Rausch, A., Schindler, I., 2013. Checking conformance with reference architectures: a case study. In: The 17th IEEE International EDOC Conference.

Hinsman, C., Sangal, N., Stafford, J., 2009. Achieving agility through architecture visibility. In: Proceedings of the 5th International Conference on the Quality of Software Architectures: Architectures for Adaptive Software Systems. Springer-Verlag, Berlin/Heidelberg, pp. 116–129.

Hofmeister, C., Nord, R., 1999. Applied Software Architecture: A Practical Guide for Software Designers. Addison-Wesley Longman, Amsterdam.

Hou, D., Hoover, H.J., 2006. Using SCL to specify and check design intent in source code. IEEE Trans. Softw. Eng. 32 (6), 404–423.

Information Sciences Institute, University of Southern California, 2006. PowerLoom Documentation. http://www.isi.edu/isd/LOOM/PowerLoom/documentation/documentation.html.

Kazman, R., 1999. A new approach to designing and analyzing object-oriented software architecture. In: Invited Talk. Conference on Object-Oriented Programming Systems, Languages and Applications (OOPSLA 1999).

Knodel, J., Lindvall, M., Muthig, D., Naab, M., 2006. Static evaluation of software architectures. In: Proceedings of the 10th European Conference on Software Maintenance and Reengineering, 2006. CSMR 2006, pp. 279–294.

Krafzig, D., Banke, K., Slama, D., 2004. Enterprise SOA: Service Oriented Architecture Best Practices. Prentice Hall International, Englewood Cliffs, NJ.

Lindvall, M., Muthig, D., 2008. Bridging the Software Architecture Gap. IEEE Comput. 41, 98–101.

Lucas, F.J., Molina, F., Toval, A., 2009. A systematic review of UML model consistency management. Inf. Softw. Technol. 51 (12), 1631–1645.

Murphy, G.C., Notkin, D., Sullivan, K.J., 2001. Software reflexion models: bridging the gap between design and implementation. IEEE Trans. Softw. Eng. 27 (4), 364–380.

Nentwich, C., Capra, L., Emmerich, W., Finkelstein, A., 2002. xlinkit: a consistency checking and smart link generation service. ACM Trans. Internet Technol. 2, 151–185.

OMG (Object Management Group), 2006. Meta Object Facility (MOF) Core Specification Version 2.0. OMG (Object Management Group).

OMG (Object Management Group), 2010. UML Superstructure Specification Version 2.3. Object Management Group (OMG). http://www.omg.org/spec/UML/2.3/.

Passos, L., Terra, R., Valente, M.T., Diniz, R., Mendonç anda, N., 2010. Static architecture-conformance checking: an illustrative overview. IEEE Softw. 27 (5), 82–89.

Patel, S., Dandawate, Y., Kuriakose, J., 2006. Architecture Recovery as First Step in System Appreciation. In: 2nd Workshop on Empirical Studies in Reverse Engineering (WESRE) at the 13th Working Conference on Reverse Engineering (WCRE 2006).

Perry, D.E., Wolf, A.L., 1992. Foundations for the study of software architecture. ACM SIGSOFT Softw. Eng. Notes. 17, 40–52.

Rausch, A., Reussner, R., Plasil, F., Mirandola Hrsg., R., 2008. In: The Common Component Modeling Example: Comparing Software Component Models, vol. 5153. Springer, Berlin.

Raza, A., Vogel, G., Plödereder, E., 2006. Bauhaus—A Tool Suite for Program Analysis and Reverse Engineering. In: Ada-Europe, vol. 4006. Springer, Berlin, pp. 71–82.

Rose, L.M., Paige, R.F., Kolovos, D.S., Polack, F.A., 2008. The Epsilon Generation Language. In: Proceedings of the 4th European conference on Model Driven Architecture: Foundations and Applications. Springer-Verlag, Berlin/Heidelberg, pp. 1–16.

Sangal, N., Jordan, E., Sinha, V., Jackson, D., 2005. Using Dependency Models to Manage Complex Software Architecture. In: Proceedings of the 20th annual ACM SIGPLAN Conference on Object-Oriented Programming, Systems, Languages, and Applications. ACM, New York, NY, pp. 167–176.

Sarkar, S., Ramachandran, S., Kumar, G.S., Iyengar, M.K., Rangarajan, K., Sivagnanam, S., 2009. Modularization of a large-scale business application: a case study. IEEE Softw. 26 (2), 28–35.

Steinberg, D., Budinsky, F., Paternostro, M., Merks, E., 2009. EMF Eclipse Modeling Framework. Addison-Wesley, Amsterdam.

Steward, D.V., 1981. The design structure system: a method for managing the design of complex systems. IEEE Trans. Softw. Eng. 28 (3), 71–74.

Van Gurp, J., Bosch, J., 2002. Design erosion: problems and causes. J. Syst. Softw. 61 (2), 105–119.

Yochem, A., Phillips, L., Martinez, F., Taylor, H., 2009. Event-Driven Architecture: How SOA Enables the Real-Time Enterprise, first ed. Addison-Wesley Longman, Amsterdam.

Zdun, U., Avgeriou, P., 2008. A catalog of architectural primitives for modeling architectural patterns. Inf. Softw. Technol. 50 (9-10), 1003–1034.

# Dashboards for Continuous Monitoring of Quality for Software Product under Development

8

**Miroslaw Staron**[1]**, Wilhelm Meding**[2]**, Jörgen Hansson**[3]**, Christoffer Höglund**[4]**,
Kent Niesel**[5]**, and Vilhelm Bergmann**[4]

[1]*University of Gothenburg, Gothenburg, Sweden*
[2]*Ericsson AB, Sweden*
[3]*Chalmers University of Technology, Gothenburg, Sweden*
[4]*Saab Electronic Defense Systems, Gothenburg, Sweden*
[5]*Volvo Car Corporation, Gothenburg, Sweden*

## INTRODUCTION

Qualities and architecture of modern software products are distinguishing excellent products from the average ones and can influence the success of software development companies. Extensible and scalable architectures of products, combined with Agile and Lean software development, can determine a long-term sustainable business models and maximize customer value. However, Agile and Lean software development methodologies come with a set of new challenges for monitoring and managing software quality in large software products (Tomaszewski et al., 2007). Continuous deliveries of customer value (features) need to be supported by extensible, reliable, and well-designed software architectures that demand shorter feedback loops, both before and after release. Combining the extensible and sustainable software architecture able to bear long-term evolution of complex software products and at the same time enabling agility can be exemplified by software products that are heavily affected by the evolution from traditional to Agile and Lean software development. These products are telecom nodes with millions of lines of executable code, embedded software in cars with millions of lines of code, or defense products with hundreds of thousands of lines of secure dependable code. In these products, monitoring quality needs to be done from two perspectives—upper management and software development teams.

The combination of extensible architectures, size of the product, and rapid feature development cause new information needs to emerge (Buse and Zimmermann, 2012), monitoring whether the desired quality level is achieved and when it is achieved, as well as monitoring that it stays at that level. These new challenges also require new ways of thinking when designing and building measurement systems visualizing large number of measures in form of dashboards (Staron et al., 2008) for both upper management and for teams. The dashboards are needed to collect the necessary information in the form of indicators and measures, visualize it in a simple way, and spread the information about the status of indicators within the organization.

In this chapter, we use the term *dashboard* to refer to a measurement system visualizing a small number of indicators (5-9) complemented with larger number of base and derived measures (>10). Dashboards contain visualization components, calculations of indicators, base and derived measures, and can be in form of MS Sidebar gadgets, web pages/portals, or Excel files with visualizations. They are available for upper management to control the company and for self-organized software development teams to monitor and communicate the status of the quality of their product under development (Sharp et al., 2009). Additional goals for the dashboards are for the teams to monitor of software econometrics (Ward-Dutton, 2011), monitor the progress of verification and validation, or visualize architectural dependencies in software products (Sangal et al., 2005).

This chapter presents a systematic overview of good examples of how dashboards are used to monitor quality of software products under development, both using multiple measures and a single indicator (combining measures of quality and development progress). In this chapter, we extract recommendations for building such dashboards for practitioners by exploring how three companies use dashboards for monitoring and controlling external and internal quality of large software products under development. The dashboards presented by each company contain a number of indicators and have different premises due to the domain of the product, its purpose, and the organization developing it. We describe a number of common principles behind a set of measures that address the challenge of quantifying readiness to deliver of software products to their end customers. The experiences presented in this chapter come from multiple case studies at Ericsson, two studies at Volvo Car Corporation (VCC), and one at Saab Electronic Defense Systems in Sweden. All companies have a long experience with software development and have undergone a transition into Agile and Lean software development; however, the length of experience with these new paradigms differs from 2 to 5 years depending on the company. This difference provides a possibility for observing that companies with longer experience tend to focus on using measures to support self-organized teams, whereas companies with shorter experience tend to focus on using measures to communicate the status from teams to management.

The experiences presented in this chapter address the following challenges of successful dashboards for monitoring quality of products under development:

- How to standardize the measures and indicators for monitoring development progress, taking into account product quality rather than schedule?
- What kind of measures and indicators should be used in dashboards to monitor the development progress?
- How to combine the need for indicators attracting attention of management, with the need to collect larger number of measures for drill-down?
- How to visualize measures in order to effectively trigger decision processes?
- How to assure high-quality information provided by the measurement systems?

The results show that dashboards can be organized either as a single indicator (release readiness), a set of measures of development progress (e.g., number of model revisions), or as a combination of internal quality and external quality (e.g., complexity and number of defects). Depending on the presentation method, the dashboards trigger different kinds of decisions at each studied company.

This chapter is structured as follows: Section 8.1 describes how the development of large software products is organized according to Agile and Lean principles at the studied companies. Section 8.2 discusses elements of successful dashboards that visualize the release readiness and software development quality progress. Section 8.3 presents how the three studied companies realized this concept, complemented with recommendations for other companies in Section 8.4. Section 8.5 provides a number of useful directions where interested readers can find more information. Section 8.6 contains the conclusions.

## 8.1 DEVELOPING LARGE SOFTWARE PRODUCTS USING AGILE AND LEAN PRINCIPLES

In software engineering in general, release management is based on the delicate balance between the market pull for new features and the technology push and company strategy (Phaal et al., 2004). One of the main activities of release management is naturally the release planning activity, which is concerned with which features should be implemented in the product and when they should be delivered to the end customers (Ruhe, 2003; Ruhe and Saliu, 2005).

In modern Agile and Lean software practices (Poppendieck and Poppendieck, 2007), once the features are planned, their development is usually in the hands of self-organized Agile software development teams, which use the products' architecture to design, implement, and test new product features. The self-organized teams are responsible for detailing the functional (FR) and nonfunctional requirements (NFR) for the feature, planning of feature development (PM), systemization and feature design (SM), implementation and detailed design (DM), and initial testing (usually functional testing) (Staron et al., 2010b; Tomaszewski et al., 2007)—all with the goal to deliver a fully functional feature to the main code branch as depicted in Figure 8.1.

In order to keep pace with market demands. multiple teams deliver their fully developed functional feature to the main code branch, where the feature is tested in the context of the real hardware and later in the context of the real execution environment, for example, telecom networks, complete vehicle manufacturers, or defense field testing.

Monitoring the *agility* can be challenging because it comprises both the functional delivery and quality of the product (both its features and its architecture). Release plans for features are developed based on experience and market needs. The plans are monitored so that the software development organizations are confident that the plans are fulfilled. Using indicators, the whole software development program (a set of self-organized development teams working on the common code base) can monitor the validity of the plan and address the issue of how confident the development program is that the plan is upheld. This monitoring of agility can be in the form of a *release readiness* indicator—an indicator

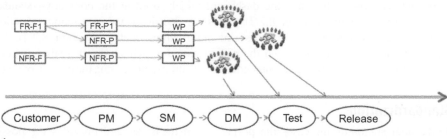

**FIGURE 8.1**

Conceptual view of software development flow in organizations with multiple, parallel cross-functional teams.

that shows when a particular set of features is ready to be released. The indicator varies from company to company, but the principles of how it is defined, calculated, and visualized are the same. The prerequisite for this indicator is that the software architecture has a good quality.

In this chapter, we use the ISO 9000:2005 (ISO, 2005a) definition of quality, that is, the degree to which a set of inherent characteristics fulfills requirements. We also distinguish between the internal and external quality as defined in ISO 25000 (ISO, 2005b) and use the external view in the rest of the chapter, except for Section 8.3.3 where we present both internal and external quality in the studied dashboards.

Monitoring the development progress is based on identifying software development phases at the company. The phases reflect how the development is organized and help to identify indicators for monitoring the progress of development of the features by monitoring the indicators. Most software development processes usually include such high-level phases as requirements breakdown, software design or modeling, and testing. Examples of weekly measures for those phases are:

- Number of requirements in the backlog during the software analysis phase
- Number of model/code check-ins for the development phase
- Number of violations of architectural rules in models/code
- Percentage of passed test cases for the test phase

The measures support the teams in communicating the status of the development and are succinct enough to be used in communication upward to project leaders and management teams. As we explore in Section 8.3, these types of measures are simple enough and together with other components are complete enough for the dashboard to be successful.

The measures of test progress include tests of nonfunctional properties of the architecture and the product, in particular performance, reliability, stability, availability, and safety of the products. As we show in the case of Saab EDS in Section 8.3, these can be presented in two levels—one for the team and one for the management—or as we show in the case of Ericsson, as part of a single indicator.

## 8.2 ELEMENTS OF SUCCESSFUL DASHBOARDS

The indicators and measures used in the dashboards for monitoring the quality of products under development often support organizations in assessing the *release readiness*—that is, when the product is to be ready to be released based on its functionality and quality. The indicators and measures are by far the most important element that determines whether the dashboard is successful. However, they have to be complemented with others to make the dashboard widely used at the company—standardization (Section 8.2.1), early warning (Section 8.2.2), focus on decisions and predictions (Section 8.2.5), succinct presentation (Section 8.2.3), and assuring information quality (Section 8.2.4). Successful dashboards lead to actions by the team and the project aimed at achieving set goals (e.g., delivery of features according to schedule, preventing unintended quality drops, monitoring the erosion of architecture).

### 8.2.1 Standardization

Using international standards increases the portability of measures and provides the possibility of showing customers that the measurement processes are planned and executed according to state-of-the-art practices. This is particularly important for Agile and Lean organizations that usually have flexible planning seen as risky for stakeholders used to plan-driven development. By using the standards, we address the following challenge:

- How can a team or company standardize the measures and indicators for monitoring development progress and release readiness taking into account product quality rather than schedule?

This challenge needs to be addressed to show that the principles of Agile planning are well implemented in the company and that there is no risk of losing the importance of long-term product quality by focusing on flexible plans and immediate delivery of customer value. The most well-known standards for measurement processes in software and systems engineering are the European standard ISO/IEC 15939[1] (International Standard Organization and International Electrotechnical Commission, 2007) and the IEEE standard 1061-1998 (IEEE, 1998). The core component of the standard is the conceptual *measurement information model*, which describes relationships between the main types of elements of measuring systems. Figure 8.2 presents an overview of this model from the standard and the two most relevant definitions for our chapter.

The information need is insight necessary for a stakeholder to manage objectives, goals, risks, and problems observed in the measured objects. These measured objects can be entities such as projects, organizations, or software products characterized by a set of attributes. ISO/IEC 15939 includes the following definitions, which are relevant. The definitions were adopted from the more general standard—JCGM vocabulary in the metrology standard (International Bureau of Weights and Measures, 1993):

- Entity: Object that is to be characterized by measuring its attributes.
- Attribute: Property or characteristics of an entity that can be distinguished quantitatively or qualitatively by human or automated means.

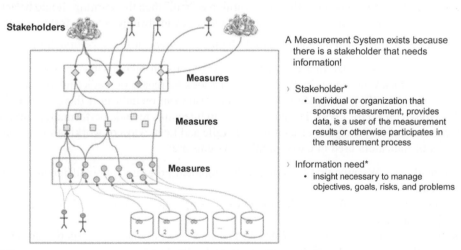

**FIGURE 8.2**

Simplified view of the measurement information model from ISO/IEC 15939.

---

[1]IEEE has adopted this standard under the same number: 15939–2008.

- Base measure: Measure defined in terms of an attribute and the method for quantifying it.
- Derived measure: Measure that is defined as a function of two or more values of base measures.
- Decision criteria: Thresholds, targets, or patterns used to determine the need for action or further investigation or to describe the level of confidence in a given result.
- Indicator: Measure that provides an estimate or evaluation of specified attributes derived from a model with respect to defined information needs.
- Information product: One or more indicators and their associated interpretations that address an information need.

ISO/IEC 15939 is not the only framework available for structuring measures in measurement systems. The most well-known non-standard framework is Goal-Question-Metric (GQM) (van Solingen and Berghout, 1999; Basili et al., 1994), which is used as a base for IEEE 1061-1998. The GQM framework is widely used in the research community and can replace ISO/IEC 15939 for structuring measures, but it does not recognize the concepts of stakeholders, information needs, or indicators.

### 8.2.2 Focus on early warning

Knowing the status of the monitored entities at a particular point of time is naturally very important for stakeholders. However, even more important is knowing what the status will be a week, month, or year ahead. This is particularly important for monitoring qualities of architectures because daily design decisions can have significant impacts on the subsequent design choices available for architects and designers. The stakeholders need indicators that warn about potential problems when the stakeholders still have the means to react and get their monitored entities back on track—for example, to prevent architecture erosion. In other words, if early warning measures are "green," then the stakeholders can focus on monitoring the current progress, but if the early warning is "red," then the warning should be acted upon and takes precedence. This requires specific kinds of measures and brings us to the following challenge:

- What kind of measures and indicators should be used to monitor the development progress?

From our experience, we found that companies usually focus on quantifying the status as step 1 in introducing indicators. When this is in place, companies look for means of predicting the outcome based on the current situation. The most mature organizations also focus on indicators linked to simulations or "what-if" analyses (Scacchi, 1999). The analyses for architectures include performance simulations or architecture modifiability analyses, crucial for the Agile and Lean ways of working in the long run.

Examples of indicators used in early warning systems are:

- Release readiness: Warning that the current development progress is not sufficient to meet the project plan.
- Test execution progress: Warning that the current test progress is not sufficient to assure that the quality goals are met.
- Requirements breakdown progress: Warning that there are not enough detailed requirements to continue software design during the current sprint for the team.
- Architecture rules violations, non-conformance, performance degradation: Warning that the current internal quality of the software product can cause external quality problem at later development stages.

There are naturally more examples, which we discuss based on the dashboards from each studied company.

### 8.2.3 **Focus on triggering decisions and monitoring their implementation**

The most important concepts from an external perspective on dashboards are *indicators* and *stakeholders*. The indicators are means for communicating the most important information about the current or predicted status of the monitored entities. The indicators are meant to trigger decision processes in the companies, including both formulating and executing decisions. This leads to the need to address the following challenge:

- How can we combine the need for indicators triggering decisions at the correct time with the need to collect a larger number of measures for drill-down and monitoring of the execution of decisions?

In order to combine a few indicators with many measures, a dashboard has to show indicators and link to a system that collects measures and stores them in a document/database (e.g., an associated Excel file). For example, a successful indicator monitoring the complexity of the product attracts the attention of the stakeholder to components that are too complex given predefined criteria. This triggers decisions from stakeholders—for example, ordering additional resources to address the rising complexity in the product. By seeing a trend in complexity development, the stakeholders can observe whether the situation is getting out of control and when they should react.

The properly chosen stakeholders are crucial for the success in adopting the dashboard in a large organization. They must have the authority to define the indicator and its threshold (decision criteria and analysis model) and have the mandate to act upon the status of the indicator. For example, the stakeholder for the release readiness indicator is the project manager who needs to constantly monitor when the product is ready to be released and has the mandate to take actions to meet the target release date if necessary—for example, order overtime.

The stakeholders usually work closely with information providers who have an interest in communicating specific information using measures and indicators. For example, a software development team could be such a provider that assures that the team's indicator objectively communicates the status of the development of a feature to the project management and to other interested entities such as line management. The team also needs to be notified about the status of the product architecture that can influence their planning.

### 8.2.4 **Succinct visualization**

In order to be effective in the communication of indicator's status to the stakeholders, the information products (according to ISO/IEC 15939) have to present the information in a concise manner. Modern tools usually support this by using apps for current operating systems such as Android, iOS, Windows, or MacOS for presenting the status of the indicator and providing the entry point for more information such as trends or statistics of base and derived measures (Staron et al., 2008). Using such simple means and focusing on presenting the most important information succinctly addresses the following challenge:

- How do we visualize measures in order to effectively trigger decision processes?

Dashboards usually contain five to nine indicators and use metaphors of the same kind to convey the message of the status of the indicators. The metaphors are important for the presentation of the status of indicators (Johansson et al., 2007; Shollo et al., 2010). Based on the previous studies we could say that the most powerful metaphors are:

- Traffic lights: Many successful indicators communicate three states: problem, warning, normal state. The traffic light metaphor is perfect[2] for this kind of communication, especially if accompanied with a number to address the status of the indicator. For an example, please see Figure 8.4.
- Gages and meters: When the focus of the indicator is primarily in the number rather than the state. Using this metaphor is suitable because it provides gradation of the status, for example, green is close to yellow.

The succinct presentation of the status of the indicator is combined with the ability (e.g., a hyperlink) to drill-down into detailed statistics to understand the cause of the status and act accordingly. The successful succinct indicator is usually supported by a number of base and derived measures directly used in calculating the status or monitoring that assumptions behind the analysis model and the indicator are upheld. The supporting base and derived measures are usually visualized as charts, for example, trends.

### 8.2.5 Assuring information quality

In large software products the number of base and derived measures per indicator can be rather large (in some cases over 10,000 data points per indicator), which means that the probability that one data point is erroneous cannot be neglected. Given that monitoring the architecture can comprise multiple indicators (as is shown in Section 8.3) and the information is spread to multiple teams, the quality of the calculations must be controlled automatically (to minimize the risk of teams making poor decisions). In this section, we elaborate on how the automated assessment of information quality addresses the following challenge:

- How do we assure that high-quality information is provided by measurement systems?

Naturally, the more data are automatically processed, the more important the question about its quality becomes (Staron and Meding, 2009a). Stakeholders need to be informed whether the information in the dashboard is, for example:

- Up-to-date
- Calculated without errors
- Within predefined limits (e.g., the number of weeks to software release must be positive)

There are frameworks that characterize information quality in a quantitative way such as the AIMQ framework (Lee et al., 2002). AIMQ provides a quality model for information that includes the following examples of characteristics:

- Accessibility: The information is easily retrievable.
- Completeness: The information includes all necessary values.
- Concise representation: The information is formatted compactly.
- Free of error: The information is correct.
- Objectivity: The information was objectively collected.
- Timeliness: The information is sufficiently current for our work.

---

[2]The metaphor of a red light for problems showed itself to be very effective to attract attention. However, one should be very careful not to abuse the red color. If the decision criteria set the red color also when the status is not "red," then the stakeholders lose trust in this problem-warning signal.

These quality attributes can be organized into two categories: (i) external quality, including how the information is perceived by the stakeholder and semiotics of information (e.g., concise representation) and (ii) internal quality, including how the information is obtained and composed from components and *internals of dashboards* (e.g., free of error). Methods used for empirical validation of measures assess the external information quality, for example, case studies with indicators. The following work is particularly useful for this purpose: Bellini et al. (2005), Raffo and Kellner (2000), Stensrud et al. (2002), Yuming and Hareton (2006), and IEEE (1998). The internal information quality can be checked during the runtime operation of measurement systems. Naturally, a lot can be measured automatically, but there are limits to how much we can control. For example, we cannot automatically check whether designers reported defects correctly in defect databases—because we do not "parse" the natural language in defect description, we can only check that defects were reported and that the database was updated.

In Section 8.3, we show how information quality is communicated to the stakeholders in practice using the case of Ericsson's release readiness dashboard.

## 8.3 INDUSTRIAL DASHBOARDS

In this section, we present how the three studied companies used the concept of release readiness in their dashboards for teams and for development projects. The approaches of the three companies are different and based on each company's history of using measures; therefore, not all elements of a successful dashboard are present in all companies. Table 8.1 presents a summary by company.

Ericsson has been the company with the longest measurement experience with respect to standardized measurement processes in software engineering; therefore, all elements are present in the dashboards at that company.

### 8.3.1 Companies

The companies operate in three different domains with commonalities (e.g., embedded software development) and variability (e.g., development methodology, dependency on suppliers). The breadth of the companies and commonalities in the presented dashboard show that similar challenges and elements of successful dashboards are applicable for each domain.

**Table 8.1** Mapping of Elements of Successful Dashboards by Company

|  | Ericsson | Volvo Car Corporation | Saab EDS |
|---|---|---|---|
| Standardization | √ | √ | √ |
| Focus on early warning | √ | √ | √ |
| Focus on decisions and monitoring | √ | √ | √ |
| Succinct presentation | √ | √ | √ |
| Information quality | √ | | |

### 8.3.1.1 Ericsson

Ericsson AB develops large software products for mobile telecommunication networks. The size of the organization during the study was several hundred engineers, and projects numbered up to a few hundred.[3] Projects were increasingly executed according to the principles of Agile software development and the Lean production system referred to as Streamline development within Ericsson (Tomaszewski et al., 2007). In this environment various teams were responsible for larger parts of the process compared to traditional processes: design teams (cross-functional teams responsible for complete analysis, design, implementation, and testing of particular features of the product), network verification and integration testing, and others.

The organization used a number of measurement systems for controlling the software development project (per project) described above, for controlling the quality of products in field (per product), and for monitoring the status of the organization at the top level. All measurement systems were developed $$using the in-house methods described in Staron et al. (2008, 2010a), with the particular emphasis on models for design and deployment of measurement systems presented in Staron and Meding (2009b) and Meding and Staron (2009).

The needs of the organization evolved from metric calculations and presentations (ca. 7 years before the writing of this chapter) to using predictions, simulations, early warning systems, and the handling of vast quantities of data to steer organizations at different levels and providing information from project and line. These needs have been addressed by action research projects conducted in the organization since 2006.

### 8.3.1.2 Volvo Car Corporation

VCC is a Swedish car original equipment manufacturer (OEM), based in Gothenburg. VCC developed software and hardware in a distributed software development environment. For a number of electronic control units (ECUs), software was developed in-house by software development teams that usually also had the responsibility for integrating the software with hardware developed by suppliers. The majority of the embedded software development, however, came from external suppliers who designed, implemented, and tested the functionality based on specifications from VCC (Eklund et al., 2012; McGee et al., 2010).

The size of the entire automotive project in terms of resources was substantially larger than the projects in the telecom domain due to the fact that both OEMs and suppliers (first and second tier) were involved, and car development projects were usually conducted using the product line approach with reference architectures (Gustavsson and Eklund, 2011). However, we studied one team, which had a comparable size to teams at Ericsson and Saab EDS.

The studied organization at VCC was a software development team responsible for software for the ECU for climate control. The team was provided a set of measures to visualize the progress of development and communicate that upward to the management.

### 8.3.1.3 Saab electronic defense systems

Saab EDS developed embedded software and graphical user interfaces for ground-based radar systems. The specific product we worked on was part of a larger product developed by several hundred developers, designers, testers, analysts, and others. The historic project developing the product was

---

[3]The exact size of the unit cannot be provided for confidentiality reasons.

driven in increments and did not utilize cross-functional teams. Project management produced some manual metrics on trouble reports.

Since this project, the organization has evolved into using more Agile processes and cross-functional teams. A lot of improvements and optimizations have also been made regarding software build and delivery times. And to improve customer value, market competitiveness, and profit, Saab AB Electronic Defense Systems in Gothenburg is going through a Lean transformation.

The organization at Saab EDS has a history of using measures and communicating quality through dashboards. The dashboard presented in this chapter shows how the organization uses one measure— number of defects —in different granularity to provide insight into the status of software development.

### 8.3.2 Dashboard at Ericsson

Ericsson chooses a dashboard that shows product release readiness in a compact form. The product release readiness indicator is intended to predict when the product under development has achieved the appropriate quality for release (Staron et al., 2012). The quality is measured by the number of open defect reports for the product—meaning that the right quality for releasing of the product is 0 defects. The defects can be related to the functionality of the software and its nonfunctional properties, in particular, performance, reliability, and availability. The properties are tested as part of regularly executed test suites.

The 0-defect criterion is sufficient only when another criterion is fulfilled—all functionality is tested and all test cases are passed. The stakeholder for this indicator is the project manager, and the software development program is the group with the need to communicate the information upward to the management teams of the program and the organization. The indicator (RR, Release Readiness) has the following form:

$$RR = \left( \frac{\#defects}{defect\_removal\_rate - (test\_execution\_rate\text{-}test\_pass\_rate)} \right)$$

where #*defects* is the number of open defects for the product,[4] *defect_removal_rate* is the average number of removed defects during the last 4 weeks, *test_execution_rate* is the average number of test cases executed during the last 4 weeks, and *test_pass_rate* is the average number of test cases passed during the last 4 weeks. The 4-week period is chosen based on statistical and empirical analyses. These analyses have shown that based on the length of the test cycles and the defect removal activities, the 4-week period is the most appropriate length for this prediction and provides the most accurate results (Staron et al., 2012).

The formula is built from a number of base measures (e.g., tests passed per week) and derived measures (e.g., test pass rate during the last 4 weeks), which show how **standardization** according to ISO/IEC 15939 is realized in practice. Each of the measures in the formula is defined according to the standard with its measurement method and measurement function. The stakeholder has the means and ability to react and get the project back on track if needed.

Figure 8.3 presents how the indicator spreads in the organization on a daily basis—in a form of an MS Vista Sidebar gadget (example of **succinct visualization**). The gadget is the dashboard where the indicator is presented. It is complemented with an Excel file with trends for the measures in the formula for RR.

---

[4]This measurement included all defects that need to be removed from the product before the release.

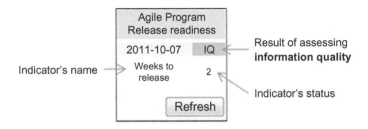

**FIGURE 8.3**

MS Vista Gadget with predicted week of release.

The content of the gadget shows 2 weeks for the project to obtain the release quality (*weeks to release*). The presentation is simple and succinct, giving the stakeholder (the manager of the studied product development project) the necessary information. The gadget also contains an information quality assurance indicator (**assuring information quality**), which is abbreviated *IQ* (Staron and Meding, 2009a). The details of the base and derived measures are available in an associated MS Excel file once the gadget is clicked on.

In addition to the gadget, the team has an auxiliary measurement system monitoring dependencies between architectural components, both explicit and implicit. The measurement system is based on monitoring how software components change over time and which components change together (Staron et al., 2013), with an example in Figure 8.4.

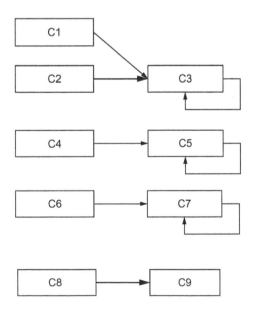

**FIGURE 8.4**

Implicit and explicit dependencies between architectural components (example of small set of components C1-C9).

The dependencies are visualized in a very succinct manner and allow teams to quickly find dependencies that are not explicit and can lead to architecture erosion. New dependencies require updating the test strategies and thus influence the release readiness indicator (new test cases to execute, thus more time needed to test the product before the release.

### 8.3.3 Dashboard at VCC

In the case of VCC, we studied how one software development team can monitor development progress using a dashboard with three components—requirement management, version control for models, and test progress. The team's interest was to communicate the status of the development of software for one ECU for a family of modern cars within the Volvo brand. The dashboard was designed and developed together with a **stakeholder** from the team who had insight into the development process and practices at the company. The stakeholder was designated by the team to represent the team's common view.

The dashboard for monitoring the development progress for the team is presented in Figure 8.5.

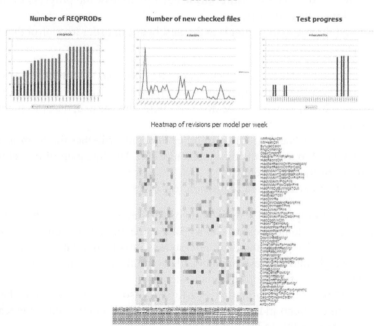

**FIGURE 8.5**

Dashboard for monitoring quality of software product under development for one team.

This dashboard presents indicators for monitoring the trend in software development by monitoring the pace of modeling of the ECU's functionality (the table under heading *Indicators*). Four indicators for check-in pace and trend have been chosen by the team to monitor:

- **Check-in trend**: The main indicator capturing the readiness of functionality defined as the difference between the moving average and the number of check-ins last week. If the number of check-ins decreases with respect to moving average, then there is a high probability that the team is moving towards the testing phase. In a succinct way it captures the readiness of the team with the implementation of the functionality.
- **Number of check-ins last week:** The indicator captured the "temperature" of the development of the functionality.
- **Number of check-ins during the current week:** The indicator monitors the activities during the current week to support the team in checking how the status develops over time.
- **Check-in pace:** The indicator showing the average level (moving average) of check-ins.
- **Heatmap of revisions per model per week:** The indicator visualizing how stable the architecture of the software is. This is a part of internal quality measurement for the team and helps to identify spots where architecture needs rework.

Due to the fact that the team is working in an Agile way with functional testing being an integral part of the development of models, the check-ins can be caused by new functionality being added or by changes to the existing functionality caused by defect fixes. Regression testing, however, was not included and therefore an additional measure was needed to control the progress of the basic quality assurance of the developed functionality.

The team monitored three auxiliary trends in the dashboard in order to control that the assumption of the indicators hold:

- Requirements elicitation and breakdown (number of REQPRODs): In order to decide about release readiness, the team assesses whether there are new requirements in the backlog. New requirements indicate that there is still new work to be done (in particular, new updates to the models or new models to be developed).
- Modeling (number of new checked files): In order to decide whether the team is ready with the product where they need to assess the development trend. The heatmap of model revisions shows the internal stability of the architecture.
- Test progress: The number of passed regression test cases.

The dashboard presented in Figure 8.5 is built based on the same principles as the gadget presented in Section 8.3.2, but the information is presented as a *flow*—three diagrams in one row instead of a single indicator. This more exhaustive presentation of release readiness is motivated by the fact that the team wanted to have more insight into the development and communicate the status visually to stakeholders outside the team, for example, sub-project managers.

The visual presentation of the information as a flow is also supposed to focus the team on **early warning**. By visualizing the trend in the number of new/changed requirements, the team can monitor whether there is still functionality to be implemented and tested.

When the trend in the requirement growth is flat, the check-in trend decreases and the number of passed regression test cases is stable or grows, then the team is close to the release (**focus on decisions**).

### 8.3.4 **Dashboard at Saab electronic defense systems**

At Saab EDS we studied two dashboards—one for monitoring the internal quality of software product under development (Figure 8.6) and one for monitoring the external quality (Figure 8.7). The dashboards are complemented with build radiators. The build radiators are used to show the current build status of products at the studied organization at Saab EDS. If a product is red (indicates a broken build) on the radiator, people react to that and perform the actions needed to make it pass again.

The dashboard in Figure 8.6 presents indicators for monitoring the current state and trend in internal software quality (ISO, 2005b), in particular the complexity of the product. This dashboard is used on a daily basis among the developers because it visualizes data that is immediately important for them. The data for the indicators is generated by a tool for static code analysis, and it shows the status of such quality indicators as the status of the complexity of source code.

The early warning for problems is provided by other views in the same dashboard by showing trends for the metrics below (as an example):

- The tree map/heatmap (in the center of the Figure 8.6 with red, intensive color pointing attention toward the problem area and green color showing high quality of the area) view is used to identify a software module with low rule compliance. The size of the rectangle is determined by lines of code. This information is used as input to decision making about whether to clean up or rewrite a certain module.[5]

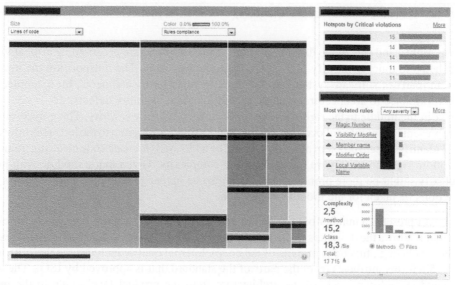

**FIGURE 8.6**

Dashboard for monitoring the internal quality (excerpt) at Saab EDS.

---

[5]Module names throughout the dashboard are grayed-out for confidentiality reasons.

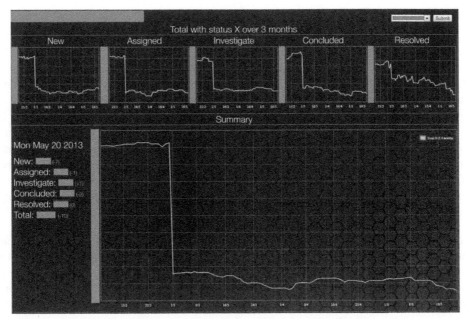

**FIGURE 8.7**

Dashboard for monitoring the external product quality at Saab EDS.

- The top, right-hand side of the dashboard (Figure 8.6) shows hotspots caused by critical violations, which helps to quickly identify high-risk code and quick wins. The hotspots are the most important parts of software systems that violate the rules set by architects, for example, non-conformance to architectural guidelines and interface visibility defects.
- The box in the middle to the right lists the most violated rules by severity. The grayed-out field represents the number of occurrences and the distribution diagram to the left. This information is used to identify certain problem areas that should be addressed (focused code clean up, training, etc.).
- The bottom right box in Figure 8.6 shows code complexity. Given that a module with high complexity might be more prone to errors and also be harder to maintain, higher values demand that actions be taken for the module in question.

The dashboard presents a number of aspects of internal quality in a succinct way and is "clickable" in the sense that it allows the designers to drill-down into detailed measures or the same measures at lower abstraction levels (e.g., functions or parts of the code). Internal quality includes the majority attributes from ISO 25000 (the attributes from the parts of the standard that is approved by ISO). The attributes are calculated at multiple levels of the architecture from the product level down to the module or function level (if applicable).

The dashboard[6] in Figure 8.7 presents indicators for monitoring trouble reports, that is, the external quality of the software product under development. The information is used to easily identify bottlenecks

---

[6]Actual numbers and organization name has been grayed-out.

in the flow of resolving the trouble reports. The small graphs represent the number of trouble reports in the corresponding state at a given time. The summary graph contains the sum of the small graphs at a given time. The colored numbers under the summary indicates the trouble report delta over 24 h.

An upward trend for resolved trouble reports, for example, can point towards both positive effects (increased quality of product) and to negative effects (unbalance between the testing resources and development resources for defect-resolution).

## 8.4 RECOMMENDATIONS FOR OTHER COMPANIES

Based on the experience with constructing dashboards for various companies, we can identify a number of recommendations for companies that intend to introduce dashboards. We divide the recommendations into two parts: constructing the dashboards (process) and indicators and measures (product).

### 8.4.1 Recommendations for constructing the dashboards

To be successful in introducing a dashboard we recommend that companies do the following:

- **When defining indicators, choose the those that match stakeholders who have the mandate and means to react upon the status of the indicators**. It is imperative that the stakeholders have the mandate to act. Without this, the dashboard is just a nice chart that perhaps can be used for discussion. With the stakeholder who has the mandate and means, the indicators become a very powerful tool for the organization to steer itself based on facts. For monitoring quality of product under development, stakeholders should be product managers and project managers. They have the mandate to order extra resources to address quality issues and to rework the architecture; they can also give assignments to architects and designers to address specific problems with architecture.
- **Limit the number of indicators.** Depending on the company's awareness and trust in measures, the dashboards should contain the appropriate number of indicators. If there is a well-established measurement culture in the organization, where measurement teams have a strong reputation for providing reliable measurement products, then one indicator is enough to communicate efficiently. However, if the organization is still gaining the awareness and the measurement team is gaining reputation, then there should be more indicators (although no more than 10 for the sake of coherence). The number of indicators usually decreases over time as organizations become more aware of the inherent dependencies between the initial set of indicators. By assigning the right test cases, companies can monitor qualities of the product (e.g., performance or reliability) by monitoring the test progress, which is one example of combining two interdependent indicators.
- **Involve multiple parts of the organization, at least product management, product development, and verification and validation** (V&V). Even when defining indicators for smaller entities, the company should keep in mind that no entity is isolated. When companies work with products, they need to understand the premises for the product (features, markets—captured by product management), software development, and requirements of the company's quality assurance (testing at different levels, customer feedback—captured by V&V). Having all three—product management, development, and V&V—allows the company to focus on the end result rather than suboptimizing toward smaller processes. This observation is particularly important for monitoring

the quality attributes of the architecture because problems with architecture can influence the extensibility of the product (thus also the agility of the company), the performance of the product, or the quality assurance effort (thus cost of the quality).

## 8.4.2 Recommendations for choosing indicators and measures

To choose the right indicators and measures for dashboards for monitoring the quality of products under development, we recommend that companies:

- **Focus on product**: The focus of the successful indicator is usually on the monitored entity, which can be a product, a process, or a project. However, in reality companies focus on products and their profitability, which demands that the indicators also focus on products. Problems with processes or projects will be visible on the product level (e.g., architecture erosion, low quality, delays in delivery) and they have to be monitored using base/derived measures as trends. However, as companies do not sell their processes or projects, the indicators should be related to products. The RR indicator at Ericsson shows how a set of process and product measures (e.g., test progress) can be packaged into a product-focused indicator. Various test cases are supposed to test both functional and nonfunctional properties, but no gradation is done on which is more important.
- **Focus on end result**: The main focus of indicators for monitoring the quality of products under development should be on the end product, that is, the software or software-hardware system and not individual artifacts. It is the end product that the software organizations provide to their customers. So, it is the end product that should have the right quality and functionality. Therefore, monitoring particular artifacts like requirements or architecture is not sufficient and can lead to suboptimizations and short-sighted decisions.

## 8.5 FURTHER READING

The dashboards for monitoring the development progress are related to monitoring bottlenecks in large software development organizations, which has been studied by Staron and Meding (2011) and Petersen and Wohlin (2011). Monitoring bottlenecks is a useful method for monitoring the capacity of the organization. In the previous work we developed and introduced a method based on automated indicators for monitoring the capacity and bottlenecks in the work flow in the large software development project—that is, the process/project view of software development in that organization.

The very rudimentary and effective first measure to be used by Agile teams to monitor quality is the RTF (Running Tested Features) measure, popular in XP (Jeffries, 2004). The metric combines three important concepts—the feature (i.e., a piece of code useful for the end user, not a small increment that is not visible to the end user), execution (i.e., adding the value to the product through shipping the features to the customer), and the testing process (i.e., the quality of the feature—not only should it execute, but it should also be of sufficient quality). This measure stimulates smart continuous deployment strategies and is intended to capture similar aspects as our release readiness indicator although in smaller projects. Monitoring the trends in RTF can provide indications of architecture erosion over time (RTF becoming longer over time).

A set of other metrics useful in the context of continuous deployment can be found in the work of Fitz (2009) in the context of market-driven software development organization. The metrics presented by Fritz measure such aspects as continuous integration pace or the pace of delivery of features to the customers. These measures complement the indicators presented in this chapter with a different perspective important for product management.

The delivery strategy that is an extension of the concept of continuous deployment was found as one of the three key aspects important for Agile software development organizations in a survey of 109 companies by Chow and Cao (2008). The indicator presented in this chapter is a means of supporting organizations in their transition toward achieving efficient delivery processes that are in line with the delivery strategy prioritized by practitioners in this survey.

The view on indicators, stakeholders, and measures presented in ISO/IEC 15939 is consistent with other engineering disciplines; the standard states that it is based on ISO/IEC 15288:2007 (Systems and software engineering—System life cycle processes), ISO/IEC 14598–1:1999 (Information technology—Software product evaluation) (International Standard Organization, 1999), ISO/IEC 9126-x (International Standard Organization and International Electrotechnical Commission, 2001), ISO/IEC 25000 series of standards, or international vocabulary of basic and general terms in metrology (VIM) (International Bureau of Weights and Measures, 1993). These standards are recommended for companies aiming at successful use of dashboards for monitoring quality of products under development.

Finally, readers interested in more details about constructing dashboards based on ISO 15939 can find more information about automation, frameworks, and modeling of measures can find more information in Staron et al. (2008, 2010a).

## 8.6 CONCLUSIONS

Qualities and architecture of modern software products are distinguishing excellent products from the average ones and can influence the success of software development companies. Extensible and scalable architectures of products combined with Agile and Lean software development can determine long-term sustainable businesses and maximize the value that customers get from these products. Agile and Lean software development methodologies change the way in which organizations work with monitoring of quality of software products under development and assessment of release readiness. Continuous development of software using these methodologies demands continuous quality management. The inherent dependability of these methodologies on self-organized teams shifts the focus from monitoring quality from the higher management to communicating the quality status. The communicated quality status triggers decision processes on all levels in the organizations and new ways of monitoring the progress of the implementation of these decisions emerge.

In this chapter, we investigated how three organizations monitor the quality of software products during development. We explored how Ericsson in Sweden works with one effective indicator of release readiness to monitor the status and trigger decisions. We studied how Saab Electronic Defense Systems combines trends for defect management with monitoring internal quality of products. Finally, we also studied how a team at VCC in Sweden can communicate the software development progress as an alternative to manual status reporting. We provided recommendations for other companies willing to use dashboards—how to construct them and how to choose indicators and measures.

# References

Basili, V., Caldiera, G., Rombach, H.D., 1994. The Goal Question Metric Approach. Available: ftp://ftp.cs.umd.edu/pub/sel/papers/gqm.pdf.

Bellini, P., Bruno, I., Nesi, P., Rogai, D., 2005. Comparing fault-proneness estimation models. In: Proceedings of the 10th IEEE International Conference on Engineering of Complex Computer Systems. ICECCS 2005, pp. 205–214.

Buse, R.P.L., Zimmermann, T., 2012. Information needs for software development analytics. In: 34th International Conference on Software Engineering (ICSE 2012 SEIP Track). Microsoft Research Report, Zurich, Switzerland.

Chow, T., Cao, D.-B., 2008. A survey study of critical success factors in agile software projects. J. Syst. Softw. 81, 961–971.

Eklund, U., Jonsson, N., Eriksson, A., Bosch, J., 2012. A reference architecture template for software-intensive embedded systems. In: Proceedings of the WICSA/ECSA 2012 Companion Volume. ACM, New York, pp. 104–111.

Fitz, T., 2009. Continuous Deployment at IMVU: Doing the impossible fifty times a day [Online]. Available: http://timothyfitz.wordpress.com/2009/02/10/continuous-deployment-at-imvu-doing-the-impossible-fifty-times-a-day/.

Gustavsson, H., Eklund, U., 2011. Architecting automotive product lines: industrial practice. In: Software Product Lines: Going Beyond, pp. 92–105.

IEEE, 1998. IEEE standard for a software quality metrics methodology. IEEE Std 1061–1998.

International Bureau of Weights and Measures, 1993. Vocabulaire International des Termes Fondamentaux et Généraux de Métrologie (International Vocabulary of Basic and General Terms in Metrology). International Organization for Standardization, Genève, Switzerland.

International Standard Organization, 1999. Information technology—software product, evaluation 14598–1:1999.

International Standard Organization & International Electrotechnical Commission, 2001. ISO/IEC 9126—software engineering—product quality Part: 1 Quality model. International Standard Organization/International Electrotechnical Commission, Geneva.

International Standard Organization & International Electrotechnical Commission, 2007. ISO/IEC 15939 Software engineering—software measurement process. International Standard Organization/International Electrotechnical Commission, Geneva.

ISO, 2005a. 9000: 2005 Quality management systems. Fundamentals and vocabulary. British Standards Institution.

ISO, 2005b. IEC 25000 Software and system engineering—software product Quality Requirements and Evaluation (SQuaRE)—Guide to SQuaRE. International Organization for Standarization.

Jeffries, R., 2004. A Metric Leading to Agility [Online]. xprogramming.com. Available: http://xprogramming.com/xpmag/jatRtsMetric, 2011.

Johansson, L., Staron, M., Meding, W., 2007. An Industrial Case Study on Visualization of Dependencies between Software Measurements. In: Arts, T. (Ed.), Software Engineering and Practice in Sweden. Göteborg, Sweden.

Lee, Y.W., Strong, D.M., Kahn, B.K., Wang, R.Y., 2002. AIMQ: a methodology for information quality assessment. Inf. Manage. 40, 133–146.

Mcgee, R.A., Eklund, U., Lundin, M., 2010. Stakeholder identification and quality attribute prioritization for a global Vehicle Control System. In: Proceedings of the Fourth European Conference on Software Architecture: Companion Volume. ACM, pp. 43–48.

Meding, W., Staron, M., 2009. The role of design and implementation models in establishing mature measurement programs. In: Peltonen, J. (Ed.), Nordic Workshop on Model Driven Engineering. Tampere University of Technology, Tampere, Finland.

Petersen, K., Wohlin, C., 2011. Measuring the flow in lean software development. Softw. Pract. Exp. 41, 975–996.

Phaal, R., Farrukh, C.J.P., Probert, D.R., 2004. Technology roadmapping—a planning framework for evolution and revolution. Technol. Forecast. Soc. Chang. 71, 5–26.

Poppendieck, M., Poppendieck, T., 2007. Implementing Lean Software Development: From Concept to Cash. Addison-Wesley, Boston, MA.

Raffo, D.M., Kellner, M.I., 2000. Empirical analysis in software process simulation modeling. J. Syst. Softw. 53, 31–41.

Ruhe, G., 2003. Software engineering decision support—a new paradigm for learning software organizations. In: Henninger, S., Maurer, F. (Eds.), Advances in Learning Software Organizations. Springer, Berlin/Heidelberg.

Ruhe, G., Saliu, M.O., 2005. The art and science of software release planning. Softw. IEEE. 22, 47–53.

Sangal, N., Jordan, E., Sinha, V., Jackson, D., 2005. Using dependency models to manage complex software architecture. In: Proceedings of the 20th Annual ACM SIGPLAN Conference on Object-Oriented Programming, Systems, Languages, and Applications. ACM, San Diego, CA.

Scacchi, W., 1999. Experience with software process simulation and modeling. J. Syst. Softw. 46, 183–192.

Sharp, H., Baddoo, N., Beecham, S., Hall, T., Robinson, H., 2009. Models of motivation in software engineering. Inf. Softw. Technol. 51, 219–233.

Shollo, A., Pandazo, K., Staron, M., Meding, W., 2010. Presenting software metrics indicators: a case study. In: The 20th International Workshop on Software Measurement IWSM.

Staron, M., Meding, W., 2009a. Ensuring reliability of information provided by measurement systems. In: Abran, A., Braungarten, R., Dumke, R., Cuadrado-Gallego, J., Brunekreef, J. (Eds.), Software Process and Product Measurement. Springer, Berlin/Heidelberg, pp. 1–16.

Staron, M., Meding, W., 2009b. Using models to develop measurement systems: a method and its industrial use. In: Abran, A., Braungarten, R., Dumke, R., Cuadrado-Gallego, J., Brunekreef, J. (Eds.), Software Process and Product Measurement. Springer Berlin/Heidelberg, Amsterdam, NL.

Staron, M., Meding, W., 2011. Monitoring bottlenecks in agile and lean software development projects—a method and its industrial use. In: Caivano, D., Oivo, M., Baldassarre, M., Visaggio, G. (Eds.), Product-Focused Software Process Improvement. Springer Berlin/Heidelberg, Torre Canne, Italy, pp. 3–16.

Staron, M., Meding, W., Nilsson, C., 2008. A framework for developing measurement systems and its industrial evaluation. Inf. Softw. Technol. 51, 721–737.

Staron, M., Meding, W., Karlsson, G., Nilsson, C., 2010a. Developing measurement systems: an industrial case study. J. Softw. Maint. Evol. Res. Pract. 23, 89–107. http://dx.doi.org/10.1002/smr.470.

Staron, M., Meding, W., Söderqvist, B., 2010b. A method for forecasting defect backlog in large streamline software development projects and its industrial evaluation. Inf. Softw. Technol. 52, 1069–1079.

Staron, M., Meding, W., Palm, K., 2012. Release readiness indicator for mature agile and lean software development projects. In: Agile Processes in Software Engineering and Extreme Programming, pp. 93–107.

Staron, M., Meding, W., Hansson, J., Höglund, C., Eriksson, P., Nilsson, J., 2013. Identifying implicit architectural dependencies using measures of source code change waves. In: Software Engineering and Advanced Applications (39th International Conference). Santander, Spain.

Stensrud, E., Foss, T., Kitchenham, B., Myrtveit, I., 2002. An empirical validation of the relationship between the magnitude of relative error and project size. In: Proceedings. Eighth IEEE Symposium on Software Metrics, pp. 3–12.

Tomaszewski, P., Berander, P., Damm, L.-O., 2007. From traditional to streamline development—opportunities and challenges. Softw. Process Improv. Pract. 2007, 1–20.

Van Solingen, R., Berghout, E., 1999. The Goal/Question/Metric Method. A Practical Guide for Quality Improvement of Software Development. McGraw-Hill, London.

Ward-Dutton, N., 2011. Software Econometrics: Challenging assumptions about software delivery. IBM.com podcast companion report [Online].

Yuming, Z., Hareton, L., 2006. Empirical analysis of object-oriented design metrics for predicting high and low severity faults. IEEE Trans. Softw. Eng. 32, 771–789.

# Domain-Specific Software Architecture and Software Qualities

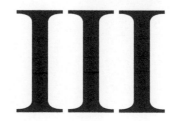

# III

# Domain-Specific Software Architecture and Software Qualities

# Achieving Quality in Customer-Configurable Products

# 9

**Martin Große-Rhode, Robert Hilbrich, Stefan Mann, and Stephan Weißleder**

*Fraunhofer Institute for Open Communication Systems, Berlin, Germany*

## INTRODUCTION

Beyond achieving pure functionality, system quality is one of the most important aspects of systems engineering. It contributes essentially to the satisfaction of customer needs, the reduction of after-sales costs, and the certification of products. Besides high quality, customers now also want products that are tailored to their needs. For this reason, configurability of products becomes more and more important, and manufacturers strive to adapt their engineering processes correspondingly. Product line engineering (Clements and Northrop, 2002) is an established approach to the development of configurable systems and gradually replaces single product engineering. The focus of this chapter is therefore on quality assurance in product line engineering with the aim to support the systematic development of high-quality configurable systems.

The series of international standards named systems and software quality requirements and evaluation (ISO/IEC, 2014) distinguishes management, modeling, measurement, requirements analysis, and evaluation as the essential activity domains to achieve system quality. One of the main insights throughout all these domains is that quality has to be addressed throughout the whole process; it cannot be added to the finished product at the end. Corresponding to this, we introduce a framework explaining how quality assurance can be established in product line engineering. We instantiate and demonstrate this framework with two quality assurance techniques that are applied at different stages of the engineering process: model-based testing (MBT) as a technique to measure both the functional suitability and the testability of the engineered systems and model-based deployment as a means to establish system reliability, availability, responsiveness, and other qualities that depend on its real-time behavior.

In this sense we understand configurability as orthogonal to other qualities such as those just mentioned. Correspondingly, the purpose of the framework is to lift a quality assurance technique—such as MBT and model-based deployment—from the level of single products to the level of product lines. This is equivalent to saying that the framework helps to achieve customer configurability as additional quality for systems whose further qualities are achieved by other techniques in that it extends these techniques to product lines instead of single products.

Product lines differ in the number of product variants and the number of products per product variant, depending on the application domain and the industrial sector. We sketch two examples in the following.

To give an initial understanding of product lines and configurability, we first consider the development of software for vehicles. There are millions of product variants, but a comparatively small number of products per product variant. Customers expect that they are able to configure their desired car, which means that they can select the equipment and functionality of the car according to their needs and desires. Today, software is embedded in almost every part of a vehicle. Consequently, the functionality as well as the equipment of the vehicle define requirements for the vehicle software. Thus, the car manufacturer has to build configurability into the software system that allows the production and delivery of the individual system requested by the customer in short time. This induces the following constraints. On the one hand, the expected time duration between the receipt of the customer's order and the vehicle's delivery is too short to allow creative or extensive development and quality assurance steps. As a consequence, the production process of an individual car, including its software, must be precisely defined and the assembly must be a matter of routine. On the other hand, the number of possible car configurations is too high to allow building and testing all variants before the market introduction: Vehicles today have more than a million variants and many of them have an impact on the software system configuration. Configurability thus means to build one generic system from which all possible individual configurations can be derived in such a way that the car manufacturer may trust in the quality of each individual configuration with respect to aspects such as safety, dependability, availability, usability, and security, for example.

As a further example, let us consider the development of software for airplanes. This domain is characterized by a small volume production. Nevertheless, configurability is required. For instance, airlines as the customers of airplane manufacturers often want to design the cabin on their own or integrate third-party systems into the airplane. Furthermore, every single end product must be approved for the target market and be certified by the authorities of the customer's states. However, the manufacturer of the airplane is responsible for the approval. In this sense, the manufacturer needs to develop a high-quality system that is configurable and compatible with the individual contributions of customers and at the same time satisfies the requirements on the integrated final system. The situation is similar for subsystem suppliers in any other domain: They typically produce solutions for different manufacturers and, therefore, have a strong interest in building systems that can be adapted to the different customer's requirements while satisfying their quality requirements.

## Outline of the chapter

Having given a rough introduction to configurable systems and an explanation of why it is important to stress the focus on quality of those systems, we detail this in Section 9.2. Furthermore, we provide a framework describing how techniques for quality assurance of configurable systems can be implemented. For this purpose, we first introduce the means to integrate the needed flexibility into a systems engineering process (Section 9.2.1). Then, in Section 9.2.2, we describe how a quality assurance concept in this context can be set up.

Afterwards we show how to apply this concept to two different quality assurance techniques: MBT is a common technique used to attain confidence in a correctly implemented functionality. We discuss in Section 9.3 how to apply MBT to configurable systems. Model-based software deployment is another quality assurance technique that provides a means to construct correct and good deployments according to predefined safety and resource constraints. By this, performance, efficiency, and reliability quality aspects can be ensured. How model-based deployment can be applied to configurable systems is discussed in Section 9.4.

We substantiate the explanations with example models that describe the properties of a flight management system (FMS), which is introduced in Section 9.1. To conclude, we give an overview of related work in Section 9.5 and summarize this chapter in Section 9.6.

## 9.1 THE FLIGHT MANAGEMENT SYSTEM EXAMPLE

A FMS is a central and important part in the aviation electronic systems (avionics) of modern airplanes. It supports a variety of in-flight tasks by providing the following set of information functions: navigation, flight planning, trajectory prediction, performance computations, and in-flight guidance. In order to implement these functions, an FMS has to interface with a variety of other avionics systems. Due to the importance of an FMS for the safe operation of an airplane, most of its functions have to be highly reliable and fault-tolerant. Although the specific implementations of an FMS may vary, it generally consists of a computer unit and a control display unit. The computer unit provides the resources for all computationally intensive calculations and establishes the interfaces to the other avionic systems. The control display unit is the primary interface for the pilots. It is used to enter data and to display the information provided by the FMS. The computer unit for small FMSs with a reduced set of functionalities can be realized as a non-standard stand-alone unit. However, for larger FMSs, the computer unit often requires the use of powerful and fault-tolerant processing resources, such as the Integrated Modular Avionics (IMA) (Morgan, 1991; Watkins and Walter, 2007) platform in modern airplanes. We use the development of a configurable FMS as running example in this chapter.

The customer-visible set of features of the envisioned product line is depicted in Figure 9.1. Each feature corresponds to a system-level function of the FMS. In Section 9.3 we focus on the application level functionality of the FMS and analyze how test cases can be derived. For that purpose the system's functionality is modeled as a configurable state chart in Figure 9.3. In Section 9.4 we discuss deployments issues. Figure 9.7 illustrates the application level of FMS by showing some of the FMS software components and their hardware requirements. In Figure 9.8 the configurable hardware architecture of the FMS is illustrated.

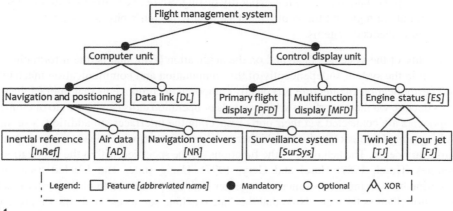

**FIGURE 9.1**

Feature model for flight management systems.

## 9.2 THEORETICAL FRAMEWORK

In this section we present the preliminaries and the theoretical framework of our approach. As indicated above, in order to achieve system quality, it must be addressed throughout the whole engineering process. Given that we focus on such complex safety-critical systems as the ones mentioned in section "Introduction", we assume that a defined software development process is given and that models are used, for instance, to capture and analyze the requirements, to design the abstract functionality of the system, or to design the software architecture. In the case of embedded systems, the development of the underlying computing platform can also be supported by models that define the topology of the system, the communication means, or the capacities of the nodes in a network. Accordingly, we discuss in this section how models can be extended to express configurability from different viewpoints and how the quality of a configurable system (under development) that is represented by such models can be assured.

### 9.2.1 Configurable models

Before we define how to express configurability in a model, we first have a closer look at which kinds of models we consider and where the distinction of different models or views comes from.

#### 9.2.1.1 System views

In this chapter, for the sake of simplicity, we consider only three views that are to be described by models.

1. The application level view in which the functionality of the system from the point of view of the user is considered.
2. The resource level view in which the computing platform (nodes, networks, hardware resources) are described.
3. And the deployment view that describes how the resources are used to realize the application functions. These views correspond to those suggested by Kruchten (1995), which we discuss below. To simplify matters, we do not explicitly distinguish between the logical and development views here, but we highlight the deployment view in Kruchten's physical view because of our emphasis on embedded systems.

The functionality of the system is designed on the application level, that is, the information flow and transformation in the system, independently of the computation and communication mechanisms, are specified. The application architecture is typically composed of components that interact via ports. The components declare via their interfaces which signals or operation calls can be sent to or emitted from a port. Components are connected via their ports respecting the interfaces. In addition, a set of components can be grouped and enclosed into a higher level component, which leads to a component hierarchy of arbitrary depth. The behavior of the functions can be specified within the application level by state machines (Harel, 1987; Harel and Gery, 1997). Using states and labeled transitions, state machines define how an input to a function, together with the present state of the system, determines an output and/or changes the state. Note that the state machine serves as an abstract representation of the functions and their dependencies. It does not define the concrete realization of the functions. In this sense, this view corresponds to the logical view or development view in Kruchten (1995).

The resource level (the physical view in Kruchten, 1995) is used to represent the computation and communication resources that are available to implement the functionality specified on the application level. Analogous to the application level, the resources are represented by components, ports, connections, and hierarchical structuring. A component thereby represents, for example, an electronic control unit with its processor(s) and storages. The ports represent the peripherals and the connections to buses and other communication lines. Behavior is usually not specified in the resource level view, but only in the capacities the resources offer.

The models of the application level and the resource level are connected by the deployment model. It defines which application components are deployed to (i.e., executed by) which computation nodes; how their interaction points are mapped to ports, peripherals, or bus connections; and how the information flow is mapped to the communication media. Deployment is part of the physical view in Kruchten (1995). An overall system model is finally given by the three integrated views: the model of the application level, the model of the resource level, and the deployment model. Model-based testing in Section 9.3 focuses on the application level, while model-based deployment in Section 9.4 deals explicitly with deployment-level aspects.

### 9.2.1.2 Variability within the views

Configurability is expressed in a model by variation points, which are locations in the model where variability is built in. In general, a variation point is a model element that carries one of the following types of additional information:

1. XOR container: The element is a placeholder for a set of other elements of the same type, its mutually exclusive alternatives. The placeholder can be replaced by one of the alternatives. Exactly one of the alternatives can be selected, which is controlled by configuration means.
2. Option: The element can be present or not, that is, a specific product variant can include or exclude the element. To decide in favor of or against the element, the selection of yes or no is controlled by configuration means.
3. Parameterized element: The element is endowed with a parameter that defines certain of its properties. The concrete value of the parameter is selected and assigned by configuration means. Usually, a set of selectable values is provided for the parameter. In this sense, the established variability is similar to XOR variability, but on a lower granularity level.

In a component model, such as the application or the resource view of a system, components can be XOR-containers, optional, or parameterized elements; ports can be optional or parameterized elements. In a state machine, both the states and the transitions can be optional. Finally, in a deployment model the links between application model elements and resource model elements must respect the variability of the elements. Additionally, alternative links can be defined in order to establish variability in the mapping. Examples for application, resource, and behavioral models with included variation points are given for the configurable FMS in Sections 9.3.2 and 9.4.3.

### 9.2.1.3 Variability view

With the growing complexity of the models the dependencies among the variation points—both within one model and across different models—also become complex. In order to reduce this complexity, a feature model can be introduced (Czarnecki and Eisenecker, 2000; Kang et al., 1990). It abstracts from the internal and overall structure of the models, that is, the components and their interconnections, the states and their transitions, and their distribution to the different views. Instead of the view-specific variation points, the feature model represents abstract features as global system variation points.

The feature model of the FMS is given in the diagram in Figure 9.1, which also illustrates the common modeling concepts of feature models (Czarnecki and Eisenecker, 2000; Kang et al., 1990). The feature model is shown by a tree that defines a hierarchy of features and specifies the common and the variable parts within the FMS product line. A feature can be decomposed by sub-features (e.g., the relationship between the control display unit and its parts primary flight display, multifunction display (MFD), and engine status). A feature can be mandatory (e.g., control display unit in Figure 9.1), optional (e.g., MFD), or an XOR-feature whose alternatives are represented as its sub-features (e.g., the control display unit has either an engine status for twin jets or for four jets, thus engine status is an XOR-feature). Finally, a feature can be a parameter feature; in this case, a data type is given from which a value can be selected. Additional constraints between features (e.g., the selection of one feature needs or excludes the selection of another one) limit the choices of the user (e.g., a option might be that FMS is equipped with the air data feature together with the surveillance systems feature only. In other words, air data would need surveillance systems). In Figure 9.1 no additional constraints are given.

### 9.2.1.4 Feature configuration, products, and resolution of model variance points

The feature model can be used to specify individual products by drawing a selection for each non-mandatory feature. That means that for each XOR-feature exactly one alternative is selected; for each optional feature yes or no is selected; and for each parameter feature a value is selected. Provided the selection is consistent with the constraints of the feature model, a feature configuration is defined.

As examples, three types of FMSs are defined in Table 9.1 via their feature configurations. The "X" sign marks selected features, "-" is used for deselected ones.

The feature model can be used to control the variability in the other models (application, resource, deployment models) by the definition of relations between the features and the corresponding elements of the other models. This feature mapping can be defined by configuration rules that are assigned to the model's elements. In the example models of Sections 9.3.2 and 9.4.3, the rules are shown as Boolean expressions that contain the features of the feature model and are attached to the corresponding model elements. The effect is that the selection of some feature induces a selection in all variation points in the related models that are related to this feature. Beyond the abstraction from the model structure, this yields another very useful abstraction mechanism to reduce complexity of variability. In order to be consistent, the relations must respect the modeled variability in the other models.

The relations of the feature model to the other models also define the model configuration, that is, the derivation of a configured model (without variation points) from the configurable, generic model

**Table 9.1** Three FMS Products Defined by Their Feature Selections

| FMS Products | FMS Features | | | | | | | |
|---|---|---|---|---|---|---|---|---|
| | AD | NR | SurSys | DL | MFD | ES | TJ | FJ |
| $P_1$: Simple FMS | - | - | - | - | - | - | - | - |
| $P_2$: FMS for Small Jets | X | X | - | - | X | X | X | - |
| $P_3$: FMS for Jumbo Jets | X | X | X | X | X | X | - | X |

(that contains variation points). Provided that the relations between the feature model and the other models cover all variation points, all variation points can be resolved in this way. Thus, for each complete selection of features (i.e., when every feature in the feature model is either selected or deselected), we obtain a configured model that no longer contains, that is, the variability has been bound and resolved by feature configuration.

### 9.2.2 Quality assurance of configurable systems

In the setting of a model-based development process, quality assurance is based on the evaluation of the models that represent the design decisions drawn so far in the process. This might either be an evaluation that is explicitly performed after the model has been created in order to prove that the quality requirements are still respected, or it may be an evaluation that is built into the construction of the model, for instance, when the model construction is machine-supported.

Given the framework described above—an overall model, a feature model, the feature-model-relations, and the model configuration mechanism based on feature selections—we discuss now how quality attributes of configurable systems can be evaluated.

Suppose a method is given that allows the evaluation of a model without variation points. In general, there are two possibilities to extend this method to a model with variation points:

1. Product-centered approaches evaluate all product models or a representative subset of them by
   a. deriving all (or sufficiently many) product models.
   b. evaluating each model.
   c. condensing the results to an evaluation of the product line.
2. Product-line-centered approaches extend the method to the evaluation of variation points, that is, they define how to integrate for example, options, alternatives, and parameters into the evaluation without resolving single product variants.

It should be noted that the evaluation criteria on the product line level may slightly differ from those on the product level. In other words, an optimal solution for the product line does not necessarily consist of optimal solutions for every single product.

Product-centered and product-line-centered approaches are illustrated in a schematic diagram in Figure 9.2. The lower layer in the figure, the product model level, represents single system evaluations: A variability-free product model $Model_P$ is evaluated by the function $evaluate_P$. The result of this evaluation is denoted by $Result_P$.

The upper layer in Figure 9.2, the product line model level, shows the variability-aware function $evaluate_{PL}$, which is used to analyze the product line model $Model_{PL}$ and produces the corresponding result $Result_{PL}$. The product line model $Model_{PL}$ includes a feature model that exhibits the supported variability of the product line, base models that represent the realization of the product line (e.g., design models) as well as the mapping model between the feature model and the base models in order to specify the presence conditions of base model's elements by features.

The function $derive_{Model}$ denotes the derivation of a product model $Model_P$ from the product line model $Model_{PL}$ for the feature configuration corresponding to product $P$. Analogously, $derive_{Result}$ represents the derivation of a product result from the product line result. The arrow set labeled $aggregate_{Results}$ stands for the inverse operation of aggregating the set of all product results $Result_P$ and building the single product-line result $Result_{PL}$.

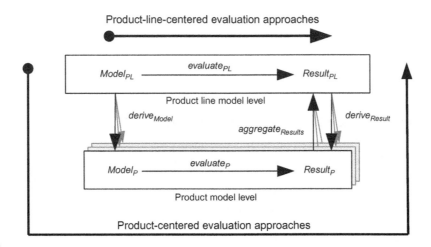

**FIGURE 9.2**

General schema.

### 9.2.2.1 Product-centered approaches

Product-centered approaches start with the product line model $Model_{PL}$ and create the product models $Model_P$ with the derivation operator $derive_{Model}$. Then the evaluation method $evaluate_P$ is applied to each $Model_P$. To get the result $Result_{PL}$ on the product-line model level, the operator $aggregate_{Results}$ is applied on the set of the individual results $Result_P$. The representation of $Result_{PL}$ (and with it the definition of $aggregate_{Results}$) depends on the concrete evaluation method. This enumerative way of the evaluation of a product line, that is, the consecutive evaluation of each single product, is sometimes called naive (von Rhein et al., 2013) because the number of (potentially) possible product variants to be analyzed are usually too large to be of practical use. Even for a small product line (e.g., option to choose from 10 freely selectable features already results in 1024 possible product variants). Furthermore, the method is inefficient because of redundant computations that result from not exploiting the commonalities between the single products.

### 9.2.2.2 Product-line-centered approaches

Product-line-centered approaches avoid the creation of single product models, that is, an evaluation method $evaluate_{PL}$ is directly applied to the product line model. The definition of the evaluation method needs to take into account the variability in $Model_{PL}$. It is supposed to be more efficient because it is aware of the commonality in the product line. However, its definition is more challenging because of the additional complexity introduced by the variability.

Between these two extremes, there are approaches that reuse analysis methods on product level, but minimize the numbers and the volume of models $Model_P$, either by selecting a representative subset of products (as done in the product-centered MBT approach in Section 9.3.4 by using a feature coverage criterion) or by reducing the projected models $Model_P$ to representative sub models, cf. for example, sample-based and feature-based methods (Thüm et al., 2012; von Rhein et al., 2013).

We have given the theoretical framework for quality assurance approaches in the context of product lines. Next, we instantiate the framework using two examples of quality assurance techniques. First, we demonstrate how configurable systems can be tested by model-based approaches in order to ensure the correctness of the single product variants (Section 9.3). Second, we discuss how the deployment of application components onto resources can be correctly constructed for configurable systems. We use the "correctness by construction" approach (Chapman, 2006) for the deployment in order to ensure safety constraints (Section 9.4).

## 9.3 MODEL-BASED PRODUCT LINE TESTING

In this section, we describe how to apply MBT for configurable systems using the schema depicted in Figure 9.2. For that, we first give an introduction to the basic concepts of MBT. Afterwards, we describe the approach of applying this technique on the product model level. Subsequently, we show how to apply it on the product line model level.

### 9.3.1 What is MBT?

Testing is a widespread means of quality assurance (Ammann and Offutt, 2008; Beizer, 1990; Myers, 1979). The idea is to compare the system under test to a specification by systematically stimulating the system and comparing the observed system behavior to the specified one. The basic approach is to first design test cases based on requirements and to execute them on the system under test afterwards. Complete testing is usually impossible due to loops and a large input data space. So, heuristics like coverage criteria are used to make a quantified statement about the relative quality of the test suite. It has been experienced in many projects that the costs for testing range between 20 and 50% of the overall system engineering costs. This is substantiated by our experiences with industrial transfer projects. For safety-critical systems, testing costs can easily reach up to 80% (Jones, 1991). Nolan et al. (2011) discovered on the basis of data collected at Rolls-Royce that around 52% of the total development effort is spent on verification and validation activities (V&V). They argue that applying a software product line approach will reduce development efforts, but not necessarily the efforts for V&V. They report that V&V can comprise up to 72% of a product's overall effort in a software product line context, and it could theoretically increase to more than 90% in cases of very low costs because of high reuse. They conclude that "the percentage is higher on a product line not because verification has increased but because the development effort has decreased making verification costs higher in relation to the overall effort," and that "testability therefore becomes critical for safety-critical product lines."

Thus, automation is a means to reduce these costs. It can be applied to test execution and to test design. Automating the test design is often implemented by deriving a formal model from requirements and by using test generators that produce a set of test cases based on this model. Corresponding approaches are also called model-based testing (Utting and Legeard, 2006; Zander et al., 2011). There are many different approaches with respect to the chosen modeling language, the modeled aspects of the system, and the algorithms for test generation (Utting et al., 2012).

In the following, we use state machines as defined in Unified Modeling Language (UML) (OMG, 2011) to describe the behavior that is used for test design. We additionally annotate the state machines with variability information and configuration rules in order to use the state machine as the base model for the MBT of product lines. There are several approaches to steer the test generation on the model level (Chilenski and Miller, 1994; Rajan et al., 2008; Weißleder, 2010). We will focus on the widespread approach of applying coverage criteria to the state machine level, for example, such as transition coverage. This criterion defines a type of model elements (here: all transitions of the model) that have to be covered by the generated test cases. There are also coverage criteria for feature models describing the coverage of feature selections and their combinations in the tested products.

### 9.3.2 Test model for the flight management system

For MBT it is necessary to use models from which test cases can be automatically generated. For our FMS example, we model the application behavior of the FMS product line as a configurable UML state machine. It describes the potential behavior of all products. By including and excluding elements of this model, it can be tailored to describe the behavior of only one product.

The UML state machine is related to the feature model in order to extract product-specific variants of the state machine according to a certain configuration. All variable elements of the state machine have been assigned with a configuration rule consisting of elements of the feature model. Configuration rules define the conditions when those elements need to be included in or excluded from state machine.

By selecting a certain product variant on the feature level (e.g., the defined products in Table 9.1), the corresponding state machine for test generation can be automatically derived using the feature mapping (i.e., by interpretation of the configuration rules).

Figure 9.3 shows the configurable state machine for the FMS as well as the configuration rules using the features from the feature model in Figure 9.1. Variation points have been explicitly marked in the state machine. For example, the transition *requestGraphics/showGraphics* between the states *computing* and *display* is only present in a product that has the *MFD* feature. Usually, the configuration rule can be any Boolean expression using features as predicates. In case of an optional state (e.g., *checkTrajectoryOnly*), all transitions to or from this state are removed from the state machine if the state's configuration rule has not been satisfied by the corresponding configuration (e.g., if feature *SurSys* has been deselected). Thus, those transitions need not be explicitly marked as optional because they depend on the existence of the states. For the sake of simplicity, we have not modeled the complete behavior in the given state machine. Also, not every feature from the feature model has been used here.

We have sketched here how to design product line models for the test generation using the 150% product line modeling approach and how to link them with the feature models. However, this only describes the static connection between the different modeling artifacts. As the framework in Figure 9.2 already depicts, there are several ways of using this information for test design automation of product lines which is explained in the following.

### 9.3.3 Applying MBT

We now instantiate the basic framework for quality assurance of configurable systems (see Section 9.2.2) for MBT. We show how MBT can be done for product-centered as well as for product-line-centered approaches. Before going into the details of both approaches, we instantiate the framework's artifacts in Figure 9.2 for the MBT context.

The product line model $Model_{PL}$ is the union of the feature model, the base model (i.e., the state machine), and the mapping between the features and base model elements as sketched in Section 9.3.2. Each $Model_i$ consists of a concrete product variant (i.e., a feature model configuration, cf. Table 9.2)

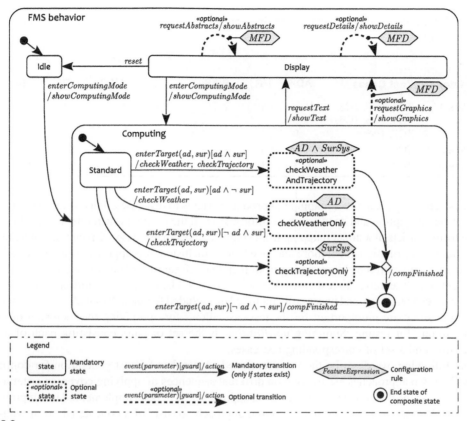

**FIGURE 9.3**

Base model of the FMS state chart including configuration rules.

**Table 9.2** Representative FMS Products for the Product-Centered MBT Approach

| FMS Products | FMS Features | | | | | | | |
|---|---|---|---|---|---|---|---|---|
| | AD | NR | SurSys | DL | MFD | ES | TJ | FJ |
| Test suite 1 | X | (?) | X | (?) | X | (?) | (?) | (?) |
| Test suite 2 | - | (?) | - | (?) | - | (?) | (?) | (?) |

and the correspondingly resolved model, that is, a state machine that describes the behavior of product $i$ only.

The direct result of test generation is the set of generated test cases. Thus, $Result_i$ describes the result for just one product. More interesting information, for example, about transition coverage, can be derived for each product. But what is the meaning of a test case on the product line model level? How should $Result_{PL}$—the result of the test generation on the product line model level—be represented? There are several possible forms of test case representations on the product line model level.

**Table 9.3** Required Configurations for the Generated Test Cases in the Product-Line-Centered MBT Approach

| Test Candidates | Test Cases | FMS Features | | | | | | | |
|---|---|---|---|---|---|---|---|---|---|
| | | AD | NR | SurSys | DL | MFD | ES | TJ | FJ |
| Candidate 1 | TC1, TC2, TC3, TC4, TC5, TC6, TC7, TC8 | ? | (?) | ? | (?) | ? | (?) | (?) | (?) |
| Candidate 2 | TC5 | X | (?) | ? | (?) | ? | (?) | (?) | (?) |
| Candidate 3 | TC9 | X | (?) | X | (?) | ? | (?) | (?) | (?) |

One extreme form is a direct mapping of product variants to test cases. This solution conforms to a product-wise description and does not show information on the product line model level. The opposite extreme form consists of a direct mapping from single features to test cases. Given that single test cases usually require information about more than one feature inclusion, this approach is not practicable. The form between both extremes is a mapping from feature configurations (i.e., the inclusion or exclusion of some but not all features) to test cases (see, e.g., Table 9.3 below). This solution allows describing the links between test cases and necessarily included or excluded features. Not making any assumptions about features that are unimportant for the test case allows for optimizing the inclusion of concrete product variants for testing. Summing up, $Result_{PL}$ is the set of pairs consisting each of a feature configuration and a set of corresponding test cases.

In the following, we describe the two mentioned approaches for test generation for configurable systems. The two approaches are focused on different sequences of applying coverage criteria for test case selection on the different test artifacts. Both approaches have been implemented in our prototypical tool chain *SPLTestbench*. The product-centered approach consists of a concatenation of well-known techniques. Consequently, it uses parts of the available information in a step-wise manner. The product-line-centered approach is aimed at combining all techniques in one step. Thus, by using all available information in one step, it bears the potential for an improved quality of the generated artifacts.

### 9.3.4 Product-centered MBT

Here, we describe the product-centered approach for MBT of configurable systems. This approach consists of three steps, each of which uses one of the three available sources—the feature model, the base model, and feature mapping. In the first step, a representative set of products is derived using feature configurations. This can be done, for example, by applying heuristics such as feature-model-based coverage criteria (Oster et al., 2011). For our FMS example, we use the feature-based coverage criterion *All-Features-Included-And-Excluded*, which is satisfied by a set of feature configurations if each non-mandatory feature is at least once included and at least once excluded. Feature configuration generation with *SPLTestbench* results in two relevant feature configurations (regarding only the features used in the state machine in Figure 9.3). See Table 9.2: The first test candidate is equipped with all features used in the state machine; the second candidate is the minimal FMS product consisting of the mandatory features only. The "(?)" sign in the table denotes features that are irrelevant for the test cases, because they have not been used in the FMS state machine example.

In the second step, the feature mapping is used to derive a resolved state machine model for each configured product variant.

The third step consists of running automated model-based test generation on each of the resolved state machines. There are several influencing factors for model-based test generation (cf. Weißleder, 2009). However, we focus on generating test suites that cover all transitions of each resolved state machine. For *All-Features-Included-And-Excluded*, satisfying transition coverage results in two test suites with a total number of 12 test cases and 63 test steps.

The product-centered approach can be implemented by standard test generators. This implementation is straightforward. It suffers, however, from the disadvantage that the available information is not used together at once, but in sequence. One consequence of this sequential use of information is that sets of model elements that are common to several product variants are tested again and again for each variant in full detail. While this repetitive approach might be useful for testing single products, it results in unnecessarily high effort for product line approaches that apply the reuse of system artifacts. Another consequence of this sequential approach is that the test effort cannot be focused on the variability. Each product variant is handled separately and the knowledge about the commonalities in their state machines is unused.

### 9.3.5 Product-line-centered MBT

Here, we describe the product-line-centered approach for MBT of configurable systems. In contrast to the product-centered approach, it is focused on using all available information together at once and not in sequence.

For implementing this approach, one typically has two options: The first choice is the invention of a new test generator; the second is an appropriate transformation of the input model. Our approach is based on the latter, that is, we use a model transformation to combine all the available information within one model. By ensuring that the model transformation results in a valid instance of UML state machines, we take advantage of using existing test generators that can be applied on this combined model.

Our model transformation works as follows: The information from the feature model and the feature mapping is used to extend the transitions of the state machine. This extension alters transitions in a way that a transition can only be fired if the features of its configuration rule have not been excluded yet. Figure 9.4 shows the result of an exemplary transformation of a transition that originally had only the guard [*Guard*] and no effect. The transformation adds two variables for each feature $f$: The variable $valueFeature_f$ marks the value of the feature selection. The variable $isSetFeature_f$ marks whether the value of the feature has been set already (i.e., if it has been already bound before). A transition that is mapped to a feature can be fired only if the feature has been included in the product variant already

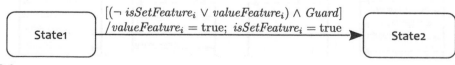

**FIGURE 9.4**

Transformation example.

(i.e., if $valueFeature == true$) or if the feature has not been considered at all (i.e., if $isSetFeature_f == false$). As the effect of the transition, both values are set to true. This means that for the current path in the model, this variable assignment cannot be undone in order to guarantee consistency of the product feature selection. For more complex configuration rules, there are corresponding transformations.

As a consequence of this transformation, the test generator only generates paths through the state machine for which there is at least one valid product variant. Furthermore, the test generator not only generates a set of paths, but also the conditions for the corresponding valid products on the feature model level (i.e. in form of feature configurations). This allows assigning the generated test cases to the product variants they are run on.

We have applied the transformation on our FMS example. The transformed state machine was used then to generate tests to satisfy transition coverage. As a result, nine test cases with a total number of 47 external steps were generated that covered all transitions. The generated test cases are shown as message sequence charts in Figure 9.5. Each test case is assigned with only the necessarily included or excluded features to make this test executable. This leaves room for optimization of the test suites such as, for example, deriving a big or small number of variants or maximizing a certain coverage criterion on the feature model. The corresponding minimal configurations for the test cases are shown in Table 9.3. The sign "(?)" denotes the features that have not been needed to be bound for running the test case. "(?)" again marks features not used in the statechart.

## 9.3.6 Comparison

Here, we describe a first comparison of both approaches. Our comparison uses two values: coverage criteria and the efficiency of the test suite to satisfy them. The application of coverage criteria is a widely accepted means to measure the quality of test suites, which is also recommended by standards

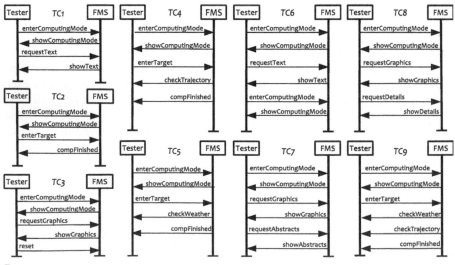

**FIGURE 9.5**

Generated test cases by the product-line-centered MBT approach.

for safety-critical systems such as the ISO 61508. We measure the test suite efficiency in terms of the numbers of test cases and test steps. The more efficient we consider the test suite, the fewer test cases and test steps are needed to satisfy a certain coverage criterion.

The current results of our evaluations are that both approaches achieve the same degree of base model coverage, which is 100% transition coverage. Furthermore, the product-line-centered approach needed only 9 test cases with a total length of 47 test steps compared to 12 test cases and 63 test steps of the product-centered approach. Based on these results, the product-line-centered approach seems to produce a more efficient test suite than the product-centered approach while guaranteeing the same degree of base model coverage.

For future work, we plan to further investigate the relations of coverage criteria on feature models and base models. For instance, there are other criteria at the feature model level such as *All-Feature-Pairs* (Oster et al., 2011). The product-centered approach is able to make a quantifiable statement about feature model coverage. Applying the *All-Feature-Pairs-and-All-Transitions* coverage criteria instead of the *All-Feature-Included-And-Excluded-and-All-Transitions* coverage in the product-centered approach have resulted in larger test suites: Testing of the FMS product line would need 6 test suites (i.e. 6 product variants) with a total number of 36 test cases and 185 test steps.

The product-line-centered approach leaves feature model coverage to the last optimization step without guaranteeing a certain degree of coverage. The meaning of feature model coverage is not yet clear here. But the most important thing to do is to test specified behavior. And the resulting question is about the impact of the feature model on testing the described behavior.

## 9.4 MODEL-BASED DEPLOYMENT

As second example of the extension of a quality assurance technique to configurable systems, we now discuss model-based deployment. A deployment model describes how the resources of a system are employed to execute the application functions. Beyond the capabilities of the resources, it is the deployment that essentially determines the runtime properties of the system, such as responsiveness, reliability, and availability. The automatic or machine-supported design of a deployment can be used to ensure the corresponding runtime qualities by construction. For that purpose the requirements specifying these qualities are fed into a deployment model builder that constructs one or proposes several deployment models that guarantee the required qualities. Such a deployment model builder for many-core systems, for instance, is described in Hilbrich (2012). In this section we discuss how a deployment model builder can be extended to systems with configurable applications and resources.

### 9.4.1 What is deployment?

Deployment is an important task within the design phase of a systems engineering process. It is concerned with the assignment of resources, for example, CPU time, memory, or access to I/O adapters for application components. The design artifact that is produced by this engineering step is referred to as a deployment model. With resource capabilities of the hardware, network, and computing components on the one hand and resource demands of the application components on the other, the deployment acts as central resource broker. A deployment is often subject to a variety of general and domain-specific constraints which determine its correctness. Generally speaking, a deployment is correct if it assigns the proper type and amount of resources to all application components at any moment during runtime of the system. It is the job of the operating system to ensure the integrity of the deployment at runtime by means of scheduling and isolation techniques.

Due to the complexity of these constraints and the intricacy of the application and resource architectures found in current software-intensive embedded systems, constructing a correct deployment is of NP-complexity. This renders a manual construction a time-consuming and error-prone task. Still, a correct deployment is an essential prerequisite for achieving high levels of system quality because it has a direct impact on the fulfillment of major system requirements. This is especially true for extra-functional requirements of embedded software, such as real-time behavior, safety, and reliability requirements. For instance, a faulty resource assignment may lead to non-deterministic latencies when a resource is erroneously "overbooked," which may eventually jeopardize the real-time behavior of the entire system.

Beyond its relevance for the fulfillment of extra-functional requirements, a deployment also helps to determine the amount of resources, for example, processing power or memory capacity, which are required. Often it is the starting point for extensive optimizations on the system level because it has direct impact on the cost and performance of the system to be built. A deployment model builder supports the optimization by providing scores for the deployments it constructs. Depending on the quality requirements and evaluation criteria that are given to the deployment model builder, it applies metrics that evaluate the deployments with respect to these requirements and criteria. The results $r_i$ can be weighted with user defined weights $w_i$, which finally defines the score of a deployment $D$:

$$\text{Score}(D) = \sum^{i} w_i.r_i$$

Evaluation criteria may encompass a variety of domain-specific and application-specific aspects of a system architecture, such as hardware cost, penalties for unused capacities, or the load distribution. The construction of a deployment therefore is not only applied to produce correct resource assignments, but it is also a vital part of the design space exploration process to find (cost-)optimal resource designs.

In addition to the relevance of a deployment for the correctness and quality of the system, it is also a central asset and synchronization point for distributed development teams. With the trend toward integrating more and more software components from different vendors into a single electronic control unit, a correct deployment proves to be an essential design artifact to prevent surprises during the integration phase.

## 9.4.2 Spatial and temporal deployment

In consideration of its NP-complexity, the construction of a deployment should be subdivided into a spatial and a temporal part. A spatial deployment focuses on the entire system architecture and yields a mapping from application components to resources. It is constrained not only by the amount and type of the resources available, but also by safety and reliability requirements. A spatial deployment determines which resources are exclusively used by some application component and which resources have to be shared.

Coordinating the access to shared resources in the temporal dimension is the objective of the temporal deployment. It addresses the question of when to execute an application component on a shared resource, so that all real-time requirements are met. Usually, a static schedule, which correctly executes all application components using shared resources, is produced as a result of a temporal deployment.

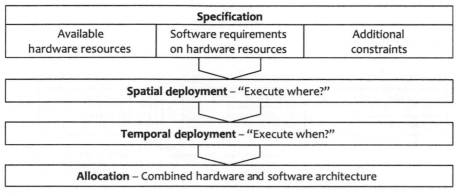

| Specification | | |
|---|---|---|
| Available hardware resources | Software requirements on hardware resources | Additional constraints |

**Spatial deployment** – "Execute where?"

**Temporal deployment** – "Execute when?"

**Allocation** – Combined hardware and software architecture

**FIGURE 9.6**

Spatial and temporal deployment.

Figure 9.6 depicts a common process model for the construction of a deployment model. The spatial deployment should be conducted first because it determines a major part of the system architecture and its properties. However, it is only feasible if a correct temporal deployment can also be constructed. Otherwise, the spatial deployment has to be modified to facilitate a temporal deployment.

In this contribution, we focus on the spatial deployment and its extension to configurable systems. Schedulability tests and tools for generating static schedules for a temporal deployment have also been extensively studied (see Section 9.5).

Their extension to configurable systems, however, is an issue for further research, which might be undertaken using the framework we present here.

### 9.4.3 Application and resource models for the flight management system

In order to construct a deployment model for the FMS, we first have to provide a resource model. Second, we have to extend the application model by the resource demands of the application components. An extract of the latter is illustrated in Figure 9.7. It shows three of the application components and their resource requirements. In order to simplify matters, we assume that each feature in our feature model (see Figure 9.1) is realized by a single application component. This defines the relation of the feature model and the application model, that is, the feature mapping. Furthermore, resource requirements and safety requirements are assigned to each application component. These requirements constrain the spatial deployment and define the valid assignments of application components to resources.

A simplified resource model is depicted in Figure 9.8. Basically, a FMS may either be built as a single, non-standard, stand-alone unit, or it may use a set of standardized IMA boxes with IMA processing boards. For our example, we assume that in the second case either one or two IMA boxes can be used. Each IMA box may host either one or two processing boards. There are two kinds of processing boards available: type A and type B. The board types differ in their processor (architecture type, vendor, and performance) and in the size of the included memory. Type A boards feature larger memories and faster processors. Boards with type B, on the other hand, are equipped with less memory and slower processors, but they are also less expensive.

At this point we do not define a relation between the variance points of the resource model and the features for two reasons. First, the deployment model that is now constructed induces a

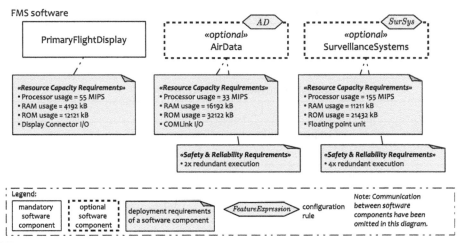

**FIGURE 9.7**

Mandatory and optional application components of the configurable FMS.

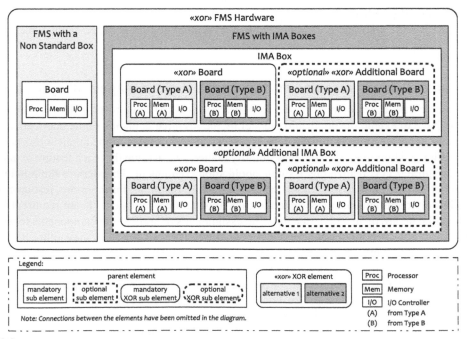

**FIGURE 9.8**

Resource components of the configurable FMS.

feature-to-resource relation by extending the feature-to-application relation with the application-to-resource relation defined by the deployment model. In this induced feature-to-resource relation a resource model element is related to a feature if there is an application model element that is (1) related to the feature and (2) deployed onto the resource model element.

Second, the resource variants are obviously not induced directly by the features we considered for the application. This is indeed a typical situation. Different parts of the system are designed with respect to different specific requirements, constraints, and features. For example, the variance drivers for the resources might be induced by supplier relations, future availability, costs, or other factors that have nothing to do with the functionality of the system. It was possible to represent this as an additional, resource-specific feature model. There is another issue here, however. In fact, the resource variants in this case represent design space alternatives rather than system variants. From the design space alternatives one or several candidates are selected for the realization of the application. The other ones are withdrawn. This is different from the variants of the application: They are all required and must all be realized.

The result of the construction of the deployment model in our example correspondingly consists of two parts: a reduction of the variance of the resource model and a feature mapping to the remaining resource model that is given by the composition of the feature mapping to the application model and the deployment model.

In Figure 9.2 we introduced our general concept for the evaluation of configurable systems. We now apply this general concept to the construction of a deployment of the FMS example and describe a product-centered and a product-line-centered approach for this engineering challenge.

### 9.4.4 Product-centered software deployment

The product-centered approach consists of three basic steps. First, sufficiently many product models are derived from product line model. These products are then individually evaluated by the deployment model builder in a second step. Finally, the results obtained from these evaluations are aggregated and combined, so that an assessment of the entire product line is achieved. In the following, these steps will be described in more detail in the context of our FMS example.

#### 9.4.4.1 Step 1: Deriving the product models

A product model is the combination of an application model, a resource model, and a deployment model. For the construction of the deployment model, the application model and the resource model must be given. So we assume to have an application model with variation points and a resource model with variation points as discussed in the previous section. In order to apply the deployment model builder (which only works for models without variation points), we have to derive all combinations of application product models and resource product models.

#### 9.4.4.2 Step 2: Evaluating the deployment candidates

Each pair of a variance-free application model and a variance-free resource model can be supplied to the deployment model builder, which either constructs a deployment for this pair that satisfies all resource requirements and safety requirements or it indicates that no valid deployment can be found. In the latter case, the resource model is deleted from the list of possible resource candidates for this application configuration. As mentioned above, the deployment model builder also attaches a score to each deployment candidate it finds. These will be used in Step 3 to find the product line deployment.

Note that all deployment candidates constructed in this way are correct, but not necessarily optimal designs for the overall configurable system.

Already, our small example has many product models, that is, pairs of configured application and resource models. So, we do not compute the whole set of pairs. Instead we use subsets of viable candidates, which is also the way one would proceed practically. There are often external criteria, obtained, for instance, from market surveys, supplier relations, or production constraints, which indicate some configurations as viable, whereas others are excluded from further consideration.

For our example we consider only three different types of flight management applications (products) that have to be developed: *Simple FMS*, *FMS for Small Jets*, and *FMS for Jumbo Jets*. These products and their features have been defined in Table 9.1.

Concerning the possible resource configurations, assume that the following set of viable variants is defined based on the resource model in Figure 9.8. Table 9.4 lists these variants together with their relative hardware cost factor, which is used as a quality evaluation criterion. Only these resource variants shall be considered as candidates for the deployment of the application and to realize the envisioned product line of FMSs.

The result of the deployment model builder for this restricted set of application and resource variants might look as represented in Table 9.5. The numbers indicate the scores that are given to the application and resource pairs by the deployment model builder. The empty set ($\emptyset$) is used to characterize a pair without a valid deployment.

For the *Simple FMS*, the stand-alone unit ($HWV_0$) is clearly an optimal choice with a score of 100. The other resource configurations for the *Simple FMS* are still viable, but they use significantly more resources, which will not be fully utilized and result in lower scores.

However, the $HWV_0$ is not a viable choice for the *FMS for Small Jets* as its *AirData* software component requires a *2x redundant execution*, which the stand-alone unit cannot provide. Score differences between $HWV_1$ and $HWV_2$ result from different costs for the processing boards of type A

**Table 9.4** Several Variants of the Resource Architecture

| Resource Variants | Resource Components | Relative Cost |
|---|---|---|
| $HWV_0$ | 1 Non-standard Box | 1 |
| $HWV_1$ | 1 IMA Box with 2 Boards Type B | 10 |
| $HWV_2$ | 1 IMA Box with 2 Boards Type A | 15 |
| $HWV_3$ | 2 IMA Boxes, each with 2 Boards Type A | 30 |

**Table 9.5** Scores of Optimal Product Candidates for All Resource and Application Combinations

| FMS Products (Application Variants) | Resource Variants | | | |
|---|---|---|---|---|
| | $HWV_0$ | $HWV_1$ | $HWV_2$ | $HWV_3$ |
| Simple FMS ($SW_{P_1}$) | **100** | 75 | 65 | 35 |
| FMS for Small Jets ($SW_{P_2}$) | $\emptyset$ | **95** | 90 | 45 |
| FMS for Jumbo Jets ($SW_{P_3}$) | $\emptyset$ | $\emptyset$ | $\emptyset$ | **75** |

and type B. Similarly, the *FMS for Jumbo Jets* can only be realized with $HWV_3$, because the *Surveillance System* requires a *4x redundant execution*.

The description of the first two steps illustrates the challenge of dealing with the combinatorial explosion in the product-centered development approach. Finding and assessing all viable product candidates exceeds the capabilities of a manual development—even for simple systems with few variation points. Instead, a tool-supported approach is required to automate these engineering steps. In Hilbrich and Dieudonne (2013), Hilbrich (2012), and van Kampenhout and Hilbrich (2013) we presented a tool that is able to construct an optimal deployment and facilitate Step 1 and Step 2.

### 9.4.4.3 Step 3: Aggregation of results

In the next step, the results from Table 9.5 have to be aggregated and combined to a deployment model for the configurable application and resource models. Instead of a formal definition of an aggregation, we discuss informally how the results of Table 9.5 for the individual application and resource model pairs without variation points can be interpreted and used to build a single, configurable deployment

The application level has already been modeled as a product line and related to the feature model as presented in Figure 9.1. The initially provided set of possible resource configurations from Figure 9.8 now can be further refined using the results of the deployment model builder. For instance, variant $HWV_2$ appears to be a suboptimal choice for all FMS products. Therefore, it may be removed from the set of viable resource variants.

However, a systems engineer may decide to use $HWV_2$ for the implementation the *FMS for Small Jets* product $(SW_{P_2})$ instead of $HWV_1$. This choice would allow for more homogeneity in the hardware components of the entire product line, because processing boards of type B would no longer be required. Taking into account this criterion implies that although using $HWV_1$ is a locally optimal choice for $SW_{P_2}$, the decision to use resource variant $HWV_2$ for $SW_{P_2}$ instead is a globally optimal choice for the entire product line and may be preferred by the systems engineer.

This aggregation of deployments based on their scores and the homogeneity criterion yields the following configurable deployment for the whole product line. First, the resource model is reduced. The boards of Type B are deleted, the XOR-boards that contained the alternative boards of Type A and Type B are replaced by the remaining boards of Type A. Inside the *FMS with IMA Boxes* we have thus the *IMA Box with one Board of Type A* and an optional. *Additional Board of Type A, and the optional Additional IMA Box* with the same internal structure.

The corresponding deployments of the three individual applications are given in Table 9.6. The additional numbers behind the application components indicate their redundant copies that are deployed to different resource components.

The mapping defined by the deployment, combined with the feature mapping to the application model, yields the feature mapping indicated in Table 9.7.

### 9.4.5 Product-line-centered software deployment

Deriving all possible products may be a very time-consuming and expensive approach for large and complex systems with many variation points. For some systems, it may not even be a viable approach at all. In these situations, optimization strategies and heuristics are needed that focus more on the product line instead of deriving all individual products. The following two strategies may be beneficial in these situations.

**Table 9.6** Product Deployments to the Reduced Resources

| Application Variants | Resource Variants | Application Components | Resource Components |
|---|---|---|---|
| $SW_{P_1}$ | $HW_0$ | Primary Flight Display | Board |
| $SW_{P_2}$ | $HW_2$ | Primary Flight Display | IMA Box. Board (Type A) |
| | | Air Data(1) | IMA Box. Board (Type A) |
| | | Air Data(2) | IMA Box. Additional Board (Type A) |
| $SW_{P_3}$ | $HW_2$ | Primary Flight Display | IMA Box. Board (Type A) |
| | | Air Data (1) | IMA Box. Board (Type A) |
| | | Air Data (2) | IMA Box. Additional Board (Type A) |
| | | Surveillance Systems (1) | IMA Box. Board (Type A) |
| | | Survelllance Systems (2) | IMA Box. Additional Board (Type A) |
| | | Surveillance Systems (3) | Additional IMA Box. Board (Type A) |
| | | Surveillance Systems (4) | Additional IMA Box. Additional Board (Type A) |

**Table 9.7** Feature Mapping of the Reduced Resource Model

| Resource Component | Configuration Rule |
|---|---|
| FMS with Non-standard Box | $(AD \lor SurSys)$ |
| FMS with IMA Boxes | $AD \lor SurSys$ |
| IMABox.AdditionalBoard | $AD \lor SurSys$ |
| AdditionalIMABox | $SurSys$ |
| AdditionalIMABox.AdditionalBoard | $SurSys$ |

### 9.4.5.1 Reuse of previously computed allocations

The first strategy is based on the assumption that it is not feasible to find and evaluate all deployments for each application and resource pair. Instead, it is assumed that finding just one valid deployment for each pair $(S,H)$ would be sufficient. The search for one deployment can be optimized by reusing parts of a previously computed deployment.

For this purpose, we start with a minimum product containing only mandatory application and resource components. The minimum product is then used to find a minimum deployment for the set of all mandatory application components. All other products with optional application components may then reuse this minimum deployment as a starting point when searching for a valid deployment.

In a best-case scenario, only the deployments for optional application components need to be constructed and there are no changes to the minimum deployment necessary. In the worst-case scenario, the selection of optional application components invalidates the entire minimum deployment, so that a reuse is not possible.

This approach still considers all application and resource combinations, so that its optimization potential for large system is limited.

### 9.4.5.2 Maximum approach

In contrast to the previous heuristic, this strategy is based on a maximum deployment. For this purpose, all optional application and resource components are assumed to be selected. Alternative application components and their requirements may be coarsened into a single application component with a superset of the requirements of all previously alternative application components. Alternative resource components, on the other hand, can be coarsened as well. This can be done by creating a single resource component instead that contains a set of resource capacities provided by all alternatives. The resulting application and resource architectures no longer contain any variability. They can then be used to compute a maximum deployment.

In order to retrieve the deployment for each individual product, the feature model is used to selectively remove application components from the system architecture. The resulting deployment of application components is still correct, but it may no longer be optimal and resource-efficient. The removal of application components may also result in entirely unused resources. These resources may be removed from the resource architecture for a specific product in order to improve its resource-efficiency.

This approach does not consider all resource and application combinations.

Therefore, it may not lead to optimal system architectures. For instance, in the FMS example, this approach would not try to use the stand-alone unit, just because it would not be sufficient for the *FMS for Jumbo Jets* product. The approach of coarsening the system architecture allows for significant process efficiency improvements, but at the cost of achieving less optimal solutions.

## 9.5 RELATED WORK

In the following we give an overview on related work with respect to product line evaluations in general, product line testing approaches, and approaches for software deployment.

### 9.5.1 General product line approaches

Beyond the basic product line modeling concepts presented in this chapter are many other approaches that we briefly sketch. They differ in how they represent variability within the various system models, whether they provide explicitly defined variability concepts in the models, and which kind of relationships between feature and system models they allow. In Voelter and Groher (2007), product line approaches have been distinguished in approaches using negative versus positive variability. An example of negative variability approaches is 150% modeling (Czarnecki and Antkiewicz, 2005; Heidenreich et al., 2008; Mann and Rock, 2009). The system models represent so-called 150% models as the base models of the product line and include all the supported variability. Options or alternatives that have been not selected for a specific product will be removed from the base models. In this chapter we have also used a 150% modeling approach. Examples for positive variability approaches are given in Apel and Kästner (2009) and Thaker et al. (2007). Here, a base model exhibits basic features only. A number of transformations are performed on the base model to add specific features and to gain the product-specific variants. Delta modeling (Clarke et al., 2010) can be used for both positive and negative variability. A general syntactic framework for product line artifacts is suggested by the common variability language CVL (OMG, 2012).

A precondition for the quality assurance of single products as well as of the complete product line is that the engineering artifacts have been consistently set up with respect to the variability dimension. Analysis and assessment methods have been developed for the various models in product line engineering approaches. The interpretation of feature models as logical formulas to be used by theorem provers, SAT solvers, or other formal reasoning have been introduced in Batory (2005) and Zhang et al. (2004), for example. A literature overview of the use of such automated analysis of feature models is given in Benavides et al. (2010). Our work is based on this because we need the ability to compute correct feature configurations for the feature coverage criterion and for the model transformations of configurable state machines in order to use standard test generators, for instance.

The idea to make the transition from single evaluation methods to variability-aware methods because of efficiency issues has been already identified within the product line community. An overview of published product-centered and product-line-centered analysis approaches is given in von Rhein et al. (2013) and Thüm et al. (2012). The authors provide a classification model in order to compare these approaches. Their model distinguishes between the dimensions of sampling, feature grouping, and variability encoding. Sampling is about which products will be selected for analysis; feature grouping is about which feature combinations will be selected; and the variability encoding represents the dimension concerning whether analysis methods are able to deal with explicit variability information.

A literature overview of approaches that consider the variability of quality attributes within a product line is given in Myllärniemi et al. (2012). The focus is set on why, how, and which quality attributes vary within a product line.

### 9.5.2 Product line testing

Testing is discussed in many scientific articles, experience reports, and books (Ammann and Offutt, 2008; Beizer, 1990; Binder, 1999). As testing usually requires much effort during system engineering, there is a trend toward reducing test costs by applying test automation. There are several approaches of test automation for test design and test execution. We focus on automated test design. Some well-known approaches in this area are data-driven or action word-driven testing that strive to use abstract elements in the test design that can be replaced by several concrete elements representing, for example, several data values or action words. The most efficient technique in this respect is MBT, which allows the use of any kind of models in order to derive test cases (Utting and Legeard, 2006; Utting et al., 2012; Weißleder, 2009; Zander et al., 2011). Many reports are available dealing with the efficiency and effectiveness of MBT (Forrester Research, 2012; Pretschner, 2005; Pretschner et al., 2005; Weißleder, 2009; Weißleder et al., 2011).

Product lines have to be tested (Lee et al., 2012; McGregor, 2001). Given that product lines can be described using models, the application of MBT is an obvious solution for testing product lines. Several approaches exist for applying MBT to product lines (Weißleder et al., 2008). For instance, coverage criteria can be applied to the feature models to select a representative set of products for testing (Oster et al., 2011). Most approaches in this area, however, are focused on product-centered evaluation approaches, that is, they apply well-known techniques for single products only. We also started the discussion about applying the product-line-centered approach to MBT (Weißleder and Lackner, 2013). Evaluations of this approach are currently under development.

### 9.5.3 **Deployment**

Deployment comprises of a spatial and temporal dimension. The temporal deployment of application software has been discussed extensively in the context of scheduling in real-time systems. Analyzing the schedulability of tasks under real-time conditions has been formally described by Liu and Layland (1973). An overview about scheduling algorithms and a variety of heuristics is presented in Buttazzo (2004), Carpenter et al. (2004), Leung et al. (2004), and Pinedo (2008). Offline scheduling approaches, because they are often used in safety-critical systems, are discussed in Baro et al. (2012) and Fohler (1994). Tools for the construction of temporal deployments, that is, static schedules, are described in Brocaly et al. (2010) and Hilbrich and Goltz (2011). A formal approach to analyze the schedulability of real-time objects based on timed automata families is introduced in Sabouri et al. (2012). Their approach fits to our category of product-line-centered approaches. Similar to our product-line-centered MBT approach, the authors transform timed automata to reuse the common state space during schedulability analysis by late decision making for feature bindings.

Spatial deployment and its challenges have been discussed in Taylor et al. (2009). Engineering approaches for a spatial software deployment for safety-critical systems have been investigated in Hilbrich and Dieudonne (2013), Hilbrich (2012), and van Kampenhout and Hilbrich (2013). A deployment of software components based on their energy consumption has been studied in AlEnawy and Aydin (2005). To the best of our knowledge, there are no solutions yet for spatial deployment that deal explicitly with configurability of the application components or the resources.

## 9.6 **CONCLUSION**

Customer-configurable systems stress the fact that manufacturers do not always have the ability to extensively conduct quality assurance measures for each single customer-specific product, but they need to have the confidence that their product line setup will achieve the quality objectives for all those single products. In this chapter, we introduced two primary ways that quality assurance can be established in this context: product-centered approaches and product-line-centered approaches as depicted in Figure 9.2. Furthermore, we pointed out that product-line-centered approaches promise to be more efficient because they can handle directly the explicitly modeled variability and can exploit the commonalities of single configured systems.

To give an idea how such approaches can be set up, we worked out two applications. We presented how the quality of customer-configurable systems can be assured by MBT and by model-based deployment approaches for both ways. This chapter does not thoroughly provide state-of-the-art techniques already usable out of the box, but rather defines research and development paths for the near future as summarized separately for the two presented applications below. The needs for these techniques, however, are very contemporary, as the sketched examples may have shown. Flexible, customer-configurable systems do exist, and high quality is an essential requirement. Thus, systematic methods for the achievement of quality in customer-configurable systems are needed.

### 9.6.1 **Model-based product line testing**

For MBT, the results of our example show that an efficiency gain is possible by using all available information together on the product-line-model level compared to the approaches of resolving a representative set of products and applying the technique to each selected product. There are, however, several aspects to discuss about such statements. For instance, there are different means to steer test generation for both approaches.

The test generation on the product-line-model level only requires defining a coverage criterion to satisfy at the base model. In contrast to that, test generation on the product-model level requires defining a coverage criterion on the feature-model level and a coverage criterion on the level of the resolved product model. This results in the obvious difference that the product-centered evaluation is focused on evaluating the quality of each selected product variant thoroughly, and the product-line-centered evaluation is focused on evaluating the behavior of all products. The product-line-centered approach bears the potential advantage of avoiding retesting elements that were already tested in other product variants. The impact of this advantage becomes stronger the more system components were reused during system engineering. If the components were not reused, however, and several product variants are developed from scratch or with a minimal reuse, then the product-centered approach has the advantage of considering all product variants independently.

Conversely, the product-line-centered approach has the potential disadvantage of missing faults that are introduced by a lack of component reuse, and the product-centered approach potentially results in testing all system components again and again in each selected variant. Consequently, the choice of the test generation approach strongly depends on the system engineering approach. This aspect is not always obvious to testers. So, the most important question for testers is whether they want to focus their tests on product line behavior or on covering product variants. A compromise is probably the best solution here.

## 9.6.2 Model-based deployment for product lines

Concerning deployment, it became apparent that the product-centered approach quickly led to a combinatorial explosion of product candidates. Tools may provide some support to automate the determination and assessment of product candidates. However, the product-centered approach is not a viable way to address the design challenges of a complex product line. Instead, powerful product-line-centered approaches are required. These may comprise strategies and heuristics to improve the efficiency of the computation or reduce the complexity of the variability in the system. Still, further research on product-line-centered approaches is necessary to overcome the shortcomings of the product-centered approaches and allow for complex, software-intensive and configurable systems with high quality.

## References

AlEnawy, T.A., Aydin, H., 2005. Energy-aware task allocation for rate monotonic scheduling. In: Proceedings of the 11th IEEE Real Time and Embedded Technology and Applications Symposium. RTAS 2005, pp. 213–223. http://dx.doi.org/10.1109/RTAS.2005.20.

Ammann, P., Offutt, J., 2008. Introduction to Software Testing. Cambridge University Press, New York, NY.

Apel, S., Kästner, C., 2009. An overview of feature-oriented software development. J. Object Technology (JOT). 8 (5), 49–84.

Baro, J., Boniol, F., Cordovilla, M., Noulard, E., Pagetti, C., 2012. Off-line (Optimal) multiprocessor scheduling of dependent periodic tasks. In: Proceedings of the 27th Annual ACM Symposium on Applied Computing (SAC 2012). ACM, Trento, Italy, pp. 1815–1820. http://dx.doi.org/10.1145/2231936.2232071.

Batory, D., 2005. Feature models, grammars, and propositional formulas. In: Obbink, H., Pohl, K. (Eds.), Proceedings of Software Product Line Conference (SPLC 2005). In: LNCS, Vol. 3714. Springer-Verlag, Berlin, pp. 7–20.

Beizer, B., 1990. Software Testing Techniques. John Wiley & Sons, New York, NY.

Benavides, D., Segura, S., Ruiz Cortés, A., 2010. Automated analysis of feature models 20 years later: a literature review. Inf. Syst. 35 (6). http://dx.doi.org/10.1016/j.is.2010.01.001.

Binder, R.V., 1999. Testing Object-Oriented Systems: Models, Patterns, and Tools. Addison-Wesley Longman, Boston, MA.

Brocaly, V., Masmanoy, M., Ripolly, I., Crespoy, A., Balbastrey, P., Metge, J.-J., 2010. Xoncrete: a scheduling tool for partitioned real-time systems. In: Proceedings of the Embedded Real Time Software and Systems Conference (ERTStextsuperscript2 2010).

Buttazzo, G.C., 2004. Hard Real-Time Computing Systems: Predictable Scheduling Algorithms and Applications. Real-Time Systems. Springer-Verlag TELOS, Santa Clara, CA.

Carpenter, J., Funk, S., Holman, P., Srinivasan, A., Anderson, J., Baruah, S., 2004. A categorization of real-time multiprocessor scheduling problems and algorithms. In: Handbook on Scheduling Algorithms, Methods, and Models. Chapman Hall/CRC, Boca, CA, pp. 1–30.

Chapman, R., 2006. Correctness by construction: a manifesto for high integrity software. In: Proceedings of the 10th Australian Workshop on Safety Critical Systems and Software. In: SCS '05, Vol. 55. Australian Computer Society, Sydney, Australia, pp. 43–46.

Chilenski, J.J., Miller, S.P., 1994. Applicability of modified condition/decision coverage to software testing. Softw. Eng. J. 9, 193–200.

Clarke, D., Helvensteijn, M., Schaefer, I., 2010. Abstract delta modeling. In: Proceedings of the 9th International Conference on Generative Programming and Component Engineering (GPCE 2010). ACM, Eindhoven, The Netherlands, pp. 13–22. http://dx.doi.org/10.1145/1868294.1868298.

Clements, P., Northrop, L., 2002. Software Product Lines—Practices and Patterns. SEI Series in Software Engineering. Addison-Wesley, Reading, MA.

Czarnecki, K., Antkiewicz, M., 2005. Mapping features to models: a template approach based on superimposed variants. In: Glück, R., Lowry, M. (Eds.), Proceedings of 4th International Conference on Generative Programming and Component Engineering (GPCE 2005). In: LNCS, Vol. 3676. Springer-Verlag, Tallinn, Estonia, pp. 422–437. http://dx.doi.org/10.1007/11561347_28.

Czarnecki, K., Eisenecker, U.W., 2000. Generative Programming—Methods, Tools and Applications. Addison-Wesley, Reading, MA.

Fohler, G., 1994, April. Flexibility in Statically Scheduled Real-Time Systems. Technisch-Naturwissenschaftliche Fakultät, Technische Universität Wien, Austria.

Forrester Research, Inc., 2012. The Total Economic Impact of Conformiq Tool Suite.

Harel, D., 1987. Statecharts: a visual formalism for complex systems. Sci. Comput. Program. 8, 231–274.

Harel, D., Gery, E., 1997. Executable object modeling with statecharts. IEEE Computer. 30 (7), 31–42.

Heidenreich, F., Kopcsek, J., Wende, C., 2008. Featuremapper: mapping features to models. In: Proceedings of Companion of the 30th International Conference on Software Engineering (ICSE 2008). ACM, Leipzig, Germany, pp. 943–944.

Hilbrich, R., 2012. How to safely integrate multiple applications on embedded many-core systems by applying the "correctness by construction" principle. Adv. Softw. Eng. 2012 (354274), 14. http://dx.doi.org/10.1155/2012/354274.

Hilbrich, R., Dieudonne, L., 2013. Deploying safety-critical applications on complex avionics hardware architectures. J. Softw. Eng. Appl. 06 (05), 229–235. http://dx.doi.org/10.4236/jsea.2013.65028.

Hilbrich, R., Goltz, H.-J., 2011. Model-based generation of static schedules for safety critical multi-core systems in the avionics domain. In: Proceedings of 4th International Workshop on Multicore Software Engineering (IWMSE 2011). ACM, Honolulu, HI, pp. 9–16. http://dx.doi.org/10.1145/1984693.1984695.

ISO/IEC, 2005. Software engineering—Software product Quality Requirements and Evaluation (SQuaRE)—Guide to SQuaRE, first ed., International Standard ISO/IEC 25000.

Jones, C., 1991. Applied Software Measurement: Assuring Productivity and Quality. McGraw-Hill, New York, NY.

Kang, K.C., Cohen, S.G., Hess, J.A., Novak, W.E., Peterson, A.S., 1990. Feature-Oriented Domain Analysis (FODA)—Feasibility Study (No. CMU/SEI-90-TR-21, ADA235785). CMU-SEI, Pittsburgh, PA.

Kruchten, P.B., 1995. The "4+1" view model of software architecture. IEEE Softw. 12 (6), 42–50. http://dx.doi.org/10.1109/52.469759.

Lee, J., Kang, S., Lee, D., 2012. A survey on software product line testing. In: Proceedings of 16th International Software Product Line Conference (SPLC 2012), vol. 1. ACM, Salvador, Brazil, pp. 31–40. http://dx.doi.org/10.1145/2362536.2362545.

Leung, J., Kelly, L., Anderson, J.H., 2004. Handbook of Scheduling: Algorithms, Models, and Performance Analysis. CRC Press, Boca Raton, FL.

Liu, C.L., Layland, J.W., 1973. Scheduling algorithms for multiprogramming in a hard-real-time environment. J. ACM 20 (1), 46–61.

Mann, S., Rock, G., 2009. Dealing with variability in architecture descriptions to support automotive product lines. In: Proceedings of 3rd International Workshop on Variability Modeling of Software-Intensive Systems (VAMOS 2009), pp. 111–120.

McGregor, J., 2001. Testing a Software Product Line. (Technical Report CMU/SEI-2001-TR-022). Software Engineering Institute, Carnegie Mellon University, Pittsburgh, PA. http://resources.sei.cmu.edu/library/asset-view.cfm?AssetID=5715

Morgan, M.J., 1991. Integrated modular avionics for next generation commercial airplanes. Aerospace and Electronic Systems Magazine, IEEE. 6 (8), 9–12. http://dx.doi.org/10.1109/62.90950.

Myers, G.J., 1979. Art of Software Testing. John Wiley & Sons, New York, NY.

Myllärniemi, V., Raatikainen, M., Männistö, T., 2012. A systematically conducted literature review: quality attribute variability in software product lines. In: Proceedings of 16th International Software Product Line Conference (SPLC 2012), vol. 1. ACM, Salvador, Brazil, pp. 41–45. http://dx.doi.org/10.1145/2362536.2362546.

Nolan, A.J., Abrahao, S., Clements, P., McGregor, J.D., Cohen, S., 2011. Towards the integration of quality attributes into a software product line cost model. In: Proceedings of 15th International Software Product Line Conference (SPLC 2011), pp. 203–212. http://dx.doi.org/10.1109/SPLC.2011.44.

OMG, 2011. Unified Modeling Language (UML). Object Management Group, Needham, MA. http://www.uml.org.

OMG, 2012, August. Common Variability Language (CVL)—OMG Revised Submission. OMG Revised Submission, OMG document: ad/2012-08-05, submitted by IBM, Fraunhofer FOKUS, Thales, and Tata Consultancy Services.

Oster, S., Zorcic, I., Markert, F., Lochau, M., 2011. MoSo-PoLiTe: tool support for pairwise and model-based software product line testing. In: Proceedings of 5th Int. Workshop on Variability Modeling of Software-Intensive Systems (VAMOS 2011), pp. 79–82.

Pinedo, M.L., 2008. Scheduling: Theory, Algorithms, and Systems, third ed. Springer, Berlin, p. 671.

Pretschner, A., 2005. Model-based testing in practice. In: Proceedings of International Symposium of Formal Methods Europe (FM 2005), pp. 537–541.

Pretschner, A., Prenninger, W., Wagner, S., Kühnel, C., Baumgartner, M., Sostawa, B., Zölch, R., et al., 2005. One evaluation of model-based testing and its automation. In: Proceedings of 27th International Conference on Software Engineering (ICSE 2005), St. Louis, MO, pp. 392–401. http://dx.doi.org/10.1145/1062455.1062529.

Rajan, A., Whalen, M.W., Heimdahl, M.P.E., 2008. The effect of program and model structure on MC/DC test adequacy coverage. In: ICSE'08: Proceedings of the 30th International Conference on Software Engineering. ACM, Leipzig, Germany, pp. 161–170. http://dx.doi.org/10.1145/1368088.1368111.

Sabouri, H., Jaghoori, M.M., de Boer, F., Khosravi, R., 2012. Scheduling and analysis of real-time software families. In: Proceedings of 36th Annual IEEE Computer Software and Applications Conference (COMPSAC 2012), pp. 680–689. http://dx.doi.org/10.1109/COMPSAC.2012.95.

Taylor, R.N., Medvidovic, N., Dashofy, E., 2009. Software Architecture: Foundations, Theory, and Practice. Wiley, New York, NY.

Thaker, S., Batory, D., Kitchin, D., Cook, W., 2007. Safe composition of product lines. In: Proceedings of 6th International Conference on Generative Programming and Component Engineering (GPCE 2007). ACM, Salzburg, Austria, pp. 95–104. http://dx.doi.org/10.1145/1289971.1289989.

Thüm, T., Apel, S., Kästner, C., Kuhlemann, M., Schaefer, I., Saake, G., 2012. Analysis Strategies for Software Product Lines (No. FIN-04-2012). University of Magdeburg, Magdeburg, Germany.

Utting, M., Legeard, B., 2006. Practical Model-Based Testing: A Tools Approach. Morgan Kaufmann Publishers, San Francisco, CA.

Utting, M., Pretschner, A., Legeard, B., 2012. A taxonomy of model-based testing approaches. Softw. Test. Verif. Reliab. 22 (5), 297–312. http://dx.doi.org/10.1002/stvr.456.

van Kampenhout, J.R., Hilbrich, R., 2013. Model-based deployment of mission-critical spacecraft applications on multicore processors. In: Keller, H.B. et al., (Eds.), Ada-Europe International Conference on Reliable Software Technologies. In: LNCS, Vol. 7896. Springer-Verlag, Berlin/Heidelberg, pp. 35–50.

Voelter, M., Groher, I., 2007. Product line implementation using aspect-oriented and model-driven software development. In: Proceedings of 11th International Software Product Lines Conference (SPLC 2007), pp. 233–242.

von Rhein, A., Apel, S., Kästner, C., Thüm, T., Schaefer, I., 2013. The PLA model: on the combination of product-line analyses. In: Gnesi, S., Collet, P., Schmid, K. (Eds.), Proceedings of 7th International Workshop on Variability Modelling of Software-intensive Systems (VAMOS 2013). ACM, Pisa, Italy.

Watkins, C.B., Walter, R., 2007. Transitioning from federated avionics architectures to Integrated Modular Avionics. In: Proceedings of IEEE/AIAA 26th Digital Avionics Systems Conference (DASC 2007), Dallas, TX, http://dx.doi.org/10.1109/DASC.2007.43918422.A.1-1–2.A.1-10.

Weißleder, S., 2009. Influencing factors in model-based testing with UML state machines: report on an industrial cooperation. In: Proceedings of 12th International Conference on Model Driven Engineering Languages and Systems (MODELS 2009), Denver, CO.

Weißleder, S., 2010. Simulated satisfaction of coverage criteria on UML state machines. In: Proceedings of International Conference on Softwarse Testing, Verification and Validation (ICST). Paris, France.

Weißleder, S., Lackner, H., 2013. Top-down and bottom-up approach for model-based testing of product lines. In: Proceedings of MBT 2013, p. 13.

Weißleder, S., Sokenou, D., Schlingloff, H., 2008. Reusing state machines for automatic test generation in product lines. In: Hajo Eichler Thomas Bauer, A.R. (Ed.), Model-Based Testing in Practice (MoTiP). Fraunhofer IRB Verlag, Berlin, Germany.

Weißleder, S., Güldali, B., Mlynarski, M., Törsel, A.-M., Faragó, D., Prester, F., Winter, M., 2011. Modellbasiertes testen: hype oder realität? OBJEKTSpektrum, 6, 59–65.

Zander, J., Schieferdecker, I., Mosterman, P.J. (Eds.), 2011. Model-Based Testing for Embedded Systems. CRC Press, Boca Raton.

Zhang, W., Zhao, H., Mei, H., 2004. A propositional logic-based method for verification of feature models. In: Proceedings of 6th International Conference on Formal Engineering Methods (ICFEM 2004). In: LNCS, Vol. 3308. Springer, Seattle, WA. http://dx.doi.org/10.1007/b102837.

# Archample—Architectural Analysis Approach for Multiple Product Line Engineering

# 10

**Bedir Tekinerdogan[1], Özgü Özköse Erdoğan[2], and Onur Aktuğ[2]**

[1]*Bilkent University, Ankara, Turkey*
[2]*Aselsan, Ankara, Turkey*

## INTRODUCTION

The benefits of adopting a product line (PL) approach has been analyzed and discussed before (Babar et al., 2004; Clements and Northrop, 2002; Pohl et al., 2005; Schmid and Verlage, 2002). The key motivation for adopting a PL engineering process is to develop products more efficiently, get them to the market faster to stay competitive, and produce with higher quality (Schmid and Verlage, 2002). In alignment with these goals, different software product line (SPL) engineering processes have been proposed, and an increasing number of companies aim to adopt a PL engineering approach.

The latest trends show that the reuse scale of current PL approaches seems to increase further with the increased size and complexity of applications that the industry is using. In this context, several authors have indicated the need for *multiple product lines* (MPLs) in which a product is defined as a composition of products from different PLs (Aoyama et al., 2003; Archer et al., 2010). Examples of MPL have been provided in the domains of e-government (Aoyama et al., 2003), car manufacturing (Hartmann et al., 2009), and healthcare (van der Linden and Wijnstra, 2001). The MPL architecture represents the gross-level structure of the system consisting of subproducts derived from separate PLs, which together form the overall product. An MPL architecture can be considered as a system-of-systems architecture that defines the systemic design decisions beyond flat PLs and likewise will have a serious impact on the overall system development.

Hence, it is important that the MPL architecture supports the software system qualities required by the stakeholders.

Architecture analysis approaches have been broadly discussed in the literature, and different methods have been proposed (Babar et al., 2004; Dobrica and Niemela, 2002; Kazman et al., 2005; Tekinerdogan et al., 2004). The goal of software architecture analysis methods is usually to understand the consequences of architectural decisions with respect to the system's quality attribute requirements and with respect to the tradeoffs between them (Babar et al., 2004; Roy and Graham, 2008; Dobrica and Niemela, 2002). Current architecture analysis approaches tend to focus on single-system architecture and appear to be limited for addressing the larger granularity and abstraction level of MPL architecture. We propose the so-called *Archample* approach for the analysis of architecture within the MPL engineering context. Unlike existing architecture analysis approaches, *Archample* focuses on the analysis of MPL architecture in particular. The goal of *Archample* is to support the decision on whether to use an MPL architecture and likewise evaluate different alternative decompositions of the MPL architecture. *Archample* also introduces architectural viewpoints for modeling and documenting MPLs and likewise supporting the analysis of the decomposition of an MPL architecture. We illustrate the analysis of alternative MPL architectures for radar and electronic warfare systems in the context of Aselsan in Turkey (Aselsan, 2011). Aselsan is a leading high-technology company in defense systems development introducing state-of-the-art equipment and software-intensive system solutions for both sophisticated military and professional applications. Using the viewpoints as defined in *Archample*, we describe the analysis of four important architecture decomposition alternatives for MPLs in Aselsan REHİS. Our study and experiences show that for analyzing the architecture of MPLs, it is necessary to describe these using appropriate architectural viewpoints. With the viewpoints we have introduced, we could describe the MPLs in a more proper way, communicate the design decisions, and select a feasible design alternative.

The remainder of the chapter is organized as follows. In Section 10.1, we describe the background including MPL engineering and software architecture analysis methods. In Section 10.2, the case study of radar and electronic warfare systems is described. In Section 10.3, we describe the architecture viewpoints for MPLs. Section 10.4 presents the *Archample* method using the introduced viewpoints. Section 10.5 describes the application of *Archample* to the industrial case study. Section 10.6 presents the related work and characterizes Archample with respect to the architecture evaluation frameworks in the literature. Finally, Section 10.7 concludes the paper.

## 10.1 BACKGROUND

### 10.1.1 Multiple product line engineering

According to ISO/IEC 42010 (ISO/IEC, 2007), the notion of *system* can be defined as a set of components that accomplishes a specific function or set of functions. Each system has an architecture, which is defined as "the fundamental organization of a system embodied in its components, their relationships to each other, and to the environment, and the principles guiding its design and evolution." When reuse is an important concern, a system can be built based on the PL approach. For very large systems, the scope of the PL can be extended further, and the product can be built using subproducts from MPLs. The notion of MPLs has been addressed earlier by different authors including Aoyama et al. (2003), Archer et al. (2010), Fritsch and Hahn (2004), van der Linden and Wijnstra (2001), van Ommering (2002), and Rosenmüller and Siegmund (2010). In this context, the terms MPLs, *nested* PLs, or PLs *of* PLs have been used to denote the same concept. Rosenmüller and Siegmund (2010) define MPLs as "a set of interacting and interdependent SPLs."

In principle, we can consider the composition of PLs as the application of a composite pattern as shown in Figure 10.1. PL could be either a flat *SPL* or a *Composite Product Line (CPL)*. *CPL* itself could contain other PLs; likewise, the PL can be built in a nested manner. Alternatively, the CPL could include only flat PLs, leading to an MPL consisting of independent PLs. In each CPL the separate PLs could use other PLs. A PL (CPL or PL) can include other reusable assets that are not PLs themselves (e.g., libraries).

The pattern in Figure 10.1 appears to be general and can model different configurations of MPLs. It should be noted that each PL is defined by a two-life cycle process including domain engineering

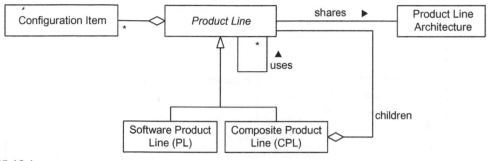

**FIGURE 10.1**

Conceptual model for system development using multiple product lines.

(with product management) and application engineering. Based on these two separate processes, the notion of architecture is usually specialized into a PL *architecture* and an *application architecture* (Pohl et al., 2005). A PL *architecture* represents the common and variant structures of a set of products of the selected PL; an *application architecture* represents the architecture of a single system. The architects who define these architectures can be called PL *architects* and *application architects*.

## 10.1.2 Software architecture analysis methods

The architecture forms one of the key artifacts in the entire software development life cycle because it embodies the earliest design decisions and includes the gross-level components that directly impact the subsequent analysis, design, and implementation. The key concerns of an architecture are defined by *stakeholders*: an individual, team, or organization with interests in, or concerns relative to, a system. Each of the stakeholder's concerns impacts the early design decisions that the architect makes. As architecture is critical for the success of a project, different architectural evaluation approaches have been introduced to evaluate the stakeholders' concerns. A comprehensive overview and comparison of architecture analysis methods have been given by, for example, Dobrica and Niemela (2002) and Babar et al. (2004). Kazman et al. (2005) have provided a set of criteria for comparing the foundations underlying different methods, the effectiveness, and usability of methods.

Figure 10.2 provides a conceptual model that we have defined to describe the architecture evaluation approach. Although different architecture evaluation approaches have been proposed in the literature, we can state that most of these follow the model in Figure 10.2. In essence, each architecture evaluation approach takes as input stakeholder concerns, environmental issues, and architecture description. Based on these inputs, the evaluation results in an *Architecture Evaluation Report*, which is used to adapt the architecture.

The proposed architecture evaluation approaches usually differ with respect to, for example, the goal of the approach, the type of inputs, the evaluation techniques, the addressed quality attributes, the stakeholders' involvement, the ordering of activities, and the output results (Babar et al., 2004; Kazman et al., 2005). It appears that no explicit approach seems to have been provided to analyze architecture within an MPL engineering context. In the following sections we show the need for a specific analysis approach for MPL engineering and the relation to the existing architecture analysis approaches.

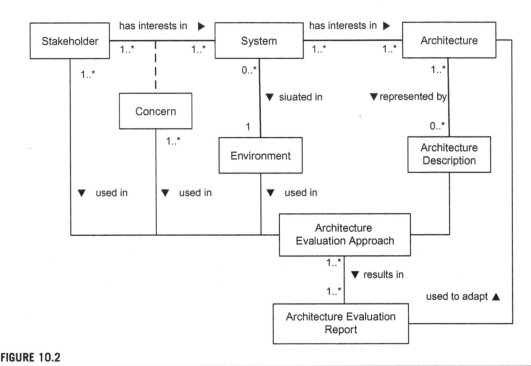

**FIGURE 10.2**

Conceptual model for software architecture analysis.

## 10.2 CASE DESCRIPTION

Figure 10.3 shows the layered reference architecture for radar and electronic warfare systems as defined in the so-called REFoRM project at Aselsan REHİS. For confidentiality reasons, the details of each layer are not given. REFoRM consists of three basic layers: *Mission Domain Applications*, *Application Support Services*, and *Application Platform Cross Domain Services*. These layers include

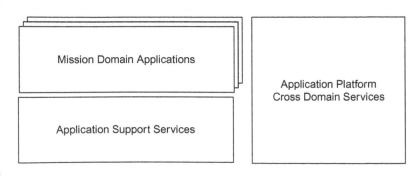

**FIGURE 10.3**

Layered reference architecture of the industrial case including multiple product lines.

different subsystems for Radar, Radar Electronic Warfare, Communication Electronic Warfare, and Self-Protection. A Radar Electronic Support system is basically an example of the Mission Domain Application. A typically product is configured by selecting different subsystems in the three distinct but interdependent layers.

Obviously, most products that Aselsan REHİS develops share lots of commonality; likewise, Aselsan REHİS has focused on systematic reuse based on PL engineering. The primary business drivers here are a faster time-to-market, higher quality, and overall cost reduction. Given that products are developed using the reference architecture in Figure 10.3, one could argue that this complete domain represents one PL. Yet, experience showed that this is far from trivial and to a large extent not feasible. Although the products are developed using the reference architecture, the separate subsystems represent different domains (Radar, Radar Electronic Warfare, Communication Electronic Warfare, and Self-Protection), are actually realized in different business groups, and as such could be considered as products derived from different product families. On the other hand, defining a PL for each (sub-)domain will increase the complexity and impede the management of the PL activities. The observation that the entire system actually consists of separate interacting product families leads to the problem of finding the right decomposition of the system into product families. For this, it is important to identify the right set and boundaries of PLs, analyze the different decomposition alternatives, and select a feasible decomposition.

## 10.3 MPL ARCHITECTURE VIEWPOINTS

Defining the proper configuration of MPLs is not trivial. To support the analysis of the MPL, first a proper documentation of the MPL architecture is required. A common practice for describing the architecture according to the stakeholders' concerns is to model different architectural views (Clements et al., 2011). An architectural view is a representation of a set of system elements and relations associated with them to support a particular concern. Usually multiple architectural views are needed to separate the concerns and as such support the modeling, understanding, communication, and analysis of the software architecture for different stakeholders. Architectural views conform to *viewpoints* that represent the conventions for constructing and using a view. Existing viewpoints for architecture (e.g., such as defined in Clements et al., 2011) can be applied to present architectural descriptions for both PL architecture and application architecture. However, if we consider MPLs, it appears that plain usage of existing viewpoints is not sufficient to represent the design and interaction of the different PLs. For reasoning about MPL decomposition, it is important make an explicit distinction among CPLs and single PLs and represent the interaction among the different PLs. This is necessary for supporting the understanding and communication among the stakeholders, the analysis of the PL decomposition, and the guidance of the product development. To cope with this issue, complementary to existing viewpoints in the literature, we define two architectural viewpoints for MPLs, the PL *Decomposition Viewpoint* (Table 10.1) and PL *Dependency Viewpoint* (not shown). We have defined these viewpoints because we are particularly interested in the composition and interaction of the PLs. To define the viewpoints, we have adopted the guidelines of the recommended standard for architecture description (ISO/IEC, 2007).

Based on the conceptual model as defined in Figure 10.1, both viewpoints distinguish between three types of development units: *CPL*, *PL*, and *Configuration Item* (*CI*). A CPL is defined as a composition

**Table 10.1** Product Line Decomposition Viewpoint

| Viewpoint Element | Description |
|---|---|
| Name | Product Line Decomposition Viewpoint |
| Overview | This viewpoint is used for decomposing a system into different product line units |
| Concerns | Optimal decomposition of the multiple product line |
| Stakeholders | Project leaders, architects, newcomers |
| Elements | • Composite Product Line Composition (CPL)—represents a composition of products lines<br>• Product Line (PL)—a single noncomposite product line<br>• Configuration Item (CI)—any reusable asset within a product line that has a defined functionality but that is not a CPL or PL |
| Relations | • Decomposition relation defines the part-of-relation between product and subproduct |
| Constraints | • A Product Line can have only one parent<br>• Only CPL can have children that can be PL, CPL, or CI<br>• A PL cannot have PLs but may include CIs |
| Notation | |

**Elements**

<<CPL>>  Composite Product Line

<<PL>>  Product Line

<<CI>>  Configuration Item

**Relations**

◇———→   part-of

of PLs or other CPLs. A PL cannot include other PLs. Both a PL and CPL are defined in fact as subsystems (Clements et al., 2011). A subsystem is defined as part of a system that "(1) carries out a functionally cohesive subset of the overall system's mission, (2) can be executed independently, and (3) can be developed and deployed incrementally." From this perspective, a CI is part of the system that cannot be considered as a subsystem that is either a CPL or PL, and it comprises the reusable assets within a CPL or PL. An example of a CI is a reusable unit that is part of the system, has a cohesive functionality, but cannot be executed independently. As it can be noted, we have chosen not to specify a separate notation for defining the composition of CIs. For this, we use the *package* construct of UML.

Figure 10.4 represents an example of the product line decomposition view for the given case study that is based on the viewpoint as shown in Table 10.1. Here, the system has been defined as one CPL that contains 3 separate CPLs (*RadEW*, *ComEW*, and *Radar*), 4 PLs (*HASP*, *VERY*, *Navigation*, and *SelfProtectionSuite*), and 12 CIs (libraries). The CPLs each consist of two PLs. The MPL architecture

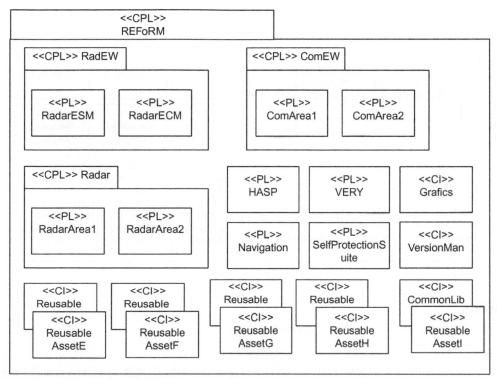

**FIGURE 10.4**

Example product line decomposition view that defines a multiple product line.

consists thus of four separate PL units (*HASP*, *VERY*, *Navigation*, and *SelfProtectionSuite*) and six other PLs that are nested in CPLs (*RadarESM*, *RadarECM*, *ComArea1*, *ComArea2*, *RadarArea1*, and *RadarArea2*). Each of these PLs will have its own domain engineering process and application engineering process. Variability management and modeling is applied within each PL. The dependency relations among different PLs are defined in the CPLs that compose the PLs.

In addition to showing the decomposition relations, it is also important to show the interactions among the PLs. For this we have defined the *PL Dependency Viewpoint*. This viewpoint adopts the same elements as the *PL Decomposition Viewpoint* but defines the *uses* relation. A PL unit uses another PL unit if its correctness depends on the correctness of the other. In fact, the relation is similar to the *uses* relation as defined in the Uses Style in the Views and Beyond approach (Clements et al., 2011). The difference is that the relation applies to a complete PL unit instead of implementation units. Further, if one PL unit uses another, there is usually also a configuration dependency. That is, the selection of features in one PL unit will have an impact on the selection of features in the other (Rosenmüller et al., 2008).

Figure 10.5 shows an example of the *PL Dependency View* that conforms to this viewpoint. Here, the dependency relations are shown using dotted arrows. Dependency relation here indicates the correct functioning of the dependent PL. As shown in the figure, the CPL *RadEW* uses the CIs, reusable assets,

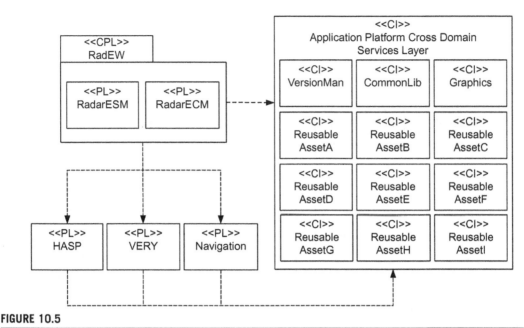

**FIGURE 10.5**

Radar and electronic warfare product line dependency view.

in the *Application Platform Cross Domain Services Layer*. Further, *RadEW* uses the product lines *PL*, *VERY*, and *Navigation*. Each of these PLs also uses the CIs from the *Application Platform Cross Domain Services Layer*. Note that the structure of the PL dependency view in Figure 10.5 follows the structure of the reference architecture of Figure 10.3.

## 10.4 *ARCHAMPLE* METHOD

The activities of the *Archample* approach are shown in Figure 10.6. As the figure shows, *Archample* consists of four phases: *Preparation*, *Design Documentation*, *Evaluation*, and *Reporting*. *Archample* is performed by a set of key stakeholders:

- *Project decision makers:* People interested in the result of the evaluation and who can affect the project's directions. These decision makers are usually the project managers.
- *MPL architect:* A person or team responsible for design of the MPL architecture and the coordination of the design of the subarchitecture.
- *PL architect:* A person or team responsible for design of a single PL architecture. The single PL architect typically informs the MPL architect about the results and if needed also adapts the architecture to fit the overall architecture.
- *Architecture stakeholders:* Developers, testers, integrators, maintainers, performance engineers, users, builders of systems interacting with the one under consideration, and others.

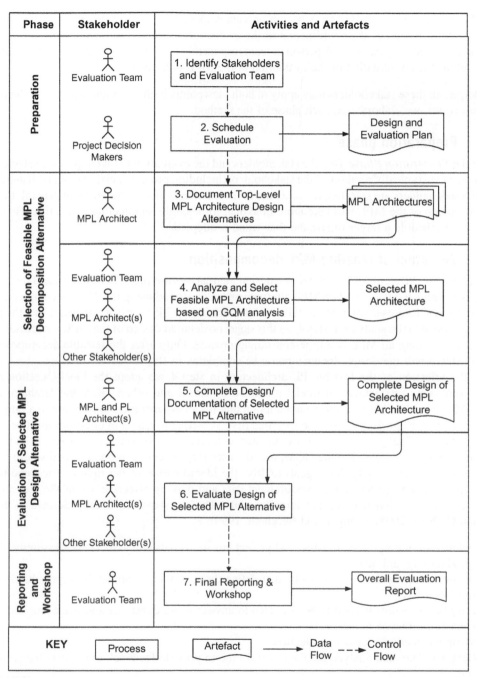

**FIGURE 10.6**

Archample process.

- *MPL architecture evaluator(s)*: A person or team responsible for the evaluation of the MPL architecture as well as the coordination of the evaluation of the PL architectures.
- *PL architecture evaluator(s)*: A person or team responsible for the evaluation of the PL architecture as well as the coordination of the evaluation of the MPL architectures.

In principle, all these stakeholders may apply to both viewpoints in the previous section. In the following subsections, we elaborate on each phase of the method.

## 10.4.1 Preparation phase

During the *Preparation Phase,* first the stakeholders and the evaluation team (step 1) are selected. The stakeholders are typically a subset of the stakeholders (including project decision makers) listed above. After the stakeholders are selected, the schedule for evaluation is planned (step 2). In general, the complete evaluation of the MPL will take more time than for a single architecture evaluation. Hence, for defining the schedule a larger timeframe than usual is adopted.

## 10.4.2 Selection of feasible MPL decomposition

In this phase the different MPL architecture design alternatives are provided (step 3), and the feasible alternative is selected (step 4). The MPL alternatives are described using the MPL decomposition and uses viewpoints. Representation of the MPL architecture in step 3 is necessary to ensure that the proper input is provided to the analysis in step 4. At this stage, no detailed design of the MPL is necessary. This is because designing an MPL is a time-consuming process. Only after the feasible decomposition is found in step 4 will the design documentation be completed in step 5.

For the selection of the feasible PL architecture in step 4 we adopt the Goal-Question-Metric (GQM) approach, a measurement model promoted by Basili and others (Roy and Graham, 2008). The GQM approach is based upon the assumption that for an organization to measure in a purposeful way, the goals of the projects need to be specified first. Subsequently, a set of questions must be defined for each goal, and finally a set of metrics associated with each question is defined to answer each one in a measurable way. For applying the GQM, usually a six-step process is recommended where the first three steps are about using business goals to drive the identification of the right metrics, and the last three steps are about gathering the measurement data and making effective use of the measurement results to drive decision making and improvements. The six steps are usually defined as follows (Roy and Graham, 2008; Solingen and Berghout, 1999):

1. Develop a set of corporate, division, and project business goals and associated measurement goals for productivity and quality.
2. Generate questions (based on models) that define those goals as completely as possible in a quantifiable way.
3. Specify the measures needed to be collected to answer those questions and track process and product conformance to the goals.
4. Develop mechanisms for data collection.
5. Collect, validate, and analyze the data in real time to provide feedback to projects for corrective action.
6. Analyze the data in a post mortem fashion to assess conformance to the goals and to make recommendations for future improvements.

### 10.4.3 **Evaluation of selected MPL design alternative**

Step 4 focuses on selecting a feasible MPL decomposition alternative. An MPL consists of several PLs and thus multiple architectures. Likewise, in step 5 of *Archample*, we focus on refined analysis of the selected MPL alternative. In fact, the selected alternative can be a single PL architecture or different MPL architectures. In case the alternative is a CPL, we apply a staged-evaluation approach in which the MPL units (PLs or CPLs) are recursively evaluated. From this perspective, we distinguish among the following two types of evaluations: (a) top-down product evaluations and (b) bottom-up product evaluations.

In the top-down evaluation, first the higher level PLs are evaluated. This is illustrated in Figure 10.7. Here, the evaluation order is indicated through the numbers in the filled circles. The evaluation starts with evaluation the top-level decomposition of the MPL architecture and continues with the subelements of the MPL, which can be again CPL or single PL.

In the bottom-up approach first the leaf PLs are evaluated, then the higher level architectures. An example bottom-up specialization is shown in Figure 10.8. Obviously, other hybrid specialization approaches that fall between top-down and bottom-up strategy can be applied. The selection of the particular evaluation strategy (top-down, bottom-up, or hybrid) depends on the particular constraints and requirements of the project. A hybrid approach can be preferred by considering the dependency relations among PLs, which are modeled in the PL dependency view.

The evaluation of the architecture can be done using any architecture evaluation method (including GQM again). Over the last decade several different architecture analysis approaches have been proposed to analyze candidate architectures with respect to desired quality attributes (Babar et al., 2004; Dobrica

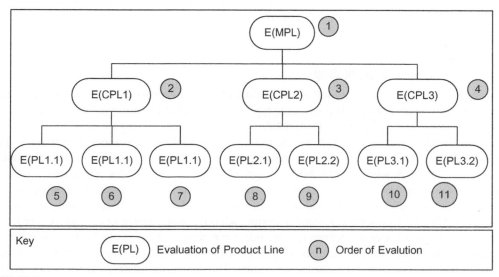

**FIGURE 10.7**

Top-down MPL evaluation.

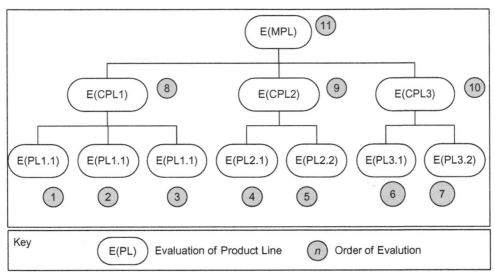

**FIGURE 10.8**

Bottom-up MPL evaluation.

and Niemela, 2002; Kazman et al., 2005). The architecture evaluation methods can be categorized in different ways. Early evaluation methods evaluate the architecture before its implementation while late architecture evaluation methods require the implementation to perform the evaluation. In principle, within *Archample* we do not restrict the selection of any method.

### 10.4.4 Reporting and workshop

In the last phase of *Archample*, a report of the evaluation results is provided and a workshop with the stakeholders is organized. The stakeholders are typically a subset of the list as defined in Section 10.4. A template for the report is given in Table 10.2.

The first Chapters 1–3 of the report provide the background information about the company and its business goals and describe the *Archample* method. Chapter 4 defines the different MPL architecture alternatives. Chapter 5 analyzes the MPL design alternatives and selects a feasible alternative. Chapter 6 presents the documentation of the selected alternative. In Chapter 7, the evaluation of the alternative is described using staged-evaluation approach (top-down, bottom-up, hybrid) and the evaluation results. Chapter 8 presents the overall recommendations, and Chapter 9 concludes the report. An appendix can consist of several sections and include, for example, the glossary for the project, explanation about standards, viewpoints, or other pertinent factors. After the first complete draft of the report, a workshop is organized to discuss the results. The discussions during the workshop are used to adapt the report and define the final version.

| **Table 10.2** Outline of the Final Evaluation Report | |
|---|---|
| Chapter 1 | Introduction |
| Chapter 2 | Archample Overview |
| Chapter 3 | Context and Business Drivers |
| Chapter 4 | MPL Architecture Alternatives |
| Chapter 5 | GQM Analysis of MPL Alternatives |
| Chapter 6 | Architecture Documentation of Selected Alternative |
| Chapter 7 | Evaluation of Selected Alternative |
| Chapter 8 | Overall Recommendations |
| Chapter 9 | Conclusion |
| Appendix | |

## 10.5 APPLYING *ARCHAMPLE* WITHIN AN INDUSTRIAL CONTEXT

In the following subsections, we describe the application of *Archample* to the REFoRM project within Aselsan REHİS.

### 10.5.1 Preparation phase

In this phase, we identified the stakeholders and the evaluation team(s) as defined in Section 10.4. These included the project decision makers, three MPL architects, a PL architect for each PL, PL evaluation team, and other stakeholders required for each PL (such as developers, testers, and customers).

### 10.5.2 Selection of feasible MPL decomposition

Within the REFoRM project of Aselsan REHİS four different MPL architecture alternatives were identified:

1. One PL: Defining the system as one PL as shown in Figure 10.9.
2. Four PLs: Defining the system as four independent PLs as shown in Figure 10.10.
3. AD PLs: Defining only the application domains as PLs as shown in Figure 10.11.
4. CPLs: Defining a CPL as it was shown earlier in Figure 10.4.

Before the analysis, the MPL architecture was not designed using the viewpoints as defined in Section 10.3. Thus, we took some time to provide a proper design of each alternative.

Evaluating four different alternatives using the GQM evaluation approach, as part of *Archample*, was carried out. Table 10.3 shows the GQM results as defined during the evaluation. The goals represent high-level business goals that were found important from the project decision makers. These goals are listed below:

– Optimize Reuse: MPL architecture should supply maximum reuse within radar and electronic warfare projects; no functionality should be repeated in different PLs.
– Increase Productivity: The MPL architecture should need minimum manpower. Where possible the need for hiring new personnel should be minimized.

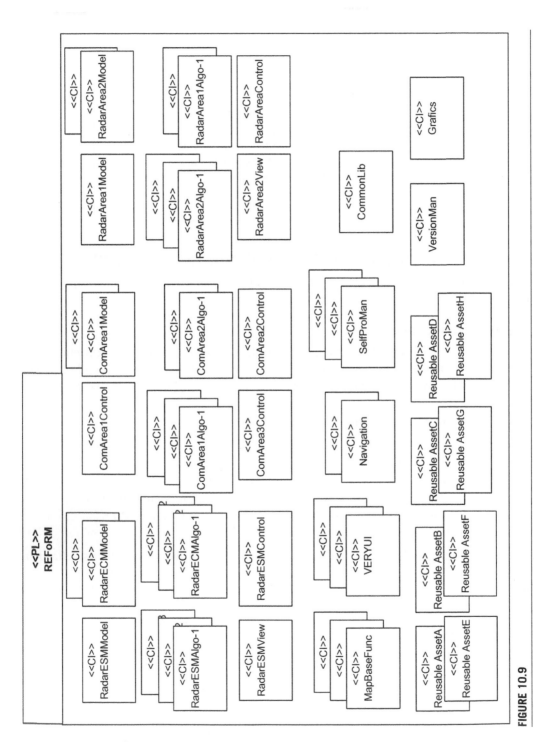

**FIGURE 10.9**

Example product line decomposition view that defines "one product line" for all types of projects.

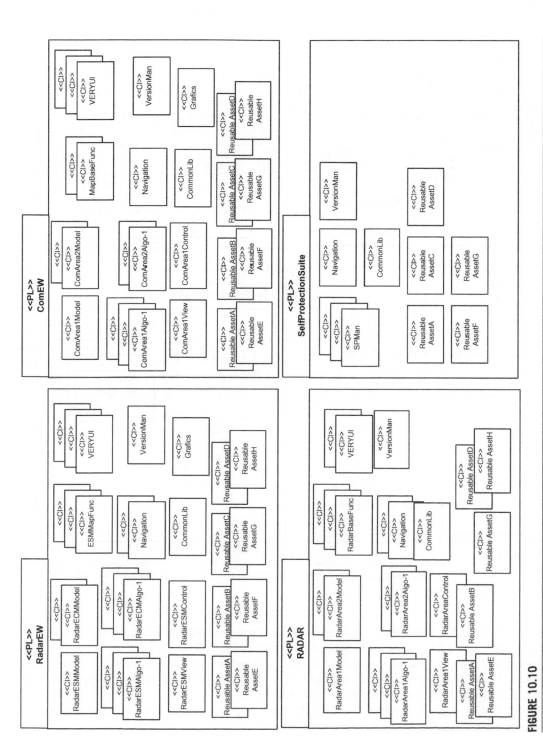

**FIGURE 10.10**

Example product line decomposition view that defines four separate independent product lines (four PLs).

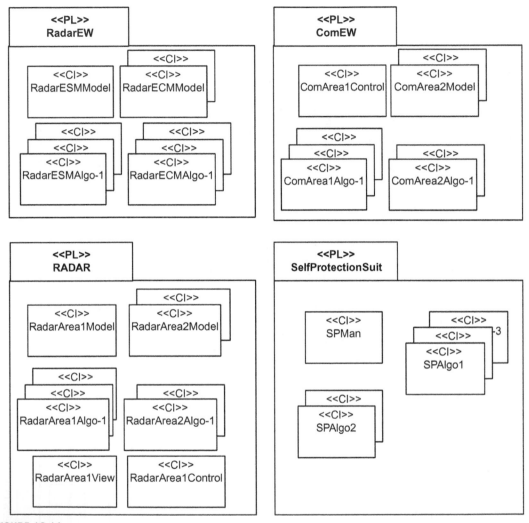

**FIGURE 10.11**

Example product line decomposition view that defines four separate independent product lines just for the Mission Domain Applications level (AD PLs).

- Manage Complexity: Due to the large domain and huge sets of features, the complexity of variability management of the PL is very high. MPL architecture should help to cope with this complexity.
- Ease Organizational Management: Aselsan is working in well-defined domains and internal business units are currently organized around these units. The MPL architecture should be in alignment with these domains and not disrupt the structure too much.
- Ease PL Management: It should be easy to add/remove/update product features within and across business units. Also, the evolution of MPL architecture should be manageable.

**Table 10.3** GQM Results for the Top-Level MPL Architecture in the REFoRM Project

| Goal | Questions | Metric |
|------|-----------|--------|
| Optimize Reuse | What is the reuse level of assets? | # % of reused assets per product |
| | What is the distribution over products for reused assets? | #asset distribution over products |
| | Is there overlapping functionality among PLs? | #common features over assets (in multiple PLs) |
| Increase Productivity | What is the required manpower for the domain engineering activities? | #man month per PL |
| | What is the required manpower for the application engineering activities? | #man month per application |
| Manage Complexity | What is the complexity of commonality and variability? | #depth of feature diagram #features |
| | Are the domain boundaries properly defined and separated over PLs? | #PL per Domain #Domain per PL |
| | Does each PL address a single domain (separation of domains over PLs)? | |
| Ease organizational management | What is the structure of the required product line organization? | Organization Hierarchy Depth |
| | Are the teams properly defined and separated over domain PL activities? | |
| | Are the PL activities properly mapped to organization teams? | |
| Ease Product Line Management | What is the effort to add/remove/update product features within PL? | #man month for total maintenance activities per PL |
| | What is the effort to add/remove/update product features across PLs? | #man month for total maintenance activities per CPL |
| | Can the organization structure cope easily when new products/domains are added? | Subjective evaluation by project management |
| Ease Composition of Products | What is the effort for composing products from different PLs? | Subjective evaluation by project management |

– Ease Composition of Products: The PL decomposition should enable combinations of products from different domains managed by related business units in the company.

Once the goals, questions, and metrics were defined, we could start the actual evaluation. The result of the evaluation of each of the four alternatives according to the presented goals is shown in Table 10.4. It was decided that all the six goals should have equal weight. For each criterion the evaluation scale includes the values $--$, $-$, $+-$, $++$, and $++$, defining a very negative evaluation to a very positive evaluation. The goals were evaluated with respect to the corresponding questions and the metrics. Below, we provide a short discussion of the alternatives.

1. One PL: As shown in Table 10.4, defining the system as one complete PL (Figure 10.9) is not favorable from the complexity management perspective and the ability to manage the organization for the resulting very large PL. In addition, the Mission Domain Applications level of the system

**Table 10.4** Evaluation Matrix for Design Alternatives of the Product Line Decomposition

| Goals | One PL | Four PLs | AD PLs | CPLs |
|---|---|---|---|---|
| Optimize Reuse | ++ | − − | −(−) | ++ |
| Increase Productivity | +(+) | − | − | ++ |
| Manage Complexity | − − | + | + | + |
| Ease Organizational Management | − − | ++ | ++ | +− |
| Ease Product Line Management | +(+) | + | − − | ++ |
| Ease Composition of Products | +(+) | − − | − | ++ |

was currently defined across different departments and from an organization point of view. Putting all the product divisions together was considered not feasible. On the other hand, this alternative was valued as positive because it would probably not include overlapping functionality, and the manpower needed would be optimized. Further, this alternative would also be beneficial for managing products and composing new products.

2. Four PLs: The second alternative of defining the system as four independent PLs (Figure 10.10) has been positively evaluated with respect to alignment with the domains because it supports the four Mission Domain Applications level. The organization management would also be distributed over the multiple divisions, thus the problems of a heavy central organization would be avoided. The product management would be easy but the composition of new products across MPLs would be severely impeded. Moreover, this alternative required that the different alternative PLs include development of similar functionality, and due to the overlapping functionality, reuse would not be optimized. Consequently, this alternative would also require more additional manpower than the other alternatives.

3. AD PLs: The third alternative (Figure 10.11) is the MPL with four separate PLs for the Mission Domain Applications level and an additional platform layer with reusable assets as libraries. For the first four criteria this alternative was evaluated like the second alternative. The motivations for the evaluations were also similar. In contrast to the second alternative, this alternative is not considered feasible for product management. The reason for this is that some critical domains are not developed as PLs but remain as libraries whose variability and architecture were not defined. Thus the composition of new products will be impeded. Regarding complexity of variability management, this was considered also similar to the second alternative. There will be less variability in the four domains because part of the functionality will reside in libraries. On the other hand, new variations would be harder to define.

4. CPLs: Defining the system as a CPL (Figure 10.4) was positively evaluated for almost all the defined criteria. The MPL could on the one hand include a hierarchical structure while still keeping the separation of domains and organizational management in the company. Overlapping functionality could be reduced or eliminated. Due to the hierarchical and composite structure, the development of new products would be supported. The only neutral result for this choice is the optimization of manpower; the manpower needed to develop the assets would be optimized as the reuse is optimized, but the manpower needed for the management of the PLs will be higher than a single PL because each PL and the CPL will need separate management.

From Table 10.4, it can be observed that defining "four PLs" and "application domain PLs" are the worst choices because they have the most negatives. Despite the increased management complexity in the PL, the alternative with one PL was more positively evaluated than was expected. After careful thought and discussion with the stakeholders, the most feasible alternative for the Aselsan REHİS case was determined to be the composite MPL alternatives. It should be noted that the evaluation of each of the alternatives was actually only possible after modeling each alternative using the architectural viewpoints in the previous section. Without the explicit architectural views, one had to rely on discussions, informal sketches, or feature modeling approaches. None of these were considered as powerful as explicitly documenting the architectural views.

### 10.5.3 Evaluation of the selected MPL design alternative

After the composite MPL was selected as the most feasible design alternative, the refined evaluation was necessary to evaluate the PL architectures in the MPL. For the refined evaluation, we adopted a top-down evaluation strategy. That is, we decided to analyze the top-level MPL first and then the sub-PLs. For some PLs it was decided not to perform an evaluation yet due to the time constraints. The strategy together with the selected evaluation methods for the various PLs are shown in Figure 10.12. The figure shows the order of the evaluation of the PLs.

As shown in Figure 10.12, it was decided to do an ATAM for the *RadEW* and a GQM for *Radar and ComEW*. For the PLs of *RadEW* an ATAM was also performed. Each ATAM evaluation took

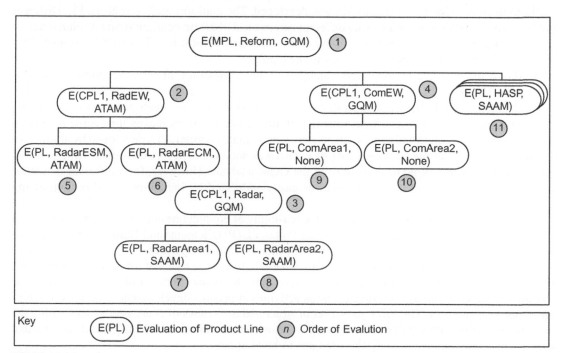

**FIGURE 10.12**

Adopted evaluation strategy for evaluation of selected CPL design alternative in REFoRM.

about 1 week. For the PLs of *Radar*, the team decided to apply SAAM, while the CPLs of *ComEW* were not evaluated yet. The separate PLs, on the right part of the figure, were either not evaluated or a quick SAAM process was applied (about two days).

### 10.5.4 Reporting and workshop

The complete design and the corresponding evaluation of the MPL alternatives were reported and written as a technical report (Tekinerdogan et al., 2012). Interactive workshops were held in step 4 (select feasible MPL using GQM) and step 6 (evaluate MPL). For the latter step, we needed more than one workshop meeting to do the evaluation for the separate PLs. The overall evaluation was completed using a final two-day workshop in which the process for selecting the MPL, the modeling of the MPL, and the modeling and evaluation of the required PLs was discussed.

## 10.6 RELATED WORK

Different industrial cases of MPL engineering have been discussed in the literature. van der Linden and Wijnstra (2001), for example, described the development of multiple product families for the Philips Medical imaging systems (PMS). Typically, several PLs are available because products are developed in different parts of the world and within different product groups. Although the products in the different lines differ a lot, there is also a lot of similar software between them. Because of this, an imaging platform to be used by the whole of PMS was developed. The platform itself was also a PL. Different product groups within Philips are using different variants and platform configurations. Within many of the product groups, software running on top of the imaging platform is built into SPL as well. This induces additional variability requirements to the platform.

In this work, we have focused on the analysis of the composition of MPL within the context of Aselsan REHİS. Each PL is developed by Aselsan REHİS, and there are no external suppliers of PLs. Several authors have indicated the fact that the required PLs could be developed and maintained by external competing suppliers. The availability of alternative suppliers makes it possible to serve a wider group of customers and avoids a dependency on a single supplier. PLs developed by alternative suppliers have been termed as *competing* PL*s*. This was not a concern for Aselsan REHİS, so it was not defined in the list of goals derived from the GQM analysis. However, for a different industrial case in which this is important, this could be easily addressed by including a goal on optimizing supplier costs.

Some authors have focused on analyzing the feasibility of product line engineering approach (PLA) for an organization. The Product Line Technical Probe (PLTP) (Clements and Northrop, 2002), as proposed by the Software Engineering Institute (SEI), aims at discovering the ability of an organization to adapt and succeed with the SPL approach. The PLTP is a diagnostic tool that uses the SEI Framework for SPL Practice as a reference model. The Framework for Software Product Line Practice divides the overall SPL process into a set of three essential activities of product development, core asset development, and management. The PLTP uses a set of structured interviews of small peer groups within the organization to identify the framework practices that need to be improved, identify the challenges that need to be addressed, and identify the strengths to build upon.

Fritsch and Hahn (2004) introduce Product Line Potential Analysis (PLPA), which aims to make a quick decision as to whether a PLA is suitable for a given set of products and target market. A PLPA is executed in a half-day workshop that includes structured interviews. The answers to the questions are compared to a set of criteria for the applicability of the PLA and result in "yes," "no," or "investigation required."

Besides analyzing the feasibility of PLA, different product line scoping approaches have been proposed to define a proper PL scope. In this context, PuLSE-Eco (Schmid and Widen, 2000) deals with defining the scope of SPL on business objectives that are identified by PL stakeholders.

Rosenmüller et al. (2008) discuss the problem of *dependent* PLs, that is, one SPL using functionality provided by another SPL. They describe that only defining constraints between the involved feature models is not sufficient in case multiple differently configured instances are used in a composition of SPLs. Thus the dependencies between the concrete instances have to be considered. Likewise, Rosenmuller et al. present an extension to current SPL modeling based on class diagrams that allows us to describe SPL instances and dependencies among them. An elaboration of this work is defined in Rosenmüller and Siegmund (2010), where the authors show the semi-automatic configuration of MPL based on so-called *composition models*. To define the MPL metrics, the notion of dependent PLs could be adopted.

Babar et al. (2004) have provided a framework for classifying and comparing software architecture (SA) evaluation methods. This framework has been developed by discovering similarities and differences among existing evaluation methods. We have used this framework to characterize *Archample* as shown in Table 10.5.

**Table 10.5** Characterization of the Approach Using Evaluation Framework as Defined in Babar et al. (2004)

| Method Criterion | Description |
| --- | --- |
| Method's activities | Seven activities in four phases +1 phase with number of activities dependent on selected architecture analysis approach (of step 6 in Figure 10.6) |
| Method's goals | – Evaluate whether it is feasible to adopt an MPL architecture<br>– Evaluate ability of MPL architecture to achieve quality attributes<br>– Combine evaluation of MPL architecture with evaluation of single PL architectures |
| Quality attributes addressed | Multiple attributes (GQM and criteria defined in adopted evaluation methods) |
| Architectural description | Using MPL architecture viewpoints and viewpoints in existing architecture frameworks |
| Maturity stage | Inception/development |
| Software architecture definition | MPL architecture, PL architecture |
| Process support | Sufficient process support |
| Applicable project stage | After MPL and PL Architecture; Early analysis |
| Evaluation approaches | Hybrid approach (GQM and existing evaluation methods) |
| Stakeholders involved | All major stakeholders |
| Support for nontechnical issues | Implicit but not explicitly addressed |
| Method's validation | Validated in one large real industrial project |
| Tool support | Not available |
| Experience repository available | No |
| Resources required | Apart from initial & postpreparation, three days. Four-person evaluation team & stakeholders |

## 10.7 CONCLUSION

Recent developments in SPL engineering show the need for MPL in which products are composed from subproducts in separate SPL. Designing and realizing the MPL approach is a challenging and time-consuming task. In this context we have in particular focused on the composition of the MPL PL from separate PLs. It is important to analyze the MPL decomposition early before large organizational resources are committed to the development. Different architecture analysis approaches have been introduced, but none of these focuses on the evaluation of MPL architectures. In this chapter, we have proposed the architecture analysis approach for MPL Engineering *(Archample)*, which has been particularly defined for the analysis of MPL architectures. *Archample* can be used to support the decision for whether to apply an MPL. Using *Archample* the possible architecture design alternatives are made explicit and the feasible design alternative is selected and evaluated. An important aspect of an evaluation method is whether it has been validated. *Archample* was designed within an industrial context and also applied for a large industrial case of Aselsan REHİS. Our experiences show that the application of *Archample* led to an increased understanding of the MPL architecture and the design decisions. *Archample* is an evaluation method itself but can also be considered as an approach to integrate evaluation approaches within an MPL context. Our future work will be focused on developing tool support to represent the architectural views and support the steps of Archample.

## Acknowledgments

We would like to thank Levent Alkışlar, Baki Demirel, Hakime Koç, Gökhan Kahraman, Şafak Şeker, Ümit Demir, and Hakan Bali for earlier discussions on the *RadEW* product line architecture. This work has been carried out as part of the Product Line Engineering for Radar Electronic Support System (PLE-RES) project under the responsibility of Aselsan REHİS and Bilkent University.

## References

Aoyama, M., Watanabe, K., Nishio, Y., Moriwaki, Y., 2003. Embracing requirements variety for e-governments based on multiple product-lines frameworks. In: Proceedings of the 11th IEEE International Requirements Engineering Conference.

Archer, M., Collet, P., Lahire, P., France, R., 2010. Managing multiple software product lines using merging techniques technical report, University of Nice Sophia Antipolis, I3S CNRS, Sophia Antipolis, France, May 2010.

Aselsan, 2011. Website: http://www.aselsan.com.tr/default.asp?lang=en (accessed February 2011).

Babar, M.A., Zhu, L., Jeffrey, R., 2004. A framework for classifying and comparing software architecture evaluation methods. In: Proceedings of 5th Australian Software Engineering Conference, pp. 309–319.

Clements, P., Northrop, L., 2002. Software Product Lines: Practices and Patterns. Addison-Wesley, Boston, MA.

Clements, P., Bachmann, F., Bass, L., Garlan, D., Ivers, J., Little, R., Merson, P., Nord, R., Stafford, J., 2011. Documenting Software Architectures: Views and Beyond, second ed. Addison-Wesley, Reading, MA.

Dobrica, L.F., Niemela, E., 2002. A survey on software architecture analysis methods. IEEE Trans. Softw. Eng. 28 (7), 638–653.

Fritsch, C., Hahn, R., 2004. Product line potential analysis. In: Proceedings of the 3rd International Conference on Software Product Lines, pp. 228–237.

Hartmann, H., Trew, T., Matsinger, A., 2009. Supplier independent feature modeling. In: SPLC 2009. IEEE Computer Society, Los Alamitos, CA, pp. 191–200.

ISO/IEC, ISO/IEC 42010 Systems and Software Engineering, 2007. Recommended Practice For Architectural Description of Software-Intensive Systems.

Kazman, R., Bass, L., Klein, M., Lattanze, T., Northrop, L., 2005. A Basis for Analyzing Software Architecture Analysis Methods. Softw. Qual. J. 13 (4), 329–355.

Pohl, K., Böckle, G., van der Linden, F., 2005. Software Product Line Engineering—Foundations, Principles, and Techniques. Springer, Berlin.

Rosenmüller, M., Siegmund, N., 2010. Automating the configuration of multi software product lines. In: Proceedings of the International Workshop on Variability Modelling of Software-intensive Systems, Linz, Austria.

Rosenmüller, M., Siegmund, N., Kästner, C., Saif ur Rahman, S., 2008. Modeling dependent software product lines. In: GPCE Workshop on Modularization, Composition and Generative Techniques for Product Line Engineering (McGPLE), Nashville, TN, pp. 13–18.

Roy, B., Graham, T.C.N., 2008. Methods for evaluating software architecture: a survey. Computing. 545, 82, no. 2008–545.

Schmid, K., Verlage, M., 2002. The economic impact of product line adoption and evolution. IEEE Softw. 19 (4), 50–57.

Schmid, K., Widen, T., 2000. Customizing the PuLSE™ product line approach to the demands of an organization. In: Proceedings of the 7th European Workshop on Software Process Technology, (EWSPT'2000), Kaprun, Austria. In: Lecture Notes in Computer Science, vol. 1780. pp. 221–238.

Solingen, R., Berghout, E., 1999. Goal/Question/Metric Method. Mcgraw Hill Higher Education, New York.

Tekinerdogan, B., et al., 2004. ASAAM: aspectual software architecture analysis method. In: Proceedings of 4th Working IEEE/IFIP Conference on Software Architecture (WICSA), pp. 5–14.

Tekinerdogan, B., Ozkose Erdogan, O., Aktug, O., 2012. Multiple product line architecture of the RadEW project, Technical report, Aselsan REHİS, 180 p.

van der Linden, F., Wijnstra, J.G., 2001. Platform Engineering for the Medical Domain. In: Proceedings PFE4, Bilbao, pp. 224–237.

van Ommering, R., 2002. Widening the Scope of Software Product Lines—from Variation to Composition. In: Proceedings of the Software Product Lines 2nd International Conference, San Diego, CA. Lecture Notes in Computer Science, vol. 2379. Springer, Berlin, p. 328.

# Quality Attributes in Medical Planning and Simulation Systems

**Matthias Galster[1] and Antoine Widmer[2]**

[1]*University of Canterbury, Christchurch, New Zealand*
[2]*University of Applied Sciences Western Switzerland, Sierre, Switzerland*

## INTRODUCTION

Medical planning and simulation (MPS) systems require the integration of resource-consuming computations and advanced interaction techniques. Examples of MPS systems include software for training surgeons in medical schools or software for preparing and planning surgeries based on simulated organs of the patient who will undergo the surgery. MPS systems often simulate human tissue as virtual objects based on complex mathematical and physical models and allow medical personnel to interact with virtual objects using a haptic device. In Figure 11.1, we show a screenshot of a simulation that allows the interaction between a virtual finger moved by a medical examiner and a virtual organ made of soft tissues. This simulation is used for training cancer screening by palpation (Galster and Widmer, 2010). The simulation in Figure 11.1 shows the human organ in 3D, provided that the user is wearing special goggles. The medical examiner would also feel the stiffness of the organ through a haptic device. This simulation teaches a medical examiner how to apply the correct force to detect embedded harder lesions in human tissue. Darker regions on the virtual object in Figure 11.1 indicate the strength of the force applied to the different regions of the virtual organ. A schematic setup of a typical MPS system is shown in Figure 11.2. The monitor in Figure 11.2 could visualize something similar as shown in Figure 11.1.

Architecting and designing MPS systems are challenging and a specialized, time-consuming, and expensive process. In particular, achieving quality in MPS systems is essential due to the criticality of those systems for human health and life. For example, poor training of surgeons may lead to misjudgments of physical conditions of patients. Through our experience with developing research and commercial MPS systems, we found that these systems impose specific constraints on "quality." This is because of the following reasons:

- Medical simulation and planning systems should replicate the real world as closely as possible, including how humans (i.e., medical practitioners) perform tasks in real time.
- Most MPS systems use physical models to represent human tissue or organs. Therefore, we need to pay special attention to the correctness of such models to provide accurate support for MPS (Galster and Widmer, 2010).

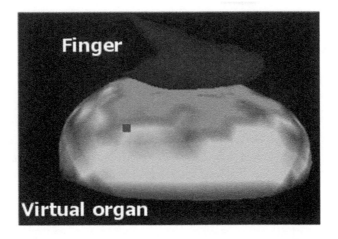

**FIGURE 11.1**

Screenshot of an application that simulates the interaction of a medical examiner (finger) with human tissue (virtual organ).

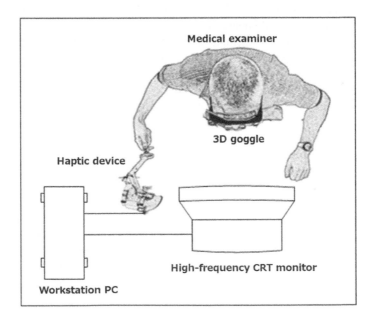

**FIGURE 11.2**

Setup of a typical MPS system.

• Various stakeholders involved in the development of such systems have different notions of quality. For example, surgeons are concerned about performance. Furthermore, surgeons are concerned about completeness of the MPS features to include all possible cases or complications that may occur in a surgical procedure. Medical research and development engineers, on the other hand, are more concerned about the accuracy of their algorithms implemented in those systems.

- When making architectural decisions for medical software, there is a need to consider complex hardware (e.g., haptic devices, stereoscopic displays, 3D goggles, and "trackable" surgical tools, such as endoscopes).

Note that most MPS systems utilize virtual reality (VR). Therefore, these characteristics may also appear in the context of other systems that utilize VR and go beyond merely visualizing virtual environments (e.g., by allowing human interaction or feedback, such as earthquake simulation systems, industrial flight simulators, or military training systems).

## 11.1 CHAPTER CONTRIBUTIONS

To the best of our knowledge, no comprehensive guidelines on how to deal with quality attributes in medical systems development exist. Therefore, in this chapter we elaborate on how quality attributes of MPS systems are exhibited in the architecture of those systems and in the architecting process. In detail, the contributions of this chapter are the following:

1. We explore challenges related to quality attributes in the development of MPS systems. These challenges can be used as pitfalls to be avoided by architects and designers involved in designing novel MPS systems.
2. We propose a set of quality attributes that should be addressed in the software architecture. Here, we focus on the quality attributes performance, usability, and correctness. These quality attributes can support architects and designers as a checklist for the quality of MPS systems. Furthermore, performance, usability, and correctness can be used as out-of-the-box architectural key drivers in medical software development projects. Based on Chen et al. (2013), these quality attributes help describe architecturally significant requirements, that is, requirements that have a measurable impact on a software architecture and shape the architecture. Even though there are other quality attributes in the context of MPS systems design, we found these three quality attributes as recurring architectural key drivers that drive architectural decisions. We acknowledge that MPS systems consist of software and hardware. However, in this chapter we only discuss issues related to the software architecture of MPS systems.
3. We report several strategies on how to handle quality attributes at the requirements and architecture stage of MPS software development. These strategies are inspired by agile development practices.

The findings presented in this chapter come from more than 8 years of researching and developing MPS systems at Canadian and Swiss research institutes and companies. We did not apply formal data collection methodologies, but recorded challenges throughout these projects and aggregate them into this chapter. Furthermore, with regard to strategies to handle quality attributes, we used final project reports to determine the level of success and satisfaction of stakeholders with the project outcome.

In Section 11.2 of this chapter, we introduce the background and related work. In Section 11.3 we elaborate on challenges related to achieving quality attributes in MPS systems. In Section 11.4 we discuss quality attributes for MPS systems. Some advice on how quality attributes could be considered during the architecting of MPS systems is provided in Section 11.5. Finally, we conclude this chapter in Section 11.6.

## 11.2 BACKGROUND AND RELATED WORK

### 11.2.1 MPS systems

MPS systems often use VR technologies. Thus, MPS systems involve resource-consuming computations because VR environments should allow human users to interact in real time with a computer-simulated environment (Kim, 2005). Advanced interaction techniques are used because MPS systems do not only integrate visual information, but also information pertinent to the sense of touch of human tissues and organs (Sorid and Moore, 2000). Thus, many MPS systems integrate complex haptic hardware systems for user-software interaction (e.g., to simulate the use of an endoscopic tool inside a human body). This is in contrast to ordinary software systems that use mouse, keyboard, or touchpads as input devices, and monitors, screens, or visual displays as output devices.

### 11.2.2 Software development for MPS systems

Developing MPS systems requires knowledge in many different areas, such as sensing and tracking technologies, stereoscopic displays, or multimodal interaction (Kim, 2005). Usually, MPS systems involve small teams and small- to medium-scale software. Close communication between users and developers of the software is essential for timely delivery of the working software. In the following paragraphs we outline some existing work on software development for MPS systems, without focusing on architecture or design activities.

- Troyer et al. (2007) applied conceptual modeling as commonly used in software engineering to the engineering of VR systems. The main goal was to reduce the complexity of VR applications by narrowing the gap between the application domain (i.e., MPS systems) and the level at which VR applications are specified by software designers. Conceptual modeling claims to involve customers in the design process of VR applications and to detect design flaws early on.
- VRID, an approach for developing VR interfaces, has been proposed by Tanriverdi and Jacob (2001). VRID divides the design process of VR systems into a low-level and a high-level phase and formally represents the environment of VR applications: It separates graphics from interaction and application data. In this sense, VRID utilizes ideas from the Model-View-Controller pattern.
- The CLEVR approach (Kim et al., 1998; Seo and Kim, 2002) utilizes UML and object-oriented design for designing VR applications. CLEVR uses simultaneous functional and behavioral modeling, hierarchical modeling and top-down creation of levels of detail, incremental execution and performance tuning, user task and interaction modeling, and compositional reuse of virtual objects.
- Geiger et al. (2000) presented an approach for developing animated and interactive media, whereas Willans and Harrison (2001) developed a toolset to separate designing interaction techniques from building a specific virtual world. Both works focus on aspects related to visualizations.
- A higher-level software engineering concept for VR has been presented by Seo, who proposed a spiral model for VR system development (Seo and Kim, 2002). This model can be viewed as a classical spiral software engineering process with requirements analysis as stage 0, system architecture "scene" modeling as stage 1, refinement as stage 2, and the development of presence and special effects as stage 3. This spiral model does not cover testing; however, some performance tuning and system simulation and validation is included.

- Focusing more on requirements-related aspects, Kim (2005) presented a requirements engineering perspective on the development of VR systems. Different levels of requirements are defined, with an internal view, interaction, and models as well as simulation parts of VR applications. The approach uses storyboards (visual scripts with informal sketches and annotations) to document requirements. These requirements are refined in UML class diagrams. UML message sequence diagrams are used to describe interactions within a VR system. Similarly, in our previous work we explored a requirements-centric perspective on the design of VR applications, following an agile-inspired approach (Galster and Widmer, 2010).

Kim, 2005 describes three factors that make the development of VR software different from other software systems:

1. Real-time performance requirements, while maintaining an acceptable level of realism and presence of virtual objects in a virtual space.
2. Modeling the appearance of objects and physical properties, including functions and behavior.
3. Consideration of different styles and modalities of interaction, according to different tasks and I/O devices.

Consequently, many system goals and drivers have to be considered simultaneously during architecting, some of which are conflicting (e.g., technology choices about I/O devices and physical properties of virtual objects). However, due to their innovative nature, most MPS systems are often developed following *ad hoc* practices or practices that are more similar to developing scientific software (Sanders and Kelly, 2008). For example, similar to scientific software development, MPS systems typically involve scientists knowledgeable in the application domain.

### 11.2.3 Quality attributes of MPS

No comprehensive study on quality attributes for MPS systems exists. However, quality attributes have been studied in the medical domain in general. For example, Wijnstra (2001) identified important quality attributes for medical imaging product lines: reliability, safety, functionality, portability, modifiability, testability, and serviceability. These quality attributes may also appear in MPS systems. As we will show later, functionality as a quality attribute (in terms of model correctness) also appears in MPS systems. Capilla and Martinez (2004) explore software architecture for VR applications and propose an architecture. However, their approach does not consider qualities such as performance, usability, and presence.

## 11.3 CHALLENGES RELATED TO ACHIEVING QUALITY ATTRIBUTES IN MPS SYSTEMS

As mentioned earlier, the challenges described in this section are based on several projects developing commercial MPS systems as well as multiple projects that developed MPS systems in an academic setting. Even though the nature of these challenges may not be unique to MPS systems and might also occur in other types of complex or unprecedented systems, we believe that making them explicit helps designers of MPS systems avoid common pitfalls. In detail, we found four different types of challenges related to achieving quality attributes:

- Constraints on the development and architecture process for MPS systems should be kept to a minimum in order to keep this process flexible. In VR as an innovative and cutting-edge discipline, creativity of developers (including architects and designers) is necessary or even desired to design useful solutions. A too-rigid process may reduce the potential of benefiting from creativity.
- During requirements engineering and architecture analysis, detailed requirements cannot simply be "gathered," but are usually "discovered" throughout development. This usually happens in tight collaboration and interactions with end users (surgeons, medical planners, physicists, etc.) rather than other stakeholders. In detail, the problems that we encountered with requirements engineering and architecture analysis are the following: First, required experts may not be available. Medical professionals, such as surgeons, usually tend to be reluctant to get involved into software engineering activities to precisely express their needs. Even in cases where they get involved, we experienced that their input is quite vague and requires lots of additional research. This additional research may result in new stakeholders and information sources. Second, not all required experts may be known early on. For example, medical planning systems may involve surgeons at early stages for requirements elicitation. At later stages, it may become necessary to involve physicists for the modeling of human tissue. This may not have been anticipated at early phases of requirements elicitation. Third, requirements and technical feasibility are closely coupled. For example, software and hardware technologies constrain how realistic simulations can be.
- We lack guidelines for how to effectively integrate various resource-consuming computations and interaction techniques (Kim, 2005) to achieve quality planning and simulation systems. In particular, trade-offs between quality attributes and quality attribute requirements need to be considered. For example, model correctness is often sacrificed for improving performance and usability in MPS systems. Architectural knowledge management (Kruchten et al., 2005) and supporting tools (Tang et al., 2010) that could help address this challenge are not or rarely used in the development of MPS systems. This means that solutions for common design problems may exist, but are not documented or shared within and across organizations. Thus, architects and designers may not be aware of these solutions and therefore cannot reuse them. As also found in other domains, architectural knowledge is not systematically managed in order to address frequently occurring challenges related to multifaceted requirements, but rather treated implicitly and informally (Tofan et al., 2013).
- The architecture of MPS systems is usually a variation of a Model-View-Controller architecture. Figure 11.3 shows a schematic view of a typical high-level architecture of MPS systems. The "Graphics module" is responsible for rendering graphics and displaying them to the user. The "Advanced I/O processing module" elements help integrate sophisticated input (haptic devices, touch screens, etc.) and output devices (haptic devices, 3D goggles, 3D screens, etc.). The "Computational module" implements algorithms necessary to simulate the behavior of tissue. However, there is no strict separation between graphics rendering (view), advanced I/O (controller), and computations (model). Instead, data and control flow appear between model elements, view elements, and controller elements. The reason for this is that performance goals are usually easier to achieve if the controller element is not in full control of all data and control flows within an MPS system. Furthermore, due to the innovative nature of MPS systems, *ad hoc* practices and quick fixes

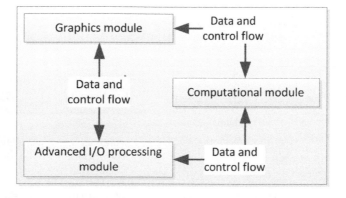

**FIGURE 11.3**

Data and control flows between major architectural elements of an MPS system.

are applied to tune quality attribute requirements. This negatively affects the maintainability of MPS and further contributes to violating design rules prescribed by the Model-View-Controller pattern.

## 11.4 QUALITY ATTRIBUTES IN MPS SYSTEMS

The notion of "quality" in the software for MPS systems is often explored from a technical perspective (e.g., the accuracy of algorithms used within the software). Quality attributes tend to be treated as high-level constraints and criteria to define test cases, rather than as explicit drivers that guide architectural decisions. Based on the experience of developing research and commercial MPS systems, Figure 11.4 shows three quality attributes and example quality attribute requirements found as most significant in the context of MPS systems. We integrated our quality attributes in the ISO 9126 model for software quality (ISO/IEC/IEEE, 2011). Thus, model correctness is a sub-quality attribute of quality attribute functionality in ISO 9126. We discuss each quality attribute in the remainder of this section. Please note that in Figure 11.4 we only show examples of quality attribute requirements to illustrate how quality attributes can be "operationalized." However, in practice each quality attribute could result in more than one quality attribute requirement.

### 11.4.1 Performance

Performance is crucial for MPS systems. Most, if not all, MPS systems are real-time applications. For medical practitioners and end-user representatives, performance refers to the smoothness of rendering objects and interaction. Usually, several performance goals for one stakeholder exist (measured in terms of response time, frame rate, etc.). Given that efficiency in ISO 9126 defines the capability of a software product to provide appropriate performance relative to the amount of resources used, we define performance as a subcategory of efficiency in ISO 9126 (ISO/IEC/IEEE, 2011).

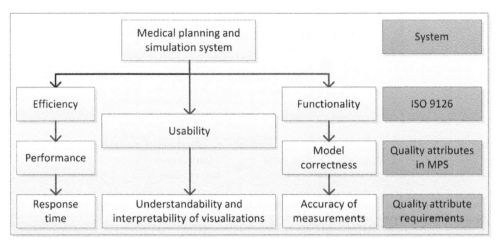

**FIGURE 11.4**

Quality attributes and example quality attribute requirements experienced in the context of medical planning and simulation systems.

## 11.4.2 Usability

Usability refers to the ease of use of an MPS system. MPS systems should be usable in an intuitive manner, and interaction with virtual objects should happen just like in a real-world setting. In ISO 9126, usability refers to the capability of a software product to be understood, learned, used, as well as its ability to attract users (ISO/IEC/IEEE, 2011). Furthermore, ISO 9126 defines understandability, learnability, and operability as a subcategory of usability. Thus, we also define usability in MPS systems as a subcategory of quality. Usability can be determined and measured using soft methods (e.g., usability tests that include test users) or hard metrics (e.g., time to learn how to use an application or the number of errors made by a novice user) (Kotonya and Sommerville, 1998). In particular, understandability and interpretability of visualizations of virtual organs are a crucial quality attribute requirement of medical examiners. Note that performance and usability affect each other. Despite being defined as similar in ISO 9126, performance is not classified as usability in our work.

## 11.4.3 Model correctness

ISO 9126 defines functionality as the capability of a software product to provide functions that meet stated and implied needs when the software is used under specified conditions. More specifically, ISO 9126 defines accuracy as the capability of a software product to provide the right or agreed results or effects with the needed degree of precision (ISO/IEC/IEEE, 2011). Thus, we define model correctness as a subcategory of functionality. Most, if not all, MPS systems use physical and mathematical models to represent real-world phenomena (such as human tissue). Such models are usually not understood by software architects and designers, but require the involvement of domain experts, such as physicists and biomedical engineers. The correctness and accuracy of those models is crucial for the applicability and reliability of an MPS system. For example, measurements obtained from mathematical models must be accurate enough to provide realistic simulations of human tissue for informed surgery planning. The meaning of "accurate enough" is usually determined by closely involving medical domain experts in the definition of quality attribute requirements.

We found that these three quality attributes describe requirements that are architecturally significant (Chen et al., 2013). According to Chen et al., a requirement or quality attribute is "architecturally significant" if it meets the following criteria:

- Has wide impact: Many different stakeholders; components are affected by performance, usability, and model correctness.
- Targets trade-offs: Trade-offs occur because no solution satisfies all requirements equally well. For example, it is usually not possible to achieve good performance and high model accuracy.
- Implies strictness: Usually, performance, usability, and model correctness are not negotiable. This means that when making architectural decisions, the quality attributes that can be satisfied by multiple design options will allow flexibility in architectural design, whereas strict requirements determine architectural decisions because they cannot be satisfied by alternative design options (Chen et al., 2013).
- Is difficult to achieve: Performance, usability, and model correctness are difficult to meet and technologically challenging.

There may be other quality attributes in the context of MPS systems (e.g., robustness, portability between different operating systems). However, we found the three quality attributes mentioned above to be the ones that appear in most MPS systems and across all projects. For example, portability may only occur in projects that develop product lines of MPS systems, and robustness tends to be of lower importance in MPS systems used for training surgeons (i.e., it would not be treated as a key driver). Consequently, these three quality attributes tend to drive trade-off analyses. Furthermore, we found them as key concerns for determining the success of an MPS system projects (e.g., to derive test cases).

Qualities that are closer to the architecture (or "intrinsic" qualities, such as maintainability, extendibility) are just as important as in other projects. However, we found them to be addressed implicitly throughout design and not considered as architectural key drivers.

## 11.5 HANDLING QUALITY ATTRIBUTES AT THE ARCHITECTURE STAGE OF MPS SYSTEMS

Our recommendations for dealing with quality attributes at the architecture stage resulted from our experience in transitioning from *ad hoc* development practices to a more agile development practice. In this section we first introduce a set of stakeholders that we found most frequently occurring in the development of MPS software (see Table 11.1). Also, we include the most typical concerns that these stakeholders have. To establish a link between these concerns and software architecture, we phrase these concerns as questions that stakeholders have and that the software architecture should help them answer. Then, we discuss the role of architecture documentation and the architecture process.

### 11.5.1 Architectural stakeholders

We found that the architect and the end-user representative (surgeon, medical examiner, etc.) are the most important stakeholders. In contrast to other types of software, the main duty of the architect is usually to have a clear understanding about the technologies used in the project, rather than to have

**Table 11.1** Stakeholders When Architecting MPS Systems

| Stakeholder | Concern |
|---|---|
| Architect | To what degree does the architecture support performance? <br> To what degree does the architecture support usability? |
| Medical examiner | How accurate are the visualizations of human tissue? <br> How accurate are analysis results from a simulation? |
| Patient | How intrusive is the MPS system when obtaining biomedical data? <br> Does the MPS ensure privacy of personal patient data? |
| Regulatory bodies | Does the MPS system comply with regulatory standards in the medical domain? |

a clear understanding about the scope and main drivers of the system. This is because many architectural decisions in the context of MPS systems are technological decisions. The architect would, for example, rely on input from 3D artists.

Furthermore, in contrast to large-scale software projects that often follow disciplined processes with clearly defined roles, architects usually reside at a client side and interact with customers closely for prioritizing user stories. These user stories are extracted from medical examiners. Patients are usually not directly involved in the development process of MPS systems. Their concerns are mostly represented by regulatory bodies. Regulatory bodies, such as standardization organizations or government agencies only have limited interests in the architecture. However, regulatory bodies have a strong interest in certifying MPS systems. For this purpose the architecture description document provides a useful source of relevant information. Other stakeholders, such as testers and product owners, make an appearance, but they do not have significant impact on architectural concerns.

### 11.5.2 MPS architecture documentation

The development process in the context of MPS systems often follows agile and heavily incremental and iterative procedures. As found in a previous study (Falessi et al., 2010), the software architecture in an agile context aims at facilitating communication among organizations involved in the development, production, fielding, operation, and maintenance of a system. The same applies for the architecture for medical simulation and planning systems. On the other hand, the architecture document of MPS systems was found less useful for supporting system planning and budgeting activities. When certifying MPS systems, the architecture document may play a significant role as a form of system documentation. This means that architecture documentation is a deliverable required by certification bodies.

As found by Babar (2009), several changes occur in software architecture documentation practices that apply agile approaches. In particular, the level of details of architecture documentation is lower compared to non-agile approaches. Also, formal architecture documentation was considered as not adding much value in MPS projects. Thus, we recommend only documenting the most important aspects for the most important stakeholders in an architecture description document. To support documenting important concerns for certain stakeholders, we recommend using architecture viewpoints and views. These help document important concerns of different stakeholders at different stages of the development process (ISO/IEC/IEEE, 2011).

### 11.5.3 **Architecture process**

Architecting in the context of MPS systems is inspired by agile development practices. For example, XP and agile practices seems to be well-suited for innovative and creative software development (Conforto and Amaral, 2008; Highsmith, 2004; Johnston and Johnson, 2003), the regulated life science industry (Fitzgerald et al., 2013) and regulated and complex industries in general (such as the automotive or aerospace domain) (Cawley et al., 2010). In this sense, MPS systems benefit from an agile architecture. In the following, we relate MPS software systems architecting to generic architecture design activities as proposed by Hofmeister et al. (2007):

- Architecture analysis: Architecture analysis defines the problem that a system architecture must solve. During architecture analysis, architectural concerns and the context of the system are examined to define a set of architecturally significant requirements. When developing MPS systems, architecturally significant requirements include requirements identified based on the quality attributes described before. In addition, project-specific key drivers can be identified (e.g., information security). Furthermore, concerns are derived from questions related to these quality attribute requirements that we would expect an architecture description document to help answer (see concerns listed in Table 11.1). Architecture analysis usually involves the architect(s) and domain experts (such as physicists) and medical examiners.

- Architecture synthesis: Architecture synthesis proposes architecture solutions (e.g., architecture candidates or decision alternatives). Architecture solutions or decision alternatives must accommodate architecturally significant requirements that were identified during architecture analysis. Common decision alternatives that occur in the context of MPS systems include what kind of programming language to use (scripting languages that do not require detailed understanding of VR concepts or lower-level programming languages), what kind of libraries to use to render graphics (OpenGL, etc.), or what authoring tools to use to develop a static scene in the world in which objects are located, including lings, viewpoints, cameras. Because the required expertise in VR and computer graphics varies significantly between these alternatives, the skills and knowledge of developers are the main decision criteria for these architectural decisions.

- Architecture evaluation: Architecture evaluation examines candidate architectural decisions against the architecturally significant requirements. Based on the outcome of the evaluation, the architecture can be revised by going back to architecture analysis and/or synthesis. Usually, architecture evaluation is done based on continuous testing rather than following strict architecture or design reviews (see below). Architecture evaluation is one of the most crucial aspects for successful MPS systems. To address the three key concerns of performance, usability, and model correctness, continuous testing was found to be useful. Here, the architecture description must support continuous testing. Furthermore, we recommend the definition of architecture viewpoints (ISO/IEC/IEEE, 2011) to provide models and other forms of description that help represent performance, usability, and correctness concerns. As shown in our previous work (Widmer and Hu, 2011), using Finite Element Method (FEM) models helped compare different implementation choices of physical models. These models could become part of an architecture view to describe the runtime behavior of a physical model used in a MPS system. This is similar to using execution viewpoints in the context of architecting MRI systems, as proposed by Arias et al. (2011). To further facilitate architecture evaluation, an approach similar to Active Reviews for Intermediate Designs (Clements, 2000) could be applied. The benefit of such approach would be that architecture evaluation could start very early in the architectural design process to ensure that the architecture of MPS is tenable. Reviews could be done before completely building a system first. Furthermore, such reviews would also ensure that the most important stakeholders are engaged early in the software development project. Early designs, or in the case of MPS also late designs, are often poorly documented and described and lack important details that would allow a proper assessment with regard to the most important architectural key drivers. Nevertheless, early reviews could already detect problems at early stages. Based on Clements (2000), we envision the following review steps:

1. Identify the most important stakeholders. These stakeholders are most likely the stakeholders listed in Table 11.1.
2. Prepare a briefing of stakeholders. This briefing should include an explanation of the most important quality attributes (such as performance, usability, and model correctness). Model correctness may not be checked through qualitative reviews, but through more formal approaches, such as model checking or testing (as explained before).
3. Identify scenarios for performance and usability. These scenarios can be used throughout the qualitative review. In Figure 11.2 we included some quality attribute requirements that could be used as starting points for scenarios to evaluate the architecture of MPS systems. Note that we do not identify scenarios for model correctness because correctness is usually checked through quantitative testing approaches.

In contrast to conventional reviews, such "active" reviews would require evaluators and reviewers to be more actively engaged in the review, rather than merely checking whether the architecture complies with certain criteria. For example, reviewers could be asked to write down exceptions for unexpected behavior of physical tissue or feedback provided through a haptic device that could occur within an MPS system, rather than simply checking whether exceptions have been defined during architecting. Exceptions written down by reviewers could then be compared with exceptions captured in the architecture.

The initial effort for architecture evaluation may be significant, but decreases with iterations. This is because in each iteration the architecture is refined. Thus, it is not required to evaluate each aspect of the architecture in each iteration. Furthermore, testing time is reduced because many problems that may occur during testing have been identified during architecture analysis.

Tang et al. (2010) also consider architecture implementation and architecture maintenance. Here, architecture implementation is about realizing the architecture by defining a detailed design (such as designing concrete algorithms to be used to simulate human tissue) and implementing a system by coding the application. Architecture maintenance is about accommodating changes once the initial system has been deployed. As argued before, MPS systems are often developed in an agile manner. Thus, we do not separate these two activities from the other activities introduced above, but rather consider them as integrated with architecture synthesis and evaluation.

During architecture maintenance and incremental synthesis, architecture refactoring is a key practice to improve or adjust the architecture to quality attribute requirements related to the three core quality attributes mentioned above. Refactoring is particularly useful to achieve performance improvements in physical models. Potential improvements are identified through reviews.

Another practice that was found useful in the context of architecting is simple design. Simple design keeps development at a low level of complexity as it aims at implementing performance and model correctness with the simplest means possible. Human tissue could be modeled in many different ways and using sophisticated algorithms. Simple design, on the other hand, requires that physical models should only be as complex as necessary to fulfill the given purpose. To compare different models and their simplicity, statistical tests were found useful (Widmer and Hu, 2010).

## 11.6 CONCLUSIONS

The training of medical students and surgical personnel in new surgical procedures and tools is becoming more important. Furthermore, simulating medical practices before the actual operation helps increase the success of an operation. However, training and planning needs to be provided without compromising patient safety. Therefore, MPS systems are becoming more important, imposing challenges on the software development of such systems.

The definition of quality attributes and architecture that help accommodate quality attributes for MPS systems is a critical endeavor to ensure a satisfactory surgical training and planning outcome. Thus, in this chapter we reported challenges related to achieving quality attributes in MPS systems. Furthermore, we introduced three quality attributes that could be used as a starting point for eliciting more detailed quality attribute requirements for MPS systems. These quality attributes represent architecturally significant requirements of MPS. Being aware of them ensures that an architecture for MPS causes fewer quality problems. We also explained how a generic software architecture process is affected by these specific quality attributes, including stakeholders and their concerns.

Even though our work focused on MPS systems, the quality attributes discussed in this chapter as well as their impact on the architecting process may also be applicable to other types of software systems. For example, considering the discussions in this chapter, our findings regarding developing and architecting MPS systems are similar to practices found in scientific software development (Ackroyd et al., 2008). For instance, the influence of agile practices can also be found in scientific software development (Ackroyd et al., 2008). Furthermore, MPS systems appear similar to critical embedded systems. Thus, trends in developing critical embedded systems (Gill, 2005) may also be applicable to MPS systems. For example, in the past, complex systems were built using centralized, distributed designs. However, new concepts for medical intensive care units and operating rooms focus on the plug and play situational usage of software and hardware components (Gill, 2005), that is, critical embedded systems are aggregated rather than based on distributed design. Exploring these directions is part of future work.

## References

Ackroyd, K., Kinder, S., Mant, G., Miller, M., Ramsdale, C., Stephenson, P., 2008. Scientific software development at a research facility. IEEE Softw. 25 (4), 44–51.

Arias, T.B.C., America, P., Avgeriou, P., 2011. Defining and documenting execution viewpoints for a large and complex software-intensive system. J. Syst. Softw. 84 (9), 1447–1461.

Babar, M.A., 2009. An exploratory study of architectural practices and challenges in using agile software development approaches. In: Paper Presented at the Joint Working IEEE/IFIP Conference on Software Architecture & European Conference on Software Architecture (WICSA/ECSA).

Capilla, R., Martinez, M., 2004. Software architectures for designing virtual reality applications. In: Paper Presented at the First European Workshop on Software Architecture.

Cawley, O., Wang, X., Richardson, I., 2010. Lean/agile Software Development Methodologies in Regulated Environments—State of the Art. In: Paper Presented at the First International Conference on Lean Enterprise Software and Systems.

Chen, L., Babar, M.A., Nuseibeh, B., 2013. Characterizing architecturally significant requirements. IEEE Softw. 30 (2), 38–45.

Clements, P., 2000. Active Reviews for Intermediate Designs, Technical Report No. CMU/SEI-2000-TN-009, SEI/CMU.

Conforto, E.C., Amaral, D.C., 2008. Evaluating an agile method for planning and controlling innovative projects. Proj. Manag. J. 41 (2), 73–80.

Falessi, D., Cantone, G., Sarcia, S.A., Calavaro, G., Subiaco, P., D'Amore, C., 2010. Peaceful coexistence: agile developer perspectives on software architecture. IEEE Softw. 27 (2), 23–25.

Fitzgerald, B., Stol, K.-J., O'Sullivan, R., O'Brien, D., 2013. Scaling agile methods to regulated environments: an industrial case study. In: Paper Presented at the International Conference on Software Engineering.

Galster, M., Widmer, A., 2010. Requirements in VR systems: The REViR approach and its preliminary evaluation. In: Paper Presented at the Workshop on Software Engineering and Architectures for Realtime Interactive Systems (SEARIS).

Geiger, C., Paelke, V., Reimann, C., Rosenbach, W., 2000. A framework for the structured design of VR/AR content. In: Paper Presented at the ACM Symposium on Virtual Reality Software and Technology.

Gill, H., 2005. Challenges for critical embedded systems. In: Paper Presented at the 10th IEEE International Workshop on Object-oriented Real-time Dependable Systems.

Highsmith, J., 2004. Agile Project Management: Creating Innovative Products. Addison-Wesley, Reading, MA.

Hofmeister, C., Kruchten, P., Nord, R.L., Obbink, H., Ran, A., America, P., 2007. A general model of software architecture design derived from five industrial approaches. J. Syst. Softw. 80 (1), 106–126.

ISO/IEC/IEEE, 2011. Systems and Software Engineering—Architecture Description (Vol. ISO/IEC/IEEE 42010). Geneva, Switzerland.

Johnston, A., Johnson, C.S., 2003. Extreme programming: a more musical approach to software development? In: Marchesi, M., Succi, G. (Eds.), Extreme Programming and Agile Processes in Software Engineering. Lecture Notes in Computer Science, vol. 2675. Springer Verlag, Berlin/Heidelberg, pp. 325–327.

Kim, G.J., 2005. Designing Virtual Reality Systems—The Structured Approach. Springer Verlag, London.

Kim, J., Kang, K.C., Kim, H., Lee, J., 1998. Software engineering of virtual worlds. In: Paper Presented at the ACM Symposium on Virtual Reality Software and Technology.

Kotonya, G., Sommerville, I., 1998. Requirements Engineering: Processes and Techniques. John Wiley & Sons, New York, NY.

Kruchten, P., Lago, P., Vliet, H.v., Wolf, T., 2005. Building up and exploiting architectural knowledge. In: Paper Presented at the 5th Working IEEE/IFIP Conference on Software Architecture.

Sanders, R., Kelly, D., 2008. Dealing with risk in scientific software development. IEEE Softw. 25 (4), 21–28.

Seo, J., Kim, G.J., 2002. Design for presence: a structured approach to virtual reality system design. Presence Teleop. Virt. Environ. 11 (4), 378–403.

Sorid, D., Moore, S., 2000. The virtual surgeon [virtual reality trainer]. IEEE Spectr. 37 (7), 26–31.

Tang, A., Avgeriou, P., Jansen, A., Capilla, R., Ali Babar, M., 2010. A comparative study of architecture knowledge management tools. J. Syst. Softw. 83 (3), 352–370.

Tanriverdi, V., Jacob, R.J.K., 2001. VRID: a design model and methodology for developing virtual reality interfaces. In: Paper Presented at the ACM Symposium on Virtual Reality Software and Technology.

Tofan, D., Galster, M., Avgeriou, P., 2013. Improving Architectural Knowledge Management in Public Sector Organizations—An Interview Study. In: Paper Presented at the 25th International Conference on Software Engineering and Knowledge Engineering.

Troyer, O.D., Kleinermann, F., Pellens, B., Bille, W., 2007. Conceptual modeling for virtual reality. In: Paper Presented at the 26th International Conference on Conceptual Modeling (ER 2007).

Widmer, A., Hu, Y., 2010. Statistical comparison between a real-time model and a fem counterpart for visualization of breat phantom deformation during palpation. In: Paper Presented at the 23rd Canadian Conference on Electrical and Computer Engineering.

Widmer, A., Hu, Y., 2011. An evaluation method for real-time soft-tissue model used for multi-vertex palpation. In: Paper Presented at the IEEE International Conference on Systems, Man and Cybernetics.

Wijnstra, J.G., 2001. Quality attributes and aspects of a medical product family. In: Paper Presented at the 34th Annual Hawaii International Conference on System Sciences (HICSS-34).

Willans, J., Harrison, M., 2001. A toolset supported approach for designing and testing virtual environment interaction techniques. Int. J. Hum.-Comput. Stud. 55 (2), 145–165.

# Addressing Usability Requirements in Mobile Software Development 12

**Rafael Capilla[1], Laura Carvajal[2], and Hui Lin[2]**

*[1]Universidad Rey Juan Carlos, Madrid, Spain*
*[2]Universidad Politécnica de Madrid, Madrid, Spain*

## INTRODUCTION

The software architecture community recognizes the importance of quality attributes for both software design and implementation methods, but such qualities are many times neglected and poorly documented. Software quality evaluation methods such as ATAM or ARID (Clements et al., 2002) are often used in the early stages of the software design process.

Today, one key relevant quality attribute for modern software development is usability because, since the 1980s, usability features have played a key role in building more usable software. Usability has been defined in various ways in literature throughout the years. One of the most widely known definitions, proposed by the ISO 9126 standard (replaced by the standard ISO/IEC 25000:2005—http://www.iso.org), describes usability as "the capability of the software product to be understood, learned, used and attractive to the user, when used under specified conditions." Other authors (Kumar Dubey and Rana, 2010; Seffah, 2004) recognize the importance of usability in multiple factors and the difficulty of putting usability into practice, but the majority of the proposed definitions consider usability as a critical aspect for interactive systems. Such relevance has been highlighted in several studies (Black, 2002; Donahue, 2001; Moreno et al., 2013) aimed at demonstrating the benefits of usabilities, including reduction of documentation and training costs, improvement of productivity, increasing morale and e-commerce revenue, and more. Accordingly, large-scale companies such as IBM and Boeing Co. have begun to consider usability as a key factor when developing and buying software.

Nonetheless, despite the obvious potential rewards, we keep falling short of producing usable software, and even when developers are convinced of the need to introduce usability features, this process is far from straightforward. One of the main reasons behind these difficulties is the lack of integration between the two communities involved in the process of building usable software, namely the human computer interaction (HCI) and Software Engineering (SE) communities. Generally speaking, the former knows which characteristics have to be included in a software system to make it usable, and the latter knows how to build software correctly. The differences in terminology and development approaches used by both communities lead to well-known HCI practices that are not integrated in SE common practices.

In addition, some application domains such as mobile software demand stringent software requirements and usability mechanisms tailored for this kind of apps. Challenges related to the size of the interface, performance, notification to users when the mobile loses the connection, and customized text entry, among others, often drive the selection and use of usability mechanisms specific to mobile software. At present, there are a number of challenges related to the integration of usability features into common SE practices and where software designers demand assessment guidelines on how to introduce and describe usability mechanisms both in the architecture and in the code.

The remainder of this chapter is organized as follows. Section 12.1 discusses the related work. In Section 12.2, we describe a taxonomy of usability mechanisms that can be applied to mobile software development. Sections 12.3 and 12.4 outline the use cases and major architectural responsibilities of two usability mechanisms presented. In Section 12.5, we analyze the impact of the two usability mechanisms selected in the architecture of a mobile application, and we discuss the implications at the design level. Finally, Section 12.6 provides a discussion of the presented approach, and in Section 12.7 we draw conclusions.

## 12.1 RELATED WORK

In order to understand the relationship between usability and software design, we describe in this section experiences and related work between usability and software architecture and related experiences in the mobile applications domain.

Bass and John (2002) describe 27 relevant usability scenarios and propose a solution to design them in the form of architectural patterns. The authors later evolved this work in John et al. (2005), introducing what they termed Usability Supporting Architectural Patterns, which propose Model View Controller (MVC)-specific sample solutions for usability concerns in Unified Modeling Language (UML). Some years later, John et al. (2009) sought to test this solution in industry. In their experiment, the authors realized that the general response was a resistance to the use of UML-based solutions. The feedback they obtained led them to remove the UML diagrams and replace them with textual descriptions that explain the structure and behavior of the solution without imposing a particular architecture. Complementarily, Ferre et al. (2003) identified 20 usability patterns and provided a design solution for incorporating them into the architecture of software applications. A different approach (Seffah et al., 2008) suggests design patterns as a solution to address concrete scenarios that illustrate how internal software components may affect the usability of the system.

Today, the importance of mobile software in many application domains requires stringent software requirements that need more and more usability attributes in order to facilitate the usage by end-users (e.g., quick reaction, interfaces easy to use, adequate feedback). Consequently, usability becomes a major concern for modern mobile applications for building highly usable interfaces. Several studies and experiences highlight the role of usability in mobile phone applications, and the evaluation and effects of usability might be different in a usability lab versus a real environment (Beck et al., 2003; Kaikkonen et al., 2005), because if the mobile user depends on location properties, physical motion (Kjeldskov and Stage, 2004), and specific contexts (e.g., mobile context), the effectiveness and efficiency as a quality of use in a particular environment may vary (Bevan and MacLeod, 1994; Kim et al., 2002; Ryan and Gonsalves, 2005; Terrenghi et al., 2005).

Moreover, the evaluation and study of HCI in mobile devices have been analyzed in Hussain and Kutar (2012a,b) in order to identify usability problems with apps installed in mobile phones (e.g., enlarge or minimize the interface). Also, the nHIMSS App Usability Work Group (2012) reported the results of the study of usability features that influence the feedback of user tasks in different scenarios because such results impact the design of the target system. Furthermore, Lundhal (2009) analyzes usability concerns in mobile apps for the NFC (Near Field Communication) technology, where usability is not only implemented in terms of usable interfaces, but also in the form of specific usability mechanisms such as a Progress Bar, which increases user satisfaction because it provides the necessary feedback during user interaction with the mobile device.

The majority of the approaches describing the relationship between architecture and usability only provide guidelines and recommendations to introduce usability patterns or mechanisms but not the details about how to perform this task or how to introduce such mechanisms in concrete architectural styles. The approach described in this chapter goes a step beyond because we define the generic and concrete architecture responsibilities for three-layered architectures and based on our previous experience using the MVC pattern. Moreover, most usability research aiming to analyze the impact of usability features in mobile apps has focused on testing and evaluating the effects of usability attributes, such as context, flexible interfaces, displaying different resolutions, and data entry methods, among others. However, they don't describe the impact of usability requirements in the software architecture and how to implement such mechanisms in the architecture of mobile systems.

## 12.2 USABILITY MECHANISMS FOR MOBILE APPLICATIONS

Based on the deficiencies summarized in the related work, we analyze the usability mechanisms that are of special interest for mobile applications in order to help software developers introduce usability mechanisms into the software architecture. Our study focused on of five PDA and Smartphone mobile applications developed at the Rey Juan Carlos University between 2005 and 2011 andanalyzed the usability features implemented on them. We also base our analysis on our previous experience of classifying usability mechanisms for the MVC pattern. As a result, we provide the following classification of usability mechanisms that we believe is suitable for mobile apps, and we include examples of use.

**System status feedback usability mechanism**: Inform users about the internal status of the system.
**Mechanisms/functionality implemented**: Status Display.
**Examples**: A status icon or bar when a Web page is being accessed using a Smartphone.
A status window to notify that a resource is not available (e.g., a Bluetooth device). Check if a connection is available before doing something. Show an icon indicating connection.

**Interaction usability mechanism**: Inform users that the system has registered a user interaction. In other words, the system has heard users.
**Mechanisms/functionality implemented**: Interaction Feedback, let user know what's going on.
**Examples**: The mobile device shakes when accessing an application.

**Warning usability mechanism**: Inform users of any action with important consequences.
**Mechanisms/functionality implemented**: Warning.
**Examples**: Warn about an unsecure Web site or inform about removing data from the agenda.

**Long Action Feedback usability mechanism**: Inform users that the system is processing an action that will take some time to complete.
**Mechanisms/functionality implemented**: Progress Indicator, let user know what's going on.
**Examples**: A bar indicating progress, an icon with a timer, a message displaying the remaining time to complete a task (e.g., progress connecting to a service).

**Global Undo usability mechanism**: Undo system actions at several levels.
**Mechanisms/functionality implemented**: Go Back One Step.
**Examples**: A mobile Web app including a questionnaire that allows you to reset values.

**Abort Operation usability mechanism**: Cancel the execution of an action or the whole application.
**Mechanisms/functionality implemented**: Go Back One Step. Emergency Exit. Cancellability.
**Examples**: A mobile Web app including a functionality to fill several questionnaires that allows you to cancel the process while filling any questionnaire going back to a specific place. Cancel sending a file.

**Go Back usability mechanism**: Go back to a particular state in a command execution sequence.
**Mechanisms/functionality implemented**: Go Back to a Safe Place, Go Back One Step.
**Examples**: Home button, Back button.

**Structured Text Entry usability mechanism**: Prevent users from data input errors.
**Mechanisms/functionality implemented**: Forms, Structured Text Entry, Structured Format, and Structured Text Entry.
**Examples**: Forms. Reduce the number of screens to introduce and display data. A phone agenda.

**Step-by-step execution usability mechanism**: Help users with tasks that require different steps with user input and correct such input.
**Mechanisms/functionality implemented**: Step-by-Step.
**Examples**: Configuration of a new mobile application that is downloaded and installed in the device.

**Preferences usability mechanism**: Record each user's option.
**Mechanisms/functionality implemented**: User preferences.
**Examples**: Configure mobile phone settings or customized settings in a mobile app.

**Favorites usability mechanism**: Record certain places of interest for the user.
**Mechanisms/functionality implemented**: Favorites.
**Examples**: Favorites Web pages only for mobile apps using a Web interface.

**Help usability mechanism**: Provide different help levels for different users.
**Mechanisms/functionality implemented**: 1-help level.
**Examples**: In contrast to standalone applications where multilevel help is common, small interfaces like those used in mobile applications often implement 1-help level.

From our previous classification of usability mechanisms that can be employed in the development of mobile software, we analyze the use and impact of such usability mechanisms in the design process, which we formulate in terms of the following research questions (RQs):

RQ1: *Which are the responsibilities of usability mechanisms from the software architecture point of view?*
RQ2: *How do usability mechanisms impact the architecture of mobile applications?*

In this research, we will focus only on two usability mechanisms that we believe represent important usability concerns demanded by modern mobile software apps. The two usability requirements we will study are:

a. **System status feedback**: Many mobile applications should inform users about the status of an action and let users know about the status of a given task, such as using a message or a warning.
b. **User Preferences**: All modern mobile devices include support to configure user preferences for a variety of configurable options such as wireless and radio settings, display, sound, privacy, and energy consumption. Therefore, users are allowed to check and change the current phone configuration and enable/disable some settings of the applications installed.

In the following sections, we outline how the aforementioned usability mechanisms impact the software architecture. We describe the functionality of each usability mechanism through use cases, and we map each use case to generic and concrete architectural elements that implement such functionality.

## 12.3 SYSTEM STATUS FEEDBACK

In this section, we focus on the system status feedback (SSF) mechanism. According to Table 12.1, the status display of a mobile application can warn users about the availability of a resource. More specifically, the use cases we identified for the SSF mechanism are described in Figure 12.1:

**SSF_UC-1 Change Status**: A status change can be triggered by a user, who must be aware of system status and its changes.

**SSF_UC-2 Handle User-initiated Status Changes**: Changes in the status initiated by the user must be handled by a specific component and the parties involved notified about the results. A status manager often takes care of such status changes and updates the status information.

**SSF_UC-3 Handle System-initiated Status Changes**: In some cases changes its status; this action must be handled similarly as in the SSF_UC-2 use case.

**SSF_UC-4 Display Status**: Changes in the status must be displayed and notified to users.

### 12.3.1 SSF generic component responsibilities

According to the use cases of Figure 12.1, the description of the major usability design guidelines and the generic component responsibilities (SSF_SR stands for Status System Feedback System responsibility) that can be used to delimit the impact of a certain usability feature in the design is as follows.

**SSF_SR-1**: Be aware of system statuses and their changes.

**Generic component responsibility**: Certain *Domain Components* can execute actions that will change one or more application statuses. A *StatusManager Component* is responsible for monitoring said *Domain Components* and listens for their status-altering actions. A *Status Component* is responsible for holding all the information relating to a particular status and for modifying it according to *StatusManager* orders (please see SSF_SR-2 and SSF_SR-3 for details on how this happens). All *Status Components* can have one active status value at any given time (i.e., "online status" can be "online," "idle," "busy," "offline," etc.). The component responsible for handling user events (*UI*) must monitor all *Status Components* and notify the user of any changes.

**Table 12.1** Usability-Enabling Design Guideline: Concrete Object Responsibilities (Three-Layered Architecture)

| System Responsibility | Objects and Layers | | | |
| --- | --- | --- | --- | --- |
| | Presentation Layer | Application Processing Layer | | |
| | Display Status | Status Manager | Status | DomainClass |
| SSF_SR-1 Be aware of system statuses (and their changes) | The *Presentation Layer* must subscribe to each *Status* object upon system initialization. | Upon system initialization, the *StatusManager* subscribes to each *DomainClass* that it knows can execute status-changing actions | The *Status* object holds all the information related to one system status and the means to change and query this information. It must notify all subscribers (*Presentation Layer*) of any changes | The *DomainClass* represents the domain object(s) responsible for executing actions that lead to system state changes. It must notify all subscribers (*StatusManager*) of any changes |
| SSF_SR-2 Handle user-initiated status changes | The *Presentation Layer* listens to user's requests for execution actions action and forwards it to the *Application Processing layer* The *Presentation Layer* displays the status display for every notification of status change received | The *StatusManager* determines the corresponding *Status* object to update and does so with the information sent forth by the *DomainClass* | The *Status* calculates the effect, if any, that the received information has on its current active status value, change it, if applicable, and notify its subscribers (*Presentation Layer*) | The *DomainClass* executes the (status-altering) action and for notifies the *StatusManager* |
| SSF_SR-3 Handle system-initiated status changes | The *Presentation Layer* changes the status display for every notification of status change received | The *StatusManager* determines the corresponding *Status* object to update and does so with the information sent forth by the *DomainClasses* | The *Status* calculates the effect, if any, that the received information has on its current active status value, change it, if applicable, and notify its subscribers | The *DomainClass* executes the (status-altering) action—triggered by an external resource or other parts of the system—and to notify the *StatusManager* |
| SSF_SR-4 Present system status notifications to users | The Presentation layer knows which type of status notification to give for each status change. It also knows how and where to display each type of status notification and does so upon notification of Status objects | | | |

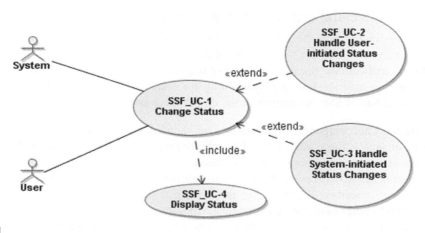

**FIGURE 12.1**

System status feedback use case model.

**SSF_SR-2**: Handle user-initiated status changes.

**Generic component responsibility**: The component responsible for handling user events (*UI*) listens for user actions and orders their execution. The component in charge of delegating actions (if any) is responsible for ordering the appropriate *Domain Component* to execute said action. Upon execution of actions that are status-changing, each *Domain Component* is responsible for notifying any interested parties (specifically the *Status Manager Component*, in this case). The *StatusManager* component then forwards the updated information on to the appropriate *Status Component*. Said *Status Component* is then responsible for determining the effect, if any, that the received information will have on its current active status value. It will, when applicable, change said value and notify any interested parties (specifically the *UI Component* in this case). The *UI Component* will update the status display for every notification of status change received.

**SSF_SR-3**: Handled system-initiated status changes.

**Generic component responsibility**: Upon execution of actions that are status-changing—invoked by any other class in the system or an external source—each *Domain Component* is responsible for notifying any interested parties (specifically the *Status Manager Component*, in this case), as is the case when such an action is invoked by the user through the UI (see SSF_SR-2). The *StatusManager* component then forward the updated information on to the appropriate *Status Component*. Said *Status Component* is then responsible for determining the effect, if any, that the received information will have on its current active status value. It will, when applicable, change said value and notify any interested parties (specifically the *UI Component* in this case). The *UI Component* will update the status display for every notification of status change received.

**SSF_SR-4**: Present system status notifications to users.

**Generic component responsibility**: The *UI Component* is responsible for knowing how and where each status (and its possible values) is displayed within the interface, and, thus, for updating the status upon receipt of notifications of status value change.

### 12.3.2 SSF architectural component responsibilities

In this section, we describe how the SSF impacts the design of the software architecture, for which we have selected a layered architecture, which is one of the most common architectural styles used in many modern software applications. Because the level of responsibility of each layer in the architecture is different, we need to map the system responsibility for each use case of the SSF mechanism. The generic responsibilities of SSF mechanism at the design level are as follows:

**Display status**: This component is responsible for showing status changes motivated by a user request or a change in the system status. The component also informs users about the new system status or the status resulting from a specific action.

**Status component**: A status component supports all the information related to one system status and notifies the subscribers of any change in a particular status.

**Status manager component**: This component handles the management of the status changes based on user and system requests, determining which new status the system must change and which information must be updated.

**Domain component**: A domain component represents the part of the system that is ultimately responsible for executing the actions requested by the user. For instance, in an e-mail program, clicking the Send button may have many intermediate effects (checking that the Subject field is not empty, loading attachments, etc.), but the part of the system that is actually responsible for *sending* the e-mail is referred to as the domain component in the context of these mechanisms

More specifically, we detail the concrete responsibilities of SSF for a layered architecture. The *display status* component is supported by the presentation layer of any client-server Web or mobile application, because the status display shows the results of the new status to the clients at the presentation layer. The *status manager* and *status component* act at the application processing layer, where the functionality of the application, accepting user and system requests, changes the status accordingly to a new one and informs the subscribers about a new status. Finally, the *Domain component* is represented by the *DomainClass*, and it must be considered an entity to be substituted at design time by the class that actually performs the requested task. Table 12.1 shows how the responsibility of each use case affects to each component for the layered architecture. However, because the data management layer does not have any responsibility in the use cases mentioned before and does not support any component regarding the SSF mechanism, we didn't represent it the table.

Figure 12.2 describes the UML package diagram of a three-layered architecture representing the distribution of the classes belonging to the SSF mechanism. As we can see, these classes should be attached to those describing the functionality of a concrete application and specify which new relationships must be added to incorporate the SSF mechanism in the software architecture.

## 12.4 USER PREFERENCES

The User Preferences usability mechanism covers user needs in a centralized place or database where the user can alter the application's settings. Different types of user preferences can be organized around categories, which lets users tailor these or set their personal preferences for a given time frame. Moreover, in case of any software problem, mobile phone users can roll back these changes and set the

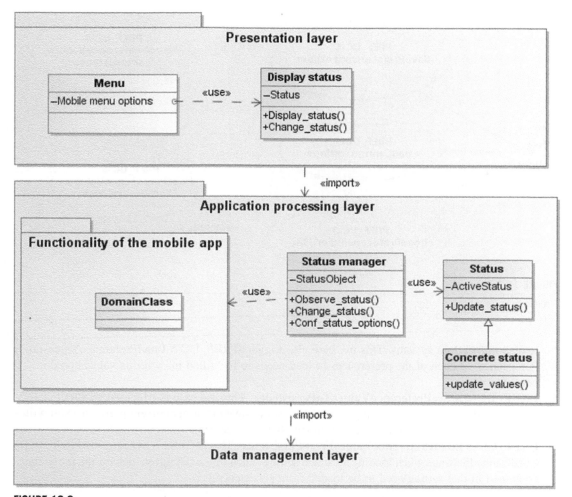

**FIGURE 12.2**

Enabling system status feedback usability mechanism in a UML package diagram.

default settings stored in the mobile phone. The use cases belonging to this mechanism are described in Figure 12.3 and are the following:

**PREF_UC-1 SavePreferencesForUser**: Upon making changes to one or more preferences, the user requests that they be saved. This will trigger the included use case PREF_UC-4 StorePreferenceValuesToPersistence.

**PREF_UC-2 LoadCannedSettings**: User request that a group of canned settings be loaded, allowing them to set a number of preferences all at once. This use case triggers PREF_UC-5 LoadPreferenceValuesFromPersistence when loading the canned settings.

**PREF_UC-3 LoadPreferencesForUser**: Users request that their preferences be loaded directly or indirectly. For example, starting the application is an indirect way to request that preferences be

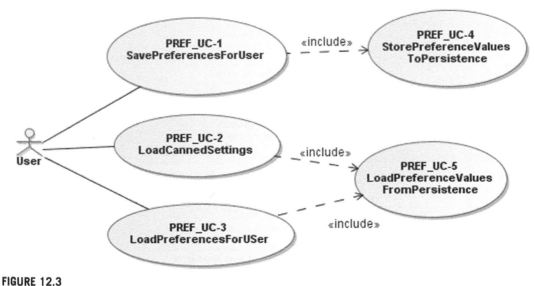

**FIGURE 12.3**

Preferences use case model.

loaded into certain systems. This use case also triggers PREF_UC-5 LoadPreferenceValuesFrom Persistence, as each of the preferences to load needs to be "filled in" with its value stored in persistence.

**PREF_UC-4 StorePreferenceValuesToPersistence**: This use case is triggered by PREF_UC-1 SavePreferencesForUser every time a user chooses to save his or her current preferences. It writes the preference values onto the predetermined physical medium.

**PREF_UC-5 LoadPreferenceValuesFromPersistence**: This use case is triggered by PREF_UC-2 LoadCannedSettings when loading a canned setting. Each of the default values for the preferences contained in that setting need to be loaded from persistence.

Like in the SSF usability mechanism, the description of the uses cases for Preferences, including the generic component responsibilities, are shown in Table 12.2.

## 12.4.1 User Preferences generic component responsibilities

Based on the use cases of Figure 12.3, the major usability design guidelines and the generic component responsibilities for the User Preferences usability mechanism are as follows (PREF_SR stands for User Preferences System responsibility).

**PREF_SR-1**: Set preferences.

**Generic component responsibility**: A *Preference* component holds the information related to a single "live" system preference, minimally its name (i.e., Background color), its possible values (i.e., green, red, blue), and its current active value. A preference is "live" once it's been loaded (as opposed to a preference *setting* that may be stored in the hard drive for later use). A *PreferencesManager* component is responsible for knowing, handling, and retrieving all live *Preference* components

**Table 12.2** Usability-Enabling Design Guideline: Concrete Object Responsibilities (Three-Layered Architecture)

| System Responsibility | Objects and Layers | | | |
| --- | --- | --- | --- | --- |
| | Presentation Layer | Application Processing Layer | | Data Mgmt. Layer |
| | User | Preferences Manager | Settings Manager | StorageFront |
| PREF_SR-1 Set Preferences | The *User* requests its *Setting* object to update all of the sent preference values Requests are forwarded to the Preferences Manager | The *Preferences Manager* orders each *Preference* to update itself with the new value Each *Preference* object updates its value to be the new value sent The *Preference* object updates itself as requested by the *Preferences Manager* | For each value sent, the *Setting* object within the *User* updates its internal *Preference* objects. The *Setting* saves itself once all of its internal *Preferences* have been updated The *Setting* object rolls itself out by loading all of its pref-value pairs from the *StorageFront* and loading them onto the "live" *Preferences*, via the *PreferencesManager* For each pref name in the received pref-value pairs, the *Setting* asks the *PreferencesManager* to update the corresponding *Preference* object with the designated value | The *StorageFront* stores the saved *Setting* object to the appropriate persistence medium |
| PREF_SR-2 Provide Default values | The *User* forwards the call to its *Setting* object | The *Preference* object, responsible for knowing and setting its default value, sets its *currentValue* to that default | The Setting orders each *Preference* to reset itself to its *defaultValue* The *Setting* saves itself via the *StorageFront* | The *Storage Front* writes the updated *Setting* to the appropriate storage medium |
| PREF_SR-3 Allow "canned settings" | The User load the canned setting via the Settings Manager object | The *Preferences Manager* orders each *Preference* to update itself with the new value The *Preference* object updates | The *Setting* object rolls itself out by loading all of its pref-value pairs from the *StorageFront* onto the "live" *Preferences*, via the *PreferencesManager* | The *StorageFront* loads all of the pref-value pairs belonging to the *Setting* in question and returns them to it |

*Continued*

**Table 12.2** Usability-Enabling Design Guideline: Concrete Object Responsibilities (Three-Layered Architecture)—cont'd

| | Objects and Layers | | | |
| --- | --- | --- | --- | --- |
| | **Presentation Layer** | **Application Processing Layer** | | **Data Mgmt. Layer** |
| **System Responsibility** | **User** | **Preferences Manager** | **Settings Manager** | **StorageFront** |
| | | itself as requested by the *Preferences Manager* | For each pref name in the received pref-value pairs, the *Setting* asks the *PreferencesManager* to update the corresponding *Preference* object (live) with the designated value | |
| PREF_SR-4 Organize Preferences | When preferences are loaded, these are displayed in groups or trees if applicable | | | |

within the system. A *Setting* Component represents a group of predetermined value pairs (preference name-preference value) that can be loaded from the hard drive (through the *Storage Front* Component) and rolled out into the live preferences. The *StorageFront* component represents the link between the application logic and the repository where the preference values are saved. A *Setting* will load its values through the *StorageFront*, because only this class has direct access to the information stored in the hard drive (or other media).

**PREF_SR-2**: Provide default values.

**Generic component responsibility**: The *Preference* component is also responsible for knowing what (if any) is its default value and for setting itself to that value if/when requested by the *UI*.

**PREF_SR-3**: Allow "canned settings."

**Generic component responsibility**: A *SettingsManager* is responsible for loading stored *Settings* when asked by the *UI*.

**PREF_SR-4**: Organize preferences.

**Generic component responsibility**: If preferences are to be grouped, a *Group Component* is responsible for holding related preferences and for providing the *UI* with them.

## 12.4.2 User Preferences architectural component responsibilities

In this section, we describe the responsibilities of the major components of the User Preferences usability mechanism and their roles in a three-layered software architecture.

**Preference component**: This component is responsible for holding the basic data related to a "live" preference where an attribute is set to a value (e.g., the wireless network provider is set to a certain "local operator").

**Settings component**: The Setting component represents a group of Preferences with an assigned value (e.g., using canned settings).

**PreferenceManager component**. This component handles individual Preferences within the system.

**StorageFront component**: The StorageFront Component stores and retrieves preference values into persistence. It can access the physical media where these values are stored.

**SettingsManager component**: This component is in charge of saving and loading Settings upon a request to the system.

**User component**: The User Component is in charge for holding and accessing a sole Settings component. This particular Settings component holds all the preference values stored for this particular User.

**Group component**: The Group component handles one or several Preference objects, where preferences are often grouped in a tree structure.

Each of the aforementioned components can be represented as classes in the architecture with the following functionality. The Preference Component is represented by the **Preference** class, and it handles the currently assigned (or active) value that the user has set or loaded. Preference objects are always contained within a Setting component, which is represented by the **Setting** class in the architecture. In addition, the so-called "canned settings" are described, for example, by a single Setting object containing a certain number of preferences with an assigned value. In multi-user systems, each User will contain a single Setting object, holding and managing all of its preferences at any time.

The PreferencesManager Component is represented by the **PreferencesManager** class, and it is responsible for ordering the Preferences that change and to retrieve these when they are requested. The SettingsManager Component represented by the **SettingsManager** class is the responsible for ordering newly created settings to be saved and to retrieve them. The User Component's responsibilities are carried out by the **User** class, in charge of holding and managing the Setting object that contains all users' preferences. Moreover, the Group Component is represented by the **Group** class for organizing and arranging Preferences according to a particular structure. Finally, the StorageFront Component is represented by the **StorageFront** parent class and by any of its subclasses. These classes are responsible for storing any saved data on a physical medium. Each subclass of **StorageFront** implements this functionality for each needed particular physical medium (e.g., a Database or a text file). The components described in Table 12.2 describe the low-level responsibilities which are mapped to classes in the layered architecture of Figure 12.4. However, in order to simplify the descriptions in Table 12.2, we have grouped some classes described before in more than one column (e.g., The PreferencesManager class includes the functionality of Preference and Group classes).

## 12.5 A MOBILE TRAFFIC COMPLAINT SYSTEM

In order to study the effects of usability in the software architecture of a real application, we describe in this section how we introduced the aforementioned usability mechanisms in a mobile application for a Smartphone. The system consists of a modern Android application for managing traffic tickets (M-ticket) issued by local police. The mobile application captures traffic infraction data and sends them to a Web server. The M-ticket application enables the police officer to capture an image and the

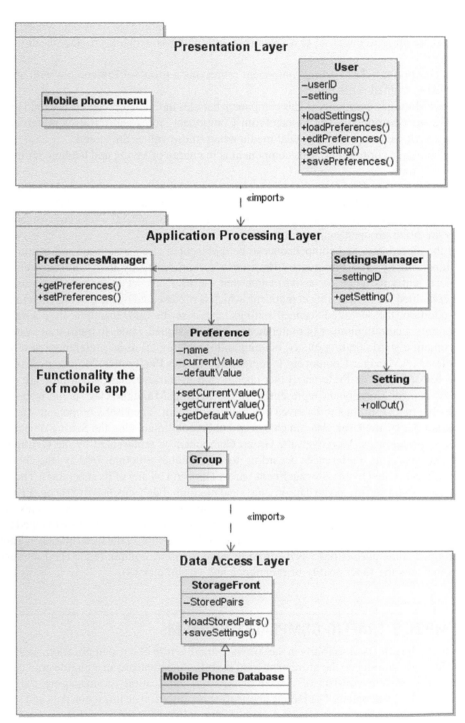

**FIGURE 12.4**

Enabling user preferences usability mechanism in a UML package diagram.

location of the infraction via GPS and record the car and the infraction data using a text form. In this chapter, we do not care about the functionality of the Web application located in the police station to manage the traffic tickets received from the mobile application—we will only focus on the usability of the mobile app.

### 12.5.1 Usability requirements

The M-ticket system was developed in 2010, but it only included usability features regarding the design of the user interface, colors, size of menu buttons, and navigation. Because none of the usability mechanisms described in Section 12.2 were included, between 2012 and 2013 we decided to add the two mechanisms described in this chapter and evaluate their impact on the architecture. Consequently, the first step was to define the following usability requirement aimed to support the introduce usability mechanisms in the M-ticket application.

**UR1**. *Alert message to users for pending tickets*: In case of a loss of the radio signal between the mobile terminal and the server, an alert message will be displayed to the user of the M-ticket application indicating that the ticket cannot be sent. In addition, the mobile M-ticket application will show in the status bar an icon advising the user that there are pending tickets to be sent.

**UR2**. *Configure alert messages*: The user can configure the following options for the alert messages in the application: activate/deactivate shaking the phone when a new alert arises, activate/deactivate a sound, and the number of times the user should be notified about an alert.

Both usability requirements must be implemented in terms of concrete usability mechanisms, such as those described in this chapter.

### 12.5.2 Impact on the software architecture

This section describes the changes we performed on the software architecture of the M-ticket system to support the usability requirements and how these impacted the existing functionality. Figure 12.5 shows the new package diagram of the modified software architecture. The three layers of the design are as follows: (a) *the presentation layer* containing the entry screen to the Android applications, (b) *the business logic layer* of the M-ticket application containing the functionality of the app and the usability mechanisms introduced, and (c) *the middleware and data access layer* supporting the connection to the GPS and images captured by the phone that are sent to the Web server database.

The three-layered architecture of the M-ticket application depicts the new classes (red color) introduced in the design and the classes that changed (blue color). It also handles the two usability mechanisms (i.e., SSF and User Preferences) introduced in the system, which we explain below:

**System status feedback**: As we can see in Figure 12.5, in the Android application we modified two of the existing classes (NewComplaint, SendComplaint) in application logic tier in order to support the SSF mechanism. The NewComplaint class allows the police officer to create a new traffic ticket using the Complaint class shown in Figure 12.5. The functionality of the M-ticket app also implements the location of the vehicle using the GPS of the mobile phone, then it sends the form, the location, and a picture of the vehicle to a remote server. The changes introduced by the "Status Feedback" mechanism affect the notifications sent to the policeman using the mobile phone. In this way, we used the android.app.NotificationManager Android library to warn the user about

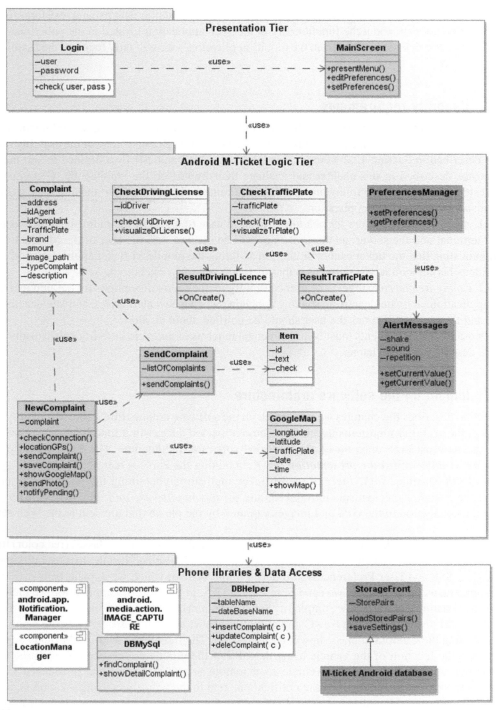

**FIGURE 12.5**

Modified software architecture of the M-ticket application including the classes for the two usability mechanisms.

events that may happen, such as a complaint already sent or no GPS signal. In addition, the changes to the SendComplaint class refer to the list of pending complaints stored in the mobile phone before they are sent to the server. In those cases of no pending complaints stored in the phone, the notifications will be removed.

**User Preferences**: Changing the user preference of the alert messages supported by the status feedback mechanism led us to introduce new classes (PreferenceManager, AlertMessages, StorageFront, and M-ticket Android database classes in Figure 12.5) in the architecture. However, this usability mechanism affected the functionality of all layers in the architecture. In the presentation layer, the MainScreen class, which acts as entry point of the mobile application once the user has logged onto the system, was modified to incorporate specific methods to set and edit the preferences of the alert messages. In the logic tier, we added two new classes, PreferenceManager and AlertMessages, which handle the specific preferences (i.e., shake, sound, and repetition) of each alert message. Finally, the implementation of the classes supporting this usability mechanism require a new class, StorageFront, located in the data access layer to store the user preferences, As we can see, there is another class in that layer, M-ticket Android database, which represents where the user preferences are stored. We added this class for the sake of clarity for designers, but in our system the storage of the user preferences data is located in a specific database of the M-ticket application.

In order to provide a better understanding of the classes we added and changed in the original architecture of the M-ticket app when usability was introduced, we describe in Tables 12.3 and 12.4 the association between the generic components of each usability mechanism and the classes that implement such functionality in our system accordingly to the architecture of Figure 12.5.

The mapping between the generic components of each usability mechanism and the concrete classes in the M-ticket application described in Tables 12.3 and 12.4 guide software designers to

**Table 12.3** Mapping Between the Classes of the SSF Usability Mechanism and Those Implemented in the Architecture of the M-ticket Application

| Usability Mechanism | Generic Component | Classes in the M-ticket Architecture | M-ticket Architectural Responsibility |
|---|---|---|---|
| System Status Feedback | Display Status | New Complaint | This class displays the status to the user |
| | Status Manager | N/A | We don't need this functionality as we only support one type of status |
| | Status Concrete Status | New Complaint | This class checks if there are pending complaints stored in the phone and updates the status when the complaints are sent to the server |
| | Domain | NotificationManager (Android) | This library performs low-level operations when the status changes and assigns an ID for the status. In case of a loss in the connection between the phone and the server, the *New Complaint* class will inform the *Notification Manager* with an ID, which will be used by the *Send Complaint* class when the notification need to be removed |

**Table 12.4** Mapping Between the Classes of the User Preferences Usability Mechanism and Those Implemented in the Architecture of the M-ticket Application

| Usability Mechanism | Generic Component | Classes in the M-ticket Architecture | M-ticket Architectural Responsibility |
|---|---|---|---|
| User Preferences | User | Main Screen | Users can configure the options of their alert messages using the Main Screen interface |
| | Preferences Manager | Preferences Manager | It handles the preferences set by the user |
| | Preference | Alert Messages | The alert message is the configurable preference supported by M-ticket |
| | Group | N/A | Not supported |
| | Settings Manager | N/A | Not supported |
| | Setting | N/A | Not supported |
| | Storage Front | Storage Front | It acts as an intermediate class to store the preferences edited by the user |
| | Mobile Phone Database | M-ticket database | This class relates the Storage Front with the access to the M-ticket database where preferences are stored |

introduce the concrete architectural responsibilities. Hence, software architects can use these mappings to determine the concrete responsibilities of new and existing classes in their application for supporting a particular usability mechanism. In our example, only one class is assigned to one component, but in more complex mechanisms, several classes can be assigned to the same component. However, we do not suggest guidelines for coding the usability mechanisms because these may depend on the current functionality of the application and the code in which the usability feature will be added.

### 12.5.3 Usability and interactions between entities

Because introducing usability in the software architecture introduces new relationships between the existing classes from the old design and the new classes supporting the functionality of both usability mechanisms, new interactions between the entities participating in the possible M-ticket scenarios arise. Because other stakeholders might be interested in the interactions that happen when a usability mechanism is activated or invoked by the system or the user, we describe in Figure 12.6 an example of a sequence diagram that exemplifies the dynamicity of the system and the calls made between the mobile user, the M-ticket application, and the server.

The aforementioned scenario shown in Figure 12.6 describes the interactions between the entities when a policeman sends a traffic ticket to the server application using the mobile device and the case where the usability mechanism SSF notifies the user if the ticket has been sent or the case when, due to a loss of the radio connection, the pending tickets have to be stored in the mobile device and the connection has to be rechecked before the tickets are resent.

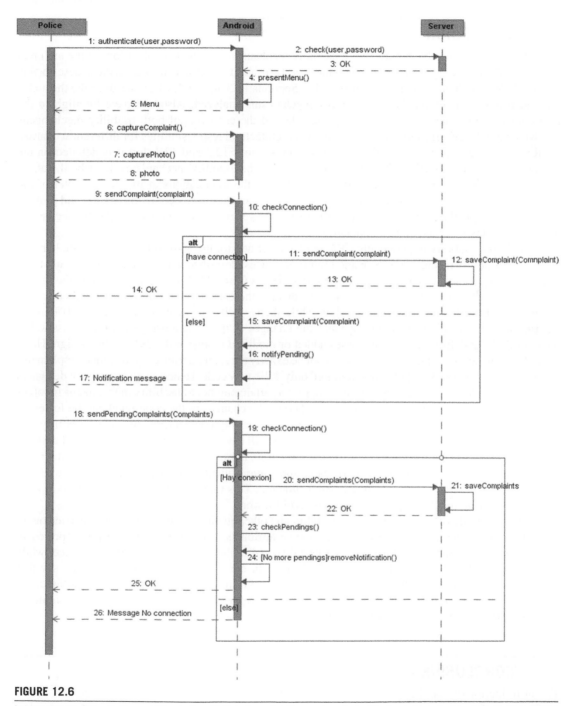

**FIGURE 12.6**

Interactions of the major entities in the M-ticket application entangled with the interaction induce by the SSF usability mechanism.

## 12.6 DISCUSSION

This chapter illustrates the importance of usability mechanisms and their implications at the architecture level when usability requirements demand specific usability mechanism, such as those described in this work. Research question RQ1 is answered in Sections 12.3 and 12.4, where we describe the architectural responsibilities for the two usability mechanisms analyzed. Also, we have highlighted the importance of this question by describing the role and the use cases of both usability mechanisms and which are the generic and concrete component architectural responsibilities for different scenarios.

Research question RQ2 is partially answered in Sections 12.3 and 12.4, but it is detailed on the example presented in Section 12.5 where we detail how the usability mechanisms describe the affect of the architecture of a mobile application. We discuss the implications at the design level of the changes that should be made for each of the usability mechanisms discussed in this chapter and provide a guiding example that shows the mappings between the generic classes of each usability mechanism and the real classes of the mobile application used.

In addition, usability requirements UR1 and UR2 defined for the M-ticket application are handled by the two usability mechanisms (SSF and User Preferences) described in the chapter. As a result, three of the existing classes were modified and four new classes were added. In order to estimate the impact of introducing both usability mechanisms in the design, the classes modified in the architecture represent around the 19% of the overall design, while the new classes represent around the 20% of the existing design. We didn't take into account the changes or new relationships between classes, but the overall design effort in terms of classes added or modified represent the 39% of the design. However, the implications at the code level might not be exactly the same, because, for instance, implementing the SSF in the M-ticket application required only 4.2% new code. Hence, even if software designers perceive that redesigning the architecture to support a certain number of usability mechanisms involves changing or adding a considerable number of classes, the changes at the code level can be lower.

In the example shown we have only addressed two usability mechanisms, but more usability features can be incorporated. However, dealing with them will have its corresponding impact and cost in a clear competition with other quality attributes. Therefore, a trade-off between usability and its implications needs to be carefully studied for each application, identifying the more relevant usability requirements from the user perspective in each situation. This usability study should be done as soon as possible during the development process to avoid rework.

Additional trade-off analysis between usability and other quality requirements can be carried out in order to address the conflicts between the quality attributes. For instance, the results reported in Henningsson and Wholin (2002) show that usability and reliability have a positive influence, while usability and efficiency exhibit a negative influence. In our M-ticket application, we can say that the usability mechanisms introduced enhance the reliability of the application because mobile users are informed when a traffic ticket cannot be sent to the server. Hence, a quality trade-off analysis aimed to balance quality attributes becomes key relevant for software and product operation.

## 12.7 CONCLUSIONS

The introduction of usability mechanisms in any software has clear implication for the design. In this chapter, we show how the architecture of a mobile application is affected when we add usability mechanisms and which classes are needed to handle the responsibilities of each usability mechanism. We have also outlined the role of the major classes in the architecture when these usability mechanisms need to be introduced in any mobile application. In order to educate software designers about the introduction of usability mechanisms in their systems, and based on our personal experience, we have described the case of a real mobile application for which two usability mechanisms were introduced.

Consequently, we provide evidence about the need and impact for considering usability requirements in mobile software development. The usability requirements we have referred to in this work are general recommendations from the HCI community aimed at improving the usability of any software system. In this sense, our approach is complementary to existing works that address usability testing in similar applications.

Regarding the generalizability of the results, we observed from our study that many of the usability mechanisms analyzed in this work can be found and used in many Web applications or in mixed Web-mobile software. More specifically for mobile apps, because many modern smartphones share a similar interface, we believe using the same usability mechanisms in other mobile apps will have the same outcomes (also for Tablet PC).

# References

Bass, L., John, B., 2002. Linking usability to software architecture patterns through general scenarios. J. Syst. Softw. 66 (3), 188–197.

Beck, E.T., Christiansen, M.K., Kjeldskov, J., 2003. Experimental evaluation of techniques for usability testing of mobile systems in a laboratory setting. In: Proceedings of OzCHI 2003, Brisbane, Australia.

Bevan, N., MacLeod, M., 1994. Usability measurement in context. Behav. Inf. Technol. 13, 132–145.

Black, J., 2002. Usability is next to profitability. BusinessWeek, Online at:http://www.businessweek.com/technol ogy/content/dec2002/tc2002124_2181.htm(Retrieved 04:10:2009).

Clements, P., Kazman, R., Klein, M., 2002. Evaluating Software Architectures: Methods and Case Studies. Addison-Wesley, USA.

Donahue, G., 2001. Usability and the bottom line. IEEE Softw. 16 (1), 31–37.

Ferre, X., Juristo, N., Moreno, A.M., Sánchez-Segura, M., 2003. A software architectural view of usability patterns. In: Proceedings of INTERACT 2003. Zurich, Switzerland.

Henningsson, K., Wholin, C., 2002. Understanding the relations between software quality attributes—a survey approach. In: 12th International Conference for Software Quality.

Hussain, A., Kutar, M., 2012a. Apps vs. devices: can the usability of mobile apps be decoupled from the device? Int. J. Comput. Sci. Issues. 9 (3), 11–16.

Hussain, A., Kutar, M., 2012b. Usability evaluation of SatNav application on mobile phone using mGQM. Int. J. Comput. Inf. Syst. Ind. Manage. Appl. 4, 92–100.

John, B., Bass, L., Sanchez-Segura, M., 2005. In: Bringing Usability Concerns to the Design of Software Architecture. In: Lecture Notes in Computer Science, vol. 3425. Springer, Hamburg, pp. 1–19.

John, B., Bass, L., Golden, E., Stoll, P., 2009. A responsibility-based pattern language for usability-supporting architectural patterns. In: Proceedings of the 1st ACM SIGCHI Symposium on Engineering Interactive Computing Systems.

Kaikkonen, A., Kekäläinen, A., Cankar, M., Kallio, T., Kankainen, A., 2005. Usability testing of mobile applications: a comparison between laboratory and field testing. J. Usability Study 1, 4–16.

Kim, H., Kim, J., Lee, Y., Chae, M., Choi, Y., 2002. An empirical study of the use contexts and usability problems in mobile internet. In: Proceedings of the 35th Hawaii International Conference on System Sciences (HICSS-35'02), Big Island, Hawaii.

Kjeldskov, J., Stage, J., 2004. New techniques for usability evaluation of mobile systems. Int. J. Hum.-Comput. Stud. 60 (5-6), 599–620.

Kumar Dubey, S., Rana, A., 2010. Analytical roadmap to usability definitions and decompositions. Int. J. Eng. Sci. Technol. 2 (9), 4723–4729.

Lundhal, O., 2009. Usability of mobile applications for near field communication. Master of Science Thesis in the Programme Design Interaction, Chalmers University of Technology, University of Gothenburg, Göteborg, Sweden.

Moreno, A.M., Seffah, S., Capilla, R., Sanchez-Segura, I., 2013. HCI practices for building usable software. IEEE Comput. 46 (10), 100–102.

nHIMSS App Usability Work Group, 2012. Selecting a Mobile App: Evaluating the Usability of Medical Applications. Online at: http://www.mhimss.org/sites/default/files/resource-media/pdf/HIMSSguidetoappusabili tyv1mHIMSS.pdf.

Ryan, C., Gonsalves, A., 2005. The effect of context and application type on mobile usability: an empirical study. In: ACSC '05 Proceedings of the Twenty-Eighth Australasian Conference on Computer Science, vol. 38. pp. 115–124.

Seffah, A.M., 2004. The obstacles and myths of usability and software engineering. Commun. ACM. 47 (12), 71–76.

Seffah, A., Mohamed, T., Habied-Mammar, H., Abran, A., 2008. Reconciling usability and interactive system architecture using patterns. J. Syst. Softw. 81 (11), 1845–1852.

Terrenghi, L., Kronen, M., Valle, C., 2005. Usability requirements for mobile service scenarios. In: Human Computer Interaction 2005 (IHCI'05), Las Vegas, USA, pp. 1–10.

# Understanding Quality Requirements Engineering in Contract-Based Projects from the Perspective of Software Architects: An Exploratory Study

**13**

**Maya Daneva**[1]**, Andrea Herrmann**[2]**, and Luigi Buglione**[3]

[1]*University of Twente, Enschede, The Netherlands*
[2]*Herrmann & Ehrlich, Stuttgart, Germany*
[3]*ETS Montréal/Engineering.IT SpA, Rome, Italy*

## INTRODUCTION

Quality requirements (QRs) for a software system define quality properties of the system, for example, scalability, security, usability, and performance (Gorton, 2011). Essentially, QRs address issues of concern to applications' users as well as other stakeholders such as the project team, the software maintainers, or the project steering committee. Getting these requirements right in the early stages of a software development project has been known to be instrumental to the design of software architecture and to lead to savings in the later phases of implementation, testing, and maintenance (Gorton, 2011; Pohl, 2011).

In the communities of software architecture and of requirements engineering (RE), the topic of engineering QRs has been investigated for more than a decade; however, primarily in terms of creating methods, representation formalisms, languages, and tools that could support in various ways the process of joint RE and software architecture (Avgeriou et al., 2011; Bachmann and Bass, 2001; Bass et al., 2003; Capilla et al., 2012; Sommerville, 2005). Only recently, this research effort was complemented with studies on the human agents conducting RE and architecture processes (Ferrari and Madhavji, 2008) and on the contexts in which RE and software architecture professionals collaborate. In turn, as noted by Ferrari and Madhavji (2008), few studies exist on the role of agents in project organizations and how these agents cope with QRs in their projects on a day-to-day basis. Specifically, empirical studies on the perspective of software architects (SAs) are relatively recent. Because they are mostly published after 2010, they address only a small number of organizational contexts in which software development might take place; namely, they report on small and mid-sized projects. Moreover, most of them do not address the contextual differences between in-house development projects and contract-based software delivery projects. Yet, in the twenty-first century, most large software system development happens in contractual settings.

In this chapter, we set about closing the gap of knowledge about how SAs cope with QRs in large and contract-based system delivery projects. We achieve this by an exploratory interview-based study with 21 SAs working in large or very large contract-based systems projects in European companies. We identified how SAs cope with the six engineering activities associated with QR, namely QRs elicitation, documentation, prioritization, quantification, validation, and negotiation. Our results revealed the roles that SAs play in these activities in a contract-based project, the interactions between SAs and other project roles, the specific actions SAs take to help discover, document, quantify, validate, and negotiate QRs, and the ways in which the contract orchestrated the QR engineering activities and encouraged the SAs do what they did. We compare our findings with previously published results and draw implications for SAs, for RE specialists, for RE tool vendors, as well as for further research.

This chapter makes three contributions: (1) to software architecture, (2) to RE, and (3) to empirical software engineering. First, whereas the interfaces between software architecture and RE have been the subject of research in the software architecture community for years, *how SAs operate in contract-based context while engineering QRs* has evaded the attention of software architecture researchers. This study narrows the gap of knowledge in the field regarding this question. Second, we inform the RE researchers and practitioners on what contributions SAs bring to the complex social and only partly understood process of engineering QRs in contact-based contexts. While the RE community has acknowledged for a long time that the RE processes are very different for contract-based projects as opposed to in-house projects (Berenbach et al., 2010; Lauesen, 2002), most of the existing empirical RE research was preoccupied with the perspectives of business users, RE specialists, vendors' marketing specialists, and managers, and in fact left the perspective of SAs almost completely unaddressed. If the RE community learns about the SAs' experiences in QR engineering, they might design new methods with and for SAs in order to help both disciplines to collaborate much easier or to collectively come up with criteria for choosing the right method. Third, our chapter responds to two explicit calls: (1) the call by the empirical SE community for more empirical research on which SE process to use in which specific context (Sjøberg et al., 2007) and (2) the particular call by the RE community for more empirical research in the sub-areas of RE (Cheng and Atlee, 2007).

The chapter is structured as follows: We first present the motivation for our study. Next, we describe the context of contract-based software development and summarize related work based on systematic literature reviews published by authors in the fields of RE and of software architecture. Then, we present our research questions, our empirical interview-based research process, its execution, and its results. We end up with our discussion on the results in the light of previously published research, on the implications of our study for practitioners and researchers, and on evaluation of validity threats.

## 13.1 MOTIVATION

Our motivation for this empirical research is rooted in the trends in the software industry for designing and deploying approaches to joint RE and architecture design (Avgeriou et al., 2011; Bachmann and Bass, 2001; Sommerville, 2005). This trend reflects the understanding that QRs are usually relevant for the architecture and, vice versa, architecture is determining QR satisfaction (Chen et al., 2013). For example, the Twin Peak model (Nuseibeh, 2001) for joint RE and architecture design reinvents the notion of the spiral life cycle for software development by viewing software architecture as a "peak" that along with the "peak" of the requirements is iterated early on. SAs and RE professionals have been experiencing such approaches as key to guiding the architecture design process, capturing design rationale, and supporting traceability between requirements and architecture. This known, both SAs and RE specialists initiated a conversation to understand how each of these professional groups reasons about QRs and contributes to the QRs engineering activities, so that these approaches are leveraged and also improved in a targeted and cost-effective fashion (Avgeriou et al., 2013). However, the concerted empirical research efforts of both research schools and practitioners on understanding the SAs' perspectives on QRs started relatively recently. Therefore, the available empirical evidence and knowledge cover only unevenly the possible range of contextual settings in which SAs and RE professionals work. Specifically, most published empirical evidence until now on how SAs and RE specialists work together has been gained in small and mid-sized projects. The context of large and contract-based software system delivery projects has remained by and large unaddressed. This knowledge gap in our understanding of the SAs' perspective on QRs motivated us to initiate empirical research by collecting and analyzing first-hand information from SAs in the field. In the next two sections, after presenting our context of interest, we report on published empirical studies and indicate that there is an important gap in knowledge.

## 13.2 BACKGROUND ON THE CONTEXT OF CONTRACT-BASED SYSTEMS DELIVERY

This section summarizes publications on contract-based software development because this is the context of interest in our study. We draw some differences between this context and the context of in-house development that relate to the work of RE staff and SAs.

For the purpose of our study, we consulted literature sources in three streams of research: (i) IT outsourcing (e.g., Furlotti, 2007); (ii) designing inter-firm contracts (Gopal and Koka, 2010; Song and Hwonk, 2012; Wu et al., 2012), and particularly, service-level agreements (SLAs) for IT projects (Goo et al., 2008); and (iii) RE for contract-based systems (Berenbach et al., 2010; Nekvi et al., 2012; Song and Hwonk, 2012). Generally, in the literature on software development contracts, a contract is understood as a legal vehicle that defines the sharing of profit and risk between a software development organization and a business client organization that is committed to delivering a project. A typical contract is composed of two parts (Furlotti, 2007): (i) a *transactional* part, which defines the parties' commitments on tasks, resources, outputs, and remuneration provisions and (ii) a *procedural* part, which defines the rights and processes designed to assist in introducing adjustments, preserving integration, and maintaining shared understanding of the terms and clauses of the contract. Brought together, these parts must address a broad array of issues such as a resulting system's quality, delivery schedule, payment schedule, escalation and termination conditions and procedures, and post-delivery services.

Based on their transactional definitions, software development contracts generally come in three alternative forms: fixed fee, time-and-material, or multistage contacts that combine components of fixed and variable prices (Berenbach et al., 2010; Gopal and Koka, 2010; Kalnins and Mayer,

2004; Lauesen, 2002; Song and Hwonk, 2012; Wu et al., 2012). A fixed-fee contract stipulates a pre-determined price that is paid to a software development organization for delivering a software system, while a variable price contract assumes the business client pays the developer the development costs topped up with some profit or payoff. Variable price contracts may differ widely in terms of levels of granularity and sophistication regarding how profit/payoff is defined. Most often, the definition of profit/payoff is tied to project performance or outcomes, and hence the payoff to the development organization depends on the quality of the delivered software system.

Each of the three contract forms is known to work well and be preferred more often in certain contexts than in others. For example, Wu et al. (2012) suggest that fixed-fee contracts fit better in a context of simple software projects that need relatively short development time. In contrast, more complex projects that bear more uncertainty, take longer time, and are tracked based on phases and critical milestones would benefit from variable price contracts, assuming efficient and effective auditing process is set up in place. Also, multi-stage contracts fit long-year large-scale projects and assist their delivery by opening up opportunities for effective use of information gathering and learning during the project, for example, by means of mid-term project evaluations, which would reduce project risk in the periods that follow and would improve team performance because they foster reflections on what works and what does not (Wu et al., 2012). Moreover, critical to the success of every contract-based project are the SLAs that form an addendum to the contract and describe the quality aspects of the products and services to be delivered by the development organization (Goo et al., 2008). They serve the purpose of establishing the parties' expectations, defining contacts in case of user problems, and defining metrics by means of which the effectiveness of the contracted services and processes as well as agreed upon deliverables will be measured and controlled.

From RE and software architecture perspectives, large contract-based systems imply massive documentation processing effort to be invested by RE staff and SAs (Nekvi et al., 2012). As an illustration of a complex project and its contract-related documentation, we refer here to the empirical report of Song and Hwonk (2012), which presents a large-scale infrastructure system that integrates numerous sub-systems, not all of which are software systems but also hardware ones like fire detection and suppression, routers, phone switches, ductwork, and fiber cable. Such a project may entail a contract containing of around 4000 clauses, and systematic processes are needed to be in place for categorizing the contractual requirements from goal-level to design-decision-level. Beyond the contract, the SLA document may well be voluminous too: The Goo et al. (2008) report, a well-designed SLA document, may include up to 11 contractual issues, and each of them might be the subject of a separate document.

Moreover, contract-based projects are usually more complex than in-house development systems because they come with project execution requirements, long-term obligations, and submittals (Berenbach et al., 2010) that are legally binding and impact how the professionals proceed at each step of the project. As these authors recommend, "*clauses dealing with the quality of deliverables must be analysed to create derived requirements that are testable and are acceptable to the client*" (p. 31). Also, these projects' requirements often have to demonstrate compliance with government regulations and standards, which becomes a key RE activity (Nekvi et al., 2012).

Furthermore, Gopal and Koka (2010) indicate that in contrast to in-house development projects, monitoring the software development organization and ensuring compliance to the project execution requirements is an explicit activity that orchestrates the vendor-client relationship at organizational level, for example, the mechanisms of how the software services vendor ensures quality and the returns on the vendor organization's investment in quality.

## 13.3 EMPIRICAL STUDIES ON THE SOFTWARE ARCHITECTURE PERSPECTIVE ON QRs

This section provides a rundown of how the software architecture perspective on QRs has been studied according to published systematic reviews and empirical studies in the fields of RE and software architecture. Although empirical research on the interplay of software architecture and QRs engineering is gaining momentum, studies in large-scale contract-based project contexts are scarce. To identify related work on SAs' perspective on QRs, we looked at the empirical studies that were included in two systematic literature reviews on QRs (Berntsson-Svensson et al., 2010; Guessi et al., 2012). We also searched the Scopus digital library (www.scopus.com) for publications that came out in the second half of 2012 and in 2013.

The two systematic reviews (Berntsson-Svensson et al., 2010; Guessi et al., 2012) provided examples of projects and organizations described in recent publications by both researchers and practitioners. We found, however, that most of these studies have taken the RE perspective exclusively. Very few studies have included the perspectives of SAs, despite the clear consensus in the RE community that the perspective of SAs is important (Ameller et al., 2012; Avgeriou et al., 2011; Bass et al., 2003; Capilla et al., 2012; Heesch van and Avgeriou, 2011; Poort et al., 2012a; Sommerville, 2005). For example, the review of Berntsson-Svensson et al. (2010) found only 18 studies to be well-documented and stating explicitly the perspectives taken in the empirical research. While preparing for this research, we reviewed these 18 studies and found that none of them considered the SAs' perspective. In the period of 2010-2013, we found six publications (Ameller and Franch, 2010; Ameller et al., 2012, 2013; Heesch van and Avgeriou, 2011; Poort et al., 2012a,b) dedicated specifically to the SAs' perceptions on QRs. These studies agree that the perspectives of SAs and RE specialists on QRs differ. However, the experiences these studies report come mostly from small- and mid-sized projects. In this chapter, we complement these results from the RE perspective and smaller projects with findings from large contract-based projects from SAs' perspective.

## 13.4 RESEARCH PROCESS

### 13.4.1 Research objective and research plan

Our study's overall research objective is to understand *how SAs cope with QRs in large and contract-based software system development projects*. We aimed to provide an in-depth understanding of the QRs' engineering activities as experienced by SAs while executing their projects.

In line with the study's objective, we defined the following research questions:

RQ1: How do SAs understand their role with respect to engineering QRs?
RQ2: Do SAs and RE staff use different terminology for QRs?
RQ3: How do QRs get elicited?
RQ4: How do QRs get documented?
RQ5: How do QRs get prioritized?
RQ6: How do QRs get quantified, if at all?
RQ7: How do QRs get validated?
RQ8: How do QRs get negotiated?
RQ9: What role does the contract play in the way SAs cope with QRs?

We note that these questions are open and explorative in nature because (as said earlier) the context of contract-based systems delivery projects is under-researched and no empirical studies on SAs' perspectives on QRs in this context have been published so far. This said, we started without any preconceived ideas about how SAs' behavior should or could be. Instead, we expected to learn such details from the lived and perceived experiences of the participating practitioners in the field. We also note that exploring such questions is a necessary first step to understand what is happening in the field concerning the phenomenon of study (i.e., QRs engineering). Only once this understanding is there, can we motivate and formulate narrower-focused questions for follow-up studies and for quantitative research.

We chose Yin's method of exploratory case study research (Yin, 2008) as the guiding methodological source to plan, execute, and report a multiple case study with 21 software project organizations. Our choice for this research methodology is justified by our research interest and commitment to explore a real-life phenomenon in the context in which it happens. As Bensabat et al. (1987) suggest, a case study is a particularly suitable research method to situations in which (1) researchers study socially constructed processes in systems development projects and seek to analyze the practice and (2) researchers want to answer "how" and "why" questions and comprehend the nature and the complexity of the processes of interest. In our exploratory case study, we expected to earn a rich and contextualized description of the practices, interactions, and roles of SAs. We also expected to understand the influences that the presence of the contract exercises on the professional behavior of the SAs (e.g., the choice of practices, interactions, and roles).

Our case study used structured open-end in-depth interviews with SAs from a wide range of companies and business sectors. The application domains where the practitioners developed software solutions represent a rich mix of fields including telecommunications, real estate management, air transportation, entertainment (online gaming, video streaming), educational services, online travel planning services (e.g., hotel/flight booking), and ERP.

The overall process of performing our study included these steps: (1) composing an interview guide following the guidelines in King and Horrocks (2010), (2) doing a pilot interview to check the applicability of the guide to real-life context, (3) carrying out interviews with practitioners according to the finalized questionnaire, (4) identifying and following up with interviews with those participants who possessed deeper knowledge or a specific perspective, (5) analyzing the data, and (6) preparing the report.

The subsections below present the practitioners involved and the data collection and analysis methods that we used.

## 13.4.2 The case study participants

The 21 SAs came from 15 companies in the Netherlands, Belgium, Finland, and Germany as presented in Table 13.1. At the time of the interviews, these companies were running large contract-based projects. There were two IT vendors that were large multinational consulting companies responsible for delivering and rolling out multicomponent and interorganizational ERP solutions based on the packaged software of SAP and Oracle. Seven of our interviewees were SAs employed by these two vendors and involved in ERP projects at these vendors' clients' sites. Furthermore, we had two SAs from a large insurance business working with internal IT staff and software development subcontractors on delivering a large custom software solution. Two other SAs were employed in a video-streaming services provider dealing with software component vendors. The rest of the companies were represented by one

**Table 13.1** Case Study Participants and Organizations

| ID | Business | System Description | Team Size (# of People) | Project Duration (months) |
|---|---|---|---|---|
| P1. | Large IT Vendor | ERP package implementation (Oracle) | 35 | 18 |
| P2. | Large IT Vendor | ERP package implementation (SAP) | 60 | 15 |
| P3. | Large IT Vendor | ERP package implementation (SAP) | 75 | 18 |
| P4. | Large IT Vendor | ERP package implementation (SAP) | 41 | 12 |
| P5. | Large IT Vendor | ERP package implementation (SAP) | 51 | 12 |
| P6. | Large IT Vendor | ERP package implementation (Oracle) | 45 | 12 |
| P7. | IT Vendor | ERP package implementation (SAP) | 40 | 18 |
| P8. | Software Producer | Online learning environment | 22 | 12 |
| P9. | Software Producer | Sensor system for in-building navigation | 35 | 12 |
| P10. | Software Producer | Online ticket booking application | 15 | 12 |
| P11. | Oil & Gas | Logistics planning application | 21 | 12 |
| P12. | Insurance | Web application for client self-service | 61 | 24 |
| P13. | Insurance | Client claim management and reimbursement app | 53 | 16 |
| P14. | Real Estate | Web application for rental contract handling | 42 | 18 |
| P15. | Air Carrier | Web app for passengers' feedback processing | 11 | 14 |
| P16. | Video Streaming | Viewer recommendation management system | 18 | 18 |
| P17. | Video Streaming | Viewer complaint management system | 45 | 9 |
| P18. | Online bookstore | Order processing system | 15 | 10 |
| P19. | Online game producer | Gaming system | 81 | 21 |
| P20. | Online travel agency | Room deal identification system | 45 | 12 |
| P21 | Online game producer | Gaming system | 97 | 19 |

participant each. We note that while there were SAs who were employed in the same company, no two or more practitioners were engaged in the same project. For example, the two SAs (see participants P12 and P13 in Table 13.1) who were employed in the insurance company were working on two different projects. This allowed us to collect experiences of a total of 21 projects.

The practitioners were selected because they (i) had professional backgrounds pertaining to our research questions and (ii) had the potential to offer information-rich experiences. Also, they demonstrated an interest in exploring similar questions from their companies' perspectives. All 21 SAs had the following backgrounds:

1. They all worked in large projects running in at least three different development locations in one country and had clients in more than two countries.
2. All SAs had at least 10 years of experience in large systems and were familiar with the interactions that happen between SAs and RE staff.

3. All SAs worked in contract-based projects where contracts between parties were established in two steps (Lauesen, 2002): first, a contract was agreed upon for the purpose to get the requirements documented in sufficient detail, so that an SA can use them to work on architecture design. Then, a second contract dealt with the system delivery itself.

4. All participants had "Software Architect" as their job titles (Gorton, 2011) and were employed full-time by their employers. Also, the RE staff and the project managers with whom these SAs worked were employed full-time in their respective jobs. The RE specialists had various job titles, such as business analysts, business system analysts, information analysts; however, they worked in these roles exclusively, in the sense that RE specialists were not senior developers who were taking on RE or project management tasks.

The pricing agreements varied across the participating companies. Some were fixed-price, others variable, and a third group combined fixed-price and variable. Five SAs worked in outsourcing contracts, and 16 were employed on projects where software development subcontractors were participating. All SAs deemed their contracts comprehensive and aligned with the spirit of their projects. (In other words: None suggested that their organization had any issue with the contract.) The projects were considered successful by both parties in the contract. The SAs got to know the first author during various business and research conferences in the period of 2001-2012. Using purposive sampling (King and Horrocks, 2010), she chose the interviewees, based on her knowledge about their typicality. The number of participants was large enough to provide a diversity in viewpoints. We planned the interviews to be "structured" (King and Horrocks, 2010) with regard to the questions being asked during the session. This means the interviewer controlled what topics would be discussed and in which order.

We note that interview-based exploratory case studies usually are intended to promote self-disclosure, and that is what we intended in this work. We collected data via one-on-one interactions of a researcher with each of the interviewees that have exposure to various application domains but also common professional values, backgrounds, and common roles in which they execute their professional duties. As in King and Horrocks (2010), interview studies are not used to provide statistically generalizable results applicable to all people similar to the practitioners in a specific study. The intention of an exploratory case study is not to infer, but to understand, and not to generalize, but to determine a possible range of views. Therefore, in this study we adopt, based on the recommendations in King and Horrocks (2010), the criterion of transferability as a useful measure of validity. Transferability asks whether the results are presented in a way that allows other researchers and practitioners to evaluate if the findings apply to their contexts.

### 13.4.3 The research instrument for data collection

Because we wanted to understand the tasks of SAs and their interactions with other project stakeholders, we looked at data collection techniques that help extract detailed information about social and cognitive processes through which a professional achieves his or her tasks' goals (Wortham et al., 2011). One prominent technique is the method of semi-structured interviews enabling the interviewer to ask predetermined questions while still remaining flexible, so that the interviewee is not prevented from elaborating on topics that may emerge but were not directly asked about by the interviewer

(King and Horrocks, 2010). Each interviewee was provided beforehand with detailed information on the research purpose and the research process. To help the subjects to verbalize their roles and tasks with respect to QRs, we asked them to think about their current contract-based project. The interviewing researcher then probed each participant for the tacit knowledge used to deal with the QRs engineering in his or her project.

Each interview lasted 35-45 min. Nine interviews took place face-to-face, and 12 on the phone. After each interview, the researcher followed up with each participant to get access to documents related to the study and that the SAs referred to during the interview, for example, job descriptions or standards.

### 13.4.4 **Data analysis strategy**

Our data analysis was guided by the Grounded Theory method of Charmaz (2008). It is a qualitative approach applied broadly in social sciences to construct general propositions (called a "theory" in this approach) from verbal data. It is exploratory and well suited for situations where the researcher does not have preconceived ideas, and instead is driven by the desire to capture all facets of the collected data and to allow the theory to emerge from the data. In essence, this was a process of making analytic sense of the interview data by means of coding and constant/iterative comparison of data collected in the case study (Figure 13.1).

Constant comparison means that the data from an interview is constantly compared to the data already collected from previously held interviews. We first read the interview transcripts and attached a coding word to a portion of the text—a phrase or a paragraph. The "codes" were selected to reflect the meaning of the respective portion of the interview text to a specific research question. This could be a concept (e.g., "willingness to pay") or an activity (e.g., "operationalization," "quantification"). We clustered all pieces of text that relate to the same code in order to analyze it in a consistent and systematic way. The results of the data analysis are presented in the next section, after which a discussion is added.

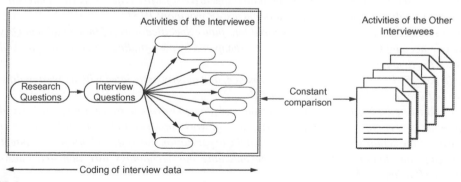

**FIGURE 13.1**

The GT-based process of data analysis.

## 13.5 RESULTS

Our findings are presented as related to each research question. As it is common in qualitative studies (Charmaz, 2008), we supplement the observations with interviewees' quotations.

### 13.5.1 RQ1: How do the software architects understand their role with respect to engineering QRs?

We found that while reflecting on their roles in QRs engineering, SAs grounded their reasoning on their job descriptions in the organizations where they were employed. In the experience of all our participants, their respective companies had job descriptions that listed the most important duties, skills, and competence levels for SAs, including those related to QRs. As said earlier, the SAs' jobs were separate (Gorton, 2011) from those of RE professionals—known as "business analysts," or "systems analysts" —and of software developers—having job titles as "programmer/analyst" or "senior programmer/analyst." This said, no SA from the 21 involved in our study has been tasked with, for example, coding or business requirements specifications.

For the purpose of illustrating the ways in which QRs are mentioned in an SA's job description, we provide below an excerpt from one participant's job description:

> *The software architect is responsible for the technical direction of a project. Makes high level design choices for the software structure, frameworks, protocols, and algorithms. Determines coding practices, development tools, and validation requirements. Performs path-finding and surveys technologies. Interacts with multiple technologists in the company and within the industry as well as between developers and project managers to evaluate feasibility of requirements and determine priorities for development. (Participant P11).*

QRs were included in a variety of responsibilities that go with the SA's job, for example, resolving technical issues related to QRs, evaluating feasibility of QRs (e.g., mapping technology limitations against desired QRs), validating QRs, and communicating technology direction in regard to QRs. These responsibilities were explicitly stated in the SAs' job descriptions, as illustrated below:

> *Understand solution performance and capabilities and drive software requirements, architecture and priorities by evaluating feasibility of requirements. (Participant P15)*
>
> *Ensure Android system needs are factored into future specifications [of functional and QRs] by taking into account Google Android feature roadmap and by path-finding usage models for Android systems. (Participant P21)*
>
> *Lead path-finding work on power, performance, and quality associated with delivering differentiating end user experiences. (Participant P19)*
>
> *Act as a trusted advisor to the business team and play a key role in transforming business plans, and product concepts [functional and QRs], into real world product architectures [software architectures]. As the senior technical leader within the organization the Systems/Software Architect will also engage our major customers in communicating our technology direction and innovative approach. (Participant P18)*
>
> *Serve as the organization's technical authority. Own and champion the product technology roadmap and ensure alignment with business, user and quality requirements. (Participant P10)*

*Provide architectural expertise, direction, and assistance to software development teams to conceive and build leading edge products based on a standard architecture. Assess the feasibility of incorporating new technologies in product designs. (Participant P11)*

*Provide technical leadership in the resolution of complex technical issues related to security, scalability, usability and privacy, across the organization. (Participant P12)*

*Make high level design choices for the software structure, frameworks, protocols, and algorithms. Determine coding practices, development tools, validation requirements, and benchmarking performance. (Participant P16)*

We note that the SAs had a wide range of duties (e.g., creating the architecture design for the system, technology road-mapping, among others) and QRs engineering was only one of the many in the range. Moreover, the SAs' job descriptions did not elaborate in detail of the exact QRs engineering tasks of the SAs. (This in itself confirmed that interviews with the SAs were indeed necessary to understand more in depth the QRs tasks; if the QRs engineering tasks were explicitly detailed in the job descriptions, one might consider carrying out a documentary study; this would be a completely different research design.)

Because all the organizations were mature in terms of project management processes and process-oriented thinking, the roles of the SAs were established and they were clearly visible for their fellow team members. We found four distinctive roles that SAs identified themselves with regarding QRs (see Figure 13.2). These roles are: (1) serving as a "bridge," (2) serving as a "gatekeeper," (3) serving as a "balance-keeper," and (4) providing "QR engineering as a service." We elaborate on these distinctive roles below.

Thirteen of the 21 SAs thought of their role as a "*bridge*" between QRs and the underlying technology that they were dealing with.

*You've got to translate what their clients want in terms of working solutions and technology choices. (Participant P1)*

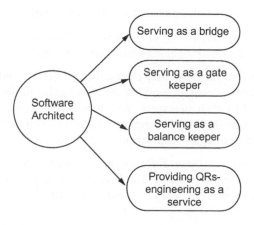

**FIGURE 13.2**

Roles that SAs play in QRs engineering in contract-based delivery projects, as perceived by the case study participants.

> *You learn pretty quickly to stretch the technology so that it works for those who you call "require-*
> *ments engineers," I mean here our Business Analysts and their "patrons," the business unit directors.*
> *(Participant P2)*
>
> *I have days when I do nothing but "translate" the language of our millions of players into the*
> *features that are technologically implementable in the next release. All I do is walk through a list*
> *of "user experiences" that our requirements folk want to launch in the market, and I make sure that*
> *it all works well at implementation level, that features build upon each other, so that the overall gam-*
> *ing experience and enjoyability are never compromised. That's why I'm coming to work every day.*
> *(Participant P19).*

Other seven SAs thought of their roles as *"review gatekeepers"* because of their active involvement in QRs reviews, contract compliance evaluation, and sign off:

> *My review is like a green light for the implementation team's work. (Participant P2)*
>
> *You are the gatekeeper in the game, and you've got to act like this so that you get them focus*
> *on the right things. If you do not tell them what the right things are, no one else will. (Participant P11)*
>
> *If you are sick, on vacation, or on a conference, there is no way this can go unnoticed; they*
> *will need you, and if there is no one to tell them that what they are doing is right [according to*
> *contract and project goals], I mean it pure architecturally; they are going to wait for me so*
> *that I give the architecture approval. Otherwise, we run a risk of screwing up things miserably.*
> *(participant P15).*

Among those seven who considered themselves as gatekeepers, there were two who explicitly thought of themselves as *"balance keepers"* as well:

> *I watch for the developers to avoid quick-fix solutions and technical debt. In our application area*
> *[gaming], this puts the qualities out of balance; you advance, only later to find out user experience*
> *is jeopardized... (Participant P19).*

Last, one SA defined his role as a provider of *"QRs engineering as a service"* because he embraced ownership and responsibility for anything related to QRs in his project.

> *I provide QRs engineering as a service to business owners and business analysts and architecture as*
> *a service to developers and integration specialists. (Participant P21).*

How did SAs get assigned to projects? Did they choose their projects or did they get assigned? All our participants thought that their interest in working on a particular project in a specific application domain has been considered by their managers. We observed a consensus that it was their domain knowledge that mattered most in the SAs' assignments to projects. Our participants explained this with the important payoffs that domain knowledge brings to a project.

> *There is little point to put you on a SAP Human Resources implementation project, if you*
> *earned your credits in Financial Accounting. You leverage your domain knowledge for your client.*
> *Unless you want to get exposure to a new domain and start building up expertise in there.*
> *(Participant P1).*

Ahead of time, the SAs signaled to the higher management their interest in a specific project. So, the project managers were aware of the willingness of the SAs to join and make a difference.

*There is no way you get assigned to a project that includes 80 people and lasts more than a year. You have to want to get there. And if you do not step in, someone else would do, and you would miss on an important opportunity to make a difference with your knowledge and experience. (Participant P7).*

### 13.5.2  RQ2: Do SAs and RE staff use different terminology for QRs?

Because all interviewees had more than 10 years of business experience in their respective sectors, they considered communication clarity with RE staff a non-issue. Even when working with less experienced RE staff, they were of the opinion that the domain knowledge they have is instrumental for spotting missing or incomplete requirements. For example, if one is to develop an online system for processing feedback of clients in the air travel sector, the obvious QR of the highest priority would be scalability.

*If your RE person says nothing about it, you are absolutely sure there is something going wrong here. And you better pick up the phone and call them ASAP (as soon as possible) because they may be inexperienced and who knows what else could go wrong beyond this point. Not doing this is just too much risk to bear. (Participant P15).*

*We do not use the term QRs, not even nonfunctional requirements, we call them ISO aspects, because we are ISO-certified and our system must show compliance to the ISO standards. Also, our requirements specialists have in their template a special section that contains these aspects. We enumerate them one after another. All relevant aspects must be there, security, maintainability, performance, you name it. It's more than 40 aspects. They [the RE staff] know them and we know them, so we have a common ground. (Participant P11).*

An interesting observation was shared by those SAs delivering large SAP systems (participants P2, P3, P4, P5, and P7, in Table 13.1). They indicated that the SAP vendor's Product Quality Handbook (SAP, 2000) includes around 400 QRs that are implemented in the SAP's standard software package and that everyone in the project team knows about. If there were QRs that are specific to a particular client in a project and that are unaddressed in the Handbook, then those should be specified and added on top of the 400 that come in the SAP's package.

*I open the ISO manual and start from there; and then a kind of expertise we do this for them. . . (Participant P7)*

We make the note that the company SAP is ISO-9001-certified and as such, they have developed and implemented three quality management systems (QMS), all certified according to ISO 9001 (ISO, 2008). These are (1) the QMS for SAP Global Development, which ensures that SAP solutions meet the highest possible standards; (2) the QSM for SAP Active Global Support, which provides tailored services to maintain the quality of installed solutions, and (3) the QMS for SAP IT, which ensures the stability and quality of SAP's internal IT infrastructure; next to this, SAP IT is certified according to the requirements specified in ISO 27001:2005. Because each QMS defines standardized, certified processes for its domain, it enables employees to share and apply best practices within their domain. The three QMSs provide common information (e.g., management review, document control, record control, audits, corrective and preventive actions, and personnel development), thereby ensuring the consistent application of this information across SAP. For more information, we refer interested readers to visit the SAP's corporate Web site (www.sap.com), which provides the current ISO certificates for SAP's QMSs.

How many SAs are enough for engineering QRs? One or two SAs have been involved in their projects. In the case of two SAs being involved, our interviewees consisted of one SA from the vendor and one SA from the client.

> *You may work with many RE people for the different subject areas, but one architect must be there to aggregate their input and evaluate what it means for the underlying architecture. (Participant P6)*

### 13.5.3 RQ3: How do QRs get elicited?

Our study revealed two types of elicitation approaches being used: (1) checklist-based elicitation and (2) user-experiment-based detection of QRs, which included a variety of techniques centered on active user involvement (see Figure 13.3).

Sixteen of the 21 SAs used checklists in eliciting QRs. These were based on a variety of sources:

 **i.** ISO standards (e.g., 25045-2010, 25010-2011, 25041-2012, 25060-2010).
 **ii.** Architecture frameworks, be they company-specific or sector-specific.
 **iii.** Internal standards (e.g., vendor/client-organization-specific).
 **iv.** Stakeholder engagement standards (e.g., AA1000SES (AccountAbility, 2011).
 **v.** The related new Knowledge Areas from the Project Management Body of Knowledge PMBOK (PMI, 2013).

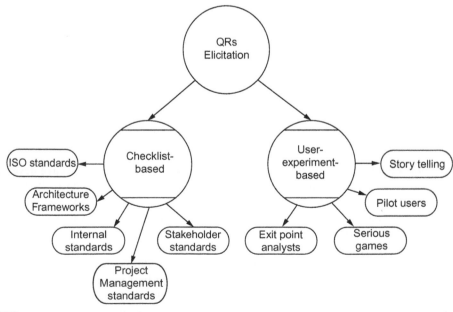

**FIGURE 13.3**

Elicitation practices as per the experiences of the SAs in the case study.

Regardless of the source, the interviewees agreed that the checklist-supported process is always iterative, because not all QRs could get 100% clear at the same time.

> *Most quality attributes are known only later, once you nail down the key pieces of functionality. I mean, you first fix the functional requirements and then let the quality stuff grow out of them. (Participant P1).*

In the participants' views, the fact that most QRs are not global to the system but act on specific pieces of functionalities imposes an order in the elicitation activities: SAs expect the functional requirements to be elicited first, so that they might use the functional requirements specification as the basis for eliciting QRs.

> *How otherwise will you know which attribute matters to what piece of functionality? (Participant P9).*
> *We do this top-down, gradually adding up more clarity to our nonfunctional requirements specs. There is no way to know all the details about them in one big batch. (Participant P8).*

Five SAs said that QRs are never elicited but are discovered or detected. For example, one SA (who worked in the gaming sector) was involved in an experimental serious-game-based process specifically designed to "detect" QRs:

> *I have a background in serious gaming for requirements acquisition, and this was instrumental to fixing scalability and repairability, which are two of our most important nonfunctional requirements. (Participant P19).*

In a computer-based environment designed for entertaining games but with non-entertainment goals, this SA has set up a QRs elicitation process with fixed starting and finishing points. In this process, users play, and then the SA, the RE staff, and other relevant roles in the project team observe the play and uncover what users want the system to do when it restores itself after a failure.

> Two other participants shared that they had "*a bunch of pilot users who volunteer to play the role of guinea pigs; they are passionate about the system and love to tell you where it fails to fulfill their expectations in terms of performance, availability, and user experience.*" (Participant P10).

> One SA said that he had been using storytelling techniques to uncover QRs, together with his RE counterpart and his clients.

> *I'm trying to collect stories from the business users that I got to know through our project meetings and this helps me understand how these users make meaning of their role as insurance claim analysts. The business analysts [the RE staff] and I then walk over these stories and analyze what they tell us. Most of the time, I ask questions in the format: "Tell me about a work day when the system worked perfectly for you. Tell me about your day when it was extremely frustrating. When the system was extremely slow, how did it affect you?..." You know, like this I can guess some common "red lines," themes if you want to call them, and I go validate them with other users. (Participant P13).*

One other SA (working in the gaming sector) indicated "*exit point analysis*" as the technique that his project team used to discover requirements. Exit points are the points in time when a player decides to stop playing a game by canceling his or her subscription. The game provider on whose projects the SA was employed made its clients fill out an exit survey in order to cancel a subscription. Analyzing the data collected in the survey served the purpose of finding out why a player is quitting a game and what requirements the project team could focus on in order to fix gameplay issues and improve the overall user experience of the game, and thus increase the "player retention rate."

### 13.5.4 RQ4: How do QRs get documented?

Sixteen of the 21 SAs specified QRs by using predefined templates. Some of them were vendor-specific. For example, in SAP projects, SAs used SAP's standard diagram notation called Technical Architecture Modelling (Groene, 2012), because it has been part of the SAP Architecture Curriculum (Groene et al., 2010). Others were derived based on (i) an ISO standard, (ii) the House of Quality (HoQ) of the Quality Function Deployment (QFD) methodology (Hauser and Clausing, 1988), (iii) the Planguage approach (Gilb, 2005), (iv) the INVEST grid approach (Buglione, 2012), and (v) the contextual design approach (Rockwell, 1999).

The other five SAs were using natural language text that provides at least the definition of each QR, plus information that is needed by the end user when testing its acceptance and the ways to demonstrate that the system meets it. The amount of detail in these specifications varied based on what the SAs deemed important to be provided to them by the RE staff or the users. For example, one SA wanted to hear a story from a user on "*how the user will know the system is slow? A user can tell you: 'If I manage to get one of my phone calls done while waiting, this means to me it's very slow.*'" (Participant P12). Other SAs said they write their QRs definitions next to the functional requirements, if these are specified in a process model or a data model.

> *This way you will know which smallest pieces of functionality and information entities are affected by which QR. (Participant P1).*

### 13.5.5 RQ5: How do QRs get prioritized?

All SAs agreed that (i) they make QRs trade-offs as part of their daily job on projects and (ii) the project's business case was the driver behind their trade-off decision making. The key prioritization criteria for making the QRs trade-offs were cost and benefits, evaluated mostly in qualitative terms but whenever possible also quantitatively, such as person-months spent to implement a QR. Perceived risk was identified as subsumed in the cost category, because SAs deemed a common practice the tendency to translate any risks into costs to estimate in a contractual agreement.

However, next to perceived cost and benefits, 12 SAs put forward two other QRs prioritization criteria: *client's willingness to pay* and *affordability*. The first is expressed as the level of readiness of client organizations to pay extra charges for some perceived benefit that could be brought by implementing a specific QR. Six SAs elaborated that this criterion alone is instrumental to split up the QRs in three groups. (i) Essential: This group includes those QRs that directly respond to why the client commissioned the system in the first place (e.g., for, a hotel reservation system). It's absolutely essential that a secure payment processing method is provided. (ii) Marginal: This group includes those QRs that are needed, despite clients being unwilling to spend much on them. For example, a user interface feature might be appreciated, but it would be and would be valued at a few hundred euro, rather than thousands of euro. (iii) Optional: This group includes QRs that clients will find enjoyable to have but would not be willing to pay for, such as flashy animation effects in a game system that are and fun, yet not truly a "*money-maker.*"

Next, affordability is about whether the cost estimation of a QR is in accordance with the resources specified in the contract and with the long-term contract spending plan of the client organization. This criterion determines whether a QR is aligned with (short-term) project goals and/or (long-term) organizational goals.

Furthermore, we found SAs' experiences differed regarding who ultimately decides on the QRs priorities. Thirteen SAs suggested that in their projects the prioritization is linked to a business driver or a key performance indicator (KPI) in the project and that it is the project's steering committee to decide on the priorities. They deemed the prioritization process *"iterative"* and a *"learning experience"* in which the SAs learn about those QRs that the business drivers *"dictate and how desperately the company needs these QRs,"* whereas the RE specialists and the business owners learn about the technical and cost limitations.

> *I educate them [the business representatives] on what risks might look like, why the things that they thought of as being simple turn out to be extremely difficult to implement on our end, and extremely costly, too. (Participant P18).*
>
> *You learn why the system must have certain qualities and how this affects the organizational bottom line... No quality, no company in business; it's that simple... (Participant P16).*

In contrast to these 13 SAs, the other 8 considered themselves as the key decision makers in setting the priorities:

> *You can stretch a technology to a certain point. No matter what your client wants, once in a while you've got to say "no" and push back decisively. The decision making on what's high priority and what's not has been delegated to you, so it's your responsibility to say "no" if you think a [QR] priority is unrealistic. (Participant P11).*

Concerning the requirements prioritization method being used in their projects, 20 SAs suggested no explicit use of any specific method other than splitting up QRs in categories of importance, namely "essential," "marginal," and "optional." SAs named these categories differently, yet they meant the same three. One SA named EasyWinWin (Boehm et al., 2001) as the group support tool that implements collaboration techniques helping the requirements prioritization and negotiation activities in a project. Three out of the 20 shared that nailing down two or three most important QRs is a non-issue, because of the obviousness of these requirements, for example,

> *If you develop a game, it's all about scalability and user experience. You have no way to make your fancy animation work if you cannot get scalable and if you jeopardize user experience. (Participant P19).*

What our participants deemed an issue is the prioritization of those QRs that take a less prominent place from user's perspective, for example, maintainability and evolvability. Such requirements make a lot of business sense from the developers' perspective; however, they are "invisible" for business users. For example:

> *You think making the system evolvable is important to business. ....But what if your project's steering committee does not care? They can be very short-term minded. And it's a downhill battle to argue over the priority of this kind of requirements. All they see is the clients' perception on it. ....The trouble is that when your manager later on wants to keep you accountable for that... for choices they made some long time ago... years ago... (Participant P13).*

### 13.5.6 RQ6: How do QRs get quantified, if at all?

All SAs agreed that expressing QRs quantitatively should not happen very early in the project. This was important in order to prevent early and not-well-thought-out commitments. Four out of the 21 said that they personally do not use quantitative definitions of QRs. Instead, they get on board an expert specializing in a specific aspect (e.g., performance, usability, or scalability) and who "*does the quantification job*" for them. For example, in the gaming application domain, one participant revealed that it is common to recruit so-called Enjoyability Evaluation Specialists who generally use quantitative models to measure enjoyability or playability of gaming software, for example, the GameFlow model (Sweetser and Wyeth, 2005) and its variants (Sweetser et al., 2012), which rest on the well-known theory of flow, or some other models that capture the "*entertainment value of a game,*" for example, the level of challenge of the task and how it matches the player's abilities (Yannakakis et al., 2006).

Ten other SAs used as a starting point the quantitative definitions that were pre-specified in the contract (e.g., a contract may state explicitly that the system should scale up to serve thousands of subscribers). However, 8 of the 10 warned that more often than not contracts address design-level requirements (Lauesen, 2002), including detailed feature specifications of how QRs are to be achieved, or a particular algorithm rather than required quality attribute value and criteria for verifying compliance. Confusing QRs with design-level requirements was deemed a critical issue in industry; it points to a mismatch in understanding what is really quantified and by using what kind of measures: Design-level requirements are quantified by using product measures and not project measures that are important for contract monitoring purposes. However, often contracts use product and project measures incorrectly, the final effect being that a number of project tasks related to implementing QRs do not get "visible" but "implicit," and therefore no budget is previewed for them and, in turn, the client does not commit to pay.

For example, when a Functional Size Measurement (FSM) method is used in a contract for the purpose of sizing the project at hand, its application would be technically "unsound" if the productivity for a project is calculated by dividing, for example, the number of Function Points (whatever the variant is used, IFPUG, COSMIC, or another ISO 14143-1:2007 compliant technique)—that's a product size measure only for sizing functional user requirements—by the overall project effort, including both functional-requirements-related effort and QRs-related effort. Because "one size doesn't fit all" (i.e., Function Points do not fit for sizing both functional requirements and QRs), what practitioners needed is at least a second unit of measure for sizing QRs (or, as termed in the ISO language, the Non-Functional Requirements). Most recently, the International Function Point User Group (www.ifpug.org) released a new technique for quantifying nonfunctional requirements, called SNAP (Software Nonfunctional Assessment Process) (IFPUG, 2013). The SNAP method adopted the ISO/IEC 25010:2011 product quality model that updated and extended the previous ISO/IEC 9126-1:2001 one. An added value for QRs analysis and sizing that all the existing FSM technique provide is the "elementary process" concept, that is, the "smallest unit of activity" perceivable from a user, self-consistent and independent. The "elementary process" concept is also included in the new SNAP method, which could help a lot when dealing with QRs because it ensures practitioners have a reference point in terms of level of granularity to be considered in QRs sizing.

Furthermore, another part of "missing" effort that becomes only evident when comparing estimates and actual values at the project closure comes from organizational/support processes in the scope of the whole project; such processes are, for example, Project Management, Measurement, Quality Assurance, which refer to another measurable entity that's the project and not its product. In that way (of using product and project measures incorrectly), there is a risk of underestimating the real effort that would be needed for QRs.

Another issue that crystallized in the interviews was the danger of specifying a QR by using a single number. Examples provided by five SAs referred to availability and performance requirements. Too often, these participants observed contracts and project teams having thought of these requirements in terms of "*99% of the time,*" "*all the time between 9 am and 5 pm,*" or "*in peak hours.*" What remains unmentioned, and in turn leads to ambiguity, is the workload and the frequency of interactions of events per period of time. Examples of interactions or events are "*requests by clients,*" "*order click by shoppers,*" "*hotel bookings per minute.*"

> *Without giving a proper context, developers cannot make much sense of availability. I need to go search and double-check what kind of context they [the business managers] are talking about when saying "99% available"; and you cannot be sure you can create a good enough design; what kind of load do they [business managers] mean? 1000 new bookings per minute with the payment processing that may go with it? Or booking cancellations? Or some other tasks the online user may want to do? (Participant P20)*

These SAs thought that suggesting only one number in quantifying a QR severely limits the search space for solution options and trade-offs between those QRs that are important to clients and to developers:

> *Of course, the team can make it work and meet what the contract wants, but that's not the point. You do not want to look myopic, meet your numbers for the sake of them, and find yourself totally out of context. You should not preclude yourself from comparing alternatives and choosing the one that makes sense for the big picture. (Participant P11)*

Next, 7 out of the 21 SAs worked with a team of systems analysts on operationalizing QRs, which in essence meant decomposing them until reaching the level of architecture design choices or of the smallest pieces of functional requirements. Once at this level, the practitioners felt comfortable starting quantifying the QRs, for example, Function Points. However, no common quantification method was observed to be used. Instead, the architect suggested the choice of a method should match the project goal (e.g., toward whatever end quantification was needed in the first place). For example, if quantification of QRs is to serve project management and contract monitoring purposes, then it might be well possible that in the future those organizations experienced in Function-Points-based project estimation would use a way to approximate them in a quantitative way as done, for example, by the newly released SNAP method (IFPUG, 2013). In this way—differently than applying the old VAF (Value Adjustment Factor) to an FP-based evaluation—it's possible to quantify only the nonfunctional-requirements side of a project, which is useful in particular for maintenance projects where the functional side is not present at all (corrective/perfective maintenance) or partly present (adaptive maintenance), as defined in the ISO/IEC 14764:2006 standard (ISO, 2006). A simple example is the adaptation of an existing Web portal to become "accessible" (i.e., the QR in question is "accessibility"), as stated in the Web Content Accessibility Guidelines 2.0 (http://www.w3.org/TR/WCAG20/) or in the Section 508 rules (https://www.section508.gov/).

### 13.5.7 RQ7: How do QRs get validated?

All SAs were actively involved in QRs validation; 17 considered it part of their job and acted as the contact point for this task, while four SAs said that it's the job of the RE staff to ensure QRs are validated. These four SAs used the RE specialists as contact points on clarifying requirements.

Fourteen SAs participated in requirements walkthroughs with clients led by an RE specialist where clients confirm the functionalities on which the QRs in question were supposed to act. The walkthroughs were deemed part of the client expectation management process that the project manager established. The SAs considered them as the opportunity to inform the clients about those QRs that could not be implemented in the system or could not be implemented in the way the client originally thought:

> You've got to educate them on what your technology can and cannot do for them and the walkthroughs are how this happens relatively easily. (Participant P1).

Two of the 14 SAs complemented the walkthroughs with inspection checklists whose purpose was to detect flaws in the QRs. These SAs said they used the checklist at their own discretion, after a walkthrough was over. The SAs did this "*for themselves,*" and not because their project managers or RE counterpart asked for it. This was a step—or "*an auxiliary means*" (as one SA put it)—to ensure they did not miss anything important for the architecture design:

> I do this myself because this way I know I did everything to ensure we do not leave out things unnoticed. This happened too many times in my past projects and I know too well the trouble it brings. (Participant P10).

The two SAs who were working in the game development business sector presented a perspective of what "the contents of a walkthrough" include in this specific domain. Unlike the other SAs who talked about walkthroughs in the context of functional requirements and quality attributes, these SAs used the term *walkthrough* as applicable at the following levels: (1) the "game play," which is the set of problems and challenges that a player must face to win a game; from RE perspective, the game play is the overarching concept that contextualizes and motivated all functional and QRs; (2) the game story, which is the plot and the character development and which determines how requirements would be grouped together; (3) the functional requirements, specific to each stage of developing of the game story; and (4) the QRs specific to each stage of developing of the game story.

> Validating your plot is what you should do first. Only after you ensure your game play and story are validated can you go into validating functionals and nonfunctionals; otherwise, it would be a premature action. (Participant P21).

Three SAs used the HoQ (Hauser and Clausing, 1988) to demonstrate the strength of the relationship between a QR statement and its operationalization in terms of either functional requirements or architecture design choices. We note that the organizations where these SAs worked have been experienced in using the QFD and the HoQ approaches in their large and ultra-large projects, so no additional training of project staff was needed for the purpose of validating the requirements in the SAs' current projects.

> Once you populate your operational terms in the house of quality, you'll know if things work or don't. If things do not work, then you've got to step back and work on one-on-one basis with those business users or developers who are affected; we do not proceed, unless we first get this done; otherwise it's too risky and you do not want risks to creep into the project. (Participant P12).

Two SAs validated QRs against internal architecture standards. Should they identify deviations from the standards, they escalate this to both managers and RE staff. In extreme cases, when QRs are grossly misaligned with the architecture standards, this should be brought to the attention of the steering committee, the program director, and the architecture office manager responsible for the project.

> *You have to inform them immediately that things have no way to work as planned, so they get back to negotiation and revise the concept. (Participant P8).*

### 13.5.8 **RQ8: How do QRs get negotiated?**

All SAs participated in requirements negotiations, but not all considered themselves as *"true negotiators."* While 16 SAs thought of themselves as the responsible person to run negotiation meetings and to push back if needed, the other five considered themselves to be *"information providers and mentors"* to the team, but not *"truly negotiators on QRs"* and that it's the project manager's responsibility to lead in the negotiation:

> *It's his job to sell it to the other parties. I'm just an internal consultant; what they do with my information is their business. (Participant P10).*

Among those 16 SAs who played the role of "true negotiators." Ten used the business case of the project as the vehicle to negotiate requirements. They considered this a common practice in enterprise systems projects.

> *If you talk money, then you talk business; that's how you get the quality attributes' voices heard. The game is lost, otherwise . . .. (Participant P20).*

Three SAs who worked on projects where user experience was the most important QR said their goal in QRs negotiation is to prevent the most important QR from becoming suboptimal if other QRs take more resources and attention. These SAs did not use the business case as such, but were considering effort and budget allocation as important inputs to negotiation meetings.

Other three SAs used the HoQ, EasyWinWin (Boehm et al., 2001), or the Six-Thinking-Hats method (de Bono, 1985) to reason about QRs in negotiation meeting. We note that the Six-Thinking-Hats is a general approach to resolving complex issues more efficiently, and companies use it for any negotiation situation, be it QRs related or not. The approach was well received and internalized in the company, and people *"had fun using it as it takes pressure off them in this kind of difficult conversations"* (Participant P16).

Does requirements negotiation happen face-to-face? Eighteen SAs relied on virtual meeting tools (e.g., a conference bridge).

> *The last time I attended a face-to-face meeting was 2 years ago. . . I can no longer imagine spending budget money on this. (Participant P2).*

Three out of our 21 participants thought of face-to-face meetings as indispensable:

> *I got to face them. Personally. To observe their faces, body language, you name it. . .. This way I know I can convince them without investing all my energy for the day in this. . .. (Participant P1)*

What is critical to the requirements negotiation outcomes? The experiences of the 21 SAs varied widely as to what makes the top-three most important skills that matter to negotiation. One common theme across the experiences of the participants was the ability to express themselves in financial terms.

> *Being able to translate architectural choices into budget figures means you are at the top of your game. (Participant P4)*
>> *Do not get emotional, get financially-savvy and they will listen. (Participant P9)*
>> *You've got to get good at it [business case terminology]. This is the only way for a large project to operate and negotiate decisions. (Participant P20).*

They suggested that the importance of being able to think in financial terms is consistent with the predominant thinking style that they use in their work, namely, that they think of software architecture as a shared "*mental model*," "*state of mind*," "*project culture*" (in the words of a few participants):

> *Your team delivers on contractual terms, this sets up the stage and the way you look at things; contracts are about money and commitments, about the bottom line, about power receivers and power losers, and you've got to think of architecture in these terms; face the big picture and use it as much as you can when negotiating nonfunctionals. (Participant P20).*

Being gatekeepers and balance keepers, does it happen that architects revise their own "architecture rules" as part of QR negotiation? Twelve of our SAs suggested this happened on regular basis. They considered this part of their job. SAs' knowledge on how to separate those rules that SAs could be flexible with from the rules that call for rigidity was deemed of paramount importance:

> *You have to know where, when, and how to break your own policies. And make sure you write down how you did this, and who you informed on this. You may desperately need this later on, if issues arise in your contractual process. (Participant P3).*
>> *If you think of yourself as a QR engineering service provider, then you know your clients and you know how to be flexible; and I do not mean it as a negative thing. Think of it as boundary-setting, as a terrain that is constantly subjected to renegotiation. . . . You have to claim and reclaim your territory and they are free to do the same. . . so I revise things in the product architecture, and I must say, we have very good reasons to do so. . . .. (Participant P12).*

## 13.5.9 RQ9: What role does the contract play in the way SAs cope with QRs?

All SAs deemed the contract "*the solid mechanisms*" for regulating the client-developer relationship. Because it determines rights, liabilities, and expectations, they thought of it as "*the specific something*" that sets the backdrop for any QRs engineering activity. Our participants revealed the following elements of the contract that in their experiences directly impacted how QRs engineering took place in their contract-based projects (see Figure 13.4): (1) service levels; (2) pricing, schedule, and payment; (3) warranty and liability; (4) project issue escalation procedures; (5) dispute resolution mechanisms; (6) termination procedures; and (7) information security, including both data security and business recovery planning.

In the SAs' experiences, there were five ways in which the contract influenced how they coped with QRs, as shown in Figure 13.4: (1) The contract enforced the cost-consciousness of the SAs and was used to evaluate the cost associated with achieving the various QRs; (2) the contract stipulated QRs

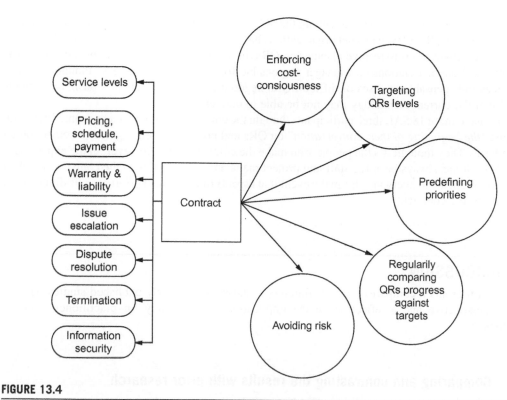

**FIGURE 13.4**

Contract elements that influenced the behavior of SAs in QRs engineering.

levels, for example, in the SLA part, that were targeted and subjected to discussions with the stakeholders; (3) the contract predefined the priorities for some small but very important set of QRs; (4) the contract instilled the discipline to regularly compare the QR levels in the project against the levels stated in the contract; and (5) the contract encouraged the SAs to practice "risk avoidance" in what they were doing (e.g., by using a checklist on their own discretion when validating QRs).

Eighteen of the 21 SAs agreed that the contract was used on an ongoing basis to stay focused on what counts most in the project. To the SAs, the contact was the vehicle to ensure the system indeed includes "*the right things,*" "*those that they needed in the first place, and that we are billing them for.*" Twelve SAs acknowledged that a contract-based context is conductive to understanding QRs as a way to maintain control because every comprehensive contract they had usually comes with SLA specifications, KPIs, and measurement plans that address multiple perspectives (of clients/vendors). For example, the Balancing Multiple Perspectives technique (Buglione and Abran, 2005) is a way to help all involved parties in understanding and validating the right amount of things to do in a contract-based project. Also, in the perceptions of these SAs, the contract helped derive mutual benefits in terms of sharing responsibilities and risks. For example, in the experience of one SAs, the precision in the definitions of those contractual clauses that referred to QRs contributed to clear understanding of risks that, if they remained unnoticed, would later on potentially have brought hidden costs.

Another conception that was shared among the 18 SAs was the role of the contract in the escalation of issues related to QRs. Eleven project organizations had in place a Contract Management Committee that was the ultimate resort to resolve disputes on QRs. In the other seven organizations, this role was played by the Vendor Relationship Manager responsible for the contract. The SAs thought of these resources as indispensable in cases of difficult QRs negotiations when the client's business depends on a QR that the current technology may not be able to deliver.

In contrast to these 18 SAs, three participants thought the contract was not that important. They said, it was just *"the beginning of their conversation"* on QRs and not the reference guide to consult on an ongoing basis. They thought it's the people who make the contract work. However, in the experiences of these SAs, it has always been RE staff and project managers who work with the contract, and they usually communicate to everyone else in the event that aspects of the project effort are misaligned with the clauses of the contract.

## 13.6 DISCUSSION

This section presents a comparison of our findings to those in previously published studies on QRs from SA perspective and a reflection on the implications of our study for practitioners and for researchers.

### 13.6.1 Comparing and contrasting the results with prior research

Our discussion is organized according to the themes behind our research questions.

#### 13.6.1.1 Role of SAs in engineering of QR

In Ameller et al. (2012), the SAs had indicated a broad diversity of tasks beyond software architecture that they took on (e.g., coding). In contrast to this, our SAs worked full-time as SAs (and not coding or carrying out any downstream development activity). Our case study is in line with Gorton's (2011) statement that *"Most of a software architect's life is spent on designing software systems that meet a set of quality attribute requirements"* (p. 23). Our findings suggest that in contract-based and large/very large projects, the SAs define their role as "a bridge" that connects clients QRs to the architecture design. This difference can be a hint that our SAs came from more regulated environments where terminology, roles, and processes are determined, well communicated, and lived up to. Our findings agree with those of Poort et al. (2012a) on the importance that SAs place on gaining a deep understanding of the QRs and using it to deliver a good quality architecture design.

Regarding how many SAs are enough for engineering QRs, we note that this question has not been yet researched in RE studies. In our interviewees' experiences, it's usually one or two SAs who operate together in a large contract-based project. This is in line with Brooks' most recent reasoning on "the design of design" of large systems (Brooks, 2010) where he explains that a two-person team can be particularly effective where larger teams are inefficient (other than for design reviews where the participation of a large number of reviewers is essential).

### 13.6.1.2 QRs vocabulary of SAs and RE staff

Our results did not indicate the use of different vocabulary of terms as the issue that preoccupied the SAs, even when communicating with other roles like RE. This contrasts the study of Ameller et al. (2012) where Spanish SAs collectively indicated a broad terminological gap between SAs and RE staff. For instance, a shared glossary of QRs types was missing and was part of the problem. We think the difference between our findings and those in Ameller et al. (2012) may well be due to the fact that our case study projects were happening in regulated organizations where standards defined terminologies that all project team members adopted (including SAs) and assumed ownership over their use.

### 13.6.1.3 QR elicitation

Our study revealed that all SAs were actively involved in elicitation. This confirms the findings from Poort et al. (2012a) and is in contrast to Ameller et al. (2012). Also, we found checklist-based techniques as the predominant approach in contract-based project context. Additionally, a variety of user-experiment-based techniques are applied for eliciting QRs from end users, like storytelling (Gruen et al., 2002; Snowden, 1999) and pilot users/players that could be considered as ethnography (Bentley et al., 1992). This shows that SAs are well aware of the variety of requirements elicitation techniques that are available and recommended for end-user involvement. This is in contrast with other studies that showed a lack of awareness about RE methods in practice, not only in SMEs (Nikula et al., 2000), but also in larger companies (Klendauer et al., 2012).

### 13.6.1.4 QRs documentation

We found that standardized forms/templates plus natural language were used most. This is in contrast with Ameller et al. (2012), where the SAs could not agree on one specific systematic way to document QRs, and natural language was the only common practice being used. Why does this difference occur? We assume that it's because of the regulated nature of the contract-based environments and of the use of standards. We think it's realistic to expect that in such contexts, a contract is monitored on an ongoing basis (e.g., all relevant SLAs are well specified and how they would be measured is explicitly defined), and its use forces IT professionals to adopt a sound template-based documentation flow throughout the project (Nicholson and Sahay, 2004). As suggested in Nicholson and Sahay (2004, p. 330), a template is "embedded knowledge" (that "resides in organizing principles, routines and standard operating procedures") and this streamlines the knowledge transfer between clients and vendor's staff (e.g., SAs in our case).

### 13.6.1.5 QRs prioritization

Two new prioritization criteria crystallized in this study: willingness to pay and affordability. These complement the well-known criteria of cost, benefits, and risk (as stated in Herrmann and Daneva, 2008). We assume that the choice of these criteria could be traceable back to the contract-based project contexts of our study where both vendors and clients have to be clear early on about scope, project duration, and the way they organize their work processes and their impact on each party.

### 13.6.1.6 QRs quantification

Our results agree with Ameller et al. (2012) on the importance of QRs quantification in practice. However, unlike Capilla et al. (2012), our SAs did not indicate that searching for new or better quantification techniques was their prime concern. Similarly to Poort et al. (2012a), our SAs warned about the pitfalls of premature quantification, meaning that early QRs quantification may be based on too many assumptions about the solution. As in Poort et al. (2012a), our SAs thought that if those assumptions turned out unrealistic, a vendor may find itself in the precarious situation of having committed resources to unachievable QRs. Regarding how quantification happens, the SAs suggest either using a standard (e.g., the ISO usability standard) or engaging an expert in specific type of QRs (e.g., security, scalability). While the first ensures that all tasks of implementing QRs are explicitly accounted for in a project, the second allows for deeper analysis on a single quality attribute and its interplay with others.

An important finding regarding quantification was the SAs' concern about the need to contextualize a QR in the terms of the domain-specific tasks that will be performed by using the system. For example, unambiguously specifying what kind of interactions a QR applies to. This topic so far has been only implicitly touched upon in textbooks in RE (Lauesen, 2002; Pohl, 2011) or in software architecture (Gorton, 2011). For this reason, we think that follow-up studies might be worthwhile to fully understand how to add contextual descriptions to enrich quantified QR definitions.

Another finding relevant to qualification of QRs is the need for a standard definition of the granularity level at which QR statements should be, in order to translate them into a value to be used for size and effort estimation purposes: Because the new SNAP technique (IFPUG, 2013) uses the "elementary process" concept (the smallest unit of activity that is meaningful to the user constitutes a complete transaction, is self-contained, and leaves the business of the application being counted in a consistent state), this concept could possibly be a good candidate to consider as a pointer on which practitioners can ground a sizing unit for properly quantifying QRs.

### 13.6.1.7 QRs validation

Unlike in QRs literature (Berntsson-Svensson et al., 2010; Capilla et al., 2012) where much accent is placed on tools and methods, we found no hint of formal and tool-based validation. No practitioner among our case study participants has even worked in a contractual agreement where a sophisticated automated (model-checking) tool for validating QRs was explicitly stated in the contract or was required by the client organization. Instead, our results suggest that simple and common-sense practices dominate the state-of-the art in engineering QRs: for example, using requirements walk-throughs, documentation reviews, building up communication processes (e.g., escalation if a QR is not timely clarified) around the artifact-development activity are down-to-earth, yet powerful ways to ensure QRs are aligned with clients' expectations and contractual agreements. One could assume the SAs' behavior to remain active and persuasive regarding QRs validation could be due to the explicit contractual agreements (e.g., SLA), controls and project monitoring procedures (e.g., KPI).

### 13.6.1.8 QRs negotiation

In contrast to RE literature (e.g., Lauesen, 2002) that offers an abundance of negotiation methods, we found that only one: EasyWinWin (Boehm et al., 2001) was mentioned (and by only one SA). SAs hinted to general purpose negotiation techniques, for example. the HoQ and the Six-Thinking-Hats method as being sufficient to help with QRs negotiation. This suggests that it might be worthwhile to explore the kind of support that negotiation methods from other fields (management science, psychology) can offer to QRs negotiation.

### 13.6.1.9 *Contract's role in SAs' coping strategies*

Our results suggest that the contract's role in the ways in which SAs executed their QRs engineering activities was fivefold:

1.  It made QRs "*first class citizens*" (as one participant put it) in the RE and AD process, as SLA and KPI automatically made them relevant part of the conversations on requirements in the very early project meetings.
2.  It instilled an artifact-related discipline in engineering QRs, for example, checklists were used in elicitation, templates were used in documentation, formal document-based walkthroughs took place to validate the QRs.
3.  It reinforced the SAs' role in a project organization and redefined how this role is included in all the RE activities concerning QRs.
4.  It reinforced SAs' thinking of progress on QRs in terms of levels achieved and also compared against targets.
5.  It encouraged SAs' thinking of QRs in terms of business cases and risk avoidance.

These results reflect that SAs are well aware of the possible impacts of a contract on their professional behavior, for example, SAs are thoughtful about what is expected in a contract and how it would be monitored, they assume responsibility to clarify QRs priorities, and they escalate to project managers and/or RE staff when they see project goals threatened. This is in line of other published results (e.g., Gopal and Koka, 2010) suggesting that the better a project organization aligns the aspects of the project effort with the clauses of the contract, the closer the project to deadline and budget.

## 13.6.2 Implications for practice

Our findings have the following implications. First, to SAs, it suggests that the conversation on QRs starts with the contract, and specifically with the SLA and the business case. Next, it provides a good reason to reflect on what skills in the already existing SAs' skillset need to be added in terms of training, so that more SAs feel at ease with contract-based systems delivery projects—for example, feel at ease with expressing QR trade-offs in financial terms. While it is well-known in the software architecture community that communication skills are the most important ones for practicing architects (Wieringa et al., 2006), these skills alone, however, might not be enough in a large-scale contract-based project. Financially savvy architects with good communication skills might turn out to be a better answer to the large project staffing needs.

Second, our research has some implications for RE practitioners. This study suggests that SAs are in the position to be RE specialists' best helpers when producing the total requirements specification documentation for a project. If organizations let RE specialists work in isolation and let them be unaware of who the SA on their project is, this may mean missing out on an important opportunity to leverage the SA's talents for the purpose of better requirements processes and artifacts. The message of our study is that RE specialists have higher chances to succeed in delivering specifications that meet contractual agreements if they reach out and actively seek the support of their respective SAs. Moreover, our study indicated that SAs have a profound knowledge of contracts and good awareness of how they influence what is happening in the RE processes related to QRs. While to the best of our knowledge there are no studies on the RE specialists' awareness of contracts, it might possibly be the case that SAs are better informed than RE staff on QRs (because SAs perceive themselves as responsible for meeting the SLAs). If this is the case, then RE specialists could tap on SAs' knowledge and consult them on evaluating contractual consequences related to any kind of requirement, both functional and QRs.

Third, to RE tool vendors, our findings suggest vendors are better off thinking about how RE tools should be better embedded into social processes and broader social interaction context. A part of any tool vendor's business is to provide education. This could possibly be positioned in the broader context of contractual agreements and large projects.

### 13.6.3 Implications for research

To RE researchers, our study suggests that instead of solely focusing on QRs methods, tools, and techniques, it makes good sense to extend existing research by including analysis of QRs processes as socially constructed ones. How a contract shapes the behavior of RE staff and SAs is an interesting question demanding future research. One could think of borrowing theories from other disciplines (e.g., behavior science and management) to explain why RE staff and SAs engineer QRs the way they do.

The line between RE tasks and architectural design is not as clear and unidirectional as is implied by current textbooks. SAs are involved in QR elicitation, prioritization, and validation. But are requirements engineers also participating in architectural design? If yes, how? The closer these two types of activities are found to collaborate, the more pressing the question of whether it makes sense to separate these activities in terms of roles, methods, and tools, or whether they should be merged into one "design" phase.

An interesting finding in our study is the observation that SAs related QRs to business drivers, business cases, KPI, and technical and business constraints, some of which were stated in the SAs' project contracts. This gives us a hint that in the minds of the SAs, interdependencies exist between QRs and the other types of nonfunctional requirements as defined by Gorton (2011) and Kassab et al. (2009), for example, project-related nonfunctional requirements that specify standards and constraints as system access, communication, user/system interface standards, budget, schedule, and scope of the project. What the nature of these interdependencies is and what tacit assumptions SAs make about them while engineering the QRs are research questions that are relevant and worthwhile investigating in the future.

It is also an interesting observation that SAs say that the elicitation of functional requirements must happen first and the QR elicitation second and that all QR must be related to functionalities. It would be interesting to investigate whether this is generally so, or only for specific systems in specific domains. RE methods should take this practical demand into account. Currently, functional and QRs are elicited using separate methods, probably simply for historical reasons. Maybe practitioners need new or integrated methods that closely link functional and QRs to each other. Exploration into this forms a line for future research.

We make the note, however, that all our case study participants were experienced in their respective domains and were well aware of the domain-specific issues and challenges that accompany the development processes in the respective business environments. We, however, did not think this is always the case. There-fore, investigating explicitly what knowledge architects need for handling QRs could be a question for further research.

## 13.7 **LIMITATIONS OF THE STUDY**

There are a number of limitations in our exploratory research. In our evaluation of them, we used the checklist of Runeson and Höst (2009) to help analyze the possible threats to validity of our observations and conclusions. Because we completed exploratory qualitative research, the key question to address when evaluating the validity of its results is (Yin, 2008): *To what extent can the practitioners' experiences in coping with QRs could be considered representative for a broader range of projects, and companies?* Our participants had at least 10 years' experience and were active in large contract-based projects. While the projects were suitable for the study, they are not representative for all the possible ways in which engineering of QRs is performed in large contract environments. Following Seddon and Scheepers (2012), we think that it could be possible to observe similar experiences in projects and companies that have contexts similar to those in our study, for example, where large and contract-based projects engage experienced SAs in teams with mature process-oriented thinking. As Seddon and Scheepers (2012) suggest, "if the forces within an organization that drove observed behaviour are likely to exist in other organizations, it is likely that those other organizations, too, will exhibit similar behaviour" (p. 12).

Moreover, we acknowledged that the application domain may have influenced the ways SAs coped with QRs, for example, the game development domain. Therefore, we think that more research is needed to understand the relationship between application domains and the way in which the QRs processes are carried out.

We also accounted for the fact that our case study participants worked on projects delivering systems falling in the class of enterprise information system, for example, only Participant P9 worked on a sensor system. The results therefore reflect the realm of information systems and may not be observable for contract-based projects delivering distributed real-time and embedded systems (e.g., software embedded in hardware components used to assemble a car). Usually, in such projects, more than one discipline deals with the system architecture, which has implications for QRs engineering. Clarifying the differences that may exist between information systems and embedded systems contexts is therefore an interesting line for research. We are willing to carry out follow-up studies and are actively searching for industry collaborators in the area of embedded systems to explore QRs process in it.

Furthermore, we note that the projects of our SAs had no issues with their contracts, nor any issues with their QRs. We assume, however, that the results might have been different if we had included problematic project cases, be it in terms of contracts or in terms of QRs and RE processes. Complementing our results with findings from such cases requires further research.

We also acknowledge the inherent weaknesses of interview techniques. The first threat to validity is whether the interviewees answered our question truthfully. We took a conscious step to minimize this threat by (i) recruiting volunteers, the assumption being that if a practitioner would not be able or willing to be honest, he or she could decline participation at any stage of the research process and (ii) ensuring that no identity-revealing data would be used in the study. Second is the threat that the researcher influences the interviewee. We countered it by paying special attention to conducting the interview in such a way that the interviewee felt comfortable in answering the question. The researcher who interviewed the participants made sure the interviewee did not avoid questions and felt at ease. This created a safer environment and increased the chances of getting a truthful answer rather than one aimed to please the interviewer. Third, it might be possible that an interviewee did not understand a question. However, we think that in our study, this threat was reduced, because the interviewer (Daneva) used follow-up questions and asked about the same topic in a number of different ways. Fourth, we accounted for the possibility that the researcher might instill his or her bias in the data collection process. We followed Yin's recommendations (2008) in this respect by establishing a chain of findings: (i) We included participants with diverse backgrounds (i.e., industry sector, type of system being delivered), and this allowed the same phenomenon to be evaluated from diverse perspectives (data triangulation; Patton, 1999) and (ii) we had the draft case study report reviewed by practitioners from the company that hosted our case study. These SAs read and reread multiple versions of the case study results.

## 13.8 CONCLUSIONS

This study makes a strong case for exploring the SA's perspective on engineering the QRs in large and contract-based software delivery projects. We reported on the internal working of QRs engineering activities as experienced and perceived by individual SAs. Although there are ample empirical studies on vendor-client relationships in IT contract-based system delivery (e.g., in the field of Information Systems Research), these studies take the level of the vendor or developer organization as a unit of study. Exploratory research at the level of individual practitioner's perspectives is very little. We are not aware of any previously published study that takes the individual SA's perspective to QRs in contract-based context. This exploratory case study therefore contributes unique empirical evidence on the ways in which SAs cope with QRs and the interaction and communication processes they actively get involved in as part of QRs engineering.

While the involvement of SAs and RE staff certainly increases the costs of a project, our study revealed that in the contract-based settings studied the SAs' involvement was a worthwhile investment. Our research found that:

1. SAs had a strong sense of identity in terms of what roles they took on and how those added value to their teams.
2. SAs had clarity on terminology used in engineering QRs and leveraged the presence of standards, business cases, and agreements for the purpose of QRs engineering activities.
3. SAs treated QRs with the same attention and attitude as the architecture design demand.
4. The relationship between RE staff/clients and SAs is actively managed, whereby the contract means embracing responsibilities over QRs (and not abdicating thereof).

Concerning the QRs engineering activities addressed in our research questions, we found that:

1. In the view of SAs, engineering functional requirements precedes and is a prerequisite for QRs engineering activities.
2. QRs elicitation happens mostly by using checklist-based techniques.
3. QRs specification happens mostly by using template-based documentation styles and natural language.
4. Willingness to pay and affordability seems as important prioritization criteria for QRs as cost and benefits are.
5. The contractual agreements and, specifically, SLAs and KPIs, play a role in deciding on QRs priorities and QRs trade-offs.

6. For quantification of QRs to make an impact, it needs to be contextualized; SAs deem knowledge of context critical for coming up with quantification that is meaningful to the project team. Often quantification is done with and by experts specialized in a specific QR (e.g., performance, scalability, enjoyability).

7. QRs validation and negotiation are considered more organizationally and in terms of social interactions with RE staff and clients than in terms of tool-supported processes.

## Acknowledgments

The authors thank the anonymous reviewers for their exceptionally helpful comments and suggestions for improving this chapter. We also thank the case study participants. Without their commitment and engaged participation, this exploration would have been impossible.

## References

AccountAbility, 2011. Stakeholder Engagement Standard (AA1000SES). http://www.accountability.org/standards/aa1000ses/index.html.

Ameller, D., Franch, D., 2010. How do software architects consider non-functional requirements: a survey. REFSQ 2010, pp. 276-277.

Ameller, D., Ayala, C., Cabot, J., Franch, X., 2012. How do software architects consider non-functional requirements: an exploratory study, RE 2012, pp. 41-50.

Ameller, D., Galster, M., Avgeriou, P., Franch, X., 2013. The role of quality attributes in service-based systems architecting: a survey. ECSA 2013, pp. 200-207.

Avgeriou, P., Grundy, J., Hall, J.G., Lago, P., Mistrík, I. (Eds.), 2011. Relating software requirements and architectures. Springer, Berlin.

Avgeriou, P., Burge, J., Cleland-Huang, J., Franch, X., Galster, M., Mirakhorli, M., Roshandel, R., 2013. 2nd international workshop on the twin peaks of requirements and architecture (TwinPeaks 2013). In: ICSE 2013, pp. 1556-1557.

Bachmann, F., Bass, L., 2001. Introduction to the attribute driven design method. In: ICSE 2001, pp. 745–746.

Bass, L., et al., 2003. Software Architecture in Practice, second ed. Addison-Wesley, NY.

Bensabat, I., Goldstein, D., Mead, M., 1987. The case research strategy in studies of information systems. MIS Quart. 11 (3), 369–386.

Bentley, R., Hughes, J.A., Randall, D., Rodden, T., Sawyer, P., Shapiro, D., Sommerville, I., 1992. Ethnographically-informed systems design for air traffic control. In: Proceedings of the 1992 ACM Conference on Computer-Supported Cooperative Work CSCW'92, pp. 123–129.

Berenbach, B., Lo, R.-Y., Sherman, B., 2010. Contract-based requirements engineering. In: RELAW 2010, pp. 27–33.

Berntsson-Svensson, R., Höst, M., Regnell, B., 2010. Managing quality requirements: a systematic review. In: EUROMICRO-SEAA 2010, pp. 261–268.

Boehm, B., Grunbacher, P., Briggs, R.O., 2001. Easy WinWin: a groupware-supported methodology for requirement negotiation. In: 9th ACM SIGSOFT FSE, pp. 320–321.

Brooks, F.P., 2010. The Design of Design: Essays from a Computer Scientist. Addison-Wesley Professional, NY.

Buglione, L., 2012. Improving estimated by a four pieces puzzle. In: IFPUG Annual Conference. http://www.slideshare.net/lbu_measure/agile4fsm-improving-estimates-by-a-4pieces-puzzle.

Buglione, L., Abran, A., 2005. Improving Measurement Plans from multiple dimensions: Exercising with Balancing Multiple Dimensions - BMP. In: 1st Workshop on "Methods for Learning Metrics", METRICS 2005.

Capilla, R., Babar, M.A., Pastor, O., 2012. Quality requirements engineering for systems and software architecting: methods, approaches, and tools. Requir. Eng. 17 (4), 255–258.

Charmaz, K., 2008. Constructing grounded theory. Sage, Thousands Oaks.

Chen, L., Babar, M.A., Nuseibeh, B., 2013. Characterizing architecturally significant requirements. IEEE Softw. 2013, 38–45.

Cheng, B.H.C., Atlee, J.M., 2007. Research directions in requirements engineering. In: Briand, L.C., Wolf, A.L. (Eds.), International Conference on Software Engineering/Workshop on the Future of Software Engineering. IEEE CS Press, pp. 285–303.

de Bono, E., 1985. Six thinking hats: an essential approach to business management. Little, Brown & Co, Toronto.

Ferrari, R., Madhavji, N.H., 2008. Architecting-problems rooted in requirements. Inf. Softw. Technol. 50 (1-2), 53–66.

Furlotti, M., 2007. There is more to contracts than incompleteness: a review and assessment of empirical research on inter-firm contract design. J. Manag. Gov. 11 (1), 61–99.

Gilb, T., 2005. Competitive Engineering: A handbook for Systems Engineering, Requirements Engineering, and Software Engineering Using Planguage. Wiley, Butterworth.

Goo, J., Huang, C.D., Hart, P., 2008. A path to successful it outsourcing: interaction between service-level agreements and commitment. Decis. Sci. 39 (3), 469–506.

Gopal, A., Koka, B., 2010. The Role of Contracts in Quality and Returns to Quality in Offshore Software Development. Decis. Sci. 41 (3), 491–516.

Gorton, I., 2011. Essential Software Architecture, second ed. Springer, Berlin.

Groene, B., 2012. TAM—The SAP Way of Combining FCM and UML, http://www.fmc-modeling.org/fmc-and-tam (last viewed on Nov 8, 2012).

Groene, B., Kleis, W., Boeder, J., 2010. Educating architects in industry—the sap architecture curriculum. In: 17th IEEE International Conference on Engineering of Computer Based Systems (ECBS), pp. 201–205.

Gruen, D., Rauch, T., Redpath, S., Ruettinger, S., 2002. The use of stories in user experience design. Int. J. Hum.-Comput. Interact. 14 (3-4), 503–534.

Guessi, M., Nakagawa, E.Y., Oquendo, F., Maldonado, J.C., 2012. Architectural description of embedded systems: a systematic review. In: ACM SIGSOFT ISARCS '12, pp. 31–40.

Hauser, J.R. & Clausing, D. (1988), House of Quality. Harvard Business Review Article, 11 pages. May 1, 1988.

Heesch, van, U., Avgeriou, P., 2011. Mature Architecting - A Survey about the Reasoning Process of Professional Architects. In: 9th WICSA, pp. 260–269.

Herrmann, A., Daneva, M., 2008. Requirements Prioritization Based on Benefit and Cost Prediction: An Agenda for Future Research. RE 2008, pp. 125-134.

IFPUG, 2013. Software Non-functional Assessment Process (SNAP)—Assessment Practice Manual (APM) Release 2.1, April.

ISO, 2006. ISO/IEC 14764:2006 Software Engineering—Software Life Cycle Processes—Maintenance. URL: http://www.iso.org/iso/catalogue_detail.htm?csnumber=39064.

ISO, 2008. ISO 9001:2008 Quality management systems—Requirements.

Kalnins, A., Mayer, K.J., 2004. Relationships and hybrid contracts: an analysis of contract choice in information technology. J. Law Econ. Org. 20 (1), 207–229.

Kassab, M., Ormandjieva, O., Daneva, M., 2009. An ontology based approach to non-functional requirements conceptualization. In: ICSEA 2009, pp. 299–308.

King, N., Horrocks, C., 2010. Interviews in qualitative research. Sage, Thousands Oaks.

Klendauer, R., Berkovich, M., Gelvin, R., Leimeister, J.M., Krcmar, H., 2012. Towards a competency model for requirements analysts. Inf. Syst. J. 6 (22), 475–503.

Lauesen, S., 2002. Software requirements: styles and techniques. Addison-Wesley Professional, NY.

Nekvi, M.R., Madhavji, N., Ferrari, R., Berenbach, B., 2012. Impediments to requirements-compliance. In: REFSQ 2012, pp. 30–36.

Nicholson, B., Sahay, S., 2004. Embedded knowledge and offshore software development. Inf. Organ. 14 (4), 329–365.

Nikula, U., Sajaniemi, J., Kalviainen, H., 2000. Management view on current requirements engineering practices in small and medium enterprises (Proceedings of the Australian Workshop on Requirements Engineering).

Nuseibeh, B.A., 2001. Weaving together requirements and architectures. IEEE Comput. 34 (3), 115–117.

Patton, M.Q., 1999. Enhancing the quality and credibility of qualitative analysis. Health Serv. Res. 34 (5 Pt 2), 1189.

PMI, 2013. A guide to the project management body of knowledge (PMBOK), fifth ed. Project Management Institute. http://goo.gl/UNbFam.

Pohl, K., 2011. Software Requirements: Fundamentals, Principles, and Techniques. Springer, Berlin.

Poort, E.R., Martens, N., van de Weerd, I., van Vliet, H., 2012a. How architects see non-functional requirements: beware of modifiability. REFSQ 2012, pp. 37-51.

Poort, E.R., Key, A., de With, P.H.N., van Vliet, H., 2012b. Issues Dealing with Non-Functional Requirements across the Contractual Divide. WICSA/ECSA. pp. 315-319.

Rockwell, C., 1999. Customer connection creates a winning product: building success with contextual techniques. Interactions 6 (1), 50–57.

Runeson, P., Höst, M., 2009. Guidelines for conducting and reporting case study research in software engineering. Empir. Softw. Eng. 14 (2), 131–164.

SAP AG, 2000. Quality Management Manual for SAP Development, Waldorf, Germany, 2000. SA, http://www.sap.com/solutions/quality/pdf/50010233s.pdf.

Seddon, P., Scheepers, P., 2012. Towards the improved treatment of generalization of knowledge claims in IS research: drawing general conclusions from samples. Eur. J. Inf. Syst. 21 (1), 6–21.

Sjøberg, D.I.K., Dybå, T., Jørgensen, M., 2007. The future of empirical methods in software engineering research. In: Briand, L.C., Wolf, A.L. (Eds.), International Conference on Software Engineering/Workshop on the Future of Software Engineering, pp. 358–378.

Snowden, D., 1999. Story telling: an old skill in a new context. Bus. Inf. Rev. 16 (1), 30–37.

Sommerville, I., 2005. Integrated requirements engineering. IEEE Softw. 22 (1), 16–23.

Song, X., Hwonk, B., 2012. Categorizing requirements for a contract-based system integration project, RE 2012, pp. 279-284.

Sweetser, P., Wyeth, P., 2005. GameFlow: a model for evaluating player enjoyment in games. ACM Comput. Entertain. 3 (3), 1–24.

Sweetser, P., Johnson, D.M., Wyeth, P., 2012. Revisiting the GameFlow model with detailed heuristics. J. Creat. Technol. 3. http://colab.aut.ac.nz/journal/revisiting-the-gameflow-model-with-detailed-heuristics/

Wieringa, R., van Eck, P., Steghuis, C., Proper, E., 2006. Competencies of IT Architects. NAF, Amsterdam, The Netherlands. http://doc.utwente.nl/68444/3/CompetencesOfITArchitects2009.pd.

Wortham, S., Mortimer, K., Lee, K., Allard, E., White, K., 2011. Interviews as interactional data. Lang. Soc. 40, 39–50.

Wu, D.J., Ding, M., Hitt, L., 2012. IT implementation contract design: analytical and experimental investigation of IT payoff, learning and contract structure. Inf. Syst. Res. 24 (3), 787–801.

Yannakakis, G.N., Lun, H.H., Hallam, J., 2006. Modeling children's entertainment in the playwre playground. In: Proceedings of the IEEE Symposium on Computational Intelligence and Games, Reno, USA, May 2006, pp. 134–141.

Yin, R.K., 2008. Case study research: design and methods. Sage, Thousand Oaks.

# Glossary

**ANP** The analytic network process (ANP) used in multi-criteria decision analysis. ANP structures a decision problem into a network with goals, decision criteria, and alternatives, then uses a system of pairwise comparisons to measure the weights of the components of the structure, and finally to rank the alternatives in the decision.

**Architectural decision** A design decision is a decision about the structure, behavior, or key properties of software system made to resolve specific problems. Architectural decisions are those decisions that impact software system's architecture and system quality. Design decisions may be reused.

**Architecture Trade-off Analysis Method (ATAM)** A scenario-based software architecture evaluation methodology developed by the Software Engineering Institute (SEI).

**Attribute Driven Design (ADD)** A systematic step-by-step design methodology based on the architecture's quality attribute requirements.

**Configurability** A property of a generic system from which a concrete system can be derived.

**Cynefin model** A general model of decision making in a specific context.

**Decision-Centric Architecture Review (DCAR)** A software architecture evaluation methodology where architectural decisions are used as first class entities to uncover and evaluate architectural rationale.

**Decision force** Any aspect of an architectural problem arising in the system or its environment (e.g., operational, development, business, organizational, political, economic, legal, regulatory, ecological, social), to be considered when choosing among the available decision alternatives.

**Decision Relationship View** A graph showing the relationships between the architecture decisions elicited during a Design-Centric Architecture Review (DCAR).

**Goal modeling** An aspect of requirements engineering that is concerned with modeling and analysis to ensure that the proposed system meets organizational goals and to verify that the proposed system is needed and how the stakeholders' interests may be addressed.

**i\*** A notation for modeling and reasoning about the goals of heterogeneous actors in business and socio-technical systems. Goal graphs serve to visualize the goals of an actor.

**MARTE** UML profile for Modeling and Analysis of Real-Time and Embedded systems, defined by the Object Management Group. This extension of UML supports modeling of performance and real-time concepts. MARTE replaced the UML profile for Schedulability, Performance, and Time specification (SPT)

**Mobile software** Software systems designed and developed to run on mobile devices such as smartphones and tablets.

**Multi-Objective Optimization (MOO)** The process of systematically and simultaneously optimizing a collection of objective functions. MOO is used whenever certain solutions or parts of solutions exist, the values of the solutions with respect to objectives are known, and there are some constraints for selecting solutions, but the complexity of the optimization problem prevents a human from figuring out the optimum or an automated selection is desired.

**Nonfunctional Requirement (NFR)** A requirement that specifies criteria that can be used to judge the operation of a system, rather than specific behaviors.

**Optimization** Finding "best available" values of some objective function, given a defined input. There is a variety of different types of objective functions and different types of inputs.

**Problem frame** A means to describe and classify software development problems. Each problem frame represents a class of software problems.

**Quality attribute** See Nonfunctional Requirement

**Quality requirement** See Nonfunctional Requirement

**Requirements interaction** Critical relationships among a set of requirements. Requirements often interact with or influence each other. These interactions may be desirable or unwanted.

**Requirements optimization**  The optimization process necessary to address the dynamic nature of technical and nontechnical requirements, customer needs, constraints, cost, etc.

**Smart grid**  To use energy in an optimal way, smart grids make it possible to couple the generation, distribution, storage, and consumption of energy. Smart grids use information and communication technology, which allows for financial, informational, and electrical transactions.

**Software architecture**  Set of principal design decisions about the system's structure, behavior, constraints, and key properties.

**Software product families**  See Software Product Lines

**Software product lines (SPL)**  A set of software-intensive systems that share a common, managed set of features satisfying the specific needs of a particular market segment or mission and that are developed from a common set of core assets in a prescribed way.

**Usability**  A measure of how easy it is to use a software system to perform prescribed tasks.

# Author Index

Note: Page numbers followed by *f* indicate figures and *t* indicate tables.

# Subject Index

Note: Page numbers followed by *f* indicate figures and *t* indicate tables.

Printed and bound by CPI Group (UK) Ltd, Croydon, CR0 4YY

03/10/2024

01040327-0006